Revolution of the Right to Education

Revolution of the Right to Education

By

A. Reis Monteiro

BRILL
SENSE

LEIDEN | BOSTON

All chapters in this book have undergone peer review.

The Library of Congress Cataloging-in-Publication Data is available online at http://catalog.loc.gov

Typeface for the Latin, Greek, and Cyrillic scripts: "Brill". See and download: brill.com/brill-typeface.

ISBN 978-90-04-46244-1 (paperback)
ISBN 978-90-04-46245-8 (hardback)
ISBN 978-90-04-46246-5 (e-book)

This book is printed on acid-free paper and produced in a sustainable manner.

Tribute to
Katarina Tomaševski
First United Nations Special Rapporteur on the Right to Education
(1998–2004)

Contents

APPENDICES

Preliminary Notes

1 There is a great diversity among languages and authors concerning the use of capital letters. Some are minimalist, others are maximalist. Where official documents and their translations are concerned, although there are professional guidelines, the criteria seem to be sometimes subjective and not always consistent. While there are general grammatical rules to be respected by all users of a language, no Grammatik can have the pretension to control its pragmatics, that is, the cultural, personal, contextual dimensions of its uses, much less on the international level. The use of capital letters should be recognised, to a large extent, as a formal dimension of the freedom of expression.

Caring for not to contribute to carelessness in the use of language, this author takes the following criterion: to use capital letters for distinguishing between different meanings of a term (such as 'state' and State, 'law' and Law); for highlighting certain concepts (Rule of Law, Ethics of Human Rights, for example); or for designating disciplines of knowledge. In any case, the options of the authors are respected when quoted, in general.

2 Nowadays, the Internet serves as an increasingly wide, accessible and frequently unavoidable documental source. Because of the kind of its most documental sources, this essay is Internet heavy. If an exclusively electronic source is quoted, it is, as a rule, referred to only as a footnote: without access date, if originated from an electronic site institutionally stable; indicating month and year of access, if the presumption of stability is uncertain. When a document included in the references is legally available electronically too, its source is indicated. Anyway, there are no immortal links … the mobility and volatility of the electronic documents are great … but it is always possible to try to find them elsewhere if they remain available.

3 While this manuscript strives to use gender-inclusive language, such a concern should not go so far as to make reading boring and unpleasant, nor to try to 'correct' the history. For example, the outdated term 'rights of man' is not changed.

4 This manuscript's spelling is, in general, British English friendly, but the quoted authors' English version is respected, as well as other writing options.

5 When quoting not English documentary sources, if no English translation is referred to, translations are this author's.

6 Each chapter of the book is self-contained: it begins with an abstract and includes its references.

7 Appendix G provides an extended overview of the book contents.
8 In such a long manuscript, with so varied documentary sources, minor inaccuracies or inconsistencies, unjustified repetitions or even unjust omissions, may remain, despite careful revisions. I apologise in advance.

I am indebted to Professor Jane Kotzmann (Deakin University Law School, Australia), for her very cordial and invaluable assistance in the linguistic revision of this book, as well to Emily Griffith, Master in Law and research assistant, who checked its linguistic accuracy. I also sincerely thank the anonymous reviewers for the hard job to read and assess this long manuscript with competence, fairness and empathy. John Bennett (Brill | Sense) was a kind interlocutor.

Abbreviations

AAVV *Autores Varii* (various authors)
ACHR American Convention on Human Rights
ACP African, the Caribbean, and the Pacific States
ACHPR African Charter on Human and Peoples' Rights
ACRWC African Charter on the Rights and Welfare of the Child
AHRC Asian Human Rights Commission
ASEAN Association of Southeast Asia Nations
AU African Union
CADE Convention against Discrimination in Education
CAT Convention against Torture and Other Cruel, Inhuman or Degrading Treatment or Punishment
CDE Convention against Discrimination in Education
CEART Committee of Experts on the Application of the Recommendation concerning the Status of Teachers
CED Committee on Enforced Disappearances
CEDAW Convention on the Elimination of All Forms of Discrimination against Women
CEDEFOP European Centre for the Development of Vocational Training
CERD International Convention on the Elimination of All Forms of Racial Discrimination
CHR/HRC Council of Human Rights (or Human Rights Council)
CIS Commonwealth of Independent States
CJEU Court of Justice of the EU
CoESCR Committee on Economic, Social and Cultural Rights
CoHR Committee on Human Rights/Human Rights Committee (HRC)
CoRC Committee on the Rights of the Child
CRC Convention on the Rights of the Child
CRPD Convention on the Rights of Persons with Disabilities
CSCE Conference on Security and Co-operation in Europe
CSW Commission on the Status of Women
ECCE Early Childhood Care and Education
ECHR European Convention for the Protection of Human Rights and Fundamental Freedoms (European Convention on Human Rights)
ECOSOC Economic and Social Council of the United Nations
ECOWAS Economic Community of West African States
ECSR European Committee of Social Rights
EFA Education for All

EIP	*Association Mondiale pour l'École Instrument de Paix* (World Association for the School as an Instrument of Peace)
ESC	European Social Charter
ESD	Education for Sustainable Development
EU	European Union
FAO	Food and Agriculture Organisation
FME	*Fórum Mundial de Educação* (World Education Forum)
GATS	General Agreement on Trade in Services
GATT	General Agreement on Tariffs and Trade
GCED	Global Citizenship Education
GDP/GNP	Gross Domestic/National Product
GEM	Global Education Monitoring
GNI	Gross National Income
HCNM	High Commissioner on National Minorities
HDP	Human Dignity Principle
HIV/AIDS	Human Immunodeficiency Virus/Acquired Immune Deficiency Syndrome
HRE	Human Rights Education
HREA	Human Rights Education Association
IACHR	Inter-American Commission on Human Rights
IACtHR	Inter-American Court Inter-American Court of Human Rights
IAU	International Association of Universities
IBE	International Bureau of Education
IBHR	International Bill of Human Rights
ICC	International Criminal Court
ICCPR	International Covenant on Civil and Political Rights
ICEPD	International Convention for the Protection of All Persons from Enforced Disappearance
ICERD	International Convention on the Elimination of All Forms of Racial Discrimination
ICESCR	International Covenant on Economic, Social and Cultural Rights
ICJ	International Court of Justice
ICMW	International Convention on the Protection of the Rights of All Migrant Workers and Members of Their Families
ICT	Information and Communication Technologies
IEL	International Education Law
IEA	International Association for the Evaluation of Educational Achievement
IGO	Intergovernmental Organisation
IHL	International Humanitarian Law
IHRL	International Human Rights Law
IIEP	International Institute for Educational Planning (UNESCO)

ILC	International Law Commission
ILO	International Labour Organisation
IMF	International Monetary Fund
INEE	Inter-Agency Network for Education in Emergencies
ISCED	International Standard Classification of Education
LDC	Least Developed Countries
LGBTQI	Lesbian, Gay, Bisexual, Transgender, Queer or Questioning, and Intersex
L.I.E.N.	*Ligue Internationale pour l'Éducation Nouvelle* (New Education International Fellowship)
MDGS	Millennium Development Goals
MOOCS	Massive Open Online Courses
NEM	New Education Movement
NGO	Non-Governmental Organisation
NHRI	National Human Rights Institution
NSA	Non-State Actor
OAS	Organisation of American States
OAU	Organisation of African Unity
ODA	Official Development Assistance
OECD	Organisation for Economic Co-operation and Development
OER	Open Education Resources
OHCHR	Office of the High Commissioner for Human Rights
OIC	Organisation of Islamic Co-operation
OIDEL	*Organisation Internationale pour le Développement de la Liberté d'Enseignement* (International Organisation for the Right to Education and Freedom of Education)
OP	Optional Protocol
OSCE	Organisation for Security and Co-operation in Europe
PCIJ	Permanent Court of International Justice
PEN	*Pour l'Ère Nouvelle* (Towards the New Era)
PISA	Programme of International Student Assessment
PPPS	Public-Private Partnerships
RPF	Respect, Protect, Fulfil
RTE	Right to Education Initiative
SADC	Southern African Development Community
SAFHR	South Asia Forum for Human Rights
SDGS	Sustainable Development Goals
STEM	Science, Technology, Engineering and Mathematics
TMB	Treaty Monitoring Body
TNC	Transnational Corporation
TVET	Technical and Vocational Education and Training
UDHR	Universal Declaration of Human Rights

UIA	Union of International Associations.
UIL	Institute for Lifelong Learning (UNESCO)
UIS	UNESCO Institute for Statistics
UK	United Kingdom
UN	United Nations
UNAIDS	Joint United Nations Programme on HIV/AIDS
UNDAF	United Nations Development Assistance Framework
UNDP	United Nations Development Programme
UNDRIP	United Nations Declaration on the Rights of Indigenous Peoples
UNEP	United Nations Environment Programme
UNESCO	United Nations Educational, Scientific and Cultural Organisation
UNEVOC	International Project on Technical and Vocational (UNESCO)
UNFPA	United Nations Population Fund
UNGEI	United Nations Girls Education Initiative
UNHCHR	United Nations High Commissioner for Human Rights
UNHCR	United Nations High Commissioner for Refugees
UNICEF	United Nations Children's Fund
UNITWIN	University Twinning Programme (UNESCO)
UNPF	United Nations Population Fund
UPE	Universal Primary Education
UPR	Universal Periodic Review
US/USA	United States of America
USSR	Union of Soviet Socialist Republics
VCLT	Vienna Convention on the Law of Treaties
WHO	World Health Organisation
WTO	World Trade Organisation

INTRODUCTION

Advent of the International Education Law

Abstract

1. Throughout centuries, education has often, somewhat paradoxically, been blamed for being the main cause of human evils and prized as the main remedy for correcting them. This proves the primacy commonly recognised to education, but what a *good education* should be, has always been a rather controversial issue.
2. An educational revolution has been increasingly claimed since the end of the 19th century. It should be, first and foremost, a normative one, concerning the truly inspiring values and aims effectively guiding education, which is purposeful, by definition. It's about what we want to become as human beings.
3. There is no timeless ideal education, but there is a universal pedagogic heritage indefinitely open to the lights of the advancements of science and conscience, for the historical perfecting of the humankind. It is condensed in the right to education.
4. The birth of the *human right* to education, after a millennia-long gestation, has opened up a new chapter in the History of Education. What is more, its normative, jurisprudential, doctrinal, and programmatic developments are constituents of an International Education Law that is now the highest source in the hierarchy of the contemporary normativity on education, to which the Education Law in States Parties should conform. Therefore, it should be recognised and studied as a new legal and educational discipline, source of the principles of legitimacy and quality of education.
5. This book offers an interdisciplinary and topical introduction to International Education Law, broadly defined. It explains in what ways the normative integrity of the right to education carries far-reaching revolutionary significance, a corollary of the Revolution of Human Rights and the Revolution of the Rights of the Child.

•••

Throughout centuries, education has often, somewhat paradoxically, been blamed for being the main cause of human evils and prized as the main remedy for correcting them. This proves the primacy commonly recognised to education, but what a *good education* should be, has always been a rather controversial issue. Already Aristotle (2000) remarked in his *Politics*:

 | DOI: 10.1163/9789004462465_001

> ... everyone looks after his own children separately and gives them separate instruction of the sort which he thinks best [...]. That education should be regulated by law and should be an affair of State is not to be denied, but what should be the character of this public education, and how young persons should be educated, are questions which remain to be considered. [...] The existing practice is perplexing: no one knows on what principle we should proceed – should the useful in life, or should virtue, or should the higher knowledge, be the aim of our training; all three opinions have been entertained. (Book VIII, 1337a)

In the early 20th century, Édouard Claparède (1931) wrote that centring education on the child was "the great principle of method that makes Rousseau the Copernicus of pedagogy" (pp. 103, 104). He thought of a psychological-didactic 'revolution', but Rousseau (1762) did not envisage a new education "better by halves" (*bonne à demi*), that is, "incorporated with the wrong methods at present in use", an alliance in which "the good is corrupted and the bad is none the better for it" (*dans cet alliage, le bien se gâte et le mal ne se guérit pas*) (p. 33). As Robert Derathé (1964) pointed out, "the problem of education is no more, from the point of view of Rousseau, a technical problem of pedagogy" (p. 109). The French Revolution pantheonised Rousseau (in 1794) but failed to revolutionise education.[1] An "Educational French Revolution" is needed, said the psychoanalyst Françoise Dolto (1985, p. 315).

An educational revolution has been increasingly claimed since the end of the 19th century. Nowadays, according to psychologist and neuroscientist Mary H. Immordino-Yang (2011):

> Neuroscientific evidence suggests that we can no longer justify learning theories that dissociate the mind from the body, the self from social context. [...]
>
> ... there is a revolution imminent in education.
>
> The past decade has seen unprecedented advances in scientists' understanding of the brain and mind, and new information about the brain is expanding the influence of cognitive neuroscience into the classroom. The neuroscientific findings from affective and social neuroscience, in particular, could have profound implications for education, eventually leading to innovations in practice and policy. (pp. 101, 102)

A landmark Report published by UNESCO (United Nations Educational, Scientific and Cultural Organisation) in the 1970s already affirmed:

> His [man's] knowledge of his own powers spreads to the knowledge of his own consciousness. Never until now has he stretched to such limits his attempts to elucidate the mystery of his inner world. Knowledge of the mechanisms of his brain, and of the conscious and unconscious sources of his own behaviour, enable him to give an account of his own and others' irrational conduct. (Faure, 1972, p. 154)

Neuroscientific findings support insights of great authors of the history of the pedagogic thought, confirming much of what the most competent, conscious and caring educators know from experience, and making evident how wrong, sterile and even pernicious many aspects of predominant education policies are. With the neuroscientific revolution, we begin to understand how education has transcendent repercussions, tangible and intangible, in individual and collective life. It is largely responsible for the emotional aridity and malformations of the personality (hypertrophies and dystrophies), which help explain, for example, the behaviour not only of 'terrorists', but also of some 'statesmen' of the world in which we live. We now also better understand why, as Condorcet warned, "men retain the errors of their childhood, their country and their time until long after the truths necessary for these errors to be removed have been recognised" (in Crampe-Casnabet, 1985, p. 14).

Calls for an educational revolution come from other knowledge perspectives. For example, in the opinion of Donald J. Cunningham (1987), Semiotics is "a genuinely new way of thinking, a way of thinking that, if adopted, cannot help but change the face of education". In effect, "if we reconceptualise the foundations of education along semiotic lines, nothing less than a revolution will occur within education [...]. Radical claims, to be sure" (pp. 214, 203). The semiotic and pedagogic fields have a common magnetic pole: the symbolic function, now illuminated by neuroscientific findings. A semiotic approach has profound repercussions throughout the field of education as a phenomenon of cultural, social, institutional, interpersonal communication of multiple contents, through multiple forms, in multiple contexts and with multiple effects. A recent example of call for education revolution is, for instance, *The Fourth Education Revolution* by Anthony Seldon (2020).

A very educational revolution should be, first and foremost, a normative one, however, concerning the truly inspiring values and aims effectively guiding education, which is purposeful, by definition. It's about what we want to become as human beings. "At all times, the major pedagogical struggles waged, not about techniques, but the deep significance of education" (Planchard, 1979, p. 30). The principal writing of Johann F. Herbart – a major reference in the history of the pedagogic thought – bears the title *Allgemeine Pädagogik aus dem Zweck der Erziehung abgeleitet* (General Pedagogy derived from the Purpose of Education, 1806). Most General Education Acts begin by setting out the overall aims of the respective school system and the goals assigned to each of its levels or cycles, to which the specific objectives of each learning contribute.

There is no timeless ideal education, but there is a universal pedagogic heritage indefinitely open to the lights of the deepening of science and conscience, for the historical perfecting of the humankind. It is condensed in the *human right* to education that has given legal form and force to the most humanist pedagogic thought. The normative, jurisprudential, doctrinal, and programmatic developments of the right to education are constituents of an International Education Law (IEL) that has inseminated the National Education Laws.

National Education Law is the Law relating or applicable to education in each country. Fundamentally, it is legally sourced in the Constitution, the Civil Law and the Administrative Law.[2] In this regard, Hans-Jürgen Töws (1970) noted:

> The determinations concerning the pedagogical action are sometimes summarised in the concept of Education Law. [...] They stem not only from different legal sources, as the Constitution, the laws, decrees and international agreements, but they also belong to different branches of the Law, especially Private Law (Family Law) or Public Law. The corresponding legal matters can be understood as a structure of rights and duties. Their subjects and addressees are parents, State and other education holders as, for example, the Church, but above all children and young. (p. 376)

A landmark date for the internationalisation of Education Law was 1934 when the International Bureau of Education (IBE) began to convene a biennial International Conference on Public Education that adopted Recommendations (see 4.1.2.4). Jean Piaget – who served as IBE Director from 1929 until 1969 – wrote in his "Introduction to the third edition" of the Recommendations:

> The recommendations which follow comprise on the whole more than one thousand clauses, and thus constitute a kind of international charter or code of public education, a body of educational doctrine of very wide scope and importance. They are not to be regarded as conventions, nor yet simply as wishes expressed by private congresses. They were passed by the duly authorized delegates of governments.
>
> They were passed, moreover, after careful preliminary inquiry and the presentation of detailed reports on the part of the Ministries of

> Education, and thus embody not merely ideal but also well-founded and practical suggestions for educational advancement. (UNESCO, 1979, p. ix)

In his "Historical Note" to the same edition, Pedro Rosselló, IBE Director-Assistant, pointed out "that the adoption of recommendations in the field of education was at that time a bold innovation" (p. xiv).

Referring to UNESCO, Pierre M. Eisemann (2007) remarked that "one might wonder what the reasons are for the relatively modest nature of the Organization's standard-setting work in this domain" (p. 291), mainly where conventional instruments are concerned. This issue was addressed in the "Report submitted by the Director-General of the United Nations Educational, Scientific and Cultural Organization on Regulations concerning Economic and Social Rights in the International Covenant on Human Rights (E/1752, 11 July 1950)",[3] prepared for the Commission on Human Rights that was drafting the 1966 International Covenants on human rights (see 2.4). It read:

> 10. In the past, the international regulation of educational affairs has met with many obstacles. For instance, when in 1921 the Assembly of the League of Nations discussed the project for setting up a Commission "with the task of studying questions of intellectual co-operation and education of international scope", it had no qualms about striking out the words "and education" from the draft resolution in order to make sure of a unanimous vote [see 4.1.2.3.2].
>
> The fact is that at that time education was still regarded as one of the chief bastions of national sovereignty and there was a fear – to quote the words of the rapporteur, Gilbert Murray – lest "the League of Nations might go so far as to interfere in domestic educational affairs".
>
> This essential reservation is therefore among the reasons why the International Institute of Intellectual Co-operation and the International Bureau of Education did not follow the International Labour Organization in evolving a system of international conventions, but embarked instead on a policy of influencing Governments indirectly by making a start on the collection of an international *corpus* of educational information and documentation, by seeking to awaken a spirit of emulation between the education authorities of the various countries and by making "recommendations" on specific educational problems.
>
> However, the situation has since developed considerably. Not only have the United Nations repaired the omission made in 1919 by making deliberate mention of education in their Charter, but the Constitution of UNESCO contains in so many words several of the principles involved

> in the right to education later promulgated in Article 26 of the Universal Declaration of Human Rights. (p. 12)

These principles have been included, to a great extent, in the Convention against Discrimination in Education (CADE) adopted by UNESCO in 1960 (see 4.2.1.2). Referring to it, Andrzej S. Nartowski (1975) said that "it is the nucleus of the International Code of Education regulating key problems of international co-operation in this field and general standards of the organization of the educational systems in the individual countries" (p. 306).

In 1983, the normative internationalisation of education as a human right was already sufficiently developed so that Angel Trapero-Ballestero, at the time Director of the Higher Education Sector in UNESCO, could affirm in his lecture on "The Right to Education and the International Law", at the symposium "The Future of the International Law in a Multicultural World" held in the Academy of International Law (The Hague, Netherlands): "There is an International Education Law [... that] will develop in the future" (Trapero-Ballestero, 1984, pp. 395, 400).[4] It was probably the first use of the term 'International Education Law', at least at such a level of authority.

International Education Law (IEL) is a term still not used frequently,[5] and its academic status is incipient, but there are examples of its formal study at the postgraduate level.[6] It can be compared with, for example, International Labour Law and International Health Law (see Monteiro, 2008a). It is far from the density reached by the former, which is older and whose scope is more immediately linked to the vital needs of individuals and societies, but its normative *corpus* is by far more developed than that of the latter. In effect, while "there is currently no overarching international recognition of international health law as a distinct field of public international law" (Töbes, 2015, p. 301), the IEL is already well identifiable as a distinct field.[7]

IEL belongs to International Human Rights Law (IHRL), which may be defined narrowly or broadly:
- Narrowly defined, the scope of the IHRL covers the legal dimensions of human rights: their sources, normative content, mechanisms of protection, case law, and doctrine.
- Broadly defined, the IHRL is an interdisciplinary field of research to which legal and other disciplines contribute, whose scope should notably include the study of the principle of human dignity, of the history of human rights and the repercussions of their recognition (and violations) in the life of individuals and peoples.

Similarly, it is submitted that the IEL may be narrowly or broadly defined:

- Narrowly defined, the scope of the IEL covers the legal dimensions of the right to education: its sources, normative content, mechanisms of protection, case law, and doctrine.
- Broadly defined, the IEL should not overlook an introduction to the human rights and to the rights of the child as a necessary general framework within which the international profile of the right to education can be outlined and its specificity understood, as well as answered all the questions the approach to education as a human right may raise; and should include the study of its origins in the history of education and human rights, as well as a conceptualisation of the legal, political, and pedagogical (theoretical and practical) outcomes from its normative content.

The first United Nations (UN) Special Rapporteur on the Right to Education (Katarina Tomaševski, 1998–2004) wrote in her "Preliminary Report" (E/CN.4/1999/49)[8]: "A simple but crucial question – what does full realization of the right to education entail? – will thus orientate the work of the Special Rapporteur" (para. 8). It is about "emphasizing differences between *education* and the *right to education* so as to create a background for advocating changes within education aimed at conformity with the human rights requirements" (para. 13). As this is an interdisciplinary challenge, in 2001 the Special Rapporteur called for "close collaboration between educationists and human rights lawyers" (E/CN.4/2001/52, para. 69).[9]

This essay offers an interdisciplinary and topical introduction to the IEL, broadly defined, drawing on this author's research and writings on the history of education, the theory of education, the education professions, human rights, rights of the child and right to education. It is submitted that the differences between 'education' and 'right to education' call for an "education revolution", as read a subtitle of the 1999 UNICEF Report on *The State of the World's Children,*[10] up to the Convention on the Rights of the Child (CRC). Colin Power, former UNESCO Assistant Director-General for Education and Deputy Director-General, published a book on *The Power of Education* whose chapter 4 is titled "Education for All – A Quiet Revolution" that is about empowering. It should be a normative revolution: "At all levels, an empowering education is one that is built on the values and principles set out in the Universal Declaration of Human Rights" (Power, 2015, p. 10).

Interdisciplinarity is risky. Criticism from academic border guards is inevitable. However, it appears to be an increasingly unavoidable path to understand and improve the human condition. All the more when it comes to human rights. As Charles Malik said at the 9th meeting of the first session of the Commission on Human Rights (E/CN.4/SR.9, 1 February 1947)[11]: "It was not politicians and diplomats alone who were concerned with this question [human rights]; the advice of poets, prophets and philosophers should be asked". Charles Foster (2011), after asking "What is Dignity?" wrote: "Lawyers and ethicists need to be anthropologists, and anthropologists need to be neuroscientists, archaeologists, sociologists, Shakespeare scholars and classicists. It would also help if they had a nodding acquaintance with the Torah, Talmud, New Testament, Koran, Upanishads, the myths of Old Iceland, and the Walmart catalogue" (p. 4). Furthermore, sight should not be lost of the Article 7 of the Declaration on the Right and Responsibility of Individuals, Groups, and Organs of Society to Promote and Protect Universally Recognized Human Rights and Fundamental Freedoms (UN, 1998)[12]: "Everyone has the right, individually and in association with others, to develop and discuss new human rights ideas and principles, and to advocate their acceptance".

Being primarily addressed to a legal and educational audience, this essay faced the following question: How much 'right' and how much 'education' should it contain? Both components have been developed as much as deemed necessary for the argument (but it has always been an insecure decision). The paramount purpose is to contribute to introducing a fundamental juridical dimension into the pedagogical culture, for the right to education to become meaningful. Hence the rationale and structure of this book:

- it begins by justifying the need for and legitimacy of introducing a juridical approach to the theorisation of the educational phenomenon (Chapter 1);
- it continues with an introduction to IHRL (Chapter 2) and the International Law of the Child (Title 3) as a necessary general framework to approach the IEL;
- the historical emergence, international profile, some distinguishing features, and controversial and topical issues of the right to education are dealt with in Chapter 4;
- the stakes of a *human right approach* to education are encapsulated in the conception of Rightful Education submitted in Chapter 5;
- the Conclusion adds a brief elaboration on two looking forwards ideas, namely: the Gordian Knot of education and the right to education as Right to Possible;
- the Appendices, which include a global summary, provide further support for study, should this essay be used as a textbook.

The polyhedric diversity of this interdisciplinary approach to the right to education aims at capturing as many juridical and conceptual nuances as possible, as well as to solve some theoretical and legal knots. The rationality fitting with its nature and scope is explained in Section 2.6.1.1. Mindful of its paramount purpose, this manuscript seeks to be balanced, appealing, didactic (for instance, by introducing informal subtitles to improve the readability and intelligibility of the text).

The birth of the *human right* to education, after a millennia-long gestation, has opened up a new chapter in the History of Education. The *travaux préparatoires* (legislative history, preparatory works or elaboration) of its major international provisions, which are auxiliary means of interpretation (according to Article 32 of the Vienna Convention on the Law of Treaties, 1969), illustrate the process of creation of International Law. The motivations of the decisions and the dissident opinions of its jurisprudence document the confrontation and evolution of educational mentalities.

What is more, IEL constitutes the highest source in the hierarchy of the contemporary normativity on education, binding for the Education Law of States Parties to it. Its superiority is based on the normative, representative and argumentative rationality of the political and diplomatic mechanisms of its drafting and approval within the institutional framework of the International Community, following the rules governing international treaty-making by States, through their Delegates and frequently with the participation of other personalities with a high moral and intellectual stature.

As a consequence, it is submitted that IEL should be recognised and studied as a new legal and educational discipline amounting to the science of the principles of legitimacy and quality of education.

Charles Baudelaire wrote in *Ébauche d'un épilogue pour la deuxième édition des Fleurs du Mal* (Draft Epilogue for the Second Edition of The Flowers of Evil, 1861)[13]: *J'ai de chaque chose extrait la quintessence* (From everything I have extracted the quintessence). It could be said that this manuscript develops as an essay of gathering and squeezing fruits of varied origins aiming to extract from them the quintessence of the human right to education.

Notes

1 And a statue of Rousseau in a roundabout at the entrance to Montmorency ('motherland' of *Émile*) was toppled by a drunk car driver in 1994 (another one had been melted down by the Nazis in 1942).

2 Referring to the USA, Michael Imber and Tyll van Geel (2004) wrote: "Educators perform their duties within a network of law [...] woven of constitutional provisions, statutes, regulations, policies, and common law" (p. 1). The Education Law origins go back to the colonial period in Massachusetts, in the 17th century, but "the birth of the field known as education

law or school law" dates back to the Federal Supreme Court's landmark decision in *Brown v. Board of Education of Topeka* (1954) that "is the most important education-related case in the history of the United States, perhaps the most important decision of all time, regardless of the subject matter. [...] Prior to *Brown*, the U.S. Supreme Court had addressed only a handful of education-related cases. However, the Court now resolves at least one school-related case almost every year" (Russo, 2008, p. xxxi) (See "U.S. Supreme Court Cases in Education", pp. 857–866).

3 https://digitallibrary.un.org/record/724469

4 *Un droit international de l'éducation existe, dont nous montrerons certains aspects significatifs.*

[...]

Considéré dans une perspective d'avenir, l'univers éducatif développe un droit de l'éducation à caractère international susceptible d'enrichir les courants positifs de droit international. Un pas supplémentaire dans la voie de ce droit a été accompli par l'adoption de conventions relatives à l'éducation. [...]

Il semble, donc, raisonnable de penser qu'un droit international de l'éducation va se développer à l'avenir si, toutefois, il est axé sur des concepts réalistes et rigoureusement construits.

5 It is found, for example, in two Doctoral Thesis: one submitted to the University of Freiburg, Switzerland, with reference to this author (Gebert, 1996), the other one submitted to the *Ludwig-Maximilians-Universität München*, Germany (Beiter, 2006).

6 For instance, the Master's Program 'Management of International Education' of the Peoples' Friendship University of Russia includes 'International Education Law'. (https://www.masterstudies.com/Master%E2%80%99s-program-Management-of-International-Education/Russia/PFUR/)

7 In December 2017, the International Organisation for the Right to Education and Freedom of Education (OIDEL) published a *Corpus sur le droit à l'éducation/Code of International Education Law*. (http://www.oidel.org/corpus)

The Doctoral Thesis submitted by this author to the University of Paris 8, discussed in 2001, titled *Un nouveau droit à l'éducation – du droit d'éducation à l'éducation de droit* (A new right to education – from the right of education to a rightful education) included a Volume II titled *Recueil d'instruments du Droit International de l'Éducation* (A Collection of International Education Law Instruments).

Jorge Miranda (2014) agrees: "There is an International Education Law, as there is an International Labour Law, an International Health Law, or an International Environment Law" (p. 9). Or an International Law of Culture as a new branch of International Law that "refers to the whole rules of international law that apply to cultural sector" (Mainetti, 2014, p. 220). Or still an International Biomedical Law, whose origins date back to the Nuremberg Trials of Nazi physicians and has evolved since the 1990s, "conceived as an *extension of international human rights law in the field of biomedicine*" (Andorno, 2016, pp. 55, 64).

8 https://undocs.org/E/CN.4/1999/49

9 http://ap.ohchr.org/documents/alldocs.aspx?doc_id=2360

10 UNICEF is the acronym for United Nations Children's Fund, as we know.

11 http://www.un.org/en/ga/search/view_doc.asp?symbol=E/CN.4/SR.9

12 https://www.ohchr.org/EN/ProfessionalInterest/Pages/RightAndResponsibility.aspx

13 http://www.public-domain-poetry.com/charles-baudelaire/draft-epilogue-for-the-second-edition-of-les-fleurs-du-mal-9090

References

Andorno, R. (2016). Droits de l'homme et bioéthique: une alliance naturelle. *Annuaire International des Droits de l'Homme, VIII*, 53–66. Retrieved December 2018, from https://www.academia.edu/24761788/Droits_de_lhomme_et_bio%C3%A9thique._Une_alliance_naturelle

Aristotle. (2000). *Politics* (Translated by Benjamin Jowett, with Introduction, Analysis and Index by H. W. C. Davis). Dover Publications, Inc. https://socialsciences.mcmaster.ca/econ/ugcm/3ll3/aristotle/Politics.pdf

Beiter, K. D. (2006). *The protection of the Right to Education by international law – Including a systematic analysis of Article 13 of the International Covenant on Economic, Social and Cultural Rights*. Martinus Nijhoff Publishers, International Studies in Human Rights, Volume 82.

Cassin, R. (1967). Vingt ans après la Déclaration universelle – 'Liberté et égalité', *Revue de la Commission Internationale des Juristes (Numéro spécial: 1968 – Année internationale des droits de l'homme, Première partie), VIII*(2), 1–17.

Claparède, E. (1931). *L'éducation fonctionnelle*. Delachaux et Niestlé.

Cunningham, D. J. (1987). Outline of an education semiotic. *The American Journal of Semiotics, 5*(2), 201–216.

Derathé, R. (1964). L'homme selon Rousseau. In AAVV (Ed.), *Pensée de Rousseau* (pp. 109–124) (Points, Vol. 168). Seuil.

Dolto, F. (1985). *La cause des enfants*. Éditions Robert Laffont.

Eisemann, P. M. (2007). Introduction (to Panel 5 – Fostering access to education and knowledge). In *Standard-setting in UNESCO – Volume I: Normative action in education, science and culture. Essays in commemoration of the sixtieth anniversary of UNESCO*. UNESCO Publishing/Martinus Nijhoff Publishers.

Elvin, L. (1972). Education. In AAVV (Ed.), *In the minds of men – UNESCO: 1946 to 1971* (pp. 53–67). UNESCO/PUF. https://unesdoc.unesco.org/search/0576314b-6646-43ba-afc1-a4b19e9431e5

Faure, E. et al. (1972). *Learning to be: The world of education today and tomorrow*. UNESCO and George G. Harrap & Co. Ltd. http://unesdoc.unesco.org/images/0000/000018/001801e.pdf

Gebert, P. (1996). *Das Recht auf Bildung nach Art. 13 des UNO-Paktes über wirtschaftliche, soziale und kulturelle Rechte – und seine Auswirkungen auf das schweizerische Bildungswesen – Dissertation – zur Eerlangung der Würde eines Doktors beider Rechte vorgelegt der Rechtswissenschaftlichen Fakultät der Universität Freiburg in der Schweiz* [The right to education according to the UN International Covenant on the Economic, Social and Cultural Rights – and its outcomes in the Switzerland's system of education]. University Dissertation. Freiburg (Schweiz).

Imber, M., & Geel, T. (2004). *Education law*. Lawrence Erlbaum Associates.

Immordino-Yang, M. (2011). Implications of affective and social neuroscience for educational theory. *Educational Philosophy and Theory, 43*(1), 98–103. Retrieved July 2019, from www-bcf.usc.edu/~immordin/papers/Immordino-Yang_EPAT_2011.pdf

Kuhn, Th. S. (1962). *The structure of scientific revolutions* (3rd ed.). The University of Chicago Press.

Mainetti, V. (2014). *La coopération culturelle internationale et l'émergence du droit international de la culture*. doi:10.4399/97888548709565

Miranda, J. (2014). Introdução ao direito da educação: direito português e direito Brasileiro [Introduction to education law: Portuguese and Brazilian law]. *e-Pública: Revista Eletrónica de Direito Público, I*(2), 1–29. Retrieved October 2018, from http://www.scielo.mec.pt/scielo.php?script=sci_arttext&pid=S2183-184X2014000200001

Monteiro, A. R. (2008). Droit International de l'Éducation: Une Discipline Nouvelle? *International Review of Education/Internationale Zeitschrift für Erziehungswissenschaft/Revue internationale l'éducation, 54*, 193–210.

Nartowski, A. (1975). The UNESCO system of protection of the Right to Education (as an example of the most rational model of the protection of human rights by an international organisation). In *Annuaire Polonais de Droit International*, VI, 1974, éd. par Académie Polonaise des Sciences/Institut des Sciences Juridiques (pp. 289–309). Maison d'Édition de l'Académie Polonaise des Sciences.

Planchard, É. (1979). *Introdução à pedagogia*. Coimbra Editora.

Plato. (1997). *Plato – Complete works* (Ed. by J. M. Cooper & D. S. Hutchinson). Hackeht Publishing Company.

Power, C. (2015). *The power of education – Education for all, development, globalisation and UNESCO*. Springer.

Rousseau, J.-J. (1762). *Émile ou de l'éducation* (Chronologie et introduction par Michel Launay). Garnier-Flammarion (1966). http://gallica.bnf.fr/ark:/12148/bpt6k5786957n/f12.image (An English translation: https://oll.libertyfund.org/titles/rousseau-emile-or-education).

Russo, Ch. J. (Ed.). (2008). *Encyclopedia of education law*. Sage Publications.

Smeyers, P. (Ed.). (2018). *International handbook of philosophy of education*. Springer International Handbooks of Education.

Töbes, B. (2015). International health law: an emerging field of public international law. *Indian Journal of International Law, 55*(3), 299–328. Retrieved July 2019, from https://link.springer.com/article/10.1007/s40901-016-0020-9

Töws, H.-J. (1970). Rechtsgrundlagen der Schule. In J. Speck & G. Wehle (Herausg.), *Handbuch Pädagogischer Grundbegriffe – Band II* (pp. 362–366). Kösel-Verlag.

Trapero-Ballestero, A. (1984). Le droit à l'éducation et le droit international. In R.-J. Dupuy (Préparé par), *L'avenir du droit international dans un monde multiculturel – Colloque*, La Haye, 17–19 novembre 1983 (pp. 391–400). Martinus Nijhof Publishers.

UNESCO. (1979). *Conférence Internationale de l'Éducation – Recommandations (1934–1977)*. http://www.unesco.org/education/pdf/34_77_F.PDF

UNESCO. (2015). *Rethinking education: Towards a global common good?* UNESCO Publishing. https://unesdoc.unesco.org/ark:/48223/pf0000232555

CHAPTER 1

Education, Power and Law

Abstract

1. A juridical approach to education as a human right raises a preliminary challenge: How to introduce it into the theorisation of the educational phenomenon?
2. Education is ultimately a form of power. Well, every power of human beings over human beings raises the question of its legitimacy.
3. The question of the legitimacy of education is that of the foundation, sense and control of the power it exerts through the contents and forms of the communication it accomplishes. It amounts to determining the very criterion of the *pedagogic* that is the traditional signifier of all validity claims concerning education. All in all, it is a matter of answering the following bold question: By what right to educate? This is the meta-question of education insofar as it underlies and overdetermines the subsequent ones.
4. Education having been elevated to the human right status – the highest one of the contemporary ethical-juridical normativity – the most legitimate response to the meta-question of its legitimacy should be researched in the right to education.
5. In order to grasp the revolutionary novelty of the right to education, we need first to understand the revolutionary significance of human rights and, in particular, of the rights of the child.

1.1 Fundamental Questions of the Theorisation of Education

Education is a complex theoretical-practical field of research, because the educational phenomenon is multidimensional, multiform, multidisciplinary, crossed by multiple interests and stakes. So much that, in the opinion of Immanuel Kant (1803), “the greatest and most difficult problem to which man can devote himself is the problem of education” (para. 12). Nevertheless, or because of that, “the most useful of all arts, the art of educating men, is still neglected”, as Rousseau (1762a) regretted (Preface).

As an object of study, education has become like an archipelago of islands of intelligibility – the ‘Sciences of Education’ – in need of an island-capital, i.e. a specific discipline whose scope should be *only, but the whole education,* to

 | DOI: 10.1163/9789004462465_002

bring about a *fundamental and global theorisation* of the educational phenomenon consisting of identifying and trying to answer the essential questions it raises. So understood, such a discipline should be, on the one hand, the centre of gravity of the *professional culture* of teachers and other educators to learn to reflect on education, and on the other, a *conceptual grid* of observation and interpretation to learn how to act and react well in every situation. After all, there is nothing more practical than a good theory ...

What name, object and method such a discipline may have?

Knowledge about education has been known by many names throughout its history. Philosophy of Education is perhaps the oldest among the Sciences of Education and continues to be preeminent. It may be, in the opinion of many authors, the discipline most fit to the specific theorisation of the educational phenomenon. However, it lacks the desirable autonomy. Pedagogy – the traditional denomination of the "science and art" of education – is, according to other opinions, the discipline that can best take the role of integrating and articulating the knowledge offered by the Sciences of Education. The term raises reservations, however, given its restrictive etymon and the historical degradation of its uses. Theory of Education is an alternative, without dependence and undesirable connotations, to identify, justify and answer the fundamental questions the educational phenomenon raises, for being the main variables of its dual dimension: scientific/descriptive and normative/prescriptive. In addition, from it can be derived principles of general methodology, i.e. valid for the diverse forms of education. The most appropriate method to such a theorisation is fundamentally philosophical-historical-dialectical, i.e. with an inherent historical dimension and using the dialectical method, typically philosophical.

This conception of a Theory of Education corresponds to the German *Allgemeine Pädagogik* (General Pedagogy), whose inaugural figure was Herbart, in the 19th century. Dietrich Benner (2010) characterised its scope as follows:

> A General Pedagogy [...] should, to deserve its name, draw up a fundamental pedagogical conception [*pädagogische Grundgedanke*] that is general in a double sense. It must claim to be valid for all fields of the pedagogical praxis and be able to be recognized in all areas of the theorisation and research of the Sciences of Education. (p. 5)

In the opinion of Peter Vogel (1998), the task of the *Allgemeine Pädagogik* is to create "a pedagogical identity", both theoretical and professional, for its "demarcation to neighbour disciplines", enabling it to "control of theoretical imports" and the articulation of the different Sciences of Education (p. 173).

What fundamental questions are involved in the educational phenomenon?

The answer is often summarised in the following main interrogations: Why? What for? What? How? Who? From the review of the main historical definitions of education, it may be concluded that they are underpinned by a conceptual trilogy that is structuring for a fundamental and global specific theorisation of education, namely: *Perfectibility* (educability), *Perfection* (ideal or purpose of education), *Perfecting* (educational contents and methods). In light of the history of the pedagogic thought and the lights of science and conscience of our times, it is submitted that the fundamental questions the educational phenomenon raises may be formulated as follows:

- Education as knowledge — *Epistemological question of scientificity*
- Education as necessity — *Anthropological question of educability*
- Education as communication — *Cognitive-methodological question of semioticity*
- Education as a power — *Political-pedagogical question of legitimacy*
- Education as a right — *Right to education*
- Education as a profession — *Teaching profession*

Karl Popper wrote in his 'Preface, 1956' to *Realism and the aim of science* (1983)[1]:

> I think there is only one way to science – or to philosophy, for the matter: to meet a problem, to see its beauty and fall in love with it, to get married to it, and to live with it happily, till death do ye part – unless you should meet another and even more fascinating problem, or unless, indeed, you should obtain a solution. But even if you do obtain a solution, you may then discover to your delight the existence of a whole family of enchanting though perhaps difficult problem children for whose welfare you may work, with a purpose, to the end of your days. (p. 8)

The *problem* of education lies in identifying the *quintessence* to which Herreweghe (1986) referred to:

> It is therefore surprising that the quintessence itself of the phenomenon of education or pedagogy, to which nobody may be insensitive, is so little an object of scientific or even metaphoric study, at the university level, in the countries of the new world, and that concerning those of the old world we must notice that, in recent decades, there has been an almost total abandonment of the problem, to give place to the study of technology, didactics, and methodology. (p. 34)

Considering that the political-pedagogical paradigms are configurations of the society-individual dialectic and that at the heart of the educational phenomenon is the paradox authority-liberty, in order to identify the *quintessence* or *problem* generating *problem children* of education it seems necessary to ask and answer the following double question:

- What is the highest interest at stake in education: that of the Society or the Individual?
- What is the highest value: Authority or Liberty?

Answering requires a dual approach, traditionally absent or marginal in the pedagogical theorisation: education as a *power* and as a *right*. It is a necessary and legitimate approach for the following main reasons:

- Education is a form of power that raises the question of its legitimacy.
- Education has become a human right.

1.2 Education as a Power

1.2.1 *Power*

There are various typologies/taxonomies of power, but the essential distinction is, perhaps, between:

- *Power to* (potentiality, ability, liberty), whose acquisition results in empowerment.
- *Power over* (things, animals, but especially the people), possibly with recourse to means which, if they are coercive, may give rise to resistance.

The predominant conception in the field of the social and political sciences is 'power over', but it always implies 'power to', i.e. sources/bases/resources necessary to exercise it. We may summarise by saying that someone's power depends on the legitimacy with which he/she is vested, or on the force at his/her disposal or on another personal resource.

From the panorama of the phenomenology of power and its theorisation by great thinkers such as Thomas Hobbes, Bertrand Russell, Michel Foucault or Pierre Bourdieu, one may take some conclusions:

1. Power is a profoundly human desire.[2] It is irreducible to its repressive meaning, to power-domination.
2. Power consists of the possibilities and means someone has at his/her disposal to get what she or he wants. Its definitions are more or less unrestricted according to the sources and forms that are taken into account.

There is, however, a very common denominator: *capacity* to produce effects, to be the cause of behaviours of others, to influence, etc.

3. The power phenomenon is a genus with many species. It has, in particular, an individual dimension (anthropological, psychological), a relational dimension (interpersonal, social, international) and a contextual dimension (cultural, temporal, spatial), with many sources and forms. It can be exerted as a means or as an end (but the end becomes means too).
4. Power is a total, ubiquitous, capillary, polymorphic, dynamic, social phenomenon, with a variable substratum: physical, psychological, cultural, religious, political, pedagogical, economic, etc. It is visible, latent or hidden. Social relations are woven by little and great struggles for power, at the inter-individual and collective levels. Power relations are, by their nature, asymmetrical, but asymmetry does not necessarily mean inequality nor always implies resistance, conflict, coercion, force.
5. The main forms of manifestation/expression of power are, perhaps, the following:
   - *Power-force*
   This is the power-domination, with recourse to violence, if necessary.
   - *Power-authority*
   This is the power vested with legitimacy, making it recognised and obeyed.
   - *Power-influence*
   This is the power of those raising admiration and desire of imitation, identification, or of those endowed with communication and persuasion skills.
6. The sources/base/resources of power are individual (attributes, talents, wealth), social (political power, organisational power) or marginal (corruption, delinquency, other crimes).

1.2.2 *Political and Pedagogical Powers*

Political and pedagogical powers are those which most deeply and extensively structure collective and individual lives, being radically consubstantial. Their primacy and interdependence are illustrated by the utopian literature: the social utopias, whatever their inspiration, are always political-pedagogical, i.e. they idealise a 'new society' through a 'new man', and vice-versa. As reads a *Ley Orgánica de Educación Intercultural* of Ecuador (Organic Law of Intercultural Education, 2011),[3] in its recitals, "a revolutionary transformation of Ecuador requires primarily a revolutionary transformation of the education of its children, adolescents, men and women of all ages, lifelong". Nathan Tarcov noted: "Philosophers have been able to stand out in the realms of both educational theory and political theory ever since the two fields of thought first flowed from their common fountainhead, the *Republic* of Plato" (as cited in Aldrich,

1995, p. 65). That is why, as wrote Raphael Lévêque and Francine Best (1969), "the philosophy of education has in common with the political philosophy the theme of power: the pedagogical relation means the *power* of the educator over the person being educated, even if the educator criticises that power, even if he intends to deny it, even if he refuses it" (p. 116).

Power is the essence of politics, whose specific scope is the *res publica* (public things), in the Latin expression, or the *koine sumpheron* (common good), in the Greek expression, as opposed to the *res privata* (private things). Political power is the power by antonomasia, i.e. the power-framework for the exercise of all other ones. It is typically the State's power to legislate and enforce laws, and if necessary, with recourse to use force.

Aristotle (2000) begins its *Politics* by saying:

> Every State is a community of some kind, and every community is established with a view to some good; for mankind always act in order to obtain that which they think good. But, if all communities aim at some good, the State or political community, which is the highest of all, and which embraces all the rest, aims, and in a greater degree than any other, at the highest good. (I.1, 1252a)

Taking up the same idea at the beginning of *The Nicomachean Ethics*, Aristotle (1925) wrote:

> ... since politics uses the rest of the sciences, and since, again, it legislates as to what we are to do and what we are to abstain from, the end of this science must include those of the others, so that this end must be the good for man. (1094b12)

Hobbes wrote at the beginning of Chapter X of *Leviathan* (1651)[4]: "The greatest of human powers is that which is compounded of the powers of most men, united by consent, in one person, natural or civil, that has the use of all their powers depending on his will; such as is the power of a Commonwealth".

However, at the basis of the pyramid of social power is the pedagogical one. Hannah Arendt (1972) noted that "from time out of mind, we have been accustomed in our tradition of political thought to regard the authority of parents over children, of teachers over pupils, as the model by which to understand political authority" (p. 244).[5]

Education is a form of personal and social power over every new-born exercised *naturally* by the family, *formally* in other institutions, especially the school, and *informally* in different contexts of the life of children and adolescents. It may be argued that the power of education is, by its resonance, the deepest and greatest human power for many reasons:

- Education is the most generalised and diffused kind of power of man over man, for being the most 'natural' and accessible: 'to have' a child is enough for exerting power over someone. In this respect, John Holt (1976) remarked: "For a very long time, ever since men formed societies in which some people bossed others, children have fulfilled this very important function. Every adult parent, however lowly or powerless, had at least someone that he could command, threaten and punish" (p. 58).
- School became an operator of the psychological and social reproduction of power relations, of the ideological legitimisation of the political power, of the cultural and technical preparation for exercising other powers. Exercising power is also one of the profound motivations of many education professionals (and other).
- Education is a power the older generations exert over the conscience, the thinking and the destination of the new ones, a power of interior impression of the values, sentiments and senses structuring the human personality. The power of parents over their children is traditionally virtually absolute, unquestionable.
- The ideal of every political power is not domination through brutal violence, but rather the internalisation of submission acquired by inculcation, persuasion, education, as one reads in the classic authors of Political Philosophy. Politically, force is the *ultima ratio* (last resort).
- Those who hold political functions have had an education, which necessarily influences their decisions and behaviour. This correlation was verified by the research of psychoanalyst Alice Miller (1980), who came to the following conclusion: "*every torturer was a victim, once*" (p. 283). In effect: "Among all the major Third Reich personages, I have not found a single one who has not suffered a harsh and severe education" (p. 83), which confirms "the reactive (and not innate) source of the destructive nature of man" (p. 169). Hitler's father's brutality resounds in the history of Nazism.

The most direct sources/bases/resources of the pedagogical power are the statute, knowledge, and personality of educators.

- *Statute*

  It is the legal statute of parents and education professionals, which includes the disciplinary power, the power to assess learning in school, the power of rewarding.
- *Knowledge*

  It is the expertise of the education professionals, without disregard for the educational capacity of parents.

– *Personality*
  It is what makes parents and other educators potentially the most influential adults in the lives of children, adolescents and young.

Well, every power of human beings over human beings raises the question of its legitimacy. As noted by the Constitutional Court of Colombia (*Case T-065/93*),[6] "all types of social domination should be constitutionalised, not only that which has its origin in the State".

1.3 Meta-Question of the Legitimacy of Education

1.3.1 *Political Legitimacy*

The legitimacy question is "the terrible question of the limits to be imposed to the powers of man over man" (Ferry, 1990, p. 16). Russell (1938) called it "the problem of the taming of power" that is "a very ancient one" and "has not yet been solved" (pp. 224, 225).

Etymologically, legitimate means 'according to Law' (*Lex,* in Latin), an obvious meaning in the English term 'lawful' and the German term *rechtsmäßig.* Rousseau (1762b) wrote at the beginning of Chapter 3 of the Book 1 of the *Social Contract:* "The strongest is never strong enough to be always the master unless he transforms strength into right, and obedience into duty", but "force does not create right and […] we are obliged to obey only to legitimate powers".

The core of the question of the legitimacy of power concerns the dominant value – the Society or the Individual? – allowing to distinguish two historical paradigms (see Dumont, 1983): the holistic paradigm, when the good of the Society prevails over the good of the Individual, and the individualistic paradigm, when the *Individual* becomes the supreme value. The USA Supreme Court evoked the holistic paradigm, illustrated by Plato's *Republic,* inspired by Sparta's regime, in *Case Meyer v. State of Nebraska, 262 U. S. 390 (1923)*[7]:

> In order to submerge the individual and develop ideal citizens, Sparta assembled the males at seven into barracks and entrusted their subsequent education and training to official guardians. Although such measures have been deliberately approved by men of great genius, their ideas touching the relation between individual and state were wholly different from those upon which our institutions rest;

Piaget (1998) referred to it when he said in a conference addressed to the 28th Swiss Congress of Elementary Teachers, in Bern (Switzerland), 1944:

> Sociology teaches us that individual liberty is a value the appearance of which was very late. Societies called "primitives" rest almost entirely in the subordination of younger generations to the "Ancients" and the general submission, both of olds and younger, to the tradition and the will of the ancestors. In the great eastern societies and ancient societies that knew the "patriarchy", children remained minors so far as the *pater familias* [father] was alive. In the political field, the multiple kinds of social coercions exerted, for centuries and even millenniums, an infinite variety of intellectual, moral and legal pressures over the conscience and the behaviour of individuals. Social life imposed for long-time to the human person compulsory conformism and blind and heteronomous submission. (p. 161)

The Greek language did not even have a word to mean the individual. Those who tried to assert their individuality were called *idiótes* (literally: idiot, without education). The Latin word *individuus* (individual) is the synonym of the Greek term *atoms* (atom), which means an inseparable part of a whole. Only in the Renaissance the term 'individual' has begun to be used.

The holistic paradigm prevailed in Western culture, *de jure* and *de facto* (by the Law and in fact), until modern times. The problematisation of the legitimacy of the political power emerged in the historical, cultural, religious, scientific, philosophical, legal and political context of the European Modernity. This refers primarily to the historical upheaval originated in the Renaissance, at the end of the 15th century and the beginning of the 16th century, due to manifold and interactive factors. Following to Alain Renaut (2002), it consisted in a subversion of the representation of Man by the Humanism of the Italian *Quattrocento* (15th century), of which an influential expression was Pico della Mirandola *Oratio De hominis Dignitate* (1486) (p. 155).

> In modernity, a new experience of time takes shape. This time can no longer be grasped as a 'period' or 'era'. Rather, the terms 'modern' and 'modernity' describe a particular mode of change that concerns all aspects of human life. Basically, modernity describes an experience of time that questions the legitimacy of prior or traditional life forms. The theological idea of 'ordo', i.e. a creational order that grants every being its place in the world, is delegitimized. This development has also to be seen in relation to the religious wars, the rise of capitalism and industrialization, as well as the scientific exploration and subjection of nature in early stages of the modern era. (Christiane Thompson, in Smeyers, 2018, p. 533)

In the opinion of Luc Ferry (1990), here is "the central problem of modernity in general: How to found the objectivity in subjectivity, the transcendence in immanence? In other words: How to think the (social, of course, but not only) ties in a society that intends to start from individuals to rebuild the collective?" (p. 42).

In the 17th and 18th centuries, the contractualistic Political Philosophy has re-founded the legitimacy of the political power on the individuals' will – the General Will – i.e. on the values of liberty and equality, giving rise to a process of subjectivation, autonomisation, emancipation, breaking the traditional holistic framework. In the opinion of Renaut (2004), it has meant, in an "age dominated by the values of the rationalism and the democracy [...] the recognition of the individual freedom as the sacred value" (pp. 25, 60). The argumentative rationality has become the political rationality *par excellence*, the democratic rationality, the source of the legitimacy of the exercise of the authority necessary for living together.

Power and authority are terms generally used as synonyms, but a distinction may be made.

Arend observed that authority is a term of Roman origin (without a Greek equivalent): the substantive *auctoritas* stems from the verb *augere* that means to increase. Authority is a *supplement* increasing power (*potestas*). The difference lies in the legitimacy that transforms the second into the first one, i.e. in the *recognition* of the right to exercise power and the *consent* of the duty to obey. Authority is, therefore, a power that may be exercised without the need for repression or persuasion, without constraints or arguments. There is not authority without power, but there are powers without authority.

We may highlight three kinds of authority:

- *Social authority*
  This is the authority of someone with the legitimacy or right to exercise the power inherent in performing a function ('figures' of such authority are, for instance, a Minister, a policeman, a father).
- *Expert authority*
  This is the authority of someone who stands up as an expert in a field of theoretical or practical knowledge ('to be an authority in ...').
- *Moral authority*
  This is the authority of someone humanly exemplary ('to have authority to ...').

In Saint-Exupéry's *The Little Prince,*[8] there is a king governing asteroid 325 who fundamentally insisted "that his authority should be respected. He tolerated no disobedience. He was an absolute monarch. But, because he was a very good man, he made his orders reasonable". As the lamplighter of the fifth planet would say: "There is nothing to understand [...]. Orders are orders". However: "That is the tragedy! From year to year, the planet has turned more rapidly, and the orders have not been changed!"

That is the *tragedy* of the pedagogical legitimacy.

1.3.2 *Pedagogical Legitimacy*

The problematisation of the traditional absolute power of the *pater familias* (father) and the legitimacy of education has emerged within the historical context of the modern problematisation of the divine origin of the monarchical power. Following the doctrine of the Catholic Church, "all power comes from God" (Saint Paul), which still inspires the *Politique tirée des propres paroles de l'Écriture Sainte* (Politics Drawn from the Very Words of Holy Scripture) by Bossuet, published posthumously in 1709. It was fought by the contractualist Political Philosophy, notably by Rousseau.

> For Rousseau, the law can only emanate from the political community itself, the only sovereign and the only one capable of expressing a general will (Social Contract, 1762). [...]
>
> The new legislative ideal sanctifies the law and culminates in the idea of code [...] with the affirmation of this principle of legality that underlies the modern conception of the Rule of Law. (Delia, 2019, pp. 28, 29)

The legitimacy of education was not at all questioned in pre-modern societies, for two main reasons:
- They were holistic societies, i.e. their dominant value was, as already noted, the Society, the collective interest, and not the Individual.
- Up to the 16th–17th centuries, education was not, in general, a very distinct social activity, with specific problems (see Ariès, 1960).

Within the modern philosophical-political framework of liberty and equality, the naturalist and sociologist assumptions of education could not keep unquestioned, for these main reasons:
- The asymmetry inherent to the educational relation favours abuses of power, and the history of education testifies how the violence of its methods is a long chapter of the history of violence and its reproduction among human beings.
- Education has been the most arbitrary, unpunished and devastating kind of power.

The history of the problematisation of the legitimacy of educational power is an aspect of the history of the *liberation of children* (Renaut, 2002), in the context of Modernity. The process of modernising their status has been, however, very slow. Renaut highlighted the contributions of Erasmus, Locke, and Rousseau.

In Erasmus, we find "a new idea of humanity, another representation of the childhood and an unprecedented conception of education", as well as a call for "moderating the power of the father" (pp. 165, 171).

Jean Bodin, in *Les Six Livres de la République* (The Six Books of the Republic, 1567), still sees in the *patria potestas* (power of the father) the model of the political power and considers that parents should keep an absolute power over their children. In the following century, Hobbes thinks that the *patria potestas* should be limited by the right to life of children. In the same century, Locke went much further, by considering, following Renaut, that "the power of parents and their rights over the child, which become only provisional and temporary, are nothing else, in fact, then the entire duties they have towards it: not only the duty to keep its life but also to educate it for the liberty as autonomy", because "they are no more in no way at all seen as owners of their children" (p. 193).

Rousseau, in his *Discourse on Inequality* (Second Discourse), was one of the three great authors (with Kant and Johan G. Fichte) who most profoundly elaborated on the idea of the perfectibility or educability inherent in the conception of the human dignity according to Pico della Mirandola. It was introduced into the pedagogical terminology by Herbart (*Bildsamkeit*: educability). Rousseau went no further than Locke concerning "all that relates to the decomposition of the paternal authority" (p. 250), but took a "contractual approach to the conjugal tie" (p. 267) where the relation to childhood is thought and practised as a dialectic of equality and difference taking into account so much its humanity as its specificity. "Leave childhood to ripen in your children" (Rousseau, 1762a, p. 68) is a formula that "revolutionises the perception of the relationship between childhood and adulthood", amounting to a "Copernican revolution (in the sense of a change of point of view or perspective on the object)" (Renaut, 2002, pp. 289, 290). Renaut concluded:

> By liberating progressively the human beings from their traditional constraints, the modernity imprinted to the relationships of power or authority a contractual dimension, according to which there is tendentially no more power that could be exercised, nowadays, without trying to get the recognition or adhesion from those over who it is exerted. […] In this sense, the liberation of children amounts to a veritable victory of the civilisation and of the Law over the barbarity and the oppression. (p. 387)

Nevertheless, the infantile identity is a paradoxical one: "the child is already a human being, but without being jet a complete being in its humanity, that is to say as liberty" (p. 281). Because of that, the relationship with the child "may not be thought other than a relationship both of equality and inequality. [...] In this sense, the dynamic of subjectivation that drove the modernisation of the childhood's status could not become accomplished without making the child itself, as a human being, a holder of rights limiting the possibility to treat it otherwise" (pp. 28, 317). This concerns education in particular.

The history of the evolution of the status of the child is closely related to the rising of the modern pedagogic thought. In effect, "the pre-humanist transformation [in the Italian *Quatroccento*] of the humanity idea questioned the representation of the education" (p. 163), having as a consequence that "the institution of the human could no more be a marginal thing but, on the contrary, should be placed at the centre of the new culture" (p. 174). Education has thus become, more and more, one of the most important issues of Modernity and its logic of liberation. By thinking the human perfectibility or educability within the modern ethical-legal framework of the liberty and equality of every human being, the problem of the legitimacy of education could not be avoided, which is "the modern problem of the legitimacy of the exercise of the pedagogical power" (*das moderne Problem der Legitimität pädagogischer Gewaltausübung*) (Benner, 2010, p. 217). It follows some outstanding moments and authors of this modern chapter of the History of Education:

- Locke questioned the legitimacy of education in *The Second Treatise of Civil Government* (1690), noted Renaut (2002): "if any man, as such, is free since his birth, how to justify his submission, even provisional, to the paternal authority?" (p. 190).
- Rousseau – for whom "the political problem and that of education are [...] deeply analogous" (p. 297) – was probably the first one to raise the question of the legitimacy of education, at least in so coherent and radical terms, when he wrote at the beginning of Chapter IV of Book I of the *Social Contract:* "Since no man has a natural authority over his fellow, and force creates no right, we must conclude that conventions form the basis of all legitimate authority among men". Consequently, as stated in Book II of *Émile*: "No one, not even its father, has the right to bid the child do what is of no use to him" (Rousseau, 1762a, p. 57). According to Renaut (2002): "The last foundation of the perspective on childhood and education adopted by Rousseau [...] is entirely included in his redefinition of humankind in terms of perfectibility and liberty" (p. 239).
- Kant (1803) put clearly the question of the legitimacy of education when he said: "One of the greatest problems of education is how to reconcile submission by legitimate compulsion with the ability to use one's freedom. As compulsion is necessary! How to cultivate freedom by means of compulsion?".[9]

- Shortly after, Herbart – Kant's successor in the Chair of Pedagogy at the University of Königsberg (Germany) – was concerned with it too, in his *Allgemeine Pädagogik* (General Pedagogy, 1806), in connection with the "government of children" (*Kinderregierung*).
- In the mid-20th century, René Hubert (1946) wrote in his *Traité de Pédagogie Génerale* (Treaty on General Pedagogy):

> The problem of the sociological antinomy is so clearly posed: there is no way other than society to reach, through education, the supreme values of civilisation and spirituality, and education does not reach them unless it rises up the particular society giving it. Such is, maybe, the most terrible problem the philosophy of education has to solve. (pp. 47, 49)

- The question of the legitimacy of education was exceptionally clearly formulated in another *Pédagogie Génerale* (General Pedagogy):

> We face now the question of the legitimacy of our action. By what right do we intervene in the present and future life of a human being? [...]
>
> A teacher who did not ask these questions and contented himself with teaching the curricular contents, because they are imposed, would not be a good educator, even so he endless worries about the methods and the processes. Here, the "how" is subordinated to the "why". (Leif & Rustin, 1970, pp. 24, 129)

The authors concluded that, although education concerns both the society and the individual, it is "in the human person that lies, in the end, the supreme, irreducible value, from which derives that of society, who comes in second place" (p. 132). As a consequence: "The educator represents more than the Society; he or she represents Humanity [...]. We have no more to ask ourselves the question of the legitimacy of our intervention: to take action is not only a right; it is a duty" (p. 141).

Summing up, following to Renaut (2002):

> ... we have to agree that one of the most complex problems of the contemporary societies is that of knowing how to live together when the power ceased being an authority referring to a source transcending individuals. More explicitly: how to keep or give again authority to powers that are necessary to provide the coexistence conditions, but have to be exercised, nowadays, more and more, as equals, between human beings proclaimed free and equal in rights? [...] In its two registers (that of the school, that

> of the family), it is just education that goes further, nowadays, in the most surprising way, into the data of this fundamental problem. (pp. 19, 20)

Indeed, the education field, particularly the family bastion, remains one of the most resistant to the modern logic of contractualising and juridifying power relations. However, as particular as the power relations inherent in education may be, in the family or in school, to consider that education could remain "or become again an island or a 'sanctuary' of the traditional universe, in a world where the values of equality and liberty assert themselves everywhere, constitutes, in fact, a singular illusion" (Renaut, 2004, p. 11).

Therefore, modernising education should mean, according to Renaut, "thinking the family and school relations according to the model of the democratic relation itself" (p. 153). It is the "difficult question of knowing to what extent the contractual re-foundation of the education power and its practices is compatible with the realities of the familial and school relations" (p. 175). We are confronted with an *aporia*: to assure the protection of the child, for being a child, while cultivating his/her autonomy, for being a person. According to the author, the key to its resolution could be the Convention on the Rights of the Child (UN, 1989), a legal international instrument "that marks a very reversal in the representation of the child, whose rights are recognised" (p. 178).

1.4 By What Right to Educate?

Educability is the primordial question of the education theorisation, but the central one has been that of the aims guiding the institutions, programmes and methods of education. The most radical, however, concerns its legitimacy, that is the question of the foundation, sense, and control of the power the education exerts through the contents and forms of the communication it accomplishes. It is the *meta-question* of education insofar as it underlies and overdetermines the subsequent ones. It is such a radical question that it has been generally *unthinkable*. For the traditional pedagogical mindset, educating is so *natural* that the question of the legitimacy of education is dissolved in this postulate: (if) education is necessary, (whatever) education is legitimate. It is fallacious reasoning, as it does not distinguish between necessity and legitimacy.

The *meta-question of the legitimacy of education* amounts to determining the very criterion of the *pedagogic* that is the traditional signifier of all validity claims concerning education:

- What is pedagogic?
- Is what is efficient? But what for?

- Is what is useful? But whom for?
- Is what parents, teachers or the Ministry of Education think, say and order? But with what legitimacy?
- By what right some human beings do what they do over other human beings in the name of education?

Boldly put: *By what right to educate?*

Education, having been elevated to *human right* status – the highest one of the contemporary ethical-juridical normativity – the most legitimate response to the meta-question of its legitimacy should be researched in the *right to education.*

In order to grasp the revolutionary novelty of the right to education, we need first to set the scene where it will be focussed, by highlighting the revolutionary significance of human rights and, in particular, of the rights of the child.

We are beginning with human rights – their history, terminology, main concepts, hard issues, revolutionary outcomes, and far-reaching challenges.

Notes

1 https://books.google.pt/books?id=VQh9BoyDBZoC&pg=PA8&lpg=PA8&dq=popper+preface+1956&source=bl&ots=5909hp935L&sig=ACfU3U20VlJVQB7a3QmnM6ClruwybA-INg&hl=pt-PT&sa=X&ved=2ahUKEwj-m6WAuZPiAhXLBGMBHR2zCxoQ6AEwGHoECAYQAQ#v=onepage&q=popper%20preface%201956&f=false

2 "… so sweet a thing is it to command and be obeyed", says the Duke to Sancho in *The ingenious Gentelman Don Quixote of La Mancha.* (http://www.spanisharts.com/books/quijote/2chapter42.htm)
In Spanish: … *por ser dulcísima cosa el mandar y ser obedecido.* (https://cvc.cervantes.es/literatura/clasicos/quijote/edicion/parte2/cap42/default.htm)

3 http://www.lexis.com.ec/wp-content/uploads/2018/07/LI-LEY-ORGANICA-DE-EDUCACION-INTERCULTURAL.pdf

4 http://etext.library.adelaide.edu.au/h/hobbes/thomas/h68l

5 See chapter at: https://thi.ucsc.edu/wp-content/uploads/2016/09/Arendt-Crisis_In_Education-1954.pdf

6 www.corteconstitucional.gov.co/relatoria/1993/T-065-93.htm

7 http://caselaw.lp.findlaw.com/cgi-bin/getcase.pl?court=us&vol=262&invol=390

8 http://www.arvindguptatoys.com/arvindgupta/littleprince.pdf

9 *Eines der größesten Probleme der Erziehung ist, wie man die Unterwerfung unter den gesetzlichen Zwang mit der Fähigkeit, sich seiner Freiheit zu bedienen, vereinigen könne. Denn Zwang ist nötig! Wie kultiviere ich die Freiheit bei dem Zwange?*

References

Aldrich, R. (1995). John Locke (1632–1704). In UNESCO (Ed.), *Penseurs de l'éducation – Volume 3* (pp. 65–82). UNESCO/BIE.

Arendt, H. (1972). *La crise de la culture – Huit exercices de pensée politique* (Trad. de l'anglais sous la direction de Patrick Lévy, les textes datant de 1954, 1956, 1957, 1958, 1960, 1961, 1963, 1967 et 1968). Gallimard.

Ariès, Ph. (1960). *L'enfant et la vie familiale sous l'Ancien Régime.* Seuil.

Aristotle. (1925). *The Nicomachean Ethics* (Translated with an Introduction by David Ross, Revised by J. L. Ackrill and J. O. Urmson). Oxford University Press.

Aristotle. (2000). *Politics* (Translated by Benjamin Jowett, with Introduction, Analysis and Index by H. W. C. Davis). Dover Publications, Incl.

Benner, D. (2010). *Allgemeine Pädagogik – Eine systematisch-problemgeschichtliche Einführung in die Grundstruktur pädagogischen Denkens und Handelns* (6. Aufgabe). Juventa Verlag.

Delia, L. (2019). Un immense désir de justice. *Les Grands Dossiers des Sciences Humains – Les Lumières: Une révolution de la pensée, 56*, septembre–octobre–novembre, 28–31.

Dumont, L. (1983). *Essais sur l'individualisme – Une perspective anthropologique sur l'idéologie moderne.* Éditions du Seuil.

Ferry, L. (1990). *Homo Aestheticus – L'invention du goût à l'âge démocratique.* Grasset.

Herreweghe, V. (1986). *Étude préliminaire sur la nature et l'importance de l'enseignement relatif aux sciences de l'éducation dans les établissements d'enseignement supérieur.* UNESCO, 11-Cahiers sur l'enseignement supérieur.

Holt, J. (1976). *S'évader de l'enfance – Les besoins et les droits des enfants* [Escape from Childhood, trad. de Laurent Jospin]. Payot. Original text: https://archive.org/details/EscapeFromChildhood

Hubert, R. (1946). *Traité de Pédagogie Générale.* PUF.

Kant, I. (1803). *Traité de pédagogie* (tr. de J. Barni, revue et actualisée, Introduction et notes par Pierre-José About). Hachette. Original text: https://de.wikisource.org/wiki/%C3%9Cber_P%C3%A4dagogik (An English translation: https://oll.libertyfund.org/titles/kant-kant-on-education-uber-padagogik).

Leif, J., & Rustin, G. (1970). *Philosophie de l'éducation – Tome 1: Pédagogie Générale.* Librairie Delagrave.

Lévêque, R., & Best, F. (1969). Pour une philosophie de l'éducation. In M. Debesse & G. Mialaret (Sous la direction de), *Traité des sciences pédagogiques – 1. Introduction* (pp. 81–120). PUF.

Miller, A. (1980). *C'est pour ton bien – Racines de la violence dans l'éducation de l'enfant* [*Am Anfang war Erziehung*] (Trad. de Jeanne Etoré). Éditions Aubier Montaigne.

Piaget, J. (1998). *De la Pédagogie* (Introduction de Silvia Parrat-Dayan et Anastasia Tryphon). Éditions Odile Jacob.

Renaut, A. (2002). *La libération des enfants – Contribution philosophique à une histoire de l'enfance.* Calmann-Lévy.

Renaut, A. (2004). *La fin de l'autorité.* Flammarion.

Rousseau, J.-J. (1762a). *Émile ou de l'éducation* (Chronologie et introduction par Michel Launay). Garnier-Flammarion. http://gallica.bnf.fr/ark:/12148/bpt6k5786957n/f12.image (An English translation: https://oll.libertyfund.org/titles/rousseau-emile-or-education).

Rousseau, J.-J. (1762b). *Du contrat social* (Édition établie par Pierre Burgelin). GF-Flammarion. https://www.rousseauonline.ch/pdf/rousseauonline-0004.pdf (An English translation: https://www.earlymoderntexts.com/assets/pdfs/rousseau1762.pdf)

Russell, B. (1938). *Power – A new social analysis*. Routledge.

Smeyers, P. (Ed.). (2018). *International handbook of philosophy of education*. Springer International Handbooks of Education.

Vogel, P. (1998). Stichwort: Allgemeine Pädagogik. *Zeitschrift für Erziehungswissenschaft*, *1*(2), 157–180.

CHAPTER 2

Human Rights

Abstract

1. Every community needs rules to regulate living together. Law is a social regulatory device that has become the most powerful driver of Civilisation. Its superior expression are human rights.
2. The human rights sentiment and ideal are as ancient and cross-cultural as human suffering and ideals, but the term and concept have appeared and been elaborated only in modern times.
3. The belief in the correlation between what is 'right' and what is 'natural' underlies the 'Natural Law' and 'natural rights' ideas, which were groundbreaking insights in the genealogy of the human rights concept.
4. International Law does not provide a definition of 'human rights'. Following the most elementary and common one, human rights are rights recognised to every human being simply because of being a member of the human species. Therefore, they are universal, by definition, and are qualified as "equal and inalienable".
5. The *Corpus Juris* (Body of Law) of International Human Rights Law includes the International Bill of Human Rights, other seven universal core human rights treaties and some hundreds of legal instruments, conventional or declaratory, with general, specific or categorical content, and universal or regional in scope.
6. Determining the structure and normative content of a human right amounts to answering the following interrogations: Who holds the right (entitlement: right-holder)? In what does it consist (object: to what is it a right)? Who has the corresponding obligations (exigibility/opposability: duty-bearers)?
7. The specificity of each right is essentially determined by its object, the content of which may be described as a normative complex composed of three layers, as it were: minimum content, full content and expanded content, to which correspond as many States' obligations levels.
8. The protection of human rights displays two faces: one turned to the inside, to national legal orders, the other one turned to the outside, to International Law. There are international systems/regimes for the protection of human rights at the universal and regional levels. Also, there are tens of thousands of Non-Governmental Organisations, international and national, devoted to human rights.
9. As a World Court of Human Rights is still lacking, there is no veritable Case Law on human rights at the universal level, but there are regional Courts (European,

 | DOI: 10.1163/9789004462465_003

American, African). Their jurisprudence contributes, to a large extent, to define and develop the normative content of human rights.

10. The history of human rights is the history of the invention of the Human Being by human beings. Of the revelation of Human Being in human beings. The Human Being is the ethical subject transcending the empirical subjects – ethnic, cultural, national, social, familial, psychological and other ones – with their roots, memberships, cradles, situations and other particularities.

11. Human rights constitute an Ethics because their source and sense are the worth and dignity of the human person, whose absolute primacy they consecrate. Here is the most profound and transcendent significance of the Ethics of Human Rights: The Human Being should be a *God* for human beings. His temple *sanctum sanctorum* (the most sacred place) is Human Dignity.

12. Human Dignity is the most brilliant star in the human rights firmament, the highest lighthouse in the ocean of the human species' indefinite destiny. It lies at the heart of Human Rights Philosophy and is the spinal column of International Human Rights Law, the supreme value of a New Constitutionalism, the axiological core of the Rule of Law, the embryo of a Law of Humanity. The Human Dignity Principle may be considered as the quintessence of Civilization.

13. While human dignity is said to be the source of human rights, it remains, paradoxically, a foundation lacking to be founded … It is submitted that:
    - *Human dignity is the principle and the sense of human rights*
    - *Human dignity hallmarks the belonging to the human species*
    - *Human dignity is an ethical invention with genetic foundation*
    - *Human dignity consists in perfectibility calling for perfecting*
    - *Human dignity is inviolable and indisposable*
    - *Human dignity is vulnerable and variable*

    Summing up: Human dignity is a *natural attribute*, a *moral status* and a *personal responsibility*.

14. The Ethics of Human Rights is an Ethics of the Recognition of Human Dignity as a Principle-Right to have Rights – rights of a living human being – which are fundamentally the Rights-Principles of Liberty, Equality, Diversity, with the consequent Responsibility. It has become the Ethics of Humanity, the Common Temple of the secular faith of the Rule of Law. And as human dignity will never be definitively protected and enhanced, the Human Rights Temple is an endless building, open to the Possible …

15. Revolution is a term frequent in human rights literature. The Revolution of Human Rights may be summarised as follows:
    - Consecration of the Individual as the highest ethical-juridical value
    - Transformation of the International Law and renovation of the Constitutional Law

   - Reconstruction of the Rule of Law
   - Inception of a Law of Humanity
16. We should be realistic without becoming pessimistic: The Revolution of Human Rights is an everyday individual, collective, endless struggle …

2.1 Origins

Every community and society need rules, written or not, to make possible the living together, according to common needs, interests and values. This is the meaning of the Latin saying, *Ubi societas, ibi jus* (Where there is society, there is Law).

Law is a social regulatory device. The legal rule is general and abstract, defending, permitting, commanding, rewarding or punishing. Its mandatory and sanctionatory nature is what distinguishes a legal rule from a moral rule.

Law has been expanding as a normative network framing the international, national and individual life, becoming the most powerful driver of Civilisation. In the contemporary world, there is no other alternative for the peaceful coexistence of cultures, peoples and the whole human diversity. The superior expression of the civilisational power of Law are human rights.

René Maheu, UNESCO's Director-General from 1962 to 1974, wrote: "Right – and the law which embodies it – represent the dialectic process whereby man strives towards a better state of his own devising", and "the mere notion of human rights introduces at the very centre of history the principle of the indefinite advancement of man by man's own efforts" (Maheu, 1972, p. 284). This is a dense and beautiful vision of Law and the human rights' ethical scope.[1]

The term 'human rights' was coined only in modern times, but the idea is not born *ex nihilo* during the European 18th century, with thinkers such as Jean-Jacques Rousseau, Thomas Paine, Immanuel Kant and others, in the aftermath of the groundbreaking elaborations of such figures as Francisco de Vitoria, Francisco Suárez, Hugo Grotius, Thomas Hobbes, Samuel von Pufendorf, John Locke. The human rights sentiment and ideal are as ancient and cross-cultural as human suffering and ideals. They have emerged slowly like the dawn, from the night of times, in East and West, in South and North, as illustrated by the anthology *Birthright of Man*, published by UNESCO in the context of the 20th anniversary of the Universal Declaration of Human Rights (UDHR) (Hersch, 1968), which contains more than 1,100 fragments of a variety of documents – proverbs, songs, literature, legislation, political treatises, religious texts, etc.

– of every latitude and longitude, dated from 3,000 BC to 1948. They testify that human rights have juridified a demand that is, following Paul Ricoeur:

> ... older than any philosophical formulation [...]. At every age and in every culture, a complaint, a cry, a proverb, a song, a tale, a treaty of wisdom said the message: if the human rights concept is not universal, the fact remains that all human beings, in all cultures, feel the need, the expectation, the sense of these rights. The demand has always been that 'something is due to the human being only for being human'. (in Ponton, 1990, p. 20)

The human rights history is thus a tapestry woven with many lines and many colours by many artisans, resounding cries and impregnated with the blood of countless victims of cruelties and injustices. Frequently mentioned historical landmarks of their millennial conquest are the following ones:
- Code of Hammurabi (Babylon, 18th century BC)
- Biblical Decalogue (13th century BC)
- Cyrus Charter (Persia, 6th century BC)
- Constitution of Medina (622)
- Magna Carta or The Great Charter of Liberties of England (1215)
- Petition of Rights (England, 1628)
- Habeas Corpus Act (England, 1679)
- Bill of Rights (England, 1689)

In Edward D. Bates (2010) view, if the history of human rights begins with the idea that every human being possesses 'natural rights', their origins go back to the Greek Stoicism. If it has begun with the first measures to protecting individuals against political power, they are born with the Magna Carta (1215). "The enduring significance of the Magna Carta, and other similar documents of this age, for the history of human rights, lies in the fact that it has come to be seen as a starting point – the beginning of the limitation of the absolute and arbitrary power of the sovereign" (p. 19).

We may distinguish three main stages in the modern and contemporary history of human rights:
- Philosophical elaboration of the 'natural rights' idea in 17th–18th centuries
- Declarations of 'rights of man' and their constitutionalisation in 18th–20th centuries
- Internationalisation and codification of human rights after World War II

2.2 Concept

The Latin word *jus* means Law, i.e. a normative system with sanctions attached.

It seems that it was by the mid-18th century that was first adjoined *subiectivum* to *jus* in order to distinguish *jus* in the subjective sense of right, i.e. *facultas* or *potestas* (faculty or power), from *jus* in the objective sense of Law (*Lex*), i.e. a system of legal norms (*complexus legum*).

However, as Thomas Mautner (2013) explains, in English 'subjective right' is tautological, a solecism. In effect, there are two English terms to distinguish between 'Law' or legal system, and 'right' or entitlement, unlike most European languages that use the same word to denote both senses. For example: *'objektives/subjektives' Recht* (in German), *Droit 'objectif/subjectif'* (in French), *Diritto 'oggettivo/soggettivo'* (in Italian), *Derecho 'objetivo/subjetivo'* (in Spanish), *Direito 'objectivo/subjectivo'* (in Portuguese), etc.

'Right' is a word used in a variety of senses, however, sometimes confusing. There are moral and legal rights. To hold a legal right means having a prerogative, i.e. a faculty/power to act or claim, and that other(s) is under the corresponding obligation(s), either negative (not acting against) or positive (doing something).

Human rights "are at the heart of the very idea of rights" (Campbell, 2006, p. 39). Their conceptual origins go back to the inception of *Natural Law* and *natural rights*.

The belief in the correspondence between what is 'right' and what is 'natural' underlies the 'Natural Law' and 'natural rights' ideas, which were groundbreaking insights in the genealogy of the human rights concept.

In Western culture, Natural Law or 'Law of Nature' (*jus natural* or *lex naturalis*, in Latin) developed from the Greek-Roman Philosophy, notably Stoicism, the Roman juridical thought, and the Christian doctrine. The first Greek philosophers, in particular Socrates, Plato and Aristotle, introduced the distinction between *φύσις* (nature) and *νόμος* (norm, customary or conventional). The Stoic Philosophy grounded the equality of human beings in their common faculty of reason. Roman Law distinguished *jus naturale* (Natural Law) and *jus civile* (Civil Law). The Christian doctrine brought a new sense of the equal moral status of all human beings as creatures of God.

The most preeminent Catholic thinker of Natural Law was St. Thomas Aquinas (13th century), who divided laws into divine, natural and human: *divine laws* are those written in the Bible and conveyed by the Catholic Church doctrine; *natural laws* are those which are inscribed in physical and human nature, being discoverable through the use of reason; *human-made laws* are written or positive laws, varying from people to people and changing over time. Natural

Law is, therefore, inherent in the whole Universe or *Cosmos* (*lex rationis*). It includes principles of good and evil, right and wrong, against which all moral and legal norms are to be assessed. Being based on nature, not on culture or customs, Natural Law is a Higher Law, permanent, trans-historical, trans-cultural, encompassing eternal and universal principles of justice. All human beings, because they are endowed with the faculty of reason, can access and live by its principles. Nevertheless, the knowledge of Natural Law's commands depends upon the evolving moral conscience and cultural contexts. They are not all evident in every era for everybody. Only the first principles of morality are immutable and within everyone's reach. Following the Thomistic conception, the most basic command regards the preservation of life (and the reproduction of it). The most general one says: "Good is to be done and pursued, and evil is to be avoided". From it, others may be derived. Consequently, Natural Law is both eternal-immutable and historical-relative. Its relativity explains historical misconceptions and wrongdoings.

During the 17th century, Natural Law theories began to secularise, i.e. to be given an immanent (not divine) foundation.

'Natural rights' are an offspring of Natural Law. When did their claim really emerge?

This is a debated issue. Following Tom Campbell (2006): "Rights talk emerged in the mediaeval period with the notion of natural rights, a by-product of the idea of natural law" (p. 5). Andrew Fagan (2005) remarked: "Many attempts have been made to identify the 'first' theorist of human or natural rights in the Middle Ages". In his opinion:

> It is perhaps best to examine the development of the theory of human rights as an incremental process. Various thinkers contributed important dimensions to its history without necessarily enunciating the idea in its final form or perhaps even appreciating the wider significance of their particular contributions.

In the opinion of James Griffin (2008), although the Latin word *jus* (Law) emerged with the meaning of subjective right during the 12th and 13th centuries, the term 'natural right' only in the 17th and 18th centuries became current (p. 9). The use of the expression *droits de l'homme* (human rights), instead of *droits naturels* (natural rights), began in the 1760s, in France. The *Déclaration des droits de l'homme et du citoyen* (Declaration of the Rights of Man and the Citizen, 1789)[2] still refers to the "*droits naturels, inaliénables et sacrés de l'homme*" (Preamble), "*droits naturels et imprescriptibles de l'homme*" (Article II), "*droits naturels de chaque homme*" (Article IV). The translation 'rights of man' entered the English language too. 'Human rights' is a term first used perhaps by Thomas Paine in his translation of the 1789 French Declaration. At the end of the 18th century, the concept of 'human right' had acquired its contemporary meaning.

However, the Natural Law idea and the term natural/human rights eclipsed, to a great extent, during the 19th century, for many reasons, in particular, because of the rise of the legal positivism that became dominant until the mid-20th century. According to it, Morals and Law ought to be kept separate. Law is only the one written or *posited* by State. It is the Law as it is, not the Law as it should be.

Whether there is a Natural (Higher) Law, to which all written, positive Law should conform to be legitimate and obeyed – this remains a central problem of the Philosophy of Law. The tension between Natural Law and Positive Law is probably insoluble. Natural Law is like "a corpse we never end to re-bury" (Henri Batiffol, as cited in Goyard-Fabre, 1988, p. 9), "a boat within which a certain conception of justice crossed the times, adapting to the demands of each era" (Tóth, 1972, p. 71). It was invoked, for instance, by Judge Kōtarō Tanaka of the International Court of Justice in his famous Dissent Opinion relating to the *Case Ethiopia v. South Africa*, in 1966[3]: "If a law exists independently of the will of the State and, accordingly, cannot be abolished or modified even by its Constitution, because it is deeply rooted in the conscience of mankind and any reasonable man, it may be called 'natural law' in contrast to 'positive law'" (p. 298).

That is why the revival of the natural/human rights claim has begun slowly after World War I and has vigorously innervated International Law in the wake of the "barbarous acts which have outraged the conscience of mankind", as reads the UDHR (second preambular paragraph).

International Law does not provide a definition of 'human rights'. They are said to be inherent in the 'human dignity', but there is no definition of human dignity either. Following the most elementary and common definition, human rights are rights recognised to every human being simply because of being a member of the human species. They are, therefore, universal, by definition, and are qualified as "equal and inalienable".

- *Equal*, because they are inherent to every human being, without any discrimination, anywhere in the world, in whatever circumstances.
- *Inalienable*, because they are never lost, i.e. they cannot be forcibly taken away (by expropriation) or voluntarily given up (by transaction).

'Imprescriptible' is another term used in 18th-century Declarations of Rights, but only 'inalienable' subsists in IHRL, subsuming the idea of imprescriptibility (inextinguishability). The scope of the inalienability needs to be nuanced, however.

Human dignity is absolutely inalienable because it is indisposable. Nobody can renounce his or her human dignity, for two reasons: it is inherent in being human, and it is not a mere individual attribute but belongs to the whole species. For example, if a human being enters a contract accepting to become a slave to someone, he/she does not cease to be human and such a contract is legally null and void. Also, in the event of conflicts of rights, they may be balanced, but this is not allowed when it comes to human dignity.

Therefore, while human dignity is absolutely inalienable, not every human right is. This becomes clearer if one takes into account the distinction between enjoyment and exercise of human rights:

– The enjoyment of human rights is inalienable because they are inherent to human dignity.
– The exercise of human rights may not be possible, may be temporarily limited or even suspended, and is not necessarily compulsory.

In effect, there is a "right of renunciation" as an expression of personal autonomy, provided that it is free (not under the pressure of a need) and enlightened (not by ignorance of its consequences) (see Schutter & Ringelheim, 2005). This does not preclude a legal system to protect individuals against themselves. For instance, in *Case Laskey and Others v. the United Kingdom* (Application 21627/93; 21628/93; 21974/93),[4] in 1997, the European Court of Human Rights said:

> 36. The Court observes that not every sexual activity carried out behind closed doors necessarily falls within the scope of Article 8 (Art. 8). In the present case, the applicants were involved in consensual sado-masochistic activities for purposes of sexual gratification. There can be no doubt that sexual orientation and activity concern an intimate aspect of private life (see, *mutatis mutandis*, the Dudgeon v. the United Kingdom judgment of 22 October 1981, Series A no. 45, p. 21, para. 52). [...]
>
> 39. The applicants submitted that their case should be viewed as one involving matters of sexual expression, rather than violence. With due regard to this consideration, the line beyond which consent is no defence to physical injury should only be drawn at the level of intentional or reckless causing of serious disabling injury.
>
> 40. For the Government [United Kingdom], the State was entitled to punish acts of violence, such as those for which the applicants were convicted, that could not be considered of a trifling or transient

> nature, irrespective of the consent of the victim. In fact, in the present case, some of these acts could well be compared to "genital torture" and a Contracting State could not be said to have an obligation to tolerate acts of torture because they are committed in the context of a consenting sexual relationship. The State was moreover entitled to prohibit activities because of their potential danger.
>
> The Government further contended that the criminal law should seek to deter certain forms of behaviour on public-health grounds but also for broader moral reasons. In this respect, acts of torture – such as those in issue in the present case – may be banned also on the ground that they undermine the respect which human beings should confer upon each other. In any event, the whole issue of the role of consent in the criminal law is of great complexity and the Contracting States should enjoy a wide margin of appreciation to consider all the public-policy options. [...]
>
> 45. The applicants have contended that, in the circumstances of the case, the behaviour in question formed part of private morality which is not the State's business to regulate. In their submission the matters for which they were prosecuted and convicted concerned only private sexual behaviour.
>
> The Court is not persuaded by this submission. It is evident from the facts established by the national courts that the applicants' sado-masochistic activities involved a significant degree of injury or wounding which could not be characterised as trifling or transient. [...]
>
> 48. Accordingly, the Court considers that the reasons given by the national authorities for the measures taken in respect of the applicants were relevant and sufficient for the purposes of Article 8 para. 2 (Art. 8-2).

Renunciation to exercise a right may be also prohibited when, also, a legitimate public interest is involved. The same European Court, in *Case D.H. and Others v. The Czech Republic* (Application N° 57325/00, 13 November 2007),[5] after noting that "the waiver of a right guaranteed by the Convention – in so far as such a waiver is permissible – must be established in an unequivocal manner, and be given in full knowledge of the facts, that is to say on the basis of informed consent", said: "In view of the fundamental importance of the prohibition of racial discrimination (see *Nachova and Others*, cited above, § 145, and *Timishev*, cited above, § 56), the Grand Chamber considers that [...] no waiver of the right not to be subjected to racial discrimination can be accepted, as it would be counter to an important public interest" (para. 204).

Human rights are not, therefore, simply interests. They are normative positions with strong moral force, making sense for everyone. "It is a great mistake to think that, because we see rights as especially important in morality, we must make everything especially important in morality into a right" (Griffin, 2008, p. 199 and p. 41). Human rights are the highest category of rights, aiming at protecting the weakest against the strongest – especially the State – as well as guaranteeing to everyone a minimum of empowerment, i.e. of autonomy and self-determination, as well as conditions for developing the human personality. As said the Human Rights Committee (CoHR) in its General Comment (GC) 24, "the human rights norms are the legal expression of the essential rights that every person is entitled to as a human being" (CCPR/C/21/Rev.1/Add.6, 1994, para. 4).[6]

Although 'human rights' is the most common term in International Law, the most used in constitutional texts is 'fundamental/basic rights', consecrated by the 1919 German Constitution of Weimar, whose Part II, echoing the 1849 Frankfurt Constitution, was titled *Grundrechte und Grundpflichten der Deutschen* (Fundamental/basic rights and obligations of Germans). There is also the term 'fundamental freedoms', frequently added to 'human rights' (example: Convention for the Protection of Human Rights and Fundamental Freedoms, best known as European Convention on Human Rights). However, no conceptual distinction can be drawn between human rights and fundamental freedoms: rights are freedoms, freedoms are rights. The UDHR[7] refers to "human rights and fundamental freedoms" (Preamble and Article 26.2), "fundamental human rights" (Preamble) and "fundamental rights" (Article 8). Other terms are 'civil rights' and *libertés publiques* (public liberties/freedoms).

It should be noted that human rights and citizens' rights are not overlapping concepts. Although they are closely tied, in general, they should not be confused. In a Rule of Law, the rights of the citizen include human rights, held simply for being human, and other rights held by virtue of being national of a given State (especially political rights).

2.3 Juridification

The first 'Declaration of Rights' has been the Virginia Declaration of Rights, drafted by George Mason and approved on 12 June 1776 as a separate document of the Constitution of Virginia (adopted on 29 June). It was used by Thomas Jefferson to draft the first part of the American Declaration of Independence (The unanimous Declaration of the Thirteen United States of America) proclaimed on 4 July 1776. It was the basis of the first Ten Amendments to the USA Constitution of 1787, which were adopted on 15 December 1791. In France, the National

Assembly adopted the *Déclaration des droits de l'homme et du citoyen* (Declaration of the Rights of Man and the Citizen) on 26 August 1789, in the context of the French Revolution (other Declarations were adopted in 1793 and 1795).

Louis Henkin (1978) pointed out: "Thomas Paine had proclaimed constitutionalism as *the* right of man and as the foundation of all rights of man", and "constitutionalism became identified with respect for individual rights" (pp. 135, 32). Thereafter, as Manfred Nowak (2003) wrote, "the development of human rights is closely linked with the era of constitutionalism" (p. 7). The 1787 American Constitution was supplemented, as above noted, with a Bill of Rights (the first Ten Amendments of 1791), and the 1791 French Constitution began with the 1789 Declaration. During the 19th century, other Constitutions included catalogues consecrating classical freedoms. The most influential one was likely the 1831 Belgian Constitution. The economic, social and cultural rights fully entered the constitutional stage in the 20th century. Landmarks of this new path were the 1917 Constitution of the Mexican United States and the 1919 Constitution of the German Reich (known as Weimar Constitution).

More than 80 % of the Constitutions adopted before 1948 included provisions concerning human rights (Bates, 2010, p. 25). Between 1949 and 1975, the percentage rose to 93 %. This tendency grew in the 1990s with the new constitutional texts of the States formerly integrated as the Union of the Soviet Socialist Republics (USSR) and Eastern Bloc.

The atrocities committed during World War II have made the international protection of universal fundamental human values and breaking the taboo of States' omnipotent sovereignty imperative. As stated in a document of the European Movement (1949):

> So long as the tyrant – or his modern counterpart, the totalitarian State – confined his activities to his own national territory, no other country claimed the right to object or interfere. [...]
>
> It needed the shock of the Nuremberg trials, with their unbelievable revelations of infamy and human degradation, to awaken the conscience of the civilized world. (p. 3)

The Organisation of the United Nations has been "created to meet the claims coming from the depths of the human conscience" (Cassin, 1951, p. 253). The UN Charter[8] – prepared by the United Nations Conference on International Organisation convened at San Francisco (USA), on 25 April 1945 – was signed by 50 States at its final plenary session, on 26 June, in the Memorial Opera House, and came into force on 24 October, the birthday of the United Nations now celebrated as United Nations Day. The Nazi Third Reich had capitulated on 8 May, after 5 years and 8 months of world war.

The UN – whose three main pillars are peace, human rights and development – is born impaired with the same original sin as the League of Nations. Its Charter echoed the Covenant of the League Article 15.8 that prevented it from taking action against the mounting domestic Nazi crimes: it is the prohibition "to intervene in matters which are essentially within the domestic jurisdiction of any State" (UN Charter Article 2.7). Nonetheless, its "Purposes" include "promoting and encouraging respect for human rights and for fundamental freedoms for all without distinction as to race, sex, language, or religion" (Article 1.3).

During the San Francisco Conference, every effort for the Charter to contain a Bill of Rights or, at least, a strong engagement with human rights protection, was made, mainly by 20 States of Latin America and Caribbean, which formed the widest geographical block in the Conference, and tens of Non-Governmental Organisations (NGOs). The UN Charter has been the first universal treaty to proclaim the principle of respect for human dignity and rights. It includes seven references to them: in the Preamble and Articles 1.3, 13.1.b, 55.c, 62.2, 68 and 76.c. The Preamble reads:

> We the peoples of the United Nations, determined to save succeeding generations from the scourge of war, which twice in our lifetime has brought untold sorrow to mankind, and to reaffirm faith in fundamental human rights, in the dignity and worth of the human person, in the equal rights of men and women and of nations large and small.

One of the UN main organs (Article 7 of the Charter) is the Economic and Social Council (ECOSOC), whose mandate includes "to set up commissions in economic and social fields and for the promotion of the human rights" (Article 68). At the Closing Session of the San Francisco Conference, President Truman stated[9]:

> Under this document, we have good reason to expect the framing of an international bill of rights, acceptable to all the nations involved. That bill of rights will be as much a part of international life as our own Bill of Rights is a part of our Constitution. The Charter is dedicated to the achievement and observance of human rights and fundamental freedoms.
>
> Unless we can attain those objectives for all men and women everywhere – without regard to race, language or religion – cannot have permanent peace and security.
>
> With this Charter, the world can begin to look forward to the time when all worthy human beings may be permitted to live decently as free people.

2.4 International Bill of Human Rights

At its first session – the first part of which was held from 10 January to 14 February 1946 in London (Central Hall, Westminster), pending the decision on the headquarters of the Organisation – the UN General Assembly elected the members of the ECOSOC. This one created, at its first meeting, on 16 February, on the basis of Articles 7.2 and 68 of the UN Charter, a 'Nuclear Commission on Human Rights', composed of nine members, preparatory of the full Commission on Human Rights that is the sole to be formally mentioned in the Charter. According to the respective Resolution 5 (I)[10]:

> 2. The work of the Commission shall be directed towards submitting proposals, recommendations, and reports to the Council regarding:
>   a. an international bill of rights;
>   b. international declarations or conventions on civil liberties, the status of women, freedom
>   of information and similar matters;
>   c. the protection of minorities;
>   d. the prevention of discrimination on grounds of race, sex, language or religion.

The Resolution 9 (II) of 21 June 1946[11] added to paragraph 2 a new subparagraph (e) reading as follows: "any other matter concerning human rights not covered by item (a), (b), (c), and (d)".

The Nuclear Commission met once, from 29 April to 21 May 1946, at Hunter College, New York, and presented a report to the ECOSOC that decided, at its second meeting (on 21 June), that the Commission should be composed of 18 representatives from the UN Members States. The Commission was elected on 11 September, at the ECOSOC third meeting (from 11 September to 10 December). Chaired by Eleanor Roosevelt (Delegate of the USA, wife of its late President), Peng Chun Chang (China) serving as Vice-Chairman and Charles Malik (Lebanon) as Rapporteur, it met, for the first time, from 27 January to 10 February 1947, at the UN Interim Headquarters, Lake Success, New York (E/CN.4/SR.1).[12] The Commission was authorised by the ECOSOC to create a subsidiary organ: the Sub-Commission on Prevention of Discrimination and Protection of Minorities (renamed Sub-Commission on the Promotion and Protection of Human Rights in 1999), composed of independent experts. Meanwhile, the UN Secretariat created a Human Rights Division, the first Director of which was John Humphrey (Canada).

The Commission requested the ECOSOC to ask the UN Secretariat to prepare a preliminary draft of International Declaration. Between February and June 1947, the Human Rights Division compiled vast documentation on human rights, forming a 408 pages volume, called *Documented Outline* (E/CN.4/AC.1/3/Add.l).[13] It included provisions from more than 50 Constitutions and drafts on human rights addressed to the UN. A "Memorandum by the Division of Human Rights" for the Commission containing an "Analysis of various draft International Bill of Rights" (E/CN.4/W.16, 23 January 1947)[14] presented and commented eighteen drafts elaborated by personalities and organisations before, during or after the World War II.[15]

Humphrey prepared a "Draft Outline of International Bill of Rights" (E/CN.AC.1/3, 4 June 1947),[16] known as the "Secretariat Outline", composed of a Preamble and 48 Articles, greatly influenced (according to his testimony) by the drafts sponsored by Chile and Panama. When it received the Humphrey draft, the Commission formed a Drafting Committee composed of eight of its members for elaborating its first draft. It met for the first time from 9 to 25 June 1947, at Lake Success, having engaged an inconclusive debate about the legal form of the text to be drafted: a Declaration or a Convention? The Drafting Committee decided to establish a small temporary Working Group (composed of four of its members) that met for three times. It asked René Cassin (Delegate of France) to write a draft Declaration based in the Humphrey draft, while the other three members were requested to examine what provisions could go into a Convention.

The Cassin draft, formed of a Preamble and 44 Articles, was discussed by the Drafting Committee, revised by Cassin, again discussed and presented to the Commission, at its second session, held in Geneva from 2 to 17 December, in the former headquarters of the League of Nations, in front of the Lake Leman (Geneva Session). The debate about the legal nature of the instrument started again and the Commission decided (E/600(SUPP), para. 18)[17] to apply the term "International Bill of Human Rights", or simply "Bill of Rights", to the set of documents being prepared – a Declaration, a Convention and implementation measures – and that the Convention should be named "Covenant on Human Rights". Three Working Groups were created to deal with the three texts.

The Working Group on the Declaration was chaired by Roosevelt, Cassin being the Rapporteur, and met nine times. Various UN specialised agencies, as well as NGOs, took part in its debates, without the right to vote, but their proposals could be taken over by members of the Working Group. It examined Cassin's draft in detail, and the draft approved was reported by the Commission to the ECOSOC that sent it to the UN Member States for comments in early 1948.

The Drafting Committee met again from 3 to 21 May 1948, at Lake Success, for redrafting the Declaration taking into account the States comments and proposals. The Commission also met for its third session from 24 May to 18 June 1948, at Lake Success too, and went on with the debate. The draft Declaration was approved for 12 votes to none against, with 4 abstentions, and was sent to the ECOSOC. After a debate, during its seventh session, from 19 July to 29 August, where each of its members could make general statements on the Report of the Commission (on 25 and 26 August), the ECOSOC transmitted to the UN General Assembly the draft Declaration, together with the draft Covenant and several proposals on implementation (including the creation of an International Court of Human Rights). On 24 September, the General Assembly, meeting for its third ordinary session at the *Palais Chaillot*, in Paris, resent the drafts to its Third Committee (Social, Humanitarian and Cultural Questions), composed of Delegates from all Member States, that examined them from 28 September to 7 December 1948.

The draft Universal Declaration of Human Rights was discussed and approved by the Third Committee, and after three plenary sessions of debate at the General Assembly (181st, 182nd, and 183rd), on 9 and 10 December, it was proclaimed on 10 December 1948, a little before the midnight, for 48 votes to none against, with 8 abstentions: S.S.R. of Byelorussia (now Belarus), Czechoslovakia (now the Czech Republic and the Slovak Republic), S.F.R. of Yugoslavia (now dissolved, giving origin to several States), Poland, Ukraine, USSR (now dissolved, giving origin to several States), South-African Union and Saudi Arabia.

Addressing the UN General Assembly (9 December), Eleanor Roosevelt said: "This Declaration of Human Rights may well become the international Magna Carta of all men everywhere".[18] Later, U. Thant (UN Secretary-General from 1962 to 1971), called it the Magna Carta of Mankind.

The drafting process of the UDHR took thus more than two years. It included:
- 18 meetings of the Nuclear Commission
- 81 meetings of the Commission on Human Rights
- 44 meetings of the Drafting Committee
- 85 meetings and more about 20 subcommittees meetings of the Third Committee
- three plenary meetings of the General Assembly

The UDHR was the first international legal instrument to give content to the principles enshrined in the UN Charter regarding human rights. It comprehends a Preamble and 30 Articles proclaiming about 40 rights: the classical civil and political liberties, including the right to asylum and the right to property

(Articles 3–21), and 'new' economic, social and cultural rights (Articles 22–27). Articles 28–30 are general provisions. The Universal Declaration has become the most translated document overall in the world: over five hundred twenty language versions are available at the website of the Office of the UN High Commissioner for Human Rights (UNHCHR). Inside the UN headquarters cornerstone, in New York, copies of its Charter and the Universal Declaration were deposited. Both became a veritable Constitution of the new international legal order emerging from the moral and material ruins of World War II.

Even though the 1948 Universal Declaration does not bear a formally binding legal status, its moral value was prized by many Delegates of the UN Member States when it was drafted and adopted. As a result of their repeated invocation in the UN documents and many constitutional texts, some of its provisions have become legally binding rules of Customary International Law. In some authors' opinion, the entire Declaration possesses this status.

Christian Tomuschat (2008) pointed out: "A new chapter of human history began" with the Universal Declaration (p. 24). Mary Glendon (2001) noted:

> Together with the Nuremberg Principles of international criminal law developed by the Allies in 1946 for the trials of German and Japanese war criminals and the 1948 genocide Convention, the Universal Declaration of Human Rights became a pillar of a new international system under which a nation's treatment of its own citizens was no longer immune from outside scrutiny. […]
>
> The Declaration marked a new chapter in a history that began with the great charters of humanity's first rights moment in the seventeenth and eighteenth centuries. […] They proclaimed that all men were born free and equal and that the purpose of government was to protect man's natural liberties. They gave rise to the modern language of rights. (pp. xvi, xvii)

The Commission on Human Rights went on to prepare the envisaged Covenant. The UN General Assembly decided, in 1950, to include in it all categories of human rights, but in 1952 it reconsidered and decided the drafting of two Covenants on Human Rights, "one to contain civil and political rights and the other to contain economic, social and cultural rights". However, they should "be submitted simultaneously" and "to contain, in order to emphasize the unity of the aim in view and to ensure respect for and observance of human rights, as many similar provisions as possible" (A/RES/543(VI), 5 February 1952).[19] Besides the Preambles, there are other similar provisions in the two Covenants, notably those laid down in their Part I and Part II.

The Commission dedicated six sessions to the Covenants (5th to 10th). Their drafting was completed in 1954, but only in 1966 the General Assembly Third Committee concluded its debates and the two Covenants were adopted:

- International Covenant on Civil and Political Rights (ICCPR), codifying and developing the provisions of UDHR Articles 3 to 21, with an Optional Protocol enabling a Committee established by the Covenant to receive individual communications.
- International Covenant on Economic, Social and Cultural Rights (ICESCR), codifying and developing the provisions of UDHR Articles 22 to 27.

The Covenants only entered into force in 1976. The UDHR, the ICCPR and the ICESCR (with their Protocols) form together the International Bill of Human Rights (IBHR) decided by the Commission at its Geneva Session.

Two landmark conferences on human rights were so far convened by the UN:

- International Conference on Human Rights, in Tehran (Iran), from 22 April to 13 May 1968, with the participation of 84 States. It adopted a Proclamation and 29 Resolutions (apart from other 18 ones especially addressed to the UN bodies).
- World Conference on Human Rights, in Vienna (Austria), from 14 to 25 June 1993. It gathered about 7000 participants, among them representatives of more than 170 States and about 800 NGOs. It adopted a Declaration and Programme of Action. According to a UN publication (United Nations, 1995): "This Conference should be regarded both as the culmination of a long process and as the point of departure for a new adventure on behalf of human rights [...] the reference document for policy and the activities of the international community for the future" (pp. 92, 97, 98).

2.5 International Human Rights Law

At the Third Committee 90th meeting, on 1 October 1948 (A/C.3/SR.90),[20] the Colombian Delegation (Augusto Ramirez Moreno) affirmed that the results of the Universal Declaration drafting process "should be of great significance, even though they might be merely the seed of a tree which would bear fruit at a much later time". The UDHR has become progressively "the source of inspiration and has been the basis for the United Nations in making advances in standard-setting as contained in the existing international human rights instruments", as reads the Preamble of the Vienna Declaration and Programme of Action (1993). It has given rise to a new branch of General International Law – International Human Rights Law (IHRL). While it is a legal field much fragmented and its autonomy is debated, its reality is beyond doubt.

2.5.1 *Specificity*

Classic International Law – originating from the Treaties of Westphalia (1648), predominant until World War II – concerned exclusively States. It was a Law of co-existence, dominated by the principles of sovereignty and consent, admitting war as means to resolve international disputes, as well as conquest as a way of territorial expansion.[21] The obligations the States accepted were contractual and reciprocal.

By contrast, IHRL is mainly concerned with the vertical relations between States and individuals, their obligations being towards all persons under their jurisdiction, which are the direct beneficiaries of IHRL. In this respect, States do not have interests on their own, but a common interest that is the protection and promotion of respect for human rights of every human being. Therefore, IHRL is not subject to the principle of reciprocity which traditionally governs the treaty-making. In this respect, the CoHR said in its GC 31 (CCPR/C/21/Rev.1/Add. 13 26 May 2004)[22]:

> 2. While Article 2 is couched in terms of the obligations of State Parties towards individuals as the right-holders under the Covenant, every State Party has a legal interest in the performance by every other State Party of its obligations. This follows from the fact that the 'rules concerning the basic rights of the human person' are *erga omnes* [towards all] obligations and that, as indicated in the fourth preambular paragraph of the Covenant, there is a United Nations Charter obligation to promote universal respect for, and observance of, human rights and fundamental freedoms. [...] To draw attention to possible breaches of Covenant obligations by other States Parties and to call on them to comply with their Covenant obligations should, far from being regarded as an unfriendly act, be considered as a reflection of legitimate community interest.

The European Court of Human Rights had said in *Case Ireland v. The United Kingdom* (Application 5310/71)[23]:

> 239. ... Unlike international treaties of the classic kind, the [European] Convention comprises more than mere reciprocal engagements between contracting States. It creates, over and above a network of mutual, bilateral undertakings, objective obligations which, in the words of the Preamble, benefit from a "collective enforcement".

Being so, human rights treaties have a normative nature, i.e. "an 'objective' character, in that they are not reducible to bilateral exchanges of advantages between the contracting states". This "produces a series of consequences in various areas related to the application of such treaties" (Scheinin, 2009, pp. 53, 54). For example, according to the Vienna Convention on the Law of Treaties (1969),[24] the reasons to terminate or suspend the application of a treaty by a State Party, as a consequence of its breach by other Party, "do not apply to provisions relating to the protection of the human person contained in treaties of a humanitarian character, in particular to provisions prohibiting any form of reprisals against persons protected by such treaties" (Article 60.5).

The deepening and expansion of the human rights idea and ideal made the second half of the 20th century the Era of Rights (*The Age of Rights*: Louis Henkin, 1990; *L'Età Dei Diritti*: Norberto Bobbio, 1990). Human rights have become a universal language.

2.5.2 *National Reception*

The relationship between international and national Law is, paradoxically, clear and complex.[25]

- It is clear because, according to the Vienna Convention on the Law of Treaties (1969)[26]:

> Article 26 (*Pacta sunt servanda*)
>
> Every treaty in force is binding upon the Parties to it and must be performed by them in good faith.
>
> Article 27 (Internal law and observance of treaties)
>
> A Party may not invoke the provisions of its internal law as justification for its failure to perform a treaty. This rule is without prejudice to Article 46.

- It is complex to the extent that:
  - The modalities of reception or entering into force of International Law in national legal orders are varying.
  - The rank of International Law in the hierarchy of the domestic legal sources is varying too.
  - In any case, conflicts may arise between international and national provisions demanding appropriate solutions.

While the first obligation of States Parties in international legal instruments is their domestication, i.e. incorporation into the domestic legal order, the modalities of legal reception or entering into force of International Law in national legal systems are traditionally two, called dualism and monism.

- *Dualism* means that national and international legal norms are considered as distinct sources of Law and, therefore, International Law is not domestically directly applicable but needs legislative transposition (more frequent in the Common Law tradition).
- *Monism* means that the norms of a treaty to which a State is Party become automatically part of the national legal order, without the need for further legislation in order to be applicable (more frequent in the Roman Law tradition).

Many Constitutions include an 'incorporation clause'. For example, according to the Constitution of the Portuguese Republic (1976, revised)[27]:

> Article 8 (International law)
>
> 1. The norms and principles of general or common international law form an integral part of Portuguese law.
> 2. The norms contained in duly ratified or approved international conventions come into force in Portuguese internal law once they have been officially published and remain so for as long as they are internationally binding on the Portuguese state.

There is also a mixed approach that has become the most frequent, most States falling somewhere in between dualism and monism, as Ineke Boerefijn (2009) remarked: "The traditional distinction between dualist and monist systems [...] is somewhat outdated, and the reality is more complex. There are various degrees of monism and dualism. More recent writings distinguish between various implementation methods that can coexist" (p. 577).

The IHRL does not contain any provision as to its national reception, but the UN Committees recommend the automatic incorporation of its treaties. For instance, the Committee on Economic, Social and Cultural Rights (CoESCR) said in GC 9 on "The domestic application of the Covenant" (E/C.12/1998/24)[28] that ICESCR "does not stipulate the specific means by which it is to be implemented in the national legal order" (para. 5), but: "In general, legally binding international human rights standards should operate directly and immediately within the domestic legal system of each State Party, thereby enabling individuals to seek enforcement of their rights before national courts and tribunals" (para. 4).

Where the rank of International Law in the hierarchy of domestic legal sources is concerned, the constitutional texts generally contain provisions regarding it, giving it supra-constitutional, constitutional or infra-constitutional (but superior to ordinary laws) normative rank. For example, the Constitution of Argentina[29] lists explicitly, at Section 75.22, several human rights international instruments to which is attributed "constitutional hierarchy"; the other treaties and conventions on human rights "shall require the vote of two-thirds of all the members of each [Parliamentary] House, after their approval by Congress". The Constitution of Bolivia provides (Article 13.IV):

> International treaties and conventions ratified by the Pluri-National Legislative Assembly (*Asamblea Legislativa*), which recognize human rights and prohibit their limitation in states of emergency, prevail over internal law. The rights and duties consecrated in this Constitution shall be interpreted in accordance with the International Human Rights Treaties ratified by Bolivia.

If the constitutional text is silent, the matter is open to judicial interpretation by the Constitutional Court or other higher one.

Conflicts may arise, however. As a State cannot invoke the domestic Law to justify non-compliance with International Law to which it is Party or with decisions of international bodies whose competence it has accepted, it should previously make sure that its domestic Law conforms to the international legal obligations undertaken. Regarding human rights, a preventive measure is the existence of a parliamentary committee to advise on the constitutionality or conventionality of legislative proposals related to human rights.

A provision could also be included in the Constitution allowing for harmonising interpretations in case of conflict of provisions on human rights, in particular, as does the Constitution of the Portuguese Republic (1976, revised),[30] for example:

> Article 16 (Scope and interpretation of fundamental rights)
>
> 1. The fundamental rights enshrined in the Constitution shall not exclude any others set out in applicable international laws and legal rules.
> 2. The constitutional precepts concerning fundamental rights must be interpreted and completed in harmony with the Universal Declaration of Human Rights.

Another way is to resort to the principle *Pro-homine/persona* (pro-human being/person) analogue to principles *In dubio pro reo* (When in doubt, for the accused) or *In dubio pro libertate* (When in doubt, for the liberty). It has triple content:

- If there are two or more norms applicable to a Case, the most protective of human rights should be applied.

- If a norm is susceptible to more than one interpretation, that offering the greatest protection should be applied.
- In the event of a necessary and legitimate limitation of a right or freedom, the least adversarial to its exercise should be applied.

Tribunals have a unique responsibility in assuring not only the respect of the domestic Law but also of the International Law to which a State is Party, through a *diffuse conventionality control* (as opposed to the *concentrated control* by especially dedicated bodies). It was the Inter-American Court of Human Rights that has introduced the concept of "conventionality control", in *Case Almonacid Arellano et al. v. Chile* (2006),[31] where it said:

> 123. ... when the Legislative Power fails to set aside and/or adopts laws which are contrary to the American Convention, the Judiciary is bound to honour the obligation to respect rights as stated in Article 1(1) of the said Convention, and consequently, it must refrain from enforcing any laws contrary to such Convention. The observance by State agents or officials of a law which violates the Convention gives rise to the international liability of such State, as contemplated in International Human Rights Law, in the sense that every State is internationally responsible for the acts or omissions of any of its powers or bodies for the violation of internationally protected rights, pursuant to Article 1(1) of the American Convention.
>
> 124. The Court is aware that domestic judges and courts are bound to respect the rule of law, and therefore, they are bound to apply the provisions in force within the legal system. But when a State has ratified an international treaty such as the American Convention, its judges, as part of the State, are also bound by such Convention. This forces them to see that all the effects of the provisions embodied in the Convention are not adversely affected by the enforcement of laws which are contrary to its purpose and that have not had any legal effects since their inception. In other words, the Judiciary must exercise a sort of "conventionality control" between the domestic legal provisions which are applied to specific cases and the American Convention on Human Rights. To perform this task, the Judiciary has to take into account not only the treaty but also the interpretation thereof made by the Inter-American Court, which is the ultimate interpreter of the American Convention.

In *Case Dismissed Congressional Employees (Aguado-Alfaro et al.) v. Peru* (2006),[32] the Court added:

> 128. When a State has ratified an international treaty such as the American Convention, the judges are also subject to it; this obliges them to ensure that the *effet utile* [utile effect] of the Convention is not reduced or annulled by the application of laws contrary to its provisions, object, and purpose. In other words, the organs of the Judiciary should exercise not only control of constitutionality but also of "conventionality" *ex officio* between domestic norms and the American Convention; evidently in the context of their respective spheres of competence and the corresponding procedural regulations. [...]

Conventionality control means, therefore, the obligation of national Judges and Courts to ensure the application of the American Convention (as well as of other human rights treaties) and its interpretation by the Inter-American Court: "The constitutionality control implies thus necessarily a conventionality control, exercised in a complementary way", as said the Inter-American Court in its Resolution of 20 March 2012 relating to the monitoring of the compliance with its judgement of the *Case Gelman v. Uruguay* (para. 88).[33] Conventionality and constitutionality form a *Block of Constitutionality*, as explained by the Constitutional Court of Colombia (*C-067/03*)[34]:

> It is well known and has been accepted by some doctrine that the constitutional normativity is not the exclusive privilege of articles formally integrating the text of the Political Charter [Constitution]. The Highest Law [Constitution] is formed of a wider group of principles, rules, and norms of positive Law that constitute the so-called "block of constitutionality" and share with the articles of the text of the Charter the highest level of normative hierarchy in the internal order. In this sense, the notion of "block of constitutionality" is intended to convey the idea that the Constitution of a State is much broader than its constitutional text because there are other provisions, contained in other instruments or compilations, which are also constitutional norms.
>
> This amplified concept of the positive Constitutional Law had its origins in the jurisprudence of the French Constitutional Council when it conferred normative value to the Preamble of the 1958 Constitution. [...]
>
> As already said, the concept of "block of constitutionality" was definitively systematized in Case C-225 of 1995 [...]. The Court defined then the block of constitutionality as being the legal unit formed "by ... norms and principles that, without formally appearing in the body of the constitutional text, are used as parameters for the control of constitutionality of

> laws, for having been integrated into the Constitution by different routes and by mandate of the Constitution itself. Therefore, they are true principles and rules with constitutional value, i.e. norms placed at constitutional level [...].
>
> The incorporation in the national legal doctrine of an institution such as the block of constitutionality arose thus from the recognition of the prevalence of international human rights treaties over the internal order [...].

2.5.3 *Sources*

According to Article 38.1 of the Statute of the International Court of Justice, annexed to the UN Charter,[35] the Court applies "international conventions", "international customs", "the general principles of law", and "judicial decisions and the teachings of the most highly qualified publicists of the various nations, as subsidiary means for the determination of rules of law". Other (soft) international sources are Resolutions, Recommendations, Declarations, and similar normative texts adopted by the UN General Assembly and other Intergovernmental Organisations (IGOs).

The universal *Corpus Juris* (Body of Law) of the IHRL is formed of three sets of instruments:

1. *International Bill of Human Rights*
   As we know, the International Bill of Human Rights (IBHR) is not a legal instrument, but the denomination of the whole composed of the UDHR (1948), the ICCPR and the ICESCR (1966), with their Protocols. As of October 2020, the ICCPR had 173 ratifications (more 6 signatures) and the ICESCR 171 (more 4 signatures).[36]
2. *Other core human rights treaties*
   Core human rights treaties are, in addition to the two 1966 International Covenants, seven other treaties adopted within the UN framework, namely:
   - International Convention on the Elimination of All Forms of Racial Discrimination (1965)
   - Convention on the Elimination of All Forms of Discrimination against Women (1979)
   - Convention against Torture and Other Cruel, Inhuman or Degrading Treatment or Punishment (1984)
   - Convention on the Rights of the Child (1989)
   - International Convention on the Protection of the Rights of All Migrant Workers and Members of their Families (1990)
   - Convention on the Rights of Persons with Disabilities (2006)

- International Convention for the Protection of All Persons from Enforced Disappearances (2006)

These treaties, which are complemented by as many Protocols, form a system of protection against the most serious violations of human rights and reinforced protection of more vulnerable categories of human beings. All were preceded by analogous declarations, adopted by the UN General Assembly, except for the International Convention on the Protection of the Rights of all Migrant Workers and Members of their Families, a field belonging to the International Labour Organisation (ILO) competence.

3. *Many other legal instruments, conventional or declaratory, with general, specific or categorical content, universal or regional in scope*
   - Conventional are legal instruments formally binding States Parties (those which undertake to apply them): they are called Treaties, Conventions, Covenants, Protocols, etc. (38 names were identified).
   - Declaratory are legal instruments that are not formally binding (Resolutions, Declarations, Recommendations, etc.) adopted by IGO's organs, as the UN General Assembly.
   - With general content are legal instruments covering all human rights or some categories of them, such as the 1966 International Covenants.
   - With specific content are legal instruments concerning a sole right (the right to education, for example).
   - With categorical content are legal instruments aiming to reinforce the protection of a more vulnerable category of persons (children, for example).
   - Universal in scope are legal instruments adopted within the UN institutional framework or under its auspices.
   - Regional in scope are legal instruments adopted within the regional framework, such as the Council of Europe or the Organisation of American States (OAS).

In the electronic site of the UNHCHR,[37] we find a "not exhaustive" list with about 100 standard-setting universal instruments on human rights, varying in nature. A UN publication (2002) recorded 94 instruments, universal and regional, conventional and non-conventional. This is not a complete compilation, however. It includes instruments adopted by UNESCO and ILO, in particular, but not all of them (ILO adopted around 200 Conventions and about as many Recommendations on different aspects of the right to work).[38] Another branch of International Law closely related to IHRL is International Humanitarian Law (IHL) that aims at 'humanising' the means of warfare.

At the regional level, the main legal instruments on human rights are:

- European Convention for the Protection of Human Rights and Fundamental Freedoms (best known as European Convention on Human Rights) Council of Europe, 1950, now with 16 Protocols
- American Convention on Human Rights (Pact of San José de Costa Rica) OAS, 1969, now with 2 Protocols
- African Charter on Human and Peoples' Rights (Banjul Charter) Organisation of African Unity (OAU, replaced by the African Union in 2001), 1981, now with two Protocols

On the European continent, there are two further instruments:
- Charter of Fundamental Rights of the European Union,[39] adopted by the European Union (EU) at the European Council meeting held in Nice (France) on 7 December 2000, which applies only to the implementation of the EU Law.
- Commonwealth of Independent States Convention on Human Rights and Fundamental Freedoms (Minsk, Belarus, 1995).[40]

The IHRL includes, therefore, two types of standard-setting instruments:
- Conventional instruments, i.e. creating international legal obligations. This is the so-called 'Hard Law'.
- Declaratory instruments, i.e. not legally binding, creating rather moral and political obligations. This is the so-called 'Soft Law' (Resolutions, Declarations, Recommendations, Principles, Directives, Codes of Conduct, etc.).

The history of human rights juridification – that is, of their moral claims becoming Law – is frequently presented as a 'generations' succession, reflecting the trilogy of the French Revolution: *Liberté, Égalité, Fraternité* (Liberty, Equality, Fraternity).
- *First generation* ('liberty rights' or 'negative rights': 'freedoms from'): they are the civil and political rights – such as the freedoms of opinion, expression, association, and participation in political life – proclaimed by the first 18th century Declarations, progressively incorporated into the constitutional texts, becoming a cornerstone of the liberal democracies.
- *Second generation* ('equality rights' or 'positive rights': 'rights to'): they are the economic, social and cultural rights – such as the rights to health, to work, to education – which emerged during the 19th century and developed in the 20th century, forwarded especially by the socialist ideologies as indispensable to exercise the 'first generation' ones.

- *Third generation* ('solidarity rights' or 'collective rights': 'new' rights): they are such rights as the right to human development, the right to a healthy environment, the right to peace, which took the floor since the 1960s. The recognition of some of them is a unique feature of the African Charter on Human and Peoples' Rights (ACHPR).

The 'generations' distinction is controversial, however, because it is neither historically nor conceptually accurate and may be misleading. In effect, if the classic freedoms were constitutionally recognised before economic, social and cultural rights, these ones internationalised first, with the establishment of ILO in 1919; a right may be recognised both as a right of 'the first generation' and of 'the second generation', as is the case of the right of trade union association; other rights have a transversal content, especially the right to life and the right to education; moreover, the distinction of rights 'generations' may have undesirable effects of hierarchisation, by suggesting that the first generation is the most important or the opposite: that the oldest generations have become obsolete. In this regard, Asbjørn Eide and Allan Rosas (2001) wrote:

> It has been asserted that economic, social and cultural rights constitute a 'second generation' of human rights, the first generation being civil and political rights, and the later or a third generation of solidarity rights has been added, such as the right to self-determination and the right to development. [...] The editors of this volume, however, do not adhere to the notion of 'generations'. The history of the evolution of human rights at the national level does not make it possible to place the emergence of different human rights into clear-cut stages. Efforts to do so would, in any case, make it necessary to distinguish also between civil and political rights, since political rights were accepted as human rights much later than some of the civil rights, in some countries even later than economic and social rights. [...] Trade union rights and property rights are often mentioned as rights which are difficult to classify according to the two-fold distinction. (p. 4)

Bertrand Ramcharan (2008) remarked: "Rights cannot be separated into generational categories except as academic classifications for the purposes of teaching or research" (p. 4).

2.5.4 *Structure and Normative Content of a Human Right*

As taught Jean Rivero (1981), "there are certain characteristics that the very notion of *right* necessarily implies: every right must have an identified holder, a precise and possible object, and must be opposable to one or several persons, which are obliged to respect it" (p. 133). In other words (as cited in Espiell, 1978):

> A right necessarily involves three elements: a holder on whom it confers a power, a defined content (of what does this power consist?) and one or several persons on whom it imposes a positive obligation (that of meeting the demands of the holder) or a negative one (that of refraining from interfering in the exercise of his right).

Determining the structure and normative content of a human right amounts, therefore, to answering the following interrogations: Who holds the right (entitlement: right-holder)? In what does it consist (object: to what is it a right)? Who has the corresponding (positive or negative) obligations (exigibility/opposability: duty-bearers)?

Right-holders

Holders of human rights are, by definition, "everyone", "every human being", "all persons", except when a legal instrument addresses a more vulnerable category of persons.

There are collective rights too. Collective is a right of a group or an individual right with a collective dimension, i.e. that can only be exercised in groups. Example of a group right is the peoples' "right of self-determination" (ICCPR and ICESCR Article 1). Example of individual rights with a collective dimension are the rights of trade unions. The CoESCR said in its GC 8 on "Article 6 of the International Covenant on Economic, Social and Cultural Rights" (E/C.12/GC/18, 6 February 2006)[41]: "The right to work is an individual right that belongs to each person and is at the same time a collective right" (para. 6).

ICCPR Article 27 refers to "persons belonging to" minorities, an expression also used in the title of the Declaration on the Rights of Persons Belonging to National or Ethnic, Religious and Linguistic Minorities (UN, 1992). This means, in particular, that: "The exercise of the rights set forth in the present Declaration shall not prejudice the enjoyment by all persons of universally recognized human rights and fundamental freedoms" (Article 8.2).

The United Nations Declaration on the Rights of Indigenous Peoples (2007)[42] addresses both dimensions when it states (Article 1): "Indigenous peoples have the right to the full enjoyment, as a collective or as individuals, of all human rights and fundamental freedoms as recognized in the Charter of the United Nations, the Universal Declaration of Human Rights and International Human Rights Law". In this connection, let us recall the wise warning of Jean Rivero (1980):

> On the rights of communities, the smoke of the crematoria throws the greatest threat because their recognition risks to give the seal of justice to the domination of the strong over the weak. […]
>
> The man should be the starting point because he is the only reality which is to survive the storms of history. […] At the heart of the concept of human right there is the intuition of the irreducibility of the human being to all its social environment. […] Without this faith in its eminent dignity, the concept of human rights can find neither foundation nor justification. […] However – and there lies the error of the individualism of 1789 – Man is inseparable from the groups, from which he takes life, substance, culture. To recognise the rights of the groups is to affirm that man, to be fully human, needs that they can fulfil their function to his service. The rights of groups are nothing more than the human right to receive from groups the means necessary for his development. (p. 23)

Object

The object of a human right states what the right-holder is entitled to. Each right proclaims a fundamental universal human value and lays down the interdictions it commands and/or actions it requires. The specificity of each right is essentially determined by its object.

Duty-bearers

Duty-bearers are those obliged to fulfil the object's normative content. They are principally States – that is, all public authorities (executive, legislative and judicial powers, as well as public administration in general) – individually and collectively, as they are the authors and direct addressees of the International Law to which they oblige themselves.

Human rights are also "a matter of priority for the international community" (Preamble of the Vienna Declaration and Programme of Action) that bears a subsidiary and supplementary role, when a State does not possess the necessary resources or when there is not the political will to meet its obligations. Although the existence of a very right to international co-operation is controversial, it is mentioned in several IHRL instruments and other international documents. For example: ICESCR (Article 2.1), CRC (Article 4), Convention on the Rights of Persons with Disabilities (Article 4.2). The CoESCR observed in its GC 3 (E/1991/23)[43] that it is "an obligation of all States" (para. 14). Its most enduring adversary is corruption, however.

It should be noted that the IHRL aims at guaranteeing a minimum of protection, and should not be invoked to justify not implementing higher national standards (see ICCPR Article 5.2, CRC Article 41, European Convention on

Human Rights (ECHR) Article 53, ACHR Article 29, Article 4 of the Protocol of San Salvador).

Moreover, the promotion and protection of human rights is a general responsibility. The UDHR has been addressed to "all peoples and all nations", to "every individual and every organ of society" (Preamble). Their responsibilities have been proclaimed by the long title of the Declaration on the Right and Responsibility of Individuals, Groups, and Organs of Society to Promote and Protect Universally Recognized Human Rights and Fundamental Freedoms (UN, 1998).[44] As individuals are concerned, both 1966 International Covenants recall that "the individual, having duties to other individuals and to the community to which he belongs, is under a responsibility to strive for the promotion and observance of the rights recognized in the present Covenant" (Preamble). Furthermore, to claim and to exercise one's rights is a duty towards the personal dignity and perfectibility, as well as towards Humanity, according to the capacity of personal responsibility.

2.5.5 *States' Obligations*

Entitlements (of rights-holders) imply obligations (from duty-bearers).

The Vienna Declaration and Programme of Action (1993)[45] has reaffirmed that the protection of human rights "is the first responsibility of Governments" (I.1). In effect: "The primacy of the state in the protection and fulfilment of internationally guaranteed human rights is the fundamental starting point of international human rights law" (Byrnes & Renshaw, 2010, p. 498).

States have general obligations towards the International Law they have accepted, as laid down in the Vienna Convention on the Law of Treaties (1969),[46] especially:
- Attitude of "good faith" (*Pacta sunt servanda*) (Article 26).
- Primacy of International Law over the domestic legal orders (Article 27).

In 2001, the International Law Commission (ILC) adopted a document on the "Responsibility of States for Internationally Wrongful Acts".[47]

States may formulate reservations concerning some treaties' provisions (if they are authorised), but a reservation cannot be "incompatible with the object and purpose of the treaty", according to the Vienna Convention (Article 19.c). Otherwise, they cannot be accepted. For example, the 1966 International Covenants were ratified by several Islamic States with reservations or declarations subjecting some of their provisions (including ICESCR Article 13 paragraphs 3 and 4, on the liberty of education) to compatibility with the *Sharia* (Islamic Law) or national legislation. This prompted various Western States to object that such reservations are not acceptable in light of International Law.

In the Vienna Declaration and Programme of Action (1993) (II.A)[48]:

> 5. The World Conference on Human Rights encourages States to consider limiting the extent of any reservations they lodge to international human rights instruments, formulate any reservations as precisely and narrowly as possible, ensure that none is incompatible with the object and purpose of the relevant treaty and regularly review any reservations with a view to withdrawing them.

The first obligation of a State in respect of International Law regards the conformity of the national legal order with the treaties it undertakes to apply (by ratifying them). After the *domestication* of International Law, the second obligation of States is to implement its provisions through consistent policies.

States' general political obligations concerning human rights were typified by the *Maastricht Guidelines on Violations of Economic, Social and Cultural Rights* (1997)[49]: "Like civil and political rights, economic, social and cultural rights impose three different types of obligations on States: the obligations to respect, protect and fulfil" (para. 6), and "each contains elements of obligation of conduct and obligation of result. The obligation of conduct requires action reasonably calculated to realize the enjoyment of a particular right. [...] The obligation of result requires States to achieve specific targets to satisfy a detailed substantive standard" (para. 7).

The *respect-protection-fulfilment* typology (proposed by Henry Shue in 1980) is applied by the UN Committees, as well as the UN International Law Commission. It's a matter of:

- Refraining from directly interfering with the enjoyment of a right (*respect*: vertical guarantee).
- Preventing and sanctioning third parties (individuals, groups, corporations) interference with the enjoyment of a right (*protection*: horizontal guarantee).
- Acting for the full realisation of a right through the adoption of all appropriate measures required (*fulfilment* that includes to facilitate, promote and provide).

For example, the CoESCR said in its GC 12 on "The right to adequate food (Art. 11)"[50]:

> 15. The right to adequate food, like any other human right, imposes three types or levels of obligations on States Parties: the obligations to *respect*, to *protect* and to *fulfil*. In turn, the obligation to *fulfil* incorporates both an obligation to *facilitate* and an obligation to

> *provide*. [...] Finally, whenever an individual or group is unable, for reasons beyond their control, to enjoy the right to adequate food by the means at their disposal, States have the obligation to *fulfil* (*provide*) that right directly. This obligation also applies for persons who are victims of natural or other disasters.

Besides the threefold obligations *to respect, to protect, and to fulfil,* as well as *obligations of conduct* and *obligations of result,* the typologies of States obligations distinguish *negative* and *positive obligations*, which is questionable. Are there purely negative obligations?

2.5.6 *Protection*

Ubi jus ibi remedium (Where there is a right, there must be a remedy) – says a Latin adage. "The principle that every right must be accompanied by the availability of an effective remedy is a general principle of law that exists across all legal systems and is enshrined in Article 8 of the Universal Declaration on Human Rights" (Schutter et al., 2012, p. 1160).

The international protection of human rights has been envisaged since the 16th century by the protection of religious, linguistic and national minorities. Religious freedom was likely the first human right internationally protected. In effect:

> In Europe, international regulations protecting minorities go back to 1555, when the Peace of Augsburg provided for the protection of religious minorities. Later the Treaty of Westphalia in 1648 and the Polish-Russian Convention of 1767 and 1775 guaranteed rights of dissidents in Poland, while the Vienna Treaty of 1815 gave religious minorities not only freedom to practise their faith but also certain civil rights. The peace treaties of 1919 required many old and new states to assure full protection to all their inhabitants without distinction of birth and nationality, language, race or religion. In subsequent years, the League of Nations worked out a procedure for the settlement of minority disputes. However, the League's treaties were only feebly enforced.
>
> After the Second World War, states in the newly created United Nations chose to focus the Organization's human rights machinery on a universal and individualistic conception of rights. (World Commission on Culture and Development, 1995, p. 57)

Other significant steps towards the internationalisation of the protection of human rights in the 19th century include the ban of slavery and slave trade, as well as the creation of the International Red Cross Committee that gave rise to the IHL. Also, the Covenant establishing the League of Nations included (Part XIII, Sect. 1) the establishment of ILO that has been the first IGO created for the protection of a human right (the right to work).

At present, there are international systems/regimes for the protection of human rights at the universal and regional levels (besides the national level). The variety of their bodies was so described by Karl J. Partsch (1991):

> The function of promotion and protection of human rights, at the international and regional level, is entrusted to a *great number* of many differentiated organs. They are own and statutory bodies of organisations, specialised conventional bodies, permanent or *ad hoc* bodies created for this effect. They distinguish themselves according to a great number of criteria: permanence, composition (Government representatives or experts), according to their procedure methods (conciliatory, almost-judicial or judicial; public or confidential) and, finally, according to the character of the act concluding their works (conciliation, friendly solution, recommendation, obligatory decision or judgment, accompanied or not by sanctions). (p. 482)

2.5.6.1 Universal Protection

The UN has been the driver of the international protection of human rights, despite its systemic defects, which are maybe the price to be paid for its longevity. Human rights are one of its three pillars, according to the Charter, alongside with peace and development. Each of them is under the responsibility of a Council, namely:

- Security Council (peace)
- Economic and Social Council (development)
- Council of Human Rights (not directly based on the Charter)

The UN universal system for human rights protection is made up of twofold mechanisms: Charter-based and Treaty-based. The distinction between them:

> ... is between those mechanisms that have grown up under the UN Charter and therefore apply to all Member States and those that are based on the human rights treaties and thus apply to the States Parties to the relevant treaties. This distinction is also sometimes described as the difference between non-conventional protection and conventional protection. (Clapham, 2009, p. 79)

- *Charter-based Mechanisms* are established by resolutions of the principal UN organs, whose authority flows from its Charter.

The main organ responsible for the promotion and protection of human rights, within the UN system, was the Commission on Human Rights, subsidiary to the ECOSOC. In 2005, the World Summit of Heads of State and Government gathered at the UN Headquarters in New York from 14 to 16 September, adopted a Resolution (A/RES/60/1)[51] where they "resolve to create a Human Rights Council" (para. 157) that "should address situations of violations of human rights, including gross and systematic violations, and make recommendations thereon. It should also promote effective coordination and the mainstreaming of human rights within the United Nations system" (para. 159). It is an intergovernmental body subsidiary to the UN General Assembly (A/RES/60/251, 15 March 2006),[52] composed of 47 Member States representatives, based in Geneva. According to the General Assembly Resolution, its work "shall be guided by the principles of universality, impartiality, objectivity and non-selectivity, constructive international dialogue and co-operation, with a view to enhancing the promotion and protection of all human rights, civil, political, economic, social and cultural rights, including the right to development" (para. 4). Its first session took place from 19 to 30 June 2006.[53]

On 18 June 2007, the Council of Human Rights (CHR) adopted the Resolution 5/1 on "Institution-Building of the United Nations Human Rights Council" by which it has established:

- A Universal Periodic Review (UPR) mechanism – the great novelty – to assess the human rights situation in every UN Member State, which takes place in cycles of four and a half years. It is a political and public peer review in which each State accounts for the fulfilment of its human rights obligations arising under the UN Charter, the UDHR, the conventional instruments to which it is Party and other obligations, in particular those derived from International Customary Law and IHL.
- A new complaint procedure, replacing the former '1503 Procedure', to address (in a confidential manner) communications submitted by individuals, groups, or NGOs claiming to be victims of human rights violations or to have direct, reliable knowledge of such violations. The complaints are examined by two working groups: Working Group on Communications and Working Group on Situations.
- An Advisory Committee, in replacement of the Sub-Commission on the Promotion and Protection of Human Rights, composed of 18 experts, which serves as the Council's 'think tank'.

Special Procedures[54] is the general name given to mechanisms established by the former Commission on Human Rights and assumed by the CHR, which Kofi Annan (former UN Secretary-General) considered to be the 'crown jewel' of the international human rights system.[55] They include Special Rapporteurs, Independent Experts, Working Groups, and Special Representatives of the Secretary-General. They are entrusted with a 'thematic mandate' (reporting and advising on a specific human right) or a 'geographic mandate' (reporting and advising on the human rights situation in a country, territory or region). The mandate-holders are independent human rights experts serving in their personal capacity and working *pro bono* (without monetary retribution).[56] As of November 2018, there were 56 Special Procedures (44 thematic and 12 geographic) with 80 mandate-holders.[57]

The Special Procedures functions, in addition to monitoring, reporting and calling the attention of public opinion, include country visits (under States' invitation); to consider allegations of violations of human rights that fall within their mandates; and to intervene directly with Governments by means of letters and, if needed, urgent appeals.

The current Charter-based bodies are, therefore, the CHR and its subsidiary bodies.

Treaty-based Mechanisms or *Treaty Monitoring Bodies* are conventional mechanisms, i.e. they are created by the human rights core treaties (all but one).

They are Committees of independent experts established to monitoring the application of the respective treaties. At present, there are nine Committees (as many as the number of core treaties) and a Subcommittee:

- Human Rights Committee (monitoring the implementation of the ICCPR, 1966)
- Committee on Economic, Social and Cultural Rights (monitoring the implementation of the ICESCR, 1966)[58]
- Committee on the Elimination of Racial Discrimination (monitoring the implementation of the International Convention on the Elimination of all Forms of Racial Discrimination, 1965)
- Committee on the Elimination of Discrimination against Women (monitoring the implementation of the Convention on the Elimination of All Forms of Discrimination against Women, 1979)
- Committee against Torture (monitoring the implementation of the Convention against Torture and Other Cruel, Inhuman or Degrading Treatment or Punishment, 1984)

- Committee on the Rights of the Child (monitoring the implementation of the Convention on the Rights of the Child, 1989)
- Committee on the Protection of the Rights of All Migrant Workers and Members of Their Families (monitoring the implementation of the International Convention on the Protection of the Rights of All Migrant Workers and Members of their Families, 1990)
- Committee on the Rights of Persons with Disabilities (monitoring the implementation of the Convention on the Rights of Persons with Disabilities, 2006)
- Committee on Enforced Disappearances (monitoring the implementation of the International Convention for the Protection of All Persons from Enforced Disappearance, 2006)
- Subcommittee on Prevention of Torture created by a Protocol to the respective Convention, which can visit detention centres in the States Parties.

The Committees are composed of 10 to 23 members and have a multidisciplinary composition, albeit most of their members are generally lawyers.[59] They meet usually in Geneva. Their functions are as follows:

- *Supervision*
  Supervision consists in examining the reports of the States Parties on the implementation of the treaties they have undertaken to apply, presented at regular intervals. The review ends with "Concluding Observations" or "Concluding Comments", which note the positive aspects and point to the negative ones of the human rights situation, followed by recommendations.
  The reports system is the classic mechanism of implementing human rights within the UN framework. States "tend to overstate their achievements and hide their shortcomings" (Power, 2015, p. 20), but the Committees collect a wide array of information.
- *Interpretation*
  The Committees are the most authoritative interpreters of the treaties whose implementation they supervise. Their interpretative function is exercised principally through 'General Comments' (GC) which are documents elaborating on a Committee's understanding of the provisions on a specific right or transversal questions of the respective treaty, with the purpose to help States Parties implement it. They are called 'General Recommendations' by two Committees (the Committee on the Elimination of Racial Discrimination and the Committee on the Elimination of Discrimination against Women). The elaboration of a General Comment or Recommendation is a largely collaborative process including usually a General Discussion Day.[60] They are adopted unanimously.

The Committees' interpretative function plays an exceptional role in the development of the normative content of human rights.

– *Quasi-judicial*

All Committees (except the Subcommittee on Prevention of Torture) can receive individual 'communications' or petitions/complaints about alleged violations by States Parties of the rights protected by the treaty whose implementation they monitor. Their decisions or conclusions (made behind closed doors) are not formally binding, because they are not true tribunals, but have some of their attributes (in particular, a legal basis, independence and motivation of decisions). They are sometimes qualified as 'quasi-jurisprudence'. Most treaties admit inter-State complaints, but States are reluctant to have recourse to them (the first three ones took place in 2018).[61] Some treaty bodies are also empowered to conduct inquiries to deal with systemic violations, which depend on the co-operation of the States Parties concerned.

The Supreme Court of Spain has been pioneering in 2018, in a case concerning the violation of the Convention on the Elimination of All Forms of Discrimination Against Women (1010/2017),[62] by ruling that "the inexistence of a specific procedure to apply the decisions of the Committee [on the Elimination of Discrimination Against Women] is, in itself, a breach of a legal and constitutional mandate by Spain". According to the Dictionary of the ACT (Australian Capital Territory) Human Rights Act,[63] International Law includes "(a) ... human rights treaties to which Australia is a party; and (b) general comments and views of the United Nations human rights treaty monitoring bodies; and (c) declarations and standards adopted by the United Nations General Assembly that are relevant to human rights".

In 1993, following a recommendation of the World Conference on Human Rights (Vienna), the UN General Assembly established a High Commissioner for Human Rights (UNHCHR), an idea already put forwards by René Cassin in 1947 and renewed by other proposals thereafter. The new body replaced and absorbed, in 1997, the Centre for Human Rights (which had been created in 1982 to replace the Division of Human Rights created in 1946). It is headquartered in Geneva, with a Delegation in New York and offices worldwide.

The UNHCHR coordinates and provides secretariat services for all UN activities in the human rights field, in particular for the Committees. The High Commissioner has the rank of Under-Secretary-General.

UNESCO, ILO, the World Health Organisation (WHO) and the Food and Agriculture Organisation (FAO) are UN "specialised agencies" for the protection of specific human rights.

The International Committee of the Red Cross plays a unique role in the protection of human rights as guardian of the IHL.

2.5.6.2 Regional Protection

The regional human rights protection systems consist of legal instruments and enforcement mechanisms that reflect the universal UN standards and system, in order to take into account historical, cultural and legal particularities, as well as issues common to a region. There are three regional systems and other organisations and instruments.

European region

The European human rights protection system is the oldest, most effective and exemplary regional one. It has been established by the Council of Europe, created on 5 May 1949, at present composed of 47 Member States, 28 of which are members of the European Union.[64] In 1950, it adopted the European Convention on Human Rights (ECHR)[65] that has come into force in 1953. As the Parliamentary Assembly of the Council of Europe recalled in its Resolution 1031 (1994),[66] "accession to the Council of Europe must go together with becoming a Party to the European Convention on Human Rights" (para. 9).

The European Convention was the first treaty adopted to protect a large set of human rights and to grant to individuals the right to address an international body for complaining of human rights violations. In effect, it was instituted a European Commission of Human Rights (1954) and a European Court of Human Rights (1959), sitting in Strasbourg (France), which have merged in a Permanent Court on 1 November 1998, to which can access individuals, groups and organisations, besides States. A European Commissioner on Human Rights was established in 1999, whose mandate is principally concerned with information and education about human rights.

A European Social Charter was adopted in 1961 (revised in 1996),[67] whose compliance is monitored by the European Committee of Social Rights through a supervisory mechanism based on a reporting system and collective complaints.[68] As the European Committee recalled in *Case International Federation of Human Rights Leagues* (*FIDH*) *v. France* (*Complaint 14/2003*)[69]:

> 27. The Charter was envisaged as a human rights instrument to complement the European Convention on Human Rights. It is a living instrument dedicated to certain values which inspired it: dignity, autonomy, equality and solidarity. The rights guaranteed are not ends in themselves, but they complete the rights enshrined in the European Convention of Human Rights.

According to the Treaty of Lisbon amending the Treaty on the European Union and the Treaty establishing the European Community, signed at Lisbon on 13 December 2007[70]: "The Union shall accede to the European Convention for the Protection of Human Rights and Fundamental Freedoms" (Article 6.2). This is also provided for in the ECHR (Article 59.2).

The Organisation for Security and Co-operation in Europe (OSCE),[71] headquartered in Vienna, is the largest regional security organisation in the world. Its approach to security is very comprehensive, dealing with a wide range of security-related issues. It includes an Office for Democratic Institutions and Human Rights (based in Warsaw, Poland) and a High Commissioner on National Minorities (based in The Hague, Holland).

American region

The American human rights protection system was created by the OAS, whose headquarters are in Washington, D.C. Its Charter was adopted by the IX American International Conference, on 30 April 1948, in Bogota (Colombia), that also was adopted the American Declaration of the Rights and Duties of Man, on 2 May 1948. In 1959, was established an Inter-American Commission of Human Rights, sitting in Washington, D.C. too. In 1969, was adopted the American Convention on Human Rights, in San José of Costa Rica, that came into force in 1978. It instituted an Inter-American Court of Human Rights that met for the first time on 29–30 June 1979 in the OAS headquarters but sits in San José of Costa Rica.

As individuals cannot access the Court (only the Inter-American Commission and the Member States), the Commission serves as an 'intermediary' (as occurred with the former European Commission of Human Rights), provided that the State concerned had recognised the adjudicatory jurisdiction of the Court. It should be noted that respect of the American Declaration is mandatory for all OAS Member States as an instrument that defines the rights referred to in its Charter (like the Universal Declaration concerning the UN Charter).

African region

The African human rights protection system was established by the OAU, which adopted the Charter on Human and Peoples' Rights[72] in 1981, in Nairobi, Kenya. In 1987, it set up an African Commission on Human and Peoples' Rights, which is headquartered in Banjul, Gambia. It receives reports from States Parties and can also receive communications from individuals or African IGOs. In 1998, a Protocol to the Charter created a Court on Human and Peoples' Rights, sitting in Arusha, Tanzania, which came into effect on 25 January 2004. Only the Commission, Member States, and African IGOs are entitled to access to the Court, but Member States may declare that they authorise it to receive complaints from individuals and NGOs. In 2008, the African Union (successor of the OAU) has adopted a "Protocol on the Statute of the African Court of Justice and Human Rights",[73] merging the Court of Justice of the African Union and the African Court of Human and Peoples Rights. It shall enter into force thirty days after the deposit of the instruments of ratification by fifteen Member States.

Other organisations and instruments

In the Asia-Pacific region, there is no system of human rights protection similar to the European, American and African ones. The main reasons for that are perhaps its extent and diversity, as well as political resistance. However, two regional IGOs include human rights in their purposes: Association of Southeast Asian Nations (ASEAN), and South Asian Association for Regional Cooperation (SAARC).

ASEAN

ASEAN was established in 1967. In 2015, it created the ASEAN Community and the ASEAN Economic Community. There is also the ASEAN Political-Security Community and the ASEAN Social-Cultural Community.

An Intergovernmental Commission on Human Rights was created in 2009. Its first task was the drafting of an ASEAN Human Rights Declaration, which was unanimously adopted in 2012, but with little participation of the civil society. Its content is not level to the universal human rights standards and contains vague and loopholes clauses, but it adds new rights: to water, to sanitation, to development, to the environment and to peace. Other declarations and conventions were adopted, such as: ASEAN Declaration on the Protection and Promotion of the Rights of Migrant Workers (2007), Declaration on the Elimination of Violence Against Women and Elimination of Violence Against Children in ASEAN (2013), ASEAN Convention Against Trafficking in Persons, Especially Women and Children (2015).

In 1993, it was agreed that ASEAN should have a regional human rights protection mechanism, but it does not exist yet. The ASEAN Intergovernmental Commission on Human Rights has only an advisory function and is not an independent body, as it is composed of members appointed by Governments. In 2007, was created an ASEAN Committee on the Implementation of the ASEAN Declaration on the Promotion and Protection of the Rights of Migrant Workers. An ASEAN Commission on the Promotion and Protection of the

Rights of Women and Children was created in 2010. It is an intergovernmental body with a mere promotion function.

SAARC

The SAARC was established in 1985. Its Charter makes only an indirect reference to human rights, but it adopted conventions addressing specific human rights, such as the SAARC Convention on Preventing and Combating Trafficking in Women and Children for Prostitution (2002). The same year was adopted the SAARC Convention on Regional Arrangements for the Promotion of Child Welfare in South Asia. In 2004, was adopted the SAARC Social Charter. In 2011, was adopted the SAARC Charter of Democracy. A Technical Committee on Women, Youth and Children also exists, composed of Governments representatives.

There is an Asia-Pacific Forum of National Human Rights Institutions, based in Sydney.

League of Arab States

The League of Arab States was established in 1945, sitting in Cairo. In 1968, it created an Arab Permanent Committee on Human Rights, composed of representatives of the Member States, with an advisory and promotion role.[74] Its sessions may be attended by NGOs and National Human Rights Institutions if granted observer status.

In 1994, the League adopted an Arab Charter on Human Rights that never entered into force for lack of sufficient ratifications. A revised Arab Charter on Human Rights was adopted in 2004, drafted with the participation of experts and civil society, that entered into force in 2008. While it improved its predecessor, it still falls below the international obligations undertaken by the Arab States, including the African Charter on Human and People's Rights (ACHPR). A Charter of the Rights of the Arab Child was adopted in 1983, with a regular reporting procedure. There is also an Arab Convention on the Status of Refugees in Arab Countries, adopted in 1994, and an Arab Convention on the Suppression of Terrorism, adopted in 1998.

The Arab Charter established an Arab Human Rights Committee, whose members are independent experts elected by States. It issues Concluding Observations regarding the human rights situation in the Member States, but cannot receive complaints regarding human rights violations. There is also an Arab Childhood Committee, assisted by the Technical Secretariat for Women, Family, and Childhood.

In 2014, the Arab League adopted the Statute of an Arab Human Rights Court to be seated in Bahrain, formed of seven judges sitting in their personal capacity. The Statute has not entered into force yet. Only States Parties shall have access to the Court. Accredited NGOs can submit complaints on behalf of individuals if accepted by States. The Court can issue opinions relating to legal issues. In the opinion of the International Commission of Jurists,[75] "the Statute of the Arab Court of Human Rights [...] must be fully amended to accord with international standards, including through a consultative and transparent process" (p. 5).

There is an Arab Network for National Human Rights.

OIC

The League of Arab States is partly overlapped by the larger Organisation of Islamic Co-operation (OIC), founded in 1969, sitting in Saudi-Arabia. In 1990, it adopted the Cairo Declaration on Human Rights in Islam that subjects human rights interpretation and application to Islamic Law. In 2005, it adopted the OIC Covenant on the Rights of the Child in Islam which included the abolition of harmful traditional practices and established an Islamic Committee on the Rights of the Child. In 2011, the OIC established an Independent Permanent Human Rights Commission that consists of 18 members and has a consultative and promotion role.

Consequently, as Fernando Urioste (1999) pointed out: "The IHRL has two visages like the god Janus: one turned to inside, the other turned to outside, representing the two national and international legal orders. The ultimate goal is respect for the dignity of the person" (p. 56). In effect, this is the double paradox of human rights: they are born against the State, against the abuses of public powers, but need protection and provisions by State; however, if States should be their main guarantors, they are often their main violators. Therefore, the protection of human rights is a responsibility of the International Community too, as the last resort. Recourse for international bodies is subject to admissibility conditions,[76] especially the exhaustion of remedies available under domestic legal systems, if they exist, are affordable and reliable.

2.5.6.3 Case Law

Access to justice is a fundamental dimension of the Rule of Law.

When the victims of violation (or threat of violation) of their rights (or someone on their behalf) can submit a complaint to an independent and impartial instance, to repair (or to prevent) it, the right is said to be justiciable. Justiciability, in a strict sense, is accomplished by Tribunals, which are the organs typically competent to give binding decisions based on laws and facts. In a broader sense, the mechanisms of the justiciability include other entities with similar power or only powers of recommendation and mediation, such as National Human Rights Institutions. In 1993, the UN General Assembly adopted "Principles relating to the Status of National Institutions (The Paris Principles)" (A/RES/48/134, 20 December 1993).[77] There are more than 120 worldwide with varying denominations and mandates: *Ombudsman* or *Ombudsperson,*

Defensor del Pueblo, *Défenseur des Droits de l'Homme*, Human Rights Commission, etc. In its GC 3, the CoESCR refers to "judicial or other effective remedies" (E/1991/23, para. 5).[78] In the GC 9 (E/C.12/1998/24),[79] it reaffirmed: "The right to an effective remedy need not be interpreted as always requiring a judicial remedy. Administrative remedies will, in many cases, be adequate", if they are "accessible, affordable, timely and effective" (para. 9).

At the universal level, there is not a veritable Case Law on human rights, as the protection of human rights still lacks a World Court, although the idea goes back to the *travaux préparatoires* of the UDHR and has recently been relaunched. In this respect, Martin Scheinin (2009b) remarked:

> The multitude of regional and international human rights instruments and monitoring mechanisms, coupled with the rapid evolution of international criminal law, may be paving the way for the future establishment of a world court of human rights. [...] With a proper design a world court of human rights could also help to remedy one of the greatest shortcomings of the present-day human rights architecture, namely the fact that only governments of nation states are held to account through the monitoring mechanisms of existing human rights treaties. A world court could – and should – be designed so as to provide monitoring of and accountability for human rights violations also in respect of other centres of power, such as intergovernmental organizations, international institutions, and even transnational corporations. (p. 620)

The International Court of Justice, established by the UN Charter as its judicial organ, pronounced several decisions relevant for the human rights protection, but it can only be seized by States.

The most comprehensive human rights international Case Law is to be found at the regional level, predominantly pronounced by the organs of the ECHR (the European Court of Human Rights and the former European Commission of Human Rights). The Inter-American Court of Human Rights is known for its comprehensive and progressive interpretation and application of the ACHR.

At the national level, the Constitutional Court of Colombia is a similar example of human rights friendly and creative jurisprudence.

Despite the Latin maxim saying *Iudicis est ius dicere non dare* (It is the judge's role to state the law, not to give it), jurisprudence and quasi-jurisprudence contribute, to a large extent, to define and develop the normative content of human rights, as already pointed out, by fleshing out abstract and general norms. Examples:

- The CoHR said in its "Views" on the *Case Toonen v. Australia* (CCPR/C/50/D/488/1992)[80] that "the reference to 'sex' in Articles 2, paragraph 1, and 26 [ICCPR] is to be taken as including sexual orientation" (para. 8.7).
- The CoESCR said in its GC 20 (E/C.12/GC/20)[81]:

> 32. "Other status" as recognized in Article 2, paragraph 2 [ICESCR], includes sexual orientation. States Parties should ensure that a person's sexual orientation is not a barrier to realizing Covenant rights, for example, in accessing survivor's pension rights. In addition, gender identity is recognized as among the prohibited grounds of discrimination; for example, persons who are transgender, transsexual or intersex often face serious human rights violations, such as harassment in schools or in the workplace.

- The same Committee has derived the right to water from ICESCR Articles 11 (right to an adequate standard of living) and 12 (right to the enjoyment of the highest attainable standard of physical and mental health). It said in GC 15 on "The right to water (Arts. 11 and 12 of the International Covenant on Economic, Social and Cultural Rights)" (E/C.12/2002/11)[82]:

> 1. Water is a limited natural resource and a public good fundamental for life and health. The human right to water is indispensable for leading a life in human dignity. It is a prerequisite for the realization of other human rights. [...]
>
> 3. Article 11, paragraph 1, of the Covenant specifies a number of rights emanating from, and indispensable for, the realization of the right to an adequate standard of living "including adequate food, clothing and housing". The use of the word "including" indicates that this catalogue of rights was not intended to be exhaustive. The right to water clearly falls within the category of guarantees essential for securing an adequate standard of living, particularly since it is one of the most fundamental conditions for survival. [...] The right to water is also inextricably related to the right to the highest attainable standard of health (Art. 12, para. 1) and the rights to adequate housing and adequate food (Art. 11, para. 1). The right should also be seen in conjunction with other rights enshrined in the International Bill of Human Rights, foremost amongst them the right to life and human dignity.

The international courts' decisions have no binding effect on third States Parties. However, as the German Constitutional Court stressed in *Case 2 BvR 2365/09, of 4 May 2011* (para. 89)[83]:

> ... the case-law of the European Court of Human Rights has at all events a *de facto* function of orientation and guidance [*faktische Orientierungs und Leitfunktion*] for the interpretation of the European Convention on Human Rights, even beyond the specific individual case in a decision (for earlier decisions on the orientation effect of the case-law of the European Court of Human Rights see BVerfGE 111, 307 <320>; BVerfGK 10, 66 <77–78>; 10, 234 <239>; in each case with further references).

Also, comparative jurisprudence is more and more influential. According to the ACT (Australian Capital Territory) Human Rights Act, Section 31(1)[84]: "International Law, and the judgments of foreign and international courts and tribunals relevant to a human right, may be considered in interpreting the human right". In the opinion of Judge Aharon Barak (former President of the Supreme Court of Israel), "comparative law is of great importance for understanding the concept of human dignity and the ideas that are derived from it. [...] Comparative law expands the interpretative horizon and thus enables each legal system to know itself better" (Barak, 2013, p. 379).

Although a judicial process is, in principle, the most effective recourse against violations of human rights, what matters most is that they are repaired (or prevented), whatever the mechanisms, judicial or other. The most effective protection is not necessarily the most coercive.

2.5.6.4 NGOs

The promotion and protection of human rights is also a general responsibility, as proclaims the long title of the Declaration on the Right and Responsibility of Individuals, Groups and Organs of Society to Promote and Protect Universally Recognized Human Rights and Fundamental Freedoms (UN, 1998),[85] also known as the "The Declaration on Human Rights Defenders". In support, the Commission on Human Rights established in 2000 the mandate of Special Rapporteur on the Situation of Human Rights Defenders.[86]

An educated world public opinion is the ultimate protection of human rights. This is the mission of tens of thousands of NGOs, international and national, devoted to human rights, such as: Amnesty International, Human Rights Watch, International Federation for Human Rights, International Commission of Jurists, World Organisation Against Torture, International Centre for the Legal Protection of Human Rights (INTERIGHTS), International

Network for Economic, Social and Cultural Rights (ESCRNet), Centre for Economic and Social Rights, etc. They are the dynamic and colourful expression of the conscience of civil society regarding its responsibilities in the promotion and protection of human rights, forming a movement increasingly strong and vigilant of the behaviour of States (by *naming and shaming*). Under Article 71 of the UN Charter, over 4000 NGOs (classified in three categories) have consultative status with the ECOSOC and other subsidiary organs. They are allowed, for instance, to present *shadow reports* to the UN Committees and to intervene in their meetings.[87] Their role was praised in the Vienna Declaration and Programme of Action (I-38)[88]:

> The World Conference on Human Rights recognizes the important role of non-governmental organizations in the promotion of all human rights and in humanitarian activities at national, regional and international levels. The World Conference on Human Rights appreciates their contribution to increasing public awareness of human rights issues, to the conduct of education, training and research in this field, and to the promotion and protection of all human rights and fundamental freedoms. While recognizing that the primary responsibility for standard-setting lies with States, the conference also appreciates the contribution of non-governmental organizations to this process. In this respect, the World Conference on Human Rights emphasizes the importance of continued dialogue and cooperation between Governments and non-governmental organizations.

In effect, NGOs play an increasing role also in the formation of International Law as spokespersons of the civil society. They had determinant participation at the San Francisco Conference and made a significant contribution to the drafting of the UDHR and the CRC. They have influenced the text of the Vienna Declaration and Programme of Action and the creation and definition of the mandate of the International Criminal Court.

The World Commission on Culture and Development (1995) summarised:

> The bonds of global non-governmental organizations, voluntary societies, grassroots organizations, churches and other religious associations, action groups, professional societies, interest groups and similar institutions stretch across national frontiers and forge links that bypass national frontiers and loyalties. They constitute the core of any future world citizenship, even though their loyalties may be confined to quite narrow issues or specialized interests. They can mobilize world opinion in order to draw attention to global problems, such as some environmental or

> human rights groups have done so successfully. Greenpeace on environmental issues or Amnesty International on human rights, or Oxfam on public education in development issues, as well as the execution of projects are examples. Other organizations provide humanitarian relief or engage in cooperation beyond state frontiers of their own, for example by linking with local self-help groups elsewhere and supporting their health, education and other projects. (p. 49)

However, the first responsibility of every one is towards himself/herself: to know, claim and exercise human rights is a duty towards the personal dignity, the communities in which we live and our common Humanity.

2.5.7 *Other Issues*

2.5.7.1 Minimum, Full and Expanded Content/Obligations

The German Basic Law (*Grundgesetz*, 1949)[89] states (Article 19.2): "In no case may the essence of a basic right be affected" (*In keinem Falle darf ein Grundrecht in seinem Wesensgehalt angetastet werden*). This provision was inspiring for Esin Orücü to propose[90]:

> The scope of each right must be analysed in terms of an outer edge, a circumjacence and a core. The essential elements of the norm which are unrelinquishable and unchangeable for the guaranteed core must be determined. This would need extensive multi-disciplinary work. Once meaningful criteria for every right have been established which can be concretised for every right, it should be possible to formulate a lowest common denominator, and perhaps even the average, or ideally the highest, common denominator of all guaranteed core. (p. 55)

This passage was quoted by Philip Alston (1987), member of the first composition of the CoESCR, who suggested that:

> ... the Committee should seek to identify some minimum core content of each right [...]. The fact that there must be such a core [...] would seem to be a logical implication of the use of the terminology of rights. In other words, there could be no justification for elevating a "claim" to the status of a right (with all the connotations that concept is generally assumed to have) if its normative content could be so indeterminate as to allow for the possibility that the right-holders possess no particular entitlement to anything. Each right must therefore give rise to an absolute minimum entitlement, in the absence of which a State Party is to be considered to be in violation of its obligations.

> The question for the Committee is how to go about identifying the core entitlement flowing from each right recognized in the Covenant. (pp. 352, 353)

The idea was taken up by the CoESCR that affirmed (italics added) in its GC 8 on "The relationship between economic sanctions and respect for economic, social and cultural rights" (E/C.12/1997/8)[91]:

> 7. ... Just as the international community insists that any targeted State must respect the civil and political rights of its citizens, so too must that State and the international community itself do everything possible to protect at least the *core content* of the economic, social and cultural rights of the affected peoples of that State (see also General Comment 3 (1990), paragraph 10).

In GC 3 on "The nature of States Parties' obligations (Art. 2, para. 1 of the Covenant) (E/1991/23),[92] the Committee had affirmed (italics added):

> 9. The principal obligation of result reflected in Article 2 (1) is to take steps "with a view to achieving progressively the full realization of the rights recognized" in the Covenant [ICESCR]. The term "progressive realization" is often used to describe the intent of this phrase. The concept of *progressive realization* constitutes a recognition of the fact that full realization of all economic, social and cultural rights will generally not be able to be achieved in a short period of time. [...] Nevertheless, the fact that realization over time, or in other words progressively, is foreseen under the Covenant should not be misinterpreted as depriving the obligation of all *meaningful content*. [...] It thus imposes an obligation to move as expeditiously and effectively as possible towards that goal. Moreover, any deliberately retrogressive measures in that regard would require the most careful consideration and would need to be fully justified by reference to the totality of the rights provided for in the Covenant and in the context of the full use of the maximum available resources.

What is more:

> 10. ... the Committee is of the view that a *minimum core obligation* to ensure the satisfaction of, at the very least, *minimum essential levels* of each of the rights is incumbent upon every State Party. Thus, for example, a State Party in which any significant number of

> individuals is deprived of *essential* foodstuffs, of *essential* primary health care, of *basic* shelter and housing, or of the *most basic* forms of education is, *prima facie* [at first look], failing to discharge its obligations under the Covenant. If the Covenant were to be read in such a way as not to establish such a *minimum core obligation*, it would be largely deprived of its *raison d'être*.

This principle keeps applied by the CoESCR.

> The concept is found in 15 of the Committee's 23 General Comments, and up to 2016, more than 100 of its Concluding Observations referenced core obligations. In deepening its commentary on core obligations, the CESCR [Committee] has aligned the concept with the International Labour Organization's conception of a 'Social Protection Floor' (SPF), emphasizing the content aspect of the concept. (Chowdhury, 2020, p. 256)

For example (italics added):

- In GC 12 on "The right to adequate food (Art. 11)" (E/C.12/1999/5),[93] the Committee referred to "the *core content* of the right to adequate food" (para. 8) and its "violations" (para. 33), as "States have a *core obligation* to take the necessary action to mitigate and alleviate hunger as provided for in paragraph 2 of Article 11, even in times of natural or other disasters" (para. 6).
- In GC 25 on "Science and economic, social and cultural rights (Article 15 (1) (b), (2), (3) and (4) of the International Covenant on Economic, Social and Cultural Rights)" (E/C.12/GC/25, 30 April 2020),[94] it said:

> 21. Some limitations on the right to participate in and to enjoy the benefits of scientific progress and its applications might be necessary, as science and its applications can, in certain contexts, affect economic, social and cultural rights. Nevertheless, limitations on the right must respect the requirements of Article 4 of the Covenant [...]. As understood by the Committee, this implies that limitations must respect the *minimum core obligations* of the right and must be proportionate to the aim pursued. [...]

Section D articulates (italics added) the "Core obligations" (Articles 51 and 52).

> 51. States Parties have to implement, as a matter of priority, *core obligations*. If a State Party fails to satisfy these core obligations, it must demonstrate that it has made every reasonable effort to comply with them,

> taking into account the totality of the rights enshrined in the Covenant, and in the context of the maximum of its available resources, individually and through international assistance and cooperation.
>
> Core obligations are laid down in Article 52.

The *Limburg Principles*[95] use the term "essence" (para. 56) and recall the rules of Articles 31 and 32 of the Vienna Convention on the Law of Treaties (1969).

The same notion is found in other UN bodies' documents and international texts, in national Constitutions and other legal texts, as well as in international and national jurisprudence. For example (italics added):

- CoHR, GC 31 (CCPR/C/21/Rev.1/Add.13, 26 May 2004)[96]: "In no case may the restrictions be applied or invoked in a manner that would impair the *essence* of a Covenant right" (para. 6).
- CoRC, GC 19 (CRC/C/GC/19, 20 July 2016)[97]: "The immediate and *minimum core obligations* imposed by children's rights shall not be compromised by any retrogressive measures, even in times of economic crisis" (para. 31).
- Committee on the Rights of Persons with Disabilities, GC 4 (CRPD/C/GC/4, 25 November 2016)[98]:

> 41. Progressive realization does not prejudice those obligations that are immediately applicable. As the Committee on Economic, Social and Cultural Rights has stated in its General Comment N°. 3 (1990) on the nature of States Parties' obligations, States Parties have a *minimum core obligation* to ensure the satisfaction of, at the very least, minimum essential levels of each aspect of the right to education.

- Commission on Human Rights (R/1993/14, E/CN.4/1993/122)[99]: States should "give effect to the *minimum core obligation* to ensure the satisfaction of *minimum essential levels* of each of the rights" (para. 7).
- African Commission on Human and Peoples' Rights, "Principles and Guidelines on the Implementation of Economic, Social and Cultural Rights in the African Charter on Human and Peoples' Rights"[100]:

> 17. States Parties have an obligation to ensure the satisfaction of, at the very least, the *minimum essential levels* of each of the economic, social and cultural rights contained in the African Charter. The minimum core obligation is the obligation of the State to ensure that no significant number of individuals is deprived of the essential elements of a particular right. This obligation exists regardless of the availability of resources and is non-derogable.

- Annual Report 1993 of the Inter-American Commission on Human Rights (OEA/Ser.L/V.II.85, doc. 9, rev., February 11, 1994, 519–534),[101] Chapter V:

> ... the obligation of Member States to observe and defend the human rights of individuals within their jurisdictions, as set forth in both the American Declaration and the American Convention, obligates them, regardless of the level of economic development, to guarantee a *minimum threshold* of these rights.

- Charter of Fundamental Rights of the European Union[102]: "Any limitation on the exercise of the rights and freedoms recognised by this Charter must be provided for by law and respect the *essence* of those rights and freedoms" (Article 52.1).
- Constitution of the Swiss Confederation, Article 36.4[103]: "The *essence* of fundamental rights is sacrosanct" (*L'essence des droits fondamentaux est inviolable*).[104]
- European Court of Human Rights, *Case "relating to certain aspects of the laws on the use of languages in education in Belgium" v. Belgium* (Applications 1474/62; 1677/62; 1691/62; 1769/63; 1994/63; 2126/64)[105]: "It goes without saying that such regulation must never injure the *substance* of the right to education nor conflict with other rights enshrined in the Convention" (B.5). The Court repeated this warning in other Cases, such as: *Campbell and Cosans v. the United Kingdom* (Applications 7511/76 and 7743/76, 25 February 1982)[106] and *Ashingdane v. The United Kingdom* (Application 8225/78, Judgement on 28 May 1985).[107]
- The USA Constitution does not include the right to education, but some State's Constitutions do, among them the Constitution of the State of New York (Article XI).[108] In the *Case Campaign for Fiscal Equity, Incl. et al. v. State of New York et al.* (Decided on June 26, 2003),[109] the Court of Appeals of New York had to decide "over the kind and amount of schooling children need in order to be assured of the constitutional minimum of educational opportunity". The term *constitutional minimum* appears several times.
- The Constitutional Court of Colombia makes large use of the core content principle.

However, core content/obligations – a notion not to be found in the Covenant – is a fuzzy and debated subject. It is "A Concept in Search of Content", as reads the subtitle of an article by Katharine G. Young (2008). The CoESCR itself is inconsistent regarding its terminology and determination (see Mechlem, 2009, pp. 940–944). The preceding considerations raise questions that may be so formulated:

- Are "core content" and "core obligation" to be distinguished?
- Are core obligations unconditional?
- Which should be the criterion to identify the core content of a human right?
- What should be the core content's scope?
- May such a concept be counterproductive?

Seeking to provide legally principled answers, the following brief conclusions are proposed.

Are "core content" and "core obligation" to be distinguished?
The CoESCR uses the terms *core content, core obligation(s), minimum core obligation(s), minimum essential levels.*

Core content and *core obligation(s)* are just two faces of the same stake: legal rights imply legal obligations or duties. If *core content* and *core obligation(s)* mean portions of the full normative content and the associated obligations, *minimum core obligation(s)* and *minimum essential levels* add nothing to the matter: *minimum* and *essential levels* are redundancy to *core content* and *core obligation(s)*. So understood, the question whether the core obligations determine the core content, or the other way around, appears meaningless. As Fons Coomans (2004) wrote:

> ... there seems to be little difference between the core content approach on the one hand, and the core obligations approach on the other, because core elements of rights of individuals need to be translated into core obligations for the State. However, it may be argued that it is crucial to retain as a point of departure the right of the individual, rather than the obligations of the State, because the latter derive from the right, at least from a human rights perspective. (p. 98)

Are core obligations unconditional?
Whereas in GC 14 the CoESCR stressed "that a State Party cannot, under any circumstances whatsoever, justify its non-compliance with the core obligations set out in paragraph 43 above, which are nonderogable" (para. 47), in GC 3 it had admitted:

> 10. ... any assessment as to whether a State has discharged its minimum core obligation must also take account of resource constraints applying within the country concerned. Article 2 (1) obligates each State Party to take the necessary steps "to the maximum of its available resources". In order for a State Party to be able to attribute its

> failure to meet at least its minimum core obligations to a lack of available resources it must demonstrate that every effort has been made to use all resources that are at its disposition in an effort to satisfy, as a matter of priority, those minimum obligations.

The normativity may be powerless facing the reality.

Which should be the criterion to identify the core content of a human right?
John Tasioulas (2017) identifies four senses of "minimum core obligations":

> (a) that sub-set of obligations corresponding to economic, social and cultural human rights that must be immediately complied with in full by all states, irrespective of differences in the level of resources that exist among them;
> (b) those human rights obligations whose content or justification bears a special connection to some underlying, high-priority ethical value, such as human dignity or basic human needs;
> (c) a sub-set of non-derogable human rights obligations, such that no competing considerations can ever justify a state's non-compliance with them, even in an emergency; and
> (d) those human rights obligations that are or should be justiciable, i.e. enforceable through domestic or supranational courts. (p. 2)

In his opinion, *immediacy* offers the best account of the concept.

As above quoted, *essence* or *substance* are terms used as synonymous with *core content*. Human dignity is the source and sense of all human rights, for the protection and promotion of which each human right is intended to contribute, in accordance with the Human Dignity Principle account to be submitted (see 2.6.2). Therefore, it can be argued that the criterion for the identification of the core content should be twofold, namely: the essence/substance of the right specific value and its feasible or affordable immediate implementation by all States, if needed "through international assistance and cooperation, especially economic and technical" (ICESCR Article 2.1).

What should be the core content's scope?
Where the concept was originally narrowly constructed by the CoESCR, in its latest GC (as of November 2020) – the GC 25 on "Science and economic, social and cultural rights (Article 15 (1) (b), (2), (3) and (4) of the International Covenant on Economic, Social and Cultural Rights)" (E/C.12/GC/25, 30 April

2020)[110] – are laid down 12 core obligations (Article 52). Another example is provided for by the extent of the "Core obligations" included in Articles 43 and 44 of the GC 14 on "The right to the highest attainable standard of health (Article 12 of the International Covenant on Economic, Social and Cultural Rights)" (E/C.12/2000/4, 11 August 2000).[111]

The question is: Could a human right core content be narrowed to the satisfaction of the basic needs necessary for survival or extended to what is necessary for life with dignity? If *human life* is dignified life, the core content of each human right should not be barely *animalising* ...

May such a concept be counterproductive?

Under the two International Covenants, civil and political rights, in general, entail stronger obligations than economic, social and cultural rights. As the CoHR stressed in its GC 31 on "The Nature of the General Legal Obligation Imposed on States Parties to the Covenant" (CCPR/C/21/Rev.1/Add. 13, 26 May 2004)[112]: "The requirement under Article 2, paragraph 2, to take steps to give effect to the Covenant rights is unqualified and of immediate effect. A failure to comply with this obligation cannot be justified by reference to political, social, cultural or economic considerations within the State" (para. 14).

Differently, economic, social and cultural rights may be realised "progressively", as reads the ICESCR Article 2.1. The doctrine of *core content/obligations* aims at safeguarding a sub-set of the normative content of each human right – minimum entitlements – protected by the Covenant that must be immediately fully satisfied by all States, in principle, for the sake of the meaningfulness of its universal object and purpose, as internationally agreed.

Therefore, the core content of a right cannot be used as an 'escape clause' for States not to comply with its full normative content. To it may apply *mutatis mutandis* (with the necessary adaptation) what is provided for in Article 5 common to the two International Covenants, so worded in the ICESCR[113] (italics added):

1. Nothing in the present Covenant may be interpreted as implying for any State, group or person any right to engage in any activity or to perform any act aimed at the destruction of any of the rights or freedoms recognized herein, or at *their limitation to a greater extent than is provided for* in the present Covenant.
2. No restriction upon or derogation from any of the fundamental human rights recognized or existing in any country in virtue of law, conventions, regulations or custom shall be admitted on the pretext that the present Covenant does not recognize such rights or that it *recognizes them to a lesser extent.*

The doctrine of the core content is a reminder of "the fact that even in times of severe resources constraints whether caused by a process of adjustment, of economic recession, or by other factors the vulnerable members of society can and indeed must be protected by the adoption of relatively low-cost targeted programmes", as the CoESCR underlined in its CG 3 (E/1991/23, para. 12).[114]

An added value of defining a human right core content is the reinforcement of its justiciability.

To conclude, whereas the *approach core obligations* is rather positivistic, the *approach core content* is more consistent with the human rights idea and ideal. It allows for the content of a human right object to be described as a normative complex composed of three layers, as it were: minimum content, full content and expanded content – a triple content that meets the initially quoted Orücü's distinction between *core, circumjacence* and *outer edge* scope, namely:

- *Minimum content* is that defining the level of guarantee of a right below which it loses its essence/substance, becoming meaningless.
- *Full content* is that including all the elements/entitlements of a human right scope, formally laid down in its standards or jurisprudentially developed.
- *Expanded content* includes all elements and obligations making up the right's full content, and others resulting from the principle of human rights interdependence.

2.5.7.2 Jus Cogens *and* Erga Omnes *Obligations*

Jus Cogens is a Latin term meaning literally 'Peremptory Law'. The denomination itself indicates that it does not express a new idea, but the concept entered International Law only with the Vienna Convention on the Law of Treaties (1969),[115] whose Article 53 bears the title "Treaties conflicting with a peremptory norm of general international law ('jus cogens')".

There is a consensus about the antiquity and superiority of *Jus Cogens*, but its sources divide the doctrine according to the classic opposition naturalism-positivism. Nonetheless, its normative uniqueness does not derive from the nature of its sources but rather from the ethical substance of its content. It transcends the conventional and customary sources of International Law. In the opinion of A. A. Cançado Trindade (2006), the *Jus Cogens* ultimately emanate "from the universal juridical conscience" (p. 176). *Conscience* and *transcendence* are, indeed, the signifiers better concentrating the ethical density of the universal fundamental norms of *Jus Cogens.* Their hard core lies in the ethical principles of human rights, which underlie the International Public Order.

As a consequence, the *Jus cogens* "introduces a material hierarchy (established by its substantial content) into the international legal order" (Dupuy, 2008, pp. 566, 567), in which there is no formal hierarchy. Following Tomuschat (2008): "It has generally been assumed, to date, that the core rights which are directly related to human existence are to be classified as *jus cogens*, i.e. as rules from which no derogation is permitted" (p. 38). Such rights, according to Olivier de Schutter (2009), "include at a minimum the prohibition of aggression, slavery and the slave trade, genocide, racial discrimination, apartheid and torture, as well as basic rules of international humanitarian law applicable in armed conflicts, and the right to self-determination" (p. 50).

The UN Charter, IHRL and the Vienna Convention may be considered cornerstones of an emerging Constitution of the International Community. *Jus Cogens* appears as the core of the constitutional dimension of International Law.

Jus Cogens norms imply obligations *erga omnes* (towards all).

Erga omnes is a category of obligations first identified by the International Court of Justice in the *Case Barcelona Traction, Light and Power, Limited* (1970),[116] when it said:

> 33. … an essential distinction should be drawn between the obligations of a State towards the international community as a whole, and those arising vis-à-vis another State in the field of diplomatic protection. By their very nature the former are the concern of all States. In view of the importance of the rights involved, all States can be held to have a legal interest in their protection; they are obligations *erga omnes*.
>
> 34. Such obligations derive, for example, in contemporary international law, from the outlawing of acts of aggression, and of genocide, as also from the principles and rules concerning the basic rights of the human person, including protection from slavery and racial discrimination. Some of the corresponding rights of protection have entered into the body of general international law (*Reservations to the Convention on the Prevention and Punishment of the Crime of Genocide, Advisory Opinion, I.C.J. Reports 1951*, p. 23); others are conferred by international instruments of a universal or quasi-universal character.

Consequently, States' obligations *erga omnes* are obligations towards the whole International Community, insofar as all States are deemed to have an interest in their being complied with. Most of them emerged within IHRL and IHL. Human rights are "a typical example of *erga omnes* obligations" (Mégret, 2010, p. 129), so that every State becomes, in some way, an "international ombudsman" of human rights (Sohn, 1982, p. 23). To the contrary: "A State that persistently violates human rights acts against the community of nations and against the ethical and legal values that guide and condition the conscience of humanity", as Julio P. Vallejo (1990, p. 70) pointed out.

The close relation existing between obligations *erga omnes* and norms *Jus Cogens* may confuse. All *Jus Cogens* norms generate obligations *erga omnes*, but these are not necessarily tied to *Jus Cogens* norms.

Jus Cogens norms and obligations *erga omnes* are notions with an open content, which develop through their concrete application.

2.5.7.3 *'Drittwirkung'*

In the second half of the 19th century, the German doctrine elaborated the concept of 'public subjective rights' as being rights opposable to the State. There are rights only opposable to the State, but there are other powers in relation to which individuals need the protection of the State. The need for protection against third parties originated the concept of *Drittwirkung*, in the 1950s, that means literally "third party effect".[117] The German Federal Constitutional Court used it, in 1958, in the *Case Lüth* (*BVerfGE 7, 198*).[118]

The *Drittwirkung* doctrine has broadened to other countries. On the American continent, the Inter-American Court of Human Rights applied it for the first time in the *Case of Velásquez Rodríguez v. Honduras* (1987), the first one submitted to its contentious jurisdiction. In this respect, the CoHR said in its GC 31 (CCPR/C/21/Rev.1/Add. 13, 26 May 2004)[119]:

> 8. The Article 2, paragraph 1, obligations are binding on States and do not, as such, have direct horizontal effect as a matter of international law. The Covenant cannot be viewed as a substitute for domestic criminal or civil law. However, the positive obligations on States Parties to ensure Covenant rights will only be fully discharged if individuals are protected by the State, not just against violations of Covenant rights by its agents, but also against acts committed by private persons or entities that would impair the enjoyment of Covenant rights, in so far as they are amenable to application between private persons or entities.

The "changing configuration of the public-private divide in human rights ordering" (Steiner, Alston, & Goodman, 2008, p. vi) has increased the need to protect human rights against their violations by powerful non-State actors (NSAs). This is a consequence of the world Globalisation, in particular. According to Catarina Krause and Scheinin (2009):

> ... globalization, with the emergence of other actors besides states as world-level agents that affect the lives of individuals in ways that traditionally were thought to be a monopoly of states, through trade, services, investments and other means, has put into question the very concept of

> human rights as a body of vertical norms between the state and the individual.
>
> If human rights are rights of the individual, should it not be for anyone who has the power to affect the enjoyment of those rights to be obliged to respect them? (p. ix)

Given that NSAs, in general, are not bound directly by IHRL, the CHR adopted in 2011 *Guiding Principles on Business and Human Rights.*[120] In 2014, it decided "to establish an open-ended intergovernmental working group on transnational corporations and other business enterprises concerning human rights, whose mandate shall be to elaborate an international legally binding instrument to regulate, in international human rights law, the activities of transnational corporations and other business enterprises" (A/HRC/RES/26/9, 14 July 2014).[121] The CoESCR adopted the "General comment N°. 24 (2017) on State obligations under the International Covenant on Economic, Social and Cultural Rights in the context of business activities" (E/C.12/GC/24).[122]

Tomuschat (2008) commented: "To advocate such a third-party effect of human rights amounts to an almost revolutionary step" (p. 108).

2.5.7.4 Private Providers

The provision by NSAs of the public services required by human rights is not incompatible with IHRL. However, in the case of decentralisation, delegation or privatisation, States are always responsible for guaranteeing that their provision respects the public service obligations, which include the universality of coverage, equality, equity, quality, continuity, neutrality, as well as affordability.

In 2002, the CoRC devoted a General Discussion Day to the theme "The Private Sector as Services Provider and its Role in Implementing Child Rights".[123] In the following year, the Committee said in its GC 5 on "General measures of implementation of the Convention on the Rights of the Child (Arts. 4, 42 and 44, para. 6)" (CRC/GC/2003/5)[124]:

> 41. The Committee reiterates that in all circumstances the State which ratified or acceded to the Convention remains responsible for ensuring the full implementation of the Convention throughout the territories under its jurisdiction. [...] Further, there must be safeguards to ensure that decentralization or devolution does not lead to discrimination in the enjoyment of rights by children in different regions.
> 42. The process of privatization of services can have a serious impact on the recognition and realization of children's rights. The Committee devoted its 2002 day of general discussion to the theme "The private sector as service provider and its role in implementing child

rights", defining the private sector as including businesses, NGOs and other private associations, both for-profit and not-for-profit. Following that day of general discussion, the Committee adopted detailed recommendations to which it draws the attention of States Parties. [...]

44. The Committee emphasizes that enabling the private sector to provide services, run institutions and so on does not in any way lessen the State's obligation to ensure for all children within its jurisdiction the full recognition and realization of all rights in the Convention (arts. 2 (1) and 3 (2)). Article 3 (1) establishes that the best interests of the child shall be a primary consideration in all actions concerning children, whether undertaken by public or private bodies.

2.5.7.5 Extraterritorial Obligations

The ICESCR does not explicitly refer to jurisdiction, a term with different uses whose meaning goes beyond the power a State exerts over a territory. States have human rights obligations outside their territory.[125]

The CoESCR alluded, in its first GC,[126] to the rights "enjoyed by all individuals within its territory or under its jurisdiction" (para. 3). In GC 24 (E/C.12/GC/24, 10 August 2017), it pointed out:

- In the ICESCR, the States' obligations "are expressed without any restriction linked to territory or jurisdiction" (para. 27).
- "Customary International Law also prohibits a State from allowing its territory to be used to cause damage on the territory of another State" (para. 27).
- States Parties are "required to take the steps necessary to prevent human rights violations abroad by corporations domiciled in their territory and/or jurisdiction" (para. 26).
- "Article 2 (1) refers to international assistance and cooperation" (para. 27).
- The International Court of Justice – in line with the UN Charter Article 55 where the Member States assume obligations under human rights treaties – "has acknowledged the extraterritorial scope of core human rights treaties, focusing on their object and purpose, their legislative history and the lack of territorial limitation provisions in the text" (para. 27). This includes situations in which a State exercises control over populations of other territories in the event of occupation or with an international mandate.

In effect, in its Advisory Opinion on the "Legal Consequences of the Construction of a Wall in the Occupied Palestinian Territory" (9 July 2004),[127] requested by the UN General Assembly, the International Court of Justice said:

> 109. The Court would observe that, while the jurisdiction of States is primarily territorial, it may sometimes be exercised outside the national territory. […]
>
> 134. To sum up, the Court is of the opinion that the construction of the wall and its associated *regime* impede the liberty of movement of the inhabitants of the Occupied Palestinian Territory (with the exception of Israeli citizens and those assimilated thereto) as guaranteed under Article 12, paragraph 1, of the International Covenant on Civil and Political Rights. They also impede the exercise by the persons concerned of the right to work, to health, to education and to an adequate standard of living as proclaimed in the International Covenant on Economic, Social and Cultural Rights and in the United Nations Convention on the Rights of the Child.

In 2005, in *Case Armed Activities on the Territory of the Congo (Democratic Republic of the Congo v. Uganda)*,[128] it reaffirmed that IHRL is applicable "in respect of acts done by a State in the exercise of its jurisdiction outside its own territory" (para. 216).

In this regard, the Joint statement by the Human Rights Committee and the Committee on Economic, Social and Cultural Rights on "The International Covenants on Human Rights: 50 years on" (CCPR/C/2016/1-E/C.12/2016/3)[129] pointed out:

> 6. … the extraterritorial implications of human rights treaties are being acknowledged: States increasingly understand that they cannot commit violations outside their borders that they would be prohibited from committing at home, and that they must refrain from taking measures that could adversely affect human rights outside their national territory. These are major advances.

The extraterritorial obligations concerning the ICESCR are addressed by the *Maastricht Principles on Extraterritorial Obligations of States in the Area of Economic, Social and Cultural Rights* (2011).[130]

2.5.7.6 Jurisprudence and Doctrine

The term 'jurisprudence' is defined in Dalloz *Lexique de termes juridique* (Lexicon of legal terms, 1988, 7th ed.) as follows:

> In an ancient sense, the science of Law.

> In a more precise and modern sense, the solution taken by a set of sufficiently consistent decisions made by the courts on a question of Law.

In the ancient sense, it is synonym with Philosophy of Law. The term is not to be found in the *Dictionary of Law* (Oxford, 1997, 4th ed.) that mentions only *Case Law*. A German *Juristisches Wörterbuch* (Lexicon of legal terms, Verlag Vahlen, 1997, 8th ed.) mentions the term *Jurisprudenz* as a synonym with *Rechtswissenschaft* (Science of Law), so defined: "Science dealing with the legal normativity" (*die rechtliche Sollensordnung betreffende Wissenschaft*). The term equivalent to *Case Law* is *Rechtsprechung*, so defined: "Decision of concrete legal issues by the competent bodies" (*Entscheidung konkreter Rechtsfragen durch die dafür zuständige Stelle*).

In the modern sense, jurisprudence, as distinguished from Case Law (claims brought before Tribunals and Courts), means, therefore, the judicial interpretation of rules (for example, the jurisprudence on the right to education). It contributes to the normative development of human rights.

Doctrine is a term whose etymology is *docere*, a Latin word meaning to teach.

The legal doctrine is the set of opinions and comments devoted to the Law, expressed in treatises, textbooks, articles, chronicles, theses, monographs, etc. It also includes Advisory Opinions of International Courts and interpretations of legal norms by other established bodies.

The Doctrine influences the Legislator and the Judges, thus participating in the creation, interpretation and evolution of the Law.

2.5.8 *Principles of Interpretation and Implementation*

Norm is a genre of which rules, standards and principles are species. Principles are norms enunciating fundamental values or ideas, with a function of generalisation or guidance; or are bases of organisation, classification, functioning or behaviour; or elementary propositions relating to a field of knowledge; or indemonstrable postulates or axioms. The term has variable uses in International and Constitutional Law. Being abstract and general, the legal principles have to be interpreted on a case-by-case basis, and their application may need metalegal contributions.

The Vienna Convention on the Law of Treaties (1969)[131] recalls, in its preamble, "the principles of international law embodied in the Charter of the United Nations", among which the principle "of universal respect for, and observance of, human rights and fundamental freedoms for all". The IHRL should be interpreted according to the rules laid down in Articles 31 and 32 of the Vienna Convention, taking into account the human rights specificity (that the Vienna Convention does not ignore). The Convention on the Rights of Persons with

Disabilities (UN, 2006) formally mentions the principles inspiring it: they are general principles and principles concerning persons with disabilities in particular. The UN Draft Convention on the Right to Development (A/HRC/WG.2/21/2)[132] also states "General principles" (Article 3).

The following categories of principles of interpretation and implementation of human rights may be distinguished: ethical principles, most general legal principles, other legal principles, jurisprudential principles, political principles. These categories are only suggested for the sake of systematisation, but they are not watertight. They form a whole whose overall sense is the guarantee of all human rights for all, as fully as possible.

In the context of this essay, only the most general legal principles and ethical principles are being addressed.

2.5.8.1 Most General Legal Principles

The following may be considered, by their very overarching nature, to be the most general legal principles of human rights interpretation and enforcement: universality, non-discrimination, interdependence, openness and evolving content.

2.5.8.1.1 *Universality*

Human rights are universal, by definition. The Vienna Declaration and Programme of Action[133] has affirmed: "The universal nature of these rights and freedoms is beyond question" (I-1). However, the human rights universality had been challenged by two regional documents preceding the Vienna Conference:
- Cairo Declaration on Human Rights in Islam, adopted by the OIC in 1990.
- Bangkok Declaration on Human Rights, approved by Ministers and representatives of Asian States meeting at Bangkok from 29 March to 2 April 1993.

The main argument opposed to the human rights universality is that they are a Western and individualistic idea, disregarding the so-called 'Asian Values' (a slogan of some authoritarian regimes). Another one is that economic, social and cultural rights should be given priority to the civil and political rights more emphasised in the Western world. Also, the principles of sovereignty and non-interference in domestic affairs must prevail. These arguments are invalidated by several facts:
- Although the concept of 'human right' is permeated with Western philosophical, legal and political thought, the UDHR was not a merely Western creature, as its legislative history documents.

  It was pointed out, for example, that freedom and tolerance are also important moral values in the Buddhist tradition, as testified by The Edicts of Ashoka (a set of inscriptions attributed to an Indian King in the 3rd century BC).

- Over 100 NGOs from 26 Asian countries, meeting at Bangkok from 24 to 28 March 1993, approved the Bangkok NGO Declaration on Human Rights highlighting the universality and unity of all human rights.
- All UN Member States undertake to respect the principle of respect for human rights included in its Charter, and all have ratified one of the core human rights treaties, at least, and more than 80% have ratified four or more.
- Several human rights have become Customary International Law and, therefore, legally binding for every member of the International Community.

Human rights are ethically individualistic, by definition too, i.e. recognised to protect and promote the worth, dignity, autonomy, and existence of each human person. The individualism of human rights does not mean, however, in any way, that individuals are considered as abstract entities, isolated from the groups indispensable for their survival and existence.

At the end of the day, what should matter is not where the moral, artistic, scientific, technological or other civilisational advancements come from, but how good and beneficial they are for the whole Humankind.

2.5.8.1.2 *Non-Discrimination*

The principle of non-discrimination is a corollary of the universality of human rights.

Non-discrimination and self-determination are the only rights formally mentioned in the UN Charter (mainly in Preamble and Articles 1, 13, 55, 76). The UDHR proclaims, in Article 1: "All human beings are born free and equal in dignity and rights". This provision must be understood in light of Articles 2 and 7, in particular. The principle of non-discrimination is a cornerstone of the 1966 International Covenants, crosses the IHRL, and is also addressed by several specific instruments, with a more or less extensive wording, but almost always open-ended. It was elaborated by the CoHR GC 18 (1989) and the CoESCR GC 20 (2009).

René-Jean Dupuy (1986) wrote: "Equality, which is a philosophical, moral and legal principle, has meaning because human beings are not identical. Thus, the fundamental, first norm, is the one that prohibits discrimination, because it assumes both the difference and the equality" (p. 176). The principle of non-discrimination is, therefore, the "new form, more perfected without a doubt and more nuanced, of the old principle of equality" (Pelloux, 1972, p. 7).

Discrimination consists of acts or omissions that affect the enjoyment and exercise of human rights. It may be *de jure* (legal) or *de facto* (actual), direct or indirect, active or passive. Notwithstanding, a slight difference is to be noticed: the UN Charter, the UNESCO Constitution, the UDHR and the ICCPR use the term 'distinction', while the ICESCR, the ILO standards, and other international instruments use the term 'discrimination' (the CRC uses both). The latter is the most appropriate as some distinctions are justified to promote equality, as said the Permanent Court of International Justice in 1935, in the *Advisory Opinion on the Minority Schools in Albania Case.*[134] Differences of treatment on the basis of need or merit are not discriminatory. In effect, the elimination of discrimination may justify measures of 'positive discrimination' (reverse discrimination or affirmative action) as long as they are objective, proportional and temporary. In this regard, the Committee on the Elimination of Racial Discrimination said in 2009, in its General Recommendation 32 (CERD/C/GC/32)[135]:

> 11. The concept of special measures is based on the principle that laws, policies and practices adopted and implemented in order to fulfil obligations under the Convention require supplementing, when circumstances warrant, by the adoption of temporary special measures designed to secure to disadvantaged groups the full and equal enjoyment of human rights and fundamental freedoms. Special measures are one component in the ensemble of provisions in the Convention dedicated to the objective of eliminating racial discrimination, the successful achievement of which will require the faithful implementation of all Convention provisions.

Notwithstanding, it should be noted that certain civil and political rights may be submitted to restrictions that are not "unreasonable" (ICCPR Article 25). In this respect, the CoHR said in 1996, in GC 21 (CCPR/C/21/Rev.1/Add.7)[136]:

> 3. In contrast with other rights and freedoms recognized by the Covenant (which are ensured to all individuals within the territory and subject to the jurisdiction of the State), Article 25 protects the rights of "every citizen". [...] Distinctions between those who are entitled to citizenship by birth and those who acquire it by naturalization may raise questions of compatibility with Article 25. [...]
> 4. Any conditions which apply to the exercise of the rights protected by Article 25 should be based on objective and reasonable criteria. For example, it may be reasonable to require a higher age for election or appointment to particular offices than for exercising the right to vote, which should be available to every adult citizen. The exercise of these rights by citizens may not be suspended or excluded except on grounds which are established by law and which are objective and reasonable. For example, established mental incapacity may be a ground for denying a person the right to vote or to hold office.

Restrictions are admitted by the ICESCR too (Article 2.3), but the CoESCR said in its GC 19 (E/C.12/GC/19)[137]:

> 36. Article 2, paragraph 2, prohibits discrimination on grounds of nationality and the Committee notes that the Covenant contains no express jurisdictional limitation. [...]
> 37. Non-nationals should be able to access non-contributory schemes for income support, affordable access to health care and family support. Any restrictions, including a qualification period, must be proportionate and reasonable. All persons, irrespective of their nationality, residency or immigration status, are entitled to primary and emergency medical care.

2.5.8.1.3 *Interdependence of Human Rights*

The principle of interdependence of human rights was hotly debated in the early 1950s, at the UN General Assembly, when began the preparatory work of the International Covenants and it was discussed whether one or two covenants should be prepared (see 2.4).

The interdependence and indivisibility of human rights have become a leitmotif in the texts adopted by the UN General Assembly (see Whelan, 2011) that, for example, approved in 1989 a Resolution on the "Indivisibility and interdependence of economic, social, cultural, civil and political rights" (A/RES/44/130).[138] The principle was restated by the two landmark conferences on human rights convened by UN: International Conference on Human Rights, Tehran (Iran), 1968, and World Conference on Human Rights, Vienna (Austria), 1993. The Vienna Declaration and Programme of Action[139] proclaimed: "All human rights are universal, indivisible and interdependent and interrelated. The international community must treat human rights globally in a fair and equal manner, on the same footing, and with the same emphasis" (I.5).[140]

The Convention on the Elimination of All Forms of Discrimination against Women, the International Convention on the Protection of the Rights of All Migrant Workers and Members of Their Families, the Convention on the Rights of the Child, and the Convention on the Rights of Persons with Disabilities include all categories of rights. Likewise, the ACHPR and the Charter of Fundamental Rights of the European Union.

The CoESCR reaffirmed, in its GC 9 on "The domestic application of the Covenant" (E/C.12/1998/24),[141] "the principle that the two sets of human rights are indivisible and interdependent" (para. 11). In 2008, the Optional Protocol to the International Covenant on Economic, Social and Cultural Rights on a Communications Procedure[142] recalled "the universality, indivisibility, interdependence and interrelatedness of all human rights and fundamental freedoms" (Preamble).

In this connection, the first joint meeting of the CoHR and the CoESCR, held on 23 June 2016, on the occasion of the 50th anniversary of the two Covenants, and their Joint Statement, were a symbolic event (CCPR/C/2016/1-E/C.12/2016/3).[143]

The interdependence of human rights is fully epitomised in the right to life, as developed by international and national jurisprudence.

The Inter-American Court on Human Rights introduced the concept of "dignified life" (*vida digna*). It said in *Case 'Street Children'* (*Villagrán-Morales et al. v Guatemala* (1999)[144]:

> 144. The right to life is a fundamental human right, and the exercise of this right is essential for the exercise of all other human rights. If it is not respected, all rights lack meaning. Owing to the fundamental nature of the right to life, restrictive approaches to it are inadmissible. In essence, the fundamental right to life includes, not only the right of every human being not to be deprived of his life arbitrarily, but also the right that he will not be prevented from having access to the conditions that guarantee a dignified existence.

The CoHR has moved in the same direction with its far-reaching GC 36 (replacing GC 6 adopted in 1982) (CCPR/C/GC/36, 3 September 2019).[145] After noting that the content of the right to life "can be informed by other human rights" (para. 2), it affirms:

> 3. The right to life is a right that should not be interpreted narrowly. It concerns the entitlement of individuals to be free from acts and omissions that are intended or may be expected to cause their unnatural or premature death, as well as to enjoy a life with dignity. Article 6 of the Covenant guarantees this right for all human beings, without distinction of any kind, including for persons suspected or convicted of even the most serious crimes. [...]
>
> 26. ... The measures called for to address adequate conditions for protecting the right to life include, where necessary, measures designed to ensure access without delay by individuals to essential goods and services such as food, water, shelter, health care, electricity and sanitation, and other measures designed to promote and facilitate adequate general conditions [...].

Other examples of Case Law on the right to life broadly understood include:
- The High Court of South Africa (North Gauteng High Court) said in *Case Stransham-Ford v Minister of Justice And Correctional Services and Others*

(27401/15) [2015] *ZAGPPHC 230; 2015 (4) SA 50 (GP); [2015] 3 All SA 109 (GP); 2015 (6) BCLR 737 (GP) (4 May 2015)*,[146] relating to assisted suicide:

> 12. … It is also worthwhile quoting what O'Reagan J had to say in the Makwanyane decision supra about the notion that the right to life must be a life that is worth living: "the right to life is, in one sense, antecedent to all other rights in the Constitution. Without life in the sense of existence, it would not be possible to exercise rights or to be the bearer of them. But the right to life was included in the Constitution not simply to enshrine the right to existence. It is not life as mere organic matter that the Constitution cherishes, but the right to human life: the right to share in the experience of humanity. This concept of human life is at the centre of our constitutional values. The Constitution seeks to establish a society where the individual value of each member of the community is recognized and treasured. The right to life is central to such a society. The right to life, thus understood, incorporates the right to dignity. So the rights to dignity and to life are intertwined. The right to life is more than existence, it is a right to be treated as a human being with dignity: without dignity, human life is substantially diminished. Without life, there cannot be dignity".

– The Inter-American Court said in *Case Sawhoyamaxa Indigenous Community v. Paraguay* (2006)[147] concerning the protection of the ancestral property right of an indigenous community involving its identity and survival:

> 156. In the instant case, there is no dispute between the parties regarding the fact that the conditions in which the members of the Sawhoyamaxa Community live are inadequate to lead a decent existence, nor regarding the fact that such conditions represent an actual and impending risk for their lives.

– The Supreme Court of India said in *Case Unni Krishnan v State of Andhra Pradesh 1993 AIR 2178; 1993 SCR (1) 594*[148] relating to private education and the link between the right to education and the right to life: "'Right to life' is the compendious expression for all those rights which the courts must enforce because they are basic to the dignified enjoyment of life. It extends to the full range of conduct which the individual is free to pursue". Therefore:

> (6) We think that the right to life includes right to live with human dignity and all that goes along with it viz., the bare necessities of life

> such as adequate nutrition, clothing and shelter and facilities for reading, writing and expressing oneself in diverse forms, freely moving about the mixing and commingling with fellow human beings. Of course, the magnitude and content of the components of this right would depend upon the extent of the economic development of the country, but it must in any view of the matter, include a right to the basic necessities of life and also the right to carry on such functions and activities as constitute the bare minimum expression of the human self.

The Inter-American Court also resorted to the concept of *life project/plan* (*proyecto de vida*) as a new dimension of non-material damage, in *Case Loayza-Tamayo v. Peru* (1998)[149] concerning a university professor imprisoned, tortured and raped for being accused of collaboration with the guerrilla *Sendero Luminoso*. Section XII (para. 144–154) is titled *Life plan*. The Court explained:

> 148. The concept of a "life plan" is akin to the concept of personal fulfilment, which in turn is based on the options that an individual may have for leading his life and achieving the goal that he sets for himself. Strictly speaking, those options are the manifestation and guarantee of freedom. An individual can hardly be described as truly free if he does not have options to pursue in life and to carry that life to its natural conclusion. Those options, in themselves, have an important existential value. Hence, their elimination or curtailment objectively abridges freedom and constitutes the loss of a valuable asset, a loss that this Court cannot disregard.

In 2007, in *Case Escue Zapata v. Colombia*[150] concerning the execution of an indigenous rights' defender, the Inter-American Court decided the following reparation:

> 169. The representatives highlighted the negative effects that the facts of the present case caused to the victim's daughter, who, with the death of his father, "lost many opportunities that could have had in her life". Considering the above, they requested a scholarship for higher studies as "reparation for the life project and a restitution of what Myriam could have". The State confirmed its will to comply with the granting of a university scholarship for the victim's daughter "in a well-known academic centre chosen by common consent between the victim and the State".

The increasing awareness of the unity of all human rights led to mentioning the human rights traditional categories in alphabetical order: civil, cultural, economic, political and social.

Human rights are interdependent because they interact (see also 2.6.2.4.2). However, a distinction should be made between interdependence and indivisibility, as stressed the former Independent Expert on the Right to Development (Arjun Sengupta) in his Fourth Report (E/CN.4/2002/WG.18/2)[151]:

> 25. The principle of indivisibility is often associated with the principle of interdependence, though they are not the same. Two rights are indivisible if one cannot be enjoyed if the other is violated. Two rights are interdependent if the level of enjoyment of one is dependent on the level of enjoyment of the other. [...]

In reality, human rights are not indivisible, in general, notably because:
- The impossibility of exercising a right does not necessarily preclude the exercise of other rights.
  For example, a sentence of imprisonment consists, by its very nature, in the deprivation of physical liberty, but does not preclude the freedom of thought. Likewise, the deprivation of the right to work does not deprive of the freedom of movement.
- Some situations may oblige one to choose between rights.
  For instance, someone may risk his or her life for the sake of liberty or accept reservations on his or her freedom of opinion or expression of the personality to gain access to a profession.
- The non-indivisibility of human rights may be better understood if a distinction between its ethical, legal and political dimensions is made:
  - Ethically, all human rights are necessary.
    All human rights are needed because all have as their source and sense the protection and enhancement of human dignity that is indivisible. As reads, for example, the preamble of the Protocol of San Salvador (1988),[152] "the different categories of rights constitute an indivisible whole based on the recognition of the dignity of the human person".
  - Legally, human rights are not equally fundamental.
    In effect, human rights were not placed by States on the same footing. There are human rights more intrinsic to human dignity than others. There is an obvious difference of urgency between, for instance, the right to life and the right to holidays. This is reflected in hierarchical and terminological differences:
    - There are human rights with customary status.

- There are human rights qualified as non-derogable.
- There are human rights whose breach is qualified as an international crime.
- There is an implicit hierarchy in the terminology itself.

For example, in the *Case Barcelona Traction, Light and Power Company, Limited (Belgium v. Spain)* (1970),[153] the International Court of Justice referred to "the principles and rules concerning the basic rights of the human person, including protection from slavery and racial discrimination" (para. 34). They are rights whose breach is a direct attack on the dignity of a human being, i.e. to his or her life, physical and psychological integrity, and moral and intellectual autonomy. In the opinion of Teraya Koji (2001), *Barcelona Traction* is "the first case which appears to recognize an emerging hierarchy in international human rights norms" (p. 931).

- Politically, it may be necessary to choose priorities.

In a situation of a humanitarian emergency, the priority is to save and to feed lives. And there are rights whose realisation is determinant for other ones.

Tasioulas (2017) rightly suggests "a more modest interpretation of the thesis" of human rights indivisibility (p. 15). Without precluding that "one part of the transition from human rights rhetoric to human rights reality is to take the indivisibility of rights seriously" (Ssenyonjo, 2016, 1.20).

2.5.8.1.4 *Open-Ended Concept and Evolving Content of Human Rights*

'Human right' is an open concept. Transformations in the world and societies change how human rights can be exercised and create the need to recognise new rights, as happened in the past. The principle of the living nature of the human rights instruments has been recalled by international bodies established for their protection and higher Courts. For example:

- European Court of Human Rights, *Case Tyrer v. the United Kingdom* (Application 5856/72, 25 April 1978)[154]: "The Court must also recall that the Convention is a living instrument which, as the Commission rightly stressed, must be interpreted in the light of present-day conditions" (para. 31). This has been frequently recalled by the European Court.[155]
- European Committee of Social Rights[156]: "The Committee interprets the rights and freedoms set out in the Charter [European Social Charter] in the light of current conditions and in the light of relevant international instruments, as well as in light of new emerging issues and situations, in other words, the Charter is a living instrument" (p. 41).
- The Federal Constitutional Court of Germany said in *Case BVerfGE 45, 187 (Lebenslange Freiheitsstrafe)* (1977)[157]: "The recognition of what is necessary

to comply with the command to respect human dignity is, however, inseparable from the historical development" (para. 146).

- The Constitutional Court of Colombia referred to "this open constitutional category that is now the fundamental right" (*T-429/92*).[158]
- The Supreme Court of India said in *Case Kesavananda Bharati v. Kerala, [1973] Supp*)[159]: "The Fundamental Rights themselves have no fixed content; most of them are mere empty vessels into which each generation must pour its content in the light of its experience". In *Case Unni Krishnan, J.P. And Ors. Etc. ... vs State Of Andhra Pradesh And Ors. ... on 4 February, 1993* (*1993 AIR 2178, 1993 SCR (1) 594*),[160] it said:

> ... great concepts like liberty and life were purposefully left to gather meaning from experience. They relate to the whole domain of social and economic fact. [...] Political, social and economic changes entail the recognition of new rights and the law in its eternal youth grows to meet the demands of society.

- The USA Supreme Court said in *Case Lawrence et al. v. Texas* (*539 U.S. 558, 2003*),[161] relating to the validity of a State of Texas law criminalizing homosexuality:

> Had those who drew and ratified the Due Process Clauses of the Fifth Amendment or the Fourteenth Amendment known the components of liberty in its manifold possibilities, they might have been more specific. They did not presume to have this insight. They knew times can blind us to certain truths and later generations can see that laws once thought necessary and proper in fact serve only to oppress. As the Constitution endures, persons in every generation can invoke its principles in their own search for greater freedom. (para. 578, 579)

- Committee on the Rights of the Child, GC 8 (CRC/C/GC/8, 2 March 2007)[162]: "But the Convention, like all human rights instruments, must be regarded as a living instrument, whose interpretation develops over time" (para. 20).
- EU Network of Independent Experts on Fundamental Rights (2006): "the international law of human rights is a living being" (p. 18).

Example of a new human right is the right to the Internet. Łukasz Szoszkiewicz (2018) argues that, just as the right to water has emancipated from the right to an adequate standard of living (Article 11 of the ICESCR), so can a right to Internet access be derived from the right to benefit from scientific progress and its applications (Article 15.1.b of the ICESCR). He notes the following: the

CHR adopted, in 2016, a Resolution on "The promotion, protection and enjoyment of human rights on the Internet" (A/HRC/32/L.20)[163]; there are frequent Internet-related issues in the texts of the UN treaty bodies; some recommendations issued by the UPR mechanism are Internet-related. In its GC 25 "on science and economic, social and cultural rights (Article 15 (1) (b), (2), (3) and (4) of the International Covenant on Economic, Social and Cultural Rights)" (E/C.12/GC/25),[164] adopted in 2020, the CoESCR includes among States' obligations "providing access to the Internet" (para. 1). Broadband Internet access has become a legal right in Finland, since 2010.

As reads the *UNESCO Medium-Term Strategy, 2014–2021* (37 C/4)[165]:

> The digital age has revolutionized freedom of expression which is a fundamental human right underpinning all other civil liberties and which is vital for open societies, the rule of law and democratic governance. It is also a key ingredient for development, for innovation and creativity. This requires a free, open and accessible Internet. (para. 1.º)

2.5.8.2 Other Principles

In addition to the most general principles just highlighted, the interpretation and enforcement of human rights involve other legal principles, jurisprudential principles, and political principles, which are only mentioned here:

- Other legal principles are, for example: Pre-eminence of Law, Primacy of International Law, Priority of National Protection, Non-abuse of Rights, Priority of Children and Women.
- Jurisprudential principles, as their denomination suggests, are principles frequently applied by Courts and Tribunals for interpreting the normative content of human rights and adjudicating their violations. Examples: Principle *Pro homine/persona*, Principle *Lex posterior derogat priori*, Principle *Lex specialis derogat generali*, Principle of Conventionality Control, Systematic Principle, Teleological Principle, Principle of Effectiveness, Principle of Equity, Principle of Reparation, Principle of Consensus, Principle of the Margin for Appreciation by States, Principle of Proportionality.
- Political principles are principles concerned with the most general national and international conditions of human rights implementation. Indisputable are principles such these: Rule of Law, Democracy, Tolerance, Development, Peace, International Co-operation.

The justification of all these principles would exceed the economy of this essay.

We are now turning to the ethical principles forming the Ethics of Human Rights, which is paramount.

2.6 Ethics of Human Rights

The history of human rights is the history of the invention of the Human Being by human beings. Of the revelation of *Human Being in human beings.* The Human Being is the ethical subject transcending the empirical subjects – ethnic, cultural, national, social, familial, psychological and other ones – with their roots, memberships, cradles, situations and other particularities. The *ethical subject* is for the field of values and the forum of conscience as the *epistemic subject* for the field of knowledge and the realm of science (as well as the *citizen* for the social diversity).

Human rights constitute an "ethics legally sanctioned" (Rivero, 1989, p. 182), because their source and sense are the worth and dignity of the human person, whose absolute primacy they consecrate. The Ethics of Human Rights concentrates the juice of the best fruits of the cultural plurality of the Humankind, expressing the quintessence of the evolution of its conscience. It is, therefore, an intercultural Ethics with juridical force and political, economic, pedagogical and other exigencies as to how every human being should be treated and should treat other human beings, by virtue of their equal worth and dignity. Adding a universal moral heritage to the genetic heritage of the human species and the cultural heritage of peoples, human rights vest every human being with a common ethical identity, making them citizens of the world. A Roman citizen could say in his defence: *Civis romanus sum!* (I'm a Roman citizen!). Now, a human being can always claim: *Civis humanus sum!* (I'm a human citizen!).

As the World Commission on Culture and Development (1995) has found:

> There is an underlying unity in the diversity of cultures, which is defined in a global ethics. [...] It is, therefore, imperative to look for a core of shared ethical values and principles. [...]
>
> One of the most encouraging trends in the last few decades has been the gradual development of international human rights standards. These standards, envisaged in the United Nations Charter and formulated in the Universal Declaration of Human Rights, have subsequently found legal and institutional expression in a number of treaties [...]. Today, the idea of human rights, though still challenged by recalcitrant governments, is a firmly entrenched standard of political conduct and will have to be a cornerstone of any global ethics. (pp. 16, 34, 36)

Skin colour, food, clothing, beliefs, music, dances, are expressions of the diversity inherent in the genetic and ethical unity of the human species, but when *ethnicity* prevails over *ethicity*, when Humanity is denied by religiosity, any barbarity is possible. And barbarity begets barbarity.

Here is the most profound and transcendent significance of the Ethics of Human Rights or Global Ethics: The Human Being should be a *God* for human beings. His temple *sanctum sanctorum* (the most sacred place) is Human Dignity.[166]

The justification of the Ethics of Human Rights that is being proposed begins with an approach to its rationality or epistemological-axiological specificity.

2.6.1 *Ethical Reason*

2.6.1.1 Normative Rationality

Rationality refers to reason, a term with two main meanings:

- The most distinctive faculty of the human being, defined as a *rational animal*.
- Justification, foundation, cause, so that to act rationally means to act based on *reasons*, even *irrational* …

As Kant (1781) wrote, the reason is the "highest faculty of knowledge" (p. 242). It "has two objects only, nature and freedom, and contains therefore both the law of nature and the law of morals […]. The philosophy of nature relates to all that is; that of morals to that only that *ought to be*" (p. 674). Ricœur (1994) remarked:

> … the whole of the human knowledge achieves in different ways the reason project following multiple regions of intelligibility, so configuring reason as an archipelago of small islands of intelligibility obeying to different rules. […] So, the word 'reason' may be kept as a term unique to say that common horizon constituting in some way the eschatology of knowledge. To become aware of that multiple functioning of the intelligibility and unique of the reason is, I think, to accede to maturity higher than that the positivistic trend of the 'unity of science' intends to support. (p. 32)

Reason is, therefore, both theoretical and practical, for knowing and living, covering all dimensions of human life.

- On one hand, human beings try to explain or interpret the world for understanding it, i.e. to find causal relations in the natural phenomena and to unveil the meanings of the human phenomena: this is the purpose of the natural sciences and the human sciences, respectively (*Naturwissenschaften* and *Geisteswissenschaften*, according to the distinction made by Wilhelm Dilthey). The latter belong "to an intelligibility regime irreducible to that

of natural sciences, where reign the ideas of verification and falsification; opposed are those of signification and interpretation" (id. p. 31). As the neuroscientist, António Damásio (2018) observes: "The sciences alone cannot illuminate the entirety of human experience without the light that comes from the arts and humanities" (p. 7).
The theoretical or cognitive reason uses two types of methods: experimental and demonstrative, typically quantitative, aiming to discover cause-effect relations; and hermeneutic and argumentative, typically qualitative, aiming to discover meanings. There are also combinations of quantitative and qualitative methods for reaching better results.

- On the other hand, human beings aim at taking practical advantage of their knowledge for living better, including the adoption of norms for individual and collective life: this is the purpose of the sciences applied to the production of instruments and other goods, as well as of the normative sciences, concerned with moral, technical and other norms.

Normative sciences
Following the definition of Georges Kalinowski (1969), a normative judgement is:

> … a specific judgement of practical reason that, by enunciating it, knows the human action to direct it, i.e. as the subject of an order, a prohibition or permission; in other words, knows what man shall, shall not or can or/ and cannot do. It matters little that it be a norm of making or a norm of acting, technical, moral or legal norm. (p. 131)

According to the author, "Lalande informs that the epithet 'normative', used in 1880 by Wallace in his *Epicureanism*, was put together with the term 'science', at the time, by Wundt who qualified ethics, aesthetics, and logic as normative sciences" (p. 3). Kalinowski distinguished three conceptions of normative science: a science that contains a coherent set of norms, a science that studies the norms, a science that derives norms from facts. He concluded that, at the end of the day, the three conceptions are complementary, and that "the normative science quarrel is practically purposeless", only remaining the underlying philosophical debate about the relationship between judgements of fact and value judgements, as well as about the possibility of a rational knowledge of norms. Some consider the concept of normative science contradictory in its terms, but others think that every science is normative, to some extent.

> It is by considering the theoretical nature of knowledge as one of the essential characteristics of science that most, if not all, of the contemporary

> theorists of science are opposed to an alleged normative science composed of assessments and norms. However, nobody goes to the point to completely reject the name 'normative science', who seems to have definitely acquired its status in the realm of contemporary metascientific terminology. (p. 79)

Aristotle is deemed to have been the first to distinguish between theoretical knowledge (*episteme*), aiming at the truth, and practical knowledge (*phronesis*), aiming at the wisdom about what kind of person to be and how to behave. In his opinion, "it is the mark of an educated man to look for precision in each class of things just so far as the nature of the subject admits; it is equally foolish to accept probable reasoning from a mathematician and to demand from a rhetorician demonstrative proofs" (Aristotle, 1925, 1094b12–1095a6).

The basic categories of morality being *right* and *wrong*, and not true and false, the moral or ethical rationality has to integrate the relativity, subjectivity, and affectivity peculiar to the values and to find a mode of production of its validity analogous to the experimentation or demonstration in the cognitive field. It is argumentation.

Argumentation

In *Traité de l'argumentation: La nouvelle rhétorique* (The New Rhetoric: A Treatise on Argumentation), published in 1958, Chaïm Perelman and Lucie Olbrechts-Tyteca faced the question: By what processes do we *reason* about values?

In 1977, Perelman wrote in *L'empire rhétorique – Rhétorique et argumentation* (The Realm of Rhetoric):

> Aristotle in his *Organon* distinguished two types of reasoning – analytic and dialectic. [...]
>
> In his *Analytics*, Aristotle studied the forms of valid inference and specifically the syllogism which allows us, certain hypotheses being given, to infer from them a necessary conclusion. [...]
>
> But this is not the case with dialectical reasoning. Aristotle tells us that dialectical reasoning presupposes premises which are constituted by general accepted opinions. [...]
>
> We can immediately see that dialectical reasoning begins from theses that are generally accepted, with the purpose of gaining the acceptance of other theses which could be or are controversial. Thus, it aims either to persuade or convince. [...] Moreover, as Aristotle noted, a persuasive argument is one that persuades the person to whom it is addressed; this means that, unlike the processes of analytical reasoning, a dialectical

> argument cannot be impersonal, for it derives its value from its actions upon the mind of some person. As a consequence, it is necessary that we clearly distinguish analytical from dialectical reasoning, the former dealing with truth and the latter with justifiable opinion. (Perelman, 1982, pp. 2, 3)

Therefore, the model of the analytical reasoning is the syllogism that derives the truth of a conclusion from the truth of its premises. The dialectical reasonings consist of discussions and deliberations. Their syllogisms are called enthymemes, whose premises are only probable.

Argumentation is the reasoning proper to practical disciplines such as Ethics, Law, and Politics, which deal with controversial matters, where analogies and metaphors are valid recourses.

> The preeminent real of argumentation, dialectic, and rhetoric is that in which values come into play. Plato, in his dialogue on piety (the *Euthyphro*) had shown that the privileged real of dialectic is the one which transcends calculation, wight, and measure, the one in which we deal with the just and the unjust, the beautiful and the ugly, the good and the bad, and in general, with the preferable.
>
> The modern conception of philosophy, which distinguishes it from the sciences, considers argumentation in all its forms as the method proper to philosophy. (p. 160)

This is "the realm of rhetoric" that "covers the vast field of nonformalized thought", so that Professor Jens of the University of Tübingen qualified rhetoric as "the once and future queen of the human sciences" (*alte und neue Königin der Wissenschaften*) (pp. 161, 162).

Accordingly, there is the *rational* and the *reasonable* (Perelman, 1979):

> The existence of two adjectives, "rational" arid "reasonable", both derived from the same noun, and designating a conformity with reason, would pose no problem if the two terms were interchangeable. But, most often, it is not so. We understand the expression rational deduction as conformity to the rules of logic, but we cannot speak of a reasonable deduction. On the contrary, we can speak of a reasonable compromise and not of a rational compromise. At times the two terms are applicable but in a different sense: a rational decision can be unreasonable and vice versa. In certain cases, the rational and the reasonable are in precise opposition. (p. 29)

A reasonable man:

> ... is guided by the search, in all domains, for what is acceptable in his milieu and even beyond it, for what should be accepted by all. Putting himself in the place of others he does not consider himself an exception but seeks to conform to principles of action which are acceptable to everyone. He considers as unreasonable a rule of action which cannot be universalized. Starting thus from a communal conception of reason, we end in a Kantian categorical imperative which makes the universal the criterion of morality. (p. 30)

Consequently, the reasonable is concerned with practical reason or practical wisdom, with reflection about how to behaviour, as opposed to theoretical reason.

In sum, following Perelman (1989):

> Argumentation is the way to present and organise the arguments; the term also designates the set of arguments which results from this presentation. [...]
>
> In spite of the importance of argumentation to the discussion, deliberation and reasonable or enlightened decision, at least, the theory of argumentation has been increasingly neglected since the Renaissance, under the influence of the rationalist, empiricist and positivist trends. [...]
>
> Argumentation being a form of reasoning without which the life of the spirit and the establishment of a human community become impossible, it seems that we need to reserve a place for the theory of argumentation within the logic, besides that assigned to the theory of demonstration, drawn up by formal logic.

His theory of argumentation has made him "the philosopher of the reasonable" – a notion "at the heart of his work" – who "contributed to refound the ethics and the philosophy of values" (Angenot, 2012, pp. 3, 4). A case in point is the human rights foundation, as Perelman (1966) pointed out:

> More and more, jurists from all corners of the world have recourse to *general principles of law,* which one might liken to the ancient *jus gentium* and which would find their real and sufficient grounding in the consensus of civilized humanity. [...]
>
> Regarding the rights of man, we find ourselves confronted with the same situation as that indicated in a previous discussion concerning the ultimate principles of morality. [...]

> The recourse to the reasonable, as a grounding for the rights of man, that defines and hierarchizes these rights in terms of their contribution to the progress of a concrete rationality, furnishes an illustration of my general thesis. [...] This example shows in what sense the undertaking is possible and demonstrates that the theory of the rights of man thus grounded would not be the expression of an irrational arbitrariness. (pp. 47, 49, 50)

Accordingly, the definition of the human being as a *rational animal* should be understood as meaning that it is an animal capable of reason (*Animal rationis capax*) whatever its expressions. Indeed, even *the heart has reasons ...* Therefore, the sociologist Raymond Boudon asked: "Can the notion of rationality itself mean something other than behaviours based on reasons?" (as cited in Pierrot, 2003, p. 32).

Arts also come under the argumentative rationality, to the extent that the recognition of their value is a matter of argumentation, according to Rainer Rochlitz[167]: "To speaking of aesthetic rationality is to consider that the aesthetic judgements and the critical discourses, both of experts and of the laity, obey the rules of an argument". It is a kind of rationality aiming at an intersubjective validity, peculiar to the "aesthetic validity, analogous simultaneously to the true and the false in the field of knowledge and to the normative rightfulness in the ethical field, but irreducible to these two types of validity" (p. 152). Following the author, nowadays, the main parameters of the aesthetic judgement are the motive or *raison d'être* of the piece of art, its effectiveness (to mean what it aims at meaning) and its originality.

The argumentative logic falls thus under rationality that is neither experimental nor demonstrative, but communicational, the validity of which was theorised by Jürgen Habermas and Karl-Otto Apel, in particular.

Communicational rationality

Habermas (1983) considered the "reductionist concept of rationality characteristic of empiricism" (p. 77) as a "pathology of modern conscience" (p. 45) because such reductions exclude practico-moral questions from the rational discussion for not being able to be held true within the epistemological framework of the positivistic rationality. He distinguished two types of rational activities: those aiming at success (through organised means) and those turned to inter-understanding. The first ones are the instrumental activity (over objects) and the strategic activity (of manipulation to gain power over people). The second one is a communicative activity aiming at a common adhesion to conclusions reached by the "unforced force of better arguments" (*zwanglose*

Zwang des besseren Arguments), that is, through a rational argumentation according to rules and without violence. The fundamental rule is the recognition of the 'other' as a person. In Habermas' view, the basis of an Ethics of Discourse is formed by "two assumptions: (a) that normative claims to validity have cognitive meaning and can be treated *like* truth claims and (b) that the justification of norms and commands requires that a real discourse be carried" (p. 68), because "the justification of norms is [...] not accidentally but *essentially* a communicative endeavour" (p. 69). The experimental and demonstrative rationality has a counterpoint in the intersubjective and argumentative rationality, that is "the rational core of moral agreements produced through argumentation" (p. 73).

According to Apel (1992), rationality is never dissociable from morality, because scientific research itself "is not only a question of subject-object relation of the cognitive act but also, simultaneously and always, a question of relation between subjects, peculiar to communication and interaction between members of a scientific community", which "has to presuppose an ethics of an ideal community of communication concerning the relation between subjects that is complementary to the relation subject-object" (p. 16). The validity of a "macro-ethics" transcending the limitations of the conventional moral – that is to say both of the (interpersonal) micro-ethics and the (social) meso-ethics – and guaranteeing, at the same time, the pluralism of differences compatible with essential universal values, depends upon the possibility of a "rational consensus" achieved by argumentation. This "consensual and communicative rationality" is possible and necessary "to overcome the scientist blockade of rationality" (Apel, 1988, p. 149).

Summing up:

Considering that the human relations are woven eminently through verbal communication – that is communication *par excellence*, through which human beings are capable of thinking and agreeing, of acting and interacting – there is communicational rationality whose logic is that of the reasonable and preferable. Their epistemological devices are inter-recognition and argumentation. The validity that results from well-regulated intersubjective communication is analogous, in terms of relations between subjects, to the truth, in terms of the well-controlled subject-object relationship. This is philosophical objectivity, according to Jean-Pierre Dupuy (2004):

> Faced with these major challenges [of our time], politics seems very helpless, incapable that it is by nature to see far in time and space. The law, on the other hand, [has a basis] very fragile. There remains the ethics, that faint spark of wisdom that nature has ignited in the heart of man.

> But in a secular society, where the social bond no longer rests on the religious, ethics can only be based on the resources of human reason. […]
>
> These and other issues can be the subject of rational philosophical debate, with arguments and objections. In other words, there is objectivity of ethics. It is the role of philosophy to found this objectivity. (pp. 5, 6)

Socrates concludes in *Meno*:

> Correct opinion is then neither inferior to knowledge nor less useful in directing actions, nor is the man who has it less than he who has knowledge. […]
>
> Since then it is not only through knowledge but also through right opinion that men are good […].
>
> Therefore, […] it is through right opinion that statesmen follow the right course for their cities. […] (Plato, 1997, *Meno*, 98c, 99c)

In this connection, Charles Malik – one of the major protagonists of the UDHR *travaux préparatoires* – observed, addressing a Conference of American Educators, at Lake Success (New York), on 26 February 1948, that the International Community moves "by free consent and persuasion. And the democratic method of free persuasion between nations, as also between individuals, requires endless discussion, reasoning, and patience" (Malik, 2000, p. 88).

Concluding remarks

Human nature explains both the universality of the faculty of reason and the diversity of its uses.

Reason is unique and multiple, theoretical and practical, cognitive and moral, technical and artistic. It consists of the aptitude to abstraction, representation, compassion, deliberation, imagination … Many stars are shinning in the firmament of the *human rationality*.

The recognition of the diversity of uses of reason implies openness to the *epistemic pluralism*, i.e. to different kinds of rationality and methods of research: there is cognitive rationality (aiming to discover the truth), normative rationality (aiming to agreements on norms), instrumental rationality (concerned with the usefulness) and even aesthetic rationality (regarding the third value of the triptych Truth-Good-Beauty).

John M. Cooper wrote, presenting *Theaetetus*, that in this dialogue Plato answers the question "What is knowledge?", being so "the founding document of what has come to be known as 'epistemology', one of the branches of philosophy". Socrates concluded that "knowledge is true judgment with an account" (Plato, 1997, *Theaetetus*, 202c), i.e. founded on reasons. Since then, "true judgment with an account" – or *justified true belief* – has become a canonical definition of knowledge, so understood:

- *Belief* consists of accepting as true a cognitive content, even without evidence.
- *Truth* consists of the correspondence of a proposition with reality, which distinguishes knowledge from belief.
- *Justification* is what distinguishes knowledge from true belief. As *Theaetetus* affirms, "true judgment without an account falls outside of knowledge" (201d).

Therefore, rational is everything based on reasons, and justification is the method of validation constituent of the rationality. As a result, a distinction should be made between scientificity, in the positivistic sense of knowledge peculiar to the natural sciences or mathematics, and rationality, which must not be reduced to the positivistic scientificity. Such a reduction would exclude from the scope of rationality the moral dimension of human life, in particular, which is all too human to stay out of the concept of rationality. A conception of rationality ignoring the human subjectivity and the affectivity is hemiplegic.

What is more, Emmanuel Lévinas (1993) argued that the primacy of the inter-human relations over the cognitive-instrumental relation with nature makes ethical rationality the "prime rationality". He considered "the face of the other man obliging the I" as "the founding inter-human" rationality. The "*re-presentation*" is the expression of a "rationality of an already derived order" (pp. 454, 455, 456). Lévinas' Ethics was qualified by Jacques Derrida as "ethics of ethics" or "metaethics" (as cited in Kovak, 1993, p. 188).

All in all, knowledge is always physically *incorporated* and historically, culturally and socially *immersed*. Therefore, borrowing a metaphor of Ernest Gellner quoted by Frédéric Vandenberghe (2008, p. 30), sentiments and values are not weeds in the Garden of Reason. When it comes to human rights, in particular, it is not enough to know the Law written in texts; it should also be written in hearts. As René Cassin (1967) said, human rights need "men and women of thought, of reason, of science. People of heart, however, are also needed" (p. 331).[168] And according to Thomas Kuhn (1962): "The competition between paradigms is not the sort of battle that can be resolved by proofs [...], the importance of aesthetic considerations can sometimes be decisive" (pp. 148, 156).

2.6.1.2 Human Morality

Axiology, Morals, Ethics – are terms belonging to the same semantic family.

Axiology or Theory of Value is the philosophical discipline that studies values, in general, i.e. what makes things desirable. Values are manifold: there are instrumental values, which are means for reaching other ones, such as wealth and power; other are both means and ends, such as health and knowledge; other are ends giving sense to or alleviating the human existence, such as happiness, justice, beauty. They are principally moral values.

Ethics and Morals are terms etymologically different (of Greek and Latin origin, respectively), but synonymous. Both refer to 'right' or 'wrong' conduct, to customs or ways of living. They are frequently used indistinctly or redundantly but may be distinguished. Some authors make the following distinction:

- Morals denotes the individual values or the values common to a group or community, which are inculcated to its members as norms of good and evil, of right and wrong behaviour. A moral judgement is one of approving or condemning decisions and behaviours in light of common values. So understood, the term has a particularistic connotation.
- Ethics is a theory or systematic reflection concerning the moral phenomenon. It is also called Moral Philosophy that Hobbes (1651) defined as "the Science of what is Good and Evil" or "the Science of Virtue and Vice" (*Leviathan*, Chapter 15).[169] It is a term with a rather intellectual meaning, without any connotation. So understood, the term has a universalistic scope.

Ethical studies are usually divided into three main areas: Meta-ethics, Normative Ethics, Applied Ethics.

- Meta-ethics addresses the most general moral questions, such as: Is the moral phenomenon specific to human beings? Moral values are absolute (transcendent) or historical (immanent)? Are there universal moral principles? Etc.
- Normative Ethics is concerned with the content of moral norms. There are three main conceptions in the history of Western Philosophy: Virtue Ethics (Aristotle), Consequentialist Ethics (Bentham) and Deontological Ethics (Kant).
- Applied Ethics is concerned with controversial moral issues, such as abortion, euthanasia, stem cell research, human cloning, human therapy and enhancement in general, animal ethics, environmental ethics, etc.

As regards the human specificity of the moral phenomenon, if the theory of evolution is scientific, there is no reason to exclude morality from it. There is research showing that the moral decisions activate archaic parts of the human brain, in the limbic region and especially in the amygdala, allowing to conclude that they are rooted in the social instinctive behaviour of mammals. It is also known that some animals – particularly those who live in groups, as chimpanzees, elephants, dolphins – seem to be able to empathy, compassion (that is, to imagine themselves in the place of others and feel what they feel) and to other apparent expressions of morality (be they innate or learnt). However, in light of the theory of evolution and of the state of research, it seems that the case of morality is similar to that of other human attributes: it has biological roots and cultural uniqueness.

According to Immordino-Yang and Damásio (2007), there is "a special kind of human innovation: the social creativity that we call morality and ethical thought" (p. 7). In the opinion of Damásio (1994): "The control of animal inclination by thought, reason, and the will was what made us human, according to Descartes' *Passions of the Soul*" (p. 139). Following Jean Guilaine: "Man is a self-domesticated social animal, since the Neolithic period" (in AAVV, 2012, p. 31), approximately ten thousand years ago, when he has become sedentary and has begun to domesticate the natural environment. Already Aristotle (2000) wrote:

> Now the reason why man is more of a political animal than bees or any other gregarious animals is evident. Nature, as we often say, makes nothing in vain, and man is the only animal whom she has endowed with the gift of speech. And whereas mere sound is but an indication of pleasure or pain, and is therefore found in other animals (for their nature attains to the perception of pleasure and pain and the intimation of them to one another, and no further), the power of speech is intended to set for the expedient and inexpedient, and likewise the just and the unjust. And it is a characteristic of man that he alone has any sense of good and evil, of just and unjust, and the association of living beings who have this sense makes a family and a state.

Being so, "when perfected, [man] is the best of animals, but, when separated from law and justice, he is the worst of all; since armed injustice is the more dangerous, and he is equipped at birth with the arms of intelligence and with moral qualities which he may use for the worst ends" (1253a). That is why José-Luis Aranguren (1900) concluded that the human being "may be defined as a moral animal, rather than as rational animal" (p. 99). Addressing the UN General Assembly, on 9 December 1948, Eleanor Roosevelt, President of the Commission on Human Rights that drafted the UDHR, cited these words of Gladstone Murray: "The central fact is that man is fundamentally a moral being".[170] In the same vein, the Constitutional Court of Colombia (*C-221/94*)[171] said that a human being is essentially an "ethical subject", i.e. whose capacity for autonomy makes it able to decide "about the most radically human, about the good and evil, about the sense of its existence". This is a haunting challenge for Humanism, since its Greco-Christian origins through the Renaissance and the *Lumières* until the transhumanism. In *Antigone* (Sophocles),[172] the Chorus sings: "Wonders are many, and none is more wonderful than man", but his skilfulness "brings him, now to evil, now to good".

Morality – the capacity and need to make moral choices – is indeed the most humanising dimension of the anthropological perfectibility. It is like a *divine* mark, with the mythical Biblical symbolism of the original sin: the first woman and the first man were expelled from the Garden of Eden for having eaten the fruit from the forbidden tree to become "as God, knowing the good and the evil" (Genesis, 3:5).[173] René Descartes wrote in the Letter-Preface to his *Principes de la Philosophie* (Principles of Philosophy, 1644)[174]:

> Thus, all Philosophy is like a tree, of which Metaphysics is the root, Physics the trunk, and all the other sciences are the branches that grow out of this trunk, which are reduced to three principals, namely, Medicine, Mechanics, and Ethics. By the science of Morals, I understand the highest and most perfect which, presupposing an entire knowledge of the other sciences, is the last degree of wisdom.

James Griffin (2008) remarked:

> From the eighteenth century to the present, most philosophers, dazzled by the success of natural scientists, pre-eminently Newton, went in search of highly systematic theory. Moral philosophers sought the reduction of all our varied moral thought to one principle, or to a small number of them. (p. 74)

This was the attempt both of the Consequentialist Ethics and the Deontological Ethics.

The Golden Rule is probably the most ancient and universal principle of morality. It may be considered the germ of the human rights idea, its millennial foundation.

2.6.1.3 Golden Rule and Human Rights

The World Commission on Culture and Development (1995) pointed out:

> There are some recurrent themes that appear in nearly all cultural traditions. They can serve as an inspiration for a global ethics. The first source is the idea of human vulnerability and the attendant ethical impulse

> to alleviate suffering where such is possible and to provide security to each individual. Some notion of this is to be encountered in the moral views of all major cultures. [...] it is part of the fundamental moral teachings of each of the great traditions that one should treat others as one would want to be treated oneself. Some version of this 'Golden Rule' finds explicit expression in Confucianism, Taoism, Hinduism, Buddhism, Zoroastrianism, Judaism, Christianity and Islam, and is implicit in the practices of other faiths. The deeply human urge to avoid avoidable suffering and some notion of the basic moral equality of all human beings together form an indispensable point of reference and a strong pillar of support for any attempt to work out a global ethics. (p. 36)

In fact, although the expression was coined only in the 17th century, perhaps, the 'Golden Rule' is a millennial commandment, having "appeared in the fifth century BC in all cultural and religious areas of the world" (Roy, 2012, p. 12), with both positive and negative formulations, like these: "Do unto others as you would have them do unto you", and "Do not do unto others what you would not have them do unto you". The second one is sometimes named the Silver Rule. Another formulation commands: "Treat others in the way that they wish to be treated". Voltaire wrote in *Remarques pour servir de Supplément à l'Éssai sur les moeurs et l'esprit des nations* (*17è Remarque: Des lois*)[175]: "The only fundamental and immutable law that exists between men is this: 'Treat men as you would expect to be treated'". It is the "great natural law", that is, "a *law mother* from which all others must be derived: *Never do harm to others*", as wrote l'Abbé Sieyès in his *Essai sur les privilèges* (Essay on privileges, 1788).[176]

In the Golden Rule come together moral traditions and philosophical wisdom, condensing a moral heritage so much ancestral and cross-cultural that it seems *natural*. According to Olivier du Roy (2012), the Golden Rule "corresponds to a kind of moral maturity of the humankind", amounting to "a universal cultural datum, the foundation of a very 'natural law'" (p. 12).

The universality of the Golden Rule is highlighted in two important contemporary documents of religious origin:

- "Declaration Toward a Global Ethic", adopted by the Parliament of the World's Religions, in 1993, in Chicago (USA), where representatives of more than 120 religions met[177]:

> There is a principle which is found and has persisted in many religious and ethical traditions of humankind for thousands of years: *What you do not wish done to yourself, do not do to others. Or in positive terms: What you*

wish done to yourself, do to others! This should be the irrevocable, unconditional norm for all areas of life, for families and communities, for races, nations, and religions.

– "The Search for Universal Ethics: A New Look at Natural Law", published by the International Theological Commission (Vatican) in 2008[178]:

> 14. … The profound altruism of the Buddhist tradition, which is expressed in a resolute attitude of non-violence, amicable benevolence and compassion, thus agrees with the Golden Rule. […]
> 24. …In his moral teaching, presented in a succinct form in the Sermon on the Mount, Jesus takes up the Golden Rule: "So, whatever you wish that men would do to you, do so to them; for this is the law and the prophets" (Mt. 7:12). This positive precept completes the negative formulation of the same rule in the Old Testament: "And what you hate, do not do to anyone" (Tob 4:15). […]
> 51. … To the Golden Rule are linked several commandments of the Decalogue, as are numerous Buddhist precepts, and, indeed, some Confucian rules, and also the greater part of the orientations of the great Charters that enumerate the rights of the person.

The moral substratum common to the Golden Rule and human rights was assumed by the *Déclaration des droits de l'homme et du citoyen* (Declaration of the Rights of Man and the Citizen, 1789) introducing the 1793 French Constitution,[179] in its Article 6: "Liberty is the power that belongs to man to do whatever is not injurious to the rights of others; it has nature for its principle, justice for its rule, law for its defence; its moral limit is in this maxim: *Do not do to another that which you do not wish should be done to you*".

The UDHR Article 1[180] may be taken as the contemporary expression of the Golden Rule: "All human beings are born free and equal in dignity and rights. They are endowed with reason and conscience and should act towards one another in a spirit of brotherhood".

Human Dignity has become the overarching principle underlying the Ethics of Human Rights.

2.6.2 *Human Dignity Principle*

2.6.2.1 Origins

The idea of 'human dignity' has numerous cultural, religious, and philosophical roots.

Dignitas (dignity) meant, in ancient Roma, a higher public status because of office, social standing, or achievements, implying corresponding posture, composure, and deference. It could also derive from personal virtue, in the Aristotelian sense.

Stoic Philosophy, originated in Athens of the 3rd century BC, contributed decisively to overcoming the traditional honorific sense of the idea of dignity, by identifying it with the faculty of reason as a common attribute of human beings. The belief in the universality of reason would be the most influential thing in shaping the modern conception of human dignity and rights.

Following the Christian doctrine, earthly creatures form a great chain (*The Great Chain of Being*, Walter Lovejoy, 1936) where the status of each one is defined by its ontological distance from the Creator. The superiority and dignity of human beings lie in their likeness with God (*Imago Dei*). According to the biblical narrative of the creation of the world, God said: "Let us make humans in our image, after our likeness" (Genesis, 1:26,27).

The Renaissance (15–16th centuries) was a vast, multiform and complex cultural movement of humanist rebirth that produced a long-term radical transformation of the Western culture. It began in Italy with the rediscovering of the Greek and Roman *humanæ litteræ* (human writings) that was earthly literature in contrast to the mediaeval *divinæ litteræ* (divine writings). The world ceased to be lamented as a vale of suffering and tears because of the sin of Adam. Pico della Mirandola famously gave expression to the new humanist faith, in his *Oratio de Hominis Dignitate* (Oration on the Dignity of Man 1486).[181] In this manifesto, the Great Artisan (God):

> ... placing him [the man] in the middle of the world, said to him:
>
> "Adam, we give you no fixed place to live, no form that is peculiar to you, nor any function that is yours alone. According to your desires and judgment, you will have and possess whatever place to live, whatever form, and whatever functions you yourself choose. All other things have a limited and fixed nature prescribed and bounded by our laws. You, with no limit or no bound, may choose for yourself the limits and bounds of your nature. We have placed you at the world's centre so that you may survey everything else in the world. We have made you neither of heavenly nor of earthly stuff, neither mortal nor immortal, so that with free choice and dignity, you may fashion yourself into whatever form you choose. To you is granted the power of degrading yourself into the lower forms of life, the beasts, and to you is granted the power, contained in your intellect and judgment, to be reborn into the higher forms, the divine".

Although, in the following centuries, the term 'dignity' kept, in general, a differentiating use – not as an attribute of all, but only of a few – the centre of gravity of the vision of human dignity has moved to the side of personal autonomy, in which are manifested the two higher human faculties that are reason and will. A movement which culminated in Immanuel Kant.

2.6.2.2 Kant

It is sometimes said that, when it comes to 'human dignity', all paths lead to Kant. He indeed represents the climax of an outstanding moral conquest in the history of Western Philosophy, being generally considered the Philosopher of Human Dignity. In his Moral Philosophy come together the most profound religious and philosophical roots of the idea of human dignity, in particular those of the Greco-Roman Stoicism, the ancient and mediaeval Christianity and the Renaissance humanism.

However, the term has a modest presence in Kant's writings. It is to be found principally in his *Grundlegung zur Metaphysik der Sitten* (Foundation of the Metaphysics of Morals, 1785) that, despite its brevity, "is one of the greatest and most influential achievements in the history of philosophy" (Wood, 1999, p. 12), and probably the most influential Kantian writing. According to it, the foundation of morality is autonomy, i.e. the aptitude and the privilege of obeying only to one's laws, endowing human beings with "an intrinsic value, that is, human dignity" (*einen innern Wert, d. i. Würde*). So, the foundation of human dignity has been inscribed inside every human being, ceasing to be social or transcendent (metaphysical or religious).

In the Preface, Kant informed that he would seek to establish rationally "the supreme principle of morality" (*Aufsuchung und Festsetzung des obersten Prinzips der Moralität*). His famous "categorical imperative" of morality is given in three main formulations, namely:

- *Principle of Autonomy* – To obey only laws imposed "to oneself" (*selbstgesetzgebung*).
- *Principle of Universality* – The laws which one obeys should be valid for all rational beings, so that each one becomes a universal legislator "in the kingdom of ends" (*ein gesetzgebend Glied im Reiche der Zwecke*).
- *Principle of Humanity* – Never treat a human being (including oneself) merely as a means, but always also as "an end in itself" (*Zweck an sich selbst sein*).

The third one (*Prinzip der Menschheit*) compensates for the "emptiness of the formalism" of the other two, being an expression of the Golden Rule, in the opinion of Ricoeur (1991, pp. 261, 262).

The social and political transformations along the 19th and 20th centuries – and especially the unprecedented events that were the two World Wars – shifted the centre of gravity of the influence of the Kantian conception of human dignity as autonomy or rational agency, and the Principle of Humanity has become the Principle of Human Dignity *par excellence*. Its fullness may be so condensed: No human being should never be treated as an animal or an object, because he/she is endowed with worth and dignity, regardless of whatever particularities and circumstances.

In short: The unequal Roman *dignitas* evolved from a differentiating social status into an equalising ethical quality, as a 'circle in expansion', but preserving and spreading the ideas of value and respect. It was this meaning that has been legally consecrated in the second half of the 20th century.

2.6.2.3 Juridification

The term 'human dignity' does not feature in the 18th century American and French Declarations of Rights. It was in the 20th century that the idea entered progressively the Constitutional and International Law, especially after World War II.

The United Nations Charter (1945)[182] was the first universal legal instrument proclaiming "faith in fundamental human rights, in the dignity and worth of the human person" (Preamble), followed some months later by UNESCO Constitution,[183] according to which "the wide diffusion of culture, and the education of humanity for justice and liberty and peace are indispensable to the dignity of man".

The UDHR (1948) – that refers to human dignity in Preamble and several articles – has become the source of its posterior torrential expansion. In the whole IBHR, we find 14 references to human dignity. If we turn to the other seven core international human rights treaties, we find the term about 30 times. Many other international instruments refer to human dignity. It is the *leitmotif* of the International Biomedical Law, in particular.

At the regional level, the term 'dignity' does not feature in the ECHR, surprisingly. Only its Protocol 13 "concerning the abolition of the death penalty in all circumstances" (2002)[184] refers to "the full recognition of the inherent dignity of all human beings". However, the European Court of Human Rights said in *Case Pretty v. The United Kingdom* (2002)[185]: "The very essence of the Convention is respect for human dignity and human freedom" (para. 65). In *Case Tyrer v. The United Kingdom* (Application 5856/72),[186] in 1978, it had referred to "an assault on precisely that which it is one of the main purposes of Article 3 (Art. 3) to protect, namely a person's dignity and physical integrity" (para. 33). Also, the European Committee of Social Rights said in *Case International Federation of Human Rights Leagues (FIDH) v. France (Complaint 14/2003)*[187]: "Human dignity is the fundamental value and indeed the core of positive European Human Rights Law – whether under the European Social Charter or under the European Convention of Human Rights" (para. 31). Human dignity is also prominent in the Charter of Fundamental Rights of the European Union (2000),[188] incorporated in the Treaty of the European Union. Its Chapter 1 bears the title "Dignity", and Article 1 is titled "Human dignity", emphatically echoing Article 1.1 of the 1949 German Constitution (see below).[189] In 2001, the Court of Justice of the European Union said in *Case Netherlands v Parliament and Council* (C-377/98)[190]: "It is for the Court of Justice, in its review of the compatibility of acts of the [European Union] institutions with the general principles of Community Law, to ensure that the fundamental right to human dignity and integrity is observed" (para. 70).

In Constitutional Law, the juridification of human dignity began during the first half of the 20th century, when it was incorporated into several European and American Constitutions, but intensified after the World War II, under the influence of the German Constitution (*Grundgesetzt*)[191] that has famously proclaimed: *Die Menschenwüde ist unantastbar* (Human dignity is inviolable). Franz J. Wetz (1998) stressed that "human dignity represents the highest legal value of our [German] Constitution and its supreme principle, with a value superior to all decisions of democratic majorities" (p. 11).

At present, human dignity is mentioned in a great number of constitutional texts worldwide. Its constitutional preeminence is reflected in abundant jurisprudence. Two examples:

The Federal Constitutional Court of Germany said in *Case BVerfGE 45, 187 (Lebenslange Freiheitsstrafe)* (1977),[192] concerning life imprisonment:

> Respect and protection of human dignity are among the constitutional principles of the Basic Law. The free human personality and her dignity represent the highest legal values within the constitutional order (vgl. BVerfGE 6, 32 [41]; 27, 1 [6]; 30, 173 [193]; 32, 98 [108]). The State in all its forms has the duty to respect and to protect the dignity of the human being. (para. 143)

The Constitutional Court of South Africa said in *Case S v Makwanyane and Another (CCT3/94) [1995] ZACC 3; 1995 (6) BCLR 665; 1995 (3) SA 391; [1996] 2 CHRLD 164; 1995 (2) SACR 1 (6 June 1995)*,[193] concerning sentences to death and long-term imprisonment:

> 328. ... The importance of dignity as a founding value of the new Constitution cannot be overemphasized. Recognizing a right to dignity is an acknowledgement of the intrinsic worth of human beings: human beings are entitled to be treated as worthy of respect and

> concern. This right, therefore, is the foundation of many of the other rights that are specifically entrenched in Chapter 3.

In countries whose Constitutions do not explicitly mention human dignity (or those who have no written Constitution), the constitutional jurisprudence often derived it from constitutional or other basic laws, for many purposes. For example, the term does not figure in the USA Constitution, but Leslie Henry (2011) notices: "For some commentators, dignity is nothing less than 'the premier value underlying the last two centuries of moral and political thought', an essential 'basis of human rights', and one of 'the great political values that define our constitutional morality'" (p. 4). For instance, in *Case Trop v. Dulles, 356 U.S. 86, 100 (1958)*,[194] the US Supreme Court said: "The basic concept underlying the Eighth Amendment is nothing less than the dignity of man" (p. 100). In *Case Hope v. Pelzer, 536 U.S. 730, 736* (*2002*),[195] it said that punishment applied to an Alabama prison inmate had been "antithetical to human dignity [...] both degrading and dangerous" (745). The Constitutions of some States (Louisiana, Illinois, Montana, for example) refer to human dignity.

2.6.2.4 Conceptualisation

Dignity is a term with many uses. It is applied not only to human beings but also to institutions, offices, professions, symbols, even to animals and plants.

Human Dignity is the most brilliant star in the human rights firmament, the highest lighthouse in the ocean of the human species' indefinite destiny. It lies at the heart of Human Rights Philosophy, is the spinal column of IHRL, the supreme moral value of a New Constitutionalism, the axiological core of the Rule of Law, the embryo of a Law of Humanity. It has become a flag of all causes and struggles against oppression and injustice, a powerful device for the international and national courts to protect and develop human rights, a *leitmotif* of the political rhetoric.

The Human Dignity Principle (HDP) may be considered as the quintessence of Civilisation.

The contemporary impressive expansion of the invocation of the HDP is not exempt from "inflation", if not "trivialisation", attributed to its conceptual vagueness. The European Court of Human Rights noted, in *Case Siliadin v. France* (Application 73316/01),[196] decided on 26 July 2005, that it is "a particularly vague concept, and one subject to random interpretation" (para. 101). Also, the Canadian Supreme Court observed in *Case R. v. Kapp, 2008 SCR 41*[197] that, "as critics have pointed out, human dignity is an abstract and subjective notion [...] confusing and difficult to apply" (para. 22). Hence two main kinds of criticism of the notion of human dignity:

- It is a too vague notion, a principle *passe-partout* (catchall), functioning as a placeholder for other more precise concepts, such as equality or autonomy.
- It is a dangerous two-edged sword that may be invoked by adversarial parts in a case or controversy, as well as used as a disguise for moralism and politically conservative stances.

The IHRL does not provide a definition of 'human dignity' (any more than of 'human rights'). Therefore: "The most fundamental problem of contemporary human rights theory" is maybe the foundational question (Freeman, 2004, p. 392).

2.6.2.4.1 *The Foundational Question*

Johannes Morsink (1999) asked: "What lies at the heart of the moral consensus about human rights that was born in the 1940s and has expanded ever since?". His answer: "During the final General Assembly debate, in December 1948, the drafters made it abundantly clear that the Declaration on which they were about to vote had been born out of the experience of the war that had just ended" (p. 36). Human dignity was the Universal Sign – a kind of Floating Signifier[198] – of the consensus that made possible the proclamation of the UDHR by the UN Member States when already blew Cold War winds. Despite their cultural, religious, and ideological heterogeneity, they had a common sentiment: human dignity is what concentration camps and their gas chambers trampled on in an appalling scale. National Socialism was "nothing but applied biology", as said Rudolf Hess at a mass meeting in 1934 (as cited ibid., p. 38). That is why, as the Ecuadoran Delegation (Jorge Carrera Andrade) pointed out, at the General Assembly 183rd plenary meeting, on 10 December 1948 (A/PV.183),[199] "ordinary people of the world [...] were not only expecting the restoration of material ruins but that of human dignity as well". Charles Foster (2011) rightly concluded that "it was the Holocaust that secured dignity's place in the pantheon of ethical principles" (p. 40).

"Human dignity is a complex principle", however, because it "extends to a broad range of human characteristics", as the Supreme Court of Israel said in *Case Commitment to Peace and Social Justice v. Minister of Finance* (*HCJ 366/03*) and *Bilhah Rubinova and Others v. Minister of Finance* (*HCJ 888/03*) (para. 14),[200] quoting prior jurisprudence. In effect, human dignity is unique and multiple, multifaceted, remaining, paradoxically, a foundation lacking to be founded ...

According to Norberto Bobbio (1990):

> There are three ways of demonstrating values: deduction from a constant objective fact, for example, human nature; their consideration as self-

> evident truths; and finally, the discovery that they are generally accepted within a given historical period (i.e. the test of consensus). [...]
>
> The third method of justifying values is that of showing that they are supported by consensus, whereby a value has greater validity the more it is agreed to. The consensus argument replaces the test of objectivity, which is considered impossible or at least extremely uncertain, with the test of inter-subjectivity. Of course, this is a historical and therefore not an absolute basis, but the historical basis of consent is the only one which can be factually proved. The Universal Declaration of Human Rights may, therefore, be considered the greatest historical test of the *consensus omnium gentium* [overall peoples' consensus] in relation to a given value system. (Chapter 2)

We may, therefore, distinguish three main accounts of human dignity and rights foundation/justification: naturalistic, axiomatic, consensus.

- The *naturalistic account* is the traditional foundation/justification of human dignity/rights. It presupposes an immutable 'human nature' with seeds of universal principles of morality.
- The *axiomatic account* conceives of human dignity and rights as self-evident, i.e. without need for justification. They speak for themselves as imperatives of the human species higher ontological status.
- The *consensus account* sustains that what has made possible the 1948 Universal Declaration was a practical universal consensus about essential common moral values to be respected and protected.

In effect, as there are historically diverging conceptions of human nature justifying contradictory values, and self-evidence is historically and individually very relative too (for example, the ban of torture only in our times became self-evident and, nevertheless, it is still practiced), it seems that there is no better alternative than the consensus account. It may be said that human dignity and rights are fruits of a double Historical Consensus, namely:

- The moral consensus of religious traditions and philosophical wisdom crystallised in the Golden Rule as a principle of reciprocity, empathy and compassion that distinguishes *humanity* from *animality*, as Charles Darwin suggests in *The descent of man, and selection in relation to sex* (1871)[201]:

  > I fully subscribe to the judgment of those writers who maintain that of all the differences between man and the lower animals, the moral sense or conscience is by far the most important [...] summed up in that short but

> imperious word *ought*, so full of high significance [Kant is evoked]. It is the most noble of all the attributes of man [...].
>
> The moral sense perhaps affords the best and highest distinction between man and the lower animals; but I need say nothing on this head, as I have so lately endeavoured to shew that the social instincts – the prime principle of man's moral constitution – with the aid of active intellectual powers and the effects of habit, naturally lead to the golden rule: "As ye would that men should do to you, do ye to them likewise"; and this lies at the foundation of morality. (pp. 97, 126)

– The legal consensus laid down in the Universal Declaration of Human Rights, whose values and principles have expanded, becoming the Law of Law, that is, a superior and indisposable Law.

The UDHR points to a foundational plurality – emotional, religious, argumentative, political, international – when it mentions, in its Preamble, "barbarous acts", "rebellion against tyranny and oppression", "rule of law", "faith", "common understanding", "common standard of achievement". Such a plurality may be illustrated with the metaphor of a four-faced head. Human dignity and rights have natural, legal, national and international faces:

– They may be said to be *natural* insofar as they are believed to be innate in every human being.
– They are *legal* because they have been given the form and force of written, positive Law.
– They are *national* because, besides several of them having been first recognised in national Constitutions, their protection and implementation depend principally upon each State.
– They are *international* because they have been recognised, expanded, and are protected by the International Community that is also co-responsible for their promotion and protection.

The Historical Consensus on human dignity and rights is a virtuous one because it is an outcome of the *ethical democracy* that alone legitimises the *political democracies*, that is, a universal consensus concerning moral values common to our Humanity that must prevail over whatever occasional political majorities. It is the consensus on "the supreme value of the human person", as said Hernan Santa Cruz, Delegate of Chile in the Commission on Human Rights that drafted the Universal Declaration (as cited in Glendon, 2001, p. 169).

During the *travaux préparatoires* of the UDHR, the question as to the source of the human worth and dignity justifying the entitlement to human rights gave rise to one of the hottest debates within the UN General Assembly Third Committee, in the autumn of 1948, revolving around the following alternative: a Creator or Nature? These two words were eventually avoided and the sole indication regarding the foundation of the human dignity and rights is laid down in Article 1 (that reproduces almost literally the first paragraph of the Preamble of the American Declaration of the Rights and Duties of Man, adopted some months before): human beings "are endowed with reason and conscience".[202] However, no agreement was reached, at the time, on "the origin of man's reason and conscience" (Hernan Santa Cruz) (A/C.3/SR.99).[203]

It is next proposed an account of the human dignity and rights foundation/justification that draws on another essay (Monteiro, 2014a), but reformulated and developed. Having recourse to the *ars philosophica* of *distinguo* (philosophical art of distinctions), it distinguishes between: 'human dignity' and 'human rights'; 'human dignity' and 'human worth'; being human and to be treated and to behave as a human being. The following propositions are being argued:

- *Human dignity is the principle and the sense of human rights*
- *Human dignity hallmarks the belonging to the human species*
- *Human dignity is an ethical invention with genetic foundation*
- *Human dignity consists in perfectibility calling for perfecting*
- *Human dignity is inviolable and indisposable*
- *Human dignity is vulnerable and variable*

2.6.2.4.2 *Human Dignity Is the Principle and the Sense of Human Rights*

The question as to whether human dignity should be qualified as a principle or a right has already sparked a debate in the course of the preparatory works of the UDHR, notably during the 96th meeting of the UN General Assembly Third Committee (A/C.3/SR.96, 7 October 1948).[204]

Human dignity is "the fundamental guiding principle of International Human Rights Law enshrined in the Preambles to the Universal Declaration of Human Rights and both Covenants", as said the CoESCR in its GC 13 (E/C.12/1999/10, para. 41).[205] The Declaration and Programme of Action of Vienna (1993)[206] have reaffirmed that "all human rights derive from the dignity and worth inherent in the human person" (Preamble). In 1986, the UN General Assembly had adopted a Resolution on 'Setting international standards in the field of human rights' (A/RES/41/120)[207] to propose "guidelines in developing international instruments in the field of human rights". One of them reads: "Be of fundamental character and derive from the inherent dignity and worth of the human person".

In Constitutional Law, human dignity is sometimes invoked in preambular texts as the foundation of all human rights, or as the central value of the whole Constitutional order, or in connection with specific human rights, or as a right in itself, or as both a right and a principle.

Human dignity is better understood as a principle in a circular relation with all human rights: respecting human rights is to respect human dignity that is the source of human rights. Human dignity and human rights are thus like the two sides of a medal so that human dignity is a principle amounting to "the right to have rights, or the right of every individual to belong to humanity" (Arendt, 1952, p. 298).

Human rights are the answer to the following question: What do human beings need to live a dignified life, free "from fear and want" (Universal Declaration, Preamble), that is, with the minimum of suffering and deprivations, and the maximum of liberty and well-being?

There are two main jurisprudential complementary visions of human dignity and the rights it requires: essential-absolute and existential-relative.

Essential-absolute human dignity

Following the Western philosophical tradition, what distinguishes the human species are the higher faculties of reason, liberty, and will. Human dignity is equated with personal autonomy (or self-determination) that consists, literally, in giving the law to oneself. The aptitude to moral liberty underlies the Kantian categorical imperative commanding never to treat a human being as simply a means to an end, but always also as an end in itself. This is an essential-absolute conception of human dignity that was somewhat synthesised by the Supreme Court of Israel when it said, in *Case HCJ 6427/02 Movement for Quality Government in Israel v. Knesset,* cited in *HCJ 2605/05 Academic Center of Law and Business v. Minister of Finance,*[208] that the essence of the dignity of a human being "lies in the sanctity of his life and his liberty" (para. 34).

The most influential jurisprudential expression of this conception is the so-called *Objektformel* (formula-object) applied by the German Federal Constitutional Court since the 1950s. For example, it said in *Case BVerfGE 45, 187 (Lebenslange Freiheitsstrafe)* (1977)[209]:

> 144. ... Therefore, it contradicts the human dignity to turn the human being into a mere object of State. The sentence "the human being must always remain an end in itself" [Kant] has unlimited validity in all areas of Law; for the dignity of man as a person, which can

> never be taken, consists particularly therein, that he remains recognized as a person who bears responsibility for himself.

In *Case 1 BvR 2378/98*,[210] it repeated: "This court has frequently expressed the view that it is inconsistent with the dignity of the individual for the State to treat him as an object" (116 (1)).

This view has been echoed by other higher Courts. For instance, the Constitutional Court of Colombia said in *Case C-221/94*,[211] concerning the legitimacy of the criminalisation of consumption of narcotic drugs:

> To consider the person autonomous has its inevitable and inexorable consequences, and the first and most important of all consists in that matters concerning only a person only by her should be decided. Deciding instead of her is to snatch her brutally from her ethical condition, to objectify her, making her a means for ends chosen outwardly to her.

The Constitutional Court of South Africa said, in *Case The State v. T Makwanyane and M Mchunu (CCT3/94) [1995] ZACC 3; 1995 (6) BCLR 665; 1995 (3) SA 391; [1996] 2 CHRLD 164; 1995 (2) SACR 1 (6 June 1995)*,[212] that the death penalty treats the convicted person "as an object to be eliminated by State" (para. 26). In the USA Supreme Court Judgement of *Furman v. Georgia, 408 U.S. 238, 1972*,[213] Justice William J. Brennan said, concurring: "The true significance of these punishments [death penalty] is that they treat members of the human race as nonhumans, as objects to be toyed with and discarded".

Another restricted of human dignity that of the USA Supreme Court jurisprudence, qualified as liberty-based for linking human dignity rather with negative freedoms, freedoms from interference by the Government. Neomi Rao (2011) commented: "American courts are restrained, if not outright hostile, to inferring and imposing positive constitutional rights. But American constitutional law is exceptional in this regard" (p. 237).

Existential-relative human dignity

This is a vision concerned with a dignified life but not unaware of its varying economic factors.

As wrote Louis Blanc, a working class leader, in 1848: "Let us say it then for once and for all: freedom consists, not only in the RIGHTS that have been accorded, but also in the power given men to develop and exercise their faculties, under the reign of justice and the safeguard of law" (as cited in Ishay, 2004, p. 140). American President Franklin Roosevelt famously stated in his so-called 'Second Bill of Rights' (1944)[214]: "Necessitous men are not free men".

Harry S. Truman, his successor, said in his closing speech at the San Francisco Conference that he wished "the time when all worthy human beings may be permitted to live decently as free people". Roosevelt's wife, Eleanor, was the President of the UN Commission on Human Rights that drafted the UDHR, whose Article 22 reads:

> Everyone, as a member of society, has the right to social security and is entitled to realization, through national effort and international cooperation and in accordance with the organisation and resources of each State, of the economic, social and cultural rights indispensable for his dignity and the free development of his personality.

The German Constitution[215] does not incorporate socio-economic rights, but its Article 20.1 states: "The Federal Republic of Germany is a democratic and social federal State". The Federal Constitutional Court refers often to an "existential minimum" (for example, in *BVerfGE 82, 60 – Steuerfreies Existenzminimum*, 1990).[216]

The Constitutional Court of South Africa said in *Case Government of the Republic of South Africa and Others v Grootboom and Others* (*CCT11/00*) [*2000*] *ZACC 19; 2001* (*1*) *SA 46; 2000* (*11*) *BCLR 1169* (*4 October 2000*)[217]: "There can be no doubt that human dignity, freedom, and equality, the foundational values of our society, are denied those who have no food, clothing or shelter" [23].

The Supreme Court of Israel said in *Case Commitment to Peace and Social Justice v. Minister of Finance* (*HCJ 366/03*) and *Case Bilhah Rubinova and Others v. Minister of Finance* (*HCJ 888/03*)[218]:

> 13. … Indeed, the human right to dignity is also the right to have living conditions that allow an existence in which he will realize his liberty as a human being.
>
> 14. … The right to human dignity, in the substantive sense, constitutes a collection of rights that need to be protected in order that dignity may exist. These are those rights without which there is no significance to a person being a free entity, since his power to develop his body and spirit in accordance with her will, within the society in which he lives, has been taken away.

The same Supreme Court of Israel referred to an intermediate conception in *Case HCJ 2605/05 Academic Center of Law and Business v. Minister of Finance*[219]:

> In the judgment in *HCJ 6427/02 Movement for Quality Government in Israel v. Knesset*, it was held that the model adopted by the Supreme Court with

> regard to the scope of application of the constitutional right to human dignity is an 'intermediate model'; in other words, the right to human dignity does not only include those clear violations that relate to a person's humanity, such as physical and emotional injuries, humiliation and defamation, but it does not encompass all human rights.

Consequently, all human rights contribute to a life with human dignity, because human beings are not abstract and isolated entities. All are required for a decent and meaningful life, by providing human beings with food, drink, shelter, health care, etc., including minimum participation in social, political and cultural life. They protect and enhance life and liberty, enabling every human being to self-determination and self-fulfilment, thus generating feelings of self-worth and self-esteem.

Concluding remarks

- *Human dignity is generally regarded as a principle and even when it is qualified as a right it is not put on the same footing of other rights.*

Human dignity is the ground of human rights, simultaneously immanent and transcendent: immanent, i.e. without metaphysical, religious or social foundation, and transcendent because, although each right is umbilically linked to dignity, there is human dignity without rights: it precedes the ability to exercise them and subsists beyond it.

- *Human dignity is protected by human rights but not all rights are equally essential.*

Not every human rights violation amounts to a direct attack on the core of the physical, psychological and moral integrity of the human person. That is why the implementation of some human rights may be progressive, some others may be restricted, and still, others may be temporally suspended. Only a few human rights are qualified as non-derogable, i.e. never allowing restriction or suspension. They are the most inherent in human dignity, which is attacked especially by slavery and torture. Other similar inhuman or degrading treatments, as well as extreme poverty and other situations of great deprivation, are serious attacks on human dignity too.

- *Human dignity is not soluble in the sum of human rights recognised at a given time.*

As the famous Justice of the USA Supreme Court William J. Brennan said in a 1985 speech on constitutional interpretation, delivered at the Georgetown University Law Center, "a comprehensive definition" of the ideal of human dignity is "an eternal quest" whose demands "will never cease to evolve" (as cited in Wermeil, 1998, p. 239) (see 2.5.8.1.4).

– *The HDP has the weakness and the virtues of principles.*
Despite the possible "function of erecting a smokescreen for disguising more profound differences", the HDP has a "heuristic function" (Habermas, 2012, pp. 66, 67). Its inherent indeterminacy allows it:
- to serve as the criterion for resolving possible conflicts between individual rights, between rights and dignity, between rights of different persons, between two positions of dignity, between individual and collective dignity;
- the flexibility required for its cultural incarnations and openness to updating the contents of human rights, as well as to the recognition of new rights, such as the jurisprudential right to personal data or the right to the Internet.

Summing up: Human dignity is better understood and protected as a principle of foundation, interpretation, and expansion of human rights.

2.6.2.4.3 *Human Dignity Hallmarks the Belonging to the Human Species*

The *sanctity of life*[220] is the biological ground of "the recognition of the inherent dignity and of the equal and inalienable rights of all members of the human family", as reads the first preambular paragraph of the UDHR. Consequently, each and every human being is endowed with human dignity, whatever their age, handicaps, merits or crimes, including unborn life, parts of the human body and deceased persons.
- There is *seminal dignity* in unborn human life. A human embryo is already vested with human dignity. In this regard, the German Federal Constitutional Court said in *Case BVerfGE 39, 1, 1975* (*Schwangerschaftsabbruch I*),[221] relating to abortion: "Where human life exists, there is human dignity. [...] The potential faculties present in the human being from the beginning suffice to ground human dignity" (para. 147).[222] The European Court of Human Rights agrees but distinguishing between having human dignity and being entitled to human rights. In *Case Vo v. France* (Application 53924/00, 8 July 2004),[223] it said that, while "there is no consensus on the nature and status of the embryo and/or fetus (see paragraphs 39–40 above)", it is recognised "that the embryo/fetus belongs to the human race. The potentiality of that being and its capacity to become a person [...] require protection in the name of human dignity, without making it a 'person' with the 'right to life' for the purposes of Article 2" (para. 84) of the ECHR.
- Human dignity is also intrinsic in little children and adults physically impaired or mentally disabled, despite their lacking effective autonomy or ability to exercise all or some human rights.

- The absolute common human dignity is not increased or decreased by individual behaviour and accomplishments. In this respect, virtuous persons and criminals are on an equal footing. The Constitutional Court of South Africa concluded in *Case S v Makwanyane and Another* (*CCT3/94*) *[1995] ZACC 3; 1995 (6) BCLR 665; 1995 (3) SA 391; [1996] 2 CHRLD 164; 1995 (2) SACR 1 (6 June 1995)*,[224] relating to sentences to death and long-term imprisonment: "What our decision does entail is a recognition that even the worst and most vicious criminals are not excluded from the protections of the Constitution" (para. 203). Justice Haim Cohn, Deputy Chief of the Israel Supreme Court, said in a concurring 'Separate Opinion' in *Case Katlan v. Prison Service* (HCJ 355/79), 1980,[225] relating to the rights of detainees: "A free and enlightened society differs from a wild and deprived society in the amount of dignity recognized for each and every person".
- There is still human dignity in a deceased person because the human body "is not simply organic", as said the Constitutional Court of South Africa in *Case S v Jordan and Others (Sex Workers Education and Advocacy Task Force and Others as Amici Curiae* (*CCT31/01*) *[2002] ZACC 22; 2002 (6) SA 642; 2002 (11) BCLR 1117 (9 October 2002)*,[226] relating to prostitution. Human beings survive physically in the genetic heritage they have transmitted to their children, affectively in the memory of their most beloved, as well as symbolically in their names, words and works (as authors' rights illustrate). Other aspects of moral survival are the online profiles and data (digital remains), whose legal statute is still generally in a limbo state. Deceased human beings may also be immortalised by their nations and by the world for the greatness of their actions or creations, to say nothing of faith in immortality. The German Federal Constitutional Court said in *Case BVerfGE 30, 173, 1971*,[227] relating to a satirical novel (*Mephisto*) describing the career of an actor during the Nazi regime:

  > It would be inconsistent with the constitutional mandate of the inviolability of human dignity, which underlies all basic rights, if a human being [...] could be belittled and denigrated after his death. Accordingly, the duty of State laid down in Article 1, paragraph 1 of the GG [Constitution], to protect the individual against assaults on his or her human dignity does not come to an end with death. (para. 61)

  The Supreme Court of Israel said in *Case Women's Association for the Future of Israel v. The Broadcasting Authority* (HCJ 6143/94, July 26, 1999),[228] relating to a play on actual historical events in which, it was claimed, there was a scene containing falsehoods defaming a woman and survivors of the Holocaust: "We must protect the dignity of the deceased and their good name". (para. 12)

In this regard, Cançado Trindade, former Judge (and President) of the Inter-American Court of Human Rights (1994–2008) and Judge in the International Court of Justice since 2009, attached to the Judgement of the *Case Bámaca-Velásquez v. Guatemala* (2000),[229] relating to the disappearance, torture and extrajudicial execution of the leader (*Comandante*) of a guerrilla group in Guatemala, a "Separate Opinion" that deserves extended citation:

> 5. ... The negligence and lack of respect for the mortal remains of the victims – disappeared or not – of violations of human rights, and the impossibility of recovering them, in various cases before the Court concerning distinct States, appear to me to configure a *malaise* [unease] of our times, disclosing the appalling spiritual poverty of the dehumanized world in which we live.
>
> 6. The point raises in me some concerns, which I feel obliged to express in this Separate Opinion since the link between the living and the dead – sustained by so many cultures, including the Maya – does not appear to me to have been sufficiently developed in the domain of legal science. I thus allow myself to focus my thoughts on four interrelated aspects of the question, from the perspective of human rights, namely: (a) the respect for the dead in the persons of the living; (b) the unity of the humankind in the links between the living and the dead; (c) the ties of solidarity between the dead and the living; and (d) the prevalence of the right to truth, in respect for the dead and the living. [...]
>
> 8. This is one of the oldest concerns of the human being, rendered immortal, e.g. more than four centuries before Christ, by the well-known tragedy of Antigone of Sophocles, which pertained precisely to the firm determination of Antigone, a courageous woman, to confront the tyranny of Creon and to give a worthy grave to one of her two dead brothers (like the other brother who had been buried). The search for an understanding of death is indeed present in all cultures and philosophical traditions of the world. This is a truly universal theme, besides being a perennial one, cultivated by the cultures of all peoples in all times. [...]
>
> 11. In fact, the respect for the dead, always cultivated in the most distinct cultures and religions, soon found expression (though insufficient treatment) also in the domain of Law. Already the ancient Roman Law, for example, safeguarded penally such respect for the dead. In the comparative law of our days, it can be found that the penal codes of numerous countries typify and sanction the crimes against the respect for the dead (such as e.g. the subtraction and

the hiding of the mortal remains of a human being). And at least one trend of the legal doctrine on the matter visualizes as the passive subject of the right to respect for the dead the community itself (starting with the relatives) which the dead belonged to.

12. Even though the juridical subjectivity of an individual ceases with his death (thus no longer being, when having died, a subject of Law or *titulaire* [holder] of rights and duties), his mortal remains – containing a corporeal parcel of humanity – continue to be legally protected (supra). The respect to the mortal remains preserves the memory of the dead as well as the sentiments of the living (in particular his relatives or persons close to him) tied to him by links of affection – this being the value legally protected. In safeguarding the respect for the dead, also penal law gives concrete expression to a universal feeling of the human conscience. The respect for the dead is thus due – at the levels of both internal and international legal orders – in the persons of the living. [...]
14. The International Law of Human Rights discloses an even wider horizon for the consideration of the question. In my understanding, what we conceive as the humankind comprises not only the living beings – *titulaires* of human rights – but also the dead with their spiritual legacy.

2.6.2.4.4 *Human Dignity Is an Ethical Invention with Genetic Foundation*

Belonging to the human species means to be a member of Humanity that is a signifier carrying two senses, so explained by Roger-Pol Droit (2005):

> On the one hand, it designates the community formed by human individuals as a whole. On the other, the notion of humanity is to be understood as the value specific to actions that are consistent with dignity. In this sense, humanity as a value stands in opposition to inhuman, unworthy and barbarous acts. The philosophical, legal and intellectual content of this idea of humanity still remains to be elaborated. (p. 18)

Understood according to the second sense, Humanity is a notion equatable to human dignity. What follows is a contribution to its elaboration.

Besides "human dignity", a frequent expression in IHRL is "dignity and worth of the human person". The term 'worth' may be interpreted as having a qualitative ethical meaning or an objective biological one. If interpreted under the first meaning, 'dignity and worth' seems redundancy. If 'worth' is taken as the ground of 'dignity', it would be more rigorous to put 'worth and dignity'. The Constitutional Court of South Africa points to this understanding as it said in

Case S v Makwanyane and Another (*CCT3/94*) [*1995*] *ZACC 3; 1995* (*6*) *BCLR 665; 1995* (*3*) *SA 391;* [*1996*] *2 CHRLD 164; 1995* (*2*) *SACR 1* (*6 June 1995*),[230] concerning sentences to death and long-term imprisonment, as above quoted: "Recognizing a right to dignity is an acknowledgement of the intrinsic worth of human beings: human beings are entitled to be treated as worthy of respect and concern" (para. 328).

As a consequence, an account of the human dignity foundation should be a matter of answering the following main questions: What is the ground of human worth? What are the qualities, attributes or faculties distinguishing the human species from other ones? What does it mean to *be human*? In short: What is Man?[231]

Throughout centuries, many answers have been given. The neuroscientist António Damásio provides the following account of the human exceptionality.

- Survival is the central value for living organisms, since about four billion years ago. Homeostasis (Walter Cannon), in its most common sense, refers to biological automatic forms of regulating life. "In humans and in numerous other species endowed with a complex nervous system, however, there is a supplementary mechanism that involves mental experiences that express a value". They are feelings (Damásio, 2018, p. 48).
- Feelings and emotions are not the same. "Feelings are the mental expressions of homeostasis" (p. 6). They may be spontaneous or provoked. The first ones "arise from the background flow of life processes in our organisms, a dynamic ground state, and constitute the natural backdrop of our mental lives. [...] Spontaneous feelings signify the overall state of life regulation of an organism as good, bad, or in between". Provoked feelings "result from a wide variety of 'emotive' responses". Emotions are action programmes activated by situations of joy, sadness, fear, fury, compassion, admiration, etc. For example:

  > When you hear a musical sound that you describe as delightful, the feeling of delight is the result of a rapid transformation of the state of your organism. We call that transformation emotive. [...] Thus provoked, emotional feelings are not quite about listening to the background music of life. Emotional feelings are about hearing occasional songs and sometimes full-regalia opera arias. (pp. 107, 108, 115)

- Feelings have triggered what is most distinctive of humankind: cultures, which are "new forms of life regulation that have the very same goal of basic automated homeostasis" (p. 46). In effect, "there is no evidence to date to suggest that intellectual processes alone can constitute the basis for what makes us distinctly human" (p. 202). It is the feeling part of human beings that "is essential to ground a considerable portion of what constitutes morality and justice and assemble the ingredients of human dignity" (p. 207). There are feelings and cultural manifestations in other animal species, but without reaching, so far, the complexity and heights of human creativity. In Damásio's opinion, lacking true feelings is the limit of the artificial intelligence programmes, of humanlike robots. Emotions are the source of what is uniquely human. Damásio would agree with the following quotation from Rousseau by Friedrich Schiller, heading his Letters *On the aesthetic education of Man* (1795)[232]: *Si c'est la raison qui fait l'homme, c'est le sentiment qui le conduit* (If it is the reason that makes man, it is the feeling that drives him).

Consequently:

> The human condition encompasses two worlds. One world is made up of the nature-given rules of life regulation, the strings of which are pulled by the invisible hands of pain and pleasure. [...]
>
> There is, however, another world. We could and did work around the conditions imposed on us by inventing cultural forms of life management to complement the basic variety. (pp. 227, 228)

Accordingly, human beings are composed of two natures, as Bernd Ladwig (2014) points out:

- The 'first nature' is that "resulting from biological evolution, without which we would lack the capabilities that make any second nature possible (Tomasello 1999)".
- The 'second nature' is that "acquired through education, shaped by culture, structured by norms, embodied in institutions, and internalized through habit (see McDowell 1996)" (p. 24).

Being so, it can be argued that human dignity has a double nature too: it is an intersubjective ethical value with an objective genetic foundation.

Genetic foundation

The Preamble of the Universal Declaration on Bioethics and Human Rights (UNESCO, 2005)[233] begins by referring to "the unique capacity of human beings to reflect upon their own existence and on their environment, to perceive injustice, to avoid danger, to assume responsibility, to seek cooperation and to exhibit the moral sense that gives expression to ethical principles". What are the biological underpinnings of such a "unique capacity"?

They are outcomes of an evolutionary chain of bio-cultural processes – interaction between bipedalism, freeing of hands, increased volume of the brain, life in groups, development of the symbolic function (especially language), rationality and imagination – which "explains why our brain, which was originally the same size as that of a chimpanzee (about 350cm3), reached a volume of 1350cm3 in just five million years!" (Henrich, 2020, p. 173). Let us summarise.

Brain and mind

As the 2005 report of an EU High-Level Expert Group on "The Human Mind Project"[234] reads, the mind "is the core of our species' uniqueness and the essence of what it means to be human" (p. 8). Its biological substratum is the human brain. Weighing about 1.3kg and formed of two main types of cells – neurons that transmit information and glial cells surrounding and supporting their activity – the human brain is probably the most complex object in the universe. Its most extraordinary property is the neuroplasticity that consists in the electrochemical dynamism of its neurons, giving it limitless potential to react to all stimuli, internal and external, creating synaptic networks and causing structural and functional changes. It is estimated that there are 80–100 billion neurons, with about 10 times more glial cells, making about 100 trillion connections or synapses between them. This is the "fourth dimension" of the neuron, whose discovery amounted to "a deep neurobiological conceptual revolution" (Marc Peschanski, in AAVV, 2012, p. 52).

Synapses are a kind of neural maps which are reflected in mental images, the manipulation of which generates symbols, thought, reflection, creativity. Feelings are the primordial mental experiences, however (see Damásio, 2020). Maps and images constitute then the basis of mind. "The images in our minds are the brain's momentary maps of everything and of anything, inside our body and around it, concrete as well as abstract, actual or previously recorded in memory" (Damásio, 2010, p. 70). Consciousness emerged as "*a state of mind in which there is knowledge of one's own existence and of the existence of surroundings*" (p. 157). It is probably not a privilege of human beings, but there is a difference in complexity, notably concerning *conscience*. The self is the single voice of a conscious brain. Damásio summarises:

> The distinctive feature of brains such as the one we own is their uncanny ability to create maps. [...] But when brains make maps, they are also creating images, the main currency of our minds. Ultimately consciousness allows us to experience maps as images, to manipulate those images, and to apply reasoning to them. (p. 63)

This is the semiotic aptitude or semioticity, especially language.

Semioticity and language

As surviving requires the ability to detecting and interpreting sensory stimuli, where there is life there is *semiosis* or production of meaning. The semiotic aptitude or semioticity of the human species consists in the ability for the creation, interpretation and use of symbols or signs, terms that may be distinguished but have in common the following characteristic: they designate something that is in place of something, represent something, linking more or less arbitrarily a signifier (for example, a word, a picture) with a meaning (feeling, idea), as two sides of a coin.

According to Damásio (2018):

> The collection of images typically related to an object or event amounts to the 'idea' of that object or event, the 'concept' of it, the meaning of it, the semantics of it. Ideas – concepts and their meanings – can be translated into the idiom of symbols and enable symbolic thought. They can also be rendered into a special class of complex symbols, the verbal idiom. Words and sentences, the latter governed by grammatical rules, execute the translation, but the translations are image based as well. All mind is made of images, from the representation of objects and events to their corresponding concepts and verbal translations. Images are the universal token of mind. (pp. 89, 90)

Ernst Cassirer (1944) called the human being an *animal symbolicum*, i.e. endowed with the ability to create and use *symbolic forms* – a concept central to his thought that includes all cultural creations. He wrote:

> Man has, as it were, discovered a new method of adapting himself to his environment. Between the receptor system and the effector system, which are to be found in all animal species, we find in man a third link which we may describe as the symbolic system. This new acquisition transforms the whole of human life. As compared with the other animals, man lives not merely in a broader reality; he lives, so to speak, in a new dimension of reality. (p. 29)

Charles Morris (1964) commented: "Ernst Cassirer called the man 'the symbolic animal' (*animal symbolicum*), instead of 'the rational animal' (*animal rationale*), and much contemporary work has shown the aptness of this conception" (p. 1). Commenting on Cassirer too, Umberto Eco (1984) asked: "Who is not, then, a semiotic animal?" (p. 6). In his opinion: "With the sign, the man comes out of the raw perception, the *hic et nunc* experience, and abstracts. Without *abstraction*, the concept does not exist, although without it the sign does not exist either" (p. 127). Henry van Lier (1980) wrote in his book titled *L'Animal Signé* (The Signed Animal):

> So the human being is rigorously defined as the semiotic animal, that is, the animal in which the sign is constructed in constructing the man. The sign is the distinctive feature of man. Or better, the sign is the man himself. In the history of the universe, sign and man have come together. (p. 17)

Morris (1964) pointed out: "Man lives in his symbols, but he often maims himself and even dies, because of them" (p. 87). Human beings are so thoroughly semiotic animals that they can even commit murder or risk and sacrifice their lives for valued symbols. In this respect, Tzvetan Todorov (2013) remarked: "Human beings aspire to symbolic recognition infinitely more than they search to satisfy their senses, and they are ready to sacrifice their lives, as A. Smith already pointed out, for so a derisory thing as a flag" (p. 63).

According to Jean Caune (1997), "the passage of the interaction mediated by gestures to interaction mediated by symbols marks the threshold of hominization" (p. 58). This was the "symbolic revolution" (Picq, 2020, p. 45) of the *Homo Erectus* (since about 2 million years).

The semiotic aptitude justifies, therefore, the definition of man as a *semiotic animal* that is probably its most profound and broad definition.

Language is the most sophisticated expression of human semioticity, and "one of the remaining and by now unassailable justifications for a bit of human exceptionalism. Nonhuman creatures, respectable as they are, do not translate their images into any word even when their minds do plenty of smart things that ours may or may not do" (Damásio, 2018, p. 146). It was the aptitude for language that led to the definition of man as a rational animal by Porphyry (3rd century BC). Sylvain Auroux (2000) called it "the support of rationality" (p. 20).

Therefore, human semioticity can be considered the 'organ' of rationality.

Rationality and liberty

Linguistic signs are abstractions from the sensible reality that allow detachment from the variety of the concrete, immediate world, giving rise to the faculty of rationality as liberty of conceptualisation and reflexivity, self-determination and morality, imagination and creativity, opening the human beings to a temporality transcending the present, made up of memory and projects, of past and future.

In Jonah Lehrer's opinion: "Imagination is a breaking point in Evolution, a turning point".

> If I should have to choose a trait defining human nature, it would be creativity. [...] What no other species is able to do, making our singularity, is that: We can see the world as it is and imagine it as it would be if it were better. This particular talent does not exist anywhere in the animal realm. We can invent our own reality. (in AAVV, 2012, p. 58)

Imagination means, literally, the ability to manipulate images. Following Yves Quéré, imagination and creativity are "specifically human", making the human species "without doubt the sole species that designs a vision of future" (ibid., p. 60), and the human being "the sole animal able to live its life as a project" (Nayla Farouki, ibid., p. 77).

Damásio (2018) sums up the 'genealogy' of the mystery of the rationality, as it were:

> Nervous systems also acquired an elaborate collection of aggregated central processors in the central nervous system, conventionally called the brain. [...] These central processors [...] manage the process of image manipulation that we otherwise know as thinking, imagining, reasoning, and decision making. Last, they manage the conversion of images and of their sequences into symbols and eventually into languages – coded sounds and gestures whose combinations can signify any object, quality, or action, and whose linkage is governed by a set of rules called grammar. Equipped with language, organisms can generate continuous translations of nonverbal to verbal items and build dual-track narratives of such items. (pp. 62, 63)

"The ability to form symbols, organize them and make social use of them is called culture" (Lenclud, 2020, p. 48). The faculty and freedom of rationality have sparked the cultural revolution.

Cultural revolution

The biological evolution of the human brain, especially the complexification of its neuroplasticity, in interaction with the internal and external environment, in increasingly larger groups, and the emergence of language and rationality, have paved the way to "the biological revolution called culture" (Damásio, 2010, p. 288). It is "a new type of evolution, the cultural evolution, at least six times faster than the genetic evolution" (Richard Dawkins, in AAVV, 2012, p. 11).

This new stage of evolution has consisted in the invention of "new devices of regulation" (Damásio, 2010, p. 26), allowing for a "sociocultural homeostasis" (p. 27). It added to the basic biological homeostasis, entirely automated, which began in unicellular living creatures, a complexity peculiar to organisms possessing "brain, mind, and consciousness" (p. 44). Sociocultural devices – such as political and economic organisations, justice systems, science, technology, art, religion, etc. through which "consciousness optimised life regulation" (p. 10) – are unique to our species. They include the discovery and use of fire, as well as the invention of writing.

François Jacob (1981), Nobel Prize Winner of Medicine in 1965 (shared with Jacques Monod and André Lwoff), concluded: "Almost everything that characterises humankind is summarised in the word culture" (p. 123).

Historical being

As Peschanski observed, the evolutionary nature of human beings overcomes "terms for a long time opposed, individuation and socialisation, innate and acquired, now reconciled in a dialectic that grounds the specification of the humankind" (in AAVV, 2012, p. 52). Therefore, Heinz Wismann concludes:

> Unlike other beings, Man has no nature. His genetic programming, which he shares with the whole living realm, does not entirely determine his existence. He has to become what he is. The Ancient Greeks had clearly distinguished between two kinds of life: natural life, *zoé*, and historical life, *bios*. [...] And this distinction is essential because it shows that Man is himself only to the extent that he still is not what he will be. He is a historical being. [...] Man is thus the artist of himself. (ibid., p. 96)

In fact, as the aforementioned UE Report (2005)[235] pointed out: "Our genome does not dictate who we are or how we will think and behave, because the function of genes is intrinsically bound up with the environmental context in which they are turned on and off" (p. 9).

Here is an unpleasant outcome of the human historical nature: We live in a mental transition between the belief in an innate human essence, of transcendent origin, destined for some immortality, and the fact that each personality is a creation of the cultural, social, educational influences of the individual existence, which dissolves with death. In *The Brothers Karamazov*, Rakitin says to Alyosha: "Humanity will find in itself the power to live for virtue even without believing in immortality. It will find it in love for freedom, for quality, for fraternity" (Dostoyevsky, 1879, Part I, Book II, Chapter VII).

Yet it is not enough to be genetically human to behave and to be treated humanely.

Ethical value

Giorgio Agamben (2002), recalling Pico della Mirandola *Oratio*, wrote: "*Homo* is constitutively not human, he can receive all natures and all faces [...]. The humanist discovery of man is the discovery of his lack of himself, of his hopeless absence of *dignitas*" (p. 30). The so-called *wolf-children* "are the messengers of man's inhumanity, the witnesses of his fragile identity and his lack of a face of his own [...] of the precariousness of the human" (p. 30). And concluded, citing Linnaeus (*System of Nature*, 1735), that "man has no specific identity other than the ability to recognize himself. [...] *man is the animal that must recognize itself as human to be human.* [...] He becomes himself only if he raises himself above man" (p. 26).

Also, Hannah Arendt (1962) noted, in *On Revolution*, that "the Latin word *homo*, the equivalent of 'man', signified originally somebody who was nothing but a man, a rightless person, therefore, and a slave" (p. 46). That's why the Greek distinction between *zoé* (animal life) and *bios politicos* (political life) was so fundamental for Arendt, and that at the centre of her political thought is the *right to have rights* – a popular slogan during the American Revolution. As a consequence in her opinion the right to citizenship must be considered as the first right, i.e. the right to legal status in a political community, which is the condition for having protected rights. The Nazis deprived their victims of legal personhood before depriving them of life.

Human dignity must, therefore, be *recognised* intersubjectively, ethically. Recognition means knowing beyond knowledge, seeing beyond what one sees, to see in each human being, first and foremost, an equal and treating him or her as one wants to be treated (Golden Rule). The racial discrimination in the USA (supported by the *Jim Crow Laws*)[236] and the *Apartheid* in South Africa were politics of non-recognition. The Constitutional Court of South Africa said in *Case S v Makwanyane and Another* (*CCT3/94*) *[1995] ZACC 3; 1995 (6) BCLR 665; 1995 (3) SA 391; [1996] 2 CHRLD 164; 1995 (2) SACR 1 (6 June 1995)*[237] concerning sentences to death and long-term imprisonment:

> 329. Respect for the dignity of all human beings is particularly important in South Africa. For *apartheid* was a denial of common humanity. Black people were refused respect and dignity and thereby the dignity of all South Africans was diminished. The new Constitution rejects this past and affirms the equal worth of all

> South Africans. Thus, recognition and protection of human dignity is the touchstone of the new political order and is fundamental to the new Constitution.

Here is then "the dual nature of human dignity as, on the one hand, objective human property and, on the other hand, an ethical value" (Pfordten, 2016, p. 65). It is clearly stated in the Universal Declaration on the Human Genome and Human Rights (UNESCO, 1997)[238] that begins by stating (Article 1): "The *human genome* underlies the fundamental unity of all members of the *human family*, as well as the *recognition* of their inherent *dignity* and *diversity*" (italics added).

2.6.2.4.5 *Human Dignity Consists in the Species' Perfectibility Calling for Its Members' Perfecting*

Human beings are "animals without a fixed nature" (*noch nicht festgestellte Tiere*), wrote Nietzsche in *Beyond Good and Evil* (1886, 62).[239] "Here is man's dignity: He is not born finished, his existence evolves!" – affirmed Ernst Bloch (1972) in his *Vorlesungen zur Philosophie der Renaissance* (Lessons on the Philosophy of the Renaissance) (p. 15).

Perfectibility essentially moral perfectibility is the most distinguishing attribute of the human species. According to Silvia Sebastiani (2019):

> [Human nature is] the question that haunts the Enlightenment, to the point that its historians will consider it the "century of the human science".
>
> ... the question of human nature, for the Enlightenment, develops around the tension between diversity and uniformity. [...]
>
> Man has a capacity for perfection, the *perfectibility*, that is a neologism introduced by Rousseau in the philosophical and political debate of the 1750s, then taken up by many philosophers with various meanings.
>
> The introduction of the concept of perfectibility into the great debate on human nature is fundamental, because it allows us to think the surpassing of the fixity of nature by man, while ensuring a clear dividing line from other animals. [...] The keyword for this route is "civilisation", another neologism also created in the 1750s. [...]
>
> The Enlightenment has finally inscribed into the notion of human species a historical notion: the "continuous creation of man by man" (I borrow the expression from Michèle Duchet) allows him to move from the wild to the civilised state, and thus to go beyond the fixity of the animal nature by becoming a moral being. (pp. 20, 21, 25)

In effect, Rousseau (1913) wrote in his *Discourse on the origin of inequality* that there is a "distinctive and almost unlimited faculty" distinguishing between men and brutes: "This is the faculty of self-improvement, which, by the help of circumstances, gradually develops all the rest of our faculties, and is inherent in the species as in the individual: whereas a brute is, at the end of a few months, all he will ever be during his whole life, and his species, at the end of a thousand years, exactly what it was the first year of that thousand". This is the human *perfectibilité* (perfectibility) (p. 60).

After quoting Claude Lévi-Strauss, who called Rousseau "the father of ethnology" because, in the Second Discourse (*Discourse on the Origin and Basis of Inequality Among Men*) he has put "the central problem of anthropology, namely the transition from nature to culture", Sebastiani (2019) remarks: "Rooted in human nature, the perfectibility is also the result of a long history: it is therefore both innate and acquired; it is the very condition of man's inscription into history" (p. 24).

Human dignity has begun to universalise when it has become equated with democratic perfectibility, and no longer with aristocratic superiority. Alexis de Tocqueville wrote in *Democracy in America* (Book I)[240]:

> It can hardly be believed how many facts naturally flow from the philosophical theory of the indefinite perfectibility of man [...]. (Chapter VIII)

> I have shown how the ideas of progression and of the indefinite perfectibility of the human race belong to democratic ages. (Book I, Chapter XVII)

At present, in light of the progress of the neurosciences, especially since the 1990s – the 'brain decade', boosted by new non-invasive techniques allowing to study the brain in operation, through a variety of brain images (SPECT, MRI, PET, fMRI) – we are discovering the genetic foundation of the human perfectibility.

Consequently, members of the human species are not born fully human. Besides recognition, they need perfecting. While, at birth, most of our 80–100 billion neurons are already in place, it is estimated that only 10% are interconnected. "The other 90% connections are progressively constructed, following the influences of family, education, culture, society" (Nicole Le Douarin, in AAVV, 2012, p. 51). Catherine Vidal to highlight:

> The brain plastic properties bring new lighting on the processes contributing to form our identities. [...] It is the interaction with the familial,

> social, cultural environment that directs the development of certain aptitudes and contributes to forming the personality traits. In this dynamic, the structuration of the cerebral material is the close reflection of the lived experience. The classic dilemma of an opposition between nature and culture is overcome. [...]
>
> That is a very revolution for the understanding of the human. (ibid., p. 53)

The individual perfecting should aim at cultivating the human capacity to rationality, holistically understood, i.e. concerned with its main dimensions, which include:
- the theoretical, cognitive reason, concerned with facts and knowledge;
- the technical, instrumental reason, concerned with the application of knowledge to producing tools and goods making human life more safe, healthy and comfortable;
- the practical, moral reason, concerned with values and behaviours, i.e. related to the human aptitude for deliberating and choosing, with autonomy and responsibility[241];
- the imagining reason concerned with possible better alternatives to the present human condition.

The vision of human dignity as perfectibility echoes in two legal pieces:
- Article 3 of the Universal Declaration on the Human Genome and Human Rights (UNESCO, 1997)[242]:

> The human genome, which by its nature evolves, is subject to mutations. It contains potentialities that are expressed differently according to each individual's natural and social environment, including the individual's state of health, living conditions, nutrition, and education.

- Decision of the South African Constitutional Court in *Cases Ferreira v Levin NO and Others; Vryenhoek and Others v Powell NO and Others (CCT5/95) [1995] ZACC 13; 1996 (1) SA 984 (CC); 1996 (1) BCLR 1 (6 December 1995)*[243] relating to winding-up proceedings:

> [49] Human dignity cannot be fully valued or respected unless individuals are able to develop their humanity, their "humanness" to the full extent of its potential. Each human being is uniquely talented. Part of the dignity of every human being is the fact and awareness of this uniqueness. An individual's human dignity cannot be fully respected or valued unless the individual is permitted to develop his or her unique talents optimally.

In sum: If the foregoing explanation is not flawed, the human dignity does not consist in an inborn divine 'soul' or ready-to-wear 'reason', but in the species' indefinite genetic perfectibility and historical perfecting through its moral and intellectual aptitude for liberty and creativity. This consciousness may contribute to the healing of the famous *narcissistic wound* caused by Darwin, Marx, Nietzsche, Freud and others.

2.6.2.4.6 *Human Dignity Is Inviolable and Indisposable*

Human dignity is inviolable

Human dignity is inviolable in a descriptive and prescriptive sense:

- In a descriptive sense, human dignity is inviolable to the extent that its genetic foundation is unexpropriatable, i.e. it cannot be taken. The German Federal Constitutional Court said in *Case BVerfGE 87, 209, 1992* (*Tanz der Teufel*)[244] relating to a film where human dignity allegedly was not respected:

  > Everybody possesses it [human dignity], regardless of his or her qualities, accomplishments or social status. It is also possessed by those who cannot act in a meaningful way because of their physical or psychological condition. It is not lost even by 'undignified' behaviour. It cannot be taken away from any human being.

  For example, a torturer may extract a confession from his victim, true or false, but will not be able to extract from him or her the genetic specific attributes underlying their dignity.
- In a prescriptive sense, human dignity is inviolable as a command, i.e. it should not be violated, as famously stated the German *Grundgesetzt* (Constitution)[245]: *Die Menschenwüde ist unantastbar* (The human dignity is inviolable).

Human dignity is indisposable

Human dignity is indisposable. The Federal Constitutional Court of Germany said in *Case BVerfGE 45, 187* (*Lebenslange Freiheitsstrafe*) (1977)[246]: "Above all, we must not lose sight of the following: Human dignity is something indisposable" (*Bei alledem darf nicht aus den Augen verloren werden: Die Würde des Menschen ist etwas Unverfügbares*) (para. 146). In *Case BVerfGE 87, 209* (*Tanz der Teufel*),[247] it said that it "is not only the individual dignity of each person but the dignity of man as a species" (para. 113: *Menschenwürde in diesem Sinne ist nicht nur die individuelle Würde der jeweiligen Person, sondern die Würde des Menschen als Gattungswesen*). Kant stated in the *Metaphysics of Morals* (Book II, § 38): *Die Menschheit selbst ist eine Würde* (Humanity is itself a Dignity). Nobody may renounce it, for example by selling himself or herself as a slave. And, if someone is involuntarily enslaved, he or she retains his or her human dignity.

This dual dimension of human dignity – as the dignity of the human species and each of its members – gives it a function both of protection and of limitation of human rights that may give rise to controversial decisions (hard cases). Some examples follow:

- The German Federal Administrative Court condemned a *Peep-Show* spectacle,[248] in *Case BVerwGe 64, 274, 1981 (Sittenwidrigkeit von Peepshows)*,[249] for being a degradation of the human person, contrary to the Constitution. The Court said:

  > Article 1.1 of the Constitution protects the personal intrinsic human value. Human dignity is violated when a person is degraded to the condition of an object. In this event, the human dignity may be attacked by private persons too, as is the case. (para. 10)
  >
  > This violation of human dignity does not become acceptable or justified for being committed by a woman who freely exposes herself in a *Peep-show*. Human dignity is an objective, indisposable value [...], the respect of which the individual cannot give up validly [...]. (para. 12)[250]

- The Constitutional Court of South Africa condemned prostitution, in *Case S v Jordan and Others (Sex Workers Education and Advocacy Task Force and Others as Amici Curiae (CCT31/01) [2002] ZACC 22; 2002 (6) SA 642; 2002 (11) BCLR 1117 (9 October 2002)*,[251] for being a commodification of the human body, contrary to the Constitution. The Court said:

  > [74] Our Constitution values human dignity which inheres in various aspects of what it means to be a human being. One of these aspects is the fundamental dignity of the human body which is not simply organic. Neither is it something to be commodified. Our Constitution requires that it be respected. [...] To the extent that the dignity of prostitutes is diminished, the diminution arises from the character of prostitution itself. The very nature of prostitution is the commodification of one's body.

- In *Case Wackenheim v France*, dwarf-throwing shows (for short distances and duly protected) were banned by the French *Conseil d'État* (Council of State, Highest Administrative Court). The decision was supported by the former European Commission of Human Rights (Council of Europe) and the CoHR. The Case is summarised in the "Views" of the Committee (CCPR/C/75/D/854/1999, 26 July 2002).[252] In its opinion:

> 3. The author affirms that banning him from working has had an adverse effect on his life and represents an affront to his dignity. He claims to be the victim of a violation by France of his right to freedom, employment, respect for private life and an adequate standard of living, and of an act of discrimination. He further states that there is no work for dwarves in France and that his job does not constitute an affront to human dignity since dignity consists in having a job. [...]
>
> 7.2 The Committee must decide whether the authorities' ban on dwarf tossing constitutes discrimination within the meaning of article 26 of the Covenant, as the author asserts. [...]
>
> 7.4 The Committee considers that the State Party has demonstrated, in the present case, that the ban on dwarf tossing as practised by the author did not constitute an abusive measure but was necessary in order to protect public order, which brings into play considerations of human dignity that are compatible with the objectives of the Covenant.

The indisposability of human dignity means, therefore, that it must prevail over individual autonomy. There are not human rights against human dignity.

2.6.2.4.7 *Human Dignity Is Vulnerable and Variable*

Human dignity is vulnerable

While human dignity is absolute, and can never be lost, the German Federal Constitutional Court noted in the aforementioned *Case BVerfGE 87, 209, 1992* (*Tanz der Teufel*)[253]: "The entitlement to respect that results from it is, however, vulnerable" (para. 113: *Sie kann keinem Menschen genommen werden. Verletzbar ist aber der Achtungsanspruch, der sich aus ihr ergibt*). It may be endangered in its objective genetic foundation or hindered as an intersubjective ethical value, by action or omission.

- The human genome may be impaired by genetic anomalies or henceforth altered through biotechnologies, as warns the Convention for the Protection of Human Rights and Dignity of the Human Being with regard to the Application of Biology and Medicine: Convention on Human Rights and Biomedicine (Council of Europe, 1997),[254] according to which "the misuse of biology and medicine may lead to acts endangering human dignity" (Preamble).
- Life, as material support of human dignity, may be annihilated by homicide, the death penalty, wars and also by suicide.

- The human beings' perfecting needs the protection and provisions of human rights that may not be assured by State or due to other causes. Human rights, in general, are not respected when human beings are victims of physical and/or psychic cruelties, disease, misery and each time they are treated simply as 'objects' and 'means'.
- Individual human dignity is also undermined if personal reputation is attacked, with reflexes in the sense of self-esteem and possible material losses. In this regard, the Supreme Court of Israel said in the aforementioned *Case Women's Association for the Future of Israel v. The Broadcasting Authority* (HCJ 6143/94, July 26, 1999)[255] relating to a play on actual historical events in which, it was claimed, there was a scene containing falsehoods defaming a woman and survivors of the Holocaust:

> 12. ... In the context of this petition, our concern is with the aspect of human dignity relating to a person's good reputation. This aspect of human dignity is vital to all people. A person's right to his or her good name is a basic value in every democratic system. It is a necessary condition for a freedom-loving society. It is predicated on the need for an internal sense of value, personal pride and personal recognition among people. [...]
>
> The significance of preserving a person's reputation also derives from the values of the State of Israel as a democratic State. One who steals my property can compensate me monetarily, but he who robs me of my good name has stolen the very reason for my existence. One's good name determines the manner in which one perceives oneself and how one's peers and society relate to one. In effect, the only asset of many people, both public servants and those working in the private sector, is their reputation, which they cherish as life itself. This applies to both the living and the dead.

- Because human beings live in families, groups, communities, societies, the discrimination, segregation, marginalisation of groups to which they belong affects the sentiment of dignity and self-esteem of their members. The Supreme Court of Canada said in *Case R. v. Keegstra,* [*1990*] *3 S.C.R. 697*[256] relating to a teacher accused of anti-Semitism:

> A person's sense of human dignity and belonging to the community at large is closely linked to the concern and respect accorded the groups to which he or she belongs. [...] The derision, hostility, and abuse encouraged by hate propaganda, therefore, have a severely negative impact on the individual's sense of self-worth and acceptance. [...] Such consequences

> bear heavily in a nation that prides itself on tolerance and the fostering of human dignity through, among other things, respect for the many racial, religious and cultural groups in our society.

Human dignity is variable

The varying conditions and levels of the perfecting of human beings explain variable incarnations and expressions of their equal dignity.

- The liberty of rationality is not operating *ab initio* (from the beginning) in little children and is absent from adults deeply mentally disabled, who are thus diminished in their possibilities for expressing their human dignity.
- Cultural, political, economic and other factors may favour or prevent the individual perfecting that the human perfectibility makes possible, which implies the right to have what one needs to have for being what one can be.
- Human dignity may be socially increased by virtues and accomplishments, eliciting respect and admiration, raising self-esteem, or decreased by undignified behaviour that affect the social respect of one's dignity, arousing disapproval or even sanctions.

Summing up, human dignity is composed of three layers, as it were:

- *Objective layer*, formed by the 'first human nature'. It can be *known*.
- *Intersubjective layer*, concerned by the 'second human nature'. It must be *recognised*.
- *Subjective layer*, depending on each one's behaviours and merits. It should be *deserved*.

All in all: Human dignity is a *natural attribute*, a *moral status*, and a *personal responsibility*.

2.6.3 *Other Ethical Principles*

The Constitutional Court of Colombia said that there are values with "a triple juridical identity: they are values, rights, and principles" (*T-363/16*).[257] Such may be considered the following values-rights-principles protecting other essential human goods-values constituent of the Ethics of Human Rights, namely: Life, Liberty, Equality, Diversity, with the correspondent Responsibility. Their pre-eminence is very briefly justified next.

Life

Life "is the supreme right", as said the CoHR in its GC 6 (1982, first paragraph),[258] to the extent that it is *sine qua non*, i.e. the biological condition of having rights, its loss being irreparable. The Constitutional Court of South Africa said in *Case S v Makwanyane and Another* (CCT3/94) [*1995*] *ZACC 3; 1995* (6) *BCLR 665; 1995*

(3) SA 391; [1996] 2 CHRLD 164; 1995 (2) SACR 1 (6 June 1995)[259] concerning sentences to death and long-term imprisonment:

> 144. The rights to life and dignity are the most important of all human rights, and the source of all other personal rights in Chapter Three [Constitution]. By committing ourselves to a society founded on the recognition of human rights we are required to value these two rights above all others. And this must be demonstrated by the State in everything that it does, including the way it punishes criminals. This is not achieved by objectifying murderers and putting them to death to serve as an example to others in the expectation that they might possibly be deterred thereby.

However, the right to life (or, more rigorously, the right to live)[260] is not absolute. The IHRL still admits the death penalty, and the Law, in general, admits intentional deprivations of life in situations of legitimate defence.

Furthermore, nowadays, the right to life has content crossing all human rights 'generations', giving it a normative density with three main dimensions (see 2.5.8.1.3):
- Protection against deprivation of the *biological life*
- Assuring the basic conditions for a *human life*
- Liberty for achieving the *life project*

Liberty and equality
Liberty is a *sacré-mot* (sacred word) of the IHRL. It underlies the Western classical conception of human dignity as autonomy, inspired by Kant, which reflects the definition of man as a rational animal. Like human life, human liberty is a *compendious expression* of various rights, because the contempt of liberty may be manifold. In *The ingenious Gentleman Don Quixote of La Mancha*, Don Quixote says: "Freedom, Sancho, is one of the most precious gifts that heaven has bestowed upon men; no treasures that the earth holds buried or the sea conceals can compare with it; for freedom, as for honour, life may and should be ventured".[261]

Following Rousseau (1762, Book II, Chapter XI): "If we ask in what precisely consists the greatest good of all, which should be the end of every system of legislation, we shall find it reduce itself to two main objects, *liberty and equality*". They are twin sisters – older daughters of human dignity, the signs-values flying most closely to it.

Equality means equal rights, equality before the law, equal protection of the law, aiming at equality in life, according to the principle of the interdependence of human rights.

Difference
Humankind is not a Palace of Mirrors, indefinitely reflecting each other, but rather a Symphony of Differences.

In reality, human beings have many cribs, many faces, many colours, as they are born in communities whose culture forms a collective identity transfused to individual identities. That is why probably the most sensitive issue raised by human rights concerns the relationship between their universality and their culturality, i.e. between abstract Human Being and concrete human beings, between ethical equality and individual and cultural diversity.

As human rights do not exist in a cultural and social *vacuum*, IHRL is not 'culture-blind'. The common language of human rights is translatable in cultural dialects that be ethically understandable. Human rights are compatible with every difference not incompatible with their values. There is a right to be different (see 5.3.2).

Responsibility
The human rights discourse is sometimes accused of individualism, forgetting duties. The debate goes back to the 1789 French Declaration and revived during the elaboration of the UDHR. This is a groundless debate, however, as there are many references to duties in IHRL. For example, in the title of the American Declaration of the Rights and Duties of Man (1948) and in the African Charter on Human and Peoples' Rights (1981, Articles 27–29). In effect, the principle of reciprocity is inherent to the concept of human rights. Rights and duties are like the two sides of a coin: if everyone holds rights, everyone bears duties. They are duties towards itself, the others and the common Humanity, including future generations.

A term without the undesirable connotations of 'duty', with more semantic amplitude and more topical, is responsibility. At the beginning of the 1990s, Geneviève Viney (1990) observed that "the word 'responsibility' has a so constant, so ordinary, so universal use, that we have difficulty to believe that it had been possible to do without it and that it does not date from far in the times" (p. 275).

The responsibility of *being human*, in its maximum exigence, is the "responsibility for the other one", in the opinion of Lévinas (1993, pp. 455, 461), for whom human rights "are originally the rights of the other human being" (Lévinas, 1989, p. 45). So much so that "*I, is another one*" [*Je est un autre*] (Lévinas, 1972, p. 98). This "absolute orientation to the Other" is the motivation to "acting without entering the Promised Land" (p. 45), renouncing "to be contemporary of one's work triumph".

> Acting for distant things, at the moment when the Hitlerism overcame, in the silent hours of this night without hours – independently of any

> assessment of the 'forces face to face' – is, no doubt, the highest nobleness. [...]
>
> Being I, means then not be allowed to escape from the responsibility, as if the whole building of creation rested on my shoulders. (pp. 47, 53)

2.6.4 *Ethics of Recognition*

The Ethics of Human Rights may be qualified as an Ethics of Recognition.

We know the ethical significance of recognition (see 2.6.2.4.4). It has become a topical and multi-purpose idea, with anthropological, political, juridical, psychological, ethical, and other stakes. It has a philosophical history which was the subject of the last book of Paul Ricoeur, titled *Parcours de la Reconnaissance* (Route of Recognition). Following Ricoeur (1994), the verb 'recognise' and the noun 'recognition' appear occasionally in René Descartes, but it was Kant who, in the 18th century, introduced the term in the philosophical glossary. Thus, begins its philosophical history, in which one may distinguish three moments: "After the Kantian moment of *Rekognition* and the Bergsonian moment of recognising images, [...] the Hegelian moment of *Anerkennung* [recognition]" (p. 239). It was "at this point that the principal conceptual revolution on the plane of philosophy took place, with the Hegelian theme of the struggle for recognition, where 'being recognised' is the horizon" (p. 25).

In the 1980s, the heuristic power of the idea of recognition has been rediscovered and attracted a great deal of interest in the social sciences field, giving rise to programmes of transdisciplinary studies and debates. A "rhetoric of recognition" (Payet & Battegay, 2008, p. 25) proliferated and "claims formulated in terms of recognition" (Ferrarese, 2008, p. 95) have multiplied. Recognition has become a normative principle of reinterpretation of morality and justice, a sign-flag of struggles of groups that aspire to acceptance of their differences and identities based on ethnicity, religion, gender, sexual orientation, etc.

Axel Honneth (2004) noted that, while the idea of recognition was always present in Ethics or Moral Philosophy, it has never been "the cornerstone of an ethics" (except for Hegel) (p. 1640). Participating in a meeting of experts on 'Ethics for the 20th Century', organised by UNESCO in 2001, he proposed an "Ethics of Recognition" as substantial Ethics, not a mere procedural one, because "every moral norm is linked to the recognition of the human being".[262] This is already true for the Golden Rule: "Most often stated as a proverbial sentence or maxim, the golden rule is, more deeply, a fundamental anthropological structure or scheme, expressing the recognition of man by man" (Roy, 2012, p. 15).

Robert Williams interpreted Hegelian Philosophy as an Ethics of Recognition. Georg W. F. Hegel considered recognition as the existential and phenomenological source of the concept of Ethics and the concept of Law, and concluded: "The absolute right is the right to have rights" (as cited in Williams, 1997, p. 240). Commenting on these words, Williams wrote: "This memorable sentence prompts a question: What is this absolute right and how is it secured? My proposal is that the absolute right is the right of recognition" (p. 240).

Indeed, recognition may be considered as the most profound need and desire of a human being.[263] It is a kaleidoscopic phenomenon generally associated with valorisation (*Aufwertung*), while non-recognition (*Aberkennung*) is connotated with devaluation (*Abwertung*) of individuals or groups. There are multiple expressions and institutions of recognition, in personal and social relations. Daily life is a theatre, at a variety of stages, of games and scenes of tacit demands, expectations, or declared and generalised competition and struggles for recognition, variable in their dramaticity, morality and geniality.

The idea of 'recognition' is also found in several fields of Law, such as Civil Law, International Law and in the IHRL, in particular. The IBHR proclaims that "recognition of the inherent dignity and of the equal and inalienable rights of all members of the human family is the foundation of freedom, justice and peace in the world" (Preambles of the UDHR, the ICCPR, and the ICESCR). Referring to the first preambular paragraph of the UDHR, Mary Glendon (2001) highlighted:

> Equally noteworthy in the first clause is the word *recognition*. Prior to World War II, legal positivism (the view that there are no rights other than those granted by the laws of the state) flourished in the United States and Europe and was dogma in the Soviet Union. But legally sanctioned atrocities committed in Nazi Germany had caused many people to reevaluate the proposition that there is no higher law by which the laws of nation-states can be judged. The declaration implicitly rejected the positivist position by stating that fundamental rights are recognized, rather than conferred. (p. 176)

Emmanuelle Jouannet (2012) even argues that:

> ... since the end of the Cold War, a new branch of International Law is emerging. We call it "International Law of Recognition" because it reflects the advent of the new social and cultural paradigm of recognition of identities that has imposed itself both at the internal and international levels since the 1990s. [...]
>
> The current phenomenon of the recognition of the Other in what makes both its dignity and its identity is rooted in an international world

> that has always been heterogeneous and multicultural, but which has only belatedly come to fully accept the reality. It includes all forms of claims related to gender, nation, languages, history, cultures or religions, and crosses the entire planet, from East to West and North to South. (p. 769)

As the author points out, recognition was an essential instrument of classical International Law "based entirely on the basic fundamental discrimination between civilised and uncivilised States", the standard of which was the Euro-American civilisation. It was "the unilateral legal act, individual or collective, by which civilised States attested to the sufficient degree of civilisation and therefore of maturity of a political entity to be part of the 'community of civilised States'" (p. 770).

After the end of the Cold War, International Law "gradually endorsed an international policy of recognition based on the right to difference and the right to preserve one's cultural identity" (p. 776). Minority rights have been addressed by several legal instruments, responding to their need for recognition, enshrining "the existence of a right to difference in equality" (p. 785). The "new paradigm of recognition" has been promoted mainly by UNESCO, having led to the gradual transformation of "the fact of plurality into a legal principle of diversity" – enshrined in its Convention on the Diversity of Cultural Expressions (2005) – that has become "a fundamental principle of International Law" (pp. 777, 780). Furthermore: "In recent years, there has been a different kind of a contemporary recognition claim that takes the form of claims for reparation of historical crimes committed as a result of racism, colonialism and imperialism" (p. 786).

As Jürgen Habermas (2012) strongly stated: "Human rights emerged from violent and sometimes even revolutionary struggles for recognition (see Honneth 1995)" (p. 73). Citizens "derive their self-respect from the fact that they are recognized by all other citizens as subjects of equal actionable rights" (p. 71).

All in all, "every consistent thought concerning human rights must start from this fundamental fact: they have not been established scientifically, but rather dogmatically", that is, "human rights are valuable because we recognise their validity" (Freund, 1972, pp. 154, 163).

Summing up: *The Ethics of Human Rights is an Ethics of the Recognition of Human Dignity as a Principle-Right to have Rights – rights of a living human being – which are fundamentally the Rights-Principles of Liberty, Equality, Diversity, with the consequent Responsibility.*

2.6.5 *Ethics of Humanity*

The Ethics of Human Rights has become the Common Ethics of Humanity.

Cultural diversity has always been a hallmark of the human Civilisation, and each people tends to believe in the superiority of its own culture, as concluded the Greek historian Herodotus, about 2,500 years ago: "For if one were to offer men to choose out of all the customs in the world such as seemed to them the best, they would examine the whole number, and end by preferring their own; so convinced are they that their own usages far surpass those of all others" (see Ishay, 2004, p. 16). In 1948, the UDHR has become "a beacon in the history of mankind", as said the Paraguayan Delegation (Carlos A. Vasconcellos) at the UN General Assembly 182nd plenary meeting, on 10 December 1948 – the day of its proclamation (A/PV.182).[264] Soon thereafter, René Cassin affirmed, by concluding a course on "The Universal Declaration and the implementation of Human Rights" at the Hague Academy of International Law (1951):

> The precedent developments have brought to the fore the revolutionary innovation the United Nations achievement means in the millennial struggle for the human rights, and the characteristics making the Universal Declaration of Human Rights, adopted in 1948, a historical document whose dynamism and influence, already immense, are destined to affirm themselves with an increasing authority along the time and the space. This monument, drawing inspiration from a practical idealism, is built on the unity of the human family and provides, in spite of its inevitable imperfections, the base of ethics without which the universal society could not organise itself at the moral, political, legal and even economic levels. (p. 360)

The universal ethical significance of human rights has been highlighted again and again. For example:

- In 1968, the International Conference on Human Rights (Teheran) adopted a Resolution (XX) on "Education of youth in the respect for human rights and fundamental freedoms"[265] in which it affirmed "that the principles set forth in the Universal Declaration of Human Rights represent ethics common to all members of the international community".
- In 1970, the UN General Assembly stated in a Declaration on the Occasion of its Twenty-Fifth Anniversary (A/RES/2627 (XXV))[266]: "The international conventions and declarations concluded under its auspices give expression to the moral conscience of mankind and represent humanitarian standards for all members of the international community" (para. 8).
- In 1993, at the opening of the World Conference on Human Rights (Vienna), the UN Secretary-General (at the time Boutros Boutros-Ghali) said:

> In sum, what I mean to say, with all solemnity, is that the human rights we are about to discuss here at Vienna are not the lowest common

> denominator among all nations, but rather what I should like to describe as the "irreducible human element", in other words, the quintessential values through which we affirm together that we are a single human community! (United Nations, 1995, p. 442)

The Vienna Declaration and Programme of Action[267] has reaffirmed: "Human rights and fundamental freedoms are the birthright [*inhérents* in French, *patrimonio inato* in Spanish] of all human beings" (I-1).

- In 1998, the UN Secretary-General (at the time Kofi Annan) said in his Message addressed to the commemorative ceremony of the 50th Anniversary of the Universal Declaration, in the *Palais Chaillot*, Paris, on 10 December: "The Declaration drew from the best of human imagination and the worst of human experience".[268]
- In 2000, the UN General Assembly adopted the *Millenium Declaration*[269] that stated:

> 3. We reaffirm our commitment to the purposes and principles of the Charter of the United Nations, which have proved timeless and universal. Indeed, their relevance and capacity to inspire have increased, as nations and peoples have become increasingly interconnected and interdependent. [...]
> 6. We consider certain fundamental values to be essential to international relations in the twenty-first century.

- In 2008, UN General Assembly stated in a Resolution on the Sixtieth Anniversary of the UDHR (A/RES/63/116)[270]: "In an ever-changing world, the Universal Declaration of Human Rights remains a relevant ethical compass that guides us in addressing the challenges we face today".

In sum: Human rights "codify universal values and establish procedures to enable every human being to live a life of dignity" (Pillay, 2012, p. 94). They amount to "a global ethic for a globalised world, based on our common humanity, the Rio principles and the shared ethos of all traditions: 'Do as you would be done by'" (United Nations, 2013, p. 6).

The principles of the Ethics of Human Rights point into five dimensions:

- A *vertical dimension*, concerning the relation between State and all persons under its jurisdiction.
- A *horizontal dimension*, concerning inter-individual relations and between individuals and other private actors.
- A *self-referential dimension*, concerning the relation of human beings and Humanity with their own dignity.

- An *environmental dimension*, concerning the relationship between human beings and nature in general.
- An *intergenerational dimension*, concerning the relationship between present and future generations.

The Ethics of Human Rights – and some dimensions of it in particular – is a common responsibility of Humankind. This is the responsibility for safeguarding its genetic, natural and cultural inheritances, as well as for its indefinite perfecting. As Blaise Pascal wrote (*Pensées*), in a different context, "man infinitely transcends man" (*Thoughts*, 1670).[271]

The Ethics of Human Rights may be represented as a millenary tree: the root is human worth; the trunk is human dignity; the main branches are further principles; other branches are the human rights forming its leafiness.

The Ethics of Human Rights may also be represented, more broadly, as a Palace of Values: human dignity is the foundation; liberty, equality and diversity are the columns; non-discrimination is the dome; the variety of human rights are the salons, intercommunicating; tolerance, responsibility, and solidarity are the gardens; democracy, peace and development are the oxygen, the bread and the music of the wellbeing and survival of the species living in it; but it might get fatally damaged if the enchanted wood surrounding is ill-treated and the arches of the heritage of its natural, genetic and cultural treasures are not preserved.

The Declaration of Independence of the USA (The unanimous Declaration of the thirteen United States of America, 4 July 1776)[272] *proclaimed*: "We hold these truths to be self-evident, that all men are created equal, that they are endowed by their *Creator* with certain unalienable Rights, that among these are Life, Liberty and the pursuit of Happiness". The Declaration of the Rights of Man and the Citizen (26 August 1789)[273] referred to "the natural, unalienable, and *sacred rights* of man" (Preamble). The UN Charter[274] reaffirms – and the UDHR recalls – "*faith* in fundamental human rights, in the dignity and worth of the human person, in the equal rights of men and women and of nations large and small" (all italics added).

In *The Hunchback of Notre-Dame* (Victor Hugo, 1831),[275] one reads that, in the middle ages, in France, until the time of Louis XII, every town had sanctuaries that "were a kind of islands, which rose above the level of human justice. Every criminal who took refuge there was saved». In Paris, one of them was the *Cathédrale de Notre-Dame*. It was there that Quasimodo – bellringer of the Cathedral, "a monster of deformity [...] with one eye, hunchback, and crooked legs" who "was but an apology for a human being" – took "the beautiful and graceful Esmeralda", supposedly a gipsy and sorceress, after pulling her off the hangman who led her to the gallows, unjustly charged with having stabbed her ardently beloved captain. And "at that moment Quasimodo was really beautiful". But King Louis XI wanted her to be hanged. "Our Lady of Paris, forgive me. I will do it but this once. That criminal must be punished. I assure you, Holy Virgin, my good mistress, that she is a sorceress who is not worthy of your kind protection. You know, madam, that many very pious princes have transgressed the privilege of churches for the glory of God and the necessity of the State". On the day Esmeralda (Agnes, her real name) was justiced, Quasimodo disappeared. His skeleton was later found closely embracing Esmeralda' skeleton, in the cemetery she had been buried in.

The Ethics of Human Rights is a Cathedral built, sculpted, embellished and illuminated by the values vesting Esmeralda and Quasimodo with an equal moral beauty, which can save the human species from itself, from its Louis XI and others who desire violently to possess or to annihilate it, such as the disgraceful Archdeacon Claude Frollo: "Thou must die, girl, or be mine".

The Ethics of Human Rights has become the Common Temple of the *secular faith* of the Rule of Law. And as human dignity will never be definitively protected and enhanced, the Human Rights Temple is an endless building, open to the *Possible*...

2.7 Revolution of Human Rights

The Ethics of Human Rights "is both radical and revolutionary" (Mégret, 2010, p. 125).

Revolution is a frequent term in human rights literature. For example:

- Bertrand Russell (1938) wrote: "The Western world, from the Reformation until 1848, was undergoing a continuous upheaval which may be called the Rights-of-Man Revolution" (p. 89).
- The modern politicisation, juridification, and institutionalisation of human rights began with the two great 18th revolutions – American Revolution and French Revolution. John F. Kennedy is officially presented as the USA President (1961–1963) who "wished America to resume its old mission as the first nation dedicated to the revolution of human rights".[276]
- The French Revolution was "the first revolution to have been founded on the theory of the rights of humanity" (Robespierre, as cited in Gauchet, 1989, Introduction).
- According to Louis Sohn (1982), one of the greatest Professors of International Law in the 20th century, who participated in the drafting of the UN Charter:

> The modern rules of international law concerning human rights are the result of a silent revolution of the 1940s, a revolution that was almost unnoticed at the time. Its effects have now spread around the world, destroying idols to which humanity paid obeisance for centuries. Just as the French Revolution ended the divine rights of kings, the human rights revolution that began at the 1945 San Francisco Conference of the United Nations has deprived the sovereign states of the lordly privilege of being the sole possessors of rights under international law. States have had to concede to ordinary human beings the status of subjects of international law, to concede that individuals are no longer mere objects, mere pawns in the hands of states. (p. 1)

- *La Révolution des Droits de l'Homme* (The Human Rights Revolution) is the title of a Marcel Gauchet essay published in 1989, the year of the Bicentenary of the *Déclaration des droits de l'homme et du citoyen* (Declaration of the Rights of Man and the Citizen).
- Other political upheavals, at the end of the 18th century, were described as *human rights revolutions*.
- *The Human Rights Revolution: An International History* is a title published in 2012 (edited by Akira Iriye, Petra Goedde, and William I. Hitchcock).
- In the opinion of Norberto Bobbio (1990), the moving from the primacy of "duties" to the primacy of "rights" meant a "Copernican revolution" (p. 57).
- Luc Ferry said that the recognition and proclamation of human rights have meant "a radical revolution that made the human being the first value, which reverses the order of priorities between man and all that, until then, had primacy over him – nature, religion, community". What counts from now on is "membership to the human species, to humanity".[277]
- In 1998 – the year of the 50th anniversary of the UDHR – the UN Secretary-General (at the time Kofi Annan), addressing the Annual Conference organised by the UN Department of Public Information (DPI) and NGOs, affirmed: "There is no turning back in the revolution of human rights".[278]

Three moments and documents should be highlighted in the history of the modern and contemporary Revolution of Human Rights:
- Declaration of the Rights of Man and the Citizen, decreed at the beginning of the French Revolution by the Constituent Assembly on 26 August 1789.
- Universal Declaration of Human Rights, proclaimed by the UN General Assembly on 10 December 1948.
- Convention on the Rights of the Child, adopted by the UN General Assembly on 20 November 1989.

The Revolution of Human Rights may be summarised in the following headings: Consecration of the Individual as the highest ethical-juridical value; Transformation of the International Law and renovation of the Constitutional Law; Reconstruction of the Rule of Law; Inception of a Law of Humanity. It follows a brief justification of these interwoven outcomes.

2.7.1 *Consecration of the Human Person as the Highest Ethical-Juridical Value*

The French Revolution "marks a moment in the history of the world", said G. del Vecchio (as cited in Morange, 1988, p. 46). Proclaiming the "immortal watchword: Liberty, Equality, Fraternity" (Report of the Scholcher Committee on the definitive abolition of slavery, 1848) (in Monchablon, 1989, p. 201), the 1789 Declaration "marks in a certain sense the triumph of the Individual", as highlighted Louis Dumont (1983, p. 120), so becoming the "supreme creation of the modern political philosophy", according to Alain Touraine (1992, p. 74). The French Declaration summarised the political individualism and contractualism by proclaiming in its two first Articles that "men are born and remain free and equal in rights" (Article 1), and that "the aim of every political association is the preservation of the natural and imprescriptible rights of man" (Article 2). Therefore: "A society in which the observance of the law is not assured, nor the separation of powers defined, has no constitution at all" (Article 16). This has been the beginning of a "legal revolution", stressed Jean Morange (1988, p. 42).

In *The Philosophy of History*[279] published in 1837, Hegel said, referring to the French Revolution: "The principle of the Freedom of the Will, therefore, asserted itself against existing Right". It was "glorious mental dawn. All thinking beings shared in the jubilation of this epoch. Emotions of a lofty character stirred men's minds at that time; a spiritual enthusiasm thrilled through the world as if the reconciliation between the Divine and the Secular was now first accomplished" (pp. 465, 466, 467). Jules Michelet wrote in the Preface to his *Histoire de la Révolution Française* (History of the French Revolution),[280] published in 1847:

> The Revolution lives in ourselves – in our souls [...].
>
> Philosophy found man without right, or rather a nonentity, entangled in a religious and political system, of which despotism was the base. And she said, "Let us create man, let him *be*, by liberty". [...]
>
> Our fathers [...] found despotism in heaven and on earth, and they instituted law. [...] It was necessary, above all things, to vindicate the rights of man [...].

> O men of the present age, is this the creed you tax with individualism – is this what you term an egotistical law? But, remember, that without these rights of the Individual, by which alone man was constituted, he really had no existence [...].
>
> Speak not of egotism. History will answer here, quite as strongly as logic. It was at the first moment of the Revolution, at the moment she was proclaiming the rights of the individual, it was then that the soul of France, far from shrinking, extended, embraced the whole world in sympathetic thought: then did she offer peace to all, and wish to participate with all her treasure – liberty. (pp. 1, 6, 7, 8)

Jean Jaurès wrote in *La Justice dans l'humanité* (Justice in Humanity)[281] in 1903:

> ... it is the honour of the French Revolution to have proclaimed that, in every individual, mankind had the same innate excellency, the same dignity and the same rights, and when it proclaimed this symbol of justice, when it declared that Governments, societies, should be submitted to rules derived from this human right idea, the Revolution made more than to shape a new world, it created a new philosophy of history: it has made law, it has made justice the spring, the supreme outcome of history and the human movement; it has created a new philosophy of history to explain through the idea of justice both the future and the past.

And in the Conclusion of his *Histoire Socialiste de la Révolution Française* (Socialist History of the French Revolution, 1903) he noted that, despite everything, "the new Law [*Droit nouveau*] had taken definitely possession of history" (ibid., pp. 229, 227). According to Jean Bart (1989), the French 1804 *Code Civil* (Civil Code), "in giving birth to a *new Law*, has implemented in the field of private relations *the principles* declared on 26 August 1789" (French Declaration) (p. 351).

The ethical-juridical individualism of the French Revolution *Droit Nouveau* was universalised by the 1948 Universal Declaration. As reads a text of the Directorate of Human Rights of the Council of Europe: "Exalting the primacy of the individual, the Universal Declaration of Human Rights continues affirming today 'the challenge of an unfinished revolution: the one that aims at putting the human being in the centre of all national and international values'" (Conseil de l'Europe, 1999b, p. 48).

The recognition and proclamation of human rights have thus consecrated "the sanctity of human personality", meaning that "State is not itself an end" and that "the individual is the final subject of all Law" (Lauterpacht, 1948, pp. 9, 10). As said the Appeals Chamber of the International Criminal Tribunal for the Former Yugoslavia, in 1995, "gradually the maxim of Roman Law *hominum causa omne jus constitutum est* (all Law is created for the benefit of human beings) has gained a firm foothold in the international community" (as cited in Buquicchio, 2006, p. 7).

The ECHR – by introducing the "revolutionary right of appeal" (Conseil de l'Europe, 1999a, p. 49), so abolishing "the radical distinction between the national order and the international order" on which was based the classical International Law (Sudre, 1990, p. 10) – was "the most accomplished expression of the specificity of the International Human Rights Law". Opening the possibility for a citizen to stand before an international body against his or her own State for alleged violations of human rights, the European Convention meant a "revolutionary advance in the legal position of the individual" (Friedmann, W.) (Velu & Ergec, 1990, p. 35). In the opinion of Cançado Trindade (2006), "the right of individual petition is undoubtedly the most luminous star in the universe of human rights" (p. 279).

2.7.2 *Transformation of International Law and Renovation of Constitutional Law*

John Humphrey (1984) – who was the first Director of the UN Division of Human Rights, as we know – wrote in his autobiography: "There has never been a more revolutionary development in the theory and practice of international law and organization than the recognition that human rights are matters of international concern" (p. 46). It has given rise to the IHRL as a new branch of International Law and to a *New International Law* claimed, since the early 20th century, but mainly after World War II, by the eminent internationalist Alejandro Alvarez (see Alvarez, 1947, 1959, 1960). Such a revolution was recalled by Humphrey in the "International meeting on the human rights" convened by UNESCO in Paris, in 1988, on the occasion of the 40th anniversary of the UDHR. He said that "the Public International Law was placed, in a certain way hierarchically, under the International Human Rights Law, what is a considerable conquest of our time and our legal evolution" (UNESCO, 1989, p. 8).

In his course on "The Universal Declaration and the realisation of human rights", at The Hague Academy of International Law, Cassin (1951) said that the Declaration gave rise to a "double legal revolution" (p. 342): the internationalisation of human rights and the establishment of international bodies to protect them. The institutionalisation of international justice has also advanced through the reaffirmation of the principle of individual international criminal responsibility and the creation of international courts to judge the most serious crimes.

The need for an international criminal court was first recognised by a UN General Assembly Resolution in 1948 (A/RES/260(III), 9 December 1948). In 1989, approving a proposal by Trinidad and Tobago, the General Assembly asked the International Law Commission to resume work on the establishment of an international criminal court. In 1993, the UN Security Council established an *ad hoc* International Criminal Tribunal for the former Yugoslavia, based in The Hague (Holland). In 1994, was established an International Criminal Tribunal for Rwanda, based in Arusha (Tanzania). The International Law Commission submitted a draft statute for an international criminal court to the General Assembly. In 1998, a UN Diplomatic Conference of Plenipotentiaries on the Establishment of an International Criminal Court met in Rome from 15 June to 17 July to adopt the Statute of the Court drafted by a Preparatory Committee on the Establishment of an International Criminal Court that met since 1996. The Statute entered into force on 1 July 2002.

The establishment of the International Criminal Court, sitting in The Hague (Netherlands), culminated an evolution of the personal responsibility conception started with the Charter of the International Military Tribunal, annexed to the London Agreement of 8 August 1945, "for the just trial and punishment of the major war criminals of the European Axis" (Article 1): crimes against peace, war crimes, crimes against humanity (Article 6). According to the Charter: "The official position of defendants, whether as Heads of State or responsible officials in Government Departments, shall not be considered as freeing them from responsibility or mitigating punishment" (Article 7). Moreover, "the fact that the Defendant acted pursuant to order of his Government or of superior shall not free him from responsibility, but may be considered in mitigation of punishment if the Tribunal determines that justice so requires" (Article 8). The Tribunal, whose permanent seat was in Berlin, held its first trials in Nuremberg.

The International Criminal Court has jurisdiction over "the most serious crimes of concern to the international community as a whole": the crime of genocide, crimes against humanity, war crimes, and crime of aggression (Article 5.1). According to Article 27 ("Irrelevance of official capacity"):

> 1. This Statute shall apply equally to all persons without any distinction based on official capacity. In particular, official capacity as a Head of State or Government, a member of a Government or parliament, an elected representative or a government official shall in no case exempt a person from criminal responsibility under this Statute, nor shall it, in and of itself, constitute a ground for reduction of sentence.

Therefore, the individual is no more just an international holder of rights – human rights – but may also be found internationally guilty of their violations.

All these advancements meant a process of "rebirth of international legality and constitutional democracy" (Antonio La Pergola, in Conseil de l'Europe, 1993, p. 4) that has given rise to "*a New Constitutional Law*" (Delperee, 1987, p.

5). It is epitomised by the 1949 *Grundgesetz* (Basic Law/Constitution) of the Federal Republic of Germany[282] that protects the intangibility and indisposability of the values and principles of human rights with the *Ewigkeitsgarantie* (eternal guarantee) of its Article 79.3: "Amendments to this Basic Law affecting the division of the Federation into *Länder* [States], their participation on principle in the legislative process, or the principles laid down in Articles 1 and 20 shall be inadmissible". In accordance with Article 1:

1. Human dignity shall be inviolable [*Die Würde des Menschen ist unantastbar*]. To respect and protect it shall be the duty of all State authority.
2. The German people, therefore, acknowledge inviolable and inalienable human rights as the basis of every community, of peace and of justice in the world.
3. The following basic rights shall bind the legislature, the executive, and the judiciary as directly applicable law.

The basic rights are laid down in Articles 2–19.

New Constitutionalism denotes recent constitutional texts especially friendly to human rights, including the rights of minorities and indigenous peoples, as is the case with several Latin American Constitutions.

2.7.3 *Reconstruction of the Rule of Law*

We may distinguish two main conceptions of the Rule of Law: one formal, qualified as thin, another one substantial, qualified as thick.

- Under its formal or thin meaning, the Rule of Law includes the rejection of the 'rule of man' in favour of controlling State's powers by Law; its application to everybody and equality before the laws; and the existence of specific institutions, especially the judiciary, to apply the laws.
- Under its substantial or thick meaning, the Rule of Law incorporates an idea of justice consubstantiated in the ideal of human rights. Its main elements are the protection of human rights, the separation of powers, the independence of judicial power, the legality of administrative acts.

According to the second conception – born after World War II – human rights are the purpose and limits of the Rule of Law. It brings together two principles:

- *The ethical principle* of the primacy of the dignity and rights of the human person.
- *The democratic principle* of the people's sovereignty or General Will.

This means the resolution of the democratic paradox, namely: No political democracy holds legitimacy against the ethical democracy in which there are no majorities and minorities but human beings equal by dignity and rights, which are "democratic principles", as affirms the UNESCO Constitution (Preamble).[283] In this respect, the European Court of Human Rights said in Case *Gorzelik & Others v. Poland* (Application N° 44158/98, 17 February 2004)[284]: "Although individual interests must on occasion be subordinated to those of a group, democracy does not simply mean that the views of a majority must always prevail: a balance must be achieved which ensures the fair and proper treatment of minorities and avoids any abuse of a dominant position" (para. 57).

In 2012, the UN General Assembly adopted a Resolution on Education for Democracy (A/RES/67/18, 28 November 2012).[285] While recognising that "there is no single model of democracy", it reaffirmed "that democracy is a universal value based on the freely expressed will of people", and "that human rights, the rule of law and democracy are interlinked and mutually reinforcing and that they belong to the universal and indivisible core values and principles of the United Nations". The CHR has established a Forum on Human Rights, Democracy and the Rule of Law.

Along the same lines, the Joint statement by the Human Rights Committee and the Committee on Economic, Social and Cultural Rights on "The International Covenants on Human Rights: 50 years on" (CCPR/C/2016/1-E/C.12/2016/3)[286] affirmed:

> 2. ... the Covenants were the expression of a consensus that, combined with the rule of law and democracy, the protection and full realization of human rights would result in better societies that would be safer, more prosperous, inclusive and respectful of diversity and that would allow each person to live a decent life.

The Constitution of South Africa (Chapter 2 – Bill of Rights – 7.1)[287] states: "This Bill of Rights is a cornerstone of democracy in South Africa. It enshrines the rights of all people in our country and affirms the democratic values of human dignity, equality and freedom".[288]

The cornerstones of the Rule of Law, so substantially understood, should be a judicial system innervated by human rights, a public health system and a public education system.

International Rule of Law is work in progress too, as proves notably the establishment of the International Criminal Court.

2.7.4 *Inception of a Law of Humanity*

As we know, human dignity and rights are not merely individual values, they concern the human species itself.

Humanity is an ancient philosophical notion that is emerging as a collective rights-holder. Although it is debated whether "humanity may be considered, in the present state of International Law, as a subject of Law" (Salmon, 2011, p. 40), some authors argue that it has been so recognised, for the first time, in the Declaration on the Prohibition of the Use of Nuclear and Thermo-Nuclear Weapons (UN, 1961). Before, the jurisdiction of the Charter of the International Military Tribunal of Nuremberg[289] included "Crimes against humanity" (Article 6.c). The word is also in the Preamble of the UNESCO Constitution[290] that refers to "the education of humanity for justice and liberty and peace". The Declaration on Race and Racial Prejudice (UNESCO, 1978)[291] affirms that "racial segregation and discrimination constitute crimes against the conscience and dignity of mankind" (Article 4.3). According to the Universal Declaration on Bioethics and Human Rights (UNESCO, 2005),[292] "it is necessary and timely for the international community to state universal principles that will provide a foundation for humanity's response to the ever-increasing dilemmas and controversies that science and technology present for humankind and for the environment"; and "cultural diversity, as a source of exchange, innovation, and creativity, is necessary to humankind and, in this sense, is the common heritage of humanity, but emphasizing that it may not be invoked at the expense of human rights and fundamental freedoms".

These and other references to humanity or humankind in IHRL imply juridical subjectivity. As said Pierre-Marie Dupuy (2007) in the International Symposium on 60 Years of UNESCO (2005c), "there is an overarching subject of law, a holder of rights to whom all countries owe obligations, namely, humanity" (p. 362).

In the context of the United Nations Climate Change Conference (COP21), in December 2015, the French President (François Hollande) entrusted Corinne Lepage, on 4 June 2015, with the mission "to take stock of the various initiatives carried out at national and international level" concerning the recognition of the rights of Humanity, "that is, the right for all the inhabitants of the Earth to live in a world whose future is not compromised by the irresponsibility of the present". The Lepage Report includes a Universal Declaration on the Rights of Humanity (Annexe 9).[293]

Trying to define Humanity starting "from the content already given to the non-derogable rights and to the crimes against humanity", Mireille Delmas-Marty (1996) concluded that crimes against humanity add a collective foundation to the individual foundation of human rights. These are the "two pillars founding humanity as a plurality of human beings that are unique". So, we seek to protect the "alterity, that is to say, the singularity of every human being, recognised as unique, and at the same time his/her equal belonging to the human community" (pp. 85, 86, 87).

Humanity is thus a concept embracing both the dignity of the human species and the uniqueness of each human being. It is an inter-spatial and intergenerational concept, postulating that human nature is not a given but rather a becoming. The Judge Cançado Trindade, at the time President of the Inter-American Court of Human Rights, agreed in his "Separate Opinion" to the Judgement of the *Case Bámaca-Velásquez v. Guatemala* (2000)[294]:

> 18. … This expression has a juridical content of its own and a strong semantic weight, seeming to conceptualize humanity itself as a subject of law. The doctrinal conceptualization of the so-called crimes against humanity – victimizing in massive scale human beings, in their spirit and in their body – has its origins, well before the Convention against Genocide of 1948, in Customary International Law itself, on the basis of fundamental notions of humanity and of the dictates of the public conscience.

Trindade (2006) recalled in his General Course at The Hague Academy of International Law, under the title "International Law for Humankind: Towards a New *Jus Gentium*", the recognition of the necessity "of the reconstruction of International Law" (p. 198) in the mid-twentieth century, motivated by the "expansion of international legal personality […] with the advent of international organizations and of the human person, individually or in groups, and of mankind as a whole, also as subjects of the law of nations" (p. 203). He made a case for "the humanization of contemporary International Law", for a reconstructed or new *Jus Gentium* as an International Law of Humankind (p. 35).

The New Law of Humanity *in statu nascendi* (emerging) is the constitutional dimension of International Law. As affirmed by American President Franklin Roosevelt in his so-called 'Second Bill of Rights' (1944),[295] the destiny of Humankind is "to move forward […] to new goals of human happiness and well-being".

2.7.5 *Being Realistic without Becoming Pessimistic*

The universal recognition, proclamation, development and protection of human rights have been a gigantic step forwards of the Civilisation – alas! not irreversible … – after the abyss where it was almost falling, in the first half of the 1940s. The UDHR is an alchemy of cross-cultural moral values that has become an ethical-juridical lighthouse and a liberation flag. However: "The human rights revolution is by definition ongoing" (Hunt, 2008, p. 29).

Contempt and violations of human rights are a daily extremely shocking reality and will remain the overwhelming picture of the world for an unpredictable long time. This may be deeply disturbing and depressing ... Nevertheless, the world being as it is, a more positive attitude may be asking: How would things be without the proclamation of the UDHR some decades ago? If it was possible to advance so much during so few decades at an increasingly faster speed, we may be less pessimistic.

The Revolution of Human Rights is an every day, individual, collective, endless struggle. One of its most enduring but decisive fronts is the Revolution of the Rights of the Child.

Notes

1 Notably in the French language: ... *la notion même de droit de l'homme introduit au cœur de l'histoire le principe d'un dépassement indéfini de l'homme par l'homme. Le droit est la dialectique par laquelle l'homme se force à un meilleur qu'il invente.*

2 http://avalon.law.yale.edu/18th_century/rightsof.asp

3 https://www.icj-cij.org/files/case-related/46/046-19660718-JUD-01-06-EN.pdf

4 https://hudoc.echr.coe.int/eng#{„itemid":[„001-58021"]}

5 https://hudoc.echr.coe.int/fre#{%22itemid%22:[%22001-83256%22]}

6 http://tbinternet.ohchr.org/_layouts/treatybodyexternal/Download.aspx?symbolno=CCPR%2fC%2f21%2fRev.1%2fAdd.6&Lang=en

7 https://www.ohchr.org/en/udhr/documents/udhr_translations/eng.pdf

8 http://www.un.org/en/sections/un-charter/un-charter-full-text/

9 www.presidency.ucsb.edu/ws/?pid = 12188.

10 https://digitallibrary.un.org/record/210598

11 http://www.un.org/en/ga/search/view_doc.asp?symbol=E/RES/9(II)

12 https://www.un.org/en/ga/search/view_doc.asp?symbol=E/CN.4/SR.1

13 http://www.un.org/en/ga/search/view_doc.asp?symbol=E/CN.4/AC.1/3/Add.1

14 https://digitallibrary.un.org/record/701860/files/E_CN.4_W.16-EN.pdf

15 Namely (in a chronological order): Dr. Alejandro Alvarez (1917), *Institut de Droit International* (1921), Herbert G. Wells (1940), Wilfred Parsons (1941), Rollin McNitt (1942), Irving A. Isaacs (1943), American Law Institute (sponsored by Panama, 1944), American Jewish Committee (1945), Hersh Lauterpacht (1945), Gustavo Gutiérrez (1945), Free World (1945), Inter-American Juridical Committee (sponsored by Chile, 1945), American Bar Association (1945), Cuba (1946), World Government Association (1946), American Association for the United Nations (1946), American Federation of Labour (1946), Commission to Study the Organisation of Peace (1946).

16 http://www.un.org/en/ga/search/view_doc.asp?symbol=E/CN.4/AC.1/3

17 http://www.un.org/en/ga/search/view_doc.asp?symbol=E/600(SUPP)

18 https://americanrhetoric.com/speeches/eleanorrooseveltdeclarationhumanrights.htm

19 http://www.un.org/en/ga/search/view_doc.asp?symbol=A/RES/543(VI)

20 https://digitallibrary.un.org/record/617781?ln=en

21 See Lider Bal, *Le mythe de la Souveraineté en Droit International – La souveraineté des États à l'épreuve des mutations de l'ordre juridique international,* Thèse de Doctorat, Université de Strasbourg, 2012: Sovereignty "is the most cursed and revered notion of international law [...] the most controversial concept in the history, doctrine and practice of public interna-

tional law" (pp. 15, 16). It has entered into crisis in a world that is no longer state-centric, but polycentric, i.e. where more and more supra-State and non-State actors intervene. (https://tel.archives-ouvertes.fr/tel-00721073/document)

22 https://tbinternet.ohchr.org/_layouts/15/treatybodyexternal/Download.aspx?symbolno=CCPR%2fC%2f21%2fRev.1%2fAdd.13&Lang=en

23 https://hudoc.echr.coe.int/eng#{%22itemid%22:[%22001-57506%22]}

24 http://legal.un.org/ilc/texts/instruments/english/conventions/1_1_1969.pdf

25 V. for instance: https://www.venice.coe.int/webforms/documents/?pdf=CDL(2014)046-e

26 https://treaties.un.org/doc/publication/unts/volume%201155/volume-1155-i-18232-english.pdf

27 https://www.parlamento.pt/Legislacao/Paginas/ConstituicaoRepublicaPortuguesa.aspx

28 https://tbinternet.ohchr.org/_layouts/15/treatybodyexternal/Download.aspx?symbolno=E%2FC.12%2F1998%2F24&Lang=en

29 http://www.biblioteca.jus.gov.ar/Argentina-Constitution.pdf

30 https://www.parlamento.pt/Legislacao/Paginas/ConstituicaoRepublicaPortuguesa.aspx

31 http://www.corteidh.or.cr/docs/casos/articulos/seriec_154_ing.pdf

32 http://www.corteidh.or.cr/docs/casos/articulos/seriec_158_ing.pdf

33 www.corteidh.or.cr/docs/supervisiones/gelman_20_03_13.pdf

34 www.corteconstitucional.gov.co/relatoria/2003/c-067-03.htm

35 https://www.icj-cij.org/en/statute

36 https://indicators.ohchr.org/

37 www.ohchr.org/EN/ProfessionalInterest/Pages/UniversalHumanRightsInstruments.aspx

38 In 2013, the CODAP (*Centre de Conseils et d'Appui pour les Jeunes en Matière de Droits de l'Homme*) issued a *Recueil d'Instruments du Droit International des Droits de l'Homme* (both universal and regional)(Available in May 2020: https://www.codap.org/documentation/CODAP/Recueil_DroitInternational_2015.pdf)

39 http://eur-lex.europa.eu/legal-content/EN/TXT/?uri=CELEX:12012P/TXT

40 Constituted by the majority of the Republics comprising the former USSR (Union of Soviet Socialist Republics). (https://www.refworld.org/docid/49997ae32c.html)

41 https://tbinternet.ohchr.org/_layouts/15/treatybodyexternal/Download.aspx?symbolno=E%2fC.12%2fGC%2f18&Lang=en

42 https://www.un.org/development/desa/indigenouspeoples/declaration-on-the-rights-of-indigenous-peoples.html

43 https://tbinternet.ohchr.org/_layouts/treatybodyexternal/Download.aspx?symbolno=INT%2fCESCR%2fGEC%2f4758&Lang=en

44 https://www.ohchr.org/en/professionalinterest/pages/rightandresponsibility.aspx

45 https://www.ohchr.org/en/professionalinterest/pages/vienna.aspx

46 https://treaties.un.org/doc/publication/unts/volume%201155/volume-1155-i-18232-english.pdf

47 https://legal.un.org/ilc/texts/instruments/english/draft_articles/9_6_2001.pdf

48 https://www.ohchr.org/en/professionalinterest/pages/vienna.aspx

49 The *Maastricht Guidelines* were adopted by more than 30 experts on International Law meeting in Maastricht (Holland) on 22–26 January 1997. They were convened by the International Commission of Jurists (Genf, Switzerland), the Faculty of Law of the University of Limburg (Maastricht, Holland), and the Urban Morgan Institute for Human Rights, University of Cincinnati College of Law (Ohio, USA), for debating the violations of the economic, social and cultural rights, and the measures to be taken as well. The meeting took place ten years after the adoption of the *Limburg Principles on the Implementation*

of the International Covenant on Economic, Social and Cultural Rights by a group of 29 experts in International Law meeting in Maastricht on 2–6 June 1986, convened by the same entities, for considering especially the nature and scope of the obligations of States Parties to the ICESCR, when the ECOSOC established the CoESCR.

50 http://tbinternet.ohchr.org/_layouts/treatybodyexternal/Download.aspx?symbolno=E%2fC.12%2f1999%2f5&Lang=en

51 https://undocs.org/A/RES/60/1

52 https://undocs.org/en/A/RES/60/251

53 https://www.ohchr.org/EN/hrbodies/hrc/pages/aboutcouncil.aspx

54 https://www.ohchr.org/en/hrbodies/sp/pages/welcomepage.aspx

55 https://www.ohchr.org/EN/HRBodies/SP/Pages/Welcomepage.aspx

56 https://www.ohchr.org/en/hrbodies/sp/pages/welcomepage.aspx

57 https://www.ohchr.org/Documents/HRBodies/SP/VisualDirectoryNovember2018_en.pdf

58 It was not established by the Covenant itself, but by ECOSOC as a subsidiary body.

59 For example, according to the CoESCR 2018 Yearbook, it is composed of 18 Members: 5 women and 13 men, 12 academics, 4 former diplomats, 2 public servants, 1 judge, 1 National Human Rights Institution representative. (https://www.gi-escr.org/latest-news/2019/7/4/now-available-the-second-edition-of-thenbspcescr-yearbooknbspfor-2018)

60 As explains the CoESCR website:

The Committee devotes regularly one day of its session to a general discussion of a particular right or of a particular aspect of the Covenant. The purpose is threefold: such a general discussion assists the Committee in developing in greater depth its understanding of the relevant issues; it enables the Committee to encourage inputs into its work from all interested parties; and helps the Committee to lay the basis for a future General Comment. (https://ohchr.org/EN/HRBodies/CESCR/Pages/DiscussionDays.aspx)

61 https://www.ohchr.org/EN/HRBodies/CERD/Pages/InterstateCommunications.aspx

62 https://www.womenslinkworldwide.org/files/3045/sentencia-angela-tribunal-supremo.pdf

63 https://www.legislation.act.gov.au/a/2004-5

64 https://www.coe.int/en/web/about-us/who-we-are

65 https://www.echr.coe.int/Pages/home.aspx?p=basictexts&c

66 http://assembly.coe.int/nw/xml/XRef/Xref-XML2HTML-EN.asp?fileid=16442&lang=en

67 https://rm.coe.int/CoERMPublicCommonSearchServices/DisplayDCTMContent?documentId=090000168048b059

68 https://www.coe.int/en/web/european-social-charter/-/new-version-of-the-digest-of-the-case-law-of-the-european-committee-of-social-rights

69 https://www.escr-net.org/caselaw/2006/international-federation-human-rights-leagues-fidh-v-france-complaint-no-142003

70 https://eur-lex.europa.eu/legal-content/EN/TXT/?uri=celex%3A12007L%2FTXT

71 https://www.osce.org/institutions-and-structures

72 http://www.achpr.org/instruments/achpr/

73 https://au.int/en/treaties/protocol-statute-african-court-justice-and-human-rights

74 https://www.cihrs.org/wp-content/uploads/2015/12/league-arab-states-manual-en-20151125.pdf

75 https://www.icj.org/wp-content/uploads/2015/04/MENA-Arab-Court-of-Human-Rights-Publications-Report-2015-ENG.pdf

76 As the European Court is concerned, see: www.echr.coe.int/Pages/home.aspx?p=applicants&c=#n1357809352012_pointer
77 https://undocs.org/en/A/RES/48/134
78 https://tbinternet.ohchr.org/_layouts/15/treatybodyexternal/Download.aspx?symbolno=INT%2fCESCR%2fGEC%2f4758&Lang=en
79 https://tbinternet.ohchr.org/_layouts/15/treatybodyexternal/Download.aspx?symbolno=E%2fC.12%2f1998%2f24&Lang=en
80 https://tbinternet.ohchr.org/_layouts/15/treatybodyexternal/Download.aspx?symbolno=CCPR%2FC%2F50%2FD%2F488%2F1992&Lang=en
81 https://tbinternet.ohchr.org/_layouts/15/treatybodyexternal/Download.aspx?symbolno=E%2fC.12%2fGC%2f20&Lang=en
82 https://tbinternet.ohchr.org/_layouts/15/treatybodyexternal/Download.aspx?symbolno=E%2fC.12%2f2002%2f11&Lang=en
83 https://www.bundesverfassungsgericht.de/SharedDocs/Entscheidungen/EN/2011/05/rs20110504_2bvr236509en.html
84 https://www.legislation.act.gov.au/a/2004-5
85 https://www.ohchr.org/en/professionalinterest/pages/rightandresponsibility.aspx
86 https://www.ohchr.org/Documents/Publications/FactSheet29en.pdf
87 For example, according to the CoESCR 2018 Yearbook, it received 150 NGOs and 11 National Human Rights Institutions parallel reports. (https://www.gi-escr.org/latest-news/2019/7/4/now-available-the-second-edition-of-thenbspcescr-yearbooknbspfor-2018)
88 https://www.ohchr.org/EN/ProfessionalInterest/Pages/Vienna.aspx
89 https://www.bundestag.de/gg
English translation: https://www.btg-bestellservice.de/pdf/80201000.pdf
90 Orücü, E. (1986). The Core of Rights and Freedoms: the Limit of Limits. In AAVV, *Human Rights: From Rhetoric to Reality* (pp. 37–59). Oxford/New York: Blackwell Pub.
91 https://tbinternet.ohchr.org/_layouts/15/treatybodyexternal/Download.aspx?symbolno=E%2fC.12%2f1997%2f8&Lang=en
92 http://tbinternet.ohchr.org/_layouts/treatybodyexternal/Download.aspx?symbolno=INT%2fCESCR%2fGEC%2f4758&Lang=en
93 http://tbinternet.ohchr.org/_layouts/treatybodyexternal/Download.aspx?symbolno=E%2fC.12%2f1999%2f5&Lang=en
94 https://tbinternet.ohchr.org/_layouts/15/treatybodyexternal/Download.aspx?symbolno=E%2fC.12%2fGC%2f25&Lang=en
95 http://www.ohchr.org/Documents/Publications/HR_P_PT_12_NHRI_fr.pdf
96 http://tbinternet.ohchr.org/_layouts/treatybodyexternal/Download.aspx?symbolno=CCPR%2fC%2f21%2fRev.1%2fAdd.13&Lang=en
97 https://tbinternet.ohchr.org/_layouts/15/treatybodyexternal/Download.aspx?symbolno=CRC%2fC%2fGC%2f19&Lang=en
98 https://tbinternet.ohchr.org/_layouts/15/treatybodyexternal/Download.aspx?symbolno=CRPD/C/GC/4&Lang=en
99 https://ap.ohchr.org/documents/alldocs.aspx?doc_id=29
100 https://www.achpr.org/public/Document/file/English/achpr_instr_guide_draft_esc_rights_eng.pdf
101 http://cidh.org/annualrep/93eng/chap.5.htm
102 http://eur-lex.europa.eu/legal-content/EN/TXT/?uri=CELEX:12012P/TXT
103 https://www.admin.ch/opc/en/classified-compilation/19995395/index.html
104 https://www.admin.ch/opc/fr/classified-compilation/19995395/201801010000/101.pdf

105 https://hudoc.echr.coe.int/eng#{„itemid":[„001-57525"]}
106 https://hudoc.echr.coe.int/eng#{%22itemid%22:[%22001-57455%22]}
107 https://hudoc.echr.coe.int/fre#{%22languageisocode%22:[%22ENG%22],%22appno%22:[%228225/78%22],%22documentcollectionid2%22:[%22CHAMBER%22],%22itemid%22:[%22001-57425%22]}
108 https://www.dos.ny.gov/info/constitution.htm
109 https://caselaw.findlaw.com/ny-court-of-appeals/1084567.html
110 https://tbinternet.ohchr.org/_layouts/15/treatybodyexternal/Download.aspx?symbolno=E%2fC.12%2fGC%2f25&Lang=en
111 https://tbinternet.ohchr.org/_layouts/15/treatybodyexternal/Download.aspx?symbolno=E%2fC.12%2f2000%2f4&Lang=en
112 https://tbinternet.ohchr.org/_layouts/15/treatybodyexternal/Download.aspx?symbolno=CCPR%2fC%2f21%2fRev.1%2fAdd.13&Lang=en
113 https://www.ohchr.org/en/professionalinterest/pages/cescr.aspx
114 https://tbinternet.ohchr.org/_layouts/treatybodyexternal/Download.aspx?symbolno=INT%2fCESCR%2fGEC%2f4758&Lang=en
115 http://www.ministeriopublico.pt/instrumento/convencao-de-viena-sobre-o-direito-dos-tratados-0
116 https://www.icj-cij.org/files/case-related/50/050-19700205-JUD-01-00-EN.pdf
117 https://papers.ssrn.com/sol3/papers.cfm?abstract_id=1481552
118 https://papers.ssrn.com/sol3/papers.cfm?abstract_id=1481552
119 https://tbinternet.ohchr.org/_layouts/15/treatybodyexternal/Download.aspx?symbolno=CCPR%2fC%2f21%2fRev.1%2fAdd.13&Lang=en
120 https://www.unglobalcompact.org/library/2
121 https://www.ohchr.org/en/hrbodies/hrc/wgtranscorp/pages/igwgontnc.aspx
122 https://tbinternet.ohchr.org/_layouts/15/treatybodyexternal/Download.aspx?symbolno=E%2fC.12%2fGC%2f24&Lang=en
123 https://www.ohchr.org/Documents/HRBodies/CRC/Discussions/Recommendations/Recommendations2002.pdf
124 http://tbinternet.ohchr.org/_layouts/treatybodyexternal/Download.aspx?symbolno=CRC%2FGC%2F2003%2F5&Lang=en
125 https://static1.squarespace.com/static/5a6e0958f6576ebde0e78c18/t/5bb39e551905f48e2cc3a9d6/1538498135136/180723+Human+Rights+Law+Sources+ETOs.pdf
126 https://tbinternet.ohchr.org/_layouts/15/treatybodyexternal/Download.aspx?symbolno=INT%2fCESCR%2fGEC%2f4756&Lang=en
127 https://www.icj-cij.org/en/case/131
128 https://www.icj-cij.org/en/case/116/judgments
129 https://undocs.org/en/CCPR/C/2016/1
130 https://www.etoconsortium.org/nc/en/main-navigation/library/maastricht-principles/?tx_drblob_pi1[downloadUid]=23
131 https://treaties.un.org/doc/Publication/UNTS/Volume%201155/volume-1155-I-18232-English.pdf
132 https://www.ohchr.org/Documents/Issues/Development/Session21/3_A_HRC_WG.2_21_2_AdvanceEditedVersion.pdf
133 https://www.ohchr.org/EN/ProfessionalInterest/Pages/Vienna.aspx
134 Albania adopted, in 1933, a constitutional amendment according to which all private schools should close; the Greek minority protested against and lodged a complaint into

the League of Nations, referring to a 1921 Albania Declaration on the protection of minorities; Albania put forward that the constitutional provision at stake concerned all private schools; the case was referred to the Permanent Court of International Justice for an Advisory Opinion. It concluded that private schools were indispensable for the satisfaction of the special needs of minorities because, "in fact, equality may imply the need of a different treatment aiming at achieving a result establishing a balance between different situations". (http://www.worldcourts.com/pcij/eng/decisions/1935.04.06_albania.htm)

135 https://tbinternet.ohchr.org/_layouts/15/treatybodyexternal/Download.aspx?symbolno=CERD%2fC%2fGC%2f32&Lang=en

136 https://tbinternet.ohchr.org/_layouts/15/treatybodyexternal/Download.aspx?symbolno=CCPR%2fC%2f21%2fRev.1%2fAdd.7&Lang=en

137 https://tbinternet.ohchr.org/_layouts/15/treatybodyexternal/Download.aspx?symbolno=E%2fC.12%2fGC%2f19&Lang=en

138 https://www.un.org/documents/ga/res/44/a44r130.htm

139 https://www.ohchr.org/EN/ProfessionalInterest/Pages/Vienna.aspx

140 By the way, what is the meaning added by the word "interrelated" in this phrase?

141 https://tbinternet.ohchr.org/_layouts/treatybodyexternal/Download.aspx?symbolno=E%2FC.12%2F1998%2F24&Lang=en

142 https://www.ohchr.org/EN/ProfessionalInterest/Pages/OPCESCR.aspx

143 https://undocs.org/en/CCPR/C/2016/1

144 https://www.corteidh.or.cr/docs/casos/articulos/seriec_63_ing.pdf

145 https://tbinternet.ohchr.org/_layouts/15/treatybodyexternal/Download.aspx?symbolno=CCPR%2fC%2fGC%2f36&Lang=en

146 http://saflii.org/za/cases/ZAGPPHC/2015/230.html

147 https://www.corteidh.or.cr/docs/casos/articulos/seriec_146_ing.pdf

148 https://indiankanoon.org/doc/1775396/

149 https://www.corteidh.or.cr/docs/casos/articulos/seriec_42_ing.pdf

150 http://www.corteidh.or.cr/docs/casos/articulos/seriec_165_ing.pdf

151 http://ap.ohchr.org/documents/alldocs.aspx?doc_id=3220

152 https://www.oas.org/juridico/english/treaties/a-52.html

153 https://www.icj-cij.org/files/case-related/50/050-19700205-JUD-01-00-EN.pdf

154 https://hudoc.echr.coe.int/eng#{%22languageisocode%22:[%22ENG%22],%22appno%22:[%225856/72%22],%22documentcollectionid2%22:[%22CHAMBER%22],%22itemid%22:[%22001-57587%22]}

155 See, for instance, Françoise Tulkens, "La Convention européenne des droits de l'homme comme un instrument vivant. Les développements récents de la jurisprudence de la Cour européenne des droits de l'homme" (https://www.ies.be/files/06110-discours.pdf).

156 https://rm.coe.int/digest-2018-parts-i-ii-iii-iv-en/1680939f80

157 http://www.servat.unibe.ch/dfr/bv045187.html

158 www.corteconstitucional.gov.co/relatoria/1992/t-429-92.htm

159 https://indiankanoon.org/doc/257876/

160 http://indiankanoon.org/doc/1775396

161 http://supreme.justia.com/us/539/558/case.html

162 https://undocs.org/CRC/C/GC/8

163 https://undocs.org/A/HRC/32/L.20

164 https://tbinternet.ohchr.org/_layouts/15/treatybodyexternal/Download.aspx?symbolno=E%2fC.12%2fGC%2f25&Lang=en

165 https://unesdoc.unesco.org/ark:/48223/pf0000227860

166 In the *Introduction* to *A Contribution to the Critique of Hegel's Philosophy of Right* (1844), Karl Marx wrote that "*man is the highest essence for man* [...] the supreme being for man", and hence "the *categoric imperative to overthrow all relations* in which man is a debased, enslaved, abandoned, despicable essence". (https://www.marxists.org/archive/marx/works/1843/critique-hpr/intro.htm)

167 Rochlitz, R. (1998). *L'Art au banc d'essai. Esthétique et critique*. Gallimard, Collection NRF Essais.

168 And people personally coherent too. In this respect, Humphrey (1984) observed: "People do not become angels simply because they are working for an international organization. In terms of human rivalry and intrigue, the United Nations Secretariat was not unlike other bureaucracies, and personal struggle for power was often compounded by international politics" (p. 8). This author could corroborate with examples of faculty members teaching human rights who did not even respond to a message from a well identified colleague devoted to human rights too.

169 https://www.gutenberg.org/files/3207/3207-h/3207-h.htm

170 www.americanrhetoric.com/speeches/eleanorrooseveltdeclarationhumanrights.htm

171 http://www.corteconstitucional.gov.co/RELATORIA/1994/C-221-94.htm

172 http://classics.mit.edu/Sophocles/antigone.html

173 http://www.capuchinhos.org/biblia/index.php/B%C3%ADblia_Sagrada

174 https://www.templeofearth.com/books/principlesofphilosophy.pdf

175 https://books.google.pt/books?id=GyQaAAAAYAAJ&pg=PA126&lpg=PA126&dq=%22Remarques+pour+servir+de+suppl%C3%A9ment+%C3%A0+l%E2%80%99Essai%22&source=bl&ots=rp849Xv7rI&sig=DgLTqJLDFtjfed_QWPV4ai1H5QA&hl=pt-PT&sa=X&ved=0ahUKEwjIxceQgaXMAhUBORoKHePSAecQ6AEIVDAJ#v=onepage&q=immuable&f=false

176 https://sites.google.com/site/revuebruissements/essais/sieyes

177 https://www.global-ethic.org/declaration-toward-a-global-ethic/

178 http://www.vatican.va/roman_curia/congregations/cfaith/cti_documents/rc_con_cfaith_doc_20090520_legge-naturale_en.html

179 https://en.wikisource.org/wiki/French_Constitution_of_1793

180 http://www.un.org/en/universal-declaration-human-rights/

181 http://pcwww.liv.ac.uk/~ndas/teaching/rendrama/PicoDellaMirandola.pdf

182 https://www.un.org/en/sections/un-charter/un-charter-full-text/

183 http://portal.unesco.org/en/ev.php-URL_ID=15244&URL_DO=DO_TOPIC&URL_SECTION=201.html

184 https://www.echr.coe.int/Documents/Convention_ENG.pdf

185 http://hudoc.echr.coe.int/sites/eng/pages/search.aspx?i=001-60448#{"itemid":["001-60448"]}

186 https://hudoc.echr.coe.int/eng#{%22itemid%22:[%22001-57587%22]}

187 https://www.escr-net.org/caselaw/2006/international-federation-human-rights-leagues-fidh-v-france-complaint-no-142003

188 http://eur-lex.europa.eu/legal-content/EN/TXT/?uri=CELEX:12012P/TXT

189 www.bundestag.de/grundgesetz

190 https://eur-lex.europa.eu/legal-content/EN/TXT/?uri=CELEX%3A61998CJ0377

191 www.bundestag.de/grundgesetz

192 http://www.servat.unibe.ch/dfr/bv045187.html

193 http://www.saflii.org/za/cases/ZACC/1995/3.html

194 https://supreme.justia.com/cases/federal/us/356/86/

195 https://supreme.justia.com/cases/federal/us/536/730/

196 https://hudoc.echr.coe.int/eng#{%22itemid%22:[%22001-69891%22]}
197 https://scc-csc.lexum.com/scc-csc/scc-csc/en/item/5696/index.do
198 *Floating Signifier* is an expression (originated from Claude Lévi-Strauss) denoting a signifier without a referent determined. Therefore, it may be used with different arguments.
199 https://undocs.org/fr/A/PV.183
200 http://versa.cardozo.yu.edu/sites/default/files/upload/opinions/Commitment%20to%20Peace%20and%20Social%20Justice%20Society%20v.%20Minister%20of%20Finance.pdf
201 http://darwin-online.org.uk/converted/pdf/1889_Descent_F969.pdf
202 https://www.ohchr.org/EN/UDHR/Pages/UDHRIndex.aspx
203 http://www.un.org/ga/search/view_doc.asp?symbol=A/C.3/SR.99
204 http://www.un.org/en/ga/search/view_doc.asp?symbol=A/C.3/SR.96
205 https://undocs.org/E/C.12/1999/10
206 www.ohchr.org/en/professionalinterest/pages/vienna.aspx
207 www.un.org/documents/ga/res/41/a41r120.htm
208 http://versa.cardozo.yu.edu/opinions/academic-center-law-and-business-v-minister-finance
209 http://www.servat.unibe.ch/dfr/bv045187.html
210 https://www.bundesverfassungsgericht.de/SharedDocs/Entscheidungen/DE/2004/03/rs20040303_1bvr237898.html;jsessionid=786C4769637859ABF326D20523675BDD.1_cid370
211 http://www.corteconstitucional.gov.co/RELATORIA/1994/C-221-94.htm
212 http://www.saflii.org/za/cases/ZACC/1995/3.html
213 https://supreme.justia.com/cases/federal/us/408/238/
214 www.ushistory.org/documents/economic_bill_of_rights.htm
215 https://www.btg-bestellservice.de/pdf/80201000.pdf
216 http://www.servat.unibe.ch/dfr/bv082060.html
217 http://www.saflii.org/za/cases/ZACC/2000/19.html
218 http://elyon1.court.gov.il/files_eng/03/660/003/a39/03003660.a39.pdf.
219 http://versa.cardozo.yu.edu/opinions/academic-center-law-and-business-v-minister-finance
220 https://link.springer.com/article/10.1007/s10677-012-9369-0
221 http://www.servat.unibe.ch/dfr/bv039001.html
222 *Wo menschliches Leben existiert, kommt ihm Menschenwürde zu* [...]. *Die von Anfang an im menschlichen Sein angelegten potentiellen Fähigkeiten genügen, um die Menschenwürde zu begründen.*
223 https://hudoc.echr.coe.int/eng#{%22itemid%22:[%22001-61887%22]}
224 http://www.saflii.org/za/cases/ZACC/1995/3.html
225 http://versa.cardozo.yu.edu/topics/prisoners%E2%80%99-rights
226 http://www.saflii.org/za/cases/ZACC/2002/22.html
227 http://www.servat.unibe.ch/dfr/bv030173.html
228 www.concernedhistorians.org/content_files/file/le/131.pdf
229 http://www.corteidh.or.cr/docs/casos/articulos/seriec_70_ing.pdf
230 http://www.saflii.org/za/cases/ZACC/1995/3.html
231 Life has appeared on Earth about 4 billion years ago. About 7 million years ago, hominids have appeared, which diversified into numerous species. The genus *Homo* has probably appeared about 2.8 million years ago in Africa, having first emigrated from this continent about 1.8 million years ago. Modern human beings have appeared in the African conti-

nent about 300 thousand years ago. They belong, therefore, to the same family as gorillas, orangutans, chimpanzees and other species of monkeys.

232 http://armytage.net/pdsdata/Friedrich%20Schiller%20translated%20with%20a%20introduction%20by%20Reginald%20Snell%20%20On%20the%20aesthetic%20education%20of%20man%20(2004%20Dover%20Publications).pdf

233 http://unesdoc.unesco.org/images/0014/001461/146180e.pdf

234 Available in February 2019: http://www.few.vu.nl/~wai/Papers/NEST05.pdf

235 Available in February 2019: http://www.few.vu.nl/~wai/Papers/NEST05.pdf

236 State and local laws legalizing racial segregation for about 100 years, from the post-Civil War era until 1968. They were named after a song insulting African Americans. (see https://www.history.com/topics/early-20th-century-us/jim-crow-laws)

237 http://www.saflii.org/za/cases/ZACC/1995/3.html

238 http://portal.unesco.org/en/ev.php-URL_ID=13177&URL_DO=DO_TOPIC&URL_SECTION=201.html

239 http://www.nietzschesource.org/#eKGWB/JGB

240 http://seas3.elte.hu/coursematerial/LojkoMiklos/Alexis-de-Tocqueville-Democracy-in-America.pdf

241 Signs and values are indissociable in the existence of the semiotic animal. Morris (1964) had the deep conviction that understanding the functioning of signs and values in human life is key to understand the emerging "new and important outlook on the nature of man" (p. viii). In his opinion: "The difficulties with the term 'meaning' in semiotic are paralleled by those with the term 'value' in axiology. Both terms have such a variety of significations and uses that they serve only to indicate in a vague way an area of investigation" (p. 16). Defining values as conceptions of the desirable, he suggested "one possible view of the relation of semiotic and axiology, conceived as the studies of sign behavior and preferential behavior" (p. 43).

242 http://www.unesco.org/new/en/social-and-human-sciences/themes/bioethics/human-genome-and-human-rights/

243 http://www.saflii.org/za/cases/ZACC/1995/13.html

244 http://www.servat.unibe.ch/dfr/bv087209.html

245 www.bundestag.de/grundgesetz

246 http://www.servat.unibe.ch/dfr/bv045187.html

247 http://www.servat.unibe.ch/dfr/bv087209.html

248 The show consists in the visualisation of scenes of sex (live or in films) by men in single cabins, through a hole, accessed by insertion of a coin. They see without being seen, unlike the traditional striptease shows, where there is direct visual contact.

249 http://www.servat.unibe.ch/dfr/vw064274.html

250 *Die Würde des Menschen ist ein objektiver, unverfügbarer Wert (BVerfGE 45, 187), auf dessen Beachtung der einzelne nicht wirksam verzichten kann (vgl. Maunz/Dürig/Herzog/Scholz, GG, Art. 1 Rdnrn. 22 und 74; von Münch, GG, 2. Aufl., Art. 1 Rdnr. 39; BGHZ 67, 119* [*125*]). [...] (para. 12).

251 http://www.saflii.org/za/cases/ZACC/2002/22.html

252 https://tbinternet.ohchr.org/_layouts/treatybodyexternal/Download.aspx?symbolno=CCPR%2FC%2F75%2FD%2F854%2F1999&Lang=en

253 http://www.servat.unibe.ch/dfr/bv087209.html

254 https://www.coe.int/en/web/bioethics/oviedo-convention

255 www.concernedhistorians.org/content_files/file/le/131.pdf

256 https://scc-csc.lexum.com/scc-csc/scc-csc/en/item/695/index.do

257 http://www.corteconstitucional.gov.co/relatoria/2016/t-363-16.htm

258 http://tbinternet.ohchr.org/_layouts/treatybodyexternal/Download.aspx?symbolno=INT%2fCCPR%2fGEC%2f6630&Lang=en

259 http://www.saflii.org/za/cases/ZACC/1995/3.html

260 Likewise: "The right to health is not to be understood as a right to be *healthy*", as noted the CoESCR in its GC 14 on "The right to the highest attainable standard of health (Article 12 of the International Covenant on Economic, Social and Cultural Rights)" (E/C.12/2000/4, 11 August 2000, para. 8). (https://tbinternet.ohchr.org/_layouts/15/treatybodyexternal/Download.aspx?symbolno=E%2fC.12%2f2000%2f4&Lang=en)

261 http://www.spanisharts.com/books/quijote/2chapter58.htm:
In Spanish: *La libertad, Sancho, es uno de los más preciosos dones que a los hombres dieron los cielos; con ella no pueden igualarse los tesoros que encierra la tierra ni el mar encubre; por la libertad así como por la honra se puede y debe aventurar la vida.*
(https://cvc.cervantes.es/literatura/clasicos/quijote/edicion/parte2/cap58/default.htm)

262 http://unesdoc.unesco.org/images/0012/001246/124626f.pdf.

263 It is implied in the popular saying "health, money and love". Even if, as one reads in *La Chute* d'Albert Camus: "Since I needed to love and be loved, I thought I was in love. In other words, I was stupid". A need also exploited by religious sects.
In a National Geographic documentary on the Australian high-security prison of Casuarina (Perth), an aboriginal inmate says: "I'm nobody here ... in my community I was someone ... was one of them ...". However, the wise 'philosophy' of the Director was that the guards should talk with the inmates ... treat them well ... because they are not there to be punished ... brutalised ... the punishment is to be imprisoned ... In other words, the inmates should be recognised and treated as human beings.

264 http://www.un.org/en/ga/search/view_doc.asp?symbol=A/PV.182

265 https://digitallibrary.un.org/record/701853?ln=en

266 http://www.un.org/Docs/asp/ws.asp?m=A/RES/2627%20(XXV)

267 https://www.ohchr.org/EN/ProfessionalInterest/Pages/Vienna.aspx

268 https://www.un.org/press/en/1998/19981210.sgsm6828.html

269 http://www.un.org/millennium/declaration/ares552e.htm

270 https://undocs.org/en/A/RES/63/116

271 https://www.ccel.org/ccel/pascal/pensees.html

272 https://www.archives.gov/founding-docs/declaration-transcript

273 http://avalon.law.yale.edu/18th_century/rightsof.asp

274 http://www.un.org/en/sections/un-charter/un-charter-full-text/

275 https://ia802602.us.archive.org/26/items/354466269.2253.emory.edu/354466269_2253.pdf

276 https://obamawhitehouse.archives.gov/1600/presidents/johnfkennedy

277 "Entretien", *Le Courrier de l'UNESCO*, 1993, 4 Avril.
(http://fr.1001mags.com/parution/le-courrier-de-l-unesco/numero-1993-4-avril)

278 *Press Release SG/SM/6697 NGO/306 PI/1079 14 September 1998*:
https://www.un.org/press/en/1998/19980914.sgsm6697.html

279 https://socialsciences.mcmaster.ca/econ/ugcm/3ll3/hegel/history.pdf

280 https://archive.org/details/historyfrenchreoomichgoog/page/n12

281 http://www.bmlisieux.com/curiosa/jaures01.htm

282 https://www.btg-bestellservice.de/pdf/80201000.pdf

283 http://portal.unesco.org/en/ev.php-URL_ID=15244&URL_DO=DO_TOPIC&URL_SECTION=201.html

284 https://hudoc.echr.coe.int/rus#{%22itemid%22:[%22001-60003%22]}

285 https://undocs.org/en/A/RES/67/18

286 https://undocs.org/en/CCPR/C/2016/1
287 https://www.gov.za/sites/default/files/gcis_document/201409/act108of1996s.pdf
288 https://www.gov.za/documents/constitution/constitution-republic-south-africa-1996-1
289 http://www.un.org/en/genocideprevention/documents/atrocity-crimes/Doc.2_Charter%20of%20IMT%201945.pdf
290 http://portal.unesco.org/en/ev.php-URL_ID=15244&URL_DO=DO_TOPIC&URL_SECTION=201.html
291 http://portal.unesco.org/fr/ev.php-URL_ID=13161&URL_DO=DO_TOPIC&URL_SECTION=201.html
292 http://unesdoc.unesco.org/images/0014/001461/146180e.pdf
293 https://www.vie-publique.fr/sites/default/files/rapport/pdf/154000687.pdf or Universal Declaration of Humankind Rights (http://droitshumanite.fr/the-declaration/?lang=en).
294 http://www.corteidh.or.cr/docs/casos/articulos/seriec_70_ing.pdf
295 www.ushistory.org/documents/economic_bill_of_rights.htm

References

AAVV. (2012). Qu'est-ce que l'Homme? – 100 scientifiques répondent. *Sciences et Avenir*, janvier.

Agamben, G. (2002). *The open – Man and animal* [*L'aperto – L'uomo e l'animale*]. Stanford University Press (2004).

Alston, Ph. (1987). Out of the abyss: The challenges confronting the new U.N. Committee on Economic, Social and Cultural Rights. *Human Rights Quarterly*, *9*(3), 332–381.

Alvarez, A. (1947). Méthodes de la codification du Droit international public (État actuel de ce droit). In *Annuaire de l'Institut de Droit International – Session de Lausanne, Août* (pp. 38–71). Ad. Goemaere.

Alvarez, A. (1959). *Le droit international nouveau dans ses rapports avec la vie actuelle des peuples*. Éditions Pédone.

Alvarez, A. (1960). *Le droit international nouveau – Son acceptation, son étude*. Éditions Pédone.

Apel, K.-O. (1988). *Discussion et responsabilité – 1. L'Éthique après Kant* [*Diskurs und Verantwortung. Das Problem des Übergangs zur postkonventionnellen Moral*] (Trad. par Christian Bouchindhomme, Marianne Charrière et Rainer Rochlitz). Les Éditions du Cerf.

Apel, K.-O. (1992). L'impératif moral. *Le Courier de l'Unesco*, juillet–août, 13–17.

Aranguren, J.-L. (1990). A Razão na Ética. In AAVV (Ed.), *Balanço do século – Ciclo de Conferências promovido pelo Presidente da República* (pp. 95–101). Imprensa Nacional-Casa da Moeda.

Arendt. H. (1951). *The origins of totalitarianism*. Harcourt Brace & Company.

Arendt, H. (1962). *On revolution*. Penguin Books. https://monoskop.org/images/b/bf/Arendt_Hannah_On_Revolution_1990.pdf

Aristotle. (1925). *The Nicomachean ethics* (Translated with an Introduction by D. Ross, Revised by J. L. Ackrill and J. O. Urmson). Oxford University Press.

Aristotle. (2000). *Politics* (Translated by B. Jowett, with Introduction, Analysis and Index by H. W. C. Davis). Dover Publications, Incl.

Auroux, S. (2000). Entretien. *Sciences Humaines – Hors-série, 27*, décembre 1999/janvier 2000, 20–22.

Barak, A. (2013). Human dignity: The constitutional value and the constitutional right. In C. McCrudden (Ed.), *Understanding human dignity* (pp. 361–380) (Proceedings of the British Academy, Vol. 192). British Academy.

Bart, J. (1989). L'individu et ses droits. In I. Théry & C. Biet (Textes réunis et présentés par), *La famille, la loi, l'État – de la Révolution au Code civil* (pp. 351–362). Éditions du Centre Georges Pompidou/Imprimerie Nationale – Éditions.

Bates, E. (2010). History. In D. Moeckli, S. Shah, & S. Sivakumaran (Eds.), *International human rights law* (pp. 18–38). Oxford University Press.

Bloch, E. (1972). *La Philosophie de la Renaissance* [*Vorlesungen zur Philosophie der Renaissance*] (Traduit de l'allemand par Pierre Kamnitzer). Petite Bibliothèque Payot.

Bobbio, N. (1990). *L'Età dei Diritti*. Einaudi. An English translation: *The age of rights* (Transl. by A. Cameron). Polity Press.

Boerefijn, I. (2009). International human rights in national law. In C. Krause & M. Scheinin (Eds.), *International protection of human rights: A textbook* (pp. 577–599). Åbo Akademi University, Institute for Human Rights.

Buquicchio, G. (2006). Introductory address. In AAVV, *The status of international treaties on human rights* (pp. 7–9). Council of Europe Publishing, Venice Commission.

Byrnes, A., & Renshaw, C. (2010). Within state. In D. Moeckli, S. Shah, & Sandesh Sivakumaran (Eds.), *International Human Rights Law* (pp. 498–517). Oxford University Press.

Campbell, T. (2006). *Rights – A critical introduction*. Routledge.

Cassin, R. (1951). La Déclaration universelle et la mise en œuvre des droits de l'homme. In Académie de Droit International, *Recueil des Cours – 1951, II, Tome 79 de la Collection* (pp. 237–367). Librairie du Recueil Sirey.

Cassirer, E. (1944). *Antropología filosófica – Introducción a una filosofía de la cultura*. Fondo de Cultura Económica.

Caune, J. (1997). *Esthétique de la communication*. Presses Universitaires de France.

Chowdhury, J. (2020). Unpacking the minimum core and reasonableness standards. In J. Dugard, B. Porter, D. Ikawa, & L. Chenwi (Eds.), *Research handbook on economic, social and cultural rights as human rights* (pp. 251–274). Edward Elgar Publishing.

Clapham, A. (2009). United Nations Charter-based protection of human rights. In C. Krause & M. Scheinin (Ed.), *International protection of human rights: A textbook* (pp. 79–103). Åbo Akademi University, Institute for Human Rights.

Conseil de l'Europe. (1993). *Les rapports entre le droit international et le droit interne – Actes du Séminaire UniDem organisé à Varsovie du 19 au 21 mai 1993 en coopération avec l'Université de Wroclaw et le Centre des droits de l'homme de Poznan et avec le soutien du Programme Phare des Communautés Européennes.* Commission européenne pour la démocratie par le droit.

Conseil de l'Europe. (1999a). *Vade-mecum de la Convention européenne des Droits de l'Homme* (Par D. Gomien). Éditions du Conseil de l'Europe, Direction des droits de l'homme.

Conseil de l'Europe. (1999b). *Bulletin d'information sur les droits de l'homme – No 45 – novembre 1998–février 1999.* Direction des droits de l'homme.

Coomans, F. (2004). Exploring the normative content of the right to education as a human right: Recent approaches. *Persona y Derecho, Revista de fundamentación de las instituciones jurídicas y de derechos humanos, 50*, 61–100.

Damásio, A. (1994). *O erro de Descartes – Emoção, razão e cérebro humano* [*Descartes' Error – Emotion, reason and human brain*] (Trad. de Dora Vicente e Georgina Segurado). Publicações Europa-América.

Damásio, A. (2010). *O Livro da Consciência – A Construção do Cérebro Consciente* [*Self comes to mind – Constructing the counscious brain*] (Trad. de Luís Oliveira Santos). Círculo de Leitores.

Damásio, A. (2018). *The strange order of things – Life, feeling, and the making of cultures.* Pantheon Books.

Damásio, A. (2020). *Sentir & Saber – A Caminho da Consciência* [*Feeling & knowing – Making minds conscious*]. Círculo de Leitores.

Delmas-Marty, M. (1996). *Vers un droit commun de l'humanité – Entretien avec Philippe Petit.* Les Éditions Textuel.

Delperee, F. (1987). Avant-Propos/Les formes de participation des citoyens au fonctionnement de l'Etat. In AAVV, *Le nouveau Droit constitutionnel – apports belges au IIe Congrès mondial de droit constitutionnel, Paris – Aix-en-Provence, 31 août–5 septembre 1987* (pp. 5–6 and 173–186). Centre Interuniversitaire de Droit public, A.S.B.L., Academia, Édition et Diffusion/Bruylant.

Dostoyevsky, F. M. (1879). *The brothers Karamazov* (Transl. by C. Garnett). The Lowell Press. http://www.gutenberg.org/ebooks/28054

Droit, R.-P. (2005). *Humanity in the making: overview of the intellectual history of UNESCO: 1945–2005.* UNESCO. https://unesdoc.unesco.org/ark:/48223/pf0000142076

Dumont, L. (1983). *Essais sur l'individualisme – Une perspective anthropologique sur l'idéologie moderne.* Éditions du Seuil.

Dupuy, J.-P. (2004). Rationalité scientifique et raison pratique. In UNESCO, *Philosophie, Science et Éthique* (pp. 5–22). https://unesdoc.unesco.org/ark:/48223/pf0000137535?posInSet=1&queryId=a5fc430d-3909-47c6-9ee4-30a1f870e505

Dupuy, P.-M. (2008). Jus cogens. In J. Andriantsimbazovina et al. (Sous la direction de) (pp. 566–570). *Dictionnaire des Droits de l'Homme*. PUF.

Dupuy, R.-J. (1986). *La communauté internationale entre le mythe et l'histoire*. Economica/UNESCO.

Eco, U. (1984). *Conceito de texto* (Trad. de Carla de Queiroz, Apresentação de Cidmar Teodoro Pais). Editora Portuguesa de Livros Técnicos e Científicos.

Eide, A., & Rosas, A. (2001). 1. Economic, social and cultural rights: A universal challenge. In A. Eide, C. Krause, & A. Rosas (Eds.), *Economic, social and cultural rights – A textbook* (pp. 3–7). Kluwer Law International.

Espiell, H. G. (1978). The right to development as a human right. In *Seminar on universalism and regionalism in the field of international protection and promotion of human rights*, Caracas, 31 July–4 August. UNESCO. Retrieved July 2019, from http://unesdoc.unesco.org/images/0003/000369/036972EB.pdf

European Movement. (1949). *European Movement and the Council of Europa* (With forewords by W. S. Churchill & P.-H. Spaak). Hutschinson & Co. (Publishers) Ltd.

Fagan, A. (2005). Human rights. In *Internet encyclopedia of philosophy*. www.iep.utm.edu/hum-rts

Ferrarese, E. (2008). Pourquoi refuse-t-on la reconnaissance? Sur les effets de la reconnaissance institutionnelle. In J.-P. Payet & A. Battegay (Dir.), *La reconnaissance à l'épreuve – Explorations socioanthropologiques* (pp. 95-102). Presses universitaires du Septentrion.

Ferry, L. (1993). Entretien. *Le Courrier de l'UNESCO*, 4–8, avril, 49–50.

Foster, Ch. (2011). *Human dignity in bioethics and law*. Hart Publishing.

Freeman, M. (2004). The problem of secularism in human rights theory. *Human Rights Quarterly*, *26*, 375–400.

Freund, J. (1972). Sociologie et Méthodologie. In AAVV, *René Cassin Amicorum Discipulorumque Liber – IV. Méthodologie des Droits de l'Homme* (pp. 153–172). Éditions Pedone, Institut International des Droits de l'Homme.

Glendon, M. A. (2001). *A world made new – Eleanor Roosevelt and the Universal Declaration of Human Rights*. Random House, Trade Paperbacks.

Goyard-Fabre, S. (1990). Le droit, tâche infinie. *Droits – Revue française de théorie juridique (Définir le droit/2)*, *11*, 25–29.

Griffin, J. (2008). *On human rights*. Oxford University Press.

Habermas, J. (1983). *Moral consciousness and communicative action* (Transl. by C. Lenhardt & S. Weber Nicholsen). Polity Press.

Habermas, J. (2012). Chapter 4 – The concept of human dignity and the realistic Utopia of human rights. In C. Corradetti (Ed.), *Philosophical dimensions of human rights – Some contemporary views* (pp. 63–79). Springer Science + Business Media B. V.

Henkin, L. (1978). *The rights of man today*. Stevens and Sons.

Henkin, L. (1990). *The age of rights*. Columbia University Press.

Henrich, J. (2020). Comment expliquer la réussite de l'espèce humaine ? *L'histoire de l'homme – Une aventure de 7 millions d'années. Et après ?* Le Monde – Hors-Série, Édition 2020, 172–174.

Henry, L. M. (2011). The jurisprudence of dignity. *University of Pennsylvania Law Review, 160*. University of Maryland Legal Studies Research Paper No. 2011-42. Retrieved July 2018, from http://ssrn.com/abstract=1928768

Hersch, J. (Dir.). (1968). *Le droit d'être un homme.* UNESCO/Robert Laffont. http://unesdoc.unesco.org/images/0021/002192/219297fo.pdf (English edition: http://unesdoc.unesco.org/images/0000/000000/000029Eo.pdf).

Honneth, A. (2004). Reconnaissance. In M. Canto-Sperber (Sous la direction de), *Dictionnaire d'Éthique et de Philosophie Morale – Tome 2* (pp. 1640–1647). PUF.

Humphrey, J. P. (1984). *Human rights & the United Nations – A great adventure.* Transnational Publishers.

Hunt, L. (2008). *Inventing human rights – A history.* W. W. Norton & Company Ltd.

Immordino-Yang, M. H., & Damasio, A. R. (2007). We feel, therefore we learn: The relevance of affective and social neuroscience to education. *Mind, Brain and Education, 1*(1), 3–10. Retrieved July 2019, from www-bcf.usc.edu/~immordin/papers/Immordino-Yang+Damasio_2007_RelevanceofNeurotoEdu.pdf

Iriye, A., Goedde, P., & Hitchcock, W. I. (Ed.). (2012). *The human rights revolution: An international history.* Oxford University Press.

Ishay, M. R. (2004). *The history of human rights: From ancient times to the globalization era.* University of California Press.

Jacob, F. (1981). *Le Jeu des possibles.* Fayard.

Jouannet, E. (2012). Le Droit International de la Reconnaissance. *Revue de Droit International Public, CXVI*(4), octobre–décembre, 769–799.

https://justiceglobale.files.wordpress.com/2015/01/article-e-jouannet-rgdip-2012-4.pdf

Kalinowski, G. (1969). *Querelle de la science normative* (*Une contribution à la théorie de la science*). Librairie Générale de Droit et de Jurisprudence, Professeurs à la Faculté de Droit et des Sciences Economiques de Paris, Volume X.

Kant, I. (1781). *Kritik of reinen Vernunft.* https://archive.org/details/kritikderreinenv19kant (An English translation: http://files.libertyfund.org/files/1442/0330_Bk.pdf).

Kant, I. (1785). *Grundlegung zur Metaphysik der Sitten.* http://gutenberg.spiegel.de/buch/grundlegung-zur-methaphysik-der-sitten-3510/1 (An English translation: www.earlymoderntexts.com/assets/pdfs/kant1785.pdf).

Kant, I. (1788). *Kritik der praktischen Vernunf.* https://archive.org/details/kritikderpraktisookantuoft (An English translation: http://pinkmonkey.com/dl/library1/book1133.pdf).

Kant, I. (1797). *Die Metaphysik der Sitten.* https://archive.org/details/immanuelkantsmeookircgoog (An English translation: https://thevirtuallibrary.org/index.php/es/?option=com_djclassifieds&format=raw&view=download&task=download&fid=7607).

Koji, T. (2001). Emerging hierarchy in international human rights and beyond: From the perspective of non-derogable rights. *European Journal of International Law, 12*(5), 917–941. Retrieved July 2019, from http://ejil.org/pdfs/12/5/1555.pdf

Kovak, E. (1993). L'Intrigue éthique. In AAVV, *Emmanuel Lévinas – L'éthique comme philosophie première (Actes du colloque de Cerisy-la-Salle sous, 23 août–2 septembre 1986)* (pp. 177–192). Les Éditions du Cerf.

Krause, C., & Scheinin, M. (2009). Preface. In C. Krause & M. Scheinin (Eds.), *International protection of human rights: A textbook.* Åbo Akademi University, Institute for Human Rights.

Ladwig, B. (2014). Chapter 3 – Human rights and human animals. In M. Albers et al. (Eds.), *Human rights and human nature* (pp. 23–42) (Ius Gentium – Comparative Perspectives on Law and Justice, Vol. 35). Springer.

Lauterpacht, H. (1948). The International Protection of Human Rights. In Académie de Droit International, *Recueil des Cours – 1947, I – Tome 70 de la Collection* (pp. 5–108). Recueil Sirey.

Lenclud, G. (2020). L'usage de la parole doit beaucoup au hasard. *L'histoire de l'homme – Une aventure de 7 millions d'années. Et après ?* Le Monde – Hors-Série, Édition 2020, 46–49.

Lévinas, E. (1972). *Humanisme de l'autre homme.* Fata Morgana, Le Livre de Poche.

Lévinas, E. (1989). Les droits de l'autre homme. In Commission nationale consultative des droits de l'homme. *Les droits de l'homme en questions – Livre Blanc* (pp. 43–45). La Documentation française.

Lévinas, E. (1993). Diachronie et représentation. In J. Greisch & J. Rolland (Dir.), *Emmanuel Lévinas – L'éthique comme philosophie première (Actes du colloque de Cerisy-la-Salle sous, 23 août–2 septembre 1986)* (pp. 447–468). Les Éditions du Cerf, La nuit surveillée.

Lier, H. (1980). *L'Animal Signé.* De Visscher.

Maheu, R. (1972). Serving the mind as a force in history. In AAVV, *In the minds of men – UNESCO: 1946 to 1971* (pp. 281–319). UNESCO/PUF. https://unesdoc.unesco.org/ark:/48223/pf0000002246?posInSet=6&queryId=74f92898-bf9a-4126-86ef-62971b78dd86

Malik, H. C. (Ed.). (2000). *The challenge of human rights: Charles Malik and the universal declaration.* Charles Malik Foundation/Centre for Lebanese Studies.

Marks, J. H. (2011). Toward a unified theory of professional ethics and human rights. *Michigan Journal of International Law.* http://papers.ssrn.com/sol3/papers.cfm?abstract_id=1818331##

Mautner, Th. (2013). How rights became 'subjective'. *Ratio Juris*, *26*(1), 111–133.

Mayerfeld, J. (2009). The democratic legitimacy of international human rights law. *Indiana International and Comparative Law Review*, *19*, 49–88. http://faculty.washington.edu/jasonm/Mayerfeld_Democratic_Legitimacy_of_International_Human_Rights_Law.pdf

Mégret, F. (2010). Nature of obligations. In D. Moeckli, S. Shah, & S. Sivakumaran (Eds.), *International human rights law* (pp. 124–149). Oxford University Press.

Monchablon, A. (Coord.). (1989). *L'esprit de 1789 et des droits de l'homme – Textes et documents (1725–1986) – Préface de Claude Nicolet*. Coédition CNDP/Larousse.

Monteiro, A. R. (2014a). *Ethics of human rights*. Springer International Publishing.

Morange, J. (1988). *La Déclaration des droits de l'homme et du citoyen*. PUF.

Morris, Ch. (1964). *Signification and significance – A study of the relations of signs and values*. The MIT Press.

Morsink, J. (1999). *The universal declaration of human rights: Origins, drafting, and intent*. University of Pennsylvania Press.

Nowak, M. (2003). *Introduction to international human rights regime*. Martinus Nijhoff Publishers.

Partsch, K.J. (1991). La mise en œuvre des droits de l'homme par l'UNESCO – Remarques sur un système particulier. In *Annuaire Français de Droit International* (pp. 482–506). Éditions du Centre National de la Recherche Scientifique, XXXVI.

Payet, J.-P., & Battegay, A. (2008). La reconnaissance, un concept de philosophie politique à l'épreuve des sciences sociales. In J.-P. Payet & A. Battegay (Eds.), *La reconnaissance à l'épreuve – Explorations socio-anthropologiques* (pp. 23–42). Presses Universitaires du Septentrion.

Pelloux, R. (1972). L'étude des droits de l'homme doit être interdisciplinaire. In AAVV, *René Cassin Amicorum Discipulorumque Liber – IV. Méthodologie des Droits de l'Homme* (pp. 9–18) (Jura Hominis ac Civis, Vol. IV). Éditions Pedone, Institut International des Droits de l'Homme.

Perelman, Ch. (1977). *L'empire rhétorique – Rhétorique et argumentation*. Librairie Philosophique J. Vrin.

Perelman, Ch. (1979). *Logique juridique – Nouvelle rhétorique*. Dalloz, Col. Méthodes du Droit.

Perelman, Ch. (1989). Argumentation. In *Encyclopaedia universalis – Corpus, 2* (pp. 937–938).

Pfordten, D. von der. (2016). *Menschenwürde*. Verlag C. H. Beck oHG.

Pic, P. (2020). C'est l'imaginaire qui a fait notre force. *L'histoire de l'homme – Une aventure de 7 millions d'années. Et après ?* Le Monde – Hors-Série, 44–45.

Pierrot, A. (2003). Sens et rationalité à l'école. Quelques réflexions librement inspirées de Wittgenstein. *Revue Française de Pédagogie*, *143*, avril–mai–juin, 31–41.

Pillay, N. (2012). Strengthening the United Nations human rights treaty body system – A report by the United Nations High Commissioner for Human Rights. United Nations – Human Rights: Office of the High Commissioner. www2.ohchr.org/english/bodies/HRTD/docs/HCReportTBStrengthening.pdf

Plato. (1997). *Plato – Complete works* (Ed. by J. M. Cooper & D. S. Hutchinson). Hackeht Publishing Company.

Ponton, L. (1990). *Philosophie et droits de l'homme de Kant à Lévinas*. J. Vrin.

Ramcharan, B. (2008). *Contemporary human rights ideas*. Routledge.

Rao, N. (2011). Three concepts of dignity in constitutional law. *Notre Dame Law Review, 86*(1), 183–271. George Mason Law & Economics Research Paper No. 11-20. Retrieved July 2018, from http://ssrn.com/abstract=1838597

Ricoeur, P. (1991). *Lectures I – Autour du politique*. Seuil.

Ricoeur, P. (1994). Entretien. In AAVV, *Éthique et responsabilité – Paul Ricoeur* (pp. 11–34). Éditions de la Baconnière.

Ricœur, P. (2004a). *Parcours de la reconnaissance*. Gallimard.

Rivero, J. (1981). *Les libertés publiques – 1/Les droits de l'homme*. Presses Universitaires de France.

Rivero, J. (1989). Une éthique fondée sur le respect de l'Autre. In AAVV, *1989 – Les droits de l'homme en questions – Livre Blanc* (pp. 179–182). La Documentation française, Commission nationale consultative des droits de l'homme.

Rousseau, J.-J. (1762). *Du contrat social* (Édition établie par Pierre Burgelin). GF-Flammarion. https://www.rousseauonline.ch/pdf/rousseauonline-0004.pdf
An English translation: https://www.earlymoderntexts.com/assets/pdfs/rousseau1762.pdf

Rousseau, J.-J. (1913). *The social contract and discourses* (Translated and introduced by G. D. H. Cole). Everyman. An English translation online: https://oll.libertyfund.org/titles/rousseau-the-social-contract-and-discourses.

Roy, O. (2012). La règle d'or, maxime universelle. *Sciences Humaines – Un siècle de philosophie – Une bibliothèque idéale, 29*, 12–15.

Russell, B. (1938). *Power – A new social analysis*. Routledge.

Salmon, J. (2011). Quelle place pour l'État dans le Droit International d'aujourd'hui?. In Académie de Droit International, *Recueil des Cours/Collected Courses of the Hague Academy of Internationl Law – 2010 – Tome 347 de la Collection*. Martinus Nijhoff Publishers.

Scheinin, M. (2001). Economic and Social Rights as Legal Rights. In A. Eide, C. Krause, & A. Rosas (Eds.), *Economic, social and cultural rights – A textbook* (2nd rev. ed., pp. 29–53). Kluwer Law International.

Scheinin, M. (2009). International mechanisms and procedures for monitoring. In C. Krause & M. Scheinin (Eds.), *International protection of human rights: A textbook* (pp. 601–620). Åbo Akademi University, Institute for Human Rights.

Schutter, O. (2009). The status of human rights in international law. In C. Krause & M. Scheinin (Eds.), *International protection of human rights: A textbook* (pp. 39–58). Åbo Akademi University, Institute for Human Rights.

Schutter, O. et al. (2012). Commentary to the Maastricht principles on extraterritorial obligations of states in the area of economic, social and cultural rights. *Human Rights Quarterly, 34*, 1084–1169. Retrieved July 2019, from https://www.etoconsortium.org/en/main-navigation/library/maastricht-principles/

Schutter, O., & Ringelheim, J. (2005). *La renonciation aux droits fondamentaux – La libre disposition du soi et le règne de l'échange*. Université Catholique de Louvain, Faculté de Droit, Centre de Philosophie du Droit, Cellule de Recherche Interdisciplinaire en Droits de l'Homme, Working Paper Series 1/2005. Retrieved July 2019, from https://sites.uclouvain.be/cridho/documents/Working.Papers/CridhoWPs012005.PDF

Sebastiani, S. (2019). À la recherche de la nature humaine. *Les Grands Dossiers des Sciences Humains – Les Lumières: Une révolution de la pensée, 56*, septembre–octobre–novembre, 20–25.

Sohn, L. B. (1982). The new international kaw: Protection of the rights of individuals rather than states. *American University Law Review, 32*.

Ssenyonjo, M. (2016). *Economic, social and cultural rights in international law.* Bloomsbury Publishing.

Steiner, H. J., Alston, Ph., Goodman, R. (2008). *International human rights in context – Law, politics, morals*. Oxford University Press.

Sudre, F. (1990). *La Convention européenne des droits de l'homme*. PUF.

Szoszkiewicz, L. (2018). Internet access as a new human right? State of the art on the threshold of 2020. *Adam Mickiewicz University Law Review*, 49–62.

https://www.researchgate.net/publication/328290234_Internet_Access_as_a_New_Human_Right_State_of_the_Art_on_the_Threshold_of_2020

Tasioulas, J. (2017). *Minimum core obligations: Human rights in the here and now*. World Bank. https://openknowledge.worldbank.org/handle/10986/29144

Todorov, T. (2013). Sous le regard des autres. *Sciences Humaines – Les Grands Dossiers – L'amour: un besoin vital, 32*, 56–63.

Tomuschat, Ch. (2008). *Human rights – Between idealism and realism* (Collected Courses of the Academy of European Law, Vol. XIII/1). Oxford University Press.

Touraine, A. (1992). *Critique de la modernité.* Fayard.

Tóth, J. (1972). Les droits de l'homme et la théorie du droit. In AAVV, *René Cassin Amicorum Discipulorumque Liber – IV. Méthodologie des Droits de l'Homme* (pp. 69–90) (Jura Hominis ac Civis, Vol. IV). Éditions Pedone, Institut International des Droits de l'Homme.

Trindade, A. A. C. (2006). International Law for Humankind: Towards a new *jus gentium* – General course on public international law. In Académie de Droit International, *Recueil des Cours/Collected Courses of the Hague Academy of International Law – 2005 – Tome 316 de la Collection*. Martinus Nijhoff Publishers.

UNESCO. (1989). *Comité consultatif sur les mesures visant à promouvoir l'application intégrale et générale de la Recommandation sur l'éducation pour la compréhension, la coopération et la paix internationales et l'éducation relative aux droits de l'homme et aux libertés fondamentales, Deuxième session (Paris, 21–25 novembre 1988) – Rapport final.*

United Nations. (1995). *The United Nations and Human Rights, 1945–1995* (The United Nations Blue Books Series, Vol. VII). https://digitallibrary.un.org/record/205690

United Nations. (2002). *Human rights – A compilation of international instruments*. Office of the United Nations High Commissioner for Human Rights.

United Nations. (2013). *A new global partnership: eradicate poverty and transform economies through sustainable development – Report of the high-level panel of experts, presented to the United Nations Secretary-General on 30 May 2013.* https://sustainabledevelopment.un.org/index.php?page=view&type=400&nr=893&menu=1561

Urioste, F. (1999). La Declaración Universal de los Derechos Humanos y el desarrollo del Derecho Internacional de los Derechos Humanos a nivel universal. In H. Gros Espiell (Coord.), *Derechos Humanos – A 50 años de la Declaración Americana de los Derechos y Deberes del Hombre y de la Declaración Universal de Derechos Humanos – Seminario organizado por la Facultad de Derecho de la Universidad Católica del Uruguay, los días 28, 29 y 30 de Setiembre de 1998, bajo la coordinación general del Dr. Héctor Gros Espiell* (pp. 51–60). Universidad Católica/Editorial y Librería Juridica Amalio M. Ferandez.

Vandenberghe, F. (2008). Sociology of the heart: Max Scheler's epistemology of love. *Theory, Culture & Society*, 25(3), 17–51.

Velu, J., & Ergec, R. (1990). *La Convention européenne des droits de l'homme*. Bruylant.

Verdoodt, A. (1964). *Naissance et signification de la Déclaration universelle des droits de l'homme* (*Préface de René Cassin*). Éditions Nauwelaerts.

Viney, G. (1990). La responsabilité. In *Archives de philosophie du droit, Tome 35 – Vocabulaire fondamental du droit* (pp. 275–292). Éditions Sirey.

Wermeil, S. J. (1998). Law and human dignity: The judicial soul of justice Brennan. *William & Mary Bill of Rights Journal*, 7(1), 223–239. Retrieved July 2018, from http://scholarship.law.wm.edu/wmborj/vol7/iss1/5

Wetz, F. J. (1998). *Die Würde der Menschen is antastbar – Eine Provokation*. Klett-Cotta.

Whelan, D. J. (2011). *Indivisible human rights: A history*. University of Pennsylvania Press.

Williams, R. (1997). *Hegel's ethics of recognition*. University of California Press.

Wood, A. W. (1999). *Kant's ethical thought*. Cambridge University Press.

World Commission on Culture and Development. (1995). *Our creative diversity.* https://unesdoc.unesco.org/ark:/48223/pf0000101651

Young, K. G. (2008). The minimum core of economic and social rights: A concept in search of content. *Yale Journal of International Law, 13*, 113–175. https://lawdigitalcommons.bc.edu/cgi/viewcontent.cgi?article=1920&context=lsfp

CHAPTER 3

Rights of the Child

Abstract

1. The recognition of the rights of the child has meant a historical deepening of the logic and ideal of human rights.
2. The history of childhood is crossed by the ambivalence of its representation and treatment by adults. A pessimistic mindset has long prevailed, underlying the lasting violence over children.
3. The Convention on the Rights of the Child has become the source of an International Law of the Child that deals with her/his human rights internationally recognised and protected, at the universal and regional levels, that is inseminating domestic legal orders.
4. Parents are naturally the first responsible for the rights of children, but legally the main responsible are States. The promotion and protection of the rights of the child are also the *cause* of thousands of international and national Non-Governmental Organisations.
5. We know why human rights constitute an Ethics of Humanity. The rights of the child have an ethical content too, fundamentally because they outlaw the discrimination of children on account of their age, and command their special protection by virtue of their age.
6. The Ethics of the Rights of the Child – inscribed in the Ethics of Human Rights – may be summarised into the following principles:
   - *Primacy of the "best interests of the child"*
   - *Love, respect and responsibility for the child*
   - *Evolving autonomy of the child*
   - *Priority of children*
7. The New International Law of the Child meant a movement from the traditional (naturalist) representation of the child-object of Law towards a new (ethical) vision of the child-subject of rights. It culminated an evolution that amounts to a revolution, as it is generally acknowledged by both its defenders and detractors. The Revolution of the Rights of the Child is, however, the most candid and peaceful one: it consists simply in fully recognising and treating children as human persons. It is an ethical and juridical revolution, but above all, it is the principle of a deeper, slow and long cultural revolution, because it must transform mentalities and customs.

 | DOI: 10.1163/9789004462465_004

8. The Convention on the Rights of the Child is a visionary text. That is why the idea of 'rights of the child' remains resisted.
9. The right to education is the Bastille of the Revolution of the Rights of the Child.

3.1 It Was Once the Rights of the Child …

The history of childhood is crossed by the ambivalence of its representation and treatment by adults. A pessimistic mindset has prevailed so far, underlying the lasting violence over children, including infanticide. The latter has been committed, for millennia, under different forms, in different cultures, echoing in mythologies, and is not a past sin (see for instance, Supino-Viterbo, 1999). Childhood literature also reflects much of the children's misfortune. In a study on *Human rights in children's literature,* Jonathan Todres and Sarah Higinbotham "found that of the two hundred best-selling children's books of all time, both hardcover and paperback, only seven feature children in intact, supportive families" (Todres & Higinbotham, 2016, p. 103). They concluded:

> Abandonment is a ubiquitous theme in children's literature. […]
>
> Children are abducted, abandoned, starved, beaten, humiliated, exiled, bullied, forced to work under exhausting and degrading conditions, plucked up by giants, lured into exploitation by witches, poisoned, fattened up to be eaten, compelled to sweep ashes, and even mutilated. Children are given menial, meaningless, and herculean work by their guardians, such as emptying a pond using only a spoon that is full of holes, sorting tiny lentils from the ashes, or spinning straw into gold. Sibling rivalry and child favouritism, weak fathers who capitulate to their new wives' jealousy, and predatory stepmothers dominate the fairy-tale genre. The favoured children are typically spoiled and pampered (and ugly), while their good-hearted but despised siblings are beaten and starved (and of course, beautiful). (pp. 104, 105)

It is submitted that the evolution of the attitudes towards children may be historically schematically divided into the following three eras, at least in the Western culture:

- *Unawareness* of the childhood specificity and despise of children, regarded as humanly inferior and property of their progenitors (for millennia). The Roman Law of the Twelve Tables (c. 450 BC), allowing the *pater familias* (father) a *vitae necisque potestas* (power of life and death) over a new-born, reflected the mentality of this very long era.

- *Awareness* of the value of childhood and dawn of a new sensitivity regarding children as developing human beings, arousing feelings of compassion and love and demanding protection and care (since the Renaissance). This evolution gained expression, to a certain extent, in the French Napoleonic Code (*Code Civil des Français*, 1804), in particular.
- *Recognition* of the child as a human person equal by dignity and rights, in the second half of the 20th century. The idea of 'rights of the child' conquered the world public opinion, has progressively transformed the status of children in many national legal systems and, despite their remaining targets of so many evils, continues to improve their lives in all continents, making the world a better place for children.

The first UN Special Rapporteur on the Right to Education wrote (E/CN.4/2002/60)[1]:

> 30. The history of human rights can be depicted through two broadening concentric circles, the first showing a gradual extension of recognized rights and the second an incremental inclusion of those previously excluded. The rights first bestowed upon adult, propertied, white men have been gradually extended to women, then to non-white adults and later also to children.

The rights of the child have become a theme of writings since the 19th century, in the context of the progress of knowledge about the childhood and the infantile medicine (the term 'paediatrics' dates back to the 1870s). For example, in 1852, it was published in the USA a paper titled "The Rights of Children" (by Slagvolk),[2] and in 1892 "Children's Rights: a Book of Nursery Logic" (by Kate D. Wiggin and Nora Smith).[3] In France, Félix Buisson affirmed in a conference at the beginning of the 20th century: "The society, which proclaimed the rights of man, also recognises the rights of the child: it assumes its assurance, takes on the responsibility of implementing them, with the family, after it, if necessary without it and, if need be, against it" (as cited in Chevallier, 1975, pp. 305, 306).

The first international legal instrument protecting children was the Minimum Age (Industry) Convention, adopted by ILO in 1919 (C05). This is the first of 46 declarations and other texts on the rights and protection of the child reproduced as appendices in a book by Phillip E. Veerman (1992).

The first Declaration of the Rights of the Child was drafted by Eglantyne Jebb and approved by the NGO *International Save the Children Union/Union Internationale de Secours aux Enfants* (Geneva), on 23 February 1923. The Declaration of Geneva (as it has come to be known),[4] with a brief preamble and five paragraphs, was broadcasted in 36 languages in the Eiffel Tower (Paris), on 21 November 1923. On 26 September 1924, it was unanimously endorsed by the League of Nations (5th session), becoming, "in a way, the Children's Charter of the League of Nations" (see Moody, 2016, Annexe 1). Although the word 'right' only appears in the title, it was the first time that a Declaration of Rights was adopted by an IGO.

The UDHR does not refer to rights of the child, but it states (Article 1): "All human beings are born free and equal in dignity and rights".[5] The ICCPR includes some children's rights in Article 24. Children are referred to also in Articles 14, 18, 23. The ICESCR addresses some children's rights in Article 10. Children are referred to also in Articles 12 and 14.

Meanwhile, on 20 November 1959, the UN General Assembly proclaimed a new Declaration of the Rights of the Child, with a preamble and ten Principles.[6] It was considered a revolutionary document, at the time. Its most significant feature is the emergence of the child's international legal personality. It included, in particular, the child's right "to a name and a nationality" (Principle 3), which were the first civil rights recognised to children. The spirit of the 'rights of the child' has begun to penetrate the national legal systems.

1979 – the year of the 20th anniversary of the 1959 Declaration – was proclaimed International Year of the Child by the UN General Assembly. Seizing the moment, Poland presented to the UN Commission on Human Rights (XXXIVth session), on 7 February 1978, a draft Convention, so that its adoption could be the great event of 1979. It didn't succeed and it took ten years for the Convention on the Rights of the Child to be adopted by the UN General Assembly, on 20 November 1989, the day of the 30th anniversary of the 1959 Declaration. It came into force on 2 September 1990.

The CRC has become the source of an International Law of the Child that deals with their human rights internationally recognised and protected, at the universal and regional levels.

3.2 International Law of the Child

3.2.1 *Sources*

3.2.1.1 Convention on the Rights of the Child

Article 1 of the Convention on the Rights of the Child (1989)[7] states: "For the purposes of the present Convention, a child means every human being below the age of eighteen years unless, under the law applicable to the child, majority is attained earlier". It is a definition covering ages with different levels of development, needs, and possibilities, requiring a modulated application of the Convention, whose main features and content are as follows:

– It is a treaty, i.e. a legally binding international instrument.

- It is the most comprehensive legal international instrument on the rights of the child. In effect:
  - it gathers together all the rights recognised to the child (which were dispersed in more than 80 international instruments, at the universal and regional levels, an abundance that was one of the arguments of the opponents to the need of a Convention);
  - it universalises rights that, until then, only had been recognised at the regional level or by jurisprudence (as the right of the child to be heard in legal or administrative cases concerning it);
  - it enhances their level of protection by making rights compulsory that, until then, had been only a matter of recommendations (as the rights of handicapped children); by imposing new obligations to States (as to abolish traditional harmful practices, and to take measures in favour of children victims); by reinforcing the interdiction of discrimination;
  - it adds new rights (as the right to preserve his/her identity, the right to enjoy his/her own culture, the right to know his/her rights).
- It is one of the most extensive treaties on human rights, enunciating civil, cultural, economic and social rights (except the political rights whose exercise is subjected to a minimum age reserve).
- It is the most universal human rights treaty, as it is in force in 196 States, including all UN Member States (except the USA that only signed it).
- It was the most quickly adopted human rights treaty (about ten months after its adoption).
- It is the most translated legal international instrument around the world, after the UDHR.

The Convention is composed of a Preamble, three Parts, and 54 Articles:
- The Preamble invokes general principles regarding human rights and the rights of children.
- Part I (Articles 1–41) sets out the rights of the child and the corresponding obligations of the States Parties.
- Part II (Articles 42–45) contains provisions on the enforcement of the Convention, in particular the establishment of a Committee on the Rights of the Child (CoRC).
- Part III (Articles 46–54) consists of final provisions.

The Convention substantial norms (Part I) form two groups of rights:
- general human rights, i.e. recognised to every human being (except political rights), such as the right to life, the right to health, the right to education, etc.
- specific rights of the child required:

- by the importance of preserving the family ties, as the right not to be separated from his/her parents without a very strong reason, and to maintain personal relations with both father and mother, in the case of separation;
- by the children' immaturity, dependence, vulnerability and needs of development, as well as their protection against all forms of negligence, violence, and exploitation;
- by the special needs of the most vulnerable groups of children, including children with disability;
- by the psychological specificity of the childhood, such as the right to play and to other activities particular to these ages.

The rights of the child are sometimes summarised in three Ps: Protection, Provision, Participation – a synthesis subscribed by the CoRC (for example, in GC 12, CRC/C/GC/2009/12, para. 3, 18).[8] A fourth 'P' could be added: *Prevention.*

In 1991, at its first session, the CoRC adopted "General guidelines regarding the form and content of initial reports to be submitted by States Parties under Article 44, paragraph 1(a), of the Convention" (CRC/C/5, 30/10/91),[9] whose paragraph 13 highlights four "general principles":

a Non-discrimination (Art. 2)
b Best interests of the child (Art. 3)
c Right to life, survival, and development (Art. 6)
d Respect for the views of the child (Art. 12)

Article 5 contains another wide-ranging principle: the evolving autonomy of children to exercise their rights (see 3.3.3).

The CRC was reinforced by two Protocols adopted by the UN General Assembly in 2000:
- Optional Protocol to the Convention on the Rights of the Child on the sale of children, child prostitution and child pornography (entered into force on 18 January 2002)
- Optional Protocol to the Convention on the Rights of the Child on the involvement of children in armed conflict (entered into force on 12 February 2002)

A third Protocol was adopted in 2011 and entered into force in 2014:
- Optional Protocol to the Convention on the Rights of the Child on a communications procedure.

3.2.1.2 Other Universal Instruments

Other relevant universal legal instruments concerning children are the following ones:

- United Nations Standard Minimum Rules for the Administration of Juvenile Justice (Beijing Rules) (UN, 1985)
- Declaration on Social and Legal Principles relating to the Protection and Welfare of Children, with Special Reference to Foster Placement and Adoption Nationally and Internationally (UN, 1986)
- United Nations Standard Minimum Rules for Non-custodial Measures (Tokyo Rules) (UN, 1990)
- United Nations Guidelines for the Prevention of Juvenile Delinquency (Riyadh Guidelines) (UN, 1990)
- United Nations Rules for the Protection of Juveniles Deprived of their Liberty (Havana Rules) (UN, 1990)
- Guidelines on Justice in Matters involving Child Victims and Witnesses of Crime (UN, ECOSOC, 2005)

As noted by the CoRC in its GC 5 (CRC/GC/2003/5),[10] "other international human rights instruments apply to all persons below the age of 18 years" (para. 23).

There are also legal instruments adopted by ILO for the protection of children,[11] such as:
- Minimum Age Convention (C138, 1973)
- Worst Forms of Child Labour Convention (C182, 1999)

The IHL also devotes special attention to children.

Children are addressed by some conventions adopted by The Hague Conference on Private International Law, an IGO dedicated to the harmonisation of Private International Law. For example:
- Hague Convention on Jurisdiction, Applicable Law and Recognition of Decrees Relating to Adoptions (1965)
- Hague Convention on the Civil Aspects of International Child Abduction (1980)
- Hague Convention on the Protection of Children and Co-operation in Respect of Intercountry Adoption (1993)
- Hague Convention on Jurisdiction, Applicable Law, Recognition, Enforcement, and Co-operation in Respect of Parental Responsibility and Measures for the Protection of Children (1996)

3.2.1.3 Regional Instruments

In the European region, the ECHR (1950) does not recognise special rights to children, which are only mentioned in Article 5 on "Equality between spouses" (twice). Nevertheless, it applies to "to everyone" within States Parties jurisdiction. Article 3 (Prohibition of torture) and Article 8 (Right to respect for private and family life) are widely applicable to children too. The 'minor' is mentioned in Article 5 (Right to liberty and security). It may be said that it was with the *Case Marckx v. Belgium* (Application 6833/74),[12] decided on 13 June 1979, recognising the legal equality between 'natural' and 'legitimate' children, that a European Children's Law is born.

There is a European Convention on the Exercise of Children's Rights (160, 1996). The European Social Charter (1996, revised) addresses children in many provisions.[13] Other European legal instruments concerning children include:
- European Convention on the Repatriation of Minors (071, 1970)
- European Convention on the Legal Status of Children born out of Wedlock (085, 1975)
- European Convention on Recognition and Enforcement of Decisions concerning Custody of Children and on Restoration of Custody of Children ("Luxembourg Convention") (105, 1980)
- Convention on Contact concerning Children (192, 2003)
- Council of Europe Convention on the Protection of Children against Sexual Exploitation and Sexual Abuse ("Lanzarote Convention") (201, 2007)
- European Convention on the Adoption of Children (202, 2008, revised)

Other European legal instruments are pertinent to the protection of children, such as:
- European Code of Social Security (048, 1964)
- European Convention on Social Security (078, 1972)
- European Convention on the Legal Status of Migrant Workers (093, 1977)
- Framework Convention for the Protection of National Minorities (157, 1995)
- Convention for the Protection of Human Rights and Dignity of the Human Being with regard to the Application of Biology and Medicine: Convention on Human Rights and Biomedicine (164, 1997)
- Convention on Cybercrime (185, 2001)
- Council of Europe Convention on Action against Trafficking in Human Beings (197, 2005)
- Council of Europe Convention on preventing and combating violence against women and domestic violence ("Istanbul Convention") (210, 2011)

The Charter of Fundamental Rights of the European Union (2000)[14] dedicates Article 24 to "The Rights of the Child", and Article 32 to the "Prohibition of child labour and protection of young people at work". Children are also mentioned in Article 14 ("Right to Education"). There are EU Directives, Regulations and Decisions concerned with the protection of children.

In the American region, children are mentioned in Articles 7 and 30 of the American Declaration of the Rights and Duties of Man (1948). The ACHR (1969) Article 19 is titled "Rights of the Child", and children are also directly addressed in Articles 4, 12, 17, 18. Article 16 of the Protocol of San Salvador (1988) holds the title "Rights of Children". There are, among other American instruments, the following ones:

- Inter-American Convention on Conflict of Laws Concerning the Adoption of Minors (OAS, 1984)
- Inter-American Convention on the International Return of Children (OAS, 1989)
- Inter-American Convention on International Traffic in Minors (OAS, 1994)

In the African region, the child is only once mentioned in the African Charter on Human and Peoples' Rights (1981, Article 18), but the former OAU had adopted a Declaration on the Rights and Welfare of the African Child (1979), and an African Charter on the Rights and Welfare of the Child was adopted in 1990.

There is also a Charter of the Rights of the Arab Child (League of Arab States, 1983) and a Covenant on the Rights of the Child in Islam (OIC, 2005).

At the national level, the influence of the CRC has also been impressive. Dozens of countries changed their laws and even their Constitutions.

3.2.2 *Protection of the Rights of the Child*

Parents are *naturally* the first responsible for the rights of their children, as the CRC recognises (mainly in Articles 5 and 18). However, the main *legally* responsible for all rights of all persons are States, as we know. The most general framework of the obligations of State Parties to the Convention is laid down in Articles 2.1, 3.2 and 4.

Like other human rights core treaties, the CRC[15] established a CoRC, as already said. Under Article 44.1, the "States Parties undertake to submit to the Committee, through the UN Secretary-General, reports on the measures they have adopted which give effect to the rights recognized herein and on the progress made on the enjoyment of those rights". With the adoption and entering into force (in 2014) of the Optional Protocol to the Convention on the Rights of the Child on a communications procedure[16]: "Communications may be submitted [to the CoRC] by or on behalf of an individual or group of individuals, within the jurisdiction of a State Party, claiming to be victims of a violation by that State Party" of the Convention and its Protocols (Article 5.1).

At the regional level, the European Convention on the Exercise of Children's Rights (1996)[17] established a Standing Committee, the first function of which is "consider any relevant questions concerning the interpretation or implementation of the Convention" (Article 16.1.2.a).

The African Charter on the Rights and Welfare of the Child (OAU, 1990)[18] established an African Committee of Experts on the Rights and Welfare of the Child. According to its Article 43.1: "Every State Party to the present Charter shall undertake to submit to the Committee through the Secretary-General of the Organization of African Unity, reports on the measures they have adopted which give effect to the provisions of this Charter and on the progress made in the enjoyment of these rights". Furthermore: "The Committee may receive communications from any person, group or non-governmental organization recognized by the Organization of African Unity, by a Member State, or the United Nations relating to any matter covered by this Charter" (Article 44.1).

In the American region, there is a Rapporteur on the Rights of the Child of the Inter-American Commission on Human Rights, as well as an OAS specialised organisation on children and adolescents: Inter-American Children's Institute, sitting in Uruguay.

At the national level, when the CRC was adopted, there were national institutions devoted to the rights of the child in only three countries (Norway, Costa Rica and New Zealand). At present, there are dozens, with different names: Children's Ombudsman, Children's Rights Commissioner, *Défenseur des Enfants*, *Defensor del Menor/de los Niños/de los Derechos del Niño*, etc. The CoRC dedicated its GC 2 to "The Role of Independent National Human Rights Institutions [NHRIS] in the Protection and Promotion of the Rights of the Child" (CRC/GC/2002/2, 15/11/2002).[19] It said:

> 1. While adults and children alike need independent NHRIS to protect their human rights, additional justifications exist for ensuring that children's human rights are given special attention. These include the facts that children's developmental state makes them particularly vulnerable to human rights violations; their opinions are still rarely taken into account; most children have no vote and cannot play a meaningful role in the political process that determines Governments' response to human rights; children encounter significant problems in using the judicial system to protect their rights or to seek remedies for violations of their rights; and children's access to organizations that may protect their rights is generally limited.

In 2000, in the Recommendation 1460 (2000) on "Setting up a European Ombudsman for Children",[20] the Parliamentary Assembly of the Council of Europe recommended to the Committee of Ministers to:

8.1. ask those Member States that have not yet done so to appoint a national children's ombudsman;

8.2. create within the Council of Europe, under arrangements to be specified, the post of European Children's Ombudsman, to be filled by a person of European standing whose task it would be to champion the cause of children.

There is a European Network of Ombudspersons for Children (ENOC)[21] that approved Standards for Independent Children's Rights Institutions.

The promotion and protection of the rights of the child is the *cause* of thousands of NGOs, at the international and national levels.

The International Community took two great initiatives concerning children:

- In 1990, a World Summit for Children, meeting in the UN Headquarters, New York, on 29–30 September, adopted unanimously a World Declaration on the Survival, Protection and Development of Children and a Plan of Action for Implementing the World Declaration on the Survival, Protection, and Development of Children in the 1990s.
- In 2002, a Special Session on Children of the UN General Assembly, meeting from 8 to 10 May to balance the implementation of the 1990 Plan of Action, adopted a new Declaration and Plan of Action for "A World Fit for Children".

In 1954, the UN General Assembly recommended that, "with effect from 1956, a Universal Children's Day shall be instituted by all countries [...] observed on the date and in the way which each considers appropriate" (Resolution 836 (IX), 14 December).[22] Within the UN framework, it is celebrated on 20 November, the day of the proclamation of the 1959 Declaration and the adoption of the 1989 Convention. This is the Universal Day, but national days vary from country to country.

3.3 Ethics of the Rights of the Child

The CRC means a "new ethical vision" of childhood (Pais, 1999, p. 7). As the CoRC said in its first GC 1 (CRC/GC/2001/1)[23]: "Children's rights are not detached or isolated values devoid of context, but exist within a broader ethical framework which is partly described in Article 29 (1) and the preamble to the Convention" (para. 7). It is an ethical framework illuminated by "the core value of the Convention: the human dignity innate in every child and his or her equal and inalienable rights" (para. 1). The CRC uses the term *dignity* in the Preamble (three times) and Articles 23, 28, 37, 39 and 40. It mentions the *values* in its Preamble (last but one paragraph) and in Article 29.1 (twice). The first GC of the Committee refers to "human rights values" (para. 2), to a "wide range of values" (para. 4) and to "the range of specific ethical values enshrined in the Convention" (para. 13). Value is a term appearing 28 times therein.

In the GC 5 (CRC/GC/2003/5),[24] the Committee reaffirmed that this is "the key message of the Convention – that children alongside adults are holders of human rights" (para. 21). In the GC 8 (CRC/C/GC/8),[25] it repeated: "The Convention asserts the status of the child as an individual person and holder of human rights. The child is not a possession of parents, nor of the State, nor simply an object of concern" (para. 47). This was echoed, for example, by the Constitutional Court of South Africa when it said in *Case M v The State Centre for Child Law (S v M (CCT 53/06) [2007] ZACC 18; 2008 (3) SA 232 (CC) (26 September 2007)*[26]: "Every child has his or her own dignity. If a child is to be constitutionally imagined as an individual with a distinctive personality and not merely as a miniature adult waiting to reach full size, he or she cannot be treated as a mere extension of his or her parents, umbilically destined to sink or swim with them" (para. 18).

As a consequence, the care and education of children must be "linked directly to the realization of the child's human dignity and rights, taking into account the child's special developmental needs and diverse evolving capacities" (CRC/GC/2001/1, para. 1).

The CRC carries an ethical significance, fundamentally because it outlaws the discrimination of children on account of their age and commands their special protection by virtue of their age. It recognises and protects, therefore, both the ethical-legal equality and the bio-psychological difference of children, i.e. the fullness of their dignity and rights, as human beings, while taking into account their immaturity, vulnerability and perfectibility, as children. The Ethics of the Rights of the Child – inscribed in the Ethics of Human Rights – may be summarised into the following principles:

- *Primacy of the "best interests of the child"*
- *Love, respect, and responsibility for the child*
- *Evolving autonomy of the child*
- *Priority of children*

These principles somewhat reflect the four aforementioned "general principles" highlighted by the CoRC in 1991. They are far-reaching in the everyday life of children – in the family, in school, in society. It follows their justification.

3.3.1 *Primacy of the "Best Interests of the Child"*

The notion of the "child's interests" emerged in the French Civil Code promulgated by Napoleon in 1804. During the 19th century, it became a principle of self-limitation of adults' power over children, in particular within the family, although in the context of a welfare approach addressing the child as an *object* of Law rather than as a *subject* of rights. The same concern inspired the legislation on nurseries and child labour, for example. The "special protection" of the child has become a principle of Childhood Law.

The progressive implementation of the principle of the best interests of the child in national legal systems paved the way for it to enter International Law. It is not found in the IBHR but in 1957, during the *travaux préparatoires* of the ICESCR, at the 12th session of the Third Committee of the UN General Assembly (A/C.3/SR.786),[27] the Syrian Delegation (Muhammad H. El-Farra) remarked, referring to the wording of the present Article 13.3, that "in the last analysis, powers recognized to parents should be used to protect the child's interests; he regrets that they are not mentioned".

The principle of the primacy of the best interests of the child entered International Law with the 1959 Declaration of the Rights of the Child. According to its Principle 2:

> The child shall enjoy special protection, and shall be given opportunities and facilities, by law and by other means, to enable him to develop physically, mentally, morally, spiritually and socially in a healthy and normal manner and in conditions of freedom and dignity. In the enactment of laws for this purpose, the best interests of the child shall be the paramount consideration.

Thereafter, it was endorsed by several international instruments, in variable formulations, such as the Convention on the Elimination of All Forms of Discrimination against Women (UN, 1979). The 1989 Convention consecrated it as a principle-guide for the exercise of public and private responsibilities concerning children. Its most general provision is in Article 3.1:

> In all actions concerning children, whether undertaken by public or private social welfare institutions, courts of law, administrative authorities or legislative bodies, the best interests of the child shall be a primary consideration.

The strongest formulation is in Article 21 (adoption of children), but the Convention refers to it in Articles 9.1, 9.3 (separation from parents), 18.1 (parental responsibilities), 20.1 (deprivation of family), 37.c (deprivation of liberty) and 40.2.b.iii (procedural guarantees).

During the drafting of the Convention, there was much discussion concerning whether the "best interests of the child" should be merely "*a* primary consideration" or "*the* primary consideration" or whether another formulation should be sought. It prevailed the indefinite article 'a' in Article 3, but the definite article 'the' is more used in the rest of the Convention. The "best interests of the child" are also mentioned in the Optional Protocols to the Convention.

The principle of the primacy of the best interests of the child is recognised by several Constitutions, as well as Acts concerning children and their rights, sometimes in stronger terms. For example, according to Section 28(2) of the Constitution of the Republic of South Africa (1996): "A child's best interests are of paramount importance in every matter concerning the child". Referring to this provision, the Constitutional Court noted: "It is notably stronger than the phrase "primary consideration" referred to in international instruments".[28] The Colombian *Código de la Infancia y la Adolescencia* (Code of Childhood and Adolescence) affirms: "It is understood that the best interests of the child and the adolescent are the imperative that obliges every person to guarantee the integral and simultaneous satisfaction of all their human rights that are universal, prevailing and interdependent" (Article 8).[29] In Goa (India), the *Goa Children's Act 2003*[30] begins by declaring that it is: "An Act to protect, promote and preserve the best interests of Children in Goa and to create a society that is proud to be child-friendly".

There is also a significant international, regional and national jurisprudence and quasi-jurisprudence on the primacy of the best interests of the child. For instance, in France, the *Conseil d'État* (Council of State) said (1997) that the best interests of the child are a higher principle of Law, directly enforceable in the internal legal order (see Dekeuwer-Défossez, 1991, pp. 5, 6). In its Concluding Observations on a Denmark Report (CRC/C/15/Add.151, 2001),[31] the CoRC "notes that the rights of parents are often found to be more important than the best interests of the child (para. 28)".

The Constitutional Court of South Africa, in an admirable decision on the *Case M v The State Centre for Child Law (S v M (CCT 53/06) [2007] ZACC 18; 2008 (3) SA 232 (CC) (26 September 2007)*,[32] suspended a sentence condemning a woman convicted of frauds to four years imprisonment by the Cape High Court and replaced it with other measures, in the best interests of her three children. The reasoning of the Constitutional Court is illuminating. It concluded that "it is clearly in the interests of the children that they continue to receive primary care from their mother", because, following the reports received, "all three boys rely on [their mother] as their primary source of emotional security, and that [her] imprisonment would be emotionally, developmentally, physically, materially, educationally and socially disadvantageous to them". If she was incarcerated, "the children would suffer: loss of their source of maternal and emotional support; loss of their home and familiar neighbourhood; disruption in school routines, possible problems in transporting to and from school; impact on their healthy developmental process; and separation of the siblings" (para. 67). The Court had been also informed that she "appears to be a devoted mother whose life revolves around her three children, that she has a loving, nurturing and caring relationship with all three boys, and that all of the children's basic needs are currently being met" (para. 68). The Court further observed that the community should not be seen "simply as a vengeful mass uninterested in the moral and social recuperation of one of its members" (para. 75), and that all should "benefit more from her being placed under correctional supervision than from her being sent back to prison" (para. 76).

The CRC does not (nor could) define the best interests of the child in abstract. The criteria of their interpretation were addressed by the CoRC in its GC 14 (2013) "on the right of the child to have his or her best interests taken as a primary consideration (Art. 3, para. 1)" (CRC/C/GC/14).[33] According to the Committee, "the child's best interests is a threefold concept" (Article 6). It is:

- "A substantive right [...] directly applicable (self-executing) and can be invoked before a court".
- "A fundamental, interpretative legal principle [...]. The rights enshrined in the Convention and its Optional Protocols provide the framework for interpretation".
- "A rule of procedure: Whenever a decision is to be made that will affect a specific child, an identified group of children or children in general, the decision-making process must include an evaluation of the possible impact (positive or negative) of the decision on the child or children concerned".

The Committee affirms:

> 4. The concept of the child's best interests is aimed at ensuring both the full and effective enjoyment of all the rights recognized in the Convention and the holistic development of the child. [...] It recalls that there is no hierarchy of rights in the Convention; all the rights provided for therein are in the "child's best interests" and no right could be compromised by a negative interpretation of the child's best interests.
>
> 5. The full application of the concept of the child's best interests requires the development of a rights-based approach, engaging all actors, to secure the holistic physical, psychological, moral and spiritual integrity of the child and promote his or her human dignity.

The principle of the primacy of the best interests of the child displays, therefore, a large amplitude. It includes all actions and omissions which, directly or indirectly, may affect children, individually or collectively. So understood, practically all policies affect children in one way or another, including "the approval of budgets, the preparation, and development of which require the adoption of a best-interests-of-the-child perspective for it to be child-rights sensitive" (para. 31). It "demands a continuous process of child rights impact assessment (CRIA)" (para. 35).

The obligations relating to the primacy of the best interests of the child concern:

> 25. … all public and private social welfare institutions, courts of law, administrative authorities and legislative bodies involving or concerning children. Although parents are not explicitly mentioned in Article 3, paragraph 1, the best interests of the child "will be their basic concern" (Article 18, para. 1).

The institutions concerned are "not only those related to economic, social and cultural rights (e.g. care, health, environment, education, business, leisure and play, etc.), but also institutions dealing with civil rights and freedoms (e.g. birth registration, protection against violence in all settings, etc.)" (para. 26).

The separation of a child from his or her parents, in particular, should not be justified just for "economic reasons" (para. 61) or "on the grounds of a disability of either the child or his or her parents" (para. 63). It should be "a last resort measure", when the protection of the child cannot be assured by "less intrusive measures" (para. 61).

The principle of the best interests of the child also serves to resolve possible conflicts between the rights of the child or between these and other interests, including those of parents. For instance:

> 83. There might be situations where "protection" factors affecting a child (e.g. which may imply limitation or restriction of rights) need to be assessed in relation to measures of "empowerment" (which implies the full exercise of rights without restriction). In such situations, the age and maturity of the child should guide the balancing of the elements. The physical, emotional, cognitive and social development of the child should be taken into account to assess the level of maturity of the child.

It is contrary to the best interests of the child "if the Law automatically gives parental responsibilities to either or both parents" (para. 67). In any case, "definitive and irreversible decisions" (para. 84) should be avoided.

74. Applying a best-interests approach to decision-making means assessing the safety and integrity of the child at the current time; however, the precautionary principle also requires assessing the possibility of future risk and harm and other consequences of the decision for the child's safety.

[...]

82. In weighing the various elements, one needs to bear in mind that the purpose of assessing and determining the best interests of the child is to ensure the full and effective enjoyment of the rights recognized in the Convention and its Optional Protocols, and the holistic development of the child.

Consequently, the principle of the best interests of the child is "a dynamic concept" (para. 11) whose "content must be determined on a case-by-case basis" (para. 32), needing "a degree of flexibility in its application" (para. 39). Having a metalegal content, it should be determined, "where possible, by a multidisciplinary team of well-trained professionals with appropriate judicial involvement" (para. 64). In this regard, the Constitutional Court of South Africa said in *Case M v The State Centre for Child Law (S v M (CCT 53/06) [2007] ZACC 18; 2008 (3) SA 232 (CC) (26 September* 2007)[34]: "In matters concerning children it is important that courts be furnished with the best quality of information that can reasonably be obtained in the circumstances" (para. 9).

Being a principle-interface between the universality and the cultural dimensions of the rights of the child, the CRC does not disregard "the importance of the traditions and cultural values of each people for the protection and harmonious development of the child" (penultimate paragraph of the Preamble). However, it must be ensured that the best interests of the child are not *familiarised* or *nationalised*, to serve as a Trojan Horse of cultural relativism or other interests incompatible with respect for the dignity and rights of the child. In effect (CRC/C/GC/14)[35]:

34. ... it may also leave room for manipulation; the concept of the child's best interests has been abused by Governments and other State authorities to justify racist policies, for example; by parents to defend their own interests in custody disputes; by professionals who could not be bothered, and who dismiss the assessment of the child's best interests as irrelevant or unimportant.

No cultural particularities may justify disrespect for the best interests of the child. The practice of sexual mutilation, for example, is not compatible with respect for the rights of the child. In Ecuador, the *Código de la Niñez y*

Adolescencia (Code of the Childhood and Adolescence)[36] states that the principle of the best interests of the child "prevails over the principle of ethnic and cultural diversity" (Article 11). The CoRC said in its Concluding Observations on a report of Nicaragua (CRC/C/15/Add.36, 1995)[37]:

> 9. The Committee is concerned that traditional cultural attitudes towards children and their role in the family and society may contribute to hampering the implementation of the Convention. In this connection, the Committee notes that an understanding of children as a subject of rights does not appear to be fully reflected in legislative and other measures in the State Party and as a result may prevent children in Nicaragua from fully enjoying their fundamental rights as recognized in the Convention.

In this respect, Philip Alston (1994) noted:

> We can conceive of the different human rights in terms of concentric circles of increasing responsiveness or flexibility to cultural factors as we move further away from the central and less flexible norms. In the centre, we might find norms relating to the physical and mental integrity of the human person. [...] In the field of children's rights a similar typology could readily be developed. While the best interests principle would be applicable across the board to all of the rights, its significance or influence will clearly be greater the further we are from the central core of survival and development rights. (p. 19)

What is the quintessence of the "best interests of the child"?

The brief preamble of the 1924 Geneva Declaration[38] proclaims that "mankind owes to the Child the best it has to give" (in French: *l'humanité se doit de donner à l'enfant le meilleur d'elle-même*; in Spanish: *la humanidad debe dar al niño lo mejor que puede darle*). These words have been revisited in the last paragraph of the preamble of the 1959 Declaration[39]: "*Whereas* mankind owes to the child the best it has to give". They were kept in the first project for a Convention on the Rights of the Child presented by Poland to the UN Commission on Human Rights, in 1978, but have been left out in the final text adopted in 1989. However, they are probably the loveliest and noblest words of the IHRL and may be considered the key to the interpretation and application of the primacy of the best interests of the child.

Indeed, is it not the *best* that Humankind has to give to its children the Ethics of Human Rights as the quintessence of its conscience and ideal? If it is so, the 1989 Convention is its best *gift*. It is like an *ethical lighthouse* that should illuminate and guide adults in their search and respect for the child's best interests. Interpreted within the framework of the 1989 Convention, the best interests of the child are superior to the cultural, national, family and other interests not compatible with his/her rights, may be superior also to his/her immediate interests, and are not different from the best interests of a democratic society and of humankind in becoming.

The best that children are entitled to expect from adults should include: not being deprived of their childhood,[40] not being abandoned to their rights, not being compelled to be in the image and likeness of mothers and fathers.

3.3.2 *Love, Respect and Responsibility for the Child*

Love is the most powerful human sentiment. The desire to be loved is the most profound expression of the most profound need of a human being, namely: to be recognised. That is why love is perhaps the most universal and lasting theme in the history of literature and arts. There is a "universal library consecrated to love", observed Lucy Vincent (2004). "All peoples sing songs of love, write poems of love, tell myths and legends founded on love, play magic to provoke love and, in extreme cases, commit suicide because of disappointed love [and homicide as well]" (pp. 9, 107).

Love is a theme also frequent in the history of childhood and education. However, loving children is not as *natural* a feeling as it is generally deemed. Philippe Ariès (1960) concluded that in Europe "a new feeling of childhood has emerged" between the 13th and the 17th centuries (p. 179). Elizabeth Badinter (1980) came to the conclusion that "love, as a familial and social value, was absent during the period of our history preceding the mid-18th century" (p. 39). Jean-Pierre Néraudau (1984) to counter, however: "The thesis is seductive, but may be reversed: And what if this natural instinct was a primary driver but capable of being overshadowed during certain historical periods?" (p. 340).

Psychoanalyst Françoise Dolto (1981) observed that, "because it is endowed with the symbolic function, the human being interiorises the code of its relationship with others, it loves itself as it is loved by others" (p. 279). Addressing the Oxford Union (University of Oxford, United Kingdom) on 6 March 2001, to lunch his initiative 'Heal The Kids',[41] Michael Jackson said that he was "the product of a lack of a childhood", and proposed a Children's Universal Bill of Rights, the first of which was: "The right to be loved, without having to earn it". Indeed, "if you don't have that memory of being loved, you are condemned to search the world for something to fill you up. But no matter how much money you make or how famous you become, you will still feel empty. What you are really searching for is unconditional love, unqualified acceptance". In the

Declaration of the Psychological Rights of the Child adopted by the 3rd Colloquium of the International School Psychology Association, held in New York on 12 July 1979 – International Year of the Child – the first right was: "The right to love, affection, and understanding" (in Veerman, 1992, p. 498).

Does the child have a right to love?

The 1959 Declaration and the 1989 Convention are not unaware of the value of affectivity for the well-being and development of the child. The Declaration[42] affirms: "The child, for the full and harmonious development of his personality, needs love and understanding. He shall, wherever possible, grow up in the care and under the responsibility of his parents, and, in any case, in an atmosphere of affection and of moral and material security" (Principle 6). The Convention[43] reaffirms: "Recognising that the child, for the full and harmonious development of his or her personality, should grow up in a family environment, in an atmosphere of happiness, love and understanding" (Preamble, para. 6). Along the same lines, the Recommendation 874 (1979) on a European Charter on the Rights of the Child (Parliamentary Assembly of the Council of Europe)[44] read: "Considering that abuse should not be taken as solely physical punishment inflicted upon children by parents, guardians or custodians but as a wider problem covering all physical and emotional ill-treatment, neglect and also denial of love and affection", Governments "must take into account the importance for children of love and affection as much as their need for material assistance" (para. 12). The Constitution of Colombia (1991) provides in its Article 44: "The fundamental rights of children are: ... care and love ...".[45] The Israel Supreme Court said in *Case Criminal Appeal 4596/98 Plonit v. A.G. 54(1) P.D.* [*2000*][46] relating to corporal punishment: "The child depends upon the parents, is entitled to parental love, protection and the parents' gentle touch".

There cannot be a *right to love*, however.

Human rights are the juridical expression of a feeling of love for our common humanity. In 1948, during the drafting of the UDHR, at the 90th meeting of the UN General Assembly Third Committee, on 1 October (A/C.3/SR.90),[47] the Delegation of Colombia (Ramirez Moreno) said that: "The Declaration expressed the same love of mankind that had moved all great political thinkers since Plato". Nevertheless, the formal recognition of a right to love would exceed the power of Law and could not guarantee the feeling of love. Transforming a need into right, passing from a moral duty to a legal obligation, implies determining who bears the correspondent obligations, as well as the possibility of appeal in case of non-compliance. Well, in the realm of feelings, there cannot be obligations or guarantees. Only in grammar, the *imperative* to love may be pronounced. As Kant said, "love, as affection, cannot be imposed".[48] Indeed: "Love is a matter of feeling, not of willing, and I cannot love because I will to, still less because I ought to (I cannot be constrained to love); so a duty to love is an absurdity' (as cited in Liao, 2009, p. 347). Friedrich Nietzsche wrote in *Human, All Too Human* (1878)[49]: "Actions can be promised, but not feelings, for these are involuntary. Whoever promises somebody to love him always [...] promises something that it is out of his power to bestow" (para. 58).

The South African High Court, Transvaal Provincial Division, observed in *Case Jooste v Botha 2000* (2) *SA 199* (*T*) *at 210C-D/E*[50] relating to an illegitimate son who claimed that he had never received from his father (who never recognised him and with whom the mother never came to live) the "parental care" to which he was entitled, in accordance with Article 28.1.b of the Constitution:

> There are two aspects of a parent-child relationship. The economic aspect of providing for the child's *physical* needs and the intangible aspect of providing for his or her psychological, emotional and developmental needs. The best interests of the child demand an environment of love, affection and consideration. This exception raises the question of whether the moral duty to provide the latter is legally enforceable.

The Court had to answer two questions: "What is the nature of this 'right'? Is it a right in the legal sense?" It concluded that "the Constitution does not state that parents are obliged to love and cherish their children". It does not recognise a "'right' of a child to be loved [...]. A bond of love was not a legal bond". Love cannot be "kindled by the Sheriff's writ". *Lex non cogit ad impossibilium*: "The law will not enforce the impossible. It cannot create love and affection where there is none".

That is why love is a term so unusual in IHRL. A rare appearance is found in the Declaration on the Promotion Among Youth of the Ideals of Peace, Mutual Respect and Understanding Between Peoples (A/RES/2037 (XX), 7 December 1965),[51] that reads:

> *Principle* VI
>
> A major aim in educating the young shall be to develop all their faculties and to train them to acquire higher moral qualities, to be deeply attached to the noble ideals of peace, liberty, the dignity and equality of all men, and imbued with respect and love for humanity and its creative achievements.

Another appearance is found in the World Declaration on Higher Education for the Twenty-first Century: Vision and Action and Framework for Priority

Action for Change and Development in Higher Education, adopted by the World Conference on Higher Education in the Twenty-First Century: Vision and Action (9 October 1998).[52] It reads: "Ultimately, higher education should aim at the creation of a new society – non-violent and non-exploitative – consisting of highly cultivated, motivated and integrated individuals, inspired by love for humanity and guided by wisdom" (Article 6.d).

The love for a child is first, naturally, a feeling of biological attachment or of compassion towards a human being so fragile and dependent, but in the era of the rights of the child it should be first and foremost a *feeling of responsibility for his/her human rights*.

Children are entitled to the responsibility of adults both for their dignity and vulnerability. It is mainly a political responsibility, but it is primarily a parental responsibility, and a general one as well.

- *Political responsibility* is concerned with the protection and implementation of the rights of the child. It is firstly a responsibility of State, of course.
  Children are not politically loved when their dignity and rights are not fully recognised or protected in national legal systems; when their respect is hindered by cultural traditions and parents' beliefs; when they suffer from undernourishment and lack of primary health care; when they are victims of wars and other forms of physical and psychological violence; when they are abandoned, abused or exploited; when they are deprived of their human right to education, etc.
- *Parental responsibility* for children is primary and paramount. It is a caring, affective and pedagogical one.
  - *Caring responsibility* for the protection and promotion of their integrity, health, and well-being.
  - *Affective responsibility* for the tenderness they vitally need to grow up happy, in harmony with themselves and others.
  - *Pedagogical responsibility* for the development of their personality, as holistic as possible, shared with education professionals.
- *General responsibility* is highlighted by the Declaration on the Right and Responsibility of Individuals, Groups and Organs of Society to Promote and Protect Universally Recognized Human Rights and Fundamental Freedoms (UN, 1998).

In sum: A child does not have a right to love but is entitled to *the love of his/her human rights*. In this sense, the entire CRC is an oath of love.

3.3.3 *Evolving Autonomy of the Child*

As a child develops, he/she becomes obviously more and more autonomous.

During the drafting of the CRC, in the context of the debate raised by participation rights, it was suggested the inclusion in it of a general clause on the evolving capacities of the child, which would eventually be worded in Article 5:

> States Parties shall respect the responsibilities, rights and duties of parents or, where applicable, the members of the extended family or community as provided for by local custom, legal guardians or other persons legally responsible for the child, to provide, in a manner consistent with the evolving capacities of the child, appropriate direction and guidance in the exercise by the child of the rights recognized in the present Convention.

The position of Article 5 in the Convention's structure is significant of the role assigned to it as a provision balancing the rights of the child and the family. These concerns are carefully articulated: in the terms' sequence – "the responsibilities, rights and duties of parents" or other persons responsible for the child – "the responsibilities" precede (because they are the justification of) both the "rights" and the "duties":
- to give the child "in a manner consistent with [his or her] evolving capacities",
- "appropriate direction and guidance in the exercise by the child of the rights recognized in the present Convention".

This idea is also mentioned in Articles 12.1 and 14.2 and is connected with other provisions. Article 12.1 indicates as the criterion "the age and maturity of the child" that is an objective (age) and subjective (maturity) one. Indeed, the needs and capacities change during the successive childhood ages, from the physical and psychological viewpoint. There is a great historic, cultural and legal diversity regarding the recognition of a child's maturity and capacities. Domestic legislation is variable concerning minimum age for the exercise of some rights. It is more reasonable to decide on a case-by-case basis, instead of fixing minimum ages in the abstract, seeking to find the right balance between the child's need for protection and his/her participatory rights laid down in Articles 12 to 15. The CoRC noticed in GC 12 (CRC/C/GC/12/2009)[53]:

> 1. Article 12 of the Convention on the Rights of the Child (the Convention) is a unique provision in a human rights treaty; it addresses the legal and social status of children who, on the one hand, lack the full autonomy of adults but, on the other, are subjects of rights. [...]
> 2. The right of all children to be heard and taken seriously constitutes one of the fundamental values of the Convention.

In its Concluding Observations on the reports presented by States Parties to the Convention, the Committee refers frequently to the right of the child to be heard, highlighting its connection with the best interests of the child. For instance, it said in its Concluding Observations on a China's report (CRC/C/15/Add.56, 1996)[54]: "It is important that awareness be developed of the child as a subject of rights and not only as a recipient of protection" (para. 33). In this respect, the Slovakian Initial Report to the Committee (CRC/C/11/Add.17, 1998)[55] read:

> 240. At the international level, it has been repeatedly emphasized that childhood should not be "life's waiting room" but it should be "life itself". That is why the legal situation, in which the child on the eve of his or her eighteenth birthday is almost "rightless" and the next day with full rights, cannot be accepted any longer. It is, therefore, necessary to create conditions for the differentiated and gradual emancipation of children in all areas of day-to-day life. [...]

The principle of the evolving autonomy of the child is expressly taken into account by the African Charter on the Rights and Welfare of the Child (1990)[56] when it refers to "the religious and moral education of the child in a manner consistent with the evolving capacities of the child" (Article 11.4). The importance of this principle was highlighted in a UNICEF's publication (2002):

> Using the concept of "evolving capacities" has avoided the need for the Convention to set arbitrary age limits or definitions of maturity tied to particular issues. The "evolving capacities" of the child is one of the Convention's key concepts – an acknowledgement that children's development towards independent adulthood must be respected and promoted throughout childhood. It is linked to Article 12's requirement that the views of children should be given "due weight in accordance with the age and maturity of the child". The concept is repeated in Article 14: parents and legal guardians may provide direction to the child, in relation to the child's right to freedom of thought, conscience and religion, in a manner consistent with his or her evolving capacities. (p. 91)

In this respect, Gerison Lansdown (2005) wrote:

> For the first time in an international human rights treaty, the Convention on the Rights of the Child introduces the concept of the 'evolving capacities' of the child. [...]

> The Convention, for the first time in international law, establishes a direct relationship between the child and the State that challenges the presumption that parents have rights of ownership over the child. It renders the child visible as a subject of rights within the family, entitled to protection on his or her own behalf, and empowers the State to intervene, when necessary, to protect the rights of the child, in recognition that the best interests of children are not always protected by parents. The rights and responsibilities of parents to provide direction and guidance to children are therefore not as a consequence of their 'ownership' of the child, but rather a function of parenthood until the child is capable of exercising those rights on his or her own behalf. (pp. ix, x)

3.3.4 *Priority of Children*

The priority of children is, in a way, an extension of the principle of the primacy of the best interests of the child. Article 3.1 of the 1989 Convention uses the singular "child" and the plural "children". These individual and collective dimensions were highlighted by the CoRC in its GC 7 (CRC/C/GC/2005/7/Rev.1),[57] where it refers to the "Best interests of individual children" and the "Best interests of young children as a group or constituency" (para. 13).

The priority of children has been recognised both before and after the 1989 Convention.

Before, the 1924 Geneva Declaration stated: "The child must be the first to receive relief in times of distress" (para. 3). The 1959 Declaration restated (but mitigatingly): "The child shall in all circumstances be among the first to receive protection and relief" (Principle 8). After the 1989 Convention, the priority of children has been reaffirmed by the International Community in various important documents.

The Declaration on the Survival, Protection and Development of Children, approved by the World Summit for Children, on 30 September 1990,[58] closed by stating: "There can be no task nobler than giving every child a better future" (para. 25). In order to achieve this, the Plan of Action for Implementing the World Declaration on the Survival, Protection and Development of Children in the 1990s stressed that the Declaration commanded "the principle of a 'first call for children' – a principle that the essential needs of children should be given high priority in the allocation of resources, in bad times as well as in good times, at national and international as well as at family levels" (para. 33). And justified:

> 3. Progress for children should be a key goal of overall national development. [...] As their individual development and social contribution

will shape the future of the world, investment in children's health, nutrition and education is the foundation for national development. [...]

36. ... There is no cause which merits a higher priority than the protection and development of children, on whom the survival, stability and advancement of all nations – and, indeed, of human civilization – depends.

The Programme of Action of the International Conference on Population and Development, approved by the International Conference on Population and Development (Cairo, Egypt, 1994)[59] recommended: "All States and families should give the highest possible priority to children" (Principle 11).

Meanwhile, the Vienna Declaration and Programme of Action (1993) had stated (I)[60]:

21 ... In all actions concerning children, non-discrimination and the best interest of the child should be primary considerations and the views of the child given due weight. [...] International cooperation and solidarity should be promoted to support the implementation of the Convention and the rights of the child that should be a priority in the United Nations system-wide action on human rights.

The priority of children has been also reaffirmed at the national level. For example, the Constitution of Paraguay[61] commands, in Article 54: "The rights of the child should prevail, in case of conflict". The Ecuadorian *Código de la Niñez y Adolescencia* (Code of the Childhood and Adolescence) states (Article 12)[62]: "When formulating and executing public policies and providing resources, absolute priority should be given to childhood and adolescence, which should be assured, in addition, preferential access to the public services and any kind of attention they may require. Special priority should be given to children under six years of age".

The document "A World Fit for Children" adopted by the Special Session on Children of the UN General Assembly (2002) includes a Declaration and a Plan of Action.[63] In the Declaration it is recognised that "the 1990s was a decade of great promises and modest achievements for the world's children" (para. 11), but: "The experience of the past decade has confirmed that the needs and rights of children must be a priority in all development efforts" (para. 13).

3. [We] are determined to seize this historic opportunity to change the world for and with children. Accordingly, we reaffirm our commit-

ment to complete the unfinished agenda of the World Summit for Children and to address other emerging issues vital to the achievement of the longer-term goals and objectives endorsed at recent major United Nations summits and conferences, in particular the United Nations Millennium Declaration, through national action and international cooperation.

[...]

5. We stress our commitment to create a world fit for children, in which sustainable human development, taking into account the best interests of the child, is founded on principles of democracy, equality, non-discrimination, peace and social justice and the universality, indivisibility, interdependence and interrelatedness of all human rights, including the right to development.

More precisely:

7. We hereby call upon all members of society to join us in a global movement that will help to build a world fit for children by upholding our commitment to the following principles and objectives:
    1. *Put children first.*
    2. *Eradicate poverty: invest in children.*
    3. *Leave no child behind.*
    4. *Care for every child.*
    5. *Educate every child.*
    6. *Protect children from harm and exploitation.*
    7. *Protect children from war.*
    8. *Combat HIV/AIDS.*
    9. *Listen to children and ensure their participation.*
    10. *Protect the Earth for children.*

The first statement of the Plan of Action reads:

14. A world fit for children is one in which all children get the best possible start in life and have access to a quality basic education, including primary education that is compulsory and available free to all, and in which all children, including adolescents, have ample opportunity to develop their individual capacities in a safe and supportive environment. We will promote the physical, psychological, spiritual, social, emotional, cognitive and cultural development of children as a matter of national and global priority.

3.4 Revolution of the Rights of the Child

The recognition of the rights of the child has meant a historical deepening of the logic and ideal of human rights.

The drafting of the CRC was crossed by the tension between two approaches: *protection-approach* (as "childhood is entitled to special care and assistance") and *rights-approach* (the child as a holder of human rights). A *child-centred approach* prevailed, giving rise to a New International Law of the Child that accomplished the movement from the traditional (naturalist) representation of the *child-object of Law* towards a new (ethical) vision of the *child-subject of rights.* In particular, the *patria potestas* (power/authority of the father) has been replaced with 'parental responsibility'.

New Law of the Child

The Law of the Child has traditionally been a Minors' Law, as a subdomain of Family Law, whose pillars are the filiation and the parental power. In this regard, Françoise Dekeuwer-Défossez (1991) wrote that, "if historically we may affirm that there has always been a Law of Childhood, it was more of a set of rights of adults over children. The Roman Law, as the ancient French Law, regarded the child as an object of parental power and the future of lineage. That is, the child was not considered as a holder of rights" (p. 4).

The 1959 Declaration and the 1989 Convention proclaimed a different conception: The Law of Childhood is no more merely about the rules applicable to children, but about their *human rights*. A child is not yet an adult but is already a human person. He/she is physically smaller, but not humanly lesser. The difference was highlighted in a UN Manual (by Santos Pais) as follows:

> In the international instruments adopted before the Convention, children were often considered as a reflexive, sometimes even invisible reality within the overall context of the family, the emphasis being essentially put on the responsibility, freedom or right of parents. The prevailing consideration was that children should be cared for, protected and guided by their parents within the unity, harmony and privacy of the family, being assumed that there was a natural coincidence of interests between parents and their children, and that the child had no legitimate interests other than those of the family as a whole.
>
> With the Convention, children's rights are given autonomy – not with the intention of affirming them in opposition to the rights of adults or as an alternative to the rights of parents, but in order to bring into the scene a new dimension: the consideration of the perspective of the child within the framework of the essential value of the family. The child is

> therefore recognized in his or her fundamental dignity and individuality, with the right to be different and diverge in his or her assessment of reality. (United Nations, 1997, pp. 445, 446)

The core of the new International Law of the Child lies in the rights and freedoms recognised in Articles 12 to 17 of the 1989 Convention: the right to express his/her own views in all matters affecting the child, duly taking into account her/his age and maturity (Article 12); the right to freedom of expression (Article 13); the right to freedom of thought, conscience and religion (Article 14); the right to freedom of association and peaceful assembly (Article 15); the right to privacy (Article 16); the right of access to information (Article 17).

The *pedigree* of the new International Law of the Child is unequivocally imprinted in four Recommendations of the Parliamentary Assembly of the Council of Europe, adopted before and after the CRC:

– Recommendation 874 (1979) on a European Charter on the Rights of the Child[64]

> I. *General principles*
> a. Children must no longer be considered as parents' property, but must be recognized as individuals with their own rights and needs;
> [...]
>
> II. *The legal position of the child*
>
> [...]
> c. The concept of "parental authority" must be superseded by "parental responsibility", and by a clear description of children's rights as individual family members,

– Recommendation 1074 (1988) on Family Policy[65]

> 9. Realising that any family policy today must face the new situation resulting from the emancipation of women and its impact on maternity, and must bear in mind two principles: first, the democratisation of the family which implies equality among its members and respect for the rights of each and, secondly, the exercise of free choice by the partners;

– Recommendation 1121 (1990) on the Rights of Children[66]

> 5. Considering that, in addition to the right to be protected, children have rights they may independently exercise themselves – even against opposing adults;

> 6. Considering that parental powers and the authority of other adults on children are derived from duty for protection and should exist only as long as they are necessary for the protection of the person and property of the child;
> 7. Considering that these powers decline as the child matures and that a child is subsequently able to exercise an increasing number of rights;

– Recommendation 1286 (1996) on a European Strategy for Children[67]

> 5. Children are citizens of the society of today and tomorrow. Society has a long-term responsibility to support children and has to acknowledge the rights of the family in the interest of the child. Responding to children's rights, interests and needs must be a political priority. The Assembly is convinced that respect for children's rights and greater equality between children and adults will help preserve the pact between generations and will contribute towards democracy.

The new International Law of the Child is thus the culmination of an evolution that means a revolution, as it is generally acknowledged by both its defenders and detractors. For example, Alain Finkielkraut, a French philosopher very critical of the Convention, wrote: "... a veritable mental revolution took place on 20 November 1989, in the UN".[68] The Revolution of the Rights of the Child (see Monteiro, 2002, 2008, 2010) is, however, the most candid and peaceful one: it consists simply in fully recognising and treating children as human persons. It is an ethical and juridical political revolution, but above all, it is the principle of a deeper cultural revolution, because it must transform mentalities and customs.

The revolutionary meaning of the rights of the child is condensed in the poem on "Children" (*The Prophet*, 1923)[69] by Khalil Gibran, a Lebanese American philosopher, writer and artist:

> And a woman who held a babe against her bosom said, "Speak to us of Children".
> And he said:
> Your children are not your children.
> They are the sons and daughters of Life's longing for itself.
> They come through you but not from you,
> And though they are with you, yet they belong not to you.
> You may give them your love but not your thoughts.

> For they have their own thoughts.
> You may house their bodies but not their souls,
> For their souls dwell in the house of tomorrow, which you cannot visit, not even in your dreams.
> You may strive to be like them but seek not to make them like you.
> For life goes not backward nor tarries with yesterday.
> You are the bows from which your children as living arrows are sent forth.
> The archer sees the mark upon the path of the infinite, and He bends you with His might that His arrows may go swift and far.
> Let your bending in the archer's hand be for gladness.
> For even as he loves the arrow that flies, so He loves also the bow that is stable.

The CRC is a visionary text. That is why the idea of 'rights of the child' remains resisted.

Resistance

The resistance to the rights of the child is illustrated by certain reservations made by States Parties to the 1989 Convention, which are incompatible with the International Law when they have a too general scope, or claim the primacy of national Law, or safeguard traditional cultural practices incompatible with respect for the child's human rights. For example, Singapore considered that Articles 19 and 37 of the Convention do not prohibit "the judicious application of corporal punishment in the best interest of the child" (2.c).[70] This kind of reservations was formally rejected by other States Parties. Finland, for instance, declared: "The Government of Finland considers that in their present formulation these reservations made by the Republic of Singapore are incompatible with the object and purpose of the said Convention and, therefore, inadmissible under Article 51, paragraph 2, of the said Convention". The CRC Article 51.2 reads as follows: "A reservation incompatible with the object and purpose of the present Convention shall not be permitted".[71] It reflects Article 19.c of the Vienna Convention on the Law of Treaties (1969).[72]

The position of the USA regarding the CRC is a surprising example of resistance.[73] It is the only UN Member State that, although having already signed the Convention (1995), has still not ratified it, despite having played an important role in its *travaux préparatoires* (as well as in the creation of the United Nations and the legislative history of the UDHR). The apocalyptic arguments of the opponents to the ratification are not shared by numerous American NGOs and eminent jurists who think like Thomas Bürgenthal (1988): "The position of the U.S. as far as international human rights are concerned is a bundle of contradictions" (p. 211). It is contradictory, for instance, to the Foreign Assistance Act (Section 116),[74] which makes assistance conditional to the respect for human rights internationally recognised.

A confrontation of mentalities also occurred in France during the debate of a *Proposition de Loi relative à l'interdiction des violences éducatives ordinaires* (*n° 1331*) (Draft law concerning the prohibition of ordinary educational violence), in the *Commission des Lois Constitutionnelles, de la Législation et de l'Administration Générale de la République* (Commission of Constitutional Laws, Legislation and General Administration of the Republic), in November 2018. According to the respective Report,[75] statements like these were made: "I find this debate ridiculous"; "It is not up to the State to tell parents how they should treat and educate their children. [...] I don't see, therefore, the interest of this law"; "If this law is adopted, can we no more say anything to children to educate them?"; "This draft law supports the weakening of parental authority!".

Underlying most resistance against the recognition of rights to children is this misunderstanding: to recognise rights to children is to take them away from parents. The rights of children are not rights against adults, they make them better human beings, instead. The rights of children and the rights of adults are in a circular relation analogous to the Möbius Ring: the protection of the rights of children begins with the protection of the rights of adults, which begins with the protection of the rights of the child. If they are respected, children will be adults more developed, conscious, creative, happy, responsible. And better citizens and better educators of their children.

If "the right to education has appeared more frequently in discussions on the international rights of the child than any other right" (Bueren, 1995, p. 232), it is because it is central in the life of a child. The right to education is the Bastille of the Revolution of the Rights of the Child.

Notes

1 http://ap.ohchr.org/documents/alldocs.aspx?doc_id=2880
2 See p. 20 in: https://shodhganga.inflibnet.ac.in/bitstream/10603/202241/1/thesis%20of%20dinesh%20kumar%20singh.pdf
3 https://www.gutenberg.org/ebooks/10335
4 www.un-documents.net/gdrc1924.htm
5 https://www.un.org/en/universal-declaration-human-rights/
6 www.abanet.org/humanrights/central/declaration_child.pdf
7 www2.ohchr.org/english/law/crc.htm

8 www2.ohchr.org/english/bodies/crc/docs/AdvanceVersions/CRC-C-GC-12.pdf
9 http://tbinternet.ohchr.org/_layouts/treatybodyexternal/Download.aspx?symbolno=CRC/C/5&Lang=en
10 http://tbinternet.ohchr.org/_layouts/treatybodyexternal/Download.aspx?symbolno=CRC%2fGC%2f2003%2f5&Lang=en
11 See https://www.ilo.org/global/standards/subjects-covered-by-international-labour-standards/child-labour/lang--en/index.htm
12 https://hudoc.echr.coe.int/fre#{%22itemid%22:[%22001-57534%22]}
13 See https://rm.coe.int/CoERMPublicCommonSearchServices/DisplayDCTMContent?documentId=090000168047 4a4b
14 http://eur-lex.europa.eu/legal-content/EN/TXT/?uri=CELEX:12012P/TXT
15 https://www.ohchr.org/en/professionalinterest/pages/crc.aspx
16 https://www.ohchr.org/EN/ProfessionalInterest/Pages/OPICCRC.aspx
17 https://www.coe.int/en/web/conventions/full-list/-/conventions/rms/090000168007cdaf
18 http://www.achpr.org/instruments/child/
19 https://tbinternet.ohchr.org/_layouts/treatybodyexternal/Download.aspx?symbolno=CRC%2FGC%2F2002%2F2&Lang=en
20 http://assembly.coe.int/nw/xml/XRef/Xref-XML2HTML-en.asp?fileid=16799&lang=en
21 http://enoc.eu/?page_id=8
22 https://undocs.org/A/RES/836(IX)
23 http://tbinternet.ohchr.org/_layouts/treatybodyexternal/Download.aspx?symbolno=CRC%2FGC%2F2001%2F1&Lang=en
24 http://tbinternet.ohchr.org/_layouts/treatybodyexternal/Download.aspx?symbolno=CRC%2fGC%2f2003%2f5&Lang=en
25 http://tbinternet.ohchr.org/_layouts/treatybodyexternal/Download.aspx?symbolno=CRC%2fC%2fGC%2f8&Lang=en
26 www.saflii.org/za/cases/ZACC/2007/18.pdf
27 https://digitallibrary.un.org/record/863167/files/A_C-3_SR-786-EN.pdf
28 Note 31 in *M v The State Centre for Child Law* (*S v M* (*CCT 53/06*) [*2007*] *ZACC 18; 2008* (*3*) *SA 232* (*CC*) (*26 September 2007*). It further observed: "The problem, then, is how to apply the paramountcy principle in a meaningful way without unduly obliterating other valuable and constitutionally-protected interests" (para. 25). (www.saflii.org/za/cases/ZACC/2007/18.pdf).
29 www.unicef.org/colombia/pdf/codigo-infancia-com.pdf
30 http://childlineindia.org.in/Goa-Children-Act.htm
31 https://tbinternet.ohchr.org/_layouts/treatybodyexternal/Download.aspx?symbolno=CRC%2FC%2F15%2FAdd.151&Lang=en
32 www.saflii.org/za/cases/ZACC/2007/18.pdf
33 https://undocs.org/en/CRC/C/GC/14
34 www.saflii.org/za/cases/ZACC/2007/18.pdf
35 https://www2.ohchr.org/English/bodies/crc/docs/GC/CRC_C_GC_14_ENG.pdf
36 http://biblioteca.defensoria.gob.ec/handle/37000/2112?mode=full
37 https://tbinternet.ohchr.org/_layouts/treatybodyexternal/Download.aspx?symbolno=CRC%2FC%2F15%2FAdd.36&Lang=en
38 http://www.un-documents.net/gdrc1924.htm
39 http://www.un-documents.net/a14r1386.htm
40 There is an International Play Association – Promoting the Child's Right to Play (http://ipaworld.org).

41 Available in January 2019: http://michaeljacksonchosenvoices.com/tag/oxford-address/
42 http://www.un-documents.net/a14r1386.htm
43 https://www.ohchr.org/en/professionalinterest/pages/crc.aspx
44 http://assembly.coe.int/nw/xml/XRef/Xref-XML2HTML-en.asp?fileid=14908&lang=en
45 http://es.presidencia.gov.co/normativa/constitucion-politica
46 https://endcorporalpunishment.org/human-rights-law/national-high-level-court-judgments/israel-2000-supreme-court-judgment/
47 https://digitallibrary.un.org/record/617781
48 *Liebe als Neigung kann nicht geboten werden.* (www.gutenberg.org/cache/epub/5682/pg5682.html)
49 www.gutenberg.org/files/38145/38145-h/38145-h.htm#HISTORY_OF_THE_MORAL_FEELINGS
50 https://dullahomarinstitute.org.za/childrens-rights/legal-resources/Cases%20and%20Judgements/High%20Courts/Jooste%20v%20Botha%20-%20Case%20No%201554-99.pdf
51 www.un-documents.net/a20r2037.htm
52 https://unesdoc.unesco.org/ark:/48223/pf0000141952/PDF/141952eng.pdf.multi
53 www2.ohchr.org/english/bodies/crc/docs/AdvanceVersions/CRC-C-GC-12.pdf
54 https://tbinternet.ohchr.org/_layouts/treatybodyexternal/Download.aspx?symbolno=CRC%2FC%2F15%2FAdd.56&Lang=en
55 https://tbinternet.ohchr.org/_layouts/treatybodyexternal/Download.aspx?symbolno=CRC%2FC%2F11%2FAdd.17&Lang=en
56 http://www.achpr.org/instruments/child/
57 www2.ohchr.org/english/bodies/crc/docs/AdvanceVersions/GeneralComment7Rev1.pdf
58 https://www.unicef.org/wsc/
59 www.un.org/popin/icpd2.htm
60 https://www.ohchr.org/EN/ProfessionalInterest/Pages/Vienna.aspx
61 http://www.diputados.gov.py/ww5/index.php/legislacion/constitucion-nacional
62 http://biblioteca.defensoria.gob.ec/handle/37000/2112?mode=full
63 https://www.unicef.org/specialsession/wffc/
64 http://assembly.coe.int/nw/xml/XRef/Xref-XML2HTML-en.asp?fileid=14908&lang=en
65 http://www.assembly.coe.int/nw/xml/XRef/Xref-XML2HTML-en.asp?fileid=15108&lang=en
66 http://www.assembly.coe.int/nw/xml/XRef/Xref-DocDetails-en.asp?FileID=15155&lang=en
67 http://assembly.coe.int/nw/xml/XRef/Xref-XML2HTML-EN.asp?fileid=15320&lang=en
68 *"La nouvelle statue de Pavel Morozov". Le Monde*, 1990, January 9. (https://archive.org/stream/LeMondeDiplomatique1990FranceFrench/Jan%2009%201990%2C%20Le%20Monde%20Diplomatique%2C%20%2313981%2C%20France%20%28fr%29_djvu.txt)
69 http://leb.net/gibran
70 https://treaties.un.org/Pages/ViewDetails.aspx?src=IND&mtdsg_no=IV-11&chapter=4&lang=en
71 https://www.ohchr.org/en/professionalinterest/pages/crc.aspx
72 https://treaties.un.org/doc/publication/unts/volume%201155/volume-1155-i-18232-english.pdf
73 www.fas.org/sgp/crs/row/RL33608.pdf
74 www.usaid.gov/sites/default/files/documents/1868/faa.pdf
75 http://www.assemblee-nationale.fr/15/pdf/rapports/r1414.pdf

References

Alston, Ph. (1994). The best interests principle: Towards a reconciliation of culture and human rights. In P. Alston (Ed.), *The best interests of the child – Reconciling culture and human rights* (pp. 1–25). Clarendon Press, UNICEF-International Child Development Center, Florence (Italy).

Ariès, Ph. (1960). *L'enfant et la vie familiale sous l'Ancien Régime*. Seuil.

Badinter, E. (1980). *L'amour en plus – Histoire de l'amour maternel (XVIIIe–XXe siècle)*. Flammarion.

Bueren, G. (1995). *The international law on the Rights of the Child* (International Studies in Human Rights, Vol. 35). Martinus Nijhoff Publishers.

Bürgenthal, Th. (1988). *International human rights*. West Publishing CO.

Chevallier, P. (1975). Le droit de l'enfant à l'éducation en France aux XIXe et XXe siècles. In *Recueil de la Société Jean Bodin pour l'histoire comparative des institutions, XXXIX – L'enfant – Cinquième partie: Le droit à l'éducation* (pp. 297–321). Éditions de la Librairie Encyclopédique.

Crampe-Casnabet, M. (1985). *Condorcet, lecteur des Lumières*. PUF.

Dekeuwer-Défossez, F. (1991). *Les droits de l'enfant*. PUF.

Dolto, F. (1981). *Au jeu du désir – Essais cliniques*. Seuil.

Hammarberg, Th. (2001). 19. Children. In A. Eide, C. Krause, & A. Rosas (Eds.), *Economic, social and cultural rights – A textbook* (pp. 353–372). Kluwer Law International.

Lansdown, G. (2005). *The evolving capacities of the child*. UNICEF. www.unicef-irc.org/publications/pdf/evolving-eng.pdf

Liao, S. M. (2009). The right of children to be loved. In M. Albertson Fineman & K. Worthington (Eds.), *What is right for children? – The competing paradigms of religion and human rights* (pp. 347–363). Ashgate.

Monteiro, A. R. (2002). *A Revolução dos Direitos da Criança* (Revolution of the Rights of the Child). Campo das Letras.

Monteiro, A. R. (2008). *La Revolución de los Derechos del Niño*. Editorial Popular.

Monteiro, A. R. (2010). *Direitos da Criança: Era uma vez ...* [Rights of the Child: It was once...]. Edições Almedina.

Moody, Z. (2016). *Les droits de l'enfant – Genèse, institutionnalisation et diffusion (1924–1989)*. Éditions Alphil-Presses Universitaires Suisses. https://archive-ouverte.unige.ch/unige:90940

Néraudau, J.-P. (1984). *Être enfant à Rome*. Éditions Payot & Rivages.

Pais, M. S. (1999). *A human rights conceptual framework for UNICEF*. UNICEF International Child Development Centre. www.unicef-irc.org/publications/pdf/essay9.pdf

Supino-Viterbo, V. (2000). *L'enfant mail-aimé*. Flammarion.

Todres, J., & Higinbotham, S. (2016). *Human rights in children's literature: Imagination and the narrative of law*. Oxford University Press.

UNICEF. (2002). *Implementation handbook for the Convention on the Rights of the Child* (prepared for UNICEF by Rachel Hodgkin and Peter Newell).

United Nations. (1997). *Manual on human rights reporting – Under six major international human rights instruments*. Geneva, HR/PUB/91/1 (Rev. 1). https://www.ohchr.org/documents/publications/manualhrren.pdf

Veerman, Ph. E. (1992). *The rights of the child and the changing image of the world*. Martinus Nijhoff Publishers.

Vincent, L. (2004). *Comment devient-on amoureux?* Odile Jacob Poches.

CHAPTER 4

Right to Education

Abstract

1. In the history of education, three eras may be roughly distinguished, before its recognition as a human right: education as mostly a familial and religious matter, the longest era; education as a national interest, from five centuries or so ago; education as an international concern, from the late 19th century. It is submitted that the major European precursors of the normative distinctiveness of the human right to education were Comenius (17th century) and Rousseau (18th century).
2. Although in the history of great concepts there is dawn when it is no longer night but day is not yet fully born either, talking about the recognition of a very 'right to education', as now understood, before the 20th century sounds anachronism.
3. The Universal Declaration Article 26 has become the source of an International Education Law that comprises provisions in much more than one hundred legal texts. Its universal most general normative framework is obviously the International Bill of Human Rights. The principal universal conventional categorical provisions are laid down in the Convention on the Rights of the Child. The Convention against Discrimination in Education remains its main specific instrument.
4. In accordance with the titles of the International Covenants on human rights, they fall into five categories: civil, political, economic, social and cultural. While the right to education has a cross-cutting content, it is generally included in 'cultural rights'.
5. The international terminology on the right to education and the respective translations are voluble and variable. Since the 1970s, the term "basic education" has begun to generalise, but there is no international consensus about its scope. Basic education/school means, in general, the segment of a school system that is compulsory and should be free.
6. As the educational phenomenon consists in learning, right to education fundamentally means right to learn. Therefore, determining its object amounts to answering the following main interrogations: Learning ... for what? ... what? ... how? ... The learnings that a right to education policy should ensure to meet the aims internationally agreed are not determined in its main provisions, but there are indications in other international texts.
7. The exigibility of the right to education concerns persons or entities with obligations or responsibilities regarding its satisfaction, i.e. to which it is opposable.

 | DOI: 10.1163/9789004462465_005

They are families, first and foremost, but the realisation of the whole object of the right to education exceeds their means. States are the principal responsible, legally and politically, for guaranteeing human rights, as we know. The International Community bears a subsidiary responsibility. The right to education is self-opposable too, i.e. a duty of each one towards himself/herself. There are also many NGOs devoted to the right to education.

8. States' obligations being paramount, they should be highlighted. They are general and specific. Their specific obligations concerning the right to education correspond to its triple normative content, following the distinction proposed. Therefore, they may be represented as three concentric circles: minimum, full, and expanded content/obligations.
9. States' full obligations regarding the right to education are generally categorised in the so-called '4-A scheme': Availability, Accessibility, Acceptability, Adaptability. Considering that acceptability and adaptability are largely overlapping and sometimes confused notions, and given the timeliness and comprehensiveness of the principle of quality education – which can subsume its acceptability and adaptability – as well as the overarching significance of the equity principle, in its relation with the principles of non-discrimination, equality and diversity, the 4-A Scheme could become: Availability, Accessibility, Quality, Equity.
10. Three paramount specific States' obligations are the following ones: all education shall be directed to the purpose of the right to education; everyone shall be guaranteed basic free compulsory schooling; private education shall be regulated and supervised.
11. The international protection of the right to education comes under general mechanisms common to other human rights, at the universal and regional levels, as well as special mechanisms set up especially by UNESCO.
12. The most important international Case Law on the right to education is that of the organs of the European Convention on Human Rights, whose jurisprudence is the most significant contribution of the European Education Law to the International Education Law.
13. The right to education displays some distinguishing characteristics. Its priority – that is relative because of the human rights interdependence – was repeatedly invoked during the *travaux préparatoires* of its major international provisions, is recognised by the International Human Rights Law, has been affirmed by jurisprudence and is supported by doctrine. It has been rediscovered, in a way, by the International Community since the last decade of the 20th century.
14. The recognition of the liberty of education preceded historically that of the right to education. With the proclamation of the latter, the relationship with the liberties of education included in its wording has become debated. Education

liberalisation and privatisation policies, from the 1980s, have revived the controversy. What is at stake is answering two main questions: Is children's education a "fundamental right" of parents? Is education privatisation compatible with the International Education Law?

15. The recognition of a "fundamental right" of parents concerning the education of their children would not be compatible with children's "human right" to education. As education privatisation is concerned, International Education Law excludes both a public monopole and the complete privatisation of education. States have an obligation to establish and to develop a public education system with a free compulsory component, as well as to adopt and supervise compliance with regulations ensuring that private provision of education meets international and national standards on the right to education.
16. The most significant feature of the UN 2030 Agenda for Sustainable Development is that it takes overtly a human rights approach (it contains more than ten references to them). So do the Incheon Declaration (2015) and the 2030 Education Agenda, which represent the most recent international vision and commitment towards the implementation of the right to education. It is a new vision pointing to an education in accordance with its human right quality, i.e. qualified by the following attributes: human right approach, humanistic, holistic, child-friendly, child-centred, empowering. It is a vision opposed, therefore, to an education captured by ethnic reflexes, religious beliefs, partisan indoctrination, or neoliberal economism.
17. Human rights indicators are quantitative/statistical and qualitative/normative references of achievement, in a complex relationship. The right to education indicators should *a fortiori* (for a still stronger reason) be both quantitative and qualitative.
18. Every education issue should be examined following a human right approach, according to which the right to education is Right to a Rightful Education.

4.1 Emergence of the Right to Education

In the history of education, three eras may be roughly distinguished, before its recognition as a human right:
- Education as mostly a familial and religious matter – the longest era.
- Education as a national interest – from five centuries or so ago.
- Education as an international concern – from the late 19th century.

This periodisation is next explained.

4.1.1 *Historical Highlights*

Along millennia, education has been taken as a *natural* extension of parents' power over their progeny-property, surrounded by the community's needs, interests and pressures, supported by religions.

Franciszek Przetacznik (1985) considered that:

> The right of an individual to education is expressed implicitly already by Plato and Aristotle, even though they treat this right in the context of the interests of the State. [...]
>
> ... Epictetus claims that individuals have the right to education, irrespective of their social and political status. The position of Epictetus concerning education constitutes a great step forward in the development of the idea of the recognition of the right to education of an individual as a basic human right. (p. 273)

In the opinion of Danielle Bonneau (1975), "in the classical Greek city we find a right to education and laws on it", but "the enormous mass of human beings in a Hellenistic realm have no right, not even moral, to education" (pp. 101, 109). Henri-Iréné Marrou (1948) noted that Plato and Aristotle deal with education in a purely subsidiary plan of their political thought. On the contrary, the Hellenistic philosophers consecrate to it autonomous treaties, following the classical doctrine of the conquest of immortality through culture, which saw in education "the most precious good that can be given to mortals", according to Plato's formula used by the poet Menandro in the following century, which "will be constantly repeated in the same terms for eight centuries" (p. 158).

A very 'right to education' was never recognised in the Greco-Roman world, however. A school law known as Law of Charondas (in the 4th century BC), referred to by the Greek historian Diodoro of Sicily (in the first century BC), seems to recognise to the child a right to education, but it is an apocryphal text (Compernolle, 1975, p. 98).

Following Jean-Pierre Néraudau (1984), the "long resistance to Greek education is the greatest originality of the Roman world" (p. 306), a fact that did not prevent Rome from playing the historical role of "implanting and rooting solidly in the Mediterranean world this Hellenist civilisation by which it had been itself conquered" (Marrou, 1948, p. 422).

With the fall of the Roman Empire in the West, in 476, the decline of urban life and the 'barbaric' occupation, the Roman municipal schools disappeared, remaining only a few libraries and preceptors in the great manor houses. It was the Catholic Church that, throughout the Middle Ages, continued to guarantee some instruction. In 529, a Catholic Council commanded bishops to create schools in the main cathedrals and parishes, but it was principally the monasteries that, since the 7th century, kept the flame of culture lit, by teaching, copying, preserving and translating manuscripts of the Greco-Roman culture. However, the monastic schools were practically limited to the teaching of the Grammar and the Bible and were attended mainly by future monks and clerics. Lay and illiterate were, at the time, practically synonymous.

In the passage from the 11th century to the 12th century, a shift occurred, as a consequence of the reanimation of cities' life and commerce, the monetarization of the economy, the Church's reforms, the evolution of mentalities and the demand of education. The school was reborn, by private initiative, a fact that led bishops to institute the *Licentia Docendi* (authorisation to teach). In the 12th century, many ancient philosophical, scientific and literary works were rediscovered and translated, and the Roman Law resurfaced in Bologna (Italy). In the 13th century, a new school institution is born: University, formed by Colleges that comprised what is, today, secondary and higher education. The mediaeval University responds to new needs for the technical preparation of an elite of clerics and jurists. Other schools are founded by new religious communities, such as the Dominicans and the Franciscans.

The discovery and revaluation of the Greco-Latin cultural heritage gave rise to a passionate rediscovery of the human and of the world, known as the Renaissance. The Renaissance humanism caused an unprecedented moral, psychological and educational interest for the child. At the end of the 14th century, Jean Gerson, Chancellor of the University of Paris, attributed to childhood "an importance that no one had ever recognised to it" (Bonneau, 1975, p. 173).

The humanists of the Renaissance were men "obsessed with education" who "originated, at the same time, the modern feeling of childhood and the modern schooling" (p. 207) – a true "school and sentimental revolution" (p. 8). Ariès (1960) underlined the relationship that was established between the "devotion to the holy childhood and the great movement of interest for childhood, of creation of small schools, of colleges, of pedagogical concern" (p. 169). The consciousness of the personal and social resonance of education had gained a definitive impetus in Europe. Instituting Man in man, through the culture of reason by a *Liberal Education* (the title of a writing by Mafeo Vegio) – this was the pedagogical ideal of the Renaissance.

The cultural humanist Revolution of the Renaissance – together with the emergence of the bourgeoisie and the capitalism, the religious Reformation and Counter-Reformation, and the scientific revolution – prompted the discovering of the economic, ideological and political value of education by the Monarchy as a political instrument of the Nation-State building, and the idea of a "national education" has emerged, competing with the centuries-long

Christian 'monopoly' of education. Morality continued to be primarily a familial and religious concern, but the school has become increasingly the specialised institution meeting the motto of Francis Bacon, in his *Novum Organum* (1620): "Knowledge is Power".

From the 16th to the 18th centuries, writings and initiatives flourish in the field of education. In the 16th century, stand up the names of Erasmus, Vivès, and Rabelais.

> The principles of Erasmus and those of his disciples formed the crucible of modern pedagogical thought, which can be found in Coménius, Jean-Jacques Rousseau, Johann Pestalozzi, and until today, in Maria Montessori, Janus Korczak, Célestin Freinet and Françoise Dolto. (Saladin, 2021, p. 19)

Gargantua and Pantagruel is "the first of these great pedagogical utopias that will abound in the two centuries that follow, among which *Émile* is only the most elaborated" (Lecercle, 1958, p. 67). In the 17th century, it stands out the name of John Locke, considered "the greatest philosopher and theorist of education of the English History" (Aldrich, 1995, p. 70). *Some Thoughts Concerning Education* is not an education treaty, nor stands out for its originality, but exerted a great influence: in the 18th century, it had more than twenty editions in England and was translated into several European languages.

Meanwhile, Departments and Ministries of Education have been established within the State apparatus of several countries. According to James Abel (1930), it was probably in China, for over 40 centuries, where the first Minister of Education was appointed to teach the people the duties in human relations. In Europe, Alcuin was Charlemagne's advisor to education, since 781. In 1580, it was promulgated in Saxony (Germany) an Ecclesiastical Constitution (*Kirchenordnung*, KO), with a code of school institution (*Schulordnung*, SO). Jean Neveux (1975) questioned: "Is this a 'right' to education or a school obligation?". In his opinion, the initiative "does not seem to be properly inscribed in the framework of the 'right to education', but rather in the right of all public powers to organise and control education as a public service of national importance". It is an obligation, not a right (pp. 238, 239, 245). In the second half of the 18th century, Prussia (Germany) takes the pioneering decision to nationalise the school and creates a Ministry of Public Education. Compulsory (but not free) school is also decreed for boys and girls from five to thirteen years old, with normal schools being created for the training of teachers.

François-Georges Dreyfus (1975) drew attention to "the pedagogical fever" of Protestant and Catholic States at the end of the 18th century (p. 257). The ideology of the Enlightenment passed the public interest of education ahead of the family interest. La Chalotais stated that "any nation has an inalienable and imprescriptible right to educate its members, because, ultimately, the State's children should be educated by States' members" (as cited in Sicard, 1975, p. 266).

The ban of the Jesuit Order in many Western European countries, in the 18th century, created an emptiness that favoured the institutionalisation of public education. It was the case of Poland, for example, where an education committee was created that put the goods confiscated from the Jesuits at the service of public education and instituted, before the division of the country (1795), a complete school system, and so may be considered the first modern Ministry of Education. Ministries of Education have been created in several European countries throughout the 19th century. At the end of the century, all Latin American countries (except Uruguay) had public school systems. In the early 20th century, other countries have established Ministries of Education.

In parallel with the *nationalisation* of education, proposals and initiatives aiming at its internationalisation have taken the scene.

4.1.2 *Internationalisation of Education*

4.1.2.1 Until the 19th Century

Education is perhaps the dimension of peoples' life most resistant to internationalisation as it is the main resource for cultivating a nation's cultural identity (and for other not good motives).

In the history of the internationalisation of education, we may distinguish three major stages.

The first one began with curiosity about other cultures and customs. Travel diaries were its main sources.

The second phase emerged with the desire to exchange and create international institutions, in modern and contemporary times. Its most notable forerunner, in the Western world, was Comenius, in the 17th century. In the opinion of Jean Piaget (1957), he was "a great precursor to contemporary attempts at international collaboration in the field of education, science and culture" (pp. 281, 282). A *Collegium Lucis* (College of Light) should constitute a kind of International Ministry of Education, within the framework of a peaceful international order. A same education for International Unity would be the task of major global institutions which – as Prévot (1981) wrote – "genially prefigure the United Nations, the U.N.E.S.C.O. or the World Council of Churches" (ibid., p. 40).

In the 19th century, Comparative Education became an autonomous discipline. Its creation is generally credited to Marc-Antoine Jullien (of Paris), with his *Esquisse et vues préliminaires d'un ouvrage sur l'éducation comparée* (Plan and preliminary views for a work on comparative education), originally published in 1817, in Geneva.

The need and calls for the establishment of international organisations in the field of education increased in Europe. Claude Henri, Count of Saint-Simon, in his project *Sur la réorganisation de la société européenne* (On the Reorganisation of European Society, 1814), provided for the existence of a Grand Parliament that would also take over public education throughout Europe (in Merle, 1966, pp. 220, 221). In 1855, on the occasion of the Universal Exhibition in Paris, the Inspector General of Public Instruction, Eugène Rendu, presented to the Minister of Public Instruction an International Education Plan that was examined by an independent committee whose report proposed, among other things, the formation of an Association of International Educational Institutions, which would apply the same curriculum in France, England, Germany, Italy and Spain. The Association would have a Higher Committee of International Education and national commissions. It was envisaged to establish an International Institute in Saint-Germain-en-Laye, in a pleasant natural setting. Unfortunately: "The International Institute of Saint-Germain did not survive the turmoil of 1870 [Franco-Prussian War]; and the general system, of which it was only a rudimentary, incomplete and partial implementation trial, is still awaiting its application" (Buisson, 1887, p. 869).

The first international congress of education took place in 1876, in Philadelphia (USA). In 1880, another one was held in Brussels (Belgium). Further initiatives aiming at the internationalisation of education include:

- Herman Molkenboer (Netherlands) proposed the establishment of a Permanent International Council of Education, as an IGO, in 1885.
- Franz Kemény (Hungary), who wrote a book on *L'enseignement International* (International Education), proposed the creation of an International Conference of Ministries of Public Instruction (1901) and drafted a project of an International Institute of Education (1905), as well as an International Review of Education, to be published in French, German, and English.
- Kurnig (his first name could not be found) (Germany) drafted, in 1904, a Project of a Consultative International Centre for Education. He wrote picturesquely: "A donkey of the Azores who adheres is worthier – from the point of view of civilisation – than a hundred decorated Ministers of State who hesitate" (as cited in Bekri, 1991, p. 38).
- Edward Peeters (Belgium) founded, in 1909, a *Bureau International de Documentation Éducative* (International Educational Documentation Office) that published a review (*Minerva*). It disappeared with the outbreak of World War I.
- E. Lebonnois (France) created, in 1911, an *Institut Pédagogique International* (International Pedagogic Institute) at the University of Caen.
- In 1921, took place in Calais (France) the first Congress of the New Education Movement that established the *Ligue Internationale pour l'Éducation*

Nouvelle (L.I.E.N. – New Education International Fellowship) and adopted its purpose and principles (see 5.1.2).

The third stage of the internationalisation of education is characterised by the gradual integration of several aspects of school education, either by normative harmonisation (of the general principles and purpose of education), or by the recognition of studies and the equivalence of diplomas, or by curricular integration. The normative harmonisation began with the recommendations of the International Conferences of Public Education in 1934, at the initiative of the IBE (see 4.1.2.4), and has been developed by UNESCO. The recognition of studies and the equivalence of diplomas were fostered after World War II by the European Communities Project with the adoption of dozens of sectoral directives, starting in 1974, and culminating in the pioneering Bologna Process, aimed at creating a "European area of Higher Education".[1] Also, the Council of Europe and UNESCO adopted normative instruments with the same purpose.

Curricular integration is the least developed method of education internationalisation. An example are the international schools (gathered in the International Schools Association since 1951), among which is the International School of Geneva that is a primary and secondary school teaching both in French and English, created in 1924 for children of parents working in the international organisations, notably the ILO. After World War II, others were established for children of the civil servants of the new international organisations, such as the European Schools created within the framework of the European Communities. International schools foreshadow the ideal of internationalisation of school education, through a common education syllabus complemented with a component of cultural diversity and individual options.

Nowadays, an indirect factor of integration of education systems is the scientific-technological Globalisation that requires similar apprenticeship and skills everywhere. The same may be said of international assessment programmes, among which the Programme for International Student Assessment (PISA) is the most known.[2]

International education, i.e. the introduction into the national school education of international spirit and contents, was fostered by the internationalist movement from the 19th century on.

4.1.2.2 Internationalist Movement

It seems that the term 'international' was first used in the 18th century by Jeremy Bentham in his *Plan for a Universal and Perpetual Peace*, written in 1789 but published only in 1831. It became popular in the second half of the 19th century. Political and technical international organisations (IGOs and NGOs) have come into existence.

In the political field, examples are the Pan-American Union (first established as International Union of American Republics, at the first International Conference of American States, on 14 April 1890, the forerunner of the Organisation of American States established in 1948); the Inter-Parliamentary Union (1889); the International Peace Bureau (1891); the International Office of Public Health (1907).

Examples in other fields are the establishment of the Universal Telegraph Union in 1865 (that has become the International Telecommunications Union in 1932); the General Union of Posts in 1874 (that has become the Universal Postal Union in 1878); the creation of the International Workingmen's Association (IWA), in 1864, at a large meeting of European trade union leaders in St. Martin's Hall, London, whose Statutes were drafted by Kar Marx. It would become known as the First International.

Following Georges P. Seeckaert (1970):

> The first few international organizations came into being gradually shortly after the Congress of Vienna: only six were created between 1815 and 1849, and twenty-nine between 1850 and 1869. The number of international congresses held during the same periods was fourteen and one hundred and twenty-two, respectively. (p. 20)

In 1900, there were 208 international organisations, most of them in Europe, 12% being IGOs. NGOs were known as international associations.

At the beginning of the 1900s, 'internationalism' was a neologism, and the term 'internationalisation' was not found in the major dictionaries. As wrote Alfred Fried in an article entitled "Internationalism as a Science", published in the 1908–1909 edition of the *Annuaire de la Vie Internationale* (Yearbook of International Life):

> Internationalism as science is of very recent origin. [... It] does not seek to abolish the homelands, but rather, through the accumulated effect of work in common, through the regular exchange of their output, to ensure that they enjoy greater wellbeing and security. In actual fact, internationalism is a higher, nobler form of patriotism. (cited ibid., p. 22)

On 29 January 1908, about twenty associations decided to set up a Central Bureau of International Associations and to convene a World Congress of International Associations, to be held in Brussels in 1910. It took place in the *Palais des Académies* (Palace of the Academies), from 9 to 11 May 1910, with the participation of Delegates representing 132 international associations, 13 Governments, as well as five Nobel Prize winners. This first World Congress led to the foundation of the Union of International Associations (UIA), whose first Secretaries-General were the three Secretaries-General of the Congress, namely: Henri La Fontaine, Paul Otlet and Cyrille Van Overbergh.

The second World Congress took place in Ghent and Brussels from 15 to 18 June 1913, attended by Delegates from 169 international associations and 22 Governments. The third World Congress was to take place in San Francisco, in 1915, but was held only in August 1920, in Brussels, because of World War I.

In 1914, the number of international organisations was about 500, most of them federated in the UIA. The internationalist movement was driven by the pacifism that inspired The Hague Peace Conferences, aiming at "a universal civilisation", as read the report of the second World Congress of International Associations (as cited in Seeckaert, 1970, p. 22).

The work accomplished by the UIA culminated in the establishment of the League of Nations, as recognised in a *Memorandum* of its Secretary-General, on 2 September 1921,[3] that gives a historical account of the UIA activities in order to justify financial support to it.

> The work accomplished by the Union of International Associations cannot be separated from the personality of its founders. In the course of a life which has been entirely devoted to the study of questions connected with the organisation of international relations in the interests of peace and humanity, M. Lafontaine and Otlet have worked for the realisation of far-reaching schemes in order to centralise methodically all the efforts put forward in the moral and intellectual sphere to establish international agreement and cooperation. The general outlines of these schemes were conceived as early as 1895 when, as a preliminary step, the International Office of Bibliography was founded. The aim of the founders was limited, but, nevertheless, of universal and practical interest. […]
>
> The principles and ambitions of the "Union of International Associations" were consecrated by the formation of the League. The very nature of the work carried out by the Union of International Associations before the war rendered it, indirectly and within the means at its disposal, one of the promoters of the League of Nations. It had already expressly declared at one of the Congresses that the "principle of a League of Nations was the ultimate end of all international movements". During the war, the leaders of the Union drew up drafts of a Covenant and of an international constitution.

Such drafts included the establishment of an international body concerned with education, but the idea was strongly resisted, as we are going to learn.

4.1.2.3 The League of Nations and Education

This is a less studied and known chapter of the history of internationalisation of education, justifying the next developments.

Pioneering projects for the promotion of peace and the collective settlement of disputes were those of William Penn: *An Essay towards the Present and Future Peace of Europe by the Establishment of a European Dyet, Parliament or Estates* (1693); of the Abbé de Saint-Pierre: *Projet pour rendre la Paix perpétuelle en Europe* (Project for Making Perpetual Peace in Europe) that included the establishment of a European Senate at Strasbourg or Dijon (1716); and of Immanuel Kant: *Zum Ewigen Friede* (For Eternal Peace, 1795).

In 1849, Victor Hugo pronounced a resonant Open Address to the Paris World Peace Congress (21 August), of which he was President. He famously said[4]:

> A day will come when your arms will fall from your hands! A day will come when war will seem as absurd between Paris and London, between Petersburg and Berlin, between Vienna and Turin, as it would today between Rouen and Amiens or between Boston and Philadelphia. A day will come when you – France, Russia, Italy, England, Germany – all you nations of the continent will merge, without losing your distinct qualities and your glorious individuality, in a close and higher unity to form a European brotherhood, just as Normandy, Brittany, Burgundy, Lorraine, Alsace, all our provinces are merged together in France.
>
> A day will come when the only fields of battle will be markets opening up to trade and minds opening up to ideas. [...]
>
> A day will come when we shall see those two immense groups, the United States of America and the United States of Europe, stretching out their hands across the sea, exchanging their products, their arts, their works of genius [...]. And to bring about that day will not take another 400 years, for we are living in a fast-moving age.[5]

Intergovernmental peace meetings were the Congress of Vienna (1814–1815), after the Napoleonic Wars, and the Hague Peace Conferences in 1899 and 1907, which established a Permanent Court of International Arbitration. A third Peace Conference was due to take place in The Hague in 1915. An offspring of the European wars was the International Committee of the Red Cross (ICRC), created in 1864 as an NGO, which launched the codification of the laws of war. In this connection, Georges Abi-Saab (2007) highlighted:

> … the distinction between the 'international law of coexistence' and the 'international law of cooperation' coined by Professor Wolfgang Friedman. In a way, the law of coexistence is traditional international law; a law that emerged with what is called the 'Westphalian system'. […]
>
> On the other hand, the idea of international cooperation – and the law of cooperation that goes with it – emerged in the second half of the nineteenth century and started to take hold at the turn of that century with the World Federalist movement, the movement for the creation of an international court and the Hague Peace Conferences, and so forth. But its concretization came in a big way after the Second World War, with the Charter of the UN. (pp. 396, 397)

International co-operation was framed by the principles of sovereignty of States and of non-intervention in domestic affairs, which were cornerstones of the classic International Law, but World War I made urgent a higher level of co-operation. This was the ideal of the League of Nations.

4.1.2.3.1 *League of Nations*

The idea of a 'society of nations' or 'concert of nations' dates back to international conferences in the second half of the 19th century.

Henri La Fontaine (Belgium), President of the International Peace Bureau (from 1907 until he died in 1943), Nobel Peace Prize laureate in 1913, proposed a pacifist Charter – *The Great Solution: Magnissima Charta, Essay on Evolutionary and Constructive Pacifism*, in 1916, and the following year a *World Constitution of the League of Nations*.

Léon Bourgeois may be considered the "spiritual father" of the League of Nations.[6] Among his numerous duties, he was Prime Minister of France (1895–1896), several times Minister, President of the French Chamber of Deputies (1902–1904) and of the Senate (1920–1923). At the international level, he was French Delegate to The Hague Conference of 1899, member of The Hague International Court of Justice (1903), French Delegate to the Paris Peace Conference (1919). In 1910, was published *Pour la Société des Nations* (Towards the League of Nations) bringing together his speeches and other texts. In 1919, he was the first President of the Council of the League of Nations and, in 1920, he was awarded the Nobel Prize of Peace.

In the USA, the American League to Enforce Peace and the Women's International League of Peace and Freedom was founded in 1915. In the United Kingdom, the League of Nations Society was founded, the same year, and a League of Nations Union in 1918. The American President (Woodrow Wilson) proposed, in January 1918, his famous "Fourteen Points" for the peace settlement (not including human rights).

On 18 January 1919, opened the Paris Peace Conference, at the Quai d'Orsay (Ministry of Foreign Affairs). On 25 January, the Conference nominated "a Commission representative of the Associated Governments to work out the details of the constitution and functions of the League" (Wilson, 1928, Appendix B). On 28 April, it was unanimously adopted the Covenant of the League of Nations that was signed as part of the Versailles Peace Treaty, on 28 June (Part I).[7] The Covenant entered into force together with the Peace Treaty on 10 January 1920. It consisted of a short Preamble, proclaiming the aims of the League, and 26 concise Articles. The overall aim was "to promote international cooperation and to achieve international peace and security". In Part XIII of the Peace Treaty (Labour – Articles 387–427), the ILO was created as a tripartite IGO – grouping Governments, employers and workers – whose Secretariat is the International Labour Office.

Geneva was chosen to be the seat of the League of Nations, defeating Brussels. The choice was favoured by Switzerland's neutrality, but it entered the League on 16 May 1920, following a favourable referendum (56.3%). The Secretariat moved from its provisional location in London to Geneva (Palais Wilson, former Hôtel National), in November. The foundation stone of its future headquarters was laid on 7 September 1929, in Ariana Park. In 1936, the League moved to its new seat – the Palais des Nations.

The main organs of the League were the Council and the Assembly, assisted by a Secretariat with twelve sections, each dealing with a specific field and headed by a Director. A Permanent Court of International Justice was established and elected by the Assembly on 30 January 1922. "For the first time, representatives from the five parts of the world went, in a spirit of friendship and harmony, to work together for the sake of solidarity and peace".[8]

The Council held its first session on 16 January 1920, in Paris (having met also in London, Rome, San Sebastian and Brussels). Its first President was Léon Bourgeois, as above mentioned. The Assembly met, for the first time, ten months later, in Geneva, from 15 November to 18 December, having taken 31 public meetings. 41 Member States were represented. Paul Hymans, Minister of Foreign Affairs of Belgium, its representative at the Paris Peace Conference and then President of the Council, was elected President of the Assembly that created six committees, whose Presidents were Vice-Presidents of the Assembly. It decided that three technical organs should be created to deal with economic and financial issues, transit issues and hygiene issues. Some temporary committees were created as well. Sir Eric Drummond (United Kingdom) was the first Secretary-General, assisted by a Deputy Secretary-General and three Under Secretaries-General, in charge of the internal administration, political affairs and international bureaux.

The *Report on the work of the League – 1942–1943 – submitted by the acting Secretary-General* (Sean Lester) noted: "The League of Nations was not at any given moment fully representative of the world. It is interesting to point out, however, that, at one time or another, though unfortunately not all at the same time, every country in the world was a Member of the League, with the exception of the United States of America" (and a few States because of their small size).[9]

The League of Nations was active for about twenty years. An overview of the scope of its action may be taken from a document prepared by the Secretariat on *The Committees of the League of Nations – Classified List and Essential Facts*, dated from 20 September 1945,[10] whose main criteria were the origin, nature and purpose of each one. Its successes include the resolution of some international conflicts; the protection of minorities and the refugees; the mandates system with the right of petition for inhabitants (not provided for in the Covenant) that was a precursor way of international human rights protection. Moreover, it created an Advisory Committee on the Traffic in Women and Children and an Advisory Commission for the Protection and Welfare of Children and Young People; it engaged with the Geneva Declaration on the Rights of the Child; it established an Advisory Committee of Experts on Slavery that drafted the Slavery Convention signed in 1926; it promoted the codification of International Law. Besides the establishment of ILO, the League also created a Health Organisation.

Nevertheless, the League of Nations was under the control of the principle of sovereignty guaranteed by the Council's unanimity rule. Also, it suffered from an original sin: despite the role played by the democrat President Wilson and his nationwide campaign, the American Senate, led by republicans, conditioned the ratification of the Covenant of the League to unacceptable reservations, and the ratification was definitely defeated by vote in March 1920, so preventing the USA from becoming a member of the League. Later, also Germany and Japan withdrew (1933), as well as Italy (1937). The Soviet Union was expelled in 1939.

Throughout World War II, a Supervisory Commission, working in close collaboration with the heads of the League Organisations, ensured the continuance of their activities, as far as possible. After the resignation of the Secretary-General (Joseph Avenol), on 31 August 1940, the Deputy Secretary-General Sean Lester (Ireland) acted as Secretary-General. He wrote in the above-mentioned *Report on the work of the League*: "We failed in our first attempt, but we are being given, at great cost, another opportunity" (p. 16).

After a meeting, in London, between the Supervisory Commission of the League of Nations and the Preparatory Commission of the United Nations set up in San Francisco (1945), the British Foreign Office took the initiative to convene the last Assembly of the League (21st) in Geneva, on 8 April 1946. It was attended by 43 States Members. On 18 April, at its closing meeting, the Assembly adopted a "Resolution for the Dissolution of the League of Nations", as well as a "Resolution concerning the International Institute of Intellectual Cooperation". It approved a "Common Plan for the Transfer of League of Nations Assets",[11] already endorsed by the General Assembly of the United Nations on 12 February, according to which:

> 1. The League of Nations agrees to transfer to the United Nations, and the United Nations agrees to receive on or about August 1st, 1946, the precise date to be determined by the administrative authorities of the two Organisations, all material assets of the League of Nations shown in column I of the attached Schedule at the valuation shown in column II.

The formal transfer was signed on 18 April by Sean Lester, who had been formally nominated, in the meanwhile, third Secretary-General of the League of Nations, and Wlodzimierz Moderow, representing the United Nations.

Thus, having handed over all of its assets to the United Nations, and having granted to it full control of its Library and Archives, the 43 Members attending this last Assembly declared by unanimous vote that, as of 20 April 1946, the League of Nations would cease to exist. Lord Robert Cecil, one of the founders of the League of Nations, said by closing the last session of the Assembly: "The League is dead, long live the United Nations!".[12] As observes the United Nations website[13]:

> Similar in many ways to the League of Nations, the United Nations sought to continue many of the operations already in place. For example, economic activities were transferred to the new Economic and Social Council; the Health Organization evolved into the World Health Organization (WHO); the Nutrition Committee became the Food and Agriculture Organization (FAO); the Committee of Intellectual Cooperation became the Educational, Scientific and Cultural Organization (UNESCO); the Permanent Mandates Commission was replaced by the Trusteeship Council; and the work of the Nansen Office was continued by the United Nations Relief and Rehabilitation Administration (UNRRA) and the United Nations High Commissioner for Refugees (UNHCR).

We are now turning to our specific interest: League of Nations work regarding the intellectual field and, in particular, education.

4.1.2.3.2 *International Committee on Intellectual Co-Operation*

The principle of sovereignty that hampered the League of Nations was especially concerned with education, as already noted.

Besides political, economic, and legal factors of international peace and security, the Covenant of the League of Nations also included health and labour as matters for cooperation, but the intellectual field, including education, was left aside. Charles Dorn (2006) remarked:

> … in David Hunter Miller's two-volume book on *The Drafting of the Covenant*, all the references during all the discussions he records in so much detail that have any bearing whatever on education could be put into a couple of his fourteen hundred pages. The only mention of international education appears to have been made by a delegation from the International Council of Women, led by Lady Aberdeen.

Indeed, the Commission for the study of the constitution of the League of Nations, at its 14th meeting, on 10 April 1919, received a delegation representing the International Council of Women and the Suffragist Conference of the Allied Countries and the United States, led by Lady Aberdeen and composed of more 16 women.

> Mrs. Schivioni asked that the League should establish an International Education Bureau.
>
> Mrs. Fanny Andrews supported her.
>
> […]
>
> President Wilson said that it had been a pleasure to hear the speeches, and that if it were not possible to accede to all requests it was only because the League could not begin by arranging all the affairs of mankind, not because the Commission did not agree that the demands were excellent.
>
> The Women's delegation then withdrew. (Miller, 1928, pp. 361, 362)

However, the League of Nations could hardly fail to include education in its activities as an unavoidable dimension of "intellectual co-operation". It was about fostering an intellectual *rapprochement*, through a *Société des Esprits* (League of Minds), as wrote Paul Valéry on 22 July 1930 in a Report.[14]

Initiatives of the Union of International Associations and others

According to a "Report from the Secretariat of the League of Nations on the proposals submitted to it with regard to intellectual cooperation by various organisations and persons",[15] they amounted to 47:

- General (6)
- Relating to co-operation in scientific research (2)
- Inter-university relations (10)
- Education (22)
- Bibliography and exchange of publications (4)
- Intellectual workers (3)

Education stands out, by far, as having been the subject of the largest number of proposals. One of the most influential was developed and highly lobbed by the Union of International Associations (UIA) and its Secretaries-General and founders (in 1907), in Brussels: Paul Otlet and Henri La Fontaine.

During the Paris Peace Conference, UIA, La Fontaine and Otlet campaigned for the Covenant of the League of Nations to include intellectual co-operation. A meeting of UIA Delegates held in Paris on 5 January 1919 approved a *Memorandum* to be addressed to the Peace Conference containing a project of *La Charte des Intérêts Intellectuels et Moraux* (World Charter of Intellectual and Moral Interests).

According to the "Proposals of the German Government for the Establishment of a League of Nations" (Foundation Principles, 1): "It is to be based upon the moral power of right and shall serve as an international community working for the intellectual and material advancement of mankind" (Miller, 1928, Volume 2, Document 35, p. 745). And the amendments proposed by the Belgian Delegation (Commission of the League of Nations, the meeting of 24 March 1919, Annexe to minutes Nº 12) included:

> Article 21 *bis*
>
> Add: Article A, the associated States will ensure, to the greatest extent possible, the development of international, moral, scientific and artistic relations between the various peoples and will prove [promote?], by all means, the formation of an international mentality.
>
> To this end, an International Commission on Intellectual Relations is established. (Miller, 1928, Volume 2, p. 522)

David H. Miller (1928, Volume 1, p. 350) reported, referring to the thirteenth meeting of the Commission:

> The Belgians also had on their amendment paper an Article for an International Commission on Intellectual Relations [...].

> There seems to have been no discussion of the proposal; the minutes do not mention it at all, though the early draft of the English minutes says that it was brought forward and withdrawn.

On 21 May 1919, the UIA sent a letter to the Secretary-General of the League proposing a collaborative relationship and inviting a Secretariat's representative to visit it, in Brussels. The invitation was accepted and a delegation consisting of Inazō Nitobe (Japan), Under-Secretary-General in charge of the International Bureaux, and E.M.H. Lloyd (Economic Section) and G.S.F.C. Kaeckenbeeck (Legal Section) visited Brussels at the end of August. Later, also the Secretary-General visited the UIA.

In September 1920, the UIA founded an International University – an idea launched in 1911 by the Central Bureau. To it contributed 15 universities and 346 professors from 23 countries. It held four sessions, in Brussels: the first one, from 5 to 20 September 1920; the second one, from 20 August to 5 September 1921; the third one, from 20 August to 3 September 1922; the fourth one, from 17 to 31 July 1927. In the first session, 50 professors from 11 countries and about 100 students from over 10 countries participated in 106 hours of lectures broken down into 53 classes and conferences. Special Chairs were entrusted to 13 international associations. The UIA invited the Secretariat of the League to send a member to hold a Special Chair. Again, Inazō Nitobe was its incumbent representative, giving lectures on "What the League of Nations has done and is doing", on 13 and 14 September 1920.

The *Memorandum* of the Secretary-General of the League of Nations above quoted[16] mentioned its financial support to the International University and the publication of the *List of Recommendations and Resolutions of International Congresses* (*Code des Voeux Internationaux*), asked by the UIA in May 1920.

During the 3rd World Congress of International Associations, in Brussels, from 5 to 20 September 1920, a plan was worked out to be submitted to the League in a report titled "On the Organisation of Intellectual Work within the League of Nations: Report and Resolution presented by the Union of International Associations". In November, the UIA published *Sur l'Organisation Internationale du Travail Intellectuel: À créer au sein de la Société des Nations* (On the International Intellectual Labour Organisation: To be created within the League of Nations), to be known before the first session of the Assembly of the League.

Another most influential proposal came from the French Association for the League of Nations. On 8 July 1920, Paul Appell, Rector of the University of Paris and Chairman of the Executive Committee of the French Association for the League of Nations, on its behalf, addressed to the League a comprehensive proposal titled "Institution of an International Office for Intellectual Intercourse and Education", to be located in Paris, accompanied by a "Draft Convention setting up a permanent organisation for the promotion of international understanding and collaboration in educational questions and in science, literature and art" (prepared by Julien Luchaire, Chief of Staff to the French Minister of Public Instruction).[17]

The proposals of the UIA and the French Association of the League of Nations were considered by the Secretariat as the most complete.

La Fontaine Report

The issue entered the League's Agenda when, at the first session of its Assembly (from 15 November to 18 December 1920), 21st plenary meeting, on 13 December 1920, three Delegates – Belgian (Prosper Poullet), Romanian (Demetre Negulesco) and Italian (Maggiorino Ferraris) – presented a proposal on the International Organisation of the Intellectual Work. The motion was approved by the plenary meeting and referred to the Second Committee of the Assembly that, on 16 December, at its 12th meeting, adopted the proposed draft resolution and appointed as rapporteur Henri La Fontaine, Senator and member of the Belgian Delegation (Grandjean, 2018, pp. 146, 147).[18] La Fontaine, on behalf of the Committee, presented his Report on "The Organization of Intellectual Labour" at the Assembly last plenary meeting, on 18 December 1920.[19] It read:

> ... the International University, which was founded in 1920, has benefited by the courteous interest shown by the Council of the League of Nations. At the Meeting at San Sebastian, the Council conveyed the expression of its sympathetic interest and its wishes for success for the work of the International University, and assured it that the Secretariat was authorised to give all possible assistance to the realisation of the work of international interest to be undertaken by the University. Active evidence of this sympathetic interest was given by the presence at the inaugural session of several Members of the Secretariat of the League of Nations, and by the participation of Dr. Nitobe in the courses organised.
>
> The International University is the product of long-sustained endeavours extending over a quarter of a century – especially by the Union of International Associations, a Union which at the outbreak of war comprised 230 International groups. The principal object of the promoters of this Union was to give to the world a centre for the accumulation, coordination and diffusion of all that the human race has thought and realised in the intellectual sphere. Its ambition is to give to the human race a memory and a brain. [...]

> It will be possible with the elements thus coordinated to create a vast educational system which will include all countries attached to the League of Nations; in particular, types of work can be created which will cover all the material laid down on the programme of the various standards of instruction in the different countries, dealing with it from a broad human standpoint. [...]
>
> The League of Nations should encourage, assist and consolidate such an effort. Beside technical organisations devoted to Labour, hygiene, economics, to communications and transit there should be placed, as their crown, a technical organisation devoted to the world's intellect.

The Poullet/Negulesco/Ferraris draft resolution was proposed for adoption, namely:

> Recommends that the Council should continue its efforts in this direction, and should associate itself as closely as possible with all methods tending to bring about the international organisation of intellectual work.
>
> The Assembly further invites the Council to regard favourably the efforts which are already in progress to this end, to place them under its august protection if it be possible, and to present to the Assembly during its next session a detailed report on the educational influence which it is their duty to exert with a view to developing a liberal spirit of goodwill and world-wide cooperation, and to report on the advisability of giving them shape in a technical organization attached to the League of Nations.

A study on the proceedings of the First Assembly (published in 1921)[20] remarked:

> The Assembly then devoted itself to the consideration of the last of the activities of the Second Committee, namely, the Resolutions upon the Organization of Intellectual Labour. These contained proposals for which the Belgian delegate, M. Lafontaine, stood sponsor. He presented a stupendous picture of the progress of international thought within the last seventy-five years. "Whilst nations have been striving with one another", he said, "thinkers have been crossing the frontiers of the various countries and meeting one another in conferences". Between 1840 and 1850, the conferences had numbered only ten. In the four years preceding the war, no fewer than five hundred of them had been held and had dealt with matters of every nature. He asked the League of Nations to give

> these movements the same kind of help that had been afforded to the manual workers of the world by the establishment of the International Labour Office.
>
> M. Lafontaine impressed his hearers powerfully, although the impressions were of opposite kinds. [...] When the British delegate, Mr. Barnes, rose to move the previous question, he found himself supported only by the votes of the other five members of the British Empire and by the delegate from Cuba. When, on the other hand, M. Lafontaine's motion was put, the representatives of thirty-four States rose to their feet. (pp. 145, 146)

In effect, the British Delegate (George N. Barnes) argued unsuccessfully that the International Labour Office could assume the intellectual labour too, so contributing to avoid the traditional but pernicious distinction between manual and intellectual labour.[21] La Fontaine answered: "It is quite possible that the intellectual workers of the world might wish to organize themselves in the same way as the manual workers have done, and such a matter would be the concern of the International Labour Office, but what we want here, and what I propose, is to give more force and more power to human thought".

The Resolution was approved by the Assembly. So, the way was paved towards the establishment of a League's committee entrusted with the intellectual labour.

At its 12th session, from 21 February to 4 March 1921, in Paris, the Council discussed a report by José Quiñones de León (Spain) on the "Organisation of the intellectual work", according to which: "Two conceptions are possible: 1st Should the Union of International Associations, which already exists, be transformed into an organization similar to the other technical organizations and be linked to the Society? 2nd Or an entirely new organization should be created?" (as cited in Grandjean, 2018, pp. 150, 151).

At the Council's 13th session, on 27 June, the Secretary-General was tasked with preparing the report asked by the Assembly. He drew up a *Memorandum* on "The Desirability of Creating a Technical Organisation for Intellectual Work",[22] according to which: "Intellectual activity is, essentially, international", and there is one form of intellectual activity from which "the League cannot remain disinterested. It is an activity which may be called educational". It was affirmed:

> The League of Nations cannot pursue any of its aims, either the general aims of cooperation as laid down in the Covenant, or even the more precise aims assigned to it by certain provisions, such as the campaign against the use of dangerous drugs and against the traffic in women and children, without, at every moment encountering educational problems,

> and without being obliged to ask for active help from those engaged in education in all countries.
>
> The Council is therefore in entire agreement with the principles of the Resolution adopted by the last Assembly. It is unanimously of opinion that the League of Nations should include in its programme the coordination of intellectual activity and international cooperation as regards education.

However, given that this is an area where a large number of private entities are already in action, "the present situation must above all be well weighed and considered" to avoid overlapping work. Therefore, another *Memorandum* was prepared on "Educational Activities and the Coordination of Intellectual Work accomplished by the Union of International Associations". It was proposed that the Council should adopt a Resolution following which the Assembly calls upon the Council to appoint a Committee to examine international questions regarding Intellectual Cooperation and Education». In the meantime, "this Committee will act as an advisory organ to the Council […]. To this Committee will also be assigned the task of examining a scheme for an International Education Office, referred to in the Council's Report".

It was in this context that:

> The UIA also convened an International Congress on Intellectual Activities, which took place from 20th to 22nd August 1921. […] After recalling the work done by the UIAI's International Centre, the congress also asked "that the League of Nations should give its consideration to the practical accomplishments already recorded, and transform them into a technical organization similar to those it has set up for Labour and Health, and the operation of which is illustrated in the project prepared by the Union of International Associations". (Seeckaert, 1970, p. 30)

Bourgeois Report

At the Council's 14th session (divided into two parts: from 30 August to 3 September, and from 12 September to 12 October 1921), Léon Bourgeois presented a Report on the "Organisation of Intellectual Work",[23] based on the documents drew up by the Secretary-General, following decisions taken by the Council in meetings of 1st March and 27 June. He proposed that the Secretary-General's reports be approved and affirmed:

> We are all agreed that the League of Nations has no task more urgent than that of examining these great factors of international opinion – the systems and methods of education, and scientific and philosophical research. […]

> To avoid all risk of the reproach of interference, a risk which the League would undoubtedly incur if it put forward on its own responsibility a scheme of organisation of intellectual activity between nations, the League should request its Members to appoint a Committee composed of the persons best qualified to deal with matters of education and science, to draw up a plan of action […].

The adoption of the following draft resolution by the Assembly was proposed:

> The Assembly calls upon the Council to appoint a Committee to examine international questions regarding Intellectual Cooperation and Education.
>
> This Committee will consist of a maximum number of twelve members, appointed by the Council. It will submit to the next Assembly a report on the measures to be taken by the League to facilitate intellectual exchange between nations, particularly as regards the communication of scientific information and methods of education.
>
> Pending the consideration of this report by the Assembly, this Committee will act as an advisory organ to the Council, which may submit to it any technical questions of this kind arising before the next session of the Assembly.
>
> To this Committee will also be assigned the task of examining a scheme for an International Education Office, referred to in the Council's Report dated March 1st, 1921.

The reports of the Secretary-General and the Resolution were adopted by the Council. In the Resolution, the term 'intellectual co-operation' appears probably for the first time in an official document of the League. The Bourgeois Report, together with the Secretariat's documents, were sent to the Assembly that met for its second session from 5 September to 5 October 1921.

The Bourgeois Report was debated by the Fifth Committee of the Assembly on 8 September. Opening the debate, La Fontaine suggested that the issue of the organisation of intellectual labour should be examined by a Sub-Committee for deeper consideration, but the Committee preferred to appoint himself to prepare proposals. La Fontaine did it on 10 September and proposed the adoption of the Resolution contained in the Bourgeois Report.

During the discussion, the President of the Fifth Committee (Charles Joseph Doherty, Canada) warned that the word 'education' could be misunderstood and interpreted as implying that the League of Nations could intervene in national education policy (see Saikawa, 2014, p. 59). The Committee agreed to drop it. Two other proposals were approved: the limitation of the committee composition to twelve members (proposed by Jonas Eliel Loefgren, Sweden) and the inclusion of the words 'men and women' after the words 'twelve members' (proposed by Kristine Bonnevie, Norway).

Gilbert Murray (British Delegate) was asked to prepare a report to be presented to the Assembly that was read at the meeting of the Fifth Committee on 20 September 1921.[24] He affirmed: "The Committee considered realises the great importance of the Organisation of Intellectual Work; it knows that the future of the League of Nations depends upon the formation of a universal conscience". It was resolved to approve and to send to the plenary meeting of the Second Assembly:

> ... the draft resolution put forward by M. Léon Bourgeois in the name of the Council: namely, the nomination by the Council of a Committee to examine international questions regarding intellectual cooperation, this Committee to consist of not more than 12 members and to contain both men and women.

Decision of the Assembly of the League of Nations (21 September 1921)
Murray presented the Report of the Fifth Committee to the plenary meeting of the Assembly on 21 September 1921. He remarked: "This whole subject of the international organisation of intellectual work suffers, I think, from a certain vagueness, or at least it causes a difficulty in some minds as to its exact meaning" (as cited in Saikawa, 2014, p. 62). He also noted that the wording of the Resolution proposed was not identical with that of the Bourgeois Report: "There is both an omission and an addition. The words 'an education' have been omitted after 'intellectual co-operation'. On the other hand, a provision has been added that women should be included on the Committee".

The removal of the term 'education' was criticised in particular by Louis Dante Bellegarde (Delegate, Secretary of State for Public Education of Haiti), who asked:

> What is our object in forming this Committee, which will have to deal with all international questions of intellectual cooperation? Our object is to collect for the information of all countries the results achieved by the human intellect. Now, if it is desired to coordinate the achievements of the human mind, how can we afford to neglect the formation of the human mind? (ibid., p. 64)

He called for the restoration of 'education' in the Resolution. Murray agreed with him but repeatedly explained the prudent omission while observing that "co-operation in intellectual work" was a field broad enough to include also educational activities. The explanation satisfied Bellegarde, who withdrew his amendment, and the Assembly unanimously adopted the Resolution proposed by the Fifth Committee,[25]:

> The Assembly
>
> approves the draft resolution put forward by M. Léon Bourgeois in the name of the Council – namely, the nomination by the Council of a Committee to examine international questions regarding intellectual cooperation, this Committee to consist of not more than twelve members and to contain both men and women.

On 14 January 1922, at its 16th session, the Council decided, "in accordance with the resolution of the Second Assembly, dated September 21st, 1921, to constitute a Committee of twelve members, which shall include women and which will be entrusted with the examination of international questions regarding intellectual cooperation". On 15 May,[26] it invited eleven persons to be members of the Committee (an American member was appointed later). They "might be asked to meet in Geneva for the first time on August 1st, 1922".

On 29 June, the Secretary-General informed the Council and Member States of the final composition of the International Committee.[27] So, was established the International Committee on Intellectual Co-operation (ICIC) as an Advisory Committee of the Council and the Assembly of the League of Nations. It was intended to foster the intellectual work and international co-operation of intellectual workers, to promote cultural internationalism, international understanding and peace.

In 1937, the ICIC was composed of 19 members. Many personalities of great stature and reputation were members or collaborated in its activities, throughout its existence, among which Albert Einstein, Marie Curie, Sigmund Freud, Paul Langevin, Léon Brunschvicg, Hendrik Lorentz, Édouard Herriot, Paul Valéry, Jules Romains, Alfred Zimmern, Thomas Mann (Nobel Prize of Literature in 1929), Gabriela Mistral (Nobel Prize of Literature in 1945), Miguel de Unamuno, Gabriel Johan Huizinga, Jean Piaget, Béla Bartók, Salvador de Madariaga, Rabindranath Tagore.

At the national level, Committees on Intellectual Co-operation emerged of themselves, since 1923.[28] They acted as connecting links between the ICIC and national intellectual circles. In 1937, they were 48 – in Europe, in the Americas (among which one in the USA that was not a member of the League), in Africa, in Asia and the Far East – including those created by the Catholic Union of International Studies and the Inter-Parliamentary Union. Since 1933, four National Committees were invited to send representatives to the ICIC sessions.

It is out of question to take stock of the diversity of activities related to "intellectual co-operation" within the League of Nations. The following offers only an overview of their evolution and, in particular, the main action in the field of education, through documented highlights, in order to realise how it evolved and to know its most outstanding actors, because the backbone of the institutions are the human beings serving them.

ICIC first sessions

The ICIC held its first session in Geneva from 1 to 5 August 1922, with ten meetings.[29] It appointed as Chairman Henri Bergson (France), as Vice-Chairman Gilbert Murray (United Kingdom), and as Rapporteur Gonzague de Reynold (Switzerland).[30] Three Sub-Committees were established: Bibliography, Inter-university relations, Intellectual property. A fourth one was created in 1925: Arts and Literature.

The Committee addressed an issue referred to it in a Resolution adopted by the Third Assembly on 21 September 1922: the teaching of Esperanto as an auxiliary international language. In the opinion of Gonzague de Reynold, three solutions were possible: an auxiliary international language could be a living language, a dead language (Latin) or an artificial language. The Committee decided not to recommend an artificial language (by 8 votes to 1).

At the Fourth Assembly (from 3 to 29 September 1923), a Report by the Fifth Committee (Rapporteur: Emilio de Palacios y Fau)[31] proposed the adoption of the following Resolution:

> The Assembly
>
> Having noted the Spanish Government's proposals concerning the equivalent recognition in all States of certain secondary educational diplomas, the creation of an International University, and the foundation of a higher educational establishment in each of the countries Members of the League of Nations, whose diplomas shall be valid in all countries Members of the League; [...]
>
> Decides to request the Council to refer these proposals to the Committee on Intellectual Cooperation for consideration, in order that this Committee may draw up a report on the subject to be submitted to the Fifth Assembly.

The Assembly adopted this Resolution on 27 September. The ICIC examined it at its third session (5–8 December 1923),[32] eighth meeting, on 8 December, and concluded: "In view of the complexity of these questions, it appeared desirable for the Committee to decide to continue its examination". At its Fifth Session, 18th plenary meeting, on 23 September 1924, the Assembly considered a Report of its Second Committee (Rapporteur: Gilbert Murray)[33] that included in its "Draft Resolutions on the Work of the Committee on Intellectual Cooperation" (third and fourth sessions) the following:

> In view of the proposals by the Spanish Government at the fourth Assembly and the suggestion made at the Second Committee by the Persian Delegate with regard to the equivalence of degrees, the Assembly asks all States to communicate what steps they have taken, or intend to take, in the direction indicated by the Committee on Intellectual Cooperation, with a view to attaining, as far as possible, the aims referred to in the said proposals. (p. 426)

The Fourth Assembly also had adopted a Resolution on the National Committees, approved by the Council on 13 December. The issue was addressed by the ICIC third session.[34] The Report to the Council (Rapporteur: Henri de Jouvenel, France)[35] read:

> At its 1923 Session, the Committee on Intellectual Cooperation was forced to recognise that it did not possess the material resources necessary to carry out the work entrusted to it by the Council. Its Chairman, voicing the unanimous opinion of the members, explained the Committee's requirements to the Fourth Committee of the last Assembly. […]
>
> The discussions of the Committee, at its 1923 session, when it appealed to the generosity of the various States and even of private associations show that it really needs some executive organ, an office or an institution to carry out the intricate work involved by the decisions of the Committee.

In fact, the ICIC was, as Jean Mistler put it: *Un cerveau qui n'avait ni muscles ni mains* (A brain that had no muscles, no hands) (cit in Bekri, 1991, p. 54).

4.1.2.3.3 *International Institute of Intellectual Co-Operation*

As read the *Monthly Summary of the League of Nations – January 1924*[36]: "M. Bergson, the Chairman of the International Committee of Intellectual Cooperation, has addressed an appeal on behalf of the national committees to all those who feel concerned at the serious conditions of present intellectual life". Answering this appeal, on 24 July 1924, the French Minister of Public Education (François Albert) made the following offer[37]:

> The appeal which you have lately made in the name of the Committee on Intellectual Cooperation, and in which you request the assistance of

> all nations in the work undertaken by the Committee, has been, I hope, favourably received. [...]
>
> In the name of the French Government, and in the conviction that I am the interpreter on this point of the whole of French public opinion, I desire to offer to the Committee on Intellectual Cooperation of the League of Nations the practical means for transforming its plans into a beautiful and concrete reality. [...]
>
> The French Government today makes an offer to the nations to establish at Paris an International Institute of Intellectual Cooperation.

The only condition of the French Government was that the organisation should have its headquarters in Paris. The Institute would be under the ICIC's jurisdiction. On 9 September 1924 (30th session), the Council decided, following the above quoted Jouvenel Report: "The Council accepts this offer in principle, and submits it to the Assembly".

The French initiative was met with some opposition within the Second Committee of the Assembly, sometimes not very diplomatic. For example, during the discussion of the Report of the Second Committee at the Fifth Assembly 18th plenary meeting, on 23 September 1924,[38] the Australian Delegate Matthew Charlton said that "the world would be putting Paris and France on a pedestal by themselves. Paris would be the seat of knowledge distributing culture to all other parts of the world" (p. 135). Frank R. Cowell (1966), who was a member of the British Delegation to the UNESCO founding Conference of London (1945), commented:

> Consistently opposed and derided by the United Kingdom and Dominion members of the League whose six delegations never voted together, as Lord Balfour tartly observed, except to oppose intellectual cooperation, it was sustained by the faith of the Latin members. Because it was a French idea, because it needed money, because more than three-quarters of the total budget was provided by the French, the United Kingdom refused to join. [...] What was harder to bear was the way the United Kingdom seemed to cover its apparent meanness by adding insult to injury with the pretext that the whole thing was just another cunning French cultural propaganda device. (pp. XII, XIII)[39]

The Fifth Assembly considered a Report of its Second Committee (Rapporteur: Gilbert Murray).[40] It affirmed that intellectual co-operation "is the very basis of our work, and not until we have won intellect to our side will the peace of the world be established on a secure foundation". Accordingly, it proposed the following Recommendation:

> The Council of the League of Nations is invited to conclude with the French Government all agreements necessary to ensure the establishment, continuity and proper working of the Institute.
>
> In accordance with these agreements, the administration of the Institute shall be entrusted to the Committee on Intellectual Cooperation, acting as a Governing Body.

On 8 December, the French Government sent to the President of the Council a letter stating the acceptance of the League's requirements and proposing the "Organic Statute of the Institute".[41] According to the letter, the Institute could "accept donations, legacies and subsidies from Governments other than the Government of the French Republic, from public or private institutions or organisations, or from private persons" ("other sources", as put in Statute's Article 10). Its purpose was so defined (Article 2)[42]:

> The principal object of this Institute shall be to prepare the work to be discussed by the Committee on Intellectual Cooperation, to assure in all countries the earning out of the decisions and recommendations of that Committee, and, under the direction of that Committee and by every means in its power, to promote, through international cooperation, the organisation of intellectual work throughout the world.

On 13 December, the Council (32nd session) decided that its acceptation of this second letter should be considered as the agreement with the French Government. The Institute would be administered by a Governing Body, a Committee of Directors, and a Director. The Governing Body should be composed of ICIC members for the time being (Article 5). It appointed, with the approval of the Council, the Committee of Directors, which included the Chairman of the Governing Body, as well as the Director and Heads of Departments (Article 7).

The International Institute of Intellectual Co-operation (IIIC) was established by a law of 9 July 1925 and installed in the fine building of Palais Royal, on 26 October. It was inaugurated on 16 January 1926, with the presence of the Prime Minister (Édouard Herriot), the Minister of Public Instruction (Édouard Daladier), the President of the Council of the League of Nations and its Secretary-General, the diplomatic corps and other personalities. It became the executive organ of the ICIC, with seven sections (General Affairs, University Relations, Scientific Relations, Literary Relations, Artistic Relations, Legal Section and Information Section), several Committees and Centres. Seeckaert (1970) remarked that it "included in its programme all sorts of tasks which were part and parcel of the UIA's activities, so causing the displacement from Brussels to Paris of the hub of the international intellectual movement" (p. 31).

The ICIC fifth session took place in Paris from 11 to 14 May 1925.[43] It was mainly dedicated to the organisation of the IIIC. At the seventh meeting (14 May), it was decided "that the Chairman of the Governing Body should be a Frenchman", following a proposal by Ganzague de Reynold (Switzerland), according to whom the Institute "had need of the large intellectual atmosphere of France" and such a decision "would seem to give to French opinion a sufficient moral guarantee". In the course of its existence, the IIIC was led by three French Directors, namely: Julien Luchaire (1926–1930), Henri Bonnet (1931–1940) and Jean-Jacques Mayoux (1945–1946).

At the ICIC sixth session (27–30 July 1925),[44] Gilbert Murray took the chairmanship in the absence of Henri Bergson for reasons of health. He said in his opening speech that he:

> … wished in the first instance to express his very sincere and very deep regret at the absence of the Chairman of the Committee, M. Bergson, whose gracious presence had constituted one of the chief charms of the Committee and whose enthusiasm for their work had kept faith alive in the Committee in spite of many disappointments.

At the ICIC seventh session (Paris, 14–18 January 1926),[45] Bergson sent a telegram informing that he was "prevented by my state of health from coming to Paris". Hendrik A. Lorentz (Netherlands) was elected Chairman.

The first ICIC President was always remembered with the utmost respect, admiration and affection, for "the brilliance of his arresting personality", as said Jacques Bardoux before the Assembly, by presenting a Report of the Fifth Committee on 26 September 1923.[46] At its 11th session (Geneva, 22–26 July 1929),[47] the ICIC sent to Bergson the following telegram: "The Committee on Intellectual Cooperation, meeting for its eleventh session, remembers with feelings of respect and friendship its former Chairman, to whom it sends its best wishes and devoted remembrances". Again, at its 13th session (July 1931), it sent a telegram: "The International Committee on Intellectual Cooperation, in the thirteenth plenary session at Geneva, offers to its eminent first Chairman its grateful homage and respectful and cordial wishes".

At the ICIC tenth session (Geneva, 25–30 July 1928),[48] Gilbert Murray had been elected Chairman, replacing Hendrik Lorentz (died). He said: "The first Chairman was the most famous and widely read of contemporary philosophers, the second the most international of all scientists. Both are among the great names of the century". Murray was the third and last ICIC Chairman (1928–1939).

4.1.2.3.4 *International Institute of Educational Cinematograph*

Although an International Institute of Educational Cinematograph (IIEC) had been a French project too, it was the Italian Government that offered to establish and fund it, in Rome, to be incorporated in the League of Nations.

The Italian offer came to the Agenda of the Assembly Eighth Session that forwarded it to the Council on 20 September 1927. On 28 September, the Council (47th session) accepted it and asked the Italian Government to submit a draft Statute. This was done on 11 February 1928.[49] The proposed "Organic Statute" was very similar to that of the IIIC that had contributed to its drafting. It was adopted by the Council on 30 August (5th session), with some amendments, that appointed the first members of its Governing Body on 26 September (52nd session).

The IIEC was inaugurated on 5 November 1928, in the presence of His Majesty the King of Italy. One of the inaugurals speeches was made by the President of the Italian Council of Ministers, Benito Mussolini. After an Assembly Resolution (12th Session), on 24 September 1931, the IIEC became part of the ICIC.

According to Article 2 of its General and Administrative Regulations approved by the Council (66th session) on 26 January 1932[50]:

> The object of the International Educational Cinematographic Institute shall be to encourage the production and promote the distribution and exchange of educational films by all suitable measures and suggestions.
>
> The Institute's main attention shall be devoted to the mutual understanding of peoples in the spirit of the League of Nations.
>
> It shall also endeavour to secure the general adoption of the best methods of utilising films from the educational point of view. [...]
>
> The organs of the Institute are:
>
> 1. The Governing Body
> 2. The Permanent Executive Committee
> 3. The Advisory and Technical Committee
> 4. The Director

The Governing Body met for the first time from 5 to 9 November 1928.[51]

The IIEC drafted a Convention on the Free Circulation of Educational Films, signed in Geneva on 11 October 1933, and published a plurilingual *International Review of Educational Cinematography.*

The Report of the first session of the Advisory Committee on League of Nations Teaching (chaired by Gilbert Murray), on 11–12 July 1934,[52] included an Annexe 4 on the "International Educational Cinematographic Institute: Report by the Director of the Institute on the Results of the International Congress of Educational and Instructional Cinematography, held at Rome in April 1934. It read:

> The International Congress of Educational and Instructional Cinematography, which sat at Rome from April 19th to 25th, 1934, laid, in its general resolution, the foundations of what might be called the future action of the Intellectual Cooperation Organisation in regard to the cinema and international relations. As this resolution makes explicit reference to the Paris Institute, the latter feels that it should submit its views to the Committee on Intellectual Cooperation. It is, naturally, the business of intellectual cooperation to utilise such new mediums of diffusion as the Press, broadcasting and the cinema, each of which would seem to be an immensely powerful agent in promoting closer intellectual intercourse, making nations more familiar with one another, and disseminating that wide knowledge of the world which must lie at the root of any international understanding.

The IIEC did not avoid being instrumentalised by the fascist propaganda.[53]

4.1.2.3.5 *Intellectual Co-Operation Organisation*

Since 1926, the IIIC was targeted by increasing criticism, with ample echo in the press. It was blamed for being *un moulin dont on ne voyait jamais sortir la mouture* (a mill from which one never saw the mill out) (as cited in Bekri, 1991, p. 71).

During the ICIC 9th session (Geneva, 20–26 July 1927),[54] at the third meeting (23 July), the IIIC Director (Julien Luchaire) presented a report on its work. He summarised the "practical results of eighteen months' activity", which were of dispersion of "our forces – multiplying our efforts and enquiries in an attempt to awaken the attention of all countries and reach all interested circles, while at the same time testing the different resources at our disposal". Now, "a change of method is necessary", namely: "for the future, we should concentrate our efforts on matters in regard to which we are determined to obtain definite results, within a definite period of time".

The IIIC Director said that, "before building a house, it was necessary to obtain the materials, and that it was mainly for this purpose that money was required to increase the activities of the Institute". The ICIC Chairman (Gilbert Murray) commented that, when he was requested to speak at meetings on the work of the Institute and the ICIC, "he experienced difficulty in convincing people of the value of the result attained".

While the IIIC shortcomings could be attributable to the discrepancy between the tasks entrusted to it and the resources at its disposal, others were deemed to have administrative and management causes. It was accused of dispersion, bureaucracy, and inefficiency. The Director was particularly targeted, as happened during the ICIC 10th session (from 25 to 30 July 1928),[55] third meeting (26 July), when he presented the General Report on its work for the year 1927–1928, which raised a general debate on the functions and management of the Institute.

Introducing the Report, the Chairman said that it "was admirably written, it was an ingenious, eloquent and imaginative document. It was not perhaps, however, strictly speaking, a report [...] such as the Committee might endorse and refer to the Council of the League of Nations. It appeared to be rather in the nature of an apologia addressed to the public by the Director". It "also seemed to be too optimistic, and occasionally appeared to meet criticisms with an air of triumph which could not perhaps in every case be justified".

Alfredo Rocco (Italy) agreed with the Chairman but concluded: "Every criticism of the Institute was due to this contradiction between the gigantic aims assigned to it and the quite insignificant means placed at its disposal. Why was there too much bureaucracy, too much red tape? Because paper replaced money". He further observed: "At the time when the League was founded, it had been asked whether there was not a danger of it becoming a super-state". Likewise, the ICIC "was agreed in thinking that the Institute could not be a sort of philosophical school or international church".

Gonzague de Reynold (Switzerland), after saying that, in the course of his travels in Europe, "had noted that the criticism of the Institute was unanimous", expressed the opinion that the underlying cause of a general unease regarding the "intellectual co-operation" was that it "had never been defined; the term was still a vague one". He recommended a principle that:

> ... could be stated in two words: great simplicity and great modesty.
>
> Simplicity was necessary because it was only thus that the best results could be obtained in moral and intellectual matters, and that action could be made proportionate to the actual means at the Institute's disposal. [...]
>
> Modesty was essential in this sense – that the Institute should not be guided by the ambition of being to the League a *pendant* in the intellectual field similar to the International Labour Office. [...]
>
> Intellectual cooperation was one of the great works of the League. It had not yet given the results expected of it, and it was time to remedy this state of affairs.

Hugo Krüss (Germany) remarked:

> The other organs of the League had been working for ten years, whereas the Institute had only been in existence for three and the criticisms which had been levelled against the work of the Institute scarcely differed, from the general point of view, from those which, up to the present, had been directed against the work of the League as a whole. It was necessary, therefore, to wait and to work for the future.

Paul Painlevé (former French Prime Minister) also made "a distinction in this criticism between the faults which could be ascribed to the Paris Institute itself and the general criticisms made against the entire organisation of the League". In effect, "the criticisms made against the Institute had been put forward on many and different occasions in almost identical terms against the League. He had read in the Press that the work of the League had yielded no practical results".

4.1.2.3.5.1 First Reform of Intellectual Co-Operation

At the ICIC ninth session (Geneva, 20–26 July 1927),[56] fifth meeting (25 July), the Chairman had "concluded that meetings of delegates of the National Committees, similar to that which had taken place in Paris in 1923, would be of great use, but thought that, for financial reasons, it was impossible to contemplate convening the next meeting until 1929 at the earliest". It took place in Geneva, from 18 to 20 July 1929, and was attended by representatives of 24 National Committees, more a representative of the Ukrainian Academic Committee, another one of the *Commission Internationale Catholique de Cooperation Intellectuelle*, 7 members of the ICIC, the IIIC Director and an Under-Secretary-General of the League of Nations. The Chairman was Gilbert Murray, and the Secretary was Georges Oprescu (Romania). The Secretary of the German Committee (Morsbach) was appointed Rapporteur. In the opinion of the Chairman, "one of the great advantages of the meeting would be that the representatives would be in a position to appreciate the international spirit of Geneva, a spirit which did not exist to the same extent in any other part of the world".[57]

According to the Report submitted to ICIC 11th session (Geneva, 22–26 July 1929)[58]:

> On the Chairman's proposal, Point 4 of the agenda was taken first. At his suggestion, the previous activities of the International Committee on Intellectual Cooperation and of the International Institute of Intellectual Cooperation were frankly discussed in the light of the impressions and

> experiences gained since the creation of the various National Committees. In particular, the following proposals were made:
>
> 1. Simplification of international cooperation by the creation of a Permanent Bureau in Geneva, under the direct control of the International Committee on Intellectual Cooperation, and a corresponding limitation of the work of the International Institute of Intellectual Cooperation.
>
> 2. Limitation of the work of the International Committee on Intellectual Cooperation and of the Institute to a few practical problems of international importance and moment, to be specified by the International Committee on Intellectual Cooperation.
>
> 3. Avoidance of all unnecessary work on the part of the Institute devoted to impracticable tasks and, if necessary, changes in the present method of work. […]
>
> The above suggestions, which were discussed with keen interest, were summarised by the Chairman in the following resolution:
>
> "This Conference of National Committees of Intellectual Co-operation respectfully begs the International Committee on Intellectual Cooperation to examine in the light of experience the practical working and the ultimate purpose of the whole organisation of intellectual cooperation, and ventures to enclose for the consideration of the International Committee on Intellectual Cooperation the Minutes of its discussions and the specific suggestions contained therein".
>
> This resolution was unanimously adopted.

Another resolution stated: "The Conference recommends that the International Committee on Intellectual Cooperation should decide to hold periodically at Geneva conferences of National Committees".

At the same ICIC 11th session, ninth meeting (26 July), the following draft resolution had been adopted:

> The International Committee on Intellectual Cooperation requests the Chairman, in consultation with the Secretary-General of the League of Nations and with the Chairman of the Governing Body of the International Institute of Intellectual Cooperation, to appoint a small committee of not more than five members of the International Committee on Intellectual Cooperation to study the programme, the work and the organisation of the International Committee on Intellectual Cooperation and of the organisations under its authority and to give opinions on improvements which might be introduced therein so as to increase the positive results of their work. The Committee shall be free to add to its number,

> after consultation with the Chairman, not more than three other persons possessed of special knowledge and experience with regard to the problems under consideration.

The appointment of a Committee of Enquiry was proposed to the Council of the League of Nations and to the Assembly, which unanimously agreed.

The Committee of Enquiry was appointed in December, chaired by Pierre-René Roland-Marcel, and was composed of five ICIC members and three experts. After three weeks of work (from 14 April to 2 May 1930), at Geneva and Paris, prepared by a consultative process since the autumn 1929, the Committee concluded its Report on 2 May 1930. Its work included an audit of the Institute's management, whose conclusions deeply displeased the IIIC Director (Julien Luchaire).

The Report was submitted to the ICIC 12th session (Geneva, 23–29 July 1930)[59] by Sir Frank Heath (United Kingdom), as the Chairman of the Committee of Enquiry could not be present. He started by saying "that he accepted this task with some hesitation, for he represented a country which had only recently shown an active interest in the movement for intellectual cooperation".

Underlying the proposals of the Committee of Enquiry was the following general definition of intellectual co-operation that would become virtually official[60]:

> The *object* of intellectual cooperation is international collaboration with a view to promoting the progress of general civilisation and human knowledge, and notably the development and diffusion of science, letters and arts. Its *purpose* is to create an atmosphere favourable to the pacific solution of international problems. Its *scope* is that of the League of Nations.

Its scope was so described:

1. To develop the exchange of ideas and to effect personal contacts between the intellectual workers of all countries;
2. To encourage and promote cooperation between institutions doing work of an intellectual character;
3. To facilitate the spread of a knowledge of the literary, artistic and scientific effort of different nations;
4. To study jointly certain major problems of international bearing;
5. To support the international protection of intellectual rights;
6. To make known by educational means the principles of the League of Nations.

A long general debate took place, followed by discussion item by item on the programme, work and organisation of the ICIC (second through ninth meetings). The Committee's conclusions were adopted unanimously.

At the fifth meeting, the Chairman of the ICIC (Gilbert Murray) recalled: "The problem of the reorganisation of intellectual cooperation as a whole was an old one. [...] A meeting of the National Committees of the various countries held in 1929 had expressed the same opinion and asked for an enquiry with the object of radical reform".

Paul Painlevé said that the French Government "had asked him to see, so far as he was able, that no attack was made on the Organic Statute of the Institute [...] and that was why he was obliged to call the Committee's attention to the serious character of certain indications given in the report of the Committee of Enquiry".

At the sixth meeting, Sir Frank Heath assured "that there had never been any question of decreasing in any way the effective role to be played by the Institute. The discussions of the Committee of Enquiry, as well as of the plenary Committee, had shown complete unanimity in regard to the advisability of leaving the Organic Statute unchanged". By closing the debate, at the ninth meeting, the ICIC Chairman concluded: "There was great promise of good results for the future".

The Committee proposed to renew all the staff of the Institute on 1 August 1930. Following conversations with the French Government and the Chairman of the Committee of Enquiry, the IIIC Director (Julien Luchaire) decided to place his position at his Government's disposal. Henry Bonnet (France) was unanimously appointed by the Administrative Council to be the new Director.

The main proposals of the Committee of Enquiry were as follows:

- Enlargement of the ICIC that meets once a year.
- Creation of an Executive Committee.
- Replacement of the Sub-Committees by Committees of Experts (three types).
- Significant reduction in staff.

These decisions were presented and approved by the Council (61st session, 9 September 1930). As this affair concerned France, in particular, the French representatives sought not to give it too much importance, starting with the French translation of the Committee's name (*Comité d'Études*, the softer French designation) and referring to the reorganisation as a mere adjustment.

According to the Rules of Procedure adopted by the Governing Body (July 1931), Article 2[61]:

> The principal object of the Institute shall be to prepare the work to be discussed by the Committee on Intellectual Cooperation, to ensure in all

> countries the carrying out the decisions and recommendations of that Committee and, under the direction of that Committee and of its Executive Committee, to promote, through international cooperation, the organisation of intellectual work throughout the world, and, generally, to develop international cooperation in literature, art and science.

The Institute should be administered by:
- A Governing Body
- A Directors' Committee
- A Director

The Governing Body was composed of members of the ICIC for the time being. It appointed the members of the Directors' Committee that consisted of the same persons as the ICIC Executive Committee. It met at least four times a year. There were many Committees of Experts: Advisory Committee on the Teaching of the Principles and Facts of Intellectual Co-operation, Permanent Committee on Arts and Letters, Directors' Committee of the International Museums Office, Directors' Committee of the Institutes of Archaeology and of the History of Art, International Commission on Historical Monuments, Committee of Scientific Advisers, Committee of Architectural Experts, Committee of Directors of Higher Education, Committee of International Students' Organisations, Committee of Library Experts, Committee of Expert Archivists, Publication Committee for the Japanese Collection, Publication Committee for the Ibero-American Collection, Committee on Intellectual Rights, International Committee for Folk Arts.

4.1.2.3.5.2 Fully Assuming Intellectual Co-Operation

The 1929 Conference of the National Committees had adopted a resolution calling, among other things, "that the Assembly expressly acknowledge the existence of the Organisation for Intellectual Cooperation". At its 13th session (Geneva, 20–25 July 1931),[62] the ICIC adopted a Resolution on "The statute of the Organisation of Intellectual Cooperation and its relations with the governing organs of the League of Nations". It read:

> The International Committee on Intellectual Cooperation,
>
> Considering the increased number and importance of the questions submitted to the Council and to the Assembly of the League of Nations which relate to the work and activity of the Organisation of Intellectual Cooperation;
>
> Noting that, after an inevitable period of trial and experiment, the work of intellectual cooperation has now reached the stage of positive achievement;

> Considering that the re-organisation in progress necessitates closer and more continuous cooperation between the Committee and the governing organs of the League of Nations;
>
> Makes the following recommendations:
>
> (a) That the Assembly should expressly recognise the existence of the Organisation of Intellectual Cooperation [...].

The Council agreed, on 4 September (64th session). On 24 September, the Assembly (12th Session) adopted a Resolution recognising[63]:

> ... the existence of the Intellectual Cooperation Organisation, comprising the International Committee on Intellectual Cooperation, which is the advisory body of the League of Nations; the commissions and committees dependent on it; the International Institute of Intellectual Cooperation, its executive organ, and the International Educational Cinematographic Institute, these two Institutes having been placed at the League's disposal under the conditions laid down in their respective statutes; and the National Committees on Intellectual Cooperation, whose representatives may be called upon to meet occasionally in conference on the proposal of the International Committee on Intellectual Cooperation.

So, the Intellectual Co-operation Organisation (ICO) came formally into existence, becoming one of the four technical bodies of the League of Nations (the others being the Hygiene Organisation, the Organisation of Communications and Transit, the Economic and Financial Organisation) (see Grandjean, 2018, pp. 480, 481), serving as an advisory organ of the Assembly and the Council. On 17 January 1934 (78th session), the Council raised the Committee's size (for the third time) from seventeen to eighteen members.

ICO now had a staff consisting of some 80 officials and employees. 44 Governments appointed each an official Delegate to the IIIC (*Délégués d'État*), including some countries not belonging to the League, as it enjoyed a certain autonomy allowing the establishment of relations with all countries.

4.1.2.3.5.3 Second Reform of Intellectual Co-Operation

The ICIC 13th session (20–25 July 1931)[64] adopted a Resolution according to which: "Requests the Council of the League of Nations and the Assembly to authorise the convening in 1934 of a Conference of representatives of National Committees". Due to an insufficient budget, it was cancelled. At its 17th session (Geneva, 15–20 July 1935),[65] the ICIC decided to convene the Conference of Intellectual Co-operation National Committees in 1937. It took place from 5 to 9 July, in Paris, with Delegations from 43 countries.[66] Its Resolution III[67] recommended:

> b) That consideration be given to the possibility of concluding an inter-Governmental agreement, in whatever form may be thought the most appropriate (convention, protocol or declaration), to enable the other Governments interested in intellectual cooperation to associate themselves with the responsibilities assumed by the French Government in providing the Intellectual Cooperation Organisation with a permanent International Institute to carry on the practical side of its work.

The proposal was transmitted by the ICIC and the IIIC to the Council that recommended it to the Assembly's attention, on 14 September 1937. On 30 September, the Assembly decided to instruct the Secretary-General "to communicate the text of the draft Act to all Members of the League and non-member States for their observations"[68]: 58 Members of the League and 6 non-members. 24 States responded favourably and, on 25 April 1938, the ICIC Executive Committee called on the Council "to plan, at its next session, the convening of the Conference charged with concluding the Convention". The Council agreed on 13 May and France took charge of the organisation of the Diplomatic Conference. It was held from 30 November to 3 December 1938, in Paris, at the Quai d'Orsay. Chaired by Édouard Herriot, President of the French Chamber of Deputies and Chairman of the Governing Body of the IIIC, with four Vice-Presidents, Henri Bonnet being Secretary-General, the Diplomatic Conference counted with the participation of Delegates from about 50 States, most of them Plenipotentiary Ministers. ICIC was represented by Gilbert Murray (its President) and Gonzague de Reynold (its Rapporteur).

On 3 December 1938, an International Act on Intellectual Co-operation was signed by 23 States present at the Conference.[69] On 1st May 1939, they were 37. Others followed. The Council of the League took "cognizance of the results of the International Conference" at its 104th session, on 18 January 1939.[70]

This was the second major reform of the intellectual co-operation within the League of Nations, after the one that led to the formalisation of the ICO in 1931. It culminated its most productive phase (mid-to late 1930s) and had a twofold unspoken purpose: to undermine the Secretariat's control and to enable the membership and financial support of non-League Member States, especially the United States with its strong foundations, notably the Rockefeller Foundation and the Carnegie Endowment. There was already a USA National Committee, headed by James T. Shotwell, who would contribute to the creation of the Division of Cultural Relations in the State Department, in July 1938, and, in 1939, together with Clark Eichelberger (USA League of Nations Association), created the Commission to Study the Organisation of Peace. He was appointed to the Presidential Advisory Committee on Post-War Foreign Policy.

As wrote the Rapporteur in the Introduction to the ICIC 20th session (Geneva, 11–16 July 1938)[71]: "During the past twelve months, from July to July, the world situation, and particularly the situation in Europe, has grown still more serious, and international relations have again become more difficult". History teaches to us that "it is more especially during periods of anarchy, turmoil and ruin that thinkers have felt an imperative need to join forces and work together to save the essentials of civilisation and prepare for the times to come". According to him, these were the ICIC principles:

- First principle: *Our Organisation has been established to serve intellectual life*
- Second principle: *Establishment of our Organisation on solid national bases*
- Third principle: *To respect the diversity and originality of all forms of culture and all aspects of civilisation*
- Fourth and last principle or, rather, supreme aim: *Universality*

> Universality is something higher than internationality. By comparison with universality, internationality – or, if the term is preferred, internationalism – is merely a means to an end, and this end itself universality. Internationalism means, etymologically, relations and exchanges between nations; universality means a superior mental quality, a supreme form of culture.
>
> We have reached the universal when we serve the life of mind itself "*dans sa belle inutilité*", as our colleague Madariaga once declared at one of our meetings.

He remarked:

> An Organisation of this kind therefore needs revising from time to time. We have now reached the end of a stage. The first – the initial – stage of research and experiment led us from 1922 to the reform undertaken in 1929/1930. The second, the stage of effective work and progress – period during which intellectual cooperation at last found its real mission and gradually spread throughout the world – brings us up to the present. At each of these stages we attempted to adapt ourselves to an ever-changing world – from 1922, the post-war world, and, from 1929, a world passing through a period of depression. What are we to do now in a world more and more divided, more and more disturbed, a world in which peace is threatened daily?

The International Act came into force on 10 January 1940, but the Second World War began on 1 September 1939, with the invasion of Poland by Germany. The German army entered Paris in June 1940.

The 1937 Conference of Intellectual Co-operation National Committees had decided that it should be held every three or four years. The Council and the Assembly agreed. However, the ICIC met for the last time in July 1939 and the IIIC was closed by the German authorities in June 1940. The IIEC had closed its doors on 31 December 1937, after Italy's withdrawal from the League of Nations. According to the *Report on the work of the League – 1941–1942 – submitted by the acting Secretary-General* (Sean Lester),[72] the Assembly and the Council met only once since the war began.

4.1.2.3.5.4 Moving to Havana?

Although Shotwell had suggested, in March 1939, that the American Government invited the League of Nations Secretariat and its IIIC to the United States, in case of war, the USA had other views (see Pernet, 2014, p. 348). Since the early 1930s, it sought to establish an Inter-American Committee on Intellectual Cooperation, a project that "Latin Americans tried their best to ignore" (ibid., p. 351). The Latin American countries always strongly supported the League of Nations – and the intellectual co-operation in particular – not only because of their European cultural roots but also as a way of escaping the USA domination.

In 1936, following an invitation of Antonio Aita, Secretary of the PEN Club of Argentina, had taken place in Buenos Aires, from 11 to 16 September, the 7th "Conversation" organised by the ICIC Committee of Arts and Letters, in connection with the XIV International Congress of the PEN Clubs that was being held there from 2 to 15 September. In 1939, took place in Santiago (Chile), from 6 to 12 January, the first Conference of American Committees on Intellectual Co-operation. At stake was saving "the holy inheritance of occidental culture and civilization", as many participants said (ibid., p. 349).

In 1941, took place the second Conference of American Committees on Intellectual Co-operation, in Havana (Cuba), from 15 to 25 November, with 19 participating countries. It was decided:

> … to offer hospitality in one of the countries of America to the Paris Institute or its Secretariat, and, if this resolution was not feasible, to organize a provisional international Centre, located on the American continent. This Centre would assume, for the duration of the war and within the possible limits, the functions of the Paris Institute.[73]

Also, the International Bureau of Education, the International Union of Academies and the International Association of Historical Sciences would move to Havana. The Havana Resolution was enthusiastically greeted, except the American Delegation that:

> ... tried hard to re-launch the notion of an inter-American committee on intellectual cooperation. The Latin Americans, however, remained deeply attached to the League and its bodies of intellectual cooperation. Apart from the deeply engrained respect for European culture, the attractiveness of reaffirming the League system lay exactly in the possibility to counter-balance US power. (Pernet, 2014, p. 351)

The Cuban Government offered the facilities and funds to set up the provisional international Centre, but it never came into being.

The IIIC remained closed from 1940 to February 1945, when it was reopened with an Interim Director (Jean-Jacques Mayoux), probably as proof of life to be known at the San Francisco Conference. The following year, it was incorporated into UNESCO (19 December 1946).[74]

4.1.2.3.6 *Educational Co-Operation*

Pedro Rosselló (1979) witnessed: "A member of the International Committee on Intellectual Cooperation had even gone so far as to write that the League of Nations would never concern itself with education!" (p. xv). Nevertheless, as we have seen, when the Report of the Fifth Committee was presented to the Assembly of the League of Nations, on 21 September 1921, it was understood that education was implicit in "intellectual co-operation". An account of the Second Assembly (by H. Wilson Harris),[75] at the time, read:

> At the 1920 Assembly a rather vague resolution was passed (the British Empire delegates forming a solid and solitary minority) in favour of the assumption by the League of some responsibility for what was termed "the organisation of intellectual work". The Secretariat having made certain investigations on the subject, the Second Assembly, on the recommendation of the Council, decided to appoint a Committee of twelve, including both men and women, to draw up a comprehensive report on the subject for the Third Assembly. The importance of this decision lies in the fact that it opens the door for the first time to action by the League in the field of Education. (p. 29)

It could be rather said that, as the Covenant of the League of Nations had closed the door for action in the education field, the "intellectual co-operation" was a window opened in the institutional building of the League through which education entered like a strong invigorating stream of air. In this regard, there is some analogy to what happened with the entry of education into the European Community project, whose founding treaties in the 1950s did not mention education (see 4.2.3.4).

Three main stages may be distinguished in the evolution of the activities of the League of Nations concerning education:

- Education approached as taboo
- Focus on international education
- Expansion of educational co-operation

4.1.2.3.6.1 Education Taboo

As intellectual co-operation had entered the scope of the League of Nations as an afterthought, a kind of illegitimate child, it was first approached with surrounding precautions, like a taboo, as evidenced by following quotations:

- According to the Report of the ICIC 1st session (Geneva, 1–5 August 1922)[76]: "During an exchange of views, it was agreed that it was not advisable to mention the possibility of adding to the proposed Institute an institute for international pedagogic studies, since the Committee had always wished to avoid every appearance of interference in national questions of education" (140).

  At the ICIC 2nd session (Geneva, 26 July to 2 August 1923),[77] 12th meeting, the representative of the Secretary-General (Inazō Nitobe, Japan):
  ... recalled the fact that a certain number of Members of the League, while appreciating at its really high value the work of the Committee, nevertheless considered that the League of Nations was first and foremost a political organisation which should not dissipate its efforts to too great an extent, above all in fields of action which were not expressly mentioned in the Covenant.

- At the ICIC 5th session (Paris, 11–14 May 1925),[78] third meeting, the Chairman (Henri Bergson) recalled again:

  In regard to the question of education, he reminded the Committee that it had not dealt with this matter up to the moment because the Assembly had decided to exclude from the terms of reference of the Committee problems concerning the education of the young. This exclusion was a formal decision.

  Also, Jules Destrée (Belgium) warned, more explicitly:

  It should not be forgotten that the League of Nations, and the Committee on Intellectual Cooperation which it had set up, were still in their youth and could not develop unless they were surrounded by all kinds of precautions. Questions of education, in the English sense of the word, were connected with the question of national sovereignty. The Committee

> could not concern itself with such a problem without appearing to interfere with the life of a nation, all the more so as within each nation questions of education were among those upon which there was most disagreement between the various parties in the country.

- Taking an opposed stance, Robert Mangin (France) affirmed "that that attitude could not long continue to be adopted by the Assembly. It was contrary to the nature of the work of the Committee". Marie Curie (France/Poland) also remarked, by presenting a proposal transmitted to her:

> The International League for New Education desired to obtain the support of the Committee on Intellectual Cooperation. [She] had not wished to discourage this institution, which was a very interesting one, although the Committee had been prevented, up to the moment, wrongly she thought, from concerning itself with educational questions.

- The Agenda of the ICIC 7th session (Paris, 14–18 January 1926)[79] included the question "Instruction of Youth concerning the Existence and Aims of the League of Nations". At the first meeting, Alfredo Rocco (Italy) referred to "a more delicate question, intervention of the League in the drafting of educational programmes and school-books". In this connection:

> The Secretary said that he would like to furnish the Committee with certain complementary information on this subject. It had been understood when the Committee on Intellectual Cooperation was created that it would not deal with questions of education. It had further been indicated [...] that, outside the special question dealt with in that report, the Committee on Intellectual Cooperation would not have to intervene in educational matters.

- Maxwell Garnett (United Kingdom) to remark: "The Committee, however, without interfering with national education, might certainly deal with the problem of international education". However, as noted the Report to the Council of the ICIC 7th session[80]:

> In examining this problem, the Committee never forgot that its competence in this sphere was strictly limited, and the part it could play was, therefore, a very small one. It must be remembered that neither the Committee nor the League itself has any compulsory powers; they can only make suggestions. National education and moral education alike lie outside, and will always lie outside, their competence. On the

> other hand, the League has every right – and, indeed, is in duty bound – to take steps to acquaint young people in every country with its existence, work and aims.
> [...]
> In reply to the request for a preliminary opinion which the Council had transmitted to it on behalf of the Assembly, it approved the suggestion that a Committee of Experts should be formed [...]. It thought that the Committee of Experts should itself determine what work it ought to undertake, but should, of course, confine itself to instruction in the existence and aims of the League and the methods to be employed in such instruction, and should not touch upon education proper.

This was repeatedly reminded when addressing international education.

4.1.2.3.6.2 International Education

Peace education was a flag of the internationalist movement and a theme of the Peace Congresses in the 19th century. School, in particular, "can bring peace to the world" by teaching "that wars can be avoided and disputes between peoples resolved such as those of individuals, by means of law or reason", an idea shared by the International Congress of Primary Education held in Liège (Belgium), in 1905, with the participation of representatives from 18 countries (Paiva, 1911, p. 9). In the 1920s, Czechoslovakia's public schools, for example, consecrated half an hour to teaching peace, on Comenius' birthday, and the Japanese Teachers' Union founded an International Education Association. Florence B. Boeckel, Education Director of the National Council for Prevention of War, published in 1928 a 591 pages volume titled *Between War and Peace – A Handbook for Peace Workers* (New York).[81] During the 1930s, Maria Montessori – one of the greatest figures of the New Education Movement (see 5.1.2) – 'preached' internationally that "education is the weapon of peace", provided it makes itself worthy of what it teaches.[82]

The Assembly of the League of Nations adopted, at its 4th Session, in 1923, the following Resolution (VIII)[83]:

> The Assembly urges the Governments of the States Members to arrange that the children and youth in their respective countries, where such teaching is not given, be made aware of the existence and aims of the League of Nations and the terms of its Covenant.

The International Union of Associations for the League of Nations organised 'Summer Schools' on the League of Nations, in Geneva. Its 1925 Congress, in Warsaw (Poland), with the participation of Delegates from 34 National

Associations, recommended the following publications: *Covenant of the League of Nations*; *Teachers and World Peace* (a short textbook to explain the League to children); *Suggestions for the Consideration of Teachers in Framing Schemes of Lessons on the League of Nations*; *Un Monde Nouveau réclame une Éducation Nouvelle* (A New World calls for New Education, a call presented to the International Council of Women at its Washington Congress, in 1925).

At the Assembly of the League 5th Session, in September 1924, the following Resolution was adopted[84]:

> The Assembly decides to place on its agenda and to refer to the sixth Assembly the proposal of the Uruguayan delegation that the Council should be requested to instruct the Committee on Intellectual Cooperation to invite all teachers and professors to collaborate in the work of the League by preparing and distributing to all scholastic institutions literature instructing the young in the aims of the League.

On 29 July 1925, the ICIC adopted a Resolution on the "Casares Proposal" (after the name of its member Julio Casares, Spain)[85] on school textbooks revision, according to which "one of the most effective methods of bringing about the intellectual *rapprochement* of peoples would be to delete or modify passages in school textbooks of a nature to convey to the young wrong impressions leading to an essential misunderstanding of other countries". This Resolution "was a milestone in the history of education for international understanding" (Saul, 2016: III – The Right to Education). A revised version was adopted in 1932.

According to the Report to the Council of the ICIC 7th session (Paris, 14–18 January 1926),[86] the following Resolution was adopted (Annexe 1):

> The International Committee on Intellectual Cooperation fully appreciates the value and importance of the invitation addressed to it by the sixth Assembly to participate in any steps which may be taken with the object of acquainting children and youth with the aims and work of the League of Nations. The Committee is fully aware of the importance of this task and of the difficulties which may arise in its execution. It accepts the suggestion of the Assembly to convene a Sub-Committee of Experts in order to discuss the means likely to spread as widely as possible the conviction that the nations must be organised in order to settle their differences by the method of peaceful understanding.

The Council appointed the Sub-Committee of Experts for the Instruction of Children and Young People in the Existence and Aims of the League of Nations that met in Geneva from 3 to 6 August 1926.

At its 9th session (Geneva, 20–26 July 1927),[87] the ICIC approved and endorsed the "Recommendations" and conclusions submitted by the Report of the Sub-Committee of Experts. According to the Report on the ICIC 12th session (Geneva, 23–29 July 1930)[88]:

> The Council's attention should also be directed to a very important proposal also submitted by the Sub-Committee of Experts for the Instruction of Youth and approved by the Committee on Intellectual Cooperation. The latter recommends an enquiry regarding school textbooks on history and geography, civics and morals and on the readers in use in the various countries. In order to avoid all possible misunderstanding, it should be emphasised that there is no question of establishing international textbooks or of asking the League of Nations to intervene in questions of national education.

The ICIC had before it (Annexe 3) a "Memorandum submitted to the International Committee on Intellectual Cooperation by its Chairman" (Gilbert Murray)[89] that justifies extended quotation, as it summarises the work already done and meant a somewhat turning point towards a larger vision of international education:

> In September 1923, the League of Nations Assembly concerned itself for the first time with the problem of the teaching of the younger generation. The resolution adopted at that time has served as a starting point for the action subsequently taken […].
>
> In 1924, the Assembly instructed the Secretariat to investigate the action which was being taken and, in 1925, it decided to take a further step and to act through the Committee on Intellectual Cooperation, thus emphasising at the outset its wish to avoid, in any action taken in the educational field, all suspicion of favouring mere propaganda.
>
> The Committee was asked to consider the summoning of a Sub-Committee of Educational Experts to go into the whole problem, which was enlarged so as to cover, not simply the teaching of the League of Nations and its Covenant, but also the question of "how to train the younger generation to regard international cooperation as the normal method of conducting world affairs". This proposal having been endorsed by the Committee on Intellectual Cooperation, a Sub-Committee of fourteen members of different nationalities was appointed and met in 1926 and 1927. It issued a report which aroused great interest and attained a wide circulation, thus showing from the very first how action in the field of education on lines

> of international understanding answered to the needs of the moment and was universally felt to be essential to the maintenance of peace.
>
> One of the recommendations of the Sub-Committee approved by the Assembly of 1927 was that an official centre should be established where information concerning the progress of the work covered by the recommendations of the experts would be available. [...]
>
> If the work undertaken at the request of the Assembly is to progress and to attain the efficiency unquestionably necessary to the prestige and authority of the League of Nations, it is essential to change the present way of dealing with it. [...]
>
> I would submit to the consideration of the Committee on Intellectual Cooperation the need for appointing at the head of this service a really qualified professional who, mindful of his duty of never interfering in national educational questions, will yet be able to direct the action of educationists and the teachers of the world towards the increasingly necessary international outlook [...].

On 23 September 1931, following a request of the Polish Government, the Secretary-General of the League of Nations transmitted to the Council, the Members of the League and the States invited to the Disarmament Conference scheduled for April 1932, in Geneva, a *Memorandum* on moral disarmament.[90] It read:

> In submitting the present memorandum to the Governments invited to the Conference, the Polish Government desires to draw attention to the value of achieving moral disarmament, and to suggest, at the same time, a few of the spheres where this is most urgently required. [...]
>
> In order to secure lasting moral disarmament, a great effort must be made to protect young people from everything capable of breeding in them hatred of a foreign nation. Schoolteachers should therefore be forbidden to abuse their position by arousing in their pupils' minds distrust and ill-will towards foreigners. Schoolbooks, particularly those dealing with history, geography, etc., would also have to be examined. On the other hand, instruction should be given to all young people so as to render them familiar with the aims and organisation of the League of Nations. The Sub-Committee of Experts of the International Committee of Intellectual Cooperation framed certain recommendations on this subject. This Committee recommended, inter alia: (1) compulsory instruction in all schools in regard to the work and aims of the League of Nations and, more generally, the development of international cooperation; (2) the formation of special League of Nations chairs in Faculties of Law; (3) the elimination from schoolbooks of everything capable of arousing hatred of foreigners, etc.

Following the *Polish Memorandum*, on 19 January 1932, the President of the ICIC (Gilbert Murray) requested the Secretary-General of the League to include information about the activities concerning the matter in the Conference documentary material on ICIC activities.[91] The following were mentioned as being "Urgent Questions": Instruction in the Work of the League, International Relations, School Textbooks, Broadcasting, Cinema. The "Educational" activities included: Collaboration in Primary and Secondary Education, Travel of Primary and Secondary School Children, Exchange of Professors and Students, Study Scholarships, Scientific Study of International Problems. Other ones included: Intellectuals in International Life, and Coordination of International Work in General. A "Memorandum on the Organisation and Working of Intellectual Cooperation from the point of view of Moral Disarmament" was annexed too.

The Political Commission of the Disarmament Conference set up a Committee on Moral Disarmament, at its meeting on 15 March 1932. On 17 November 1933, it adopted a document[92] following which:

> Article 1
>
> The High Contracting Parties undertake to use their powers or their influence to see that education at every stage, including the training of teachers, is so conceived as to inspire mutual respect between peoples and to emphasise their interdependence, which makes international collaboration a necessity.

In accordance with a Decision of the Council, on 22 September 1933 (76th session),[93] the ICIC appointed an Advisory Committee on League of Nations Teaching (chaired by Gilbert Murray) to replace the former Sub-Committee of Experts on the Instruction of Youth in the Aims of the League of Nations. It held its first session in Geneva, on 11–12 July 1934. Following the Report of the ICIC 16th session (Geneva, 16–21 July 1934)[94]:

> The Committee concludes that, although it should remain a subject of instruction, the League of Nations, and particularly its basic principles, should not be regarded as a separate subject but should be incorporated, according to the requirements of the different disciplines and national mentalities, in the general curricula of the various grades. […]
>
> … efforts might be more effective if they were closely associated with the endeavours made to propagate the international spirit, to promote a knowledge of other countries and of the mutual duties of nations, and more generally any instruction designed to bring out the value of the

> special contribution of the genius of the several nations as a part of the common heritage of civilisation.

The Report included Appendix 5 with "Extracts from the General Report of the Director of the International Institute of Intellectual Cooperation to the International Committee". In the Introduction to the IIIC Report it was affirmed:

> All bear witness to the interest of the intellectual world, and of its best representatives, in a movement directed towards ensuring the recognition of a universal moral doctrine – those ethical principles which must constitute the basis of a flourishing League of Nations – and towards the prevention of the dangerous excesses and warped mentality that are born of hatred. [...]
>
> But if ever unanimity has been reached during the discussions which the Intellectual Cooperation Organisation has devoted to the issues of the day, it is surely on the part played by education and the fundamental importance of the problems of teaching. This problem is generally regarded as the key to the future; this is not the place to discuss it or to attempt to discover how sound educational methods can be substituted for dangerous forms of instruction and their natural orbit extended. It may be noted, however, that, in the work of intellectual cooperation, the place reserved for everything relating to education has, this year again, been considerable.

At its 17th session (Geneva, 15–20 July 1935),[95] the ICIC adopted a Resolution on "Revision of School Textbooks", following a proposal by Émile Borel (France) and an IIIC Draft Declaration regarding the Revision of History Textbooks. The Declaration was approved by the Assembly of the League on 2 October 1937, at its 16th session.[96] According to it:

> The Governments ...
>
> Declare that they agree, each for its own part, upon the following principles: [...]
>
> 3. It is desirable that in every country a committee composed of members of the teaching profession, including history teachers, should be set up by the National Committee on Intellectual Cooperation, where such exists, in collaboration with other qualified bodies. [...]
>
> They would, in particular, be empowered, should they think the revision of school textbooks necessary, to follow the procedure provided for in the resolution adopted on July 29th, 1925, by the International

> Committee on Intellectual Cooperation, on the proposal of M. Casares, the recommendations of which were confirmed and amplified in 1932 and 1933 by the International Committee on Intellectual Cooperation and approved by the Assembly of the League of Nations.
>
> 4. The present Declaration [...] shall bear this day's date and shall be open for signature on behalf of any Member of the League of Nations or of any non-Member State to which a draft of the said Declaration has been communicated.
>
> 5. The present Declaration shall be registered by the Secretary-General of the League of Nations when it has received two signatures, on which date it shall come into force.

The Council was requested to communicate the Declaration to the States Members and non-Members. In 1938, the Report of the ICIC 20th session[97] informed: "The Declaration concerning the teaching of history [...] came into force on November 24th, 1937. Up to the present, fourteen countries have acceded to the Declaration".

At its 2nd session, held in Geneva on 10–11 July 1935, the Advisory Committee on League of Nations Teaching adopted a long programmatic Resolution, according to which[98]:

> a. The object of teaching on the subjects of the League of Nations and international relations must be not only to give the younger generation an objective knowledge of the international aspects of a great many problems of contemporary affairs. It must also be based on moral considerations, with a view to fostering sentiments of justice and human solidarity. [...]
>
> c. The Committee's task is not simply to promote instruction on the organisation and work of the League of Nations as a separate subject, but to propagate a certain 'spirit', and 'international sense ', with which education as a whole should be imbued.
>
> Among the branches of instruction which appear to be best calculated to bring out the importance of international life today, the Committee, recalling its previous resolutions on this matter, considers that, at the present time, special attention should be paid to history, geography and modern languages.

The Advisory Committee held its 3rd session in Geneva, on 8–9 July 1936. The respective Report was annexed (Appendix 2) to the Report of the ICIC 18th session (Geneva, 13–18 July 1936).[99] In 1937, according to the Report of the ICIC

19th session,[100] the Advisory Committee and the ICIC thought it desirable a change of the title of the Advisory Committee, created in 1933, to become "Advisory Committee on the Teaching of the Principles and Facts of International Cooperation".

So, the scope of international co-operation was limited no more to only the League of Nations and, what is more, it could not be confined to a kind of school enclave without touching the whole education system.

4.1.2.3.6.3 Expansion of Educational Co-Operation

The Report of the ICIC 16th session (Geneva, 16–21 July 1934)[101] included, as already mentioned, an Appendix 5 with "Extracts from the General Report of the Director of the International Institute of Intellectual Cooperation to the International Committee". In the Introduction of the IIIC Report, it was affirmed: "The work done has related to all stages of education, from universities down to elementary schools".

Another Appendix (6) to the Report of the ICIC 17th session (Geneva, 15–20 July 1935),[102] referring to the "Conversation" held in Nice (1935), whose agenda called for a discussion of "The Training of Modern Man and the Aims of Education", remarked:

> From the discussions which had been conducted by an exchange of "Open Letters" and by "Conversations", there had emerged one specific point, which had engaged general attention from the very beginning. What, it was asked, are, or what should be, the function and aims of education? [...]
>
> Side by side with so many other international problems, there arises today the international problem of education. [...]
>
> In order, therefore, that the discussion held at Nice may be continued, it would be necessary to arrange a larger meeting of longer duration, which would be asked to express an opinion on definite educational problems, in accordance with an agenda prepared in detail and which would bring together the necessary groups of specially qualified persons.

The Report of the ICIC 20th session (Geneva, 11–16 July 1938)[103] read:

> When the *Advisory Committee on League of Nations Teaching* was attached to us, its mandate was based on the Assembly Resolution of September 24th, 1924, which brought it into existence: "To invite all teachers and professors to collaborate in the work of the League by preparing and distributing to all scholastic institutions literature instructing the young in the

> aims of the League". Having followed that programme for several years, the Sub-Committee decided to extend its scope. The new stage reached in 1937 was marked by a change of name: since then the Sub-Committee has been known as the *Advisory Committee on the Teaching of the Principles and Facts of International Cooperation.* [...] The Advisory Committee has studied the principles and facts of international cooperation successively in the spheres of history, geography, and, during the past year, modern languages. For the coming year the question of instruction in civics has been placed on its programme.

The Report of the ICIC 21st session (Geneva, 17–22 July 1939)[104] announced:

> Every year there are numerous educational problems which are considered and discussed by the Committee and on which it has to take decisions. [...] Among the questions to which the Committee devoted special attention this year were problems affecting higher education, the development of an international spirit amongst students, the teaching of history, civic instruction and courses of general culture in secondary education. [...]
>
> In the forthcoming administrative period, the first meeting of the Committee on Higher Education will be held. [...]
>
> The Advisory Committee on the Teaching of the Principles and Facts of Intellectual Cooperation has for some years past been devoting each of its sessions to the study of a single problem; the teaching of modern languages, the teaching of geography, etc.
>
> This year it will meet in December. The Committee on Intellectual Cooperation has retained a subject already chosen in 1938 – namely, civic education. The Institute is preparing the way for the discussions by conducting a comparative enquiry into this type of education in the different countries.

The IIIC and ICIC last Agendas offer an overview of the expansion of the "intellectual co-operation" regarding education from 1922 to 1938:

- The IIIC Agenda reported to the ICIC 18th session (Geneva, 13–18 July 1936)[105] included: Organisation of Higher Education; International Relations between Universities; University Exchanges; Students abroad; Holiday Courses in Europe; Committee of International Student Organisations; Collaboration with China; National Educational Information Centres; Bibliography; Teaching of History; Revision of School Textbooks; School Broad-

casting; International School Correspondence; Travel and Exchanges of Young People; Liaison with the Major International Associations.
- The IIIC Agenda reported to the ICIC 21st and last session (Geneva, 17–22 July 1939)[106] included: The Teaching of History; Civic Instruction; Coordination of Systems of Secondary Education; Enquiry on the Organisation of Higher Education; Standing Committee on Higher Education; The Student and the International Student Organisations; International Conversations for Students; Holiday Courses in Europe; Students abroad; International University Documentation; National Educational Information Centres; International School Correspondence; Liaison with the Major International Associations.
- The Agenda of the ICIC 20th session (Geneva, 11–16 July 1938)[107] included: Revision of School Textbooks and History Teaching; Secondary Education; Permanent Committee on Higher Education; Unemployment of University Graduates; Students' International "Conversation".
- The Agenda of the ICIC last session (Geneva, 17–22 July 1939)[108] included: International Studies Conference; Study of Social Sciences; Application of the Convention for facilitating the International Circulation of Films of an Educational Character; Unemployment among Intellectuals; Committee on Higher Education; International Student Organisations; Diffusion of Scientific Information.

Other facts illustrate the expanded work concerning intellectual co-operation in respect of education:
- Among other numerous publications,[109] the IIIC published an *Educational Survey* (1929–1934), later the *Bulletin of League of Nations Teaching* (1935–1938); a bilingual International Educational Bibliography (French and English); a list of educational works and articles published in 31 countries; a reference book for teachers titled *Aims and Organisation of the League of Nations.*
- A Report by the ICIC Chairman (Gilbert Murray) informed, at its 13th session (20–25 July 1931),[110] that two communications had been received from the Chinese Ministry of Education (1931) requesting the League of Nations to send a mission of experts to China to aid in the reorganisation of its education system. A mission was sent and, in 1933, a mission of Chinese educationists came to Europe to study the organisation of public education.
- Even an International Sanatorium for Students was envisaged, taking as starting point the experience gained by the Swiss University Sanatorium opened in 1922, in Leysin, for students and professors of the institutions of higher education in Switzerland, without distinction of nationality. It was

visited by university professors, writers, and other personalities, who gave lectures for the patients.[111]

Concerning intellectual co-operation in general:
- Between 1933 and 1935, were published "Open Letters" on topical questions exchanged between renowned intellectuals: Einstein, Freud, Paul Valéry, Aldous Huxley, André Maurois, J. Huizinga, Gilbert Murray, Salvador Madariaga, Henri Focillon, Robert Waelder, Miguel Ozorio de Almeyda, Alfons Reys, Tsai Yuan Pei, J. Strzygowski, Rabindranath Tagore, Johan Bojer.
- Between 1932 and 1938, the Permanent Committee on Arts and Letters organised "Conversations" gathering distinguished intellectuals in different European cities: Frankfort (in 1932, on "Goethe"), Madrid (1933, on the "Future of Culture"), Paris (1933, on "Future of the European Culture"), Venice (1934, on "Art and Reality, Art and State"), Nice (1935, on "The Training of Modern Man" and "The Methods of Education"), Budapest (1936, on "What is meant by 'Humanities' and by 'Humanism'?"), Paris (1937, "The Letters near Destiny"), Nice (1938, on "Quality of Modern Life"). Another one took place in Buenos Aires (1936, on "Europe-Latin America"), as above said. An International Students "Conversation" took place at Luxemburg, in 1938, on "University Education, its Aims and Methods".

Summing up: The above quoted Report of the ICIC 20th session (1938) noted that "it appears that the Committee's sphere of action has constantly increased". And the Report of its 21st session (Geneva, 17–22 July 1939)[112] also remarked that "the methods of intellectual cooperation are applied to an ever-broader field".

4.1.2.3.7 *In Concluding*

The League of Nations did not succeed politically, because it failed to avoid World War II, but its internationalist legacy survived and should be acknowledged and valued. What can be concluded from the precedent outlook concerning the place of education in its short history?

The following general assessment is proposed:

1. The Covenant of the League of Nations aimed "to promote international cooperation and to achieve international peace and security",[113] without qualifying and circumscribing the scope of "international cooperation". Therefore, it did not expressly exclude intellectual and educational co-operation. How to "achieve international peace" without sowing and cultivating it in minds through education? The Report of the ICIC 16th session (Geneva, 16–21 July 1934)[114] stressed:

> No attempt to organise the world on an international basis, to establish an international order and thereby ensure abiding peace, could be durable or even possible were it not accompanied by a corresponding effort in the realm of the mind. The one is the body and the other is the soul: a League of Nations is inconceivable without intellectual cooperation.

The peaceful aims of the League were the juridical window through which education entered its co-operation framework.

2. The bodies of international co-operation set up within the League of Nations launched initiatives touching virtually all dimensions of the internationalisation of education developed after World War II by the new normative and institutional landscape drawn by UNESCO, Council of Europe, European Communities and other regional IGOs. This was reminded by the Director of the Office of International Standards and Legal Affairs of UNESCO (Abdulqawi Yusuf) in his Introduction to the publication of the essays presented at the first Symposium ever organised on UNESCO's standard-setting action that was held in Paris from 9 to 10 March 2006, on the occasion of its 60th anniversary:

> The emphasis given to standard-setting functions in the UNESCO Constitution may have been inspired by the activities undertaken by the International Institute of Intellectual Cooperation (IIIC) [...].
>
> In the realm of standard-setting, the IIIC was responsible for two major international conventions, which entered into force, and four draft conventions which, albeit adopted by various sub-committees of the League of Nations, never became operative. The first of the two conventions was the *Convention to Facilitate the International Circulation of Films of an Educational Nature*, which entered into force in January 1935. [...] The second one was the *International Convention concerning the Use of Broadcasting for Peace*, adopted also in Geneva by an international conference in 1936. [...]
>
> The draft international conventions proposed by the IIIC were: a *Draft International Convention on the Rights of Scientists*, a *Draft Universal Statute on Copyright*, a *Draft International Convention for the Protection of National Art and Historical Collections*, and a *Draft International Convention for the Protection of Ancient Monuments and Works of Art During Periods of Armed Conflict*. In addition to these conventions, the IIIC also drafted and proposed to Member States of the League of Nations a *Declaration on the Revision of*

> *School Textbooks*, and a number of suggested rules and statements on archaeological excavations, on the organization of international art exhibitions and on international competitions in architecture, town planning, and allied arts. (p. 16)

However, they were met with the resistance of States' sovereignty reflexes concerning domestic affairs, especially the educational cradle of the national cultural *soul*.

3. The International Act concerning Intellectual Co-operation (3 December 1938)[115] aimed, as read its preamble, at "giving increased effect" to the International Institute of Intellectual Cooperation" as an organisation of States instrumental to "the mission incumbent upon them of preserving the cultural heritage of mankind and of promoting the development of science, arts and letters", which "depends in a large measure upon intellectual cooperation" that should possess "the threefold character of universality, permanence and independence". The Report of the IIIC Governing Body dated from 26 July 1939,[116] referring to the International Act, pointed out:

> It is rare in these days to find so many States taking part in a Diplomatic Conference, whatever its purpose; the eagerness of nearly every Government in the world to collaborate in the work of intellectual cooperation proves that its activities stand in the very first rank among questions of urgent importance at the present day. The Governing Body unanimously expressed its gratification at that success, which has endorsed the methods of work followed by the Intellectual Cooperation Organisation, methods based on universality and the collaboration of all interested in intellectual work.

This reinforced international legal framework to intellectual co-operation would allow for it to go further, but the dark and brutal night of World War II fell. The Agenda of the third Conference of Intellectual Co-operation National Committees, scheduled to 1940, in Paris, would include: "Intellectual cooperation in the field of education: (a) At the level of the university; (b) In the primary and secondary schools".[117]

Corinne A. Pernet (2014) noted "the recent re-evaluation of the League of Nations, which has stressed the important role its technical organisations have played", emphasising "the connections – ideologically as well as institutionally – between pre- and post-war organisations" (p. 342).

The foregoing pages have documented the connections between UNESCO and the IIIC activities. Another UNESCO's forerunner was the International Bureau of Education.

4.1.2.4 International Bureau of Education

4.1.2.4.1 *First Education Non-Governmental Organisation*

In 1919, the establishment of a body similar to the International Labour Office created by the Versailles Peace Treaty was an idea widely shared.

For example, Fanny Fern Andrews (USA), who founded the American School Peace League in 1908, developed a project for an International Bureau of Education supported by her country's Government, whose statutes were approved at the 18th Stockholm Peace Congress in 1910. It was expected to be approved by an International Education Conference in The Hague (Netherlands). The USA asked the Dutch Government to call it. Several European Governments (and Japan) were invited, on 14 January 1913, but only France and Switzerland answered. The Conference was postponed until September 1914, from 7 to 12. The second invitation included the draft statutes of an International Bureau of Education. Under pressure from the USA diplomacy, 16 countries replied, but World War I broke out.

As above said, in 1919 the International Council of Women and the Suffragist Conference of the Allied Countries and the United States proposed to the League of Nations Commission the establishment of an International Bureau of Education. Also, the third Conference of the International Union of Associations for the League of Nations (Brussels, December 1919) invited the League to set up a technical organisation for education and science. On 27 September 1920, the Japanese Association of Teachers submitted to the First Assembly of the League of Nations a proposal that an International Education Council should be convened under the auspices of the League, and that it should adopt a plan to set up a permanent Bureau of International Education, with various committees. In October, the fourth Conference of the International Union of Associations for the League of Nations (Milan) requested the League to set up, at the earliest opportunity, an International Bureau of Education. An International Congress on Intellectual Activities convened by the UIA from 20 to 22 August 1921 examined the draft statutes of an International Confederation of Intellectual Workers that was set up in Paris on 8 April 1923. On a proposal by Adolphe Ferrière, it expressed the hope that "in liaison with the League of Nations and the proposed Intellectual Activities Organization, an International Bureau of Education should be set up for the comparative analysis of information on modern teaching methods" (Seeckaert, 1970, p. 30).

The League of Nations resisted all proposals, but the idea remained alive. The third International Congress on Moral Education (in 1922, Geneva), presided by Ferrière, proposed the creation of an International Bureau of Education (IBE) in The Hague. It was founded in Geneva, at the end of December 1925, by some personalities, notably the psychologist Édouard Claparède (who had founded the Jean-Jacques Rousseau Institute in 1912), with the financial support of the Foundation Rockefeller.[119] The first Director was Pierre Bovet, having as Deputy Directors two prominent leaders of the New Education Movement: Adolphe Ferrière and Elisabeth Rotten. The Steering Committee included Albert Einstein. It met for the first time on 19 January 1926. In May, "the permanent committee of the International Congress of Moral Education acknowledged the IBE as a successor of its International Bureau of Moral Education, in The Hague, entrusting it to pursue its own enterprise" (Hofstetter & Schneuwly, 2013, note 3).

4.1.2.4.2 *Four Stages*

There are four clear-cut phases in IBE history:

1. 1925–1929: First years as NGO
2. 1929–1939: Activity as IGO until the outbreak of World War II
3. 1939–1945: Wartime
4. 1945 onwards: Incorporation into UNESCO

1925–1929: First years as NGO

Here is "the founding principle of IBE: international understanding, a goal that spans all the documents like a leitmotiv" (id. p. 225). Among its first initiatives, a children's literature section was set up, with American financial support, to developing a spirit of international co-operation through children's books. It organised, for six years, summer courses on "How to make the League of Nations Known and Develop the Spirit of International Cooperation", attracting teachers from many countries. In 1927, it organised the Congress "Peace by School", in Prague.

Besides children's books, the IBE library grew with school textbooks, educational journals, legislative texts and collections of other works on comparative education. It published a *Bulletin of Educational News and Bibliography*, issued four times a year, with an increasing number of pages and of copies.

1929–1939: Activity as IGO until the outbreak of World War II

As IBE not afforded to survive, it was obliged to become an IGO, on 25 July 1929. The first Member States were Poland, Ecuador, and the Republic and

Canton of Geneva, the only private member being the Institute J.-J. Rousseau. The Republic and Canton of Geneva was some years later replaced with Swiss Confederation. Other States progressively joined. In 1938, on the eve of World War II, Member States were 17. "For the first time in history, representatives of governments signed a document in which they undertook to collaborate in the field of education" (Rosselló, 1979, p. xii). Jean Piaget was appointed Director, a position he held until 1969, with Pedro Rosselló as Assistant Director.

According to IBE Statutes (Article 2):

> The aim of the International Bureau of Education is to serve as an information centre for all matters relating to education. The Bureau, which aims at promoting international cooperation, will maintain an entirely neutral position with regard to national, political and religious questions. As an organ of information and investigation, it will work in a strictly scientific and objective spirit. Its activities will be twofold: to collect information relating to public and private education, and to undertake experimental or statistical research and to make the results known to educationists.

In 1932, the IBE decided to open its annual summer session to representatives of non-Member States, and to convene International Conferences on Public Education that took their future form in 1934. They have convened annually (except during World War II), through the intermediary of the Swiss Federal Council, gathering Ministers, diplomats, educationists, researchers. States were asked to present, each year, reports on their education systems. These official reports served as the basis for an *International Yearbook of Education*. In 1937, began a Permanent Exhibition of Public Education, where each country could display its educational progress.

Recommendations were adopted by the International Conferences, addressing administrative and pedagogical questions of interest for most countries, generally dealing with primary and secondary education, but also with international understanding, notably the following ones:

- "The development of international understanding among young people and teaching about international organizations" (1948)
- "The teaching of geography as a means of developing international understanding" (1949)
- "The international interchange of teachers" (1950)
- "Education for international understanding as an integral part of the curriculum and life of the school" (1968)

The adoption of the Recommendations was prepared by international inquiries on the respective subjects, as well as monographs. These Recommendations were "the IBE's main achievement" (Rosselló, 1979, p. xi).

The IBE and the ICIC of the League of Nations, both seated in Geneva, collaborated. For example, in 1938, the Report of the fifth session of the ICIC Advisory Committee on the Teaching of the Principles and Facts of International Cooperation[120] informed:

> In 1935 the Committee requested the International Education Bureau to collect from Ministries of Education documentation concerning the teaching of modern languages as a means of promoting mutual understanding between nations. The International Education Bureau, which had at that time also undertaken a general investigation into the teaching of modern languages, agreed to extend the scope of its enquiry in order to comply with the Advisory Committee's request. The Committee was therefore anxious to hear a statement on the results of that enquiry by Professor Jean Piaget, Director of the International Education Bureau, before discussing the various items on its agenda.
>
> Professor Piaget's account of the existing situation in a large number of countries added usefully to the information at the Committee's disposal.

Piaget was Assessor of the Advisory Committee on League of Nations Teaching.

1939–1945: Wartime

During the war, most of IBE ordinary activities had to be interrupted, because of the difficult international relations and communications, but it set up a Service of Intellectual Assistance to Prisoners of War that, between 1939 and 1945, sent over half a million books to prisoners of detention camps.

1945 onwards: Incorporation into UNESCO

After the war, it became clear that the IBE *raison d'être* was taken over by the new UN "specialised agency" created in 1945: United Nations Educational, Scientific and Cultural Organisation (UNESCO). As a result, on 28 February 1947, the two Organisations reached an interim agreement, confirmed and enlarged on 28 February 1952. In 1968, another agreement was signed to integrate IBE into UNESCO. Governed by a Council consisting of representatives of Member States, the IBE became an international centre of comparative education, but retaining its name, headquarters (Geneva) and enjoying a large autonomy.[121] Its Director (Jean Piaget) was Under Director-General for Education of UNESCO in 1949/1950.

In 1970, the name of the International Conference on Public Education was changed to become the International Conference on Education, open to the participation of education providers other than States. Later, the IBE focus was adjusted too:

- In the 1990s, it became an international centre for developing contents and methods of education.
- In 2011, it was transformed into a global Centre of Excellence in Curriculum.

As read the inaugural issue of *IBE In Focus – 2015*, a new annual magazine[122]: "The 20th century will easily go down in history as the century of the 'institutionalization of the international' in the field of education. It all started in 1925, with the establishment of the IBE" (p. 21). UNESCO took over.

4.1.2.5 UNESCO's Advent

Early 1940, a United States Committee on Educational Reconstruction to develop an International Education Organisation was formed by professional educators meeting in Princeton, New Jersey. The Committee was chaired by E. George Payne, Dean of the New York University School of Education. In January 1943, it appointed a special commission, chaired by Alonzo Myers (New York University), to develop plans for an International Education Office. Grayson Kefauver, Dean of Stanford University School of Education, participated in the project. Kefauver and Sir Ernest Simon, a member of the British Parliament and Chairman of the University of Manchester Board of Trustees, collaborated in developing "A Proposal for the Establishment of an International Commission on Education", drawing on the American and European educational internationalism (see Dorno, 2006, p. 301 ff.).

Kefauver, who was Vice-Chairman of the American Council on Education (1938–1939), Vice-President of the Progressive Education Association (1939–1942), President of the National Society for the Study of Education (1942–1943), and would play a leading role in the USA participation in the founding of UNESCO, had influent contacts and access to Governmental officials. His campaign for a post-war international education organisation culminated in an international conference held in Harpers Ferry, West Virginia, in September 1943. It was convened by the Liaison Committee for International Education, composed of representatives of some 20 American educational organisations interested in international education, chaired by Kefauver. Among them were the Educational Policies Commission, the International Education Assembly, the Institute of International Education, the American Council of Learnt Societies, and the American Association for an International Office of Education.

The international conference was attended by over 30 American professional organisations and 70 invited participants from 26 nations. An Observer of the State Department (Ralph Turner) was present. Its conclusions – *Education for International Security: Proposals of the International Education Assembly* – included the establishment of an International Organisation for Education and Cultural Development, whose functions were outlined. Turner collaborated in their drafting and they were welcomed by the USA Office of Education.

4.1.2.5.1 *The Sound Report of a British Joint Commission*

In 1943, the American Council on Public Affairs published *Education and the United Nations: A Report of a Joint Commission of the Council for Education in World Citizenship and the London International Assembly*[123] with a short Introduction by Kefauver. The London International Assembly (LIA) was an unofficial body formed of people from all the United Nations (those fighting the Axis Powers), constituted in September 1941 "to serve the common cause of all those nations that are resisting aggression" (p. 7). At the time, its President was Lord Robert Cecil (Viscount Cecil of Chelwood, since 1923) and the Deputy President was Henri Rolin, Belgian Senator, member of the Permanent Court of Arbitration. The Council of Education in World Citizenship (CEWC) was a body formed of representatives of the British associations of education authorities, of teachers and other educational organisations. The Chairman was Gilbert Murray, former ICIC President, as we know. In January 1941, the Council held a conference with representatives of Allied Ministries of Education, academics and teachers from Allied countries.

The Joint Commission had been appointed at the end of 1941, on a proposal by Murray. It was formed of 56 members and observers from the Board of Education, the British Council, and the Royal Institute of International Affairs. Murray was appointed Chairman and the Secretary was C. W. Judd. It held its first meeting on 4 February 1942 and since then met twelve times, at the Hilda's College, Oxford. According to the Chairman, "our Commission has been principally concerned with three main problems, the restoration of education in the countries that have been under Axis oppression, the re-education of Germany, and international arrangements for the advancement of education" (p. 15).

The Report of the Joint Commission included, after the Introduction, three short Comments. The author of one of them (William G. Carr, Secretary of the Educational Policies Commission, established by the National Education Association and the American Association of School Administrators) said that both his Commission and the British Joint Commission "urge that peacemakers after this war realize that the shaping of the minds of men is no less important than political and economic arrangements". While noting that the two Commissions "supplement on another", he noted:

> On only one important matter is there disagreement, namely, on the question of compulsory control of education in post-war Germany by educational officials of the United Nations. The British Joint Commission favours such control. The Educational Policies Commission's report does not.

To justify the compulsory control of German education, the Report included large quotations about Nazi education mainly taken from a paper titled "Minds in the Making" (Eric Robertson Dodds) (pp. 13–15). Passages of Hitler's *Mein Kampf* were recalled too (p. 21). In this respect, it was mentioned the German newspaper *Frankfurt Zeitung* of 31 May 1939 informing:

> … that according to the estimate of a German official 45 per cent of the entire teaching staff of the universities and technical colleges was replaced between 1933 and 1939. Moreover, it is known that in 1933 special committees examined the political records of 160,000 schoolteachers, and that large numbers of them were dismissed. (p. 51)[124]

Therefore:

> This is the nature of the problem that must be faced and, in our own examination of it, we have not ignored the fact that its roots lie further back in the history of the German people. […] Nazism is undoubtedly only the latest and most violent form of the vaunted *Kultur* of the German people, of their militarist tradition, Pan-Germanism and disastrous worship of their own race. […]
>
> We have considered the task allotted to us to include much more than the mere reconstruction of educational and cultural systems and institutions as part of the general process of reconstruction after the war. It seemed to us proper to consider also the *kind* of education that should be provided in all countries in order that a new generation may be able to create the new world proclaimed in the Atlantic Charter and other statements of our war aims. […] It should in our view be one of the primary aims of education to prepare the hearts and minds of men for the winning of the peace that should follow the winning of the war. (pp. 15, 16)

Before such a “moral crisis” it was asked: Should education have “a sound religious foundation”? There were different views. “But, however we may differ in this, we all agree that all truly civilised men hold in common certain principles. They believe in the dignity of the human person and the oneness of the human family. These principles and the rules of conduct derived from them should be inculcated” (p. 76).

Here are the Joint Commission’s principal recommendations:

> 1. That Governments be asked to recognise that the urgent tasks of educational reconstruction in the occupied countries, as soon as they have been set free, must be one of the chief responsibilities of the United Nations, and
> 2. That, for this reason, a United Nations’ Bureau for Educational Reconstruction should be appointed now to prepare, and so far as possible put into operation, the necessary plans for meeting those needs which are too great for any nation to bear alone.
> 3. That, in any period during which Germany may be occupied, the occupying powers should exercise their control over education through a High Commissioner for Education who should be appointed in advance by the United Nations and be ready to start work at the moment the occupation begins. [...]
> 6. That for the advancement of education generally and for the promotion of education in world citizenship it is urgently necessary that the United Nations should agree to establish as soon as may be practicable an International Organisation for Education and should forthwith undertake the necessary preparations for that act. (pp. 104, 105)

Upon minor alterations, the Report was approved by the LIA and the CEWC on 10 February 1943 and commended to the Governments and other authorities of the United Nations, because these are “the hard facts”:

> First, that the task of restoring what has been destroyed is far beyond all private enterprise and charity and must call for concerted action of the Governments. And secondly, that civilisation could hardly survive a third world war. Truly men must *learn or perish*. (pp. 103, 104)

The Report was transmitted to the Conference of the Allied Ministers of Education.

4.1.2.5.2 *Conference of the Allied Ministers of Education*

Early 1941, the LIA had taken the initiative to lunch a forum for the Ministers of Education of the European Governs exiled in London during World War II. On 11 February 1942, the British Council[125] organised an informal meeting between the President of the Board of Education (British Ministry of Education) and the foreign Ministers of Education. On 28 October 1942, at the request of the President of the Board of Education (Richard A. Butler), the Chairman of the British Council (Malcolm R. Richard) invited the Ministers of Education for a meeting on 16 November to discuss "educational questions affecting the Allied countries of Europe and the United Kingdom".[126] Besides the United Kingdom, it was attended by representatives of eight Governments (Belgium, Czechoslovakia, Greece, Luxembourg, Netherlands, Norway, Poland, Yugoslavia) and a representative of the French National Committee (renamed "French Provisional Government" after the return of De Gaulle to Paris in 1944), who was René Cassin, its Commissioner for Justice and Education.

So, the Conference of the Allied Ministers of Education (CAME)[127] was born, referred to in the report of its first session as "Conference of Ministers of Education of the Allied Governments and the French National Committee".[128] The initial countries were joined by Luxemburg in 1943 (March), the year when the USA and URSS sent observers (May), as well as China, British Dominions (Canada, Australia, New Zealand, South African Union) and India (July). The USA became a member in 1944 (April). So, they were 17 countries.

The CAME was primarily concerned with the material needs of the future rebuilding of the education systems of liberated European countries, through a relief and reconstruction agency. A first list of the equipment required amounted to about 10,000 items.[129] As a Latin sentence says, *primum vivere, deinde philosophari* (to do philosophy, we need first be alive, that is, material conditions are needed to pursue ideals). Its agenda evolved, however, from the problems of rebuilding the education systems destroyed by war to general issues of co-operation in the field of education in the post-war times.

It should be noted that the backdrop of the CAME existence were the steps towards the establishment of the Organisation of the United Nations, namely[130]:

- *Atlantic Charter*, issued on 14 August 1941 by Franklin D. Roosevelt and Winston Churchill as a statement "of certain common principles in the national policies of their respective countries on which they based their hopes for a better future for the world".
- *Declaration by the United Nations*, first signed by USA, URSS, United Kingdom and China on 1 January 1942, by more 22 countries on the next day

and by almost 50 countries until the end of the war. It was the first use of the term "United Nations", suggested by the American President Franklin Roosevelt.

- *Moscow Declaration*, signed on 30 October 1943 by the Foreign Ministers of USA, United Kingdom, URSS, and the Chinese Ambassador in Moscow, where it was recognised "the necessity of establishing at the earliest practicable date a general international organization".
- *Dumbarton Oaks Proposals for a General International Organisation – to be the subject of the United Nations Conference at San Francisco, April 25, 1945*, adopted by the USA, URSS, United Kingdom and China (the Big Four), on 7 October 1944.[131]

The CAME met, from 1942 to 1945, every two months and held 21 plenary meetings, and its Bureau 37 meetings. It set up 7 commissions, 4 committees, 7 sub-committees and a centre. It follows an account of its three years history conducting to the foundation of UNESCO in 1945, highlighting the decisive influence of the USA, documented and commented by the exchange of telegrams between the State Department and the Embassy in London.[132]

At the CAME 2nd meeting, on 19 January 1943, a Commission on Cultural Conventions was set up, following a proposal by the Belgium representative (Julius P. Hoste). Others came into being, namely (see Cowell, 1966, p. IX): Books Commission (January 1943), Science Commission, Audio-Visual Aids Commission (July 1943), Commission for the Protection and Restitution of Cultural Material (April 1944), Basic Scholastic Equipment Commission (May 1944), Commission for Special Problems in Liberated Countries (February 1945), Committee on the Belgian Memorandum (de-nazification, March 1945). The Book Commission included a History Committee (March 1943) and an Inter-Allied Book Centre (September 1944).

On 27 July (5th meeting), the CAME approved a document titled *The Origins of the Conference* that included in its aims: "Studying plans for the establishment of a permanent organization for international cooperation in education for the post-war period". An *ad hoc* committee was appointed to examine the above presented Joint Commission Report and other proposals. On 25 August, it concluded that the proposed organisation "is currently premature" (Bekri, 1991, pp. 96, 97).

A reorganisation was decided. A Planning Committee chaired by the President of the British Board of Education (Butler) was set up. A telegram from the American Ambassador in the United Kingdom (John Gilbert Winant) to the Secretary of State (Cordell Hull), on 30 July, informed[133]:

> At Fifth Meeting of Conference of Ministers of Education on July 27 questions of reconstructing Conference on broader basis, establishing Standing Committee or Bureau of Conference and of financing Conference activities were raised. [...] All delegates to Conference were invited to send representatives to Planning Committee and nations represented by observers were invited to send either accredited representatives or observers. [...]
>
> Embassy was approached informally prior to Conference meeting by officials of British Board of Education and British Council as to possible American attitude toward full participation in work of Conference or Bureau.

On 1 September, the Secretary of State asked "advice" on some matters concerning the scope of the Conference and the relation with the United Nations. On 4 September, the Ambassador answered:

> Scope of activity of conference as outlined by Butler, President Board of Education, is to promote closer cultural collaboration between Allied nations, to assist in cultural rehabilitation of war-torn Allied nations and to lay ground work for organization of permanent international Secretariat or Bureau of Education. Butler is preparing statement outlining aims in greater detail. This will be presented to plenary session on October 5 for approval.

The telegram included other information and mentioned the sending of "a report on the proposed reorganization of the Conference which was discussed by a Conference committee yesterday". This committee would meet again on 23 September, "and a plenary session of the Conference will be convened on October 5 to consider the plan forwarded by the Committee and probably to issue formal invitations to the other Allied nations to send fully accredited representatives to the Conference".

On 2 October, the Acting Secretary of State (Adolf A. Berle) informed that "Department is considering sending representatives to be accredited to the Conference in time for its December meetings". To prepare for their arrival, Ralph E. Turner (Division of Cultural Relations) would arrive in time for October 5 meeting and attend other meetings as an observer. He was authorised "to explore possibilities of cooperation" regarding various fields, including "Organization of Conference as United Nations Agency". Also, John W. Studebaker, USA Commissioner of Education, would arrive in London in the second half of the month. Two months later, the State Department appointed Kefauver Consultant to the Division of Cultural Relations.

Following a "Report on the Reorganization of the Conference of Allied Ministers of Education", an Executive Bureau was set up on 5 October (6th meeting), formed of 11 representatives and observers from the USA, URSS, China, United Kingdom and the British Dominions, to meet more frequently for coordinating the Committees. A Report on the "Origin of the Conference" was issued, according to which: "The Conference has formed the view that in its establishment and organization lies the germ of a future international organization for education and it deems to be one of its duties to consider upon what practical lines such an organization can be formed and made to function in the post-war period" (as cited in Capello, 1970, p. 6).

A new phase had begun.

On 7 October, the American Ambassador informed the Secretary of State:

> The Conference of Ministers of Education of the Allied Governments at the meeting of October 5 set up a bureau of 11 members to coordinate the work of its commissions and sub-committees. [...]
>
> Butler, the President of the Board of Education, as Chairman, desires to develop the Conference, step by step, into a United Nations agency in the educational and cultural fields. [...] The British seem willing to adapt themselves to an American viewpoint. These circumstances appear to offer an opportunity for taking steps to transform the Conference into a United Nations body.
>
> The first step in this transformation should be the determination of a principle of representation. It seems clear that until the end of the war membership should be restricted to the United Nations. [...]
>
> Turner believes that the United States Government should favor the representation of states on an equal basis. In the educational and cultural fields, democratic cooperation and international goodwill require the free and equal association of peoples.

The Ambassador observed: "The matter of Mr Studebaker's proposed visit requires consideration. American educators, recently here, have tended to create a confused state of mind about American policy and plans".

On 28 October, the Acting Secretary of State (Edward R. Stettinius, Jr.) confirmed that Studebaker would arrive in London at the beginning of November for an approximately two weeks stay. His observations should "supplement those of Turner". Later, a telegram informed the Ambassador that, due to trip difficulties, the departure of the American Commissioner of Education was delayed until approximately 7 December.

On 9 December, the *Chargé* of the American Embassy in the United Kingdom (Howard Bucknell) forwarded to the Secretary of State a communication from the Foreign Office. It informed that, following a recent CAME *Memorandum*, "the scope of its activities has been gradually extended", so that "the Conference should now be transformed into an official organization, on the basis of full membership", and "all the United Nations should be asked to appoint official delegates and to assume the financial and other responsibilities of full membership". Therefore: "His Majesty's Government in the United Kingdom accordingly has the honour to convey to the United States Government, on their own behalf and on behalf of the other Allied Governments already officially represented, an invitation to participate in the Conference on the basis of full membership". Similar invitations were addressed "to the Soviet and Chinese Governments, to His Majesty's Governments in the Dominions and to the Government of India".

On 16 and 30 December, the Ambassador informed the Secretary of State that China and URSS observers at the Conference had approached the Embassy requesting "to be kept informed about the United States' policy with regard to participation in the Conference of Allied Ministers of Education". The Ambassador noted: "Throughout the discussion the observer for the U.S.S.R. displayed a somewhat deprecatory attitude toward the Conference [...] at least as it is now organized [...] and is evidently apprehensive that the U.S.S.R. may be isolated".

On 31 December, the Secretary of State (Hull) ordered the Ambassador to "transmit the following reply to the appropriate British authorities: '[...] It is considering asking Congress for authorization to participate in the Conference and for an appropriation of funds in order to meet the costs of such participation'". On 6 January 1944, similar telegrams were sent to the Soviet and Chinese Ambassadors.

At the CAME meeting in February 1944, a little sub-committee was charged with a preliminary review of the various proposals for the establishment of an intergovernmental body. It recommended further study of the possibilities they outlined.

On 13 February, the Under Secretary of State (Stettinius) presented a *Memorandum* to President Roosevelt answering a presidential request.[134] It was affirmed:

> This Department's Division of Science, Education and Art (formerly the Division of Cultural Relations) has been and is giving this important subject active attention. [...]

To these ends we purpose to take the following steps in the immediate future:

1. Appoint an outstanding leader from the field of intellectual and educational organizations as Chief of the Department's Division of Science, Education and Art. [...]

2. Make a public statement of the Department's and this Government's general policies in respect to these matters [...]. Attached hereto is a proposed statement which, with any changes you may care to suggest, will be issued by the Department.

3. Submit proposals to the British Government and the other governments having members or observers in the existing Conference of Allied Ministers of Education in London for the transformation of the present Conference into a United Nations Advisory Commission for Educational and Cultural Reconstruction. To date, we have not participated in the existing Conference, but have sent observers. [...]

If these three proposed steps have your approval, we shall go forward on these lines immediately.

4.1.2.5.3 *USA Steps Into*

On 21 March, the Secretary of State (Hull) ordered the Ambassador (Winant) to transmit to the British Government the following reply also sent to all Governments having members or observers in the Conference:

> The United States Government acknowledges the important preliminary work done by the Conference of Allied Ministers of Education, and recognizes it as a useful agency for the further emergency development of international cooperation in educational and cultural reconstruction.
>
> The United States Government also recognizes the great importance of the reestablishment of essential educational and cultural facilities in the war-torn countries, and, therefore, proposes, for the present, to collaborate with the Conference of Allied Ministers of Education, pending the development of a United Nations Organization in this field.
>
> In undertaking such collaboration, it would be the view of this Government:
>
> First, that the Governments collaborating in the Conference should study and formulate recommendations for action on the emergency problems of rebuilding the educational and cultural facilities of the war-torn countries [...].
>
> Second, that the governments collaborating in the Conference should take steps with other interested governments to seek the best means for

> establishing a United Nations agency for educational and cultural reconstruction, organized and administered along democratic lines.
>
> The United States Government proposes to send representatives to collaborate with the Conference of Allied Ministers of Education for the session of April 5, 1944, upon which occasion initial recommendations covering the above points will be made.

On 22 March, the Secretary of State presented to President Roosevelt a *Memorandum* with a list of persons to make up the American Delegation to the April CAME meeting, namely:
- *J. William Fulbright* (Representative and member of the Committee on Foreign Affairs), Chairman of Delegation
- *Archibald MacLeish* (Librarian of Congress)
- *John W. Studebaker* (Commissioner, USA Office of Education)
- *Grayson N. Kefauver* (Dean of School of Education of Stanford University, Consultant to Department of State's Division of Science, Education and Art)
- *Ralph E. Turner* (Assistant Chief, Division of Science, Education and Art, Department of State)

Later, another name was added: C. Mildred Thompson, Dean of Vassar College.

On 31 March, the day of the departure of the Delegation to London, the Department of State released a statement of policy on the participation of the United States in the CAME. As said Ralph Turner and Hope French in a 1944 conference[135]:

> The Department of State concluded that the participation of the United States Government in an international program to provide assistance to liberated countries in re-establishing their essential educational and cultural facilities would be an important service to world security and hence to our national interest. (p. 2)

Raymond E. Wanner (2015) to comment:

> Great power politics ultimately drew US government leaders fully into the CAME process. [...] France was working assiduously to counteract Anglo-Saxon influence and promote French language and culture by seeking to have the Paris-based International Institute for Intellectual Cooperation (IICI) approved as the new organization's secretariat. Washington also grew uncomfortable with what it considered overly aggressive British leadership in the creation of the new educational and cultural

> organization. It was time for Washington to take CAME seriously. It did so with vigour. (p. 12)

At the CAME 10th meeting (April 1944), the high-level and well-prepared American Delegation carried "Suggestions for the Development of the Conference of Allied Ministers of Education into the United Nations Organization for Educational and Cultural Reconstruction" (Capello, 1970, p. 9). They were discussed during two "open-meetings" with the CAME, on 12 and 14 April, and the reactions were not unanimous. Reconstruction assistance was deemed more urgent than the creation of an international organisation.

A Drafting Committee, chaired by Fulbright, was formed to review the "Suggestions" in light of the debates. It met on 16 April, at the hotel of the American Delegation, and quickly agreed on another "tentative draft for the establishment of a United Nations Educational and Cultural Reconstruction Organization".

On 17 April, the American Ambassador informed the Secretary of State that open meetings were held on 12 and 14, with excellent progress "toward drafting a plan for a United Nations organization for educational and cultural reconstruction". General principles were agreed, and a small committee was appointed to prepare a final draft to be presented to the Conference meeting of 19 April. The Drafting Committee completed in one meeting a draft with seven sections. The Ambassador noted: "The delegation has been greatly impressed by the fine spirit of cooperation and genuine international goodwill which members of the Conference of Allied Ministers of Education have manifested". In a telegram dated from the same day (midnight), the Secretary of State (Hull) instructed the Ambassador: "We believe it essential for us to have an opportunity to go over plan with you on your return here before it is formally approved and submitted by Conference to this Government. Please make our position on this clear to Conference members and observers".

On 19 April, the revised tentative draft, merging the CAME and the USA proposals, was submitted to the Conference and approved, with minor amendments. It was informally transmitted to all "United and Associated Nations" for comments. They were informed that, when 20 Governments had favourably replied, a conference would be convened to transform the CAME into a United Nations organisation.

> Although this projected Organization for Educational and Cultural Reconstruction would at first be concerned with the emergency work of restoring essential educational facilities and cultural institutions destroyed by the Axis powers, this experience would be expected to create a basis for lasting international cooperation in educational and cultural fields.[136]

On 20 April, the Ambassador informed the Secretary of State:

> Conference of Allied Ministers of Education today accepted with minor textual amendments tentative draft of constitution of a United Nations organization for educational and cultural reconstruction prepared at open meetings convened by joint invitation of conference and the United States delegation. Conference also decided to send tentative draft constitution to all United Nations and Associated Nations for study and comment. [...] Copies of tentative draft constitution as accepted by Conference are being submitted by airmail.

Wanner (2015) summarises:

> Drawing on the existing constitutions of the UN Relief and Rehabilitation Administration (UNRRA), the Food and Agriculture Organization (FAO) and the International Labor Organization (ILO), [the American Delegation] produced a new document entitled "Suggestions for the Development of the Conference of Allied Ministers of Education into the UN Organization for Educational and Cultural Reconstruction" [...]. The Fulbright team's draft soon became the meeting's working text. After two open meetings with CAME participants, Fulbright chaired a small drafting committee that made minor revisions to the text. It was then sent as a CAME document to 44 governments for comment. (p. 13)

A *Memorandum* by the American Delegation, dated from 29 April and signed by all its members, made Recommendations, among which the following:

> 1. The Department act immediately to approve, with the amendments it may see fit to make, the tentative draft constitution of a United Nations Organization for Educational and Cultural Rehabilitation accepted by the Conference of Allied Ministers of Education on April 19, 1944.
> 2. The Department, through diplomatic channels, consider with other governments but especially with those of Great Britain, Russia, and China, their respective acceptances of the tentative constitution and the convening of the assembly provided for therein.
> 3. The Department maintain a small staff in London to collaborate with the Conference of Allied Ministers of Education in the preparation for educational rehabilitation of the war-torn countries until a United Nations Organization for Educational and Cultural Reconstruction is constituted. [...]

4. The Department, on the basis of studies undertaken by the staff in London, request an appropriation from Congress to cover the contribution of the United States Government to (*a*) the initial costs of educational rehabilitation programs, (*b*) the administrative expenses of a United Nations Organization, and later (*c*) to the Emergency Rehabilitation Fund.

On 3 May, the Secretary of State announced that most members of the Delegation had returned home, but Turner remained in London until September, and Kefauver until October 1944.

On 10 August, the Secretary of State (G. Howland Shaw on his behalf) sent to the Ambassador in London further instructions (also later sent to Moscow and Chungking):

> You are requested to bring informally to the attention of Mr. Eden [Anthony Eden, British Secretary of State for Foreign Affairs] the enclosed tentative draft of a United Nations Organization for Educational and Cultural Reconstruction. [...]
>
> The attached draft, which is slightly modified from the one originally adopted by the Conference of Allied Ministers of Education and the American Delegation, when adopted, will bring about the creation of such an organization on a temporary basis. The Department does not propose at this time to consider the matter of a permanent organization in this field.

On 23 November, the Acting Secretary of State (Stettinius) reported to President Roosevelt "on the present status of the planning for the United Nations Organization for Educational and Cultural Reconstruction, the preliminary plans for which were developed by the American Education Delegation in London in cooperation with the Conference of Allied Ministers of Education". The Report read:

> The tentative draft constitution which was developed in London last April was sent to the governments of the United Nations for their reaction. Thirteen governments have given reactions to this tentative draft constitution, all of which were favorable. The Department of State considered this draft constitution on the return of the Delegation to Washington and made certain revisions. This revised draft was sent to our Ambassadors for informal discussions with the governments of the Soviet Union, Great Britain and China concerning their position on the establishment of the United Nations Organization for Educational and Cultural Reconstruction.

> It also seemed desirable to discuss the matter with Congressional leaders before reporting back this Government's suggestions for revision of the draft constitution to the Conference of Allied Ministers of Education. […]
>
> In the meantime, this Government has continued its active collaboration with the Conference of Allied Ministers of Education through Dr Kefauver, a member of the original Delegation, who remained in London to carry on our relations with the Conference.

On 28 November, the Ambassador sent to the Acting Secretary of State a letter and a *Memorandum* from the British Foreign Office. The letter began by deeply regretting the delay in replying to the American letter from 18 August relating to the revision of the tentative draft constitution. "We are, however, in complete agreement with the general trend of your proposed modifications", which would be discussed "as soon as 20 Governments have expressed their views on the tentative draft". The British Foreign Office suggested that it could be "helpful if we were both, without further delay, to accept the project in principle on the lines of the enclosed draft memorandum" that stated:

> His Majesty's Government in the United Kingdom accepts in principle the project for a United Nations Organization for Educational and Cultural Reconstruction as set forth in the tentative draft constitution, on the understanding that:
>
> (1) they intend to propose a number of amendments to the draft when it comes before the meeting foreshadowed in the explanatory note which was circulated with it to the Governments;
>
> (2) the immediate task of the proposed Organization will be to promote practical and concrete measures to meet the urgent educational needs of liberated territories;
>
> (3) as regards other fields of educational and cultural cooperation, the activities of the proposed Organization will be directed to the preparation of plans for the establishment of a continuing organization.

On 16 December, the Secretary of State communicated to the Ambassador that the Department was "reviewing earlier plans for United Nations organization in the educational and cultural field in view of changes in general situation since last April and the clarification of the framework of international organization developed by the Dumbarton Oaks Conference". The exchange of views with the British Government should wait for the return of Kefauver to London at the beginning of 1945.

The Department of State organised meetings with dozens of national agencies, organisations and associations, on 2 March, 24 and 26 September, and 6 December, seeking their opinions on the draft constitution. Frank R. Cowell (1966) remarked:

> The weight of American public opinion was reflected and supported by the State Department and it influenced members of Congress. Practical effect was given to it by an entirely new draft for UNESCO's Constitution elaborated in the State Department and sent to London. [...]
>
> Such were the manifold and mighty influences which combined to induce the Conference of Allied Ministers of Education to supersede their limited project for what was to have been a predominantly relief and reconstruction agency and to prepare instead proposals based upon the new American draft constitution for an 'educational and cultural organisation of the United Nations'. (pp. XV, XVI)

In the opinion of Charles Dorn (2006):

> Three important international developments led the United States, in the spring of 1945, to withdraw its earlier support for the United Nations Organisation for Educational and Cultural Reconstruction. First, the United Nations Relief and Rehabilitation Administration (UNRRA), established in November 1943 and financed primarily by the United States, had become active in providing hundreds of millions of dollars in emergency aid to European nations for basic human needs such as food, clothing, medicine and the rebuilding of public utilities. [...] Negotiations at the Dumbarton Oaks conferences redirected the State Department's attention towards creating a United Nations security organization, to which an educational and cultural body was considered secondary.
>
> Perhaps even more importantly, the military situation in Europe changed radically throughout the second half of 1944. [...]
>
> When Kefauver returned to the United States in October 1944, he met with State Department officials to discuss 'certain educational and cultural problems which the changing military situation' was 'bringing to the fore'. They informed him that, in light of recent developments, the United States had moved away from its previous agreement with CAME and drafted new proposals for establishing a permanent body of educational and cultural exchange as a specialized agency within the Economic and Social Council of the United Nations' organization. (pp. 311, 312)

On 28 March 1945, the draft was revised by the Drafting Committee, taking into account the comments received from Governments. On 11 April, the Secretary of State (James F. Byrnes) informed the Ambassador[137]:

> The Department has practically completed its study of this draft and has decided to propose the establishment of a permanent international educational and cultural agency.
>
> Attached is the revised draft constitution approved by the United States Government as its proposal for an international organization for education and cultural cooperation. The draft may still be slightly modified to emphasize somewhat more the cultural as distinct from the educational functions, but the main lines are fixed. The draft is being explained to the Conference of Allied Ministers of Education in London at its meeting on April 11, 1945.

At the CAME 17th meeting (11 April), France and other European Governments objected to some American proposals.

On 19 April, as read a telegram from the American Ambassador, the Drafting Committee "decided to drop its draft proposal for a constitution and to use the United States draft as a basis for formulating working proposals to be presented by the Conference to Governments concerned and to the international conference to be called later". On 24 April, the Ambassador reported to the Department of State:

> Drafting Committee yesterday came much closer to complete acceptance of American draft, approving all main features. Revisions they have made are minor. [...]
>
> Richardson [Acting Assistant Secretary in the British Ministry of Education] yesterday made a Drafting Committee approved proposal that Conference and US Government jointly present revised statement of proposals for consideration by Governments and by the international conference to be called after the San Francisco meetings. [...]
>
> Immensely pleased with the spirit of the discussions and the agreement reached. The US document stood up very well under analysis and as the discussions advanced, there was a growing respect for the US formulation. It is a high tribute to these men that they acknowledged the higher quality of the US document accepting it as the basis of operation and modified their position on a considerable number of important points without irritation or resistance.

The San Francisco Conference took place from 25 April to 26 June 1945 to draft the United Nations Charter.

The 1944 *Dumbarton Oaks Proposals for a General International Organisation* included in its "Purposes" (Chapter I) "international cooperation in the solution of international economic, social and other humanitarian problems", without reference to cultural, intellectual and educational co-operation. However: "The Organization should have such subsidiary agencies as may be found necessary" (Chapter IV.2), as well as "promote respect for human rights and fundamental freedoms" (Chapter IX, Section A).

It was in this context that the Inter-American Conference on Problems of War and Peace, meeting in Mexico City from 21 February to 8 March 1945 (Chapultepec Conference), recommended the establishment of an "International Organization for Intellectual and Moral Cooperation between Nations". Venezuela sent to the San Francisco Conference a draft recommendation for the establishment of an International Institute for Educational and Intellectual Co-operation. Chile and Guatemala proposed the establishment of a Pan-American Institute of Education.

The reference to education in the Charter of the United Nations was met with resistance, echoing those of the time of the creation of the League of Nations. The American Delegation itself was initially hesitant, but the favourable attitude of the American Congress and the campaign of the NGOs present in San Francisco was decisive. 42 NGOs representatives of different social sectors (ABLE: Agriculture, Business, Labour, Education) had been invited to advise the American Delegation. Those of education included the National Congress of Parents and Teachers, the American Association of University Women, the American Council on Education, and the National Education Association whose Secretary Executive (William Carr) was their spokesperson. Their campaign resulted in education being referred to 9 times in the Charter signed on 26 June and, in particular, its inclusion among the ECOSOC "Functions and Powers" (Article 62.1)[138]:

> The Economic and Social Council may make or initiate studies and reports with respect to international economic, social, cultural, educational, health, and related matters and may make recommendations with respect to any such matters to the General Assembly, to the Members of the United Nations, and to the specialized agencies concerned.

On 2 May, at the 6th plenary session of the San Francisco Conference, Georges Bidault (French Minister of Foreign Affairs), speaking for the first time, announced that "France will advance suggestions to the Conference with a view to maintaining and reorganizing the Institute of Intellectual Cooperation".[139] The Report of the 12th meeting of Committee II/3 (Doc. 579, II/3/28, 25 May 1945) included a "Recommendation proposed by the French Delegation on Cultural Cooperation" (by Henri Bonnet),[140] according to which:

> The Delegations taking part in the San Francisco Conference
>
> recommend that the Member Governments should convene within the next few months a General Conference to draw up the Statute of an International Organization on Cultural Cooperation. All Governments members of the United Nations should be invited to take part in this Conference, in which the existing international Organizations specialised in the study of the same problems should participate in an advisory capacity.

At the Closing Session of the Conference, on 26 June 1945,[141] the American President Harry S. Truman declared:

> We must set up an effective agency for constant and thorough interchange of thought and ideas. For there lies the road to a better and more tolerant understanding among nations and among peoples.
>
> All Fascism did not die with Mussolini. Hitler is finished, but the seeds spread by his disordered mind have firm root in too many fanatical brains. It is easier to remove tyrants and destroy concentration camps than it is to kill the ideas which gave them birth and strength. Victory on the battlefield was essential, but it was not enough. For a good peace, a lasting peace, the decent peoples of the earth must remain determined to strike down the evil spirit which has hung over the world for the last decade.

Meanwhile, on 12 June, the American Acting Secretary of State (Joseph Grew) had instructed the Ambassador in London:

> Dept suggests that you, in your judgment, informally express view of the US Govt that it would be glad to have the Govt of UK call the international conference to establish an international organization for education and cultural cooperation. [...]
>
> Events in San Francisco have made it clear that all govts represented there want an organization formed in this field as soon as possible. Both Houses of the American Congress have so expressed themselves in identical resolutions unanimously adopted. At San Francisco, the French Delegation, particularly interested in the Paris Institute of Intellectual Cooperation, announced "French will probably take the initiative in calling this Conference in agreement with the interested govts and especially with the Brit Govt since it was in London, at the beginning of this war, that the ministers of National education of a certain number of Allied countries held their first conference".

> This Govt does not object in principle to a conference called by France. But before France, or any other govt, should issue such a call, it is considered vitally important that it accept as a kind of Dumbarton Oaks plan for the conference the present draft of a proposed constitution developed by the Conference of Allied Ministers of Education. If the UK would promptly call the conference this would be assured.

After the Bureau's 35th meeting, on 27 June, and the CAME 19th meeting, on 12 July, it was decided to send the draft adopted to the United Nations Member States, together with an explanatory document, on 1 August. A Preparatory Committee was set up, composed of representatives of the States participating in the Conference. On the same day, the Ambassador informed the Secretary of State:

> British Minister of Education issued following news release yesterday on behalf of Conference Allied Ministers of Education without consultation [...] and without discussion at meeting of Conference:
>
> "A conference is to be held in London on Nov 1 next to consider the establishment of a United Nations educational and cultural organization.
>
> The Conference of Allied Ministers of Education under the chairmanship of Mr. Richard Law, Minister of Education, at a meeting in London today unanimously agreed that the UK Govt be asked to invite on its behalf the Govts of all United Nations to send delegates to this conference.
>
> A working committee will be set up in London to make preparations for the conference and to assemble and collate opinions and proposals as to the scope and methods of operation of the organization.
>
> Draft proposals for the constitution of the organization prepared by the Conference of Allied Ministers of Education will be issued shortly and will form the basis of discussion at the forthcoming conference".
>
> Kefauver [American representative in the CAME] has expressed informally dissatisfaction with this action without preliminary discussions and failure to indicate in last paragraph that draft constitution was prepared by Conference in cooperation with US Govt.

The British unilateral announcement did not please France either. At the CAME 19th meeting, on 12 July (see Bekri, 1991, p. 113), Henri Laugier said that "it would not be in accordance with the international spirit of the Conference for the invitations to be issued by the British Government, which might lead other Governments to call similar conferences elsewhere" (as cited in Capello,

1970, p. 16). This provoked a violent reaction by Richard Law (the new CAME British President).

The British Government agreed to regard the French Government as inviting power. France also succeeded that French was an official working language and that proposals other than American could be examined. On 21 August, it had ready an alternative project named "Proposals for the Constitution of the United Nations Organisation of Intellectual Cooperation", drafted after the International Act of 1938 (see 4.1.2.3.5.3), according to which the new Organisation would be tripartite, like the International Labour Office, i.e. with Delegations composed of Governments, National Commissions and NGOs representatives. The IIIC would be the Secretariat of the Organisation, and its Director the Secretary-General.

On 12 September, the American Ambassador was instructed to accept the invitation to be represented at the Conference. The draft Constitution was presented and explained to the American people in numerous meetings all over the country, culminating in a meeting in Washington, on 24 September, attended by about 50 national organisations, chaired by William Benton, then Assistant Secretary of State who, as Senator, would lead two American Delegations to UNESCO's General Conferences and be a member of its Executive Board.

On 29 September, the Acting Secretary of State (Dean Acheson) asked the Ambassador to communicate to the British Government some observations regarding the draft Constitution, "which we assume will be the basic document for consideration at the November Conference". Substantive changes were suggested, and others proposed to spell out certain implicit matters. They concerned the role of scientific collaboration and interchange, as well as the relationship between the future Organisation and NGOs. In addition, "there should be textual changes to make this Constitution conform more closely to the United Nations Charter".

On 10 October, the American *Chargé* in the United Kingdom (Waldemar J. Gallman) informed the Secretary of State that the Foreign Office had received a letter from the Soviet Embassy that its Government was of the opinion that the establishment of the envisaged Organisation should be an initiative of the future Economic and Social Council of the United Nations, in accordance with Article 59 of its Charter. The *Chargé* to observe:

> It will be noted that arguments Soviets advance for postponement Conference are identical with those originally proposed by French when they argued British alone should not convene Conference. Foreign Office does not propose to reply to Soviet letter but will make statement at meeting of working committee Oct 12 defending propriety of British Govt and

> French Govt convening Conference and urging that present timetable be followed.

On 12 October, the Working Committee decided that five Commissions should be set up for the Conference, as well as a Drafting Committee and an Executive or Steering Committee composed of the President of the Conference, five Vice-Presidents and Chairmen of the Commissions. On 16 October, the Secretary of State (Byrnes) telegraphed to the *Chargé*:

> Concerning basic document for discussion at Conference, it has always been view of the Department that this would be the CAME draft as transmitted with British invitation. You were right in position taken in working committee on reference in agenda to French draft. [...] The Department believes the French draft should be treated with the complete respect it deserves when the Conference convenes. But it would very much confuse and retard deliberations to present the Conference with two official drafts. [...] It is our hope that they will not do so, but rather seek amendment of the CAME draft, which should be the basic working document unless the Conference makes a different decision.

4.1.2.5.4 *United Nations Conference for the Establishment of an Educational and Cultural Organisation*

4.1.2.5.4.1 Constitution

The "United Nations Conference for the Establishment of an Educational and Cultural Organization" took place from 1 to 16 November 1945 at the Institute of Civil Engineers, near Westminster Abbey, the Houses of Parliament and St. James' Park. It was the only building in Central London large enough and with minimum material facilities, after the Nazi bombings, to receive it. The Conference was attended by representatives of 44 countries,[142] the largest group being the Latin American one. The URSS was absent, for reasons already mentioned, but three Eastern countries (Czechoslovakia, Poland and Yugoslavia) attended the Conference. Observers of 8 international organisations (Governmental and Non-Governmental) were present, namely[143]: ILO, UNRRA, IBE, ICIC, IIIC, League of Nations Secretariat, Preparatory Commission of the United Nations Organisation and Pan-American Union (the oldest and then only regional IGO).

The largest Delegations were those of the USA and France. The American Delegation came together, for the first time, in Washington, on the weekend of October 26–28, for reviewing the 'Draft Proposals', before embarking to

London, where most of its members arrived on the evening of 31 October. They were 34 people, including Archibald MacLeish (Chairman, Consultant of the Department of State, former Librarian of Congress and Assistant Secretary of State), William Benton (Assistant Secretary of State), Chester E. Merrow (House of Representatives, Committee on Foreign Affairs), and James E. Murray (Senate, Chairman of the Committee on Education and Labour). During the Conference, they met twice almost every day. Wanner (2015) remarked:

> Capable of grand vision, the MacLeish delegation was also firmly grounded in reality. It is remarkable, given the difficulty in travel and communications during the turbulent first weeks of transition from war to peace, that the State Department had reached out to the American academic and scientific communities for the specialized advice, expertise and intellectual diversity needed. The delegation's composition demonstrated this. [...]
>
> The delegation's views on the draft constitution were influenced by broad consultation with civil society, in particular the nine consultative meetings on the envisioned new ECO [Educational and Cultural Organization] arranged by the Department of State during September and early October 1945 in Denver, San Francisco, Chicago, Philadelphia, New York and Washington. (p. 15)

The French Delegation was composed of 25 members, among them personalities such as Léon Blum, René Cassin, Henri Bonnet, Joliot-Curie, Henri Wallon, Étienne Gilson, Lucien Febvre, Henri Laugier, Roger Seydoux, Jean Thomas. The British and the Chinese Delegations were composed of 18 members each. Several Delegations were chaired by the respective Ministers of Public Instruction, such as the British (Ellen Wilkinson) and Mexican (Jaime Torres Bodet). The IBE was represented by Jean Piaget and Pedro Rosselló. In a *Memorandum* sent to the Secretary of State, Benton informed[144]: "The only comparable delegation was that of the French. The British magazines ran severe criticisms of the bungling of their own Government in the appointment of a delegation obviously inferior to ours in reputation and stature".[145]

Ellen Wilkinson ('Ellen the Red': feminist and former suffragette and communist) was elected President. Léon Blum – Head of the French Delegation, socialist politician who had been deported to Dachau and then to Buchenwald, in 1943, having been liberated in 1945 – was elected Co-President. Among the 12 Vice-Presidents were Archibald MacLeish and Jaime Torres Bodet.

In his Welcoming Address, on 1 September, 2nd plenary meeting, the British Prime Minister (Clement Richard Attlee) said[146]:

> The conception of an international organisation for educational and cultural collaboration is of course a great deal older than the Conference of Allied Ministers of Education; indeed, I believe that in one form or another it has been before the world since the days of the French Revolution or even earlier. France has indeed steadily kept this aim before the world and we would all, I know, wish to acknowledge the lead she has given, notably by promoting the work of intellectual cooperation undertaken by the League of Nations. But the meetings of the Conference of Allied Ministers of Education during the last three years have undoubtedly brought this idea much nearer to its practical fulfilment.

The main proposals to be debated were the following ones:
- *Draft Proposals for an Educational and Cultural Organisation of the United Nations framed by the Conference of Allied Ministers of Education*
- *French Proposals for the Constitution of the United Nations Organisation of Intellectual Co-operation*

The Conference met six times in plenary sessions (three at the beginning and three at the end). On 5 November, it divided itself into five Technical Commissions.

The purpose of the Conference was expressed by the Delegate of India (Rajkumari Amrit Kaur), at the third plenary meeting, in this way: "We are met to consider a very vital issue – the proper education of mankind. Culture and civilisation stand today at the brink of disaster".[147] Edwin Letts (Peru) said at the fifth plenary meeting[148]: "Now, more than ever, we feel in our innermost consciences the imperative necessity of making a supreme and concerted effort to avoid the recurrence of another catastrophic war, which would inflict the final mortal wound to humanity and to our concept of civilisation". More precisely, said Jaime Torres Bodet (Mexico) during the same meeting, it was a question of "the imperative necessity of pronouncing decisively on the general aims implied in the education of man".[149] Therefore, a key point debated by the First Commission of the Conference was the following: "Education must be considered within a framework of ethics: the moral and spiritual aspects were all-important" (5).[150]

The "Constitution of the United Nations Educational, Scientific and Cultural Organisation" (UNESCO) was signed by 44 States[151] on 16 November 1945, Friday, at the tenth plenary session of the Conference, opened at 3 p.m., exactly three years after the CAME first formal meeting. Besides a Covenant, the Conference adopted its Final Act and the Agreement creating a 'Preparatory

Educational, Scientific and Cultural Commission' entrusted with preparing the first General Conference.

According to the Final Act,[152] 44 Governments were represented at the Conference, but Jan Opocensky (1950), representative of Czechoslovakia at the CAME, Vice-President of the Preparatory Commission of UNESCO and member of its Executive Board from 1946 to 1948, reported 43 (the same, except Argentina), and that the Final Act was signed by 42 (including Argentina but not El Salvador and Poland (pp. 466, 468). In UNESCO's texts, it is frequently said that the Final Act was signed by 37 States, probably because some Delegates were not fully empowered to do so.

The Preparatory Commission was set up. It was composed of representatives of the participating Governments, similar to that of the Preparatory Commission of the United Nations. Under the pressure of the USA, it was decided that it should meet immediately after the final plenary session. Because many Delegations were still not fully empowered to represent their Governments, the first regular meeting of the Commission was scheduled on 1 February 1946. Meanwhile, meetings were held on 16 and 19 November, and on 3 and 4 December. An Executive Committee of 15 members was elected and a Secretariat was set up. The Executive Secretary was Sir Alfred Zimmern, Chief of the British Minister of Education Office, former Deputy Director of the IIIC, who had been the Secretary-General of the Conference. The American representative (Walter Kotschnig) served as Deputy Executive Secretary until 15 February. As Zimmern was hospitalised for surgery, in January 1946, he was replaced by Julian Huxley, from 1 March on.

The main task of the Preparatory Commission was to prepare a draft programme for the first General Conference. It created seven committees to address the following areas: Education, Social Science, Natural Science, Mass Media, Libraries and Museums, Fine Arts, Letters and Philosophy.

UNESCO was thus born as a "specialised agency" of the United Nations. It was mainly a creature of the Big Three: the USA was most influential in the drafting of its Constitution; the French proposals attracted little support, but France succeeded in claiming its siege; the United Kingdom, where the Founding Conference took place, won the position of first Director-General for his candidate.

Three issues are highlighted next.

4.1.2.5.4.2 Highlighting Three Issues

Name

As we saw (italics added):

- On 5 October 1943, following the "Report on the Reorganization of the Conference of Allied Ministers of Education", the purpose was the creation of a *United Nations Bureau of Education.*
- On 12 April 1944, the American Delegation submitted "Suggestions for the Development of the Conference of Allied Ministers of Education into the *United Nations Organization for Educational and Cultural Reconstruction*".
- On 8 March 1945, the American Delegation proposed *Draft Proposals for an International Organisation for Educational and Cultural Cooperation.*
- On 25 May 1945, the Resolution adopted by the San Francisco Conference recommended to the Member Governments to convene "a General Conference to draw up the Statute of an *International Organization on Cultural Cooperation*".
- On 1 August 1945, the British Minister of Education announced a conference to consider the establishment of a *United Nations Educational and Cultural Organisation.*
- In November 1945, the CAME and French proposals discussed during the UNESCO founding Conference, referred to, respectively, an *Educational and Cultural Organisation of the United Nations* and a *United Nations Organisation of Intellectual Co-operation.*

Accordingly, the acronyms changed successively: UNEO (United Nations Education Office), UNECRO (United Nations Educational and Cultural Reconstruction Organisation), UNECCO (United Nations Educational and Cultural Co-operation Organisation), UNECO (United Nations Educational and Cultural Organisation) (see Bekri, 1991, p. 91).

As the words 'science' and 'scientific' were completely absent from the draft then adopted, the Science Commission (chaired by E. F. Armstrong) approved a proposal aiming for the inclusion of 'science' in the title of the new organisation (ibid., p. 128). At the CAME 19th meeting (12 July 1945), it was sent to the Drafting Committee but was opposed by the American representative (Kefauver), in particular. Following the meeting record: "The Drafting Committee did not share this view (to include Science) for two reasons: (1) because it was desirable that the title be as short as possible; (2) because the word culture does include science" (ibid. 103). Indeed, even for some scientists the term 'science' was subsumed within 'culture'. For others, education included all disciplines.

Eventually, the words 'science' and 'scientific' were included in the text several times, but the name remained unchanged.

On 29 September, the American Acting Secretary of State (Dean G. Acheson) asked the Ambassador in London to communicate to the British Government some suggestions concerning the draft Constitution made public on 1 August. Among them, "role of scientists, scientific collaboration and interchange of scientific knowledge should be emphasized and made more explicit", though remarking: "This suggestion obviously has no bearing on scientific research for military purposes, which has always been carefully guarded without preventing extensive cooperation and exchange of information among scientists". The CAME *Draft Proposals* were spelt out in greater detail, notably the Preamble and Article 1, but the title remained unchanged.

Among the eminent scientists adamant that 'Science' be included, were Joseph Needham and Julian Huxley.

Needham was a biochemist at Cambridge University (1920–1942). After receiving three Chinese students in his University (later married one of them), he learnt Chinese and served as the scientific counsellor at the British embassy in China from 1943 to 1946. In three *Memoranda* sent to politicians, diplomats and scientists of the allied countries he proposed the creation of an International Science Co-operation Service. His proposal was supported by the British Association for the Advancement of Science and the Association of Scientific Workers. It was in one of the *Memoranda*, dated 15 March 1945,[153] that the acronym UNESCO appeared for the first time in a published document.

Huxley wrote in a letter sent to Philip Noel-Baker (British Foreign Office) on 14 August[154]:

> Culture does *not* cover all of science, any more than science covers all of culture. To use an Americanism, we want to put the S in UNESCO. This, it seems to us, could be achieved (1) by inserting 'Scientific' in the title, (2) by having the organization essentially tripartite, one section dealing with education in the narrow sense, the second with culture in the sense of the humanities and arts, the third with science, pure and applied [...].

In her Opening Address as President of the Founding Conference, at the second plenary meeting, on 1 November, Ellen Wilkinson announced[155]:

> Though Science was not included in the original title of the Organisation, the British delegation will put forward a proposal that it be included, so that the title would run 'Educational, Scientific and Cultural Organisation'. In these days, when we are all wondering, perhaps apprehensively, what the scientists will do to us next, it is important that they should be linked closely with the humanities and should feel that they have a responsibility to mankind for the result of their labours.

At the First Commission second meeting, on 5 November: "The United States Delegate submitted a proposal that the Organisation be called United Nations Educational, Scientific and Cultural Organisation".[156] The proposal was voted and unanimously approved, the next day, at the Commission third meeting.

The change of mind was probably caused by both the news on the atrocities committed by medical experiments in the Nazi concentration camps, and the mushroom clouds of the atomic bombs of Hiroshima and Nagasaki, released on 6 and 9 August 1945.

Needham was invited by Huxley, in April 1946, to join the UNESCO Secretariat. He would become the first Head of the Natural Sciences Section of UNESCO (1946–1948). According to Patrick Petitjean (2006):

> Needham was part of an idealistic generation of scientists who wanted to use discoveries and their applications to improve living conditions for all and to develop democracy. […]
>
> One of Needham's most original concepts was the 'periphery principle'. He believed that the most scientifically advanced nations must share their knowledge and resources with less developed countries – that is, countries 'on the periphery' – in order to reduce disparities between the different regions of the world. […]
>
> Needham believed that the 'social function of sciences' had to be part and parcel of UNESCO's science programmes. […] Behind Needham's thinking was the idea of the universality of science and its subsequent internationalism. (pp. 44, 45, 46).

Also, communication and information are UNESCO's areas of expertise and action from the beginning, as said Julian Huxley during the presentation of the Report of the Preparatory Commission mentioned above to the first session of the General Conference[157]:

> Let us first recall that UNESCO's aims, as laid down in its Constitution, are twofold – to contribute to peace and security, and to promote the general welfare of mankind. This twofold purpose must of course be carried out in relation to the three fields of activity – Education, Science and Culture – embodied in its title, as well as to the fourth field of Mass Communications, expressly mentioned in its Constitution.

Preamble

The First Commission of the Founding Conference, chaired by R. C. Wallace (Canada), was in charge of the Title, Preamble and Article 1 (Purposes and

Principal Functions of the Organisation). It set up a Drafting Committee composed of representatives of the USA (Archibald MacLeish), United Kingdom (Theodora Bosanquet), France (René Cassin), Mexico (Jaime Torres Bodet), India (Amarnath Jha) and Poland (Bernard Drzewieski). The latter testified at the tenth plenary meeting, on 16 November[158]:

> One of my pleasantest experiences during this Conference was my work in the Drafting Committee on the Preamble. We were a mixed crowd. The Chairman was Mr. MacLeish. He says he is an American, but I think he would be more correctly described as a representative of world citizenship. Then we had an Indian, an English lady, a Mexican, a Pole and a Frenchman. We were people from different continents, of different denominations, different races, different nations, and probably different political opinions. During our work we did not argue on these matters. We all tried merely to find the best expression for our common feelings and our common longings [...].

According to Jan Opocensky (1950): "The author of the text of the Preamble was Mr. MacLeish, from the United States delegation", drawing on different proposals. For example, the second and most famous sentence – *That since wars begin in the minds of men, it is in the minds of men that the defences of peace must be constructed* – "is taken from the speech of Rt. Hon. C. R. Attlee, Prime Minister of Great Britain and Northern Ireland, in the Second Meeting of the Conference on November 1, 1945" (pp. 228, 229). Indeed, Atlee asked: "Do not wars, after all, begin in the minds of men?"[159] Shortly thereafter, the future first UNESCO Director-General wrote: "The preamble begins with Mr. Attlee's noble words 'since wars begin in the minds of men, it is in the minds of men that the defences of peace must be constructed' " (Huxley, 1946, p. 5). In a book published the same year, titled *Between Two Wars – The Failure of Education: 1920–1940*, its author had even written in the Dedication that "war begins in the nurseries" (Sargent, 1945). Wanner (2015) remarked: "According to Evans's notes for November 9, 'Mr. MacLeish presented the fifth draft of the Preamble ... He had the agreement of the British, French, Mexican and other delegates ... When he had finished reading it aloud the general reaction was that it was magnificent'" (pp. 16, 17).

This famous sentence of the UNESCO Constitution's Preamble is engraved, in ten languages, on a stone wall erected in the gardens of UNESCO's siege – Square of Tolerance – inaugurated in 1996. In this connection, Cowell (1966) witnessed:

> Where so much has been forgotten it is pleasant for the author of this brief account to recall a cold November morning in a small, unheated room, where the Drafting Committee was preparing the final version of the Constitution and endeavouring to ensure equivalent French and English texts. The energetic chairmanship of Mr Archibald MacLeish, leader of the United States delegation, the deeply thoughtful contributions of Dr Jaime Torres Bodet, and the fecund inspiration of M. Etienne Gilson from France aroused an admiration which the passage of years has not dimmed. It was then that Mr MacLeish picked up Prime Minister Attlee's remark, as he welcomed the delegates, 'Wars begin in the minds of men' and added the more than pertinent corollary: 'It is in the minds of men that the defences of peace must be constructed.' It was also at that time that M. Gilson minted the happy phrase, 'the fruitful diversity of cultures', and that, on a more pedestrian level, this writer persuaded the Committee to include the promotion of 'the rule of law' among the primary purposes of the Organisation. (pp. XIX, XX)

Still concerning the Preamble to UNESCO's Constitution, Cowell remarked:

> Just as the war revealed the depths to which man can still sink, so it also provoked eager efforts to serve the best in humanity with an intensity of idealism now difficult to characterise convincingly to those who never experienced it. [...]
>
> The ordeal of war had revealed the imminent perils threatening those values which are the motive forces of civilisation because they endow life with meaning and worth. It was to enforce this solemn lesson that the references to war were included in the preamble to the Constitution of UNESCO. (pp. XIV, XXXI)

Headquarters

In closing his Address, as Associate-President of the Founding Conference, at the second plenary meeting, on 1 November 1945, Léon Blum said[160]:

> I have only one word to add. The French delegation intends to ask you to decide on Paris as the seat of the new Organisation and desires to state this quite simply at this first meeting. [...] We crave this honour, we ask it of you, because it would be infinitely dear to us, because we feel ourselves not unworthy of it, and because we shall endeavour by all the means in our power to prove that it has been well deserved.

The British Government was of the opinion that all the United Nations Specialised Agencies should be located at the Organisation's headquarters, for economic and efficiency reasons, but there was a change of mind.

At the Fourth Commission third meeting, on 9 November, the British Delegate, reverting to the question of the seat of the future Organisation, proposed "that Paris be selected, a city which had rendered unforgettable services to the cause of human culture". This "should be interpreted also, essentially, as a tribute to the work that France had accomplished in the past". The proposal was supported by the American and Chinese Delegations. "The delegate of Belgium said that the distinguished delegates of Great Britain, the United States and China had just expressed in a few words the feeling they all shared for France". The Delegate of Brazil added that: "Paris was the great centre which had done so much for humanity". The Delegate of Turkey stressed that Paris was "the cradle and shrine of human rights". The Chairman of the Commission (Jan Opocensky, Czechoslovakia) "associated himself whole-heartedly with what had been said to the glory of France and in gratitude to that country, which had been throughout history the great disseminator of ideas". The Commission greeted "with unanimous applause" a proposal by the Brazilian Delegate that the decision "should be not only passed, but passed by acclamation".[161]

The American Ambassador in London reported to the Secretary of State, on 15 November 1945[162]: "The French delegation regards the delegation of the United States as having won for it a most important point and the British delegation regards that of the United States as having successfully resolved a difficult situation between it and the French delegation". Yet, Jean Thomas (1962), who was a member of the French Delegation to the Conference, Executive Under-Secretary of the Preparatory Commission and Deputy Director-General of UNESCO, testified that "the decision was not made without reservations or without conditions. [...] The discussion, always courteous, was tight". Finally, it was agreed that the seat provision should not be incorporated into the UNESCO Constitution, but be the object of a Resolution added to the Conference's Final Act, so worded: "This Resolution shall not in any way affect the right of the General Conference to take decisions in regard to this matter by a two-thirds majority".[163] As a counterpart, "it was tacitly agreed that at least in the early days [France] wouldn't nominate a candidate for Director-General or President of the Executive Council" (pp. 15, 16, 17).

The Paris siege did not become final until 2 July 1951, when the General Conference decided to build the permanent headquarters of the Organisation and an agreement was reached with the French Government to that effect. The present UNESCO House (Place Fontenoy) was inaugurated on 3 November 1958.

The plans for the new buildings were drafted by three great international architects and approved by an international panel that included Le Corbusier. Many countries and great artists such as Henry Moore, Pablo Picasso, Joan Miró, contributed to the construction and embellishment of this *Global Village*.[164]

4.1.2.5.4.3 Some Further Notes

An official explanation of the origins of the UNESCO logo/emblem seems to be nowhere to be found.[165] The first one, in 1946, was modelled according to the UN one[166]: a map of the world seen from the North Pole, surrounded by two olive branches, the acronym UNESCO at the top and the inscription 'Paris 1946' at the bottom. In 1947, the Director-General authorised – and the eighth General Conference (1954, Montevideo) confirmed and adopted – "the emblem and distinctive sign" now used, inspired by the façade of the Parthenon, Athens Acropolis (evoking the cradle of Western Civilisation), whose columns are the letters of the acronym UNESCO (IV.1.8.2).[167]

Richard A. Butler, the President of the Board of Education, who was at the origin of the CAME, did not participate in the Founding Conference of UNESCO, because his Conservative Party, led by Winston Churchill, had been defeated by the Labour Party in the general election of July 1945.[168] When the Conference began, the Prime Minister was Clement Richard Attlee and the Minister of Education was Ellen Wilkinson.

Four personalities participated in the London Conference, who would become Director-Generals of UNESCO, namely: Julian Huxley (Preparatory Commission), Jaime Torres Bodet (Chairman of the Mexican Delegation, former Mexico's representative to IIIC), Luther Evans (a member of the American Delegation), and René Maheu (a member of the Secretariat).

Grayson Kefauver, a leading actor of the USA stepping into the CAME, member of the American Delegation in the London Conference and of the UNESCO Preparatory Commission, returned home on 11 December 1945 and began a speaking tour arranged by the State Department to present the new Organisation to the American people. On 3 January 1946, after addressing the United Nations Association of Southern California, he walked back to his hotel to interview an applicant for a position with the Secretariat of the UNESCO Preparatory Commission. During the interview, he got sick and a doctor was called. When he arrived, Kefauver was paralysed on his left side and unconscious. He was taken to a hospital and was diagnosed with a severe cerebral haemorrhage. Kefauver died the following day at age 45 (see Dorn, 2006, p. 317). So early disappeared one of the greatest UNESCO founding fathers, and maybe a future great UNESCO servant was missed.

On 5 December, the Assistant Secretary of State (William Benton) addressed a *Memorandum* on the London Conference to the Secretary of State. It read, among other things:

> I have reported to you that Mr. MacLeish served most effectively as chairman, winning not only the confidence of the American delegation but the respect of the delegations of the other forty-three countries. The American delegation itself was outstanding at the Conference and did us much credit. It worked hard and worked harmoniously. Senator Murray and others on the delegation were enthusiastic in their reports to me. [...]
>
> The charter is good and provides an excellent framework but UNESCO will amount to very little, and will fall far short of the high hopes many groups in this country have for it, unless it is backed by men and by money. Perhaps the more important of the two is the men. [...]

And to conclude:

> I believe it would be a mistake for us in the Department to minimize the potential significance of UNESCO. True, it may not reach the stratosphere. But the hopes of millions of people are centered in it. Many believe that it is the principal instrument through which the world may hope to achieve better understanding and thus minimize the risks of future wars.

A "Summary Report on the UNESCO Conference – The London Conference, November 1 to 16, 1945", dated from 3 December, was enclosed.

The CAME was dissolved on 31 December 1945, after a final formal meeting.

4.1.2.5.5 *First General Conferences*

In September 1946, the Preparatory Commission moved from London to Paris, having been installed at the former Hotel Majestic (Avenue Kléber, close to the Arc de Triomphe), a historic building.[169] It issued a *Report on the Programme of the United Nations Educational, Scientific and Cultural Organisation.* On 4 November, when Greece became the 20th State to deposit instruments of acceptance of its Constitution with the United Kingdom Government, UNESCO legally came into being.

UNESCO's first General Conference was convened from 19 November to 10 December by the Preparatory Commission that held its final session on 14–15. The inaugural session took place in the Sorbonne, on 19 November, in the presence of the President of the French Provisional Government (Georges Bidault), the Minister of Education (Marcel-Edmond Naegelen) and the Rector of the Sorbonne (Gustave Roussy). Ellen Wilkinson (British Minister of Education), President of the Preparatory Commission, was unable to be present because of illness, and she was represented by David Hardman M.P., Parliamentary Under-Secretary of the Ministry of Education, who was to lead British Delegations to the first six sessions of the General Conference.

One of the speakers was Jean-Paul Sartre, whose subject was "The responsibility of the writer".[170] He began with a quote: "Dostoyevsky has said: Every man is responsible towards everyone for everything. This statement becomes truer from day to day". And affirmed, notably: "So that phrase, dear to the Americans – 'one world' – means many things, but among others, it means that everyone is responsible for everything that goes on in the world".

> Thus, we can, at this stage, define in wide terms the responsibility of the writer. If the writer is a maker of literature; in other words, if he writes, it is because he is assuming the function of perpetuating, in a world where freedom is always threatened, the assertion of freedom and the appeal to freedom. [...]
>
> That is why a body like UNESCO is necessary.

48 Governments were represented in the First General Conference of UNESCO. France stood out due to the high level of its Delegation, chaired by Léon Blum, which included names such as René Cassin, Frédéric Joliot-Curie, François Mauriac, Lucien Febvre, Étienne Gilson, Paul Langevin, Henri Wallon, Roger Seydoux, Gaston Berger.

On 20 November, the Conference started its meetings at the Hotel Majestic. 39 UN Member States participated, but only 34 had ratified UNESCO Constitution and were qualified to vote. Sweden and Switzerland sent observers. Léon Blum was elected President of the General Conference that also elected the Executive Council, composed of 18 members. Half of them had participated in the CAME or the Preparatory Commission. Its first President was Victor Doré (Canada). It met daily during the General Conference. One of its competencies was to elect UNESCO Director-General. This turned out to be a troubled diplomatic game.

An obvious candidate was Zimmern, the first appointed Executive Secretariat of the Preparatory Commission. After recovering from his illness, he hoped to regain his former position as Executive Secretary of the Preparatory Commission, probably legitimately looking forwards to his appointment as a candidate to be the first Director-General of UNESCO, but he was only offered the post of Adviser. It seems that the opportunity was taken by Minister Ellen

Wilkinson and her Secretary John Redcliffe-Maud to dismiss a conservative and anti-scientist personality, lacking large views for the new Organisation. Cowell (1966) testified that Sir Alfred Zimmern "was a man of great personal charm, unfailing good nature and boundless enthusiasm for UNESCO's cause, to which he devoted himself unceasingly". However, he was then sixty-six years old and tended to regard UNESCO as a more effective IIIC. "I remember that he said to me during one of our very frequent, almost daily discussions, that he thought that the staff of the new Organisation would perhaps grow to fifty or sixty people" (p. XXV). In the second half of September 1946, he learnt that the British candidate for Director-General was Julian Huxley.

"Lady Zimmern, who was bitter over her husband's illness and the resulting loss of his position on the Commission [...], started spreading rumours that Huxley was a Communist" (Dronamraju, 1993, p. 65), probably because of the ideas he had exposed in *On living in a revolution* (1944) and *UNESCO – Its Purpose and its Philosophy* (1946) (see below). The second one was a "pamphlet" (as Huxley called it) written in the 1946 summer, during a two-week holiday, after he was appointed Secretary-General of the Preparatory Commission. When it was presented to the Preparatory Commission to be approved and printed as an official document, one of its members, the historian and churchman Sir Ernest Barker, close to Zimmern, persuaded other members that Huxley proposed an atheist conception disguised as humanism that should be circulated only as a personal view. In his *Memories*, Huxley agreed: "Looking back, I think he was right. Though UNESCO has in fact pursued humanistic aims, it would have been unfortunate to lay down any doctrine as a basis for its work. Further, a purely humanist tone would have antagonised the world's major religious groups".[171]

> As it turned out, the humanist attitude which I adopted led various delegates (quite erroneously) to think that I was anti-religious, while my liberal views were taken by others to be communistic. When I found during the Conference that one of my previous colleagues was spreading this allegation of my communist leanings, I became very angry and formally asked the Executive Board to expel him, failing which I would resign. (in Dronamraju, 1993, p. 181)

On 3 October, Zimmern was sent to London to carry out a study on international intellectual co-operation and was advised not to return for the General Conference. After the end of his contract with UNESCO, in 1947 the couple Zimmern emigrated to the USA where he worked at Trinity College (Hartford, Connecticut).

The British interest in the first UNESCO Director-General to be a British personality was met with the American opposition. In addition to the ideas exposed by Huxley in his writings and the ideological suspects spread by the Zimmern couple, especially by the "abrasive nature" of Lucie Zimmern (Toye & Toye, 2010, p. 313), already on 5 December 1945 the Assistant Secretary of State (William Benton) remarked in a *Memorandum* on the London Conference addressed to the Secretary of State:

> The United States has asked for nothing thus far. The Preparatory Commission is located in London. The executive secretary is an Englishman. The headquarters of UNESCO are to be in Paris. It is generally understood that the United States Government can nominate the permanent secretary-general if it so desires. The choice of this man is crucial. I know you will agree with me that, unless we turn up with a candidate of stature and capacity, we do not want to press for an American in this role.

Wanner (2015) comments:

> ... the Americans supported Paris as the site of UNESCO's headquarters, albeit with the provisos that the General Conference "be ambulatory" – that it meets elsewhere on occasion – and the understanding that the first Director-General be English-speaking. For their part, the French abandoned the idea of having the Paris-based IIIC serve as the UNESCO Secretariat and agreed to an international staff. They saw a kindred intellectual spirit in Archibald MacLeish and signalled informally that they would welcome him as the first Director-General. (p. 18)

Archibald MacLeish was invited but declined, preferring to fully devote his time to the literary creativity. *I prefer to be a poet* – he would have said (see Maurel, 2006, p. 43). The Secretary of State proposed Francis Biddle to President Truman. Biddle was a lawyer who had been a member of the Nuremberg International Military Tribunal and Attorney General of President Roosevelt. He was persuaded to accept but even the Americans agreed that he was not a strong candidate. The British Foreign Office advised the Prime Minister to support him but, despite the pressures of the American Delegation (chaired by Benton), including the threat to cut the financial support to UNESCO, Attlee kept supporting the British candidate. France did not object, in recognition of the British attitude concerning the UNESCO headquarters.

Eventually, Julian Huxley was elected on 6 December by 22 votes to 3, but on condition that his tenure would be barely two years (allegedly at his request), instead of the six years provided for in the Convention creating UNESCO (Article VI.2).

The second session of UNESCO's General Conference met in Mexico City in 1947. Its opening took place at the *Palacio de Bellas Artes* (Palace of Fine Arts, Mexico City) with the presence of the President Miguel Alemán and more than 2,500 people. The meetings were held in the *Escuela Nacional de Maestros* (National School for Primary Education Teachers).

At the inaugural meeting, on 6 November 1947, Jacques Maritain, French philosopher, Ambassador to the Vatican and head of his country's Delegation (replacing Léon Blum, who was sick), gave a resounding speech on "The Way of Peace" (written in Rome and read by Léon Blum during his transit in Paris). He said[172]:

> The first questions that arise when seriously pondering the conditions for a just and lasting peace are, of course, those raised by the idea of a supranational organization of peoples. [...] At present, a supranational organization of the world is out of the realm of possibilities. A philosopher would betray his duty if he did not add that this now impossible thing is however necessary, and that without it the building of a just and lasting peace cannot be conceived. Hence, it follows that the first obligation for men of this time is to work with all their might to make possible what is so necessary. [...]
>
> My last considerations will relate to another problem that refers to UNESCO's own work and the kind of agreement it implies within diversity. (pp. 10, 13)

This is a paradoxical task, because it "involves an agreement of thought between men whose conceptions are different or even opposed". Not being possible "to agree on either a common *speculative* ideology or on common principles of *explanation*", the alternative is to borrow a "fundamental *practical* ideology and fundamental principles of *action*" (p. 14) which constitute:

> ... a kind of common unwritten law, at the point of practical convergence of the most different theoretical ideologies and spiritual traditions. [...] This is how, in my opinion, the paradox that I just pointed out may be resolved. [...]
>
> That is why I believe that one of the major tasks undertaken by the United Nations is this new Declaration of Human Rights, to which UNESCO contributes. (pp. 22, 16)

He asked: "Doesn't it seem obvious that the knowledge of man and the development of a new humanism are in the order of science and culture what matters most in the preparation of a lastingly established peace?" (p. 16).

Maritain addressed a *Solemn Appeal against the Idea that War is Inevitable* "to all who are concerned for the dignity of Man and the future of civilization, particularly educationalists, scientists, artists, writers and journalists throughout the world", approved by the General Conference on 29 November 1947".[173]

Let us recall that, in connection with the drafting of the UDHR, he later wrote (UNESCO, 1948):

> It is related that at one of the meetings of a UNESCO National Commission where Human Rights were being discussed, someone expressed astonishment that certain champions of violently opposed ideologies had agreed on a list of those rights. "Yes", they said, "we agree about the rights but on condition that no one asks us why". That "why" is where the argument begins. (Introduction)[174]

The UNESCO General Conference met every year until 1952 (Paris), when it was decided that General Conferences would be held every two years, except when there was a need to convene an extraordinary session.

4.1.2.5.6 *Outstanding Directors-General*

So far, UNESCO was led by eleven Directors-General, namely: Julian Huxley (1946–1948), Jaime Torres Bodet (1948–1952), John Taylor (1952–1953), Luther Evans (1953–1958), Vittorino Veronese (1958–1961), René Maheu (1961–1974), Amadou-Mahtar M'Bow (1974–1987), Federico Mayor (1987–1999), Koïchiro Matsuura (1999–2009), Irina Bokova (2009–2017), Audrey Azoulay (2017-). Huxley, Bodet and Maheu may be considered as the most outstanding ones, for different reasons. It follows a mere documented glimpse of their convergent visions for UNESCO.

4.1.2.5.6.1 Julian Huxley

Julian Huxley – a grandson of the famous Darwinist biologist Thomas Henry Huxley, brother of Aldous Huxley, the author of *The Best of the Worlds* (1932) – was a "charismatic and fascinating personality" (Maurel, 2006, p. 57), as well as a distinguished scientist and thinker, having been also a prominent populariser of science who was awarded, in 1953, the UNESCO Kalinga Prize. Quoting Alison Bashford (2013):

> In *The Humanist Frame* he listed the challenges ahead that would be catastrophic if not addressed. In his words:

> ... the threat of over-population; the threat of super-scientific war, nuclear, chemical, and biological; the rise and appeal of Communism especially in the under privileged sectors of the world's people; the over-exploitation of natural resources; the erosion of the world's cultural variety; the widening gap between the haves and the have-nots between the rich and poor nations. (p. 164)

Among his numerous publications on scientific and humanist matters are the writings abovementioned, in connection with the American reserves on his suitability to be UNESCO Director-General: *On Living in a Revolution* (1944) and UNESCO – *Its Purpose and its Philosophy* (1946).

On Living in a Revolution

On Living in a Revolution (published in 1944) is the title of the first (published in 1942) of a set of 15 essays, the second one (published in 1941) was titled *Economic Man and Social Man*. Huxley (1944) affirmed: "The world's most important fact is not that we are in a war, but that we are in a revolution", in the sense of a "*historical transformation*" (p. 1). He considered that never "has the process of re-thinking been as intense as in these past four years. There has been the re-thinking of old problems, the transvaluation of values". It was "a revolution of thought, both reinforcing and reinforced by the revolution of economic and social fact" (p. vii). In his opinion: "This revolution is the first in which scientific knowledge and conscious planning is able to play a part. History is being made at greater speed than ever before, and if we are willing to make the effort, we who live in this revolution have the privilege of helping history" (p. xii). How?

It is not easy "to visualize a new kind of society", but we need to try and to act towards achieving it, even "at the cost of giving up many ideas which once seemed illuminating and inspiring" (p. 16). It will be through a truly democratic revolution.

> The only universal criterion of democracy and the democratic method is the satisfaction of the needs of human individuals, their welfare, development, and active participation in social processes. A further democratic criterion, applicable in the immediate future, is equal cooperation in international organization, including the treatment of backward peoples as potential equals. (pp. 1, 2)

A democratic society is, therefore, a society of rights and responsibilities. With the emotions of its collective beliefs, but without aggressive nationalism and the individualism allowing property rights "to override human needs" (p. 18).

Huxley quoted the book by Peter Drucker titled *The End of Economic Man – The Origins of Totalitarianism* (1939) and concluded that:

> ... it is clear that the present is the end of an age – in Peter Drucker's words, the end of economic man. We think and believe that the new epoch of civilization will best be described as the age of social man, in which society will be much more of an organic whole, tied together mainly by the living relations of human beings and organized groups of human beings instead of mainly by the cold impersonal forces of profit and economic competition. (p. 16)

However, "we must make sure that the new social order is also a democratic order", but "to fit in with the new framework, the expression of democracy will have to be radically transformed. Many of our old ideas must be retranslated, so to speak, into a new language" (p. 17). This implies putting in second place a lot of what is in the first place in our lives. "There are powerful forces working against any such change. But there are also reservoirs of sanity and idealism that can be mobilized for it" (p. 27).

In sum: "I would say that the new phase of history should be styled the Age of Social Man" (p. 5), meaning each human being together with the whole society. "Liberty, Equality, Fraternity – these will always constitute democracy's triple crown" (p. 12), understood in light of each epoch's conditions.

UNESCO – *Its Purpose and its Philosophy*

UNESCO – *Its Purpose and its Philosophy*, published on 15 September 1945, was a bold and visionary essay of "A Philosophy for UNESCO" (p. 6) that should be "a world philosophy, a unified and unifying background of thought for the modern world" (p. 41), in order to promote "the emergence of a single world culture" (p. 60). In Huxley's opinion, it should be a scientific evolutionary humanism and "a world humanism, both in the sense of seeking to bring in all the peoples of the world, and of treating all peoples and all individuals within each people as equals in terms of human dignity, mutual respect, and educational opportunity" (p. 7). Huxley's thought necessary reflects epochal mental frontiers, but some views deserve to be contextually highlighted to better appreciating their rigour and broad-mindedness.

Over-population and environment

> The recognition of the idea of an optimum population-size (of course relative to technological and social conditions) is an indispensable first step towards that planned control of populations which is necessary if

man's blind reproductive urges are not to wreck his ideals and his plans for material and spiritual betterment. The recognition of the fact that the wildlife of the world is irreplaceable, but that it is being rapidly destroyed, is necessary if we are to realise in time that areas must be set aside where, in the ultimate interests of mankind as a whole, the spread of man must take second place to the conservation of other species. (p. 43)

Eugenics

Still another and quite different type of borderline subject is that of eugenics. It has been on the borderline between the scientific and the unscientific, constantly in danger of becoming a pseudo-science based on preconceived political ideas or on assumptions of racial or class superiority and inferiority. It is, however, essential that eugenics should be brought entirely within the borders of science, for, as already indicated, in the not very remote future the problem of improving the average quality of human beings is likely to become urgent; and this can only be accomplished by applying the findings of a truly scientific eugenics. [...]

Thus, the application of genetics in eugenics immediately raises the question of values – what qualities should we desire to encourage in the human beings of the future? (pp. 37, 38)[175]

Equality and differences

... we come to a difficult problem – that of discovering how we can reconcile our principle of human equality with the biological fact of human inequality. Perhaps the problem is not so difficult as it appears when stated in this paradoxical form; for the contradiction largely disappears as soon as it is realised that equality is used in two very different senses. The democratic principle of equality, which is also UNESCO's, is a principle of equality of opportunity – that human beings should be equal before the law, should have equal opportunities for education, for making a living, for freedom of expression and movement and thought. The biological absence of equality, on the other hand, concerns the natural endowments of man and the fact of genetic difference in regard to them. (p. 18)

The Individual and the community

The two opposing philosophies of today differ essentially on one point – the relation between the individual and the community. But this one central difference provides differences in every field with which UNESCO has to deal, as well as in many others. It engenders different moralities and systems of ethics; different methods of education; different conceptions of the role of art in society; different economic systems; different ways of integrating science with national life; different interpretations of the fundamental human freedoms; different conceptions of the possibilities and limits of international cooperation.

... They can be reconciled along the lines of some such evolutionary humanism as I have sketched in my opening sections, in which, though the full development of the individual is recognised as the central aim and criterion of further evolutionary progress, the proper organisation of society is recognised as the indispensable mechanism of that progress. Put another way, society as such embodies no values comparable to those embodied in individuals; but individuals are meaningless except in relation to the community (though that community transcends the nation both in space and in time), and can only achieve fullest self-development by self-transcendence, by interpenetration of the self with other reality, including other selves. [...] I believe that this reconciliation can be approached from two directions. It can be approached from above and from outside, as an intellectual problem, a question of agreement in principle; and it can also be approached from below and from within, as a practical problem, a question of agreement through action. (pp. 61 62)

Education

Education (apart from the few limited and rudimentary instances to be found in lower mammals and in birds) is a distinctively human activity: in its developed form, as a cumulative social process, it is entirely confined to Man. It is the process by means of which knowledge, skill, technique, understanding, ideas, emotional and spiritual attitudes, are transmitted from individual to individual and from generation to generation. It is also a major part of the process by which the latent potentialities of the individual are actualised and developed to their fullest extent. It includes the broad sense of adult education and self-education as well as the narrow sense of schooling and training. [...]

These things being so, it becomes clear that the approach of UNESCO must adopt certain general principles concerning education – not only that it should equip the growing human being to earn a livelihood, not only that it should fit him to take his place as a member of the community and society into which he is born, but certain further principles, which have been lacking in many previous (and existing) systems of education.

First, that education can be and should be a permanent and continuing process: the mind is capable of growth throughout life, and provision must be made for assisting its growth – in other words for education – among adults of all ages and not only in children and young people.

Next, that education has a social as well as an individual function: it is one of the means by which society as a whole can become conscious of its traditions and its destiny, can fit itself to make adjustment to new conditions, and can inspire it to make new efforts towards a fuller realisation of its aims.

Thirdly, that scientific research is capable of improving the technique of education to a very large extent, and that accordingly UNESCO must give every encouragement to research in this field, and to the full dissemination of its results. (p. 30)

Scope of education

… education must seek not only to confer knowledge, skills, habits, and outlook upon individuals, but also to bring out and develop their inherent qualities and aptitudes, and to help them to realise their potentialities to the fullest degree possible. And finally, that education must not confine itself to objectives which are practical in the restricted sense of having immediate utility, whether for the individual or for society. On the contrary, it must include in its scope activities which are valued for their own sake, whether in the intellectual, the aesthetic, or the moral sphere – knowledge for the sake of knowing, discovery for the sake of discovering, beauty because it is beautiful, art and music and literature for their power of moving the human spirit, morality for the sake of living a good life, nobility of character because it is an end in itself. (p. 29)

Fundamental education

Thus, mass campaigns against illiteracy and for a common fundamental education must form part of UNESCO's programme. Further, a satisfactory common scale of values can obviously not be attained so long as large sections of mankind are preoccupied with the bare material and physiological needs of food, shelter, and health. […]

On reflection, however, it is speedily seen that a campaign for mere literacy is not enough. It needs to be linked with the general system of education, and, among illiterates above school age, to be coupled with general social education, notably in relation to health, current methods of agriculture, and citizenship. That is why, in UNESCO's programme, literacy campaigns have been merged in a more comprehensive study of Fundamental Education. (pp. 17, 29)

International education

An educational system, for instance, can just as readily be made to promote the idea of a chosen race or of a privileged caste as it can that of the dignity of men and the equality of their opportunity.

... UNESCO must pay special attention to international education [...].

Nor is literacy, once achieved, necessarily going to lead either to democracy or, even if it does so, to a right development of society. Nazi Germany demonstrated all too clearly the way in which one of the most literate and most thoroughly educated peoples of the world could be led into false ways and anti-democratic developments; and in democratic countries the manipulation of the press and the debasement of literature and the cinema for financial or political ends is all too possible. Nor, finally, if literacy helps to achieve international awareness and knowledge, will this necessarily promote peace and international goodwill. [...]

... at the moment two opposing philosophies of life confront each other from the West and from the East, and not only impede the achievement of unity but threaten to become the *foci* of actual conflict.

You may categorise the two philosophies as two super-nationalisms; or as individualism versus collectivism; or as the American versus the Russian way of life; or as capitalism versus communism; or as Christianity versus Marxism; or in half a dozen other ways. [...] Can this conflict be avoided, these opposites be reconciled, this antithesis be resolved in a higher synthesis? [...] Since another war would be so appalling as to set back the march of human progress by centuries, I am convinced that the task of achieving this synthesis in time to forestall open conflict must be the overriding aim of UNESCO. (pp. 18, 30, 31, 61)

Art in education

UNESCO intends to make a basic study of the role of art in general education, and of the methods involved. The scattered experiments which have been made in this field show that art in general education has two main functions. First, to give the developing human being not merely some intellectual understanding of art, but that real understanding which is at the same time love, and desire for further satisfaction through art. And secondly, to secure the development of a fuller and more solid personality in the child. (p. 51)

The Preparatory Commission set up a Basic Education Commission, chaired by Sir Fred Clarke (Professor at the University of London), which produced the Report *Fundamental education: Common ground of all peoples* (issued in 1946).[176] It was defined by the General Conference 1st Session (1946),[177] in Resolution "B – Fundamental Education":

> Fundamental Education is a long-term, world-scale, "attack upon ignorance". It is a many-sided undertaking ranging from primary education to work with adult illiterates. It includes education for better health and agriculture, for economic improvement, for artistic and cultural development, for citizenship and for international understanding. It is the concern of schools and many other agencies, and requires the use of the new media of mass communication. (p. 270)

This UNESCO's primordial costly operational project did not accomplish its ambitions. In 1958, the General Conference (10th Session, Paris)[178]:

> *Recognizing* that the term 'fundamental education' has led to confusion.
> *Instructs* the Director-General to take immediate steps to secure that a proper terminology which can be applied all over the world be used by UNESCO for all kinds of education of adults and young people and to discontinue as rapidly as feasible the use of the term 'fundamental education' in all official documents of UNESCO.

Yet, the *Centro Regional de Educación Fundamental para la América Latina* (CREFAL: Regional Centre for Fundamental Education in Latin America, Pátzcuaro, Mexico), created in 1951, is still a heritage of it, and its vision resounds in the Jomtien Declaration (1990) (see below).[179]

Huxley wrote in his *Memories* (1970): "If I am to be remembered, I hope it will not be primarily for my specialized scientific work, but as a generalist; one to whom, enlarging Terence's words, nothing human and nothing in external nature was alien" (Dronamraju, 1993, p. XXI).

4.1.2.5.6.2 Jaime Torres Bodet

Jaime Torres Bodet studied in the National Preparatory School and the Faculty of Jurisprudence and High Studies of the National University of Mexico

(UNAM), and was the personal secretary of its Rector, José Vasconcelos (Minister of Education from 1921 to 1924). He was teacher of literature, writer, Public Education and Foreign Affairs Secretary, and diplomat. As we know, he chaired the Mexican Delegation to the UNESCO London Founding Conference, in November 1945. Speaking on 2 November, at the third plenary meeting (pp. 35–39),[180] he exposed principles for the new UN Organisation:

> Let us face the fact squarely: what would be the fate of this age on which we are just entering if we neglected the intellectual and moral basis of education?
>
> War is invariably the logical result in great part of some inadequacy or some lamentable mis-shaping of the national educational system.
>
> ... the opposition between the rights of the individual and the rights of the collective body must be replaced by some form of organisation in which the best citizen shall also be the best man. [...]
>
> How are we to reconcile such assistance with the duty which devolves upon us of respecting the freedom of each nation in the choice of methods for organising education in its own territory? And how shall we coordinate that freedom, which we regard as inalienable, with the imperative necessity of pronouncing decisively on the general aims implied in the education of man? [...]
>
> What is to be the ideal which shall inspire true education? [...]
>
> An education based upon unassailable principles cannot possibly yield its full fruits if it is required to operate within an economic and political system which underestimates the tremendous importance of these principles.
>
> The question how we are to educate ourselves is therefore closely linked with two other questions: how are we to live? What is to be the system for the world of tomorrow? [...]
>
> Those who accuse education of having failed intime to restrain the passions which brought about the war, are making a partial but profound mistake. Undoubtedly schools and books can do much, but clearly, they cannot do everything. If all that the peoples expect from education by their teachers in schools is promptly contradicted by the acts of these same peoples in the fields of trading, banking, diplomacy, and judicial administration, what in such conditions can schools achieve in the matter of moral reformation? [...]
>
> No schools or school teachers can in fact educate more than does life itself.

At the General Conference 3rd Session (Beirut), on 26 November 1948, Bodet was elected UNESCO's Director-General. In addressing the General Conference after his nomination, on 10 December, he said[181]:

> In Mexico, I have been Minister of Education and Minister of Foreign Affairs. In these two posts, I came to realize that there could be no sharp dividing line between the duties of the educationist and the obligations of the diplomat. […]
>
> The United Nations are the body politic of a new world, and UNESCO is its conscience. Unless that conscience triumphs, it will be difficult for the new World order to assert itself durably.
>
> In pondering over the present world crisis, we realize that the discords of the time constitute the most eloquent proof of the distress of the peoples in their efforts to attain, at one bound, to the three aims: Liberty, Equality, Fraternity, proclaimed by the French Revolution. […]
>
> We never sought to hide the formidable difficulties inherent in the fulfilment of its purpose: "to determine the general aims of man's education" […].
>
> Of all the various international bodies which have been established, UNESCO is the only one which claims to touch man directly. […]
>
> Our one wish is to set a fair and just goal to private ambitions, namely, service to man as man.

He paid tribute to Julian Huxley: "In naming that eminent representative of contemporary learning, I realize how much UNESCO has lost by his departure. For us, the memory of Dr. Huxley's gifts and authority will be imperishable. UNESCO owes him the highest possible tribute". It was reported that[182]:

> As UNESCO's General Conference drew to its end on December 11, 1948, in the last hour of the last Plenary Session, the announcement came that the United Nations General Assembly in Paris had adopted the International Declaration of Human Rights. […]
>
> The entire Conference rose to its feet and applauded for five minutes to mark the solemn occasion.

The General Conference adopted a Resolution on the dissemination of information about the Declaration and its incorporation in UNESCO's programme activities.[183]

In 1949, Torres Bodet was invited by the USA National Commission for UNESCO to address its Second National Conference, in Cleveland (Ohio), that began on 30 March. It was attended by representatives from hundreds of national organisations, various national and international personalities, and officials and observers from many countries. Bodet spoke on "UNESCO: A Personal Faith", before almost 10,000 persons, on 1 April. His speech was published in *The UNESCO Courier* of the same month.[184] He said:

> For centuries, the peoples have lived in a world of isolated cultures which they regarded as mutually incompatible. But we now know that all cultures can and must harmonize, without excluding or distorting each other, in order to contribute to the emergence of a world civilization.
>
> Harmony does not imply uniformity.

Therefore, he thought that "of all UNESCO's undertakings, the one relating to education for international citizenship is the most original and the most significant". The world civilisation calls for world citizenship that should be fundamentally citizenship of human rights, as symbolically meant by the presence in Cleveland of Eleanor Roosevelt just to speak on the Universal Declaration of Human Rights proclaimed less of four months earlier. She wrote in *My Day* (a daily newspaper column published almost without interruption from 1935 until she died in 1962) on 4 April[185]: "The new Director-General of UNESCO, Dr. Jaime Torres Bodet of Mexico, spoke on 'UNESCO – A Personal Faith' and made a deep impression. Everyone seemed very happy and the general feeling seemed to be that Dr. Bodet was taking hold of his job and the organization on UNESCO very well".

In 1950, addressing the General Conference 5th Session (Florence),[186] Torres Bodet said:

> … for freemen the longing for the lost fatherland is but the aspiration to another fatherland that may always be won – humanity itself. […]
>
> Our authority is only of a moral character. It cannot by itself produce the political and economic decisions which could limit armaments and halt preparations for war. […]
>
> Are not freedom of the individual, and respect for the dignity of man, the very bases of the system set up by the United Nations? […]
>
> The universality of the human spirit is not a matter of arithmetic but consists essentially in a unity with diversity of opinions, systems, and points of view. Without that diversity UNESCO will not be universal and unless in fact it does seek to be universal, I can see no significance in it.

Continuing, he stressed:

> As every year, the fate of our Organization is in your hands. […]

> A programme without a budget is a voice crying in the wilderness. [...]
>
> I have spoken of the financial effort that devolves on Member States. There is also the moral effort. [...]
>
> Everywhere we see conflict, or provocation to conflict, between ideologies which consider themselves irreconcilable. [...]
>
> As I said to you in Beirut when accepting the position to which you had elected me, it is our duty to make of UNESCO the conscience of the United Nations, and conscience can never stand aside from the main stream of history. [...]
>
> UNESCO is fighting for a fellowship of free men, a fellowship of human beings capable of full self-expression and genuine self-realization. It is only with men thus worthy of the name of man that we shall be able to assure a true peace.
>
> May your debates, gentlemen, be inspired by the ideal of such a peace!

The proposed budget was cut by the Delegates. Deeply frustrated by UNESCO's budget as compared with military budgets, Torres Bodet resigned. Nevertheless, he was persuaded to remain in tenure. Eleanor Roosevelt wrote in *My Day* on 9 Mai 1951[187]:

> Jaime Torres-Bodet, Director of UNESCO, has a deep conviction that no democracy can exist without education. Little can be done, he maintains, to improve living standards of people throughout the world or to make human rights a reality and use them to bring about peace unless education is made available to every child and some kind of basic education made possible for every adult who is at present illiterate. It is quite obvious that for many countries this is a long-term program.

On 22 November 1952 (7th Session, Paris),[188] Torres Bodet resigned for good. On 26, he said goodbye in his native Spanish language[189]:

> Que la UNESCO logre desarrollar algún día sus programas, como lo soñamos en Londres – en 1945 – quienes tuvimos el privilegio de asistir a su nacimiento. Y que, a pesar de todos los obstáculos, la paz asegure al mundo – merced a la educación, a la ciencia y a la cultura – un destino digno para el hombre. Señoras y señores: Adiós.

His successor testified (René Maheu)[190]:

> The session had begun well, however, and the general debate had ended in a triumph for the Director-General, whose leadership, ideas and general

> policy objectives had all been unanimously approved by the Conference. [...] Nevertheless, a few days later, the delegates disagreed over the question of means, by which I mean the budget, and, after heated discussions, a majority declared themselves against the Director-General's proposals [...].

In Maheu's opinion, "the figures in question seem derisory" but Torres Bodet was also unhappy with the decision of the General Conference admitting Franco's Spain as a member of UNESCO, after the UN General Assembly has adopted, on 4 November 1950, a resolution in favour of its admission as a member of the United Nations. "UNESCO had disappointed him all the more because he had loved it so ardently" (id.). He felt his internationalist idealism defeated. *El desierto internacional* (International desert) is the title of the third volume of his *Memories*.

On the same day[191]:

> The General Conference
>
> Considering that Mr. Jaime Torres Bodet, Director-General of UNESCO, has rendered the most admirable services to the Organization in every way [...];
>
> Declares:
>
> [...]
>
> 2. That the Conference wishes to pay a deep and genuine tribute to Mr. Torres Bodet for the four years of his creative leadership of UNESCO.

Jaime Torres Bodet was also the author of the reform of Mexico's Constitution Article 3 on the right to education (see Latapí, 1992, pp. 31, 32). The previous Constitutional wording on education (1917, 1934) did not define the purpose of education. On 14 December 1945, the Secretary of Public Education released a Press Statement informing:

> The draft reform of the Constitution Article 3º sent today to Congress of the Union by President Avila Camacho is first and foremost inspired by the purpose of clarifying clearly what the objectives of our public education should be.
>
> As defined by the proposed wording, these objectives coincide with those supported by Mexico at the Educational, Scientific and Cultural Conference held in London in November of this year and also respond to the principles solemnly proclaimed there, on behalf of their peoples, by 43 United Nations Governments.

> Comprehensive education. [...]
>
> Fight against ignorance. [...]
>
> Understanding what is ours; but not to raise the mistakes of blind and ignorant nationalism, but to secure our life and advancement for the sake of universal solidarity and to contribute, ever more broadly, to the peace of the world.
>
> In the spirit of the best efforts in our history, and the most genuine and firm aspirations of our Revolution, these are, in short, the purpose that points to public education the project that the Executive has just submitted to the study and resolution of our Congress. (quoted from Nuria & Tejada, 2016, p. 97).

It is worth noting that the Constitution's Article 3 is in tune with the UDHR proclaimed about three years later.

In the opinion of Torres Bodet, a comprehensive education should include music as "an international art par excellence" and "a true ethical discipline", as he said addressing the First General Assembly of the International Music Council, on 30 January 1950.[192]

On 13 May 1974, *The New York Times* reported[193]:

> Dr. Jaime Torres Bodet, the father of modern Mexican education and the Director General of the United Nations Educational, Scientific and Cultural Organization from 1948 to 1952, shot and killed himself at his home tonight, the police announced. He was 72 years old. Dr. Torres Bodet was suffering from cancer of the prostate...
>
> In a suicide letter he wrote that because of illness, he was "waiting for death on a day to day basis" and "I prefer to call on death myself at the right time", spokesman for the family reported.

A week later, on 20 May 1974, paying tribute to Bodet in a meeting at UNESCO's headquarters, Maheu offered a first-hand and insightful synopsis of the contribution "in some respects decisive [...] to the Organization at a particularly difficult time in its uncertain early years" of a man "so open to all the horizons of the mind, so sensitive to all the world's appeals", who was an exceptional representative "of Latin American humanism"[194]:

> The signal value of his contribution was immediate evident, for he played an important and highly significant part in drawing up the Constitution of the Organization. [...] It is, for instance, to him that we owe the famous statement in the preamble to the Constitution that peace "must... be

founded… upon the intellectual and moral solidarity of mankind", which is, in my view, the clearest possible definition of the Organization's *raison d'être* and means of action. […]

First and foremost, he brought to hit his own very lofty conception of the originality and the greatness of UNESCO's mission. […]

Secondly, Jaime Torres Bodet gave UNESCO's work a resolutely humanistic inspiration and approach which have not only never been repudiated but have steadily gained in depth and strength. By humanism, I mean in this context the view of man as "a living centre of self-determination", to use his own words; and the belief in the absolute dignity of the individual in which that freedom takes specific form. In point of fact, Julian Huxley, the first Director-General, was a humanist too, and they were both profoundly convinced rationalists. Nevertheless, in comparison with Huxley's scientific humanism whose evolutionism, however flexible and inventive, could not disengage the freedom of the mind from the determinism of nature, the essentially moral humanism of Torres Bodet undeniably brought with it an enlargement of scope which allowed UNESCO to take in the whole estate of man with its interests ranging from fundamental education for the great numbers of the most deprived to cooperation among specialists at the highest level of intellectual and artistic activity.

Hence the fundamental importance which he attached to the promotion and observance of human rights. On the very day that Jaime Torres Bodet took the oath of office at Beirut, on 10 December 1948, the General Assembly of the United Nations adopted the Universal Declaration of Human Rights in Paris. There could have been no more propitious coincidence, since this Declaration became the foundation of all that he did. He realized that it solved that notorious problem of UNESCO's ideology or philosophy in which his predecessor had become embroiled, and over which, for a while, the Organization seemed to be in danger of foundering, amid the fury of doctrinal disputes, before ever putting out to sea. It was accepted, once and for all, that UNESCO's ideology must be that of human rights, as the only ideology on which it could base militant but non-partisan action on behalf of justice and peace. […]

The third thing that Jaime Torres Bodet gave us – and what a novel idea it was at the time! – was the appreciation of the duty that the international community has, for the sake of justice, towards those peoples whom he described as being robbed of their heritage by history and geography. […]

It was in this way that he was able to save UNESCO from the temptation of elitism which has so often proved fatal to even the best-intentioned intellectual enterprise. […]

> This novel conception of the aims of international cooperation was primarily inspired by the desire to relieve the world's want in an effective and practical way, and to establish the internal conditions for the emancipation of the most deprived peoples and classes. [...]
>
> I accompanied Mr. Torres Bodet to the meetings held by the Administrative Committee on Coordination during 1950 in Geneva and New York to prepare the first outlines of the Programme. I remember what high hopes he had and how enthusiastically he entered into the discussions to show that man, in the fullness of his personality, must be central to the development process [...].

Jaime Torres Bodet is buried in the *Rotonda de las Personas Ilustres* (Rotunda of Illustrious Persons), Mexico City. There is a UNESCO-UNAM Jaime Torres Bodet Prize in Social Sciences, Humanities and Arts, created in 2014.

4.1.2.5.6.3 René Maheu

René Maheu, a teacher of philosophy, was Professor at the University of Cologne from 1931 to 1933, witnessing the rise of Nazism in Germany. He taught from 1933 to 1939 in the French Institute of London, where he also was cultural *Attaché* with the French Embassy. He was hired by Huxley for the Secretariat of the Preparatory Commission. Later, he became Director of the Executive Office of Torres Bodet, Assistant Director-General, Deputy Director-General, Acting Director-General in 1961, and Director-General for two successive terms. After years "conceptually quite empty (1953–1961), UNESCO enters, from its takeover by René Maheu in 1961, a major conceptual renewal which leads to the advent of a period of intense radiation" (Maurel, 2006, p. 122).

It was a time of UNESCO turning to practical action when the majority in the General Conference gradually became formed by new States resulting from the decolonisation wave: from 1956 to 1964, the Member States increased from 70 to 117. In 1960, 16 new African States participated, for the first time, in the General Conference, the first one with a Third World majority. It was the *African Conference.*[195] The next Director-General would be African (Amadou-Mahtar M'Bow, Senegal).

After the UN General Assembly has called for a "New International Economic Order", in 1974, UNESCO called for a "New World Information and Communication Order". The Director-General set up the International Commission for the Study of Communication Problems, in 1977, chaired by Seán MacBride (Ireland), whose Report *Many Voices One World* was published in 1980. This Report was among the causes of the USA, United Kingdom and Singapore withdrawal from UNESCO in 1984 and 1985. The Organisation's budget suffered a 30% cut.

Development aid became a priority for the United Nations, the World Bank came into play (1962), an International Institute of Educational Planning (IIEP) was created in 1963 (in 1999, UNESCO established the Institute for Statistics: UIS), but within UNESCO the relationship between intellectual action and operational action (direct or indirect) was an issue greatly debated. The tension was mentioned by René Maheu in the Introduction of his Report, as Acting Director-General, to the General Conference of 1962 (where he would be elected Director-General on 14 November 1962)[196]:

> Although there is unanimous recognition that operational action is a necessity in the present state of world affairs and that there can be no question, now that the United Nations General Assembly is launching the Development Decade, of checking this necessary trend, anxiety over the suddenness and scope of the changes it has brought about has occasionally been voiced. The discussions of the General Conference, however, showed that there was general agreement that the 1963–1964 programme reflected a reasonably fair balance between operational activities and intellectual cooperation. (p. XIV)

The true nature and mission of UNESCO as envisaged by Maheu favoured the intellectual side, in all its splendour, which led him to create in 1966 a Division of Philosophy, entrusted with Jeanne Hersch (Swiss philosopher)[197] and, following the 1960s *world education crisis* due to the *school explosion* and the wave of students' unrest, to set up the International Commission on the Development of Education that prepared the Faure Report (1972) (see below).

The UNESCO Courier published in October 1976[198] excerpts from his speeches (pp. 24–30),[199] which summarise his views on UNESCO's mission. They deserve a large quotation:

> Development as we understand it today means the development of man by man and for man. [...]
>
> Development is more than a tool to be used for creating a final product. This product is human dignity. [...]
>
> In fact, the only kind of economy which can be qualified as humanist is one which considers man to be both the alpha and omega of development. [...]
>
> Nothing at the present time is as important as education. I am not just speaking from an ethical or moral point of view, but rather from a realist and even political one; for educational problems have now acquired political dimensions. [...]

> Thus, the purpose of education is not so much to provide once and for all a fixed sum of knowledge as to teach the art of learning: and to make learning a lifelong process. [...]
>
> We need to evolve a new form of humanism which will strike a balance between science and culture, between science and technology, and within the confines of science itself between the natural and human sciences. [...] Man's existence only has meaning as a total concept.
>
> At the present time there is not task more urgent than to provide modern man with a new meaning embracing the whole range of his ideals. [...]
>
> It has often been said – but it cannot be said too often – that UNESCO is an organization concerned with man and his destiny. [...]
>
> UNESCO is thus, by its very nature, committed [... to a] humanistic vocation which is inseparable from its ethical mission. [...]
>
> UNESCO is founded on the belief that in the long run it is the freedom of man which decides the path of history, [...] so that there can only be true peace as long as the mind abides by an order which it respects.
>
> What is this order? It is that of the dignity of man, which finds its expression as specified in the various human rights; whose authority in society is called justice; and whose prevalence in people's hearts is called love, or at least tolerance. [...]
>
> It is Human Rights, as defined in the Universal Declaration of 1948, which inspire the whole of UNESCO's work, and give it its meaning; [...] in fact all its activities are designed to facilitate the advent of a civilization of the universal.
>
> Peace itself has no value and, strictly speaking, no reality for UNESCO unless it is founded on justice, which is nothing other than human rights in action. [...]
>
> International cooperation is both a necessity and an ideal.
>
> It is a necessity for modern civilization [...]. It is also an ideal – and by that I do not mean a dream, but a moral imperative – for men are coming to realize more and more that they are morally as well as physically interdependent.

According to Maurel (2006):

> Of all UNESCO's leaders, René Maheu appears unquestionably as the strongest personality. The period during which he led UNESCO proved to be very fruitful in new conceptual developments. It gives the organisation new breathing both in terms of ideas and action. [...]

> The Maheu's period appears in the collective memory of contemporaries as the golden age of UNESCO. [...]
>
> This impression of *golden age*, this atmosphere of idealism and renewal, are not only due to Maheu's charisma, but have an objective basis: they correspond to a real UNESCO's conceptual mutation towards the needs of the Third World, which gives the organisation much greater importance on the international stage. [...]
>
> Maheu succeeds in the difficult challenge of making this real transformation of UNESCO characterised by a massive development of operational action, while avoiding that the organisation does not completely topple into this task and abandon its intellectual, philosophical, and ideological initial vocation. He thus manages to make a radical change in the definition of UNESCO's functions, without losing its identity. On the other hand, it strives to reconcile universalism and multiculturalism. (pp. 122, 127, 129, 145)

At the end of his second term, he was seriously ill and died on 19 December 1975. Like Julian Huxley, he was an idealistic personality "whose religion was the human", as witnessed his son Jean Maheu (as cited ibid., p. 127).

4.1.2.5.7 *UNESCO's Ideology and Mission*

The October 1985 special issue of *The UNESCO Courier*, dedicated to celebrating its 40th anniversary, was titled "Birth of an Ideal".[200] Maybe it would have been more accurate to put "Renaissance of an Ideal" – the ideal of "The precursors" recalled in its pages 6 and 7. UNESCO's precursors brought together over about two decades intellectual and moral figures of outstanding stature, imbued with the idealism of the French illuminism and/or a Christian humanism, which echoed in the London Founding Conference, impregnating UNESCO's Preamble and Article 1, inspiring its most outstanding Directors-General, and resounding in the first General Conferences, where were present such great personalities as Bertrand Russell (1949), Helen Keller (1950), Maria Montessori (1950 and 1951), Jean Piaget[201] or Cardinal Roncalli, the future Pope John XXIII, appointed Observer of the Holy See to UNESCO in 1952.

During the London Conference, at the extraordinary plenary meeting of 16 November,[202] Étienne Gilson declared: "The San Francisco Charter created the United Nations as a body; the Charter of our Organisation will give that body a soul". What is UNESCO's *soul*?

The Introduction to Appendix 5 included in the Report of the ICIC 17th session (Geneva, 15–20 July 1935),[203] with "Extracts from the General Report of the Director of the International Institute of Intellectual Cooperation to the

International Committee", read: "All bear witness to the interest of the intellectual world, and of its best representatives, in a movement directed towards ensuring the recognition of a universal moral doctrine – those ethical principles which must constitute the basis of a flourishing League of Nations".

At the opening of the International Seminar on "Nehru, the man and his vision", UNESCO House, 27 September 1989, the General Director (at the time Federico Mayor) recalled[204]:

> In his [Jawaharlal Nehru, leader of the Indian independence movement and Prime Minister from 1947 until 1964] speech to the ninth session of UNESCO's General Conference held in New Delhi in 1956, he spelt out his commitment to the Organization when he said: "Man does not live by politics alone, nor indeed wholly by economics. And so, UNESCO has come to represent something that is vital to human existence and progress. Even as the United Nations General Assembly represents the political will of the world community, UNESCO tries to represent the finer and deeper sides of human life and indeed might be said to represent the conscience of humanity".

As said Pierre-Marie Dupuy (2007) in the International Symposium on 60 Years of UNESCO (2005c): "Humanity is, if I may say so, UNESCO's speciality" (p. 362). The same idea has been put forwards by the Director-General (at the time Koïchiro Matsuura) in his inaugural address to the same International Symposium: "I would suggest that the best definition of UNESCO's mission is nothing but the perpetual search for the human in the humankind" (p. 61). This is the stake of the Ethics of Human Rights. UNESCO's ideology – understood as an ensemble of values and principles – is the "ideology of Human Rights" (Maheu, 1972, p. 284).

The primary, albeit indirect, legal basis for UNESCO's human rights work is Article 1.3 of the United Nations Charter, read together with Articles 55 and 56. The direct legal basis lies in its Constitution,[205] mainly in Article 1.1. In its Preamble, the word 'dignity' appears twice, and Article 1 mentions "the human rights and fundamental freedoms". It was involved in the UDHR and International Covenants on human rights drafting. The General Conference 1st Session (1946) included in "Other Projects and Activities" concerning "E – Philosophy and Humanistic Studies" the following[206]:

> 2. Rights of Man
>
> UNESCO will obtain from Governments, National Commissions and individuals, contributions toward a modern formulation of human rights with a view to:

a. Drafting, with the aid of a small conference of experts, a statement on the subject for the United Nations Commission on Human Rights.
b. Promoting the publication of a symposium on the subject. (p. 275)

This was the task of the Committee chaired by Jacques Maritain, referred to above.[207]

UNESCO's ideology may be condensed in these conceptually interwoven values: humanism and universalism, implying pacifism and internationalism, opposite to a small-minded nationalism. It is an ideology of the unity and diversity of Humanity, calling for an International Rule of Law and even a Word Government, dreaming of world citizenship.

Humanism and universalism

In 1951, during a "Discussion on the Cultural and Philosophical Relations Between East and West" held in New Delhi (India), from 13 to 20 December, a new holistic humanism was proposed.[208] In March 2011, the UNESCO High Panel on Peace and Dialogue among Cultures, meeting at the UN headquarters in New York, agreed that "rethinking peace and reconciliation resonated with the quest for a New Humanism for the 21st Century". It should be recalled that the IIIC published in 1937 *Vers un nouvel humanisme* (Towards a New Humanism), collecting the papers of the Budapest 'Conversation' (1936).

In April 2009, Irina Bokova submitted to UNESCO's Executive Board (181st session), in conjunction with her candidacy for the post of Director-General, a text where she stated: "My understanding of a NEW HUMANISM for the 21st century will guide all my activity".[209] What was her understanding?

In her speech delivered at the UNESCO General Conference 35th Session, on 23 October 2009, she said: "Respect for fundamental rights, for the dignity of every individual and for diversity, thus a humanity that is mutually supportive and responsible – this is my message".[210] In an address delivered at the University of Malaya, Kuala Lumpur (Malaysia), on 21 May 2013, she restated: "This is what I mean by calling for a new humanism. This is really an appeal to invest in the dignity and capabilities of every woman and man. We need today a new humanism rooted in a profound respect for human dignity, fundamental rights and the diversity of cultures".[211] As she wrote in the Editorial of *The UNESCO Courier*, October-December 2011[212]:

> Humanism is an age-old promise, as well as an idea that is always new, endlessly reinventing itself. The humanist project has been part of our history since Antiquity, yet it shines like new in every epoch. [...]
>
> Respect for cultural diversity is a core element of 21st century humanism. It is a vital constituent during these times of globalization. [...]

> Humanist values form the very foundations of the philosophy of UNESCO. Written into its constitution, they have been guiding the actions of our Organization for 65 years [...].
>
> Building the ramparts of human dignity in everyday life is not a Utopian quest. Humanism is a promise we must all keep.

The same issue included a contribution titled "Towards a humanist turn", by Oliver Kozlarek (Mexico), who wrote:

> Instead of looking for the universal in biological nature, a recent humanist turn in the social sciences and humanities is focusing on what all human beings around the globe share, without neglecting their differences. And instead of thinking that a universal humanist culture has to be invented or imposed on other cultures, the new approach believes that universal ideas and values are already present in all cultures. It also acknowledges that people everywhere on the planet are sharing dehumanizing experiences – which should encourage us to consider what it means to live a humane and dignified life.

In sum: "This principle of constant 'attuning' is central to the New Humanism. [...] As stated frequently in this booklet: humanism is in the DNA of UNESCO".[213]

As education is concerned, the *UNESCO Education Strategy – 2014–2021* states (Chapter 2 – Towards a new education agenda after 2015)[214]:

> UNESCO advocates *a humanistic and holistic vision of education* [italics added] as a fundamental human right that is essential to personal and socio-economic development. The objective of such education must be envisaged in a broad lifelong learning perspective that aims at empowering people to realize their right to education, fulfil their personal expectations for a decent, healthy life and work, and contribute to the achievement of their societies' socio-economic development objectives. In addition to the acquisition of basic knowledge, attitudes and cognitive, social and emotional skills, the content of learning must promote problem-solving and creative thinking; understanding and respect for human rights; inclusion and equity; and cultural diversity, all of which are essential to the realization of peace, responsible citizenship and sustainable development. (p. 25)

UNESCO's universalism is an ethical outcome of its humanism. Already Article 1 of the International Act on Intellectual Co-operation signed on 3 December

1938 within the framework of the League of Nations read: "The High Contracting Parties note that the work of Intellectual Cooperation is independent of politics and based entirely on the principle of universality".[215]

Pacifism and internationalism

Pacifism and internationalism are logic outcomes of humanism and universalism. In its 1st Session (1946),[216] UNESCO's General Conference adopted the Resolution "C – Education for International Understanding".

It should go without saying that pacifism and internationalism are not compatible with "the nationalist tendencies which have invaded education in almost every country", as said Murray by presenting the Report of the Fifth Committee to the Second Assembly of the League of Nations on 21 September 1921 (as cited in Saikawa, 2014, p. 63). Johan Huizinga warned against it at the meeting "Towards a New Humanism" in Budapest (1936):

> It will do us no good to go on talking about humanism and agreeing that it must be preserved if we do not oppose its mortal enemy, nationalism, which I consider to be the scourge of our time. By nationalism I mean exaggerated patriotism, that is, a great virtue become a vice. If nationalism continues to spread throughout the world as it has for some ten or twelve years now, it will end by engulfing all our fine humanism. (as cited in Droit, 2005, p. 32)

It was certainly this nationalism that Paul Valery had in mind when he wrote in reply to Salvador de Madariaga in 1933: "I regard the political need to exploit all that is psychologically of the lowest order in human beings as the gravest danger currently facing us" (ibid., p. 38). Einstein answered an interviewer when asked if he considered himself a German or a Jew, in 1929: "It is possible to be both. I look upon myself as a person. Nationalism is an infantile disease. It is the measles of mankind".[217]

In this regard, the Report of the ICIC 17th session (Geneva, 15–20 July 1935)[218] read:

> Nationalism and internationalism […] are complementary, if by nationalism is meant the need which a people feels for regrouping and for a realisation of its own originality, and by internationalism, the impossibility of living in isolation, the need for exchanges of thought, the interdependence which is the very essence of modern life. The work of intellectual cooperation is an attempt at synthesis between these two very legitimate tendencies. The difficulties which it encounters are proof of their inevitability.

World citizenship

Resonating with Kantian *Jus Cosmopolitum* (Cosmopolitan Law), Victor Hugo wrote in the preface to his play *The Burgraves*, dated from 25 March 1843[219]:

> Let us hope that one day the entire globe will be civilized, all areas of human habitation will be enlightened, and then the magnificent dream of intelligence will be realized: to have the world as one's country and humanity as one's nation.

President Roosevelt said in a broadcasting Address to the International Student Assembly, on 3 September 1942,[220] that "the old term 'Western civilisation' no longer applies. World events and the needs of all humanity have joined the culture of Asia with the culture of Europe and the Americas to form the first time a real world civilisation".

Already in 1928, William G. Carr had published *Education for World Citizenship*. The Report of the Preparatory Commission presented to UNESCO First General Conference,[221] on 20 November 1946, recommended "the creation of World Citizenship Clubs in schools" (p. 24), inspired by "an ideology with the most universal basis possible, namely, the existence of common human needs and the necessity for satisfying them" (p. 24). Indeed: "Perhaps the most overall principle governing our activities is that they should be directed towards the creation of *One World* in the things of the mind and spirit" (p. 25).

At the first meeting of the Sub-Commission on Education, on 26 November: "The Delegate of Brazil pointed out that, to justify faith in secular education, the latter must create an ideal; that ideal must be universal and human and be based on a deep knowledge of man. The aims of secular education must be to love, know and serve humanity" (p. 149). During the fourth meeting, on 27 November: "The Delegate of Ecuador suggested that a competition should take place throughout the world for a textbook of civic education, which would deal with man's duties towards: (1) his country, (2) the cultural group to which he belongs, (3) humanity" (p. 155).

Torres Bodet said in his 1949 speech in Cleveland (Ohio)[222], as above quoted, that education for international citizenship "sums up UNESCO's highest mission". Global Citizenship Education (GCED) has become a UNESCO strategic area. Its website reads[223]:

> While the world may be increasingly interconnected, human rights violations, inequality and poverty still threaten peace and sustainability.
>
> Global Citizenship Education (GCED) is UNESCO's response to these challenges. It works by empowering learners of all ages to understand

> that these are global, not local issues and to become active promoters of more peaceful, tolerant, inclusive, secure and sustainable societies.
>
> GCED is a strategic area of UNESCO's Education Sector programme and builds on the work of Peace and Human Rights Education. It aims to instil in learners the values, attitudes and behaviours that support responsible global citizenship: creativity, innovation, and commitment to peace, human rights and sustainable development.
>
> UNESCO's work in this area is grounded in its own Constitution [...].

World Government?

Huxley (1946) wrote:

> The moral for UNESCO is clear. The task laid upon it of promoting peace and security can never be wholly realised through the means assigned to it – education, science and culture. It must envisage some form of world political unity, whether through a single world government or otherwise, as the only certain means for avoiding war. However, world political unity is, unfortunately, a remote ideal, and in any case does not fall within the field of UNESCO's competence. (p. 13)

During the general discussion of the Report of the Preparatory Commission of UNESCO, in November 1946, Sir Sarvepalli Radhakrishnan – Delegate of India, philosopher, academic and statesman who would be chair of the UNESCO's Executive Board and become President of his country – said: "The Executive Secretary's report gives us the blueprints for the development of what one may call a world brain, a world mind, or a world culture, which alone can be the basis of a world authority or a world government" (p. 27).

The dream of a *universal civilisation*, a *world culture*, a *world citizenship*, even a *World Government*, was shared by many personalities. In the post-World War II times, it was so much in the air that the President of the University of Chicago (Robert Hutchins) formed, in 1945, a *Committee to frame a World Constitution.*[224]

World Ministry of the Right to Education

We know the States' reluctance regarding international intervention in their domestic affairs and, in particular, education. For instance, the USA Ambassador in the United Kingdom (Winant) reported to the Secretary of State on 30 December 1943,[225] informing about the CAME, that "the observer for the U.S.S.R. approached the Embassy's observer yesterday" and:

... also raised the question of the establishment of an International Education Office which the Conference has listed as one of its objectives. He indicated that the U.S.S.R. might not feel great hesitancy about participating in the work of such an office as long as its activities were confined to the exchange of purely technical information, but that the U.S.S.R. would be extremely reluctant to participate in an International Education Bureau which undertook to deal with the subject matter introduced in the curricula of national schools.

The famous Article 2.7 of the Charter of the United Nations states[226]:

> Nothing contained in the present Charter shall authorize the United Nations to intervene in matters which are essentially within the domestic jurisdiction of any state or shall require the Members to submit such matters to settlement under the present Charter;

This provision is replicated in Article I.3 of the UNESCO Constitution[227]:

> With a view to preserving the independence, integrity and fruitful diversity of the cultures and educational systems of the States Members of the Organization, the Organization is prohibited from intervening in matters which are essentially within their domestic jurisdiction.

In spite of the diversity of national school systems, they rise similar questions. Moreover, like the UN Charter Article 2.7 was superseded by the international responsibility to protect and promote human rights, if the values and principles enshrined in the UN Charter and the UNESCO Constitution are to be protected and promoted, the concern underlying the recommendation included in the LIA and CEWC Joint Commission Report (1943), above quoted, was legitimate: "That, in any period during which Germany may be occupied, the occupying powers should exercise their control over education through a High Commissioner for Education who should be appointed in advance by the United Nations and be ready to start work at the moment the occupation begins". Dorn (2006) noted in this respect:

> The State Department's ambivalence towards assigning UNESCO a strong 'active function' resulted, in part, from the extreme differences between America's war experience and that of many of its allies. Countries that had suffered severely under Nazi occupation, such as Poland, lobbied for immediate economic assistance in rebuilding their educational

> infrastructure and demanded that Germany's educational system be controlled by an external, international authority, preventing its future use as a training ground for German militarism and aggression. (p. 320)

So, the General Conference First Session (1946) took over its constitutional legitimacy when it included in "Other Projects and Activities" concerning "Education" the following[228]:

> 5. Re-Education of Ex-Enemy Countries
> An enquiry will be made into the possibility of opening up ex-enemy countries to programmes consistent with the objectives of UNESCO. (p. 273)

The question has, therefore, at times arisen: Should UNESCO be a kind of Universal Ministry of Education?

Torres Bodet said in his speech to the General Conference 3rd Session (Beirut), on 10 December 1948, after being elected Director-General[229]: "UNESCO has no right to interfere in the domestic affairs of Governments. We have neither the power nor the wish to transform the Organisation into a World Ministry of Education". But immediately added: "Our work must be based, above all on two factors for which no substitute has so far been found: the good faith of governments and the persuasive force of principles". It was about – as he had said at the London Conference third plenary meeting, on 2 November 1945 (pp. 35–39)[230] – how to reconcile each nation's freedom concerning education "with the imperative necessity of pronouncing decisively on the general aims implied in the education of man? [...] What is to be the ideal which shall inspire true education?".

Obviously, UNESCO could not aim at unifying the contents of education in the plurality of the world's nations but, as Elfert (2016) notices, "the 1989 OECD report *Education and the Economy in a Changing Society* 'became a bible for Ministers of Education' (Rubenson, 2008, p. 255)" (p. 205). In effect, OECD has become like a World Ministry of Education, as it is sometimes written, in the sense explained, for example, by Pasi Sahlberg – the most mediatic ambassador of Finland's worldwide praised education system – who compared its influence with a pandemic[231]:

> When I look around the world, I see competition, choice, and measuring of students and teachers as the main means to improve education. This market-based global movement has put many public schools at risk [...].
>
> One thing that has struck me is how similar education systems are. Curricula are standardized to fit to international student tests; and students

> around the world study learning materials from global providers. Education reforms in different countries also follow similar patterns. So visible is this common way of improvement that I call it the *Global Educational Reform Movement or GERM*. It is like an epidemic that spreads and infects education systems through a virus. It travels with pundits, media and politicians. Education systems borrow policies from others and get infected. As a consequence, schools get ill, teachers don't feel well, and kids learn less.
>
> GERM infections have various symptoms.
>
> The first symptom is more competition within education systems. [...]
>
> The second symptom of GERM is increased school choice. [...]
>
> The third sign of GERM is stronger accountability from schools and related standardized testing of students. [...]
>
> We should instead restore the fundamental meaning and values of school education. Without public schools, our nations and communities are poorly equipped to value humanity, equality and democracy. I think we should not educate children to be similar according to a standardized metric but help them to discover their own talents and teach them to be different from one another. Diversity is richness in humanity and a condition for innovation.

In this connection, the Report Delors (1996) remarked:

> Humanity can hardly recognize itself in the distorting mirror in which the ills affecting our societies take the form of marks and scars. The new direction in which history has been moving since 1989, a direction determined by the triumph of an implacable economic logic based on the law of the strongest and subjected to the dictates of a *soulless neo-liberalism* [italics added] make it essential that there should be *a reawakening of consciences, a moral revival* to tackle the fundamental social issue of worsening inequality in the world. (p. 201)

To counter these realities, it was stressed that:

> ... UNESCO's ethical mission, to which its Constitution assigns priority, is today enhanced by the new tasks required of education in the modern world, be it promoting sustainable development, ensuring social cohesion, encouraging democratic participation at every level, or responding to the demands made by globalization. In all these areas, the ultimate societal aims of education should never obscure the primacy of the human individual and the ideals proclaimed by the international

> community when the United Nations was founded. The ethical imperative, then seen as primordial, thus turns out in the final analysis to be what attunes the work of UNESCO most profoundly to present realities, with all their doubts and uncertainties. (p. 188)

In a world driven by science and technology, increasingly globalised but largely dominated by neoliberal policies, for acting "as a global education think-tank and moral compass", UNESCO "needs to rediscover its heart, its ethical roots" (Power, 2015, pp. 248, 263). Without breaking the balance between pragmatism and idealism, it must reflect and foster the advancement of the Ethical Conscience of Humanity, even when political and financial constraints do not allow it to be more than a bird with divine singing but short wings.

In sum: UNESCO should strive to be more and more recognised as a World Ministry of the Right to Education and the Culture of Human Rights.

4.1.3 *Education: Human Right*

Fernando Volio (1979) wrote:

> Certain eminent pedagogues and philosophers in the sixteenth and seventeenth centuries adumbrated the existence of an individual right to education when they focused their attention on the pupil and his needs. For example, John Amos Comenius (1592–1670) in *The Great Didactic*, wanted education for all men together, as well as for each one individually, i.e. young and old, rich and poor, noble and common, men and women, because the point was to be able to educate 'each and every person whose destiny was to be born as man'. […]
>
> For their part, John Locke (1632–1704) and Jean-Jacques Rousseau (1712–78) also came close to the modern conception.
>
> Locke, in his *Second Treatise of Government*, where he speaks of paternal power, highlights parents' obligation to educate their children until they become able to make full and proper use of their freedom, which is theirs by virtue of the simple but fundamental fact that they are people; there exists the 'equal right that every man hath to his natural freedom'. […]
>
> Thus, the parents' power of guardianship is matched by the children's right to education.
>
> Rousseau, in *Émile*, also recognizes and asserts children's freedom and sees their happiness as dependent on the exercise of such freedom. […] Here, as in the case of Locke, children's right to be educated is a result of their right to be able to enjoy their freedom to the full in due course and,

> likewise, of every human being's vital need to be given an education in order to be able to use his faculties: 'All that we lack at birth, and need in adulthood, we owe to education'. (pp. 20, 21)

It is submitted that the major precursors of the normative distinctiveness of the *human right* to education were Comenius and Rousseau, for these main reasons: Comenius pointed to the universality of education as imperative of the human essential educability, Rousseau questioned the legitimacy of the educational power, alongside with that of the political power. The argument is briefly summarised next.

4.1.3.1 Major Precursors

4.1.3.1.1 *Comenius*

Comenius is the prominent European name of the history of education in the 17th century. Gabriel Compayré called it the "Bacon of Pedagogy", and Jules Michelet the "Galileo of education" (in Château, 1980, note 189). He was "the world's first great international educator" (Dobinson, 1970, Preface).

Comenius was the greatest precursor of the right to education under the anthropological angle of its universality (including women). He wrote in his *Didactica Magna* (The Great Didactic, 1657)[232] that man is an "educable animal", because "it is only by a proper education that he can become a man", referring to cases of 'wild children' (Chapter VI).

Comenius's philosophical-theological view of man evolved so that he came to place the will at the core of the human uniqueness. "Comenius defines man as a rational animal, whose highest faculty is the mind", but "the central and the noblest faculty of the human mind was the will" (Čížek, 2016, pp. 202, 182). His unique nature "permits his existential open-endedness that is founded on his free and unlimited will. In Comenius's definition, man is a being that creates himself endlessly and eternally". In consequence: "For Comenius, education is the tool of man's ultimate *humanisation* and a way to regulate his self-creation. Only education, whose goal is to teach man how he should use his reason, will, and agency, can make man truly human" (p. 203).

Comenius's *pedagogical optimism*, however, was tempered by an *anthropological realism*, as Jan Hábl (2017) points out. Human dignity is not prevented from depravity.

> Comenius's distinction between the ontological and moral nature of the human being realistically captured the complexity and ambivalence of humanity. Humans are endowed with both positive and negative potential. The ontological value of a person (humanity) is firmly anchored.

> The moral nature (humaneness) is open. [...] A person is capable of both humanity and inhumanity. (p. 133)

That is why it can be concluded that Comenius “claimed that each man on this earth has a right to education” (Jean Aubá, in Dobinson, 1970, p. 59). Also, according to Piaget (1957), the starting point of his pedagogic thought is the “affirmation of the right to education for all and in full equality” (p. 280).

Comenius “is fully aware of the devastation of this permanent plague of teaching which is the verbalism or pseudo-knowledge”, wrote Piaget, who noted: “in a century in which the ferule constitutes a pedagogical instrument (it is still recommended by Locke!), and in which the only school morality is a moral of obedience, [...] Comenius is radically against corporal punishment” (pp. 274, 276, 277). Many of its methodological recommendations could be written “in gold letters on the entrance door of all schools today, so much they remain valid and are unfortunately still little applied” (p. 272). The right to education is the right to another education.

Moreover, Comenius was “the first to conceive a science of education in all its breadth”, and this “is undoubtedly its main title of glory” (pp. 266, 282). He has been the precursor of the developmental psychology and was probably the first to use illustrations didactically in a schoolbook, in his *Orbis sensualium pictus* (The Sensitive World Illustrated), published in 1658 in Nuremberg (Germany).

During the 1945 UNESCO Founding Conference, in London,[233] in the fourth plenary meeting (November 2), the representative of Czechoslovakia (Jan Opocensky) affirmed his nation proud of:

> ... John Amos Comenius, who was the first to show clearly the way to democracy in education in his *Didactica Magna*. He not only asks for the common education of every child without difference of sex or social origin; but he gave a wonderful plan of the comprehensive school, from the 'Mother School' – *école maternelle* – up to the University. (pp. 45, 46)

Comenius dreamt of a new world regenerated by a universal right to humanist education. His “pedagogical modernism sounds a little like a miracle” (Prévot, 1981, p. 14).

4.1.3.1.2 *Rousseau*

In the 18th century, Rousseau was the genius of the “movement from the old to the new world in education”, as Pestalozzi said in 1826 (as cited in Soëtard, 1995). *Émile* – his main work and probably the masterpiece of the history of the pedagogic thought – is “the founding text of the modern pedagogy” (Soëtard,

1997, p. 100). Despite its disorder and paradoxes, it should be "regarded as the culminating point, in the pedagogical field, of the liberation efforts of a whole series of humanistic thinkers" (Lecercle, 1958, p. 67).

Rousseau was the most powerful influence, perhaps, on the formation and triumph of the juridical individualism of the French Revolution. His work configures, in the profoundness of its complexity, an individualistic political-pedagogical paradigm, i.e. centred on the individual's ethical primacy. He never loses sight of the political framework of human existence. His pedagogic thought is indissociable from his political thought. A comparison between *Émile* and the *Republic* reveals that this vision is the great affinity and motive of Rousseau's admiration for Plato. Eugenio Garin (1957) concluded that, "stripped of its paradoxical aspects, the work of Rousseau gains all its value for its revolutionary content. Human education is not possible except in a renewed society, a society of free and equal men [...]. The myth of *Émile* is the myth of the new Adam in the new earthly paradise. And the strength of *Émile* consists in being a revolutionary manifesto" (pp. 248, 249).

The most revolutionary content of Rousseau's pedagogic thought has, indeed, the same source as the revolutionary content of his political thought. It lies in these words from the *Contrat Social* (Social Contract, 1762b), Book III, Chapter XV: "Where right and liberty are everything, disadvantages count for nothing". However, Rousseau considered the *Émile* as "the most useful, the most significant of my works, and the one that holds me more in the heart than did all others", as he wrote to Duchesne, his Parisian publisher, on 21 November 1761.[234] In a letter to another correspondent, he said that *Émile* and the *Contrat Social* "together make a complete whole", but the second one "must be taken as a sort of appendix" to the first one. Michel Soëtard to comment: "And it is a fact that the substance of *Du contrat social* is recapitulated in Book V of *Émile* [...]. It is here that politics' roots in the educational sphere become palpable" (p. 7).[235]

Rousseau (1762a) wrote: "I am showing what we should try to attain, I do not say we can attain it, but I do say that whoever comes nearest to it is nearest to success" (p. 114). In effect, he resorted to the *Utopian method* consisting of a mental experience analogous to that which he mentions in the introduction to his Second Discourse (*Discourse on the Origin and Basis of Inequality Among Men*). In this regard, Rousseau is for the pedagogical experimentation as Galileo for experimental science. *Émile*'s education is a fiction (analogous to that of a primordial *state of nature*) intending "to show what education could do for man [...] so as to see what a difference education may make in the individual" (pp. 319, 331). He employs the term *force de l'éducation* (force of education). "Use force with children and reasoning with men; this is the natural order; [...] If there is something he should not do, do not forbid him; prevent him without explanation or reasoning" (p. 109). This language may be shocking for a certain social narcissism but, as lucidly observed Guy Avanzini (2003), the idea of "natural goodness", in Rousseau, has been misunderstood. It means rather "the denial of the Christian dogmatic of the original sin" (p. 58). *Émile* implores: "Oh, my friend, my protector, my master! [...] make me free by guarding me against the passions which do me violence; do not let me become their slave; compel me to be my own master and to obey, not my senses, but my reason" (p. 426).

While education is indeed a form of power, it should not degenerate in a relationship of forces. Rousseau binds the exercise of family power to the contractual principle, the founding legal act, civilising and legitimising both the political and the pedagogical authority. He did not underestimate the strength of family ties but, as he said in *A Discourse on Political Economy*, "as the reason of each man is not left to be the sole arbiter of his duties, Government ought the less indiscriminately to abandon to the intelligence and prejudices of fathers the education of their children, as that education is of still greater importance to the State than to the fathers". It is even "certainly the most important business of State" (Rousseau, 1913, pp. 148, 149). This is, in the opinion of Elisabeth Badinter (1980), "a radically new theory of the family", which "still disturbs our present values" (pp. 156, 157).

Consequently, moved by the sense of principles that is a trait of genius, Rousseau did not stop the logic of the juridical individualism at the door of the family home. He did not exclude the pedagogical power from the problematisation of the legitimacy of every power of man over man, so raising the meta-question of the legitimacy of education (see 1.3.2).

Rousseau has not always been a man of principles in his troubled life, but he is one of the liveliest sources of the European and universal culture. To paraphrase what Sagnac wrote, in 1898, concerning the "Law of the Revolution", the education vision of Rousseau "only had the defect of appearing too early" (as cited in Mulliez, 1989, p. 428). *Émile* continues to be a guiding map in the palace of *fantasies* and games of mirrors of education, to avoid "dangerous shortcuts" (p. 419) that threaten it to become perverted in *pedagogical infanticide*, in a hazardous unreality or a desperate marginality. The lights of his ethical *utopia* are still the most luminous on the horizon of the pedagogic thought. He has pointed to the normative content of the "right to education" *avant la lettre* (*before the term and concept coming into existence*).

4.1.3.2 Constitutionalisation

4.1.3.2.1 *Freedom of Education*

Education is a word absent from the French Declaration of the Rights of Man and the Citizen (1789),[236] as well as from the precedent American Bills of Rights, but the ascending phase of the French Revolution (about 1789–1793) was driven by the utopia of a *new people* and a *new man*, fuelled by the belief in the indefinite human perfectibility and in the omnipotence of an education of reason (by Enlightenment in a transfigured school) and of the heart (by learning republican virtues through civic feasts, in particular). However, the revolutionary action on education was a "very complex game of continuity and rupture, modernity and archaism, etc." (Baczko, 2000, p. 12), crossed by the religious debate on freedom of education. "Everything happens as if, throughout the revolutionary period, the same problems were debated, the same hopes were revived, ending up the same dead ends" (p. 11).

Among the hundreds of texts aimed at education radical reform, produced during the revolutionary period, three projects are representative of the revolutionary momentum and utopia.

Mirabeau Project (April 1791)
Mirabeau's Project was explained in four speeches to be made at the National Assembly, found after his death and published by Cabanis. It was "the first great attempt to think about the revolutionary experience in terms of education, to define its new goals and new paths" (p. 13). The central idea was: "Nothing in the political space should escape a public education system that reflects the overall project of a regenerated society" (p. 15). According to Rabaut Saint-Étienne: "the child who is not born already belongs to the Motherland" (p. 32). Following Danton: "After the bread, education is the first need of the people… So, let us go to the common education. Everything shrinks in domestic education, everything grows in common education. And I too am a father, but my son does not belong to me: he belongs to the Republic" (p. 37).

Condorcet Project (April 1792)
Condorcet was, a member of the Committee of Public Education established on 14 October 1791 by the Legislative Assembly. His project for education, reflected his *Mémoires sur l'instruction publique* (Memoirs on Public Education), published in 1791. "Condorcet's Project, one of the most remarkable texts on education produced during the revolutionary period, is distinguished by its intellectual rigour, the breadth and modernity of its ideas, its coherent and complete character" (p. 179). Public education would be secular and free, but without school obligation, because he did not consider it necessary to make such a benefit an obligation.

Lepeletier Project (July 1793)
Lepeletier was a member of the National Convention (Assembly), stabbed by a royalist on 20 January 1793. His project for education was presented by Robespierre to the Convention. "It takes as a principle that the child belongs to the Motherland and that parents are only his/her custodians" (p. 35). According

to it, in tune with Mirabeau's Project and echoing the Platonic Republic: "So, from five to twelve years, that is, in this part of life so decisive to give to the physical and moral being the modification, the impression, the habit he will always keep, everything that must compose the Republic will be thrown into a republican mold" (p. 370).

Nevertheless, contrary to what Balzac wrote metaphorically in *Mémoires de deux jeunes mariées* (Memoirs of two Young Married Women, 1841),[237] the Revolution did not "cut off the heads of all fathers". Bronislaw Baczko (2000) to conclude:

> No revolution marks the total break with the society that precedes it, none makes the time of the history to restart from zero, none satisfies the hopes it awakens and realises the utopias it stimulates. [...] Through its projects, dreams and experiences, the revolutionary period bequeaths to the social imagination the representation and hope of education for freedom and democracy [...].
>
> Having made the fusion, at the symbolic level, of education and democracy, one necessarily having to secure the future of the other, was, in the end, the great invention, both political and pedagogical, of the revolutionary period. (pp. 53, 54)

The great principles of secular, free and compulsory schooling survived the contradictions and impasses of the French Revolution and crossed the 19th century to culminate in the 1880s Jules Ferry Laws (see below).

The liberty of education was constitutionalised before the right to education as an element of "The free communication of ideas and opinions" proclaimed by the 1789 French Declaration (Article 11). It was recognised by the French Constitution of 1795[238] and the Constitutional Charter of 1830.[239] The 1831 Belgian Constitution[240] – which recognised the liberty of education (*L'enseignement est libre*) and mentioned public education (*L'instruction publique*) in its Article 17 – was influential for the introduction of the liberty/freedom of education in other constitutional texts, such as the French Constitution of 1848.[241] What was mostly meant, in the opinion of Imre Szabo (1974), was "precisely an education free from the Church and not one 'free' from the State and carried on by Church" (p. 13).

However, Jean Rivero wondered "why the freedom of education, direct application of the law, affirmed by the Declaration of 1789, to speak freely, an element of this free communication of thoughts and opinions of which it makes one of the most precious human rights, [...] does it not arouse the same fervour among some of those who claim the liberal legacy?".[242] Indeed, it has become "the least beloved among the liberties of expression", he suggested (as cited in Morange, 1985, p. 286). Why? Probably because of the following double fact: the monopoly of education by the Catholic Church, replaced with the almost monopoly by the State.

Indeed, the Catholic Church condemned, sometimes with truculent terms, the French revolutionary freedoms, before claiming them later, in turn.

Pope Pius VI issued the Encyclical *Quod aliquantum*, on 10 March 1791,[243] declaring that the effect of such freedoms was "to destroy the Catholic religion, and with it, the obedience due to kings". The freedoms of thought, opinion, conscience and religion, in particular, were "monstrous". In effect, "what could there be more outrageous than to establish among men this equality and this unbridled liberty which will snuff out reason, the most precious gift that nature has given to man, and the only one which distinguishes him from the animals?".

The most famous of the Church's texts against the liberal and socialist thought was the *Syllabus* annexed to the Encyclical *Quanta cura* (1864)[244] of Pope Pius IX, which anathematised in 80 statements "the prominent, most grievous errors of the age". Pope Leo XIII affirmed, notably in the Encyclical *Libertas praestantissimum* (1888),[245] "that it is quite unlawful to demand, to defend, or to grant unconditional freedom of thought, of speech, or writing, or of worship, as if these were so many rights given by nature to man" (para. 42), freedoms from which "follows the fatal theory of the need of separation between Church and State" (para. 18). According to the Pope:

> 39. ... Many wish the State to be separated from the Church wholly and entirely, so that with regard to every right of human society, in institutions, customs, and laws, the offices of State, and the education of youth, they would pay no more regard to the Church than if she did not exist; and, at most, would allow the citizens individually to attend to their religion in private if so minded. Against such as these, all the arguments by which We disprove the principle of separation of Church and State are conclusive; with this super-added, that it is absurd the citizen should respect the Church, while the State may hold her in contempt.

In 1929, "Pope Pius XI exulted Mussolini as a man sent by 'providence' to liberate his country from the false doctrine of liberalism" (Kershaw, 2015, p. 336). Valentine Zuber (2021) notes: "The doctrinal evolution of the Church towards a Catholic conception of human rights did not take place until after the Second World War" (p. 31).

Another front of the war for control of education was compulsory schooling. First envisaged in the 16th century in Europe, it was decreed by the French revolutionary Convention in December 1793 (from 6 to 8 years old), but was never applied. Despite all the resistance, the needs of the industrial revolution and the ideological movements it generated converged to make the expansion of education an imperative and a flag: economy and democracy needed educated workers and citizens.

The Guizot Act of 28 June 1833 – which was the first Charter of primary education in France – established a school in each village, whose attendance was free for the needy, but without imposing a school obligation. Minister François Guizot wondered, as read his *Memoirs*,[246] "whether to make primary education for all children an absolute obligation, imposed by law on all parents and punishable by certain penalties in case of negligence, as is done in Prussia and most States of Germany".

At the time, resistance to school obligation was stronger than support, motivated mainly by the defence of class and religious interests and privileges, but also by anti-democratic conservatism (compulsory education was a powerful Republican ideological resource), as evidenced by these words of Adolphe Thiers, during the elaboration of the Falloux Act on denominational education, in 1850: "And what madness that obligation! Who, then, in the countryside wants his children to be taught? [...] Primary education should not be accessible to all. Education is a beginning of ease and ease is not reserved for all" (as cited in Sicard, 1975, p. 303).

On the one hand, for the countrymen, sending children to school was to deprive themselves of their work, on the other hand, the bourgeoisie feared the abandonment of manual trades and claimed the public costs of the generalisation of education. The Catholic Church also opposed, in support of the freedom of parents. Freedom was, in fact, the ideological pole of the controversy. Guizot to argue (ibid.):

> Popular education is today in England, on the part of national and municipal powers as well as of ordinary citizens, the object of a zealous and persevering effort; yet no one proposes to order it to parents absolutely and by law. It thrives in United States of America; local governments and individual associations are making great sacrifices to multiply and perfect schools; we do not think of entering the interior of families to forcefully recruit schoolchildren. It is the character and honour of the free peoples to be both confident and patient, to count on the empire of enlightened reason, of interest well understood, and to know how to wait for its effects. I don't care about rules that bear the imprint of the convent or the barracks; I decidedly ruled out the constraint from my primary education bill, and none of my collaborators insisted on introducing it, not even those who felt any regret about it.

Compulsory schooling gradually became a social imperative, however, culminating, in France, with the famous Jules Ferry Laws: Law of 16 June 1881 on free primary education, Law of 28 March 1882 on secular and compulsory primary education,[247] and the replacement of the "Moral and religious education" by "Moral and civic education". It was Condorcet – the "great thought" of Condorcet, "heritage of the Revolution", as Jean Jaurès wrote (as cited in Crampe-Casnabet, 1985, pp. 124, 126) – who had the greatest influence in the organisation of public education in France. In pleading for the secularism of the school, before the Chamber of Deputies, in 1880, Ferry argued:

> Yes, 1789 secularised all institutions, and especially the family institution [...], and I say that the secularistion of institutions should necessarily lead, sooner or later, to the secularisation of the public school. [...]
>
> One hundred years ago, Gentlemen, civil power was secularised. Two hundred years ago, the world's greatest minds, Descartes, Bacon, secularised human knowledge, philosophy. We, today, come to follow this tradition; we are merely obeying the logic of this great movement, begun several hundred years ago, by asking you to secularise the school.

Before (in 1870), in a speech on the equality of education, Ferry said that education is "the very law of human progress", whose "last aim" is "to reduce more and more, through the ages, the primitive inequalities given by nature", among which "the most formidable" is "educational inequality" because it prevents "equal rights", which is "the very substance and essence of democracy", being thus "the greatest obstacle that can meet the creation of truly democratic customs" (in Monchablon 1989, pp. 219, 220).

The debates leading up to the approval of the Ferry Laws were the last battle of a long war, but the recognition of a 'right to education' was yet to come.

4.1.3.2.2 *Right to Education*

Education has always been regarded as a (*natural*) *right of the Family*, based on procreation. The Roman Law, originated in the *XII Tables Law* (about 450 BC), recognised the absolute *patria potestas* (power of the father). In the Western world, over centuries, only the Catholic Church was able to assure formal education that was practically a privilege of its clergy.

As we know, from the Renaissance on, by the advent of the modern Nation-State, education has become also a (*political*) *right of the State*, for the sake of General Interest (see Garin, 1957). The Catholic Church monopole was progressively challenged, Ministries of Instruction were created, and compulsory schooling was constitutionalised, because *De l'instruction naît la grandeur des nations* (Jules Ferry: Instruction is the source of the greatness of nations), as it is inscribed in the frontispiece of the *Bâtiment des Écoles Communales* (Building of Communal Schools, MDCCCLXXV), at the Bd. Jules Guesde, in Saint-Denis, France. *Letteris et Patriae* (To Letters and the Motherland) – is also written on the frontispiece of the *Palais Universitaire* (Palace of the University) of Strasbourg.

That there is a right to education – this has become progressively clearer.

Towards the end of the 19th century, Jules-Gabriel Compayré (1893) expressed his faith in the power of education this way:

> In all countries, it is now recognised that every human creature has the right to a minimum of education, and that primary education is a debt that society has virtually incurred towards each of its children, a debt it must pay, either by promoting the opening of free schools or by paying the costs of popular education itself. As has been said, "primary education is a kind of redemption of humanity". It is obviously not a cure for all the ills that suffers and will always suffer the human species. But it must be blessed as one of the greatest benefits of modern civilisation. The 19th century can undoubtedly be called the century of the railways, the century of electricity; but its greatest title will be to have been the century of the creation of primary schools. [...]
>
> The future of humanity depends in large part on the progress of pedagogy. [...]. Let us remain convinced [...] that the benevolent action of pedagogy will grow more and more, that enlightened by science it will become the mistress of the world, being the ever-increasing expression of the human will and reflection fighting against the blind forces of nature. (p. 219)

In the meanwhile, Georg W. F. Hegel wrote in *Elements of the Philosophy of Right* (1821)[248]:

> § 174
>
> Children have a right to be *brought up* and *supported* at the expense of the family. The right of the parents to their children's *services*, as services, is based on and limited to the common concern of caring for the family in general. In the same way, the right of the parents over the *arbitrary will* of the children is determined by the end of bringing them up and subjecting them to discipline. The end to which punishments are directed is not justice as such; it is rather of a subjective and moral nature, seeking to have

> a deterrent effect on a freedom which is still entrammelled in nature and to raise the universal into the children's consciousness and will.
>
> *Addition* (H). Human beings do not arrive by instinct at what they are destined to become; on the contrary, they must attain this by their own efforts. This is the basis of the child's right to its upbringing. [...]
>
> § 175
>
> Children are free *in themselves*, and their life is merely the immediate existence [*Dasein*] of this freedom; they therefore do not belong as things [*Sachen*] either to others or to their parents. [...]
>
> The need for an upbringing is present in children as their own feeling of dissatisfaction within themselves at the way they are – as the drive to belong to the adult world whose superiority they sense, or as the desire to grow up.

John Adams, second USA President (1797–1801) thought that "liberty cannot be preserved without a general knowledge among the people who have a right, from the frame of their nature, to knowledge, as their great Creator, who does nothing in vain, has given them understanding, and a desire to know".[249] In 1872, a German handbook on education stated that "the right of children to an education and the duty of parents towards them in this respect is incontestable".[250]

At the beginnings of the following century, Compayré (1911) wrote:

> Christianity, by its dogmas, came again to proclaim, with more sharpness and sparkling, the principles that were already contained and germinating in the doctrine of stoicism; it affirmed the equality of all human creatures, and thus, implicitly, their right to education; it highlighted the dignity of the person and freed her from the State despotism by calling man to take his place, not only in the earthly city, but in the city of God. But the generous ideas of Christianity, which, when applied, should have profoundly altered education, did not flourish right away. [...]
>
> Finally, and this is perhaps the true characteristic of nineteenth-century pedagogy, statesmen put improving public education at the forefront of their duties. Education at all levels becomes a State's responsibility, a public service. [...] Without abolishing private initiative, State, that is, the majority of the nation, appropriates the right to direct the education of young people according to its own principles.

The constitutionalisation of education was a great step towards its recognition as a 'human right'.

Some American constitutional texts in late 18th century already contained provisions on education: North Carolina (1776), Pennsylvania (1776), Georgia (1777), Massachusetts (1780).

The first French Constitution (1791)[251] – headed by the Declaration of the Rights of Man and the Citizen – provided: "Public instruction for all citizens, free of charge in those branches of education which are indispensable to all men, shall be constituted and organized, and the establishment thereof shall be apportioned gradually, in accordance with the division of the kingdom" (Title I: Fundamental provisions guaranteed by the Constitution).

The new Declaration introducing the 1793 Constitution stated (Article 22): "Education is necessary for everyone. Society must promote with all its power the advancement of public reason, and must place education within reach of all citizens". The Constitution's Article 122 guaranteed "general instruction", as well as "the enjoyment of all the rights of man".[252]

The Declaration of the Rights and Duties of Man and Citizen heading the 1795 French Constitution[253] did not refer to education, but the constitutional text granted the whole Title X (Articles 296–301) to "Public Instruction", noting in particular: "There are in the Republic primary schools where the pupils may learn reading, writing, the elements of computation and those of morality. The Republic provides for the expense of the lodgings of the instructors who preside over these schools" (Article 296). There should also be "schools higher than the primary schools, the number of which shall be such that there shall be at least one of them for every two departments" (Article 297). Moreover: "Citizens have the right to form private establishments for education and instruction as well as free societies to promote the progress of science, letters, and the arts" (Article 300).

The 1848 French Constitution[254] proclaimed, in the preamble, that "the Republic should [...] put within the reach of each one the education indispensable to all men" (VIII). In Chapter II (Citizens' Rights guaranteed by the Constitution), Article 9 recognised the liberty of teaching "under the surveillance of State". Article 13 provided that "the society favours and encourages the development of the work by means of the free primary education, professional training [...]".

In the *Verfassung des Deutschen Reiches* (Constitution of the German Empire), adopted on 28 March 1849 by a revolutionary Parliament, known as *Frankfurter Reichsverfassung* (Frankfurt Constitution of the Empire) or *Paulskirchenverfassung* (Constitution of St. Paul's Church), Article VI was titled *Die Grundrechte des Deutschen Volkes* (Basic Rights of the German People), provisions 152 to 158 being devoted to education.[255] Education was seen as a function of the State, aiming to harmonise the different interests involved in it, including restricting religious influence and protecting the children from parents (see Nowak, 1995, p. 191). Although acknowledging that the poor were entitled to free education, the State was not explicitly obliged to create educational institutions. The freedom to create schools and to educate children at home was recognised. This Constitution was Germany's first democratic constitutional text, but never formally entered into force, because of opposition from Emperor Friedrich Wilhelm IV, who invoked the traditional divine legitimacy of the monarchies. However, it exerted a great influence in German and European constitutionalism.

The Constitution of the Mexican United States (1917)[256] prescribed, in its Article 3 (Title I, Chapter I), that "primary education shall be compulsory". Public education "will stay absolutely moved away from any religious doctrine and, based on the results of the scientific progress, will fight against the ignorance and its effects, the servitudes, the fanaticism and the prejudices. Moreover [...] it will contribute to a better human understanding".

The German Constitution of Weimar (1919)[257] declared, in its Article 120 (Second Section): "The rearing of the rising generations to physical, mental and social fitness is the supreme duty and natural right of the parents, over whose activities the political community watches". The Fourth Section was titled "Education and Schools" (Articles 142–150). Article 144 declared: "The entire school system stands under the supervision of the State". Article 145 commanded "universal compulsory education". In accordance with Article 148:

> In all schools, moral training, civic sentiment, personal and vocational efficiency are to be aimed at, in the spirit of German nationality and of the reconciliation of nations.
>
> In the instruction in public schools care is to be taken not to hurt the feelings of persons of a different way of thinking.
>
> Civics and labour are to be taught in schools. Every pupil shall receive a copy of the Constitution upon completion of the compulsory education.

The USSR Constitution of 31 January 1924[258] provided: "The Union of Socialist Soviet Republics through its supreme organs has the following powers: [...] To establish the general principles regarding public instruction" (Article 1.q). Every territory member of the Republic should have a "Commissioner of the People for Public Instruction" (Article 67.k).

The short-lived 1934 Brazilian Constitution[259] affirmed [Title V, Chapter II (Education and Culture), Article 149]: "Education is a right of everyone and owes to be provided by family and Public Powers, the latter being in charge of providing it to Brazilians and foreigners residing in the Country [...]".

The USSR Constitution of 5 December 1936 recognised (Chapter X: Fundamental Rights and Duties of Citizens – Article 121)[260]:

> Citizens of the U.S.S.R. have the right to education. This right is ensured by universal, compulsory elementary education; by education, including higher education, being free of charge; by the system of state stipends for the overwhelming majority of students in the universities and colleges; by instruction in schools being conducted in the native language, and by the organization in the factories, state farms, machine and tractor stations and collective farms of free vocational, technical and agronomic training for the working people.

Under the Constitution of the Republic of Ireland of 1 July 1937 (Article 42)[261]: "The State acknowledges that the primary and natural educator of the child is the Family", but shall, "as guardian of the common good, require in view of actual conditions that the children receive a certain minimum education, moral, intellectual and social". Moreover, if needed, "by appropriate means shall endeavour to supply the place of the parents, but always with due regard for the natural and imprescriptible rights of the child".

The French Constitution of 1946 reaffirmed, in its Preamble, the rights and freedoms proclaimed in 1789, but adding, among "the political, economic and social principles" considered as "especially necessary to our times", the following: "The Nation guarantees equal access for children and adults to instruction, vocational training and culture. The provision of free, public and secular education at all levels is a duty of the State".[262]

The Italian Constitution of 1947[263] provided in its Part I (Citizens' Rights and Duties), Title II (Ethical-social Relationships), Article 34: "Schools are open to everyone. / Primary education, given for at least eight, is compulsory and free of tuition. / Capable and deserving pupils, including those lacking financial resources, have the right to attain the highest levels of education".

When the *travaux préparatoires* of the UDHR began, in 1947, the volume prepared by the UN Human Rights Division (*Documented Outline/Project Annotated,* 2 June 1947) (E/CN.4/AC.1/3/Add.1)[264] included 42 constitutional texts and other documents almost all containing provisions relating to education, notably to compulsory and free education. Only in the Soviet (Article 121) and Cuban (Article 8) Constitutions was found the term "right to education", which was also used by three draft international Declarations on human rights, namely:

– American Law Institute (Article 11): "Everyone has the right to education".

- American Federation of Labour (Article 36): "Everyone has the right to education".
- Inter-American Juridical Committee (Article XVII): "Every person has the right to education".

When, then, was a true *right to education* recognised, for the first time?

Gonzalo J. Olmeda (1989), while noting that it was necessary to reach "until well entered our century to see explicitly included in many constitutional texts the term 'right to education'" (p. 282), saw in the last paragraph of the Preamble to the French Constitution of 1848 "a programme of social rights, among which is enshrined the right to education". He quoted one author who said that "this term is already contained in Article 121 of the USSR Constitution of 1936; the Preamble to the French Constitution of 1946; Articles 34 and 38 of the Italian Constitution of 1947" (p. 301). Nevertheless, in the Preamble to the 1946 French Constitution, there is no formally worded right to education. The 1947 Italian Constitution recognised that entities and private persons have "the right to establish schools and institutions of education, at no cost to the State" (Article 33), but a general human 'right to education' is not recognised, while health, for instance, was expressly recognised "as a fundamental right of the individual and as a collective interest" (Article 32). Only the 1936 Soviet Constitution clearly recognised a "right to education".

Nowak (2001) pointed out: "An explicit human right to receive an education with a corresponding duty of the state to provide education was, therefore, laid down for the first time in Article 121 of Stalin's Soviet Constitution of 1936" (p. 248). Yet, the 1934 Brazilian Constitution, as quoted above, provided (Article 149): "Education is a right of everyone".

In effect, the constitutional guarantee of public education did not necessarily entail the recognition of a very subjective right. In this connection, Franciszek Przetacznik (1985) wrote:

> To the philosophers, who recognized expressly the right to education of an individual, belong, *inter alia*, Hegel [...]. Hegel asserts that 'children have the right to ... education at the expense of the family's common capital'. This statement of Hegel is of paramount importance, because he expressly states that an individual has the right to education. In this respect Hegel is a precursor of the Universal Declaration of Human Rights, which recognized and consecrated the right of an individual to education. [...] According to Hegel, the right to education of an individual has a restricted character, because such individual can claim only this right against his family and not against the State. Accordingly, even

> though the formulation by Hegel of the right to education of an individual is very important, because he is one of the first philosophers, if not the first one, who explicitly recognized the right to education of an individual as such, however, his formulation of this right is not satisfactory, for he does not state that the individual has a right to education at the expense of the State. (p. 272)

In the opinion of Szabo (1974):

> Early constitutions cover not so much the right to instruction but rather *public education*, and that *with a certain reserve*. [...] A study of some constitutions suggests that the regulation of the family's or the parents' rights in constitutions with regard to instruction served the purpose, first of all, *to diminish the State's concern and burden* while providing for private schools relatively more readily. The constitutions adopted in the inter-war period cannot be said to regulate the right to instruction in an elaborate form; a major development is discernible only in *post-war constitutions*. [...]
>
> It may be said with a degree of generalization that what these constitutions emphasize is the *supervisory authority* of the States, their powers of direction, *influence on instruction* and its various types, rather than their duties to provide instruction facilities. [...]
>
> *The right to the institutional formation*, generally speaking, *has not found its way into* these constitutions; [...]
>
> It appears that, contrary to the Universal Declaration of Human Rights and to the Covenants on human rights, the *right to instruction has not yet been interlocked* with, or developed into, the *right to education*; not even the initial traces of such a process can be discerned. As regards the right to culture as an independent right, traces of some of its elements can rarely be discovered. [...]
>
> If it was national law that gave momentum to the emergence of the relevant international legal rules, now *a reverse process is going on*. (pp. 70–72)

At the international level, education was first recognised as a human right on the American continent: In 1948, the OAS Charter[265] included the "right to education" in its Article 49, which has been proclaimed by the American Declaration of the Rights and Duties of Man (Article XII). At the universal level, it was first proclaimed in UDHR Article 26, some months later. UNESCO took an active part in the drafting of this provision (and of other provisions falling within its field of competence, especially Articles 19 and 27, but its mission is also particularly concerned with Articles 1 and 2).

Consequently, although in the history of great concepts there is a time when it is no longer night but day is not yet fully born, talking about the recognition of the 'right to education', as now understood, before the 20th century, sounds anachronism. Indeed, right to education:

- is not just a (*natural*) *right* of children morally opposable to parents;
- is not only a (*social*) *right*, increasingly vital for the political existence and economic subsistence and development of a nation, justifying compulsory schooling;
- is rather an (*individual*) *right* internationally and nationally recognised and protected as a *human right* essential for the personal flourishing of beings endowed with perfectibility and the aptitude for rationality, morality, creativity and responsibility.

At the beginning of the 1970s, Herbert L. Elvin, at the time Director of the Institute of Education of the University of London and former Director of the UNESCO Department of Education, wrote:

> The most powerful single idea that has spread through the world in relation to education in the last twenty-five years is that it is a right. [...] Its bible has been the Universal Declaration of Human Rights, adopted by the General Assembly of the United Nations on 10 December 1948. The relevant Article is number 26, which begins with the phrase (stirring, sweeping and sufficiently lacking in analysis to be worthy of Rousseau): "Everyone has the right to education". (p. 55)

The 1948 Universal Declaration gave rise to an International Education Law (IEL), whose existence has been justified in Introduction, and a definition proposed. The international profile of the right to education is addressed next.

4.2 International Profile of the Right to Education

4.2.1 *Legal Sources*

The IHRL is composed of varied instruments, as we know: their scope may be universal or regional, their legal force may be conventional or declaratory, their content may be general, specific or categorical. Accordingly, the *Corpus Juris* (Body of Law) of the IEL may be systematised as follows:

Universal normative framework

1. Universal most general normative framework
2. Universal conventional specific normative framework
3. Universal conventional categorical normative framework
4. Provisions in the other universal human rights core treaties
5. Other provisions in other human rights universal treaties
6. Universal declaratory specific instruments adopted within the UNESCO framework
7. Other specific texts adopted within the UNESCO framework
8. Provisions in other universal or regional conventional or declaratory instruments adopted within the UNESCO framework
9. Other important universal declaratory specific instruments and documents, adopted in various contexts
10. Other provisions in declaratory instruments and documents approved within the UN framework or in conferences it organised or sponsored
11. Provisions in conventional or declaratory instruments adopted by ILO
12. International Law of Refugees
13. International Humanitarian Law
14. International Criminal Law

Regional normative framework

15. European region
16. American region
17. African region
18. Asian region
19. Other organisations and instruments

4.2.1.1 Universal Normative Framework

The UN Charter refers to education 9 times (Articles 13.1.b, 55.b, 57.1, 62.1, 73.a, 73.e, 76.b, 83.3 and 88), but the principal universal normative framework of the right to education – most general, categorical and specific – is composed of the following instruments and provisions.

Universal most general normative framework

The universal most general normative framework of the right to education is obviously the International Bill of Human Rights (IBHR), formed of the UDHR (1948), the ICESCR (1966) and the ICCPR (1966) (see Appendix A).

- In the UDHR, the right to education is laid down in Article 26.
  Education is also referred to in the Preamble of the Declaration and is implied in other provisions, especially in Article 27 (cultural rights) and

Article 18 (freedom of thought, conscience and religion). Moreover, Article 26 must be interpreted in light of Article 2 (non-discrimination), of Article 22 (realisation of the economic, social and cultural rights), and Article 30 (interpretation of the provisions of the Declaration), in particular.

- In the ICESCR, the right to education is laid down in Articles 13 and 14.
  These Articles develop the content of UDHR Article 26. Education is also mentioned in Article 10.1 concerning the protection and assistance to the family "for the care and education of dependent children". Article 6.2 mentions "technical and vocational guidance and training programs" for "the full realisation" of the right to work.
- In the ICCPR, education is mentioned in Article 18.4.
  According to this provision, States Parties "undertake to have respect for the liberty of parents and, when applicable, legal guardians to ensure the religious and moral education of their children in conformity with their own convictions". This wording replicates ICESCR Article 13.3, with the justification that a State may be a Party to the ICCPR without being Party to the ICESCR. The liberty of individuals to establish and direct educational institutions is indirectly recognised.

Universal conventional specific normative framework
UNESCO is the main source of international normativity on the right to education (see Daudet & Singh, 2001). Conventions, Charters, Recommendations, Declarations, Programmes of Action, are adopted by its General Conference, as well as International Conferences under its auspices or jointly with other international organisations. The following conventions concerning the right to education have been adopted:

- Convention against Discrimination in Education (1960), with a Protocol Instituting a Conciliation and Good Offices Commission to be responsible for seeking a settlement of any disputes which may arise between States Parties to the Convention against Discrimination in Education (1962)
  This Convention is the principal instrument of the IEL, having been ratified by 106 States (as of December 2020).
- Convention on Technical and Vocational Education (1989)
  This Convention did not succeed, as it was ratified by only 19 States (as of December 2020).
- Global Convention on the Recognition of Qualifications Concerning Higher Education (2019)
  This Convention aims at complementing and enhancing the cohesion among the existing regional Conventions.[266]

Main universal conventional categorical provisions

The main universal conventional categorical provisions on the right to education are in CRC Articles 28 and 29. They are the most detailed conventional provisions, laying down "the full scope of the right to education", as noted the first Special Rapporteur on the Right to Education (E/CN.4/1999/49, para. 43).[267] Education is also concerned with many other provisions of the Convention and is mentioned in its two first Protocols. By defining a child as "every human being below the age of eighteen years unless, under the law applicable to the child, majority is attained earlier" (Article 1), the CRC covers all children and adolescents attending primary and secondary schools.

Provisions in the other universal human rights core treaties

Education is referred to in the other six core human rights treaties (in addition to the 1966 International Covenants and the CRC).

Other provisions in universal human rights treaties

The right to education is mentioned in other universal human rights treaties, such as the Convention relating to the Status of Refugees (UN, 1951).

Universal declaratory specific instruments adopted within the UNESCO framework

- Recommendation against Discrimination in Education (1960)
- Recommendation concerning the Status of Teachers (adopted by a special Conference convened jointly by UNESCO/ILO, 1966)
- Recommendation on Education for International Understanding and Cooperation and Peace and Education relating to Human Rights and Fundamental Freedoms (1974)
- Recommendation on the Recognition of Studies and Qualifications in Higher Education (1993)
- Declaration and Integrated Framework of Action on Education for Peace, Human Rights and Democracy (1995)
- Recommendation concerning the Status of Higher Education Teaching Personnel (1997)
- International Charter of Physical Education, Physical Activity and Sport (2015, replacing the International Charter of Physical Education and Sport adopted in 1978 and revised in 1991)
- Recommendation concerning technical and vocational education and training (2015, replacing the Recommendation concerning Technical and Vocational Education adopted in 1962 and revised in 1974 and 2001)

- Recommendation on adult learning and education (2015, replacing the Recommendation on the Development of Adult Education adopted in 1976)
- Recommendation on Open Educational Resources (2019)

Other specific texts adopted within the UNESCO framework
The right to education is addressed by other specific texts approved within UNESCO's framework, in particular the numerous texts adopted by the International Conference on Education and the regional Conferences of Ministers of Education (of Member States).

Provisions in other universal or regional conventional or declaratory instruments adopted within the UNESCO framework
Examples: Declaration on Race and Racial Prejudice (1978, especially Articles 5, 6 and 9); Declaration of Principles on Tolerance (1995, Article 4 and also in Preamble and Articles 3, 5 and 6); Convention on the Protection and Promotion of the Diversity of Cultural Expressions (2005, Article 10 and also in Preamble); Recommendation on Science and Scientific Researchers (2017, replacing the 1974 Recommendation on the Status of Scientific Researchers).

Following the "Comprehensive report by the Director-General on UNESCO's standard-setting instruments (207 EX/23.I.INF, 7 August 2019),[268] UNESCO has adopted:
- 37 Conventions and Agreements (12 relating to education)
- 34 Recommendations (8 relating to education)
- 14 Declarations and Charters (1 relating to education)[269]

Other important universal declaratory specific instruments and documents, adopted in various contexts
- World Declaration on Education for All: Meeting Basic Learning Needs, and Framework for Action to Meet Basic Learning Needs: Guidelines for implementing the World Declaration on Education for All (1990)
  World Conference on Education for All, Jomtien (Thailand)
- Salamanca Statement and Framework for Action on Special Needs Education (1994)
  World Conference on Special Needs Education: Access and Quality, Salamanca (Spain)
- World Declaration on Higher Education for the Twenty-First Century: Vision and Action, and Framework for Priority Action for Change and Development in Higher Education (1998)
  World Conference on Higher Education – Higher Education in the Twenty-First Century: Vision and Action, Paris (France)

- Technical and Vocational Education and Training: A Vision for the Twenty-First Century – Recommendations (1999)
  Second International Congress on Technical and Vocational Education, 'Technical and Vocational Education and Training: A Vision for the Twenty-First Century', Seoul (Republic of Korea)
- Dakar Framework for Action – Education for All: Meeting Our Collective Commitments (2000)
  World Education Forum, Dakar (Senegal)
- Declaration of Amsterdam on the Right to and the Rights in Education (2004)
  World Conference on the Right to and the Rights in Education, Amsterdam (Netherlands)
- The Right to Basic Education as a Fundamental Human Right and the Legal Framework for its Financing (2005)
  International Conference, Jakarta (Indonesia)
- United Nations Declaration on Human Rights Education and Training (2011)
  UN General Assembly
- Incheon Declaration (2015)
  World Education Forum, Incheon (Republic of Korea)
- Education 2030 Framework for Action (2015)
  High-level Meeting at UNESCO

Other provisions in declaratory instruments and documents approved within the UN framework or in conferences it organised or sponsored
An example is the Declaration of the Rights of the Child (1959, especially Principle 7).

Provisions in conventional or declaratory instruments adopted by ILO
The vocational element of the right to education falls into the ILO's field of action. In a *Memorandum of Understanding between the International Labour Organisation* (*ILO*) *and the United Nations Educational, Scientific and Cultural Organisation* (*UNESCO*), signed on 14 October 1954 and updated in 2014,[270] the following sharing of competences was agreed: the vocational training integrated into the educational systems comes under UNESCO's competence, the practical job training comes under ILO's competence.[271]

Education is referred to in various ILO's legal instruments relating to aspects of the right to work, including the work of children and the rights of indigenous peoples. They are, among others:

- Convention concerning the Night Work of Young Persons Employed in Industry (C06, 1919, revised in 1948 by C90)

- Recommendation concerning Night Work of Children and Young Persons in Agriculture (R014, 1921)
- Recommendation concerning Vocational Training (R057, 1939)
- Recommendation concerning Vocational Guidance (R087, 1949)
- Recommendation concerning the Vocational Training of Adults including Disabled Persons (R088, 1950)
- Recommendation concerning Vocational Training in Agriculture (R101, 1956)
- Convention concerning the Protection and Integration of Indigenous and Other Tribal and Semi-Tribal Populations in Independent Countries (C107, 1957)
- Convention concerning Basic Aims and Standards of Social Policy (C117, 1962)
- Recommendation concerning Vocational Training (R117, 1962)
- Recommendation concerning Vocational Training of Seafarers (R137, 1970)
- Convention concerning Minimum Age for Admission to Employment (C138, 1973)
- Convention concerning Paid Educational Leave (C140, 1974)
- Convention concerning Vocational Guidance and Vocational Training in the Development of Human Resources (C142, 1975)
- Convention concerning Indigenous and Tribal Peoples in Independent Countries (C169, 1989)
- Convention concerning the Prohibition and Immediate Action for the Elimination of the Worst Forms of Child Labour (C182, 1999)
- Recommendation concerning the Prohibition and Immediate Action for the Elimination of the Worst Forms of Child Labour (R190, 1999)

The right to education is still indirectly concerned in legal instruments addressing education professionals. In addition to the abovementioned Recommendations on teaching personnel (1966 and 1997), there are "ILO Policy Guidelines on the promotion of decent work for early childhood education personnel" (2013), which is "the first international text dealing specifically with the status of early childhood education personnel" (Foreword).[272] Most education professionals are also concerned with ILO legal instruments addressing public servants.

International Law of Refugees

The right to education is addressed by the International Law of Refugees, based on the Convention Relating to the Status of Refugees (UN, 1951). In 2016, the UN General Assembly adopted the New York Declaration for Refugees and Migrants.

International Humanitarian Law
The International Humanitarian Law includes provisions concerning students, education personnel and school buildings.

International Criminal Law
There are provisions relating to education in the International Criminal Law, whose most recent instrument is the Statute of Rome of the International Criminal Court (1998).

As the Convention against Discrimination in Education (CADE) remains the principal instrument of the IEL, it is being highlighted.

4.2.1.2 Convention against Discrimination in Education

In 1954, following an ECOSOC Resolution, the former Sub-Commission on Prevention of Discrimination and Protection of Minorities designated a Rapporteur for preparing a study about discrimination in the education field, the first such a study decided by the Sub-Commission. In his *Study of Discrimination in Education,*[273] published in 1957, the Rapporteur (Charles D. Ammoun) formulated some principles and recommended the adoption of a Convention. UNESCO was placed in charge of doing it, and its General Conference agreed in 1958. The development of a Recommendation was also decided in order to meet the concerns expressed by some States that, given their federal nature, may have difficulty in ratifying a Convention on a matter coming under the jurisdiction of the provincial authorities. Both instruments would have the same content, except for the formal differences due to their different legal nature.

The Convention against Discrimination in Education (CADE)[274] drew inspiration from the ILO Convention concerning Discrimination in Respect of Employment and Occupation (C111). In the opinion of Nartowski (1975), "both of them played the role of a pacemaker in the process of codification of the general principles of international protection of human rights, especially the anti-racialist norm, which was soon given the highest priority in the United Nations work" (p. 299). This priority was given solemn expression with the UN Declaration on the Elimination of All Forms of Racial Discrimination (1963) and with the International Convention on the Elimination of All Forms of Racial Discrimination (1965). In 1978, UNESCO adopted the Declaration on Race and Racial Prejudice.

The CADE's scope is much broader than its title suggests because it involves everything that matters to equality in education. As reads the Preamble, it is intended "not only to proscribe any form of discrimination in education but also to promote equality of opportunity and treatment for all in education". According to Article 4 – its framework provision – States Parties "undertake furthermore to formulate, develop and apply a national policy which, by methods appropriate to the circumstances and to national usage, will tend to promote equality of opportunity and of treatment in the matter of education".

In Article 5, they agree: "Education shall be directed to the full development of the human personality and to the strengthening of respect for human rights and fundamental freedoms; it shall promote understanding, tolerance and friendship among all nations, racial or religious groups, and shall further the activities of the United Nations for the maintenance of peace". It provides for the respect of the freedom of parents or legal guardians concerning the education of children, and of the education rights of members of national minorities.

The Convention doesn't permit reservations (Article 9) and is applicable "to all non-self-governing, trust, colonial and other territories for the international relations of which they [States Parties] are responsible" (Article 15).

The CADE doesn't include any special measures in favour of certain categories of persons, but its *travaux préparatoires* admitted them,[275] as well as separate education for the two sexes, for religious or linguistic reasons, and private education. As non-nationals are concerned, States Parties undertake: "To give foreign nationals resident within their territory the same access to education as that given to their own nationals" (Article 3.e). This goes further than other international instruments, in particular the Convention relating to the Status of Refugees (UN, 1950, Article 22) and the Convention relating to the Status of Stateless Persons (UN, 1954, Article 22). In its GC 20 on "Non-discrimination in economic, social and cultural rights (Art. 2, para. 2, of the International Covenant on Economic, Social and Cultural Rights)" (E/C.12/GC/20 2 July 2009),[276] the CoESCR pointed out:

> 30. The ground of nationality should not bar access to Covenant rights, e.g. all children within a State, including those with an undocumented status, have a right to receive education and access to adequate food and affordable health care. The Covenant rights apply to everyone including non-nationals, such as refugees, asylum-seekers, stateless persons, migrant workers and victims of international trafficking, regardless of legal status and documentation.

Moreover, the right to free primary/basic education having become Customary International Law (see 4.3.6), it obliges every State, regardless of its international conventional obligations.

In 1962, was adopted a Protocol Instituting a Conciliation and Good Offices Commission to be responsible for seeking a settlement of any disputes which may arise between States Parties to the Convention against Discrimination in Education.

Contrary to what the chronology might suggest, the preparatory work of the CADE was influenced by the draft International Covenants adopted in 1966 and not the other way around. Indeed, the draft Covenants were concluded by the Commission on Human Rights as early as 1954.[277]

4.2.1.3 Regional Sources

At the international regional level – Council of Europe, Organisation of the American States (OAS), Organisation of African Unity (OAU, African Union since 2000), the Asian region and other regional IGOs – there are the following principal legal instruments with provisions on the right to education:

European region

- Additional Protocol to the European Convention for the Protection of Human Rights and Fundamental Freedoms
  Council of Europe, 1952, Article 2, the first international binding instrument to include the right to education.
- European Social Charter
  Council of Europe, 1961 (revised in 1996, with a Protocol adopted in 1965), principally Articles 7, 9, 10, 15, and 17, 19
- European Charter for Regional or Minority Languages
  Council of Europe, 1992, Article 8
- Framework Convention for the Protection of National Minorities
  Council of Europe, 1995, Articles 12, 13 and 14
- European Charter on Education for Democratic Citizenship and Human Rights Education
  Council of Europe, 2010
  Within the Council of Europe framework, there are also the texts adopted by the Committee of Ministers, the Parliamentary Assembly and the Permanent Conference of Ministers of Education.
  Still on the European continent:
- The Charter of Fundamental Rights of the European Union (2000) addresses the right to education in Article 14, mentioning education also in Article 32 and "teaching" in Article 10.
- The Commonwealth of Independent States Convention on Human Rights and Fundamental Freedoms (1995) addresses the right to education in Articles 27 and 28.[278]

American region

- Charter of the Organisation of American States
  OAS, 1948, principally Article 49, but with many other references to education: Articles 3.n, 30, 31, 34.h, 47, 48, 50, 51, 52, 94, 95.2 and 111

- American Declaration on the Rights and Duties of Man
  OAS, 1948, Articles XII and XXXI
- American Convention on Human Rights
  (Pact of San José)
  OAS, 1969, Preamble and Articles 12.4, with references to education in Preamble and Articles 23, 26 and 42
- Additional Protocol to the American Convention on Human Rights in the Area of Economic, Social and Cultural Rights
  (Protocol of San Salvador)
  OAS, 1988, Article 13 and also in Articles 7, 10, 16 and 19
- Inter-American Democratic Charter
  OAS, 2001, Articles 16 and 27

African region
- African Charter on Human and Peoples' Rights
  (Banjul Charter)
  OAU, 1981, Article 17, education being also mentioned in Article 25
- African Charter on the Rights and Welfare of the Child
  OAU, 1990, Articles 11, 14, 16 and 20
- Protocol to the African Charter on Human and Peoples' Rights on the Rights of Women in Africa
  African Union, 2003, Article 12 and others
- African Youth Charter
  African Union, 2006, principally Articles 10.3.d, 13 and 23

Other organisations and instruments
- ASEAN Human Rights Declaration
  ASEAN, 2012, Article 31
- Arab Charter on Human Rights
  League of Arab States, 2004, Article 41 and also Articles 30, 34, 39 and 40
- Arab Charter on the Rights of the Child
  League of Arab States, 1983 (available in Arabic only)
- Cairo Declaration on Human Rights in Islam
  OIC, 1990, Articles 7 and 9
- SAARC Social Charter
  SAARC, 2004, principally Article V.1
- Covenant on the Rights of the Child in Islam
  OIC, 2005, principally Article 12

Summing up: There are provisions on education/right to education in much more than one hundred treaties and other international legal texts, but the

main universal normative framework of the right to education is formed of the following provisions (in chronological order):
- UDHR Article 26 (1948)
- Convention against discrimination in education (1960)
- ICESCR Articles 13 and 14 (1966)
- CRC Articles 28 and 29 (1989)

It may be added that, according to the former Special Rapporteur on the Right to Education (Kishore Singh) (A/HRC/23/35, 10 May 2013)[279]:

> 25. The right to education is enshrined in the Constitutions of a large number of countries – it is one of the most universally recognized rights in national constitutions in the world today. A study of national Constitutions found that 90 percent of Constitutions in the world contain a provision on the right to education. Of those Constitutions that contain education provisions, 56 percent require that education be compulsory up to a certain level. Additionally, 65 percent of these Constitutions stipulates that education should be free up to a certain level. Moreover, national legislation on education exists in most States.[280]

4.2.1.4 Nature, Definitions and Terminology

4.2.1.4.1 *Nature*

In accordance with the titles of the 1966 International Covenants, there are five categories of human rights: civil, political, economic, social and cultural rights. "Economic, social and cultural rights are those human rights relating to the workplace, social security, family life, participation in cultural life, and access to housing, food, water, health care and education".[281] They are laid down in ICESCR Part III (Articles 6–15).

The ICESCR does not draw a distinction between 'economic', 'social' and 'cultural' rights, which are closely intertwined but fall within the mandate of different UN specialised agencies: ILO, FAO, WHO, UNESCO. The right to education is generally included in the 'cultural rights' to which also pertain the rights laid down in Article 15.

Cassin (1953) informed that the drafters of the UDHR were "obliged to arrange the rights to education and culture – or, at least, their principal attributes – into the same category of the economic and social rights" to mark their difference from others "that are above all liberties implying for third-parties and for the collectivity a negative obligation of respect" (p. 4). In this regard, during the drafting of the 1966 Covenants, at the 7th session of the Commission on Human Rights, 226th meeting (E/CN.4/SR.226, 27 June 1951),[282] the representative of the World Jewish Congress (Frank R. Bienenfeld) questioned "whether it could properly be called a cultural right. It should be counted as one of the civil and political rights, and one of the greatest importance, because it was fundamental to the exercise of all economic, social and political rights" (p. 18). Education is mentioned also in ICCPR Article 18, as already said.

Within the European framework, it is included in the first Protocol to the ECHR, whose principal scope are civil and political rights. Marc Bossuyt (1975) noted: "In the context of the Council of Europe, the right to education appears then as a socio-economic right 'civilised', i.e. a right enjoying the same protection as a civil right" (p. 811).

The right to education is generally considered as the main cultural right, like the right to an adequate standard of living is the most comprehensive social right, and the right to work is the most basic economic right. It is usually set out in autonomous provisions, immediately before other cultural rights, but some Constitutions put them together. Sometimes, it was laid down together with the right to work.

The right to education is, however, a cross-cutting right. Mehedi commented (E/CN.4/Sub.2/1999/10)[283]:

> 51. It is generally accepted in the literature that the right to education, on account of its dual nature, belongs to both the first and the second generations of human rights. However, some authors even maintain that, on historical grounds and for reasons linked to the formulation of international and regional instruments, the right to education is a specific and possibly unique case of a right that belongs not only to the first two generations of rights but also to what is termed the third generation of human rights, namely collective rights and solidarity rights.

Novak (1995), for example, remarked: "As the historical background and the wording of the right to education in various universal and regional human rights instruments show, the right to education is probably the only right that reveals aspects falling under all three generations" (p. 196). The third-generation dimension is illustrated by CRC Article 28.3 that refers to international co-operation. The CoESCR said in its GC 11 (E/C.12/1999/4)[284]:

> 2. The right to education [...] has been variously classified as an economic right, a social right and a cultural right. It is all of these. It is also, in many ways, a civil right and a political right, since it is central to the full and effective realization of those rights as well. In this

> respect, the right to education epitomizes the indivisibility and interdependence of all human rights.

Consequently, the normative content of the right to education includes elements of:

- *Liberty-rights* ('first generation') – whose guarantee calls firstly for legislative measures.
- *Equality-rights* ('second generation') – whose implementation needs resources.
- *Solidarity-rights* ('third generation') – that call for international co-operation.

Despite the "complex legal relationships" of the normative content of the right to education, Nowak (2001) concluded: "The second generation right of every human being, and of children in particular, to receive education constitutes the core of the right to education under international law" (p. 255).

4.2.1.4.2 *Definitions*

Education means a process and the outcome of the process. The integration of children into the communities and cultures where they are born – through learning the values and skills necessary to their survival – is a need and a phenomenon as old as human communities.

There are dozens of definitions of education in the history of the pedagogic thought, varying from larger to narrower conceptions:

- The educational phenomenon, broadly considered, includes all experiences and influences, intentional and unintentional, formal and informal, which contribute to forming the personality of each human being.
- Education, strictly considered, is mainly school education, i.e. an organised communication process of learning the values, competencies (knowledge, capacities, skills), sentiments, attitudes, behaviours, through which the human communities ensure their survival, reproduce their identity and each of their members form his/her personality.

During the drafting of the 1966 Covenants, at the 7th session of the Commission on Human Rights, 226th meeting (E/CN.4/SR.226, 27 June 1951),[285] the representative of UNESCO (Lionel Elvin):

> ... noted that the Commission had made no attempt to define the general concept of education. He therefore assumed that the Commission wished UNESCO to submit a definition of the right to education, and proposed the following formula:

> "The right of access to the knowledge and training which are necessary to full development as an individual and as a citizen". (p. 14)

At the 228th meeting (E/CN.4/SR.228, 28 June 1951),[286] the Delegation of Australia (Harry F. E. Whitlam) observed: "The problem before the Commission was that of finding a precise definition of 'education' which would present no possibility of misinterpretation" (p. 7). No definition was agreed.

At present, we find some definitions in international legal instruments and other texts, as well as in jurisprudence. For instance:

- Convention against Discrimination in Education (UNESCO, 1960)[287]

> Article 1
>
> [...]
>
> 2. For the purposes of this Convention, the term 'education' refers to all types and levels of education, and includes access to education, the standard and quality of education, and the conditions under which it is given.

- Recommendation on Education for International Understanding and Co-operation and Peace and Education relating to Human Rights and Fundamental Freedoms (UNESCO, 1974)[288]

> 1. For the purposes of this Recommendation:
>
> a. The word 'education' implies the entire process of social life by means of which individuals and social groups learn to develop consciously within, and for the benefit of, the national and international communities, the whole of their personal capacities, attitudes, aptitudes and knowledge. This process is not limited to any specific activities.

- European Court of Human Rights, *Case Campbell and Cosans* (1982)[289]

> 32. ... The Court would point out that the education of children is the whole process whereby, in any society, adults endeavour to transmit their beliefs, culture and other values to the young, whereas teaching or instruction refers in particular to the transmission of knowledge and to intellectual development.

- Committee on the Rights of the Child, first GC (CRC/GC/2001/1)[290]

> 2. ... The education to which every child has a right is one designed to provide the child with life skills, to strengthen the child's capacity to enjoy the full range of human rights and to promote a culture

> which is infused by appropriate human rights values. The goal is to empower the child by developing his or her skills, learning and other capacities, human dignity, self-esteem and self-confidence. "Education" in this context goes far beyond formal schooling to embrace the broad range of life experiences and learning processes which enable children, individually and collectively, to develop their personalities, talents and abilities and to live a full and satisfying life within society.

The Recommendation Concerning Technical and Vocational Education and Training (UNESCO, 2015)[291] and the Recommendation on Adult Learning and Education (UNESCO, 2015) also contain their respective definitions.[292]

The International Standard Classification of Education (ISCED-2011)[293] includes an expanded Glossary where the following definition of education is provided: "The processes by which societies deliberately transmit their accumulated information, knowledge, understanding, attitudes, values, skills, competencies and behaviours across generations. It involves communication designed to bring about learning".

Carmen M. V. Puig (1979) remarked: "The Declaration [UDHR] uses the term 'education', not 'instruction' [...]. So, the meaning St. Thomas had given to education is reiterated, comprising *nutritio, instructio* and *discipline*" (p. 568). Similar was Kant's (1803) understanding: "by education we must understand nurture (the tending and feeding of the child), discipline (*Zucht*), and teaching, together with culture" (para. 1).

4.2.1.4.3 *Terminology*

The international terminology on the right to education and their translations are variable and voluble.

Notes from the travaux préparatoires

Droit à l'instruction (Right to instruction) is the term to be found in the first drafts of the Universal Declaration, in French: those of John Humphrey (Secretariat), René Cassin (Drafting Committee of the Commission on Human Rights) and of the Group for the Declaration formed during the second session of the Commission (Geneva, 1947). It was Cassin who proposed, during the third session of the Commission (Lake Success, 1948), the replacement (in the French version) of the word *instruction* with *éducation*, for being a broader concept. This amendment may have been influenced by the American Declaration of the Rights and Duties of Man proclaimed on 2 May 1948 by the IX American International Conference, meeting in Bogota (Colombia), whose Article XII bears the title "Right to education".[294] Later, during the debates in the UN General Assembly Third Committee, also the Delegation of Guatemala

(García Bauer) "pointed out a defect in the Spanish translation of the text of Article 23 [now 26]. The word *instrucción* meant education in a limited intellectual sense; he thought that the word *educación* was more correct" (A/C.3/SR.146, 19 November 1948).[295]

Eleanor Roosevelt (USA Delegate and President of the Commission) proposed, in the Drafting Committee of the Declaration, the replacement of the term "primary" education with "elementary" education, which was accepted by the Commission, but "primary" has prevailed in the CADE, in the ICESCR, as well as in the CRC.

Another amendment proposed by Roosevelt in the Drafting Group of the Declaration was the replacement of the words "for children" by "everyone", in order to include adults. In the Commission, the UNESCO representative (Pierre Lebar) and the China Delegation (Peng Chun Chang) proposed to add the term "fundamental", having in view the courses for adults who have not been able to attend or complete elementary schooling.[296] The proposal was approved. In the General Assembly Third Committee, the drafting Subcommittee proposed to replace the term "elementary education" by "fundamental education" (used by the UNESCO Preparatory Commission in 1946), but the two terms (elementary and fundamental) were kept. The ICESCR includes the "fundamental education" in its Article 13.2.d.

English, French, Spanish and German versions and translations

The English version of international legal instruments only uses, in general, the word 'education'. In the Preamble of the UDHR is found the expression "teaching and education". The French versions use *éducation*, *instruction* and *enseignement* (UDHR Article 26 and ICESCR Articles 13 and 14), which are also found in the Spanish official versions, probably because their bases were the French versions (as is the case with the Portuguese translations, for instance). However, the Spanish versions use *instrucción* in UDHR Article 26 (the term appearing also in the CADE) and *enseñanza* in ICESCR Article 13 and CRC Article 28. In the Portuguese translation of the ICESCR, the term *instrução* appears once (Article 13.2.d).

Regarding the CADE's title, it is translated in French as *Convention concernant la lutte contre la discrimination dans le domaine de l'enseignement*. This is reflected in the official Spanish version: *Convención relativa a la Lucha contra las Discriminaciones en la Esfera de la Enseñanza* (and in the Portuguese translation: *Convenção relativa à luta contra a discriminação no campo do ensino*). In this Convention, while the term "education" prevails, the terms "teaching" and "religious instruction" also appear. The French version uses the term *enseignement* more often than éducation, but also appears the term *instruction*.

The Spanish version also uses more *enseñanza* than *educación,* and the term *instrucción* still appears.

The English version of the CRC only uses the term "education", with a reference to the "teaching methods". In the French version, in addition to the terms *éducation* and *enseignement,* the term *élever* is used, typically French (that is the etymological root of *élève*: pupil).

It should be added that in the English version of Article 2 of the first Protocol to the ECHR, besides "right to education", the term "teaching" is used. The French version uses the term *droit à l'instruction* and also mentions *enseignement.*

The French preference for the term *enseignement* is due, perhaps, to a concern for rigour in the delimitation of the legal object of the UNESCO Convention and Recommendation. Apparently, in the French versions of the legal international instruments, *enseignement* is considered as the main component of the *droit à la éducation.* ICESCR Article 13 refers to the different levels of *enseignement* necessary "to achieving the full realisation of" the *droit à l'éducation.*

The difference between the English term 'education' and the French term *enseignement* sparked debate during the 4th meeting of the Special Committee of Governmental Experts on the Preparation of a Draft International Convention and a Draft Recommendation on the Various Aspects of Discrimination in Education (1960).[297] In the opinion of the Legal Counsel of UNESCO Secretariat (Hanna Saba): "The Universal Declaration Article 26, which uses both terms, seems to give to éducation the sense of moral education, and to *enseignement* that of school education" (27.2). In the following session, another representative of the Secretariat (Jean Guiton) offered the following explanation:

> 2.2 If we refer to the texts that have inspired the preparation of the drafts of international instruments currently under study, we note, in effect that:
>
> – in the UNESCO Constitutive Act, the term éducation is always used, preferably to the term *enseignement*;
> – in the texts emanating from the Commission on Human Rights and from the Sub-Commission on the fight against the discriminatory measures, *enseignement* is almost the only term used (and almost never éducation);
> – in the Universal Declaration of Human Rights, the two words are used almost interchangeably.
>
> 2.3 Although there is, in this respect, a certain ambiguity in French thought, [the representative of the Secretariat] has the impression that

> the word *enseignement* should only normally be used to designate an essentially intellectual process leading to the acquisition of knowledge. Regarding *éducation*, it could be defined, in his opinion, as "the sum of all the actions – including *enseignement* – which tend to develop the physical, intellectual, moral and emotional faculties".

As the main Western languages are concerned, there is still the case of the German translations where we find the terms *Erziehung*, *Bildung*, *Ausbildung* and *Unterricht*.[298]

The distinction between *Erziehung* and *Bildung* is much debated in the German education field. The two are often used as synonyms, but the first is more densely tied to the human educability. "*Erziehung* refers to the whole of the pedagogical phenomenon" (Eggeersdorfer, 1962, p. 478). *Bildung* has a rather school, cognitive connotation. According to Hans-Jürgen Töws (1970):

> The *Recht* [*right*] *auf Erziehung* und das *Recht* [*right*] *auf Bildung* have indeed a different historical profile but are conceptually difficult to separate. The *Recht auf Erziehung* concerns primarily the help to the formation of the personality and lifestyle. The *Recht auf Bildung*, on the contrary, is more concerned with acquiring knowledge and skills for the professional, economic and social life, or generally refers to a certain socially relevant status. (p. 378)

Bildung is a broader concept than *Ausbildung* that means vocational training. *Unterricht* means teaching (in French: *enseignement* or *instruction*).

In the German translations of international legal instruments, however, the most used expression is *Recht auf Bildung*. The term *Unterricht* is used in UDHR Article 26: for example, the *Grundschulunterricht* (elementary/primary school education) is part of the *Recht auf Bildung*. The Preamble refers to *Unterricht und Erziehung*. ICESCR Article 6.2 mentions *Ausbildungsprogramme* (training programmes) in relation to the right to work. Article 13.3 and ICCPR Article 18.4 mention *die religiöse und sittliche Erziehung ihrer Kinder* (the religious and moral education of their children). *Erziehung* is also found in ICESCR Article 10.1. In the CRC, besides *Bildung*, other terms are used: *Erziehung* (Articles 18, 20, 23, 32), *Ausbildung* (Article 23), *Unterrichtsmethoden* (Article 28.3).

In the short Article 2 of the first Protocol to the ECHR[299] we find *Bildung*, *Erziehung* and *Unterricht*.

The United Nations Declaration on Human Rights Education and Training is officially translated in French as *Déclaration des Nations Unies sur l'éducation et la formation aux droits de l'homme* and in Spanish as *Declaración de las*

Naciones Unidas sobre educación y formación en materia de derechos humanos. The title of the German translation[300] is: *Erklärung der Vereinten Nationen über Menschenrechtsbildung und -ausbildung.*

In summary:

- The most comprehensive terms in English, French, Spanish and German are, respectively: *right to education, droit à l'éducation, derecho a la educación, Recht auf Erziehung.*
- The term *education* is translated as:
  - French: *éducation, enseignement* or *instruction*
  - Spanish: *educación, enseñanza* or *instrucción*
  - German: *Bildung* or *Erziehung*
- The term teaching is translated as:
  - French: *enseignement* or *instruction*
  - Spanish: *enseñanza* or *instrucción*
  - German: *Unterricht*
- The term *training* is translated as:
  - French: *formation*
  - Spanish: *formación*
  - German: *Ausbildung*

Basic education

Since the 1970s, has begun to generalise the term "basic education" (*éducation de base* in French), but there is no international consensus about its scope:

- it may be synonymous with elementary/primary education/school;
- it may have a component of pre-school education and/or secondary education/school;
- it may cover the entire school education, except higher education;
- it may include the education of adults.

In 2005, the International Conference on the Right to Basic Education as a Fundamental Human Right and the Legal Framework for its Financing, convened by UNESCO and the Ministry of National Education of Indonesia, adopted the Jakarta Declaration.[301] An Experts' Consultation on the Operational Definition of Basic Education took place on 17–18 December 2007, at UNESCO headquarters (ED/BAS/RVE/2009/PI/1),[302] with the aim to harmonise the variety of names of the early years of school education, within the UN system. This would facilitate the monitoring of the implementation of the right to basic education, through the adoption of a flexible and universally applicable definition, broad-minded, including its duration, purpose, content, as well as its free and compulsory scope. The experts concluded, *inter alia*:

> For the purposes of this definition, basic education covers notions such as fundamental, elementary and primary/secondary education. [...]
>
> Beyond pre-school education, the duration of which can be fixed by the State, basic education consists of at least 9 years and progressively extends to 12 years. Basic education is free and compulsory without any discrimination or exclusion.
>
> Equivalent basic education is offered for youth and adults who did not have the opportunity or possibility to receive and complete basic education at the appropriate age. [...]
>
> Basic education is directed to the full development of the human personality. It develops the capability for comprehension and critical thinking, and it inculcates the respect for human rights and values, notably, human dignity, solidarity, tolerance, democratic citizenship and a sense of justice and equity. [...]
>
> Basic education is provided in the mother tongue, at least in its initial stages, while respecting the requirements/needs of multilingualism. In those States where basic education is also provided by private schools, the State ensures that such schools respect fully the objectives and content as mentioned in the present definition.

In 2008, the *EFA Global Monitoring Report* (UNESCO, 2008) informed:

> More and more countries, especially in the developing world, are using the term 'basic education' in official documents. At the end of the 1970s, 14% of national education systems employed the term; by the 1990s, 38% did so. Between 2000 and 2006, almost two-thirds (63%) of the 182 countries with data referred to some segment of their education system as basic education. In most instances, the term is meant to capture a country's commitment to the universalization of a cycle beyond primary education. [...]
>
> An analysis of 113 national definitions of basic education in relation to the formal education system shows that, in two-thirds of the countries, the term follows the ISCED and covers primary and lower secondary education. In the remaining third, the term is equivalent to primary education only or to primary plus some pre-primary or secondary education. (p. 25).

According to ISCED 2011[303]:

> 123. Programs classified at ISCED level 1 may be referred to in many ways, for example: primary education, elementary education or basic education (stage 1 or lower grades if an education system has

> one program that spans ISCED levels 1 and 2). For international comparability purposes, the term 'primary education' is used to label ISCED level 1.

Following to the Education 2030 Framework for Action (see 4.6), basic education includes "pre-primary, primary and lower secondary education" (para. 6).

We may, therefore, conclude that, on the one hand, 'education' and 'instruction' are not separable concepts. It is not right to say, for example, that family educates, and school teaches. Both educate and teach. On the other hand, basic education/school means, in general, the segment of a school system that should be free and compulsory.

Secondary education has become a grey zone, with variable geometry, between primary/basic and tertiary education.

The remainder of this essay seeks to argue the following general conception: Education, as a human right, is right to *access* a specific education *quality*, supported by the needed general and particular *conditions*, as internationally agreed.

4.2.2 *Normative Content*

The constituent elements of the structure and normative content of a right are its entitlement, object and exigibility, as we know. What follows is a presentation of the normative content of the right to education, in accordance with its legal sources.

4.2.2.1 Entitlement

Like all human rights, the right to education is a right of "everyone": children and adults, women and men, white, black or whatever their colour and belongings, differences and other circumstances. Although the ICESCR does not formally states that it applies "to all individuals within its territory and subject to its jurisdiction", as reads ICCPR Article 2.1, the CoESCR confirmed in its GC 13 (E/C.12/1999/10)[304] "that the principle of non-discrimination extends to all persons of school age residing in the territory of a State Party, including non-nationals, and irrespective of their legal status" (para. 34). The CRC Article 2.1 reads too: "States Parties shall respect and ensure the rights set forth in the present Convention to each child within their jurisdiction without discrimination of any kind".[305]

Three major priorities remain in the Agenda of the International Community:

- *Children*, given the intensity of their educability and the resonance of their education. They cannot wait to grow[306] and it is in the dawn of life that a whole life may be won or lost.

This was stressed by the first Special Rapporteur on the Right to Education (E/CN.4/2004/45)[307]: "Children cannot wait to grow, hence their prioritised right to education in international human rights law. The damage of denied education while they are growing up cannot be retroactively remedied" (para. 8). The (probably) most quoted poem by Gabriela Mistral, Chilean teacher and Nobel Prize Winner of Literature in 1945, titled *Su Nombre es Hoy* (His Name is Today),[308] reads:

> We are guilty of many errors and many faults,
> but our worst crime is abandoning the children,
> neglecting the fountain of life.
> Many of the things we need can wait.
> The child cannot.
> Right now is the time his bones are being formed,
> his blood is being made,
> and his senses are being developed.
> To him we cannot answer 'tomorrow',
> his name is Today.

- *Girls*, because of their enduring discrimination and of the repercussion of mothers' education on the family planning, health, well-being and development of children, as well on the welfare of society at large.[309]
- *Illiterate adults*, who are hindered in their ability for "learning to read (understand) and writing (transform) their own reality", in order "to be people", as said Paulo Freire (1975, p. 35).

Some more vulnerable groups of children, in particular, often left behind or discriminated against, deserve special attention and protection too. They include: children with disability, children affected by HIV/AIDS, pregnant girls, LGBTQI children, working children, street children, children living in remote rural areas, orphaned children, children institutionalised, children hospitalised, imprisoned children, children affected by armed conflicts, internally displaced children, indigenous and belonging to minorities (ethnic, linguistic, religious and other) children, migrant (nomadic, immigrant, refugee, asylum-seeker) children, children with learning difficulties, etc.

As a child is dependent on adults, "by reason of his physical and mental immaturity" (Preambles of the 1959 Declaration and the 1989 Convention), and because every human being lives in communities "in which alone the free and full development of his personality is possible" (UDHR Article 29.1), families and States are co-holders of the right to education of children. However, their rights are merely functional, i.e. they are not own and competing rights, but assigned to fulfil their responsibilities. Parents' (descending) legitimacy derives, therefore, from the (descending) inability of children to exercise their rights autonomously.

The right to education bears a particular collective dimension when it comes to more culturally vulnerable communities, such as indigenous peoples, but "none of the rights protected under Article 27 [minority rights] of the Covenant [ICCPR] may be legitimately exercised in a manner or to an extent inconsistent with the other provisions of the Covenant", as underlined the CoHR in its GC 23 (CCPR/C/21/Ver.1/Add.5, para. 8).[310] Also, the right to education bears a general collective dimension evoked by the Third International Conference on Adult Education (Tokyo, 1972)[311] in its Recommendation 7 that refers to "the right of individuals and nations to education" (Preamble). The CoESCR also observed in its CG 21 (E/C.12/GC/21, 21 December 2009),[312] echoing the Jomtien Declaration (see 4.2.2.2.4), that "States should recall that the fundamental aim of educational development is the transmission and enrichment of common cultural and moral values in which the individual and society find their identity and worth" (para. 26). The Constitutional Court of Colombia rightly said in *Case T-085/17*[313] that the right to education: "Enhances the subject and, through him, humanity" (para. 17).

In effect, it is through education that are transmitted and improved "the cultural instruments with which we can make the world better: ethics, law, art, science, technology" (Damásio, 1994, p. 246). Therefore, because of, and in addition, to be a human right: "The notion of education as a 'common good' reaffirms the collective dimension of education" (UNESCO, 2015b, p. 78).

In this context, it should be noted that, while the purpose of education carries both individual and social dimensions, and although learning to know, to respect and to appreciate the wealth of cultural heritages and identities of the Humankind should be a permanent concern of education, cultural beliefs, values, traditions and practices should not impair the ethical, subjective core of the right to education, which shall never be sacrificed to collective interests. Furthermore, public school, in particular, shall not be indoctrinating, except for human rights, which are recognised as Common Ethics of Humanity that States undertake to promote especially through education.

According to the *Global Education Monitoring Report – 2017/8*,[314] in 2015 there were 264 million primary and secondary age children and youth out of school, and about 6 out of 10 children and adolescents did not reach minimum proficiency in reading and mathematics. And there are about 700 million adults deprived of basic reading, writing and numeracy skills. Regarding girls, in particular, their school attendance is hindered by particular causes, such as early marriage and pregnancy: each year 12 million girls are married before the age of 18.[315] Also, they are frequently victims of sexual abuse by their teachers.

The International Commission on Financing Global Education Opportunity (2016) "recommends that, when balancing spending across different levels of education and population groups, decision-makers should prioritize the poor and early years where social returns are highest, and minimize household spending on basic education by the poor" (p. 20).

4.2.2.2 Object

Each human right aims at protecting and fostering a fundamental universal value.

The educational phenomenon consists globally in learning. Already Aristotle (1998) said: "By nature, all men long to know" (980a). François Jacob (1981), Nobel Prize Winner of Medicine, wrote: "Like any living organism, the human being is genetically programmed, but programmed to learning" (p. 132). The aptitude to learning amounts to *the* intelligence or *mother* of the plurality of intelligences developed by learnings accomplished by each and every one, lifelong, according to their needs, interests and possibilities. There are as many intelligences as differences of intelligence.

Consequently, the right to education fundamentally means the right to learn. It is through education that human beings learn all they need to survive and live peacefully together. Therefore, determining the object of the right to education amounts to answering the following main interrogations: Learning ... for what? ... what? ... how? ...

So understood, the object of the right to education comprehends its purpose and mediations: the purpose commands the values which should inspire and the aims which should guide education; the mediations include persons, learnings, methods, institutions, implying obligations for duty-bearers.

The object of the right to education is described principally in UDHR Article 26, ICESCR Articles 13 and 14, and CRC Articles 28 and 29 (see Appendix A). These provisions set up its purpose and are focussed on the main obligations of the principal duty-bearer, State: establishment, maintenance and expansion of a public school system. Liberties of education are included too.

4.2.2.2.1 *Purpose*

Education is always purposeful, by definition. The normative content of the object of the right to education could not fail to determine the purpose to which education shall be directed. Its main universal provisions are set out in UDHR Article 26.2, ICESCR Article 13.1 and CRC Article 29.1. By comparing them, it appears that:

- ICESCR Article 13.1 adds two new aims to Article 26.2:
  - to develop "... the sense of its human dignity"

  - and "… enable all persons to participate effectively in a free society".
  Furthermore, "ethnic" groups are added to the groups among which understanding, tolerance and friendship are to be promoted.
- CRC Article 29.1 – the most detailed conventional provision on the purpose of the right to education – includes the following new elements:
  - paragraph (b) mentions "the principles enshrined in the Charter of the United Nations";
  - paragraph (d) mentions "the preparation of the child for responsible life in a free society" and refers to "equality of sexes", "national" groups and "persons of indigenous origin".

  The following paragraphs are very innovative:

> c. The development of respect for the child's parents, his or her own cultural identity, language and values, for the national values of the country in which the child is living, the country from which he or she may originate, and for civilizations different from his or her own;
>
> […]
>
> e. The development of respect for the natural environment.

The values which should inspire and the aims which should guide education, as agreed in these main international provisions, have been endorsed and expanded in other international instruments and texts.

At the regional level, the ECHR (first Protocol Article 2, 1952) does not mention the purpose of education. The European Social Charter (Revised, 1996)[316] refers to "the right of children and young persons to grow up in an environment which encourages the full development of their personality and of their physical and mental capacities" (Article 17). The ACHPR (1981)[317] only refers to "the promotion and protection of morals and traditional values recognized by the community" (Article 17.3), but the African Charter on the Rights and Welfare of the Child (1990)[318] devotes eight paragraphs of its Article 11.2 to the aims of education. The Protocol of San Salvador (1988)[319] includes the following elements (Article 13.2):

- "… strengthen respect for human rights, ideological pluralism, fundamental freedoms, justice and peace";
- "… enable everyone to participate effectively in a democratic and pluralistic society";
- "… achieve a decent existence".

The Cairo Declaration on Human Rights in Islam (1990),[320] adopted by the Islamic Conference of Foreign Ministers, provides:

Article 7

[...]

b. Parents and those in such like capacity have the right to choose the type of education they desire for their children, provided they take into consideration the interest and future of the children in accordance with ethical values and the principles of the Shari'ah.

(c) Both parents are entitled to certain rights from their children, and relatives are entitled to rights from their kin, in accordance with the tenets of the Shari'ah.

Article 9

(a) The quest for knowledge is an obligation, and the provision of education is a duty for society and the State. The State shall ensure the availability of ways and means to acquire education and shall guarantee educational diversity in the interest of society so as to enable man to be acquainted with the religion of Islam and the facts of the Universe for the benefit of mankind.

(b) Every human being has the right to receive both religious and worldly education from the various institutions of education and guidance, including the family, the school, the university, the media, etc., and in such an integrated and balanced manner as to develop his personality, strengthen his faith in God and promote his respect for and defence of both rights and obligations.

Significantly, the Parliamentary Assembly of the Council of Europe has adopted the Resolution 2253 (2019) on "Sharia, the Cairo Declaration and the European Convention on Human Rights".[321] In its Resolution:

4. The Assembly considers that the various Islamic declarations on human rights, adopted since the 1980s, while being more religious than legal, fail to reconcile Islam with universal human rights, especially insofar as Sharia is their unique source of reference. This includes the 1990 Cairo Declaration on Human Rights in Islam, which, while not legally binding, has symbolic value and political significance in terms of human rights policy under Islam. [...]
6. The Assembly recalls that the European Court of Human Rights has already stated in *Refah Partisi (The Welfare Party) and others v. Turkey* that the institution of Sharia law and a theocratic regime are incompatible with the requirements of a democratic society. [...]

9. The Assembly calls on the member States of the Council of Europe to protect human rights regardless of religious or cultural practices or traditions on the principle that, where human rights are concerned, there is no room for religious or cultural exceptions. [...]

11. The Assembly calls on Council of Europe member States and those whose parliaments enjoy partner for democracy status with the Assembly to:

 [...]

11.4. engage in the process of revision of the Cairo Declaration launched by the Organisation of Islamic Cooperation (OIC) so as to ensure that the future OIC Declaration on Human Rights is compatible with universal human rights standards and the European Convention on Human Rights, which is binding on all Council of Europe member States and a source of inspiration for those whose parliaments enjoy partner for democracy status.

The aims of the right to education may be summarised as follows:
- Developing the human personality – freely, fully, harmoniously – and the sense of the personal worth, dignity and uniqueness.
- Sowing the Ethics of Human Rights and other cultural values compatible with its respect.
- Preparing for an autonomous and responsible life – as human being, parent, citizen, worker – in a democratic, pluralistic society and a globalised world.

4.2.2.2.2 *Public School System*

Family and school are the main education institutions. Family continues to be paramount for children's care and education, but school has become the principal institutional mediation of education in modern and contemporary societies, a place where children and young people spend most of their days.

The CoESCR underlined in its GC 13 (E/C.12/1999/10)[322]: "Article 13 regards States as having principal responsibility for the direct provision of education in most circumstances" (para. 48). This requires a public school system. ICESCR Article 13.2 is a "portrait-robot of an educational system" (Kiss, 1975, p. 427). It indicates its structure, which is more detailed in the ISCED 2011[323] that distinguishes the following levels:

Level 0 – Early childhood education
Level 1 – Primary education
Level 2 – Lower secondary education
Level 3 – Upper secondary education
Level 4 – Post-secondary non-tertiary education

Level 5 – Short-cycle tertiary education
Level 6 – Bachelor's or equivalent level
Level 7 – Master's or equivalent level
Level 8 – Doctoral or equivalent level

Let us highlight some passages of CoESCR GC 13 on Article 13 (E/C.12/1999/10)[324] regarding school education levels.

Primary education

9. The Committee obtains guidance on the proper interpretation of the term "primary education" from the World Declaration on Education for All which states: "The main delivery system for the basic education of children outside the family is primary schooling. Primary education must be universal, ensure that the basic learning needs of all children are satisfied, and take into account the culture, needs and opportunities of the community" (Art. 5). "[B]asic learning needs" are defined in Article 1 of the World Declaration. While primary education is not synonymous with basic education, there is a close correspondence between the two. In this regard, the Committee endorses the position taken by UNICEF: "Primary education is the most important component of basic education".

Secondary education

13. According to Article 13 (2) (b), secondary education "shall be made generally available and accessible to all by every appropriate means, and in particular by the progressive introduction of free education". The phrase "generally available" signifies, firstly, that secondary education is not dependent on a student's apparent capacity or ability and, secondly, that secondary education will be distributed throughout the State in such a way that it is available on the same basis to all. [...]
14. ... "progressive introduction of free education" means that while States must prioritize the provision of free primary education, they also have an obligation to take concrete steps towards achieving free secondary and higher education. For the Committee's general observations on the meaning of the word "free", see paragraph 7 of General Comment No. 11 on Article 14.

Technical and vocational education

15. Technical and vocational education (TVE) forms part of both the right to education and the right to work (Art. 6 (2)). Article 13 (2) (b) presents TVE as part of secondary education, reflecting the particular importance of TVE at this level of education. Article 6 (2), however, does not refer to TVE in relation to a specific level of education; [...] Accordingly, the Committee takes the view that TVE forms an integral element of all levels of education.
16. An introduction to technology and to the world of work should not be confined to specific TVE programs but should be understood as a component of general education. [...]

Higher education

19. The third and most significant difference between Article 13 (2) (b) and (c) is that while secondary education "shall be made generally available and accessible to all", higher education "shall be made equally accessible to all, on the basis of capacity". According to Article 13 (2) (c), higher education is not to be "generally available", but only available "on the basis of capacity". The "capacity" of individuals should be assessed by reference to all their relevant expertise and experience.

Fundamental education

22. In general terms, fundamental education corresponds to basic education as set out in the World Declaration on Education For All. [...]
23. Since everyone has the right to the satisfaction of their "basic learning needs" as understood by the World Declaration, the right to fundamental education [...] extends to all those who have not yet satisfied their "basic learning needs".
24. It should be emphasized that enjoyment of the right to fundamental education is not limited by age or gender; it extends to children, youth and adults, including older persons. Fundamental education, therefore, is an integral component of adult education and lifelong learning. [...]

The Committee further observed that:

25. ... a State Party is obliged to have an overall developmental strategy for its school system. The strategy must encompass schooling at all levels, but the Covenant requires States Parties to prioritize primary education [...].
26. ... the fellowship system should enhance equality of educational access for individuals from disadvantaged groups.

Comparing ICESCR Article 13 with UDHR Article 26, we see that, in the former, paragraph 13.2.b adds secondary education (not mentioned explicitly in the UDHR) and paragraphs 13.2.d and 13.2.e are new too. Paragraphs 13.3 and 13.4 complement Article 26 third paragraph.

Comparing ICESCR Article 13.2 and CRC Article 28.1, some provisions of the latter are articulated lower than the corresponding ones in the former, but new elements are added.

Lower provisions are the following ones (italics added):
- ICESCR Article 13.2 reads "with a view to *achieving the full realisation* of this right", while in the CRC "the right of the child to education" is to be achieved "*progressively*" (28.1).
- CRC Article 28.1.b, concerning secondary education, refers to "appropriate measures *such as* introduction of free education", while ICESCR Article 13.2.b refers to "every appropriate means, and *in particular* by the progressive introduction of free education".
- ICESCR Article 13.2.c uses the same formula for higher education, while Article CRC 28.1.c omits the goal to make it progressively free.
- In the CRC there is no provision similar to ICESCR Article 14.

CRC Article 41 is a saving clause, however, providing: "Nothing in the present Convention shall affect any provisions [national or international], which are more conducive to the realisation of the rights of the child".

New elements are the following ones:
- the *chapeau* of Article 28(1) includes "on the basis of equal opportunity";
- "educational and vocational information and guidance" (28.1.d);
- "to encourage regular attendance at schools and the reduction of drop-out rates" (28.1.e), addressed in Article 32 too;
- "school discipline" (Article 28.2);
- "international co-operation" (Article 28.3).

The right to education also entails the *effet utile* (useful effect) of the official recognition of the studies successfully accomplished. As the European Court of Human Rights underlined in *Case "relating to certain aspects of the laws on the use of languages in education in Belgium" v. Belgium* (Applications 1474/62; 1677/62; 1691/62; 1769/63; 1994/63; 2126/64)[325]:

> For the "right to education" to be effective, it is further necessary that, *inter alia*, the individual who is the beneficiary should have the possibility of drawing profit from the education received, that is to say, the right to obtain, in conformity with the rules in force in each State, and in one form or another, official recognition of the studies which he has completed. (B.4)

4.2.2.2.3 *Liberties of Education*

The CADE (1960) provides for liberties of education (Articles 2 and 5), as well as the third and fourth paragraphs of the ICESCR Article 13. They are:

- Liberty of parents and legal guardians "to ensure the religious and moral education of their children in conformity with their own convictions" (Article 13.3).
- Liberty of parents and legal guardians "to choose for their children schools, other than those established by public authorities" (Article 13.3).
- Liberty "to establish and direct educational institutions" on condition that they observe "the principles set forth in paragraph 1 of this Article and [...] conform to such minimum standards as may be laid down by the State" (Article 13.4).

The liberty of parents and legal guardians "to ensure the religious and moral education of their children in conformity with their own convictions" is literally reaffirmed in ICCPR Article 18.4, as we know.

There is still the academic freedom that is only implicit in ICESCR Article 13. In the opinion of the CoESCR, it falls also within the scope of Article 15, paragraphs 3 and 4. It said in its GC 13 (E/C.12/1999/10)[326]:

> 38. ... the Committee has formed the view that the right to education can only be enjoyed if accompanied by the academic freedom of staff and students. Accordingly, even though the issue is not explicitly mentioned in Article 13, it is appropriate and necessary for the Committee to make some observations about academic freedom. [...]
>
> 39. Members of the academic community, individually or collectively, are free to pursue, develop and transmit knowledge and ideas, through research, teaching, study, discussion, documentation, production, creation or writing. Academic freedom includes the liberty

> of individuals to express freely opinions about the institution or system in which they work, to fulfil their functions without discrimination or fear of repression by the State or any other actor, to participate in professional or representative academic bodies, and to enjoy all the internationally recognized human rights applicable to other individuals in the same jurisdiction. [...]
>
> 40. The enjoyment of academic freedom requires the autonomy of institutions of higher education. Autonomy is that degree of self-governance necessary for effective decisionmaking by institutions of higher education in relation to their academic work, standards, management and related activities.

Nowak (1995) remarked that academic freedom is also concerned with ICCPR Articles 9, 12, 18, 19, 21, 22.

The academic freedom is addressed, in particular, by the Recommendations on the teaching personnel of 1966 (para. 61) and 1997 (several paragraphs, in particular: "VI. Rights and freedoms of higher education teaching personnel", para. 25–30).[327] Eisemann (2007) regretted "that the fundamental principle of the independence of higher education teaching personnel has to date not been affirmed through any treaty instrument" (p. 292).

It should be noted that academic freedom is two-dimensional: it denotes both individual freedom and institutional autonomy. The latter is condition of the former, but it may condition it as well.

In the European continent, the Parliamentary Assembly of the Council of Europe adopted the Recommendation 1762 (2006) on "Academic freedom and university autonomy".[328] The European Court of Human Rights underlined, in Case *Sorguç v. Turkey* (Application 17089/03, Judgement on 23 September 2009), "the importance of academic freedom, which comprises the academics' freedom to express freely their opinion about the institution or system in which they work and freedom to distribute knowledge and truth without restriction" (para. 35). The *Case Mustafa Erdogan and Others v. Turkey* (Applications 346/04 and 39779/04, on 27 May 2014)[329] allowed the Court "to refine its conception of academic freedom and to recognize its specificity".[330] Academic freedom is mentioned in the Charter of Fundamental Rights of the European Union (Article 13). In the American continent, there are provisions on the liberties of education in the ACHR (1969, Article 12), and in the Protocol of San Salvador (1988, Article 13). In the African continent, they are recognised in the Charter on the Rights and Welfare of the Child (1990, Article 11.4).

Liberties of education are widely recognised at the national level as well (see Jenker, 1994).

4.2.2.2.4 *What School Learnings?*

The main international provisions on the right to education do not spell out the learnings basic education should ensure,[331] but there are indications in various international documents, among them the following ones are highlighted: A General Comment, three documents approved by three major conferences and three UNESCO Reports.

General Comment

The UN Committees on Human Rights are the most authoritative bodies to interpret the treaties whose implementation by States Parties they monitor, as we hnow. This is done by means of General Comments (GC) or Recommendations, in particular. The main GCs on the right to education are those devoted by the CoESCR to ICESCR Articles 13 and 14, and the first one of the CoRC, devoted to CRC Article 29.1 (aims of education). The Committee on the Rights of Persons with Disabilities and the Committee on the Elimination of Discrimination against Women adopted similar documents. Other GCs relevant for the right to education are the CoESCR GCs 1, 3, 5, 6, 9, 14, 16, 18, 20, 21 and the CoRC CGs 3 a 12, 14, 17.

The CoRC first GC (CRC/GC/2001/1)[332] is the most relevant in the present context. According to it:

> 9. … the curriculum must be of direct relevance to the child's social, cultural, environmental and economic context and to his or her present and future needs and take full account of the child's evolving capacities; teaching methods should be tailored to the different needs of different children. Education must also be aimed at ensuring that essential life skills are learnt by every child and that no child leaves school without being equipped to face the challenges that he or she can expect to be confronted with in life. Basic skills include not only literacy and numeracy but also life skills such as the ability to make well-balanced decisions; to resolve conflicts in a non-violent manner; and to develop a healthy lifestyle, good social relationships and responsibility, critical thinking, creative talents, and other abilities which give children the tools needed to pursue their options in life.

Three documents approved by major international conferences

1. *World Declaration on Education for All: Meeting Basic Learning Needs*

This Declaration has been approved by the World Conference on Education for All, Jomtien (Thailand), in 1990,[333] gathering representatives of

155 Governments, 33 IGOs and 125 ONGs (national and international). It stated:

Article 1 – Meeting basic learning needs

1. *Every person – child, youth and adult – shall be able to benefit from educational opportunities designed to meet their basic learning needs.* These needs comprise both essential learning tools (such as literacy, oral expression, numeracy, and problem solving) and the basic learning content (such as knowledge, skills, values, and attitudes) required by human beings to be able to survive, to develop their full capacities, to live and work in dignity, to participate fully in development, to improve the quality of their lives, to make informed decisions, and to continue learning. The scope of basic learning needs and how they should be met varies with individual countries and cultures, and inevitably changes with the passage of time.
2. The satisfaction of these needs empowers individuals in any society and confers upon them a responsibility to respect and build upon their collective cultural, linguistic and spiritual heritage, to promote the education of others, to further the cause of social justice, to achieve environmental protection, to be tolerant towards social, political and religious systems which differ from their own, ensuring that commonly accepted humanistic values and human rights are upheld, and to work for international peace and solidarity in an interdependent world.
3. Another and no less fundamental aim of educational development is the transmission and enrichment of common cultural and moral values. It is in these values that the individual and society find their identity and worth.
4. Basic education is more than an end in itself. It is the foundation for lifelong learning and human development on which countries may build, systematically, further levels and types of education and training.

Article 2 – Shaping the vision

1. To serve the basic learning needs of all requires more than a recommitment to basic education as it now exists. What is needed is an "expanded vision" that surpasses present resource levels, institutional structures, curricula, and conventional delivery systems while building on the best in current practices. New possibilities exist today which result from the

> convergence of the increase in information and the unprecedented capacity to communicate. We must seize them with creativity and a determination for increased effectiveness.

2. *Dakar Framework for Action – Education for All: Meeting Our Collective Commitments*

This Framework for Action was approved by the World Education Forum, Dakar (Senegal), in 2000. It reaffirmed:

> 3. … the vision of the World Declaration on Education for All (Jomtien 1990), supported by the Universal Declaration of Human Rights and the Convention on the Rights of the Child, that all children, young people and adults have the human right to benefit from an education that will meet their basic learning needs in the best and fullest sense of the term, an education that includes learning to know, to do, to live together and to be.

And proclaimed six goals:

1. Expanding and improving comprehensive early childhood care and education, especially for the most vulnerable and disadvantaged children;
2. Ensuring that by 2015 all children, particularly girls, children in difficult circumstances and those belonging to ethnic minorities, have access to a complete free and compulsory primary education of good quality;
3. Ensuring that the learning needs of all young people and adults are met through equitable access to appropriate learning and life skills programs;
4. Achieving a 50 percent improvement in levels of adult literacy by 2015, especially for women, and equitable access to basic and continuing education for all adults;
5. Eliminating gender disparities in primary and secondary education by 2005, and achieving gender equality in education by 2015, with a focus on ensuring girls' full and equal access to and achievement in basic education of good quality;
6. Improving all aspects of the quality of education and ensuring excellence of all so that recognized and measurable learning outcomes are achieved by all, especially in literacy, numeracy, and essential life skills.

In order to implement these goals, a global movement was launched, led by UNESCO, called *Education for All* (EFA), and for its monitoring, a High-Level Group was created that prepared *EFA Global Monitoring Reports,* published every year (from 2002 to 2015).

In the same year (2000), the UN General Assembly adopted the *Millenium Declaration*[335] with eight *Millenium Development Goals* (MDGS)[336] to be reached until 2015:

1. Eradicate extreme poverty and hunger
2. Achieve universal primary education
3. Promote gender equality and empower women
4. Reduce child mortality
5. Improve maternal health
6. Combat HIV/AIDS, malaria and other diseases
7. Ensure environmental sustainability
8. Develop a global partnership for development

MDGS 2 and 3 met the *EFA Goals.*

The 2015 *EFA Global Monitoring Report Education 2015 – Education for All 2000–2015: Achievements and Challenges* began with this conclusion (Foreword): "There has been tremendous progress across the world since 2000 – but we are not there yet. Despite all efforts by Governments, civil society and the international community, the world has not achieved Education for All" (UNESCO, 2015a). A new impetus was needed to achieve the unfinished Agenda.

3. *Incheon Declaration*

This Declaration was approved by the World Education Forum, Incheon (Republic of Korea), in 2015. In November, the Education 2030 Framework for Action was adopted. The two documents contain the most recent international vision and commitments towards the implementation of the right to education (see 4.6).

Three UNESCO Reports

1. *Learning to be – The world of education today and tomorrow*

This Report (Faure Report, 1972) was prepared by an International Commission created by UNESCO, chaired by Edgar Faure, former French Prime Minister and Minister of Education. Its Chapter 6 (Goals) ends with a sub-section titled "Towards the complete man" that reads:

Respect for the many-sidedness of personality is essential in education, especially in schools, if the individual is to develop as he should, both for himself and his associates. Complex attitudes, indispensable for balanced development of all personality components, must be stimulated and given form in the course of the individual's education. [...]

The physical, intellectual, emotional and ethical integration of the individual into a complete man is a broad definition of the fundamental aim for education.

We find this pedagogic ideal throughout history, in almost all countries, among philosophers and moralists, and among most theoreticians and visionaries of education. It has been one of the fundamental themes for humanist thought in all times. It may have been applied imperfectly, but it has been fruitful and helped to inspire many of the noblest educational enterprises. [...]

Every learner is indeed a remarkably concrete being. He has his own history which cannot be confused with any other. His personality is determined, more and more so with age, by a complex of biological, physiological, geographical, sociological, economic, cultural and professional data, which are different for each individual. How can we fail to allow for this in determining the ultimate aims, the content and the methods of education? Entering the educational process is a child with a cultural heritage, with particular psychological traits, bearing within him the effects of his family environment and surrounding economic conditions. And, involved in continual education, we have the adult – producer, consumer, citizen, parent – and a happy or unhappy creature.

Recognizing this evidence must lead to a radical change in educational practices, wherever this has not already taken place. (pp. 155, 156, 157)

2. *Learning: The treasure within*

This Report (Delors Report, 1996) was prepared by another International Commission created by UNESCO, chaired by Jacques Delors, former President of the European Commission (European Union). It summed up the goals of education in the known *four pillars* of the "Pointers and recommendations" of its Chapter 4:

Education throughout life is based on four pillars: learning to know, learning to do, learning to live together and learning to be.

– *Learning to know*, by combining a sufficiently broad general knowledge with the opportunity to work in depth on a small number of subjects.

This also means learning to learn, so as to benefit from the opportunities education provides throughout life.

- *Learn to do*, in order to acquire not only an occupational skill but also, more broadly, the competence to deal with many situations and work in teams. It also means learning to do in the context of young peoples' various social and work experiences which may be informal, as a result of the local or national context, or formal, involving courses, alternating study and work.
- *Learning to live together*, by developing an understanding of other people and an appreciation of interdependence – carrying out joint projects and learning to manage conflicts – in a spirit of respect for the values of pluralism, mutual understanding and peace.
- *Learning to be*, so as better to develop one's personality and be able to act with ever greater autonomy, judgment and personal responsibility. In that connection, education must not disregard any aspect of a person's potential: memory, reasoning, aesthetic sense, physical capacities and communication skills.

Formal education systems tend to emphasize the acquisition of knowledge to the detriment of other types of learning, but it is vital now to conceive education in a more encompassing fashion. Such a vision should inform and guide future educational reforms and policy, in relation both to contents and to methods.

3. *Rethinking education: Towards a global common good?*

This new Report (UNESCO, 2015b) was prepared by a Senior Experts' Group, in the context of the preparation of the Incheon World Education Forum. It reads:

This book enhances the vision provided by the two landmark UNESCO publications: *Learning to Be: The world of education today and tomorrow* (1972), the 'Faure Report', and *Learning: The treasure within* (1996), the 'Delors Report'. [...]

Education alone cannot hope to solve all development challenges, but a humanistic and holistic approach to education can and should contribute to achieving a new development model. [...] it means going beyond narrow utilitarianism and economism to integrate the multiple dimensions of human existence. [...] It requires an open and flexible approach to learning that is both lifelong and life-wide: an approach that provides the opportunity for all to realize their potential for a sustainable future and a life of dignity. This humanistic approach has implications for the

> definition of learning content and pedagogies, as well as for the role of teachers and other educators. It is even more relevant given the rapid development of new technologies, in particular digital technologies. [...]
>
> A humanistic vision reaffirms a set of universal ethical principles that should be the foundation for an integrated approach to the purpose and organization of education for all. Such an approach has implications for the design of learning processes that promote the acquisition of relevant knowledge and the development of competencies in the service of our common humanity. A humanistic approach takes the debate on education beyond its utilitarian role in economic development. [...]
>
> We need a holistic approach to education and learning that overcomes the traditional dichotomies between cognitive, emotional and ethical aspects. Overcoming the dichotomy between cognitive and other forms of learning is increasingly being recognized as essential to education. [...]
>
> International development discourse often refers to education as both a human right and a public good. The principle of education as a fundamental human right that enables the realization of other human rights is grounded in international normative frameworks. It denotes a role for the State in ensuring the respect, fulfilment and the protection of the right to education. Beyond its role in the provision of education, the State must act as a guarantor of the right to education. (pp. 9, 10, 37, 39, 75)

The indications offered by the just quoted documents point to an education accounting for the many-sidedness of the personality and existence of the human beings – their physical, emotional, aesthetic, ethical, intellectual, professional, familial, civic, international dimensions – generally summed up in the quoted "four pillars" or learnings. Accordingly, a sound basic education should include:

Common learnings
- learning tools: literacy, numeracy and digitalcy (possible neologism);
- fundamental learnings: universal and shared values, essential knowledge and competencies (capacities, skills), notably capacities for critical thinking, creative problem-solving, wise decision-making, interpersonal and collaborative work, as well as languages.

Optional learnings
They are learnings meeting the diversity and wealth of individual aptitudes and interests, for the sake both of everyone and the society at large.

In addition to purpose, learnings and institutions, the mediations of the right to education include, as above noted, persons and methods, which will be addressed in other sections. They imply obligations for duty-bearers, which are next identified.

4.2.2.3 Exigibility

The exigibility of the right to education concerns persons or entities with responsibilities or obligations concerning its satisfaction, i.e. to which it is opposable. They include families, States, International Community and the right-holders themselves.

4.2.2.3.1 *Opposability*

Responsibility for the education of children is firstly *naturally* incumbent on their parents or substitutes, supported and supervised by State. Their responsibilities, as well as the corresponding rights, are affirmed in the IBHR (UDHR Article 16.3, ICESCR Article 10, ICCPR Article 23.1), in the CRC (especially in Preamble and Articles 3.2, 5, 18.1, 23.3 and 24.2.f), and in other international legal instruments. The role of family is unique. It should be valued and treated as the most deeply touching influence on the life and destiny of a human being. In its Recommendation 1074 (1988) on Family Policy,[337] the Parliamentary Assembly of the Council of Europe stressed that "the family is still the place where human relationships are most intense and rich, and the best place for bringing up children and providing care for its elderly, lonely or sick members" (para. 5).

However, the satisfaction of the whole object of the right to education exceeds families' means. States hold the principal responsibility – legally and politically – for the implementation of all rights for all. The mission of school is far-reaching.

The International Community carries a subsidiary responsibility regarding human rights, as we know (see 2.5.4). Concerning the right to education, the World Declaration on Education for All (Jomtien, Thailand, 1990)[338] stated (Article 10.1): "*Meeting basic learning needs constitutes a common and universal human responsibility. It requires international solidarity and equitable and fair economic relations in order to redress existing economic disparities*". The CoESCR said in GC 13 (E/C.12/1999/10)[339]:

> 56. In its General Comment No. 3, the Committee drew attention to the obligation of all States Parties to take steps, "individually and through international assistance and cooperation, especially economic and technical", towards the full realization of the rights recognized in the Covenant, such as the right to education.

International co-operation is an obligation expressly referred to in the CRC, whose Article 28.3 provides: "States Parties shall promote and encourage international cooperation in matters relating to education [...]".[340] Therefore, according to the CoRC, in its GC 5 on "General measures of implementation of the Convention on the Rights of the Child (Arts. 4, 42 and 44, para. 6)" (CRC/GC/2003/5)[341]: "When States ratify the Convention, they take on obligations not only to implement it within their jurisdiction but to contribute, through international cooperation, to global implementation (see paragraph 60 below)" (para. 7).

The promotion and protection of the right to education is self-opposable too, i.e. a duty of each one towards him/herself, mentioned in the American Declaration of the Rights and Duties of Man (OAS, 1948),[342] Article XXXI: "It is the duty of every person to acquire at least an elementary education". Finland's Constitution (1999)[343] refers to "the duty to receive education" (Section 16). The Declaration of Amsterdam on the Right to and the Rights in Education (2004) refers to "the right and the obligation to be educated". Education is a right-duty, more than any other human right, because at stake is the *humanisation* itself (see 4.4.3). Indeed, is there a more transcendent individual duty than the duty of education to accomplish the personal perfectibility or educability as fully as possible? It is about "working out the nature of our own soul" (Plotinus, *The Six Enneads*, 3rd century),[344] about sculpting *La statue intérieure* (The Statue Within: An Autobiography, François Jacob, 1987).

As States are the authors and direct addressees of International Law, their obligations should be highlighted.[345]

4.2.2.3.2 *States' General Legal Obligations*

ICCPR Article 2.1 reads: "Each State Party to the present Covenant undertakes to respect and to ensure ...".[346] In the ICESCR, the most used term is "recognise". Coomans (2002) noted:

> The drafting history of the Covenant in general and of Article 13 in particular shows that the use of the term "to recognise" is closely linked to the idea of progressive realisation. The opening words of the original draft of paragraph 2 of Article 13 did not contain the term "recognise", but rather the expression "it is understood". It was subsequently changed into the clause "the State Parties to the Covenant recognise", in order to have a term with stronger legal significance. The meaning of the term "recognise" was expounded by the representative of UNESCO in 1951 during the preparatory work in the Commission on Human Rights as follows: "recognition meant first and foremost that States should accept the obligation to do all in their power to achieve certain clearly defined aims, without, however, undertaking to attain them in a specified period. Admittedly, they could be achieved only by slow degrees, and the time

> involved would vary according to the relative magnitude of the problems of each country and the means at its disposal" [E/CN.4/AC.14/SR.1, 17 May 1951]. (p. 221)[347]

Other terms used to express the international commitments of State Parties to the ICESCR[348] are 'promote', ''agree', 'undertake', 'ensure', 'guarantee'. Their principal general legal obligations are laid down in Article 2 (italics added):

> 1. Each State Party to the present Covenant undertakes to *take steps*, individually and through *international assistance and cooperation*, especially economic and technical, to the *maximum of its available resources*, with a view to *achieving progressively the full realization* of the rights recognized in the present Covenant *by all appropriate means*, including particularly the adoption of *legislative measures*.
> 2. The States Parties to the present Covenant undertake to guarantee that the rights enunciated in the present Covenant will be exercised *without discrimination of any kind* as to race, colour, sex, language, religion, political or other opinion, national or social origin, property, birth or other status.

CRC Article 4 refers to "all appropriate legislative, administrative and other measures", applied "to the maximum extent of their available resources", including "international co-operation".[349]

The CoESCR devoted its GC 3 (E/1991/23)[350] to the first paragraph of ICESCR Article 2. The Committee begins by affirming that this provision "must be seen as having a dynamic relationship with all of the other provisions of the Covenant. It describes the nature of the general legal obligations undertaken by States Parties to the Covenant. Those obligations include what may be termed (following the work of the International Law Commission) obligations of conduct and obligations of result" (para. 1), which are immediate or progressive.

There are two particular obligations "of immediate effect": prohibition of discrimination and "to take steps". In respect of the obligation of non-discrimination, the Committee said in GC 13 (E/C.12/1999/10)[351]:

> 31. The prohibition against discrimination enshrined in Article 2 (2) of the Covenant is subject to neither progressive realization nor the availability of resources; it applies fully and immediately to all aspects of education and encompasses all internationally prohibited grounds of discrimination. The Committee interprets Articles 2 (2) and 3 in the light of the UNESCO Convention against Discrimination in Education, the relevant provisions of the Convention on

the Elimination of All Forms of Discrimination against Women, the International Convention on the Elimination of All Forms of Racial Discrimination, the Convention on the Rights of the Child and the ILO Indigenous and Tribal Peoples Convention, 1989 (Convention No. 169), and wishes to draw particular attention to the following issues.

32. The adoption of temporary special measures intended to bring about *de facto* equality for men and women and for disadvantaged groups is not a violation of the right to non-discrimination with regard to education, so long as such measures do not lead to the maintenance of unequal or separate standards for different groups, and provided they are not continued after the objectives for which they were taken have been achieved.

33. In some circumstances, separate educational systems or institutions for groups defined by the categories in Article 2 (2) shall be deemed not to constitute a breach of the Covenant. In this regard, the Committee affirms Article 2 of the UNESCO Convention against Discrimination in Education (1960).

To take steps means adopting measures that "should be deliberate, concrete and targeted as clearly as possible towards meeting the obligations recognized in the Covenant" (para. 1 and 2). They should include legislative measures and judicial remedies (para. 5).

Concerning progressive realisation, the Committee commented in GC 3 (E/1991/23)[352]:

9. ... The concept of progressive realization constitutes a recognition of the fact that full realization of all economic, social and cultural rights will generally not be able to be achieved in a short period of time. In this sense, the obligation differs significantly from that contained in Article 2 of the International Covenant on Civil and Political Rights which embodies an immediate obligation to respect and ensure all of the relevant rights. Nevertheless, the fact that realization over time, or in other words progressively, is foreseen under the Covenant should not be misinterpreted as depriving the obligation of all meaningful content. It is, on the one hand, a necessary flexibility device, reflecting the realities of the real world and the difficulties involved for any country in ensuring full realization of economic, social and cultural rights. On the other hand, the phrase must be read in the light of the overall objective, indeed the *raison d'être*, of the Covenant which is to establish clear obligations for States Parties in respect of the full

> realization of the rights in question. It thus imposes an obligation to move as expeditiously and effectively as possible towards that goal.

The Committee observed that the "available resources" include "international cooperation and assistance" (para. 13).

4.2.2.3.3 *States' Specific Legal Obligations*

Where the right to education is concerned, States' obligations are enunciated in CADE (see Appendix A) that is in line with ICESCR Articles 13 and 14, to which the CoESCR devoted the GC 13 (E/C.12/1999/10)[353] that describes its normative content (para. 4–42), points out the corresponding obligations (para. 43–57), gives examples of violations (para. 58–59) and addresses obligations of other international actors (para. 60). Three categories of obligations are distinguished: "General legal obligations" (para. 43–48), "Specific legal obligations" (para. 49–56) and a "minimum core obligation" (para. 57).

States' obligations with regard to the right to education may be summed up as follows:

- To respect, protect and fulfil each of its elements, with obligations concerning their availability, accessibility, acceptability, adaptability (see below), which are of result or of conduct.
- Some obligations are immediate, such as to act without discrimination and to take steps aiming at its full realisation, if needed with international assistance.
- Primary free compulsory education must be the immediate priority, but a complete school system should be developed.
- Whole education must be directed to the purpose internationally agreed for the right to education, and minimum standards should be prescribed to private education.
- States may fail to comply with their international commitments concerning the right to education both by action or inaction.

With regard to respect-protection-fulfilment obligations (see 2.5.5):

- Respecting includes, for example, to respect the liberty of parents and private education establishments.
- Protecting includes, for example, to protect children against possible abuses of parents' or private actors' liberty.
- Fulfiling includes, for example, to support disadvantaged groups by means of financial and other appropriate egalitarian measures.

According to the Committee: "There is a strong presumption of impermissibility of any retrogressive measures taken in relation to the right to education, as well as other rights enunciated in the Covenant" (para. 45). Cases in point are a decrease in the education budget and the (re)introduction or increasing of fees. If retrogressive measures become absolutely unavoidable, they should not affect the minimum content of the right to education, should be proportionate, temporary, non-discriminatory (directly or indirectly) and safeguard the rights of the most vulnerable groups. Decreasing the scope of satisfaction of a right or part thereof, if such a measure envisages raising an insufficient level of satisfaction of another right or part thereof, may be exceptionally justifiable.

Following the distinction proposed (see 2.5.7.1), States' obligations may be represented as three concentric circles, regarding three levels of content: minimum, full and expanded.

4.2.2.3.3.1 Minimum Content

The CoESCR identified in its GC 13 (E/C.12/1999/10)[354] the minimum content/obligations concerning the right to education as follows:

> 57. In its General Comment 3, the Committee confirmed that States Parties have "a minimum core obligation to ensure the satisfaction of, at the very least, minimum essential levels" of each of the rights enunciated in the Covenant, including "the most basic forms of education". In the context of Article 13, this core includes an obligation:
>
> – to ensure the right of access to public educational institutions and programs on a non-discriminatory basis;
> – to ensure that education conforms to the objectives set out in Article 13 (1);
> – to provide primary education for all in accordance with Article 13 (2) (a);
> – to adopt and implement a national educational strategy which includes provision for secondary, higher and fundamental education;
> – and to ensure free choice of education without interference from the State or third parties, subject to conformity with "minimum educational standards" (Art. 13 (3) and (4)).

The African Commission on Human and Peoples' Rights reinforces in its "Principles and Guidelines on the Implementation of Economic, Social and Cultural Rights in the African Charter on Human and Peoples' Rights",[355] as a matter of "Minimum Core Obligations" (para. 71):

> a. To ensure that all children enjoy their right to free and compulsory primary education. No children should be denied this right because

> of school fees or related costs of education. Special measures may be required to ensure that children belonging to disadvantaged or vulnerable groups receive free primary education. To achieve this objective States are bound to progressively increase the amount of national resources allocated to education.

Arguably, the core content of the right to education should entail two further elements, with the corresponding obligations.

Learning the and in the mother tongue

The main international provisions on the right to education do not include a linguistic dimension. However, if a child involved in a judicial proceeding should be guaranteed "at least", among other things, "free assistance of an interpreter if the child cannot understand or speak the language used" (CRC Article 40.2.b.vi),[356] why is he/she not entitled to be instructed in a familiar language? This is a view shared by, for instance, Angelina Fisher (2017, p. 17).

Referring to ECHR first Protocol Article 2, Luzius Wildhaber (1993), who was President of the European Court of Human Rights, said that:

> … it appears somewhat too harsh to claim that the right to education 'contains in itself no linguistic requirement'. In my opinion, it remains open whether a denial of a right to be educated in a language which is spoken in a State but not defined as a national language should not be considered as a violation of Article 2.

At stake is "the substance of the right to education" (p. 541).

The Parliamentary Assembly of the Council of Europe addressed the issue diplomatically in its Recommendation 1740 (2006) on "The Place of the Mother Tongue in School Education"[357]:

> 1. In the Parliamentary Assembly's view, considerations of various kinds influence the place of the mother tongue in schools. There is the question of rights, both the right to education and the right to a cultural identity; there is the preservation of linguistic heritage, at both European and world levels; there is the promotion of dialogue and exchange through linguistic diversity; and there are pedagogical factors, to say nothing of the political use which is often made of the issue.

In this regard, see 5.3.4.

Vocational education

As already quoted, the CoESCR "takes the view that TVE [technical and vocational education] forms an integral element of all levels of education" (E/C.12/1999/10, para. 15).[358] It "is understood as being part of both the universal right to education and the right to work", as notes (Preamble) the *Recommendation concerning technical and vocational education and training* (TVET) (UNESCO, 2015).

Because the right to education is instrumental in earning a decent livelihood, vocational education should be part of basic education (see 4.2.2.2.4) and taken as an element of quality education (see 4.6.2). Paivi Gynther (2007), for example, also held the view that "vocational skills should be incorporated into the core of the right to education" (p. 63).

4.2.2.3.3.2 Full Content

Full content/obligations regarding the right to education include all the elements formally set out in its main international standards or jurisprudentially elaborated.

In its GC 4 on "The right to adequate housing (Art. 11 (1) of the Covenant)" (E/1992/23),[359] the CoESCR used an analytical framework identifying several determinant factors for its realisation, in particular the following ones (para. 8): *legal security of tenure*; *availability of services, materials, facilities and infrastructure*; *affordability*; *habitability*; *accessibility*; *location*; *cultural adequacy*. In GC 12 on "The right to adequate food (Art. 11)" (E/C.12/1999/5),[360] the Committee used the terms *availability* and *accessibility* to characterise "the core content of the right to adequate food" (para. 8). In the same year, the Special Rapporteur on the Right to Education wrote in her Preliminary Report addressed to the former UN Commission on Human Rights (E/CN.4/1999/49)[361]:

> 50. ... To portray the complexity of Governmental obligations corresponding to the right to education, the Special Rapporteur has structured them into a 4-A scheme, denoting the four essential features that primary schools should exhibit, namely availability, accessibility, acceptability and adaptability.

In 2002, the Special Rapporteur "further elaborated her 4-A scheme so as to make it suitable for generating data based on parameters of rights-based education. It is presented in the table *Translating the 4-A scheme into rights-based indicators*" (E/CN.4/2002/60, para. 28).[362] According to the Special Rapporteur:

- *Availability* "relates to ensuring that primary schools are available for all children" (para. 51).

- *Accessibility* "relates to ensuring access to available public schools, most importantly in accordance with the existing prohibition of discrimination" (para. 57).
- *Acceptability* relates to the State's obligation "to ensure that all schools conform to the minimum criteria which it has developed as well as ascertaining that education is acceptable both to parents and to children" (para. 62).
- *Adaptability* relates to the imperative "that the best interests of the child be given prominence" and to "the need for the educational system to become and remain adaptable" (para. 70).

The CoESCR has endorsed and expanded, in its GC 13 (E/C.12/1999/10),[363] the '4-A scheme': "education in all its forms and at all levels shall exhibit the following interrelated and essential features" (para. 6), namely: availability, accessibility, acceptability, adaptability. Let us summarise their scope:

- *Availability*

  Availability fundamentally means the existence of an education system with the infrastructures, facilities, resources (material, financial, human), indispensable for the provision of the public service necessary to the satisfaction of the right to education. Schools are needed in sufficient number, which are safe, healthy, decent, functional learning environments, minimally comfortable, desirably beautiful, with clean drinking water, gender-sensitive sanitation, convenient playgrounds, electricity if possible. The school equipment should include, as far as possible, refectory, sports halls, a library, computers, etc. Class sizes should be acceptable and the teaching-learning materials should be free from gender stereotypes or ethnic prejudices. Last but not least, teachers with the qualities, qualifications and status required.
- *Accessibility*

  Accessibility includes the following main dimensions: legal, economic, geographic, architectural, linguistic.
  - *Legal accessibility*

  Legal accessibility means, first of all, that there is no legal discrimination as defined in CADE Article 1. It is the right to attend school, in particular for categories of children more vulnerable (see Ringelheim, 2016). One aspect of legal accessibility is administrative accessibility, i.e. not being conditioned by undue or unachievable requirements, such as certificates of birth or residence. However, there may be no discrimination *de jure* (legal), active, but remaining *de facto* (real), passive discrimination, in public policies, in the practice of schools and the behaviour of teachers.

  - *Economic accessibility*

    Economic accessibility or affordability means, not only the absence of direct costs to attend basic schooling, but also the absence of 'hidden fees' and indirect costs in general, which may be an obstacle to its attendance, such as transport, school uniforms, study materials or other, and that access to other levels of schooling is progressively free. Affordability implies the possibility of support, if needed, and may justify other measures in favour of groups traditionally discriminated against.
  - *Geographical accessibility*

    Geographical accessibility means that the distance between the place of residence and the school is not excessive or dangerous and that there is transport if needed, or even accommodation for children who live too far away from the school. Accessibility may also be ensured under the form of distance learning, using appropriate technological means.
  - *Architectural accessibility*

    Architectural accessibility means that school facilities are prepared to receive children with mobility limitations.
  - *Linguistic accessibility*

    Linguistic accessibility means that the language used especially in pre-school education and primary education is not a barrier to learning (see 5.3.4).
- *Acceptability*

  Acceptability of education refers mainly to its substance and form, i.e. contents and methods. The contents should meet the aims stipulated by the right to education international provisions, be individually relevant and respect the cultural particularities not incompatible with them. The methods should exclude everything not compatible with the respect for the dignity and rights of the subjects of the right to education and encourage their participation in learning, in school life and social life in general.
- *Adaptability*

  Adaptability of learnings means that they should respond to the individual diversity of aptitudes and needs, as well as to the collective particularities and necessities, as well as have the flexibility allowing them to be up to the advancement of knowledge and technologies, and to adapt to unpredictable factors.

By defining acceptability in its GC 13 (E/C.12/1999/10),[364] the CoESCR referred to the relevancy and quality of "the form and substance of education", taking as the criterion "the educational objectives required by Article 13 (1) [of the ICESCR] and such minimum educational standards as may be approved by the

State (see Art. 13 (3) and (4))". Concerning adaptability, it refers to the flexibility and satisfaction of the needs of students, with their diversity (para. 6.c and d.).

Considering that acceptability and adaptability are largely overlapping and sometimes confused notions, and given the timeliness and comprehensiveness of the principle of quality education – which can subsume its acceptability and adaptability – as well as the overarching significance of the equity principle, in its relation with the principles of non-discrimination, equality and diversity, the *4-A* could be categorised as follows:

- *Availability*
- *Accessibility*
- *Quality*
- *Equity*

Quality and equity education will be addressed below (see 4.6.2 and 4.6.4).

4.2.2.3.3.3 Expanded Content

The expanded content/obligations concerning the right to education, as here understood, cover full content/obligations, all commitments internationally assumed by States regarding the right to education, and other obligations derived from the general principle of human rights interdependence, and the dialectical relationship education-society. As said the CoESCR in its GC 11 on "Plans of action for primary education (Article 14 of the International Covenant on Economic, Social and Cultural Rights)" (E/C.12/1999/4, 10 May 1999),[365] "the right to education epitomizes the indivisibility and interdependence of all human rights" (para. 2).

In reality, children and adolescents, in particular, are not abstract entities, 'pupils/students' without body and cradle; they are sons and daughters of mothers and fathers who live within cultural, social and economic horizons involving their destinies. For example, unhealthy or hungry children are diminished in their ability and willingness to learn; young educated and trained for a profession they have chosen, but have not the opportunity to exercise, suffer an unfair frustration and limitation of their horizons of life, with prejudice also for their communities and society at large; illiterate mothers and fathers or with little education, or unemployed, or education professionals undermined in their professionality and professionalism, are affected in their ability to be responsible for the right to education.

When the human rights interdependence is lost sight of, the right to education may be a chimaera ...

> Educational rights cannot be divorced from wider socioeconomic rights. Achieving curricular goals, and the rights of a child to a meaningful

> quality education, will depend, for example, upon confronting patterns of child poverty, illness and malnutrition, discrimination, spatial inequality, and social exclusion. We cannot expect children to come to school ready to learn if they are without parents, if they are hungry, if they have been evicted from their homes, if they spend many hours walking to school, or if they lack light by which to read at night. Related issues concern safe public transportation where schools are not within walking distance, adequate nutrition for learners, and sufficient facilities and infrastructure in schools. Issues of poverty and inequality are important and have a profound impact on achieving education rights. (Salim Vally, in Mehendale & Mukhopadhyay, 2018, p. 44)

In this respect, the first Special Rapporteur on the Right to Education noticed (E/CN.4/2000/6)[366]:

> 64. Opportunities for working children to "learn and earn" have been grounded in the necessity for poor people – including children – to work so as to be able to survive. Full-time education then appears to be a luxury rather than a basic right of the child, and changing that cruel reality requires a great deal of political and financial commitment. The Supreme Court of India has accepted this "learn and earn" approach for non-hazardous employment of children below 14 years of age, mandating a reduction of daily working hours to six, coupled with at least two hours of education at the expense of the employer. For hazardous work, the Court has recalled that child labour could not be eliminated without tackling underlying poverty and suggested ensuring work for an adult member of the family in lieu of the child or, if this is impossible within the limits of the economic capacity of the State, the provision of a minimum income to the family in order to enable them to send the child to school payable as long as the child is attending school.

These, and other factors of the realisation of the right to education, are put together and quantified in the *World Development Report 2018: Learning to Realise Education's Promise*, the first-ever World Bank Report "devoted entirely to education"[367] which states: "This is a moral and economic crisis that must be addressed immediately" (Foreword). It begins with two quotations: "Education is the most powerful weapon we can use to change the world" (Nelson Mandela); "If your plan is for one year, plant rice. If your plan is for ten years, plant trees. If your plan is for one hundred years, educate children" (Kuan Chung, 7th century BC). It observes: "The recent expansion in education is impressive by historical standards" (p. 4). Part I starts by reaffirming: "Education is a basic human right, and it is central to unlocking human capabilities. It also has tremendous instrumental value" (p. 38). However, "schooling is not the same as learning". Moreover, "education cannot do it alone" (pp. 3, 44).

States' obligations relating to human rights outside their territory may be included in the concept of expanded obligation. Extraterritorial obligations also include international aid and co-operation (see 2.5.7.5).

4.2.2.3.4 *Three Paramount Specific Legal Obligations*

According to ICESCR Articles 13 and 14, three States' obligations stand out:
- All education shall be directed to the purpose of the right to education.
- Everyone shall be guaranteed basic free compulsory schooling.
- Private education shall be regulated and supervised.

These are unqualified obligations, that is, not subject to "available resources" and to be achieved "progressively".

4.2.2.3.4.1 All Education Shall Be Directed to the Purpose of the Right to Education

The CoESCR affirms in its GC 13:

> 49. States Parties are required to ensure that curricula, for all levels of the educational system, are directed to the objectives identified in Article 13 (1). They are also obliged to establish and maintain a transparent and effective system which monitors whether or not education is, in fact, directed to the educational objectives set out in Article 13 (1).

During the *travaux préparatoires* of the UDHR, at the 3rd session of the Commission on Human Rights (Lake Success, 1948), the representative of the World Jewish Congress (Bienenfeld) said that (E/CN.4/SR.67)[368]: "It was necessary to stress the importance of article devoted to the spirit of education, which was possibly greater than that of all the other articles of the declaration".

During the *travaux préparatoires* of the ICESCR, at the 8th session of the Commission (E/CN.4/SR.285, 23 May 1952),[369] the inclusion of the aims of education in Article 13.1 was not consensual. Following a UN Document (A/2929)[370]:

> 37. Some doubt was expressed as to the desirability of including the definition of the aims of education which appears in paragraph 1.

> It was argued that that definition confused elements which were not all of equal importance and that no similar definition appeared in other articles. It was felt, however, that, in the light of the widely differing ends to which education could be used, it was important to state what those ends ought to be. (pp. 322, 323)

The inclusion and the legal force of the aims of education were objected again by some Delegations during the 12th session of the UN General Assembly Third Committee, in 1957, when it examined the draft Covenants concluded by the Commission on Human Rights at its 10th session, in 1954. It prevailed the concern expressed by UNESCO Director-General (René Maheu) who stated that: "It was not enough for States Parties to the Covenant to recognize the right to education; it should be specified that the type of education recognized was one which would dispose the pupils towards good and not towards evil" (A/C.3/SR.786, 22 October 1957).[371] In this respect, Eleanor Roosevelt wrote in *My Day* on 9 May 1951[372]: "On Friday we had long discussion in the Human Rights Commission on the right to education and what that right should mean. In the covenant it does not seem practical to go into detail, but where education is concerned most of the delegates feel it so important that it is difficult to condense all the things they want to say".

Nevertheless, as reads a Report of UNESCO (2000):

> In the early decades following the proclamation of the Universal Declaration of Human Rights, the international context was not favourable to the exchange of views and experience among countries concerning the purposes and contents of education, at least in the areas specifically mentioned by the Declaration. [...]
>
> At the national level, as observed in the preceding chapters, the emphasis of educational policies in probably the majority of countries was primarily quantitative rather than qualitative: expansion of access to education at all levels and adjustment of educational structures, contents and methods mainly with a view to facilitating this. [...] The themes treated at the annual International Conferences on Public Education during this period are indicative: in the twenty years following the adoption of the Universal Declaration of Human Rights, the purposes of education spelled out in Article 26 were the main focus of discussion and debate just twice. (pp. 76, 77)

The aims of education have been, progressively, legally enhanced and densified, being now strong established:

- In UDHR Article 26, they are laid down in the second paragraph.
- In ICESCR Article 13, they are laid down in the first paragraph, immediately after the right to education entitlement.
- In CRC, they are expanded in an autonomous Article (29.1).

It should also be noted that Article 13 of the Protocol of San Salvador (1988) divided into two paragraphs what in Article 13 of the ICESCR is stated in one (Article 13.1): the first proclaims the entitlement, the second describes the purpose of the right to education.

The CoESCR included the respect for the aims laid down in Article 13.1 into the "minimum core obligation" of the States Parties obligations (E/C.12/1999/10, para. 57).[373] The "General guidelines regarding the form and contents of periodic reports" adopted by the CoRC (CRC/C/58, 20/11/96)[374] devote to the aims of education some long paragraphs (112 to 116). The fact that the Committee has dedicated its first GC to Article 29.1 (aims of education) is also telling.

The aims internationally agreed for the right to education are compulsory for private education too, according to ICESCR Article 13.4 (1966), almost literally reproduced in CRC Article 29.2 (1989) and Article 11.7 of the African Charter on the Rights and Welfare of the Child (1990), as well as in Article 13.5 of the Protocol of San Salvador (1988) that expressly states (Article 13.4)[375]: "In conformity with the domestic legislation of the States Parties, parents should have the right to select the type of education to be given to their children, *provided that it conforms to the principles set forth above*" (italics added).

Alexander Kiss (1975) stressed that the aims of the right to education "could be opposed to the more extremist totalitarian regimes we ever knew", as well as, "if necessary, to parents that used their right of guiding the education of their child in a sense very different from the provisions of the international instruments, and above all to education institutions not respecting the fundamental aims so prescribed" (p. 438).

The purpose of education should be, therefore, the overarching criterion of quality education (see 4.6.2).

4.2.2.3.4.2 Everyone Shall Be Guaranteed Basic Free Compulsory Schooling

The CoESCR observed (E/C.12/1999/10)[376]:

> 51. ... Given the wording of Article 13 (2), States Parties are obliged to prioritize the introduction of compulsory, free primary education. This interpretation of Article 13 (2) is reinforced by the priority accorded to primary education in Article 14. The obligation to provide primary education for all is an immediate duty of all States Parties.

Article 14 reinforces "the principle of compulsory education free of charge for all", amounting to an "extraordinary provision", as noted Cassin (1953): "*The fight against the illiteracy is such an essential thing and its success, in a reasonable future, would have such a value for the humanity that the Commission on Human Rights understood to print it a particularly vigorous character*" (p. 10). When the draft Article 14 was examined by the UN General Assembly Third Committee, at its 12th session, in 1957 (A/C.3/SR.791),[377] the Ghana Delegation remarked: "It was said that Article 15 [now 14] gave in a way a superiority to education, to the detriment maybe of the other rights, such as the right to social security. But this superiority is entirely justified if one considers that education commands the social progress and that those without a minimum of instruction are unable to exercise their social and political rights". In its GC 11 (E/C.12/1999/4),[378] the CoESCR said: "Where a State Party is clearly lacking in the financial resources and/or expertise required to "work out and adopt" a detailed plan, the international community has a clear obligation to assist" (para. 9).

As stated by the World Declaration on Education for All: Meeting Basic Learning Needs (Jomtien, 1990),[379] Article 1.4: "Basic education is more than an end in itself. It is the foundation for lifelong learning and human development on which countries may build, systematically, further levels and types of education and training".

In this respect, the Constitutional Court of South Africa stressed in *Case Governing Body of the Juma Musjid Primary School & Others v Essay N.O. and Others (CCT 29/10) [2011] ZACC 13; 2011 (8) BCLR 761 (CC) (11 April 2011)*[380]:

> 37. It is important, for the purpose of this judgment, to understand the nature of the right to "a basic education" under section 29(1)(a). Unlike some of the other socio-economic rights, this right is immediately realisable. There is no internal limitation requiring that the right be "progressively realised" within "available resources" subject to "reasonable legislative measures". The right to a basic education in section 29(1)(a) may be limited only in terms of a law of general application which is "reasonable and justifiable in an open and democratic society based on human dignity, equality and freedom".

However, there is no normative instrument or programmatic text determining the duration of compulsory education/school, which is variable from country to country, depending upon economic development. It has increased progressively, over the decades, with a tendency to absorb secondary schooling.[381] The only existing formal consensus, in this respect, is that the age of its term shall not be under the minimum age for access to employment, according to the Convention concerning Minimum Age for Admission to Employment (C138),[382] adopted by ILO in 1973, that provides: "The minimum age specified in pursuance of paragraph 1 of this Article shall not be less than the age of completion of compulsory schooling and, in any case, shall not be less than 15 years" (Article 2.3). The Convention admits exceptions.

Following a recent publication (UNESCO/Right to Education Initiative, 2019, p. 100), there are 191 countries with legal provisions on compulsory school, being their minimum duration of 5 years and the maximum 15 years.

Whatever its duration, compulsory education/school should be free (see 4.3.3).

4.2.2.3.4.3 Private Education Shall Be Regulated and Supervised

The Education 2030 Framework for Action (see 4.6) states: "The role of the State is essential in setting and regulating standards and norms" (para. 10).[383]

As said the European Court in *Case "relating to certain aspects of the laws on the use of languages in education in Belgium" v. Belgium* (Applications 1474/62; 1677/62; 1691/62; 1769/63; 1994/63; 2126/64),[384] the right to education, "by its very nature calls for regulation by the State, regulation which may vary in time and place according to the needs and resources of the community and of individuals" (B.5). The Recommendation CM/Rec(2012)13 of the Committee of Ministers to Member States on ensuring Quality Education (Council of Europe, 2012)[385] affirms: "Both public and private provision may be a part of national education systems. In all cases, public authorities are responsible for the national education system, for setting the general framework within which education is provided and for ensuring its quality" (para. 20).

In its GC 13 (E/C.12/1999/10),[386] the CoESCR recalled:

> 54. States Parties are obliged to establish "minimum educational standards" to which all educational institutions established in accordance with Article 13 (3) and (4) are required to conform. They must also maintain a transparent and effective system to monitor such standards.

The minimum educational standards "must be consistent with the educational objectives set out in Article 13 (1)" (para. 29).

The CHR has reaffirmed States' obligations concerning this matter in its Resolution 38/9 (5 July 2018)[387]:

> 5. *Urges* States to put in place a regulatory framework to ensure the regulation of all education providers, including those operating independently or in partnership with States, guided by international

> human rights law and principles, that establishes, at the appropriate level, inter alia, minimum norms and standards for the creation and operation of educational services, addresses any negative impact of the commercialization of education and strengthens access to appropriate remedies and reparation for victims of violations of the right to education;

As the State has an obligation to protect human rights against third parties, and there are more and more private actors providing education services, for-profit or not, the regulatory framework should be sufficiently robust and efficient for, if necessary, "prohibit a completely partial, intolerant and totalitarian education" (Wildhaber, 1976, p. 161) and close private education institutions, if needed, as did the Government of Ecuador to 14 Universities in 2012 (see A/69/402, para. 90).[388]

The European Court further said in the Case above quoted: "It goes without saying that such regulation must never injure the substance of the right to education nor conflict with other rights enshrined in the Convention" (B.5). The CoESCR also noted that the minimum educational standards should not be a pretext for purposes not provided for in PIDESC Article 4, which lays down the criteria for the legitimacy of limitations to any right recognised therein.

4.2.3 *Protection*

The international protection of the right to education comes under general mechanisms common to other human rights, at the universal and regional levels, as well as special mechanisms within the UNESCO framework (and of ILO concerning the professional element of its normative content).

4.2.3.1 Universal Protection

In the universal UN system, the CHR mechanisms include the UPR, a complaint procedure and Special Procedures, among which a Special Rapporteur on the Right to Education nominated by the former Commission on Human Rights, in 1998 (Resolution 1998/33).[389] The first Special Rapporteur (Katarina Tomaševski) developed a broad-minded doctrine, in her reports and other writings, that has been largely endorsed by the CoESCR. In 2004, in her sixth annual Report (E/CN.4/2004/45),[390] "the Special Rapporteur recommends that the Commission on Human Rights decide not to renew the mandate on the right to education" (para. 1). In the Summary, she began by explaining:

> This is the sixth – and the last – annual report of the Special Rapporteur on the right to education. When her mandate was established in 1998, its key purposes were enhancing the visibility of the right to education and

> eliminating obstacles and difficulties in its realization. This has proved to be an impossible task because obstacles and difficulties in the carrying out of her mandate have considerably increased each year.

It was the first time a Special Rapporteur recommended the respective mandate not be renewed. It was regrettable, but more unfortunate was her premature death in 2006. The mandate continued and another Special Rapporteur was appointed.[391]

Treaty monitoring bodies have 'communications' or petitions/complaints procedures. The most directly concerned with the right to education are the CoHR, the CoESCR, the CoRC, the Committee on the Elimination of All Forms of Discrimination against Women and the Committee on the Rights of Persons with Disabilities. Until 2018, ten complaints were submitted to these Committees, alleging violations of different aspects of the right to education. In three of them were found violations (C/82/D/1155/2003, C/36/D/4/2004, C/71/D/40/2007).

In 2017, the CoESCR adopted "Working methods concerning the Committee's follow-up to Views under the Optional Protocol to the International Covenant on Economic, Social and Cultural Rights".[392]

Regarding the ILO, it has a regular system and special procedures to protect the right to work[393]:

- Under the regular system, Member States are required to submit reports to its Committee of Experts on the Application of Conventions and Recommendations.
- Special procedures are the Committee on Freedom of Association, 'Representations' (allowing for complaints submitted by employers or workers organisations against States) and an inter-States complaint mechanism.

It should be noted that the Statute of the International Criminal Court (1998) mentions among the war crimes: "Intentionally directing attacks against buildings dedicated to [...] education, art, science [...]" (Article 8(2)(b)(ix)).[394]

4.2.3.2 UNESCO's Mechanisms

Within UNESCO's specialised framework, there are constitutional mechanisms, a procedure created by the Executive Board and bodies established by some instruments.[395]

According to the UNESCO Constitution (Article VIII)[396]:

> Each Member State shall submit to the Organisation, at such times and in such manner as shall be determined by the General Conference, reports on the laws, regulations and statistics relating to its educational, scientific

> and cultural institutions and activities, and on the action taken upon the recommendations and conventions referred to in Article IV paragraph 4.

Article IV.4 reads:

> The General Conference shall, in adopting proposals for submission to the Member States, distinguish between recommendations and international conventions submitted for their approval. In the former case, a majority vote shall suffice; in the latter case, a two-thirds majority shall be required. Each of the Member States shall submit recommendations or conventions to its competent authorities within a period of one year from the close of the session of the General Conference at which they were adopted.

Consequently, the approval of a convention (legally binding) requires a two-thirds majority, whereas for approval of a recommendation or declaration (not legally binding) a simple majority is sufficient. In any case, every instrument adopted by the General Conference shall be submitted to the national political organs concerned, even those a State has not approved, and every Member State is required to report on the respective follow-up.

There is a Committee on Conventions and Recommendations (CR)[397] that is a permanent subsidiary body of the Executive Board now composed of 30 from among its members. It meets in closed sessions, in principle twice a year, on the occasion of the sessions of the Executive Board. Its tasks are:

- examining reports received from the Member States concerning the implementation of UNESCO's standard-setting instruments, according to "Framework guidelines for the preparation of reports on the implementation of conventions for the monitoring of which the CR Committee is responsible".
- examining communications relating to cases and questions concerning the violation of human rights in UNESCO's fields of competence.

The right of communication of States is implicit in the Rules of Procedure of the General Conference (Rule 10.d) and the Executive Board (Rule 5.2),[398] but there was no procedure to deal with other individual or collective communications. In 1976, France submitted to the 19th session of the General Conference (in Nairobi) a project aiming at creating a general mechanism to deal with the violations of the human rights falling within its field of competence. In its Resolution 19 C/12.1,[399] the General Conference, "*Noting*, in particular, that violations of human rights in UNESCO's fields of competence are increasingly frequent and are the subject of numerous complaints sent to the Organisation", invited the Executive Board and the Director-General to consider the creation of a procedure to deal with "cases and questions" concerning the violation of human rights in its fields of competence.

In 1978, the Executive Board adopted the 104 EX/Decision 3.3 (inspired in the ECOSOC '1503 Procedure' and in the ILO mechanism to protect the trade union freedom).[400] In this Decision, based on a "Study of the procedures which should be followed in the examination of cases and questions which might be submitted to UNESCO concerning the exercise of human rights in the spheres of its competence, in order to make its action more effective":

> The Executive Board,
>
> 1. *Mindful* that the competence and role of UNESCO in the field of human rights derive primarily from Article I.1 of the Constitution of UNESCO [...].
>
> 10. *Considering* that, in the exercise of its competence in the field of human rights, UNESCO is called upon to examine:
>
> a cases concerning violations of human rights which are individual and specific,
>
> b questions of massive, systematic or flagrant violations of human rights which result either from a policy contrary to human rights applied *de jure* or *de facto* by a State or from an accumulation of individual cases forming a consistent pattern,
>
> 11. *Considering* the terms of reference of the Committee on Conventions and Recommendations in Education, [...]
>
> 13. *Decides* that the Committee will henceforth be designated 'the Committee on Conventions and Recommendations';
>
> 14. *Decides* that the Committee will continue to carry out its functions with respect to conventions and recommendations and will consider communications received by the Organization concerning cases and questions of violations of human rights within UNESCO's fields of competence in accordance with the following conditions and procedures [...].

The so-called '104 Procedure' has the following main features:
- it is a mechanism established by the Executive Board, not treaty-based;
- it covers any UNESCO's Member State;
- it is completely confidential;
- it aims at a friendly outcome, avoiding a conflictual and accusatory context.

Janusz Symonides (2000), former Director of the UNESCO Division of Human Rights, Democracy and Peace (1989–2000),[401] commented:

> The Executive Board decision did not specify which human rights fall within UNESCO's fields of competence. In practice, it has been accepted that the following belong to this category:
>
> - the right to education,
> - the right to share in scientific advancement and enjoy its benefits,
> - the right to participate freely in cultural life, and
> - the right to information, including freedom of opinion and expression.
>
> These rights may imply the exercise of others, in particular:
>
> - the right to freedom of thought, conscience and religion,
> - the right to seek, receive and impart information and ideas through any medium and regardless of frontiers;
> - the right to protection of the moral and material interests resulting from any scientific, literary or artistic production, and
> - the right to freedom of assembly and association for the purposes of activities connected with education, science, culture and information. (pp. 215, 216)

The victims may be teachers, students, researchers, artists, writers, journalists and intellectuals in general. The CR begins by examining the conditions of admissibility of the communications as set out in the '104 Procedure'. There are ten, including the following ones:

- not being anonymous;
- not being manifestly ill-founded;
- not being offensive;
- not being an abuse of the right to submit communications;
- containing relevant evidence;
- not being based exclusively on mass media information;
- to be submitted within a reasonable time limit following the facts which constitute its subject matter, or within a reasonable time limit after the facts have become known.

More than 600 communications were examined by the CR.

The Decision on the '104 Procedure' recalled the discreet diplomatic, intercession, humanitarian role the Director-General can also play concerning the promotion of human rights in UNESCO's fields of competence, especially in cases demanding an urgent intervention.

Despite its confidential nature, the '104 Procedure' provides, at last:

18. … that questions of massive, systematic or flagrant violations of human rights and fundamental freedoms – including, for example, those perpetrated as a result of policies of aggression, interference in the internal affairs of States, occupation of foreign territory and implementation of a policy of colonialism, genocide, apartheid, racialism, or national and social oppression – falling within UNESCO's fields of competence should be considered by the Executive Board and the General Conference in public meetings;

This provision was never applied.

The General Conference can invite a Member State to withdraw from UNESCO.[402]

Beyond these mechanisms, there are two bodies concerned, directly or indirectly, with the right to education:

- Conciliation and Good Offices Commission to be responsible for seeking a settlement of any disputes which may arise between States Parties to the Convention against Discrimination in Education (1962)
  The "Good Offices" of the Commission were never requested.
- Joint ILO/UNESCO Committee of Experts on the Application of the Recommendations concerning Teaching Personnel (CEART), first called Joint Committee UNESCO/ILO for controlling the implementation of the Recommendation concerning the Status of Teachers. This is a Joint Committee because, as Beiter (2006) remarks, both Recommendations "deal with international labour law as well as international education law" (p. 282). It monitors States' compliance with the abovementioned 1966 and 1997 Recommendations on the teaching personnel, based on States' reports answering a questionnaire. Its mandate includes the examination of allegations from national and international teachers' organisations on violations of the Recommendations in ILO and UNESCO Member States.

4.2.3.3 Regional Protection

At the regional level, there are three systems of human rights protection, as we know (European, American, African).

In the European region, the right to education was added to the ECHR in 1952 by the laconic and twisted wording of its first Protocol Article 2 (see Appendix C) – a *Formulierungsanomalie*, noted Bannwart-Maurer (1975, p. 74). The European Social Charter addresses the right to education in Article 17.1, but education is mentioned in other provisions (Articles 9, 10, 15.1).[403] Its application is monitored by the European Committee of Social Rights that, with the CoESCR, are the two international bodies dedicated exclusively to the protection of economic, social and cultural rights.

In the American region, according to Article 19.6 of the Protocol of San Salvador,[404] the right to education (Article 13) is one of the economic, social and cultural rights (besides Trade Union Rights, Article 8) to which applies the system of individual petitions governed by Article 44 through 51 and 61 through 69 of the ACHR.[405] There is a Special Rapporteur on Economic, Social, Cultural, and Environmental Rights.

In the African region, the mandates of the African Commission on Human and Peoples' Rights and the Court on Human and Peoples' Rights include the protection of the right to education as laid down in the African Charter on Human and Peoples' Rights and in the African Charter on the Rights and Welfare of the Child. The latter established an African Committee of Experts on the Rights and Welfare of the Child too. The Economic Community of West African States (ECOWAS) Court of Justice can also examine claims on human rights violations. The East African Court of Justice (EACJ)[406] is one of the organs established by the Treaty for the Establishment of the East African Community (2001), according to which: "The Partner States undertake to abide by the principles of good governance, including adherence to the principles of democracy, the rule of law, social justice and the maintenance of universally accepted standards of human rights" (Article 7.2). However: "The Court shall have such other original, appellate, human rights and other jurisdiction as will be determined by the Council at a suitable subsequent date. To this end, the Partner States shall conclude a protocol to operationalise the extended jurisdiction" (Article 27.2).

In the Asia-Pacific region, a regional system of human rights protection was not yet established, but there is the ASEAN Intergovernmental Commission on Human Rights, the ASEAN Commission on the Promotion and Protection of the Rights of Women and Children,[407] and the SAARC Technical Committee on Women, Youth and Children.[408]

Within the context of the League of Arab States,[409] there are the Arab Permanent Committee on Human Rights, the Arab Human Rights Committee, and the Arab Childhood Committee (see 2.5.6.2).

Within the context of the OIC,[410] there are the Independent Permanent Human Rights Commission and the Islamic Committee on the Rights of the Child.

4.2.3.4 Case Law

The justiciability of economic, social and cultural rights has been controversial for a long time, in the context of the Cold War, growing from the 1950s (see Chatton, 2013), which influenced the dissociation of the two International Covenants in 1952 (instead of just one, as the UN General Assembly had first decided). In effect, while Western countries (market economies) put civil and political rights first, the Eastern bloc of socialist/communist countries (centrally planned economies) put economic, social and cultural rights first.

The main arguments voiced against the justiciability of economic, social and cultural rights are the following ones: they are vaguely worded, they demand high investments, being only societal goals, programmatic; the intervention of Courts infringes upon the separation of powers. The controversy became legally groundless, especially after the adoption, in 2008, of the Optional Protocol to the International Covenant on Economic, Social and Cultural Rights on a communications procedure.[411] It dismantled "a myth whereby economic, social and cultural rights, including the right to education, are not justiciable and thus 'not-quite-rights'", remarked Tomaševski (2005b, p. 226). There are not *bourgeois* and *socialist* rights, but simply *human* rights. The denial of economic, social or cultural rights is not merely a *social injustice* against the poorest members of society, but a *violation of their rights.*

The CoESCR noted, in its GC 9 on "The domestic application of the Covenant" (E/C.12/1998/24)[412]: "The Covenant [ICESCR] contains no direct counterpart to Article 2.3 (b) of the International Covenant on Civil and Political Rights which obligates States Parties to, *inter alia*, 'develop the possibilities of judicial remedy'" (para. 3). Nevertheless:

> 10. ... The Committee has already made clear that it considers many of the provisions in the Covenant to be capable of immediate implementation. Thus, in General Comment N°. 3 it cited, by way of example, Articles 3, 7 (a) (i), 8, 10.3, 13.2 (a), 13.3, 13.4 and 15.3. [...] While the general approach of each legal system needs to be taken into account, there is no Covenant right which could not, in the great majority of systems, be considered to possess at least some significant justiciable dimensions.

An indirect way for judicial appeal may be the principle of the interdependence of human rights, if demonstrated the connection between the exercise of an economic, social or cultural right and the exercise of another right whose justiciability is indisputable. In effect, some civil and political rights have mixed content, i.e. their implementation calls for measures in the field of the economic, social and cultural rights.

There is already a significant Case Law on economic, social and cultural rights, in all continents.

In its Resolution 37/13 of 22 March 2018,[413] the CHR:

> 14. *Welcomes* the steps taken at the national level to implement economic, social and cultural rights, including the enactment of

> appropriate legislation and adjudication by national courts, and in this regard underlines the need to consider justiciability when determining the best way to give domestic legal effect to the rights in the International Covenant on Economic, Social and Cultural Rights;

The most important international Case Law on the right to education is that of the ECHR (see European Court of Human Rights, 2020), being the most significant contribution of the European Education Law to International Education Law. It represents a kind of "'Crucial experiments' – those able to discriminate particularly sharply between the two paradigms" (Kuhn, 1962, p. 153), having a far-reaching significance for the interpretation of the right to education in general.

The jurisprudence of the ECHR was pronounced by its organs (the former European Commission of Human Rights and the European Court of Human Rights, now merged in a permanent Court). Its principles were established mainly in the following classical Cases:
- *Case "relating to certain aspects of the laws on the use of languages in education in Belgium"* (1968)
- *Case Kjeldsen, Busk Madsen and Pedersen* (1976)
- *Case Tyrer* (1978)
- *Case Campbell and Cosans* (1982)

Also, the Case Law of the European Committee of Social Rights is already significant (see Council of Europe, 2015).

Within the European Union, the founding treaties of the European Communities, in the 1950s, did not refer to education. However, the progress and needs of the European integration project compelled the increasing community intervention in the overall field of education. The Court of Justice of the European Communities (now Court of Justice of the European Union), after having laid down the foundations of a community legal system of protection of the fundamental rights, in its decision on the *Case Stauder* (1969), recognised a community right to education, based principally on Articles 118 and 128 of the European Economic Community Treaty, in the following main cases:
- *Case Donato Casagrande* (1974)
- *Case Forcheri* (1983)
- *Case Gravier* (1985)
- *Case Barra and Case Balizot* (1988)

The jurisprudence of the Court of Justice of the European Communities caused a turn in the community status of education.

It is worth noting that the ACHR (Article 63.1) gives the Inter-American Court of Human Rights broad competence to decide on reparations for human rights violations. The Court has produced an abundant, original and diverse jurisprudence that goes far beyond traditional compensation (see Appendix D.10).

Constitutional jurisprudence has often played a decisive role in protecting and developing the right to education. Here are some examples:

- The Constitution of India[414] refers to education several times, but a right to education was not formally provided for, although it had initially been listed as a fundamental right by the Fundamental Rights Subcommittee of the Constituent Assembly, in 1947. In 1992, however, the Supreme Court of India said in *Case Miss Mohini Jain vs State Of Karnataka And Ors on 30 July, 1992 (1992 AIR 1858, 1992 SCR (3) 658)*,[415] concerning fees charged by private schools: "The right to education flows directly from right to life. The right to life under Article 21 and the dignity of an individual cannot be assured unless it is accompanied by the right to education" (1.07).

  In 1993, in *Case Unni Krishnan, J.P. And Ors. Etc. ... vs State Of Andhra Pradesh And Ors. ... on 4 February, 1993 (1993 AIR 2178, 1993 SCR (1) 594)*,[416] by answering the question "Whether the Constitution of India guarantees a fundamental right to education to its citizens?", the Supreme Court said:

  > 31. Right to education is not stated expressly as a fundamental right in Part Ill [of the Constitution]. This Court has, however, not followed the rule that unless a right is expressly stated as a fundamental right, it cannot be treated as one. Freedom of Press is not expressly mentioned in Part III, yet it has been read into and inferred from the freedom of speech and expression.

  In the wake of this jurisprudence, the Constitution of India was amended in 2002, and an Article 21A was added, so worded: "The State shall provide free and compulsory education to all children of the age of six to fourteen years in such manner as the State may, by law, determine". However, the Right of Children to Free and Compulsory Education Act (RTE Act)[417] was passed only in 2009, coming into effect in 2010.
- In 2008, the Constitutional Court of the Republic of Indonesia concluded in *Case N°13/PUU-VI/2008*[418]:

  > [3.16] Considering that as long as the Constitution still requires to prioritize the education budget of 20% of the State Budget (APBN) and the Regional Budget (APBD), regardless of the calculation method, then for the Court – as the protection of the 1945 Constitution – cannot but state

> that a norm of law is contrary to the 1945 Constitution if such norm of law does not respect the obligation. [...] Therefore, in order to uphold the authority of the Constitution as the highest law in accordance with the principle of constitutionalism in the nation of laws, as referred to in Article 1 paragraph (3) of the 1945 Constitution, the Court must declare that all provisions of the 2008 APBN-P Law concerning the education budget is contrary to the Constitution 1945. As a result of not meeting the calculation of the education budget of at least 20% of the State Budget (APBN), the overall calculation of the budget in the 2008 APBN-P Law is unconstitutional.

- In 2010, the Constitutional Court of Colombia (*C-376-10*)[419] found that an Education Act allowing to charge fees for primary education was unconstitutional. Complying with the Court's Decision, the Government decreed that education shall be free in public institutions at the primary and secondary levels.
- In 2013, in *Case Movimento Creche para Todos vs Municipality of São Paulo*, the Court of Justice of the State of São Paulo, Brazil, reversed a lower court's ruling and decided (N° 0150735-64.2008.8.26.0002, 16/12/2013)[420] that the city of São Paulo should provide at least 150,000 new places in early childhood education units by 2016, for children aged five years old and under.
- In 2015, the Eastern Cape High Court, Grahamstown, South Africa, in *Case Tripartite Steering Committee and Another v Minister of Basic Education and Others (1830/2015) [2015] ZAECGHC 67; 2015 (5) SA 107 (ECG); [2015] 3 All SA 718 (ECG) (25 June 2015)*,[421] recalling previous Case Law, agreed "that the right to basic education, in order to be meaningful, includes 'such issues as infrastructure, learner transport, security at schools, nutrition and such related matters'" ([17]). In effect: "The right to education is meaningless without teachers to teach, administrators to keep schools running, desks and other furniture to allow scholars to do their work, textbooks from which to learn and transport to and from school at State expense in appropriate cases" ([18]).

Besides the jurisprudence of international and national Higher Courts,[422] several GCs/GRs of the UN Committees, notably the CoESCR and the CoRC, have also contributed to the normative development of the right to education. The same should be said of the doctrine elaborated by the first Special Rapporteur on the Right to Education, in particular, as well as of the *Limburg Principles on the Implementation of the International Covenant on Economic, Social and Cultural Rights* (1986) and the *Maastricht Guidelines on Violations of Economic, Social and Cultural Rights* (1997).

4.2.3.5 NGOs

There are plentiful NGOs dedicated to the right to education. Among them are:

- *Right to Education Initiative*
  At the origins of the Right to Education Initiative was the Right to Education Project launched by the first Rapporteur on the Right to Education, Katarina Tomaševski, in 2000. After her death, it was relaunched in 2008 by five NGOs. Its multilingual electronic site[423] is an exceptional source of information and documentation.
- *Platform NGOs – Droit à l'Éducation*
  This large NGO Platform for the Right to Education, based in Geneva, includes among its objectives to support the work of the Special Rapporteur on the Right to Education.[424]
- *Global Campaign for Education*
  It is an active movement in about 100 countries.[425]
- *Human Rights Education Association* (HREA)
  HREA presents itself as a global human rights education and training centre.[426]
- *Organisation Internationale pour le Droit à l'Éducation et la Liberté d'Enseignement* (OIDEL)
  The OIDEL (International Organisation for the Right to Education and Freedom of Education) has been created in 1985 by forty political personalities, educational experts and parents.[427]
- *Association Mondiale pour l'École Instrument de Paix* (EIP)
  The EIP (World Association for the School as an Instrument of Peace) was founded in Geneva in 1967 by Jacques Mühlethaler. In 1987, it created the International Training Centre for Human Rights and Peace Teaching (CIFEDHOP) that is now focused on training on the Universal Periodical Review (UPR).[428]
- *Fórum Mundial de Educação* (FME)
  The FME (World Education Forum) took place, for the first time, in 2001, in Porto Alegre (Brazil). It defines itself as "a movement for planetary citizenship and the universal right to education".[429]

There is an "NGO-UNESCO Liaison Committee",[430] whose legal base is Article XI of UNESCO's Constitution, as well as the "Directives concerning UNESCO's partnership with non-governmental organizations".[431]

4.3 Singularity of the Right to Education

The right to education displays some distinguishing features:

- It is the most complex human right
- It is the most empowering human right
- It is the only human right with a formally free element
- It is the only human right with a compulsory component
- Its normative content is among the most internationally developed
- Its normative content includes elements of all international legal sources

4.3.1 *It Is the Most Complex Human Right*

The right to education is the most complex human right for two main reasons: plural entitlement claims and multidimensional scope.

Nowak (2001) noted that "the right to education is one of the most complex human rights under present international law" (p. 268), because of the plurality of interests involved. Kiss (1975) remarked that the right to education "is a complex right" especially in the case of children, because "children are really its holders and beneficiaries, but its realisation is in charge of State, and parents have the choice of the modes of its practice" (p. 432). In effect:

- Parents claim that children are *their* children and they are *naturally* the first legitimately responsible for them.
- States claim that citizens are *their* citizens and they are *legally* the principal responsible for their human rights and the General Interest as well.
- Children and young, however, are the first and most legitimate holders of *their* right to education.

In addition to these three main players or constituencies, religions claim legitimacy too, in the name of their divine mission, as the right to education is subsidiary to the liberty of religion of parents.

As we know, the right to education entails a multiple normative content, demanded by the plurality of its aims that are inseparably individual and social, moral and instrumental, national and international.

4.3.2 *It Is the Most Empowering Human Right*

Human rights are qualified as empowerment rights. "Empowerment of the individual is the very essence of human rights" (Nowak, 2003, p. 25). They aim at endowing every human being with a minimum of power – the power to survival and self-determination – by conferring on them faculties to claiming and acting, with corresponding obligations (active or passive) from other(s), principally the State.

Jack Donnelly and Rhoda Howard (1988) identified a "set of ten essential rights that separately are intrinsically essential and together provide good proxies for almost all other rights", ranged in four categories (pp. 214, 215):

- *Survival rights*: rights to life, food and health care.

- *Membership rights*: family rights and the prohibition of discrimination.
- *Protection rights*: rights to *habeas corpus* and an independent judiciary.
- *Empowerment right*: rights to education, a free press, and freedom of association.

Where the right to education is concerned, they wrote:

> The key to social action in defence of rights, in our view, is an educated citizenry, able to spread its ideas and to organize in defence of its rights. [...]
>
> Empowerment rights are concerned principally with the goals of personal autonomy and efficacity; they allow the individual to determine the shape and direction of his or her life. Education provides much of the basic intellectual capacity that enables the individual to think seriously and critically about what it means to live a good life; to examine and appraise actions, institutions and ideas; and to choose a course of action on the basis of such appraisals.
>
> Schools are often used as an instrument of social control rather than personal liberation, as a mechanism to enforce intellectual conformity rather than foster creativity and autonomy. [...]
>
> Beyond the liberating potential of education, we have chosen the right to education as a key of measure of national human rights performance because of its link to other empowerment rights. [...]
>
> Education can also make important contributions to social mobility and thus to combatting class-based discrimination. [...]
>
> Finally, education can be important even to the protection of survival rights. [...] (pp. 234, 235, 236)

Indeed, the right to education may be considered the most empowering human right. In this regard, the CoESCR said in CG 13 (E/C.12/1999/10)[432]:

> 1. Education is both a human right in itself and an indispensable means of realizing other human rights. As an empowerment right, education is the primary vehicle by which economically and socially marginalized adults and children can lift themselves out of poverty and obtain the means to participate fully in their communities. [...] Increasingly, education is recognized as one of the best financial investments States can make. But the importance of education is not just practical: a welleducated, enlightened and active mind, able to wander freely and widely, is one of the joys and rewards of human existence.

In his inspiring book on *The Power of Education*, Power (2015) evokes Paulo Freire's *Pedagogy of the Oppressed*.

> According to Paulo Freire (1970), the process of learning is necessarily accompanied by the learner's increasing consciousness of his or her existential situation and the possibility of changing it, a process he called "conscientisation", but which today is more likely to be called "empowerment". His focus was on the human potential for creativity and freedom in the midst of politically, economically and culturally oppressive structures. In most basic education programmes, formal and non-formal, the focus is on the knowledge and life skills required for daily life. However, one should remember that an empowering education is one that deepens our awareness and understanding of the socio-cultural reality that shapes our lives and of one's capacity to transform that reality. Freire's *Pedagogy of the Oppressed* is to be understood as the dialectic relationship between action and reflection, as teaching that leads to critically reflective action. [...]
>
> In our shrinking global village, our collective well-being, even survival, will increasingly be dependent on the extent to which education contributes not only to the empowerment of individuals and nations, but to the entire global community. [...]
>
> There is much to be done to ensure that all (regardless of age, gender, ethnicity, nationality or social class) are empowered through an education based on the intellectual and ethical principles enshrined in the Constitution of UNESCO and the Universal Declaration of Human Rights. (pp. 4, 10, 13)[433]

4.3.3 *It Is the Only Human Right with a Formally Free Element*

Human rights are universal, by definition. They should, therefore, be universally accessible without discrimination, not only because of their human fundamentality but also because they are global public or common goods (see 4.8.7). However, the satisfaction of the rights requiring more expenditure and resources depends on the economic development of each country. That is why the ICESCR admits that their "full realisation" may be progressive (Article 2.1). There is, however a "minimum content" that must be assured (see 2.5.7.1).

The right to education is the only human right with a formally free element: primary education. The term 'free' is also used in Article 14.3.f of the ICCPR (and in Article 40.2.vi of the CRC) regarding the need for an interpreter in court, if necessary. In also appears in CRC Article 23.3, in respect of the rights of children with a mental or physical disability, but the gratuity is conditioned by "whenever possible".[434]

Primary free compulsory education is such a decisive priority that in ICESCR[435] Article 14 States Parties undertake "to work out and adopt a detailed plan of action for the progressive implementation [...] of the principle of compulsory education free of charge for all", where it is not yet assured. As far as other levels of the school system are concerned, as long as their attendance is not free, costs should not be an obstacle to their accessibility that should be fostered "by every appropriate means" (ICESCR Article 13.2).

It should be noted that previously the Declaration on Social Progress and Development (UN, 1969)[436] had proposed as objectives (italics added): "The eradication of illiteracy and the assurance of the right to universal access to culture, to free compulsory education at the elementary level and to *free education at all levels*; the raising of the general level of life-long education" (Article 10.e).

There are countries where the gratuity covers the whole public school system; 190 countries with legal provisions on free primary education; and 161 countries with legal provisions on free primary and secondary education (UNESCO/Right to Education Initiative, 2019, p. 100). According to the revised European Social Charter (Council of Europe),[437] States Parties undertake "to provide to children and young persons a free primary and education" (Article 17.2). The *Global Education Monitoring Report – 2017/8*[438] informs that less than one in five countries guarantee 12 years of free and compulsory education. This is a target (in part) proclaimed by the *Incheon Declaration* (see 4.6.1).

How free should basic education be? There are narrow and broad views.

Example of a narrow view is that expressed by the Constitutional Court of the Czech Republic in its Decision on *Case PL.US 25/94*, 13 June 1995[439]:

> The right to a free education means that the State shall bear costs for establishing schools and school facilities and also for their operation. Primarily this means that no tuition fees shall be charged, i.e. primary and secondary education shall be provided free of charge.
>
> The right to a free education cannot, however, mean that the State will bear all costs arising in connection with the implementation of the right to education. The specification of the extent to which schoolbooks and fundamental materials will be provided free of charge by the Government cannot be subordinated to the notion of free education.

Example of a broad view was the Decision, already quoted, of the Eastern Cape High Court, Grahamstown, South Africa, in *Case Tripartite Steering Committee and Another v Minister of Basic Education and Others* (*1830/2015*) [*2015*]

ZAECGHC 67; 2015 (5) SA 107 (ECG); [2015] 3 All SA 718 (ECG) (25 June 2015),[440] in 2015, saying "that the right to basic education, in order to be meaningful, includes 'such issues as infrastructure, learner transport, security at schools, nutrition and such related matters'" ([17]).

The Constitution of the Federative Republic of Brazil devotes to education generous provisions (Chapter III, Section I, Articles 205–214),[441] which include "assistance to students in all grades of basic education, by means of supplementary programmes providing school materials, transportation, food, and health care" (Article 208.VII).

The "Principles and Guidelines on the Implementation of Economic, Social and Cultural Rights in the African Charter on Human and Peoples' Rights"[442] adopted by the African Commission on Human and Peoples' Rights include:

> b. To implement policies to eliminate or reduce the costs of attending primary school which include the provision of stipends, providing free or subsidised uniforms (or lifting of uniform requirements), provision of free textbooks, provision of free or subsidised transportation or free school meals to encourage the attendance of poor children at school.

In a "Resolution of 13 November 2018 on "EU development assistance in the field of education" (2018/2081(INI)),[443] the European Parliament considered "that the condition of being 'free of charge' should apply not only to schooling itself but also to hidden costs, such as school supplies, transport and food" (para. 12).

In Finland[444]:

> In addition to free education, textbooks and other materials are free. Pupils also get a free school meal every day. Health care services are free as well; there are school nurses and dentists in schools. In addition, welfare services are free for pupils; schools have psychologists and social workers for those who need these services. If the school is not near home pupils get free school transportation.

Together with fighting poverty, relevant school learning and a teaching profession professionally and socially valued, an effective way to promote school attendance and to prevent school drop-out is making it really free, in particular by providing for transports, textbooks and other learning material, individual support, meals, health care, every necessary affirmative action, as well as a respectful and friendly environment.

4.3.4 *It Is the Only Human Right with a Compulsory Component*

Israel's Supreme Court Sitting as The High Court of Justice noted in *Case Abu Libdeh v. Minister of Education* (*HCJ5373/08*),[444] in 2011, quoting a previous Case:

> 27. ... The right to education is a complex right. It has an aspect of a human right, against which stands a "human duty" which must be exercised within the framework of compulsory education. [...] Rarely does the law enforce the realization of human rights. Such is the right to education.

Elementary/primary education/school must be "compulsory", as provided for by UDHR Article 26.1, CADE Article 4.a, ICESCR Article 13.2 and 14 and CRC Article 28.1.[445] Nowak (1995) underlined that "the right to education is the only human right for which international law stipulates a corresponding duty, that is, *compulsory education* until the end of primary education" (p. 204). He noted: "This phenomenon may be explained by the fact that in many Western States compulsory education was introduced long before education was recognized as a human right" (Nowak, 2001, p. 253). And to add: "Compulsory education is an important means by which the state protects children against their parents and all forms of economic exploitation" (p. 262). The term 'compulsory' is applied also in the Convention on the Elimination of All Forms of Discrimination against Women (UN, 1979)[446] that commands "to make the registration of marriages in an official registry compulsory" (Article 16.2).

However, the term was challenged within the Commission on Human Rights, during the *travaux préparatoires* of the UDHR, in particular at its 3rd session (Lake Success, May-June 1948). The Indian Delegation (Hansa Metha) objected that the term was not suitable in a Declaration of Rights; also, it could undermine the liberty of parents. René Cassin explained that it meant only that nobody could, primarily the family and the State, make access to elementary education difficult for children, any other idea of constraint being excluded. Eleanor Roosevelt (President of the Commission) and Pierre Lebar (UNESCO's representative) further explained that the term did not question the right of parents to choose their children's schools. Nevertheless, its inclusion was approved by only eight votes in favour, against seven. The CoESCR reaffirmed in its GC 11 (E/C.12/1999/4)[447]: "The element of compulsion serves to highlight the fact that neither parents, or guardians, or the State are entitled to treat as optional the decision as to whether the child should have access to primary education" (para. 6).

A human right is not necessarily undermined if an element of its content is made compulsory when it is at stake a legitimate public interest not incompatible with the respect of the substance of that right. Also, vaccination and voting, for instance, might be made compulsory. Danton said, intervening at the French National Convention in 1793: "In the Republic, no one is free to be ignorant: a child belongs to the Republic before belonging to his father" (in Baczko, 2000, p. 416). In this regard, Karl J. Partsch (1966) observed: "A democracy without compulsory education is, therefore, unthinkable. [...] The right of the individual to education does not include then the right to spiritual abstinence" (pp. 232, 238). The Constitutional Court of Colombia remarked (*C-309/97*)[448] that "the compulsory basic education clearly aims to strengthen the choice capacities of the person when she reaches adulthood". Summing up: Education, especially basic education, is both a human right and a common good.

Notwithstanding, the principle of compulsory schooling has not ceased to be put in question, particularly its duration. The first Special Rapporteur on the Right to Education informed (E/CN.4/2002/60)[449]: "The Special Rapporteur is receiving increasing numbers of letters questioning the notion of compulsory education from the human rights perspective" (para. 48). In effect, "as was implicitly recognized when the Universal Declaration of Human Rights was being drawn up [...] there is obviously a limit in every country beyond which education cannot be made compulsory without at the same time offending the very idea of education as a 'right'" (UNESCO, 2000, pp. 51, 52).

To sum up: The rationale of the principle of compulsory education, as an element of the right to education, is the protection of the best interest of the child (even if he/she is not aware of it), against opposing parents, whatever their motives, and against her/his exploitation as workforce or for other harmful and unlawful purposes (as provided for by CRC Article 32.1). There is also a legitimate public interest in it, without making education a monopoly of State.

4.3.5 *Its Normative Content Is among the Most Internationally Developed*

The CoESCR observed in its GC 13 (E/C.12/1999/10): "Article 13, the longest provision in the Covenant [ICESCR], is the most wide-ranging and comprehensive Article on the right to education in international human rights law" (para. 2). CRC Articles 28 and 29 are also among its most extensive provisions. The IEL is one of the most developed branches of IHRL, as Pius Gebert (1996) highlighted (with reference to this author):

> With the exception of the International Labour Law that, thanks to the legislative and jurisdictional action of the ILO, during decades, is perhaps the specific human rights field having the densest international normative network, also the International Education Law presents already today an extensive normative density. Especially thanks to the UNESCO's

> normative action, it is nowadays being shaped an "International Code of Education Law". (p. 63)[450]

As already said, there are many more than a hundred international instruments with provisions concerning the right to education.

4.3.6 *Its Normative Content Includes Elements of All International Legal Sources*

Some international sources of the right to education are *hard Law* (formally binding), but they are mostly *soft Law* (not formally binding). Its normative content includes non-derogable elements, others that have become Customary Law and some others qualifying as General Principles of Law and *Jus Cogens* (Peremptory Law).

Non-derogable elements

The ICCPR[451] includes among its non-derogable provisions Article 18, according to which (para. 4): "The States Parties to the present Covenant undertake to have respect for the liberty of parents and, when applicable, legal guardians to ensure the religious and moral education of their children in conformity with their own convictions". This liberty is also recognised in the ICESCR that doesn't include a clause on reservations or derogations (see HRI/MC/2005/5, 2005[452]; Ssenyonjo, 2016, 1.86–1.96). The CADE doesn't admit "any reservation" (Article 9). The ACHR includes the rights of the child among its non-derogable rights.

Customary Law

Following Gebert (1996), "it is safe to say that there are two educational principles that have become part of Customary Law, namely the right to free and compulsory primary education, and the right not to be discriminated against in the enjoyment of educational rights" (p. 45). This opinion is shared by Al-Samman (1987) and Beiter (2006, p. 17), for instance. In the opinion of Pierre-Marie Dupuy (2007) too: "Thus, to the extent that UNESCO's promotion of respect for human dignity encourages States to acknowledge equal access to education as an imperative aim and to promote such equality of access in practice, it further strengthens the right to education as a high-priority principle of customary law" (p. 355).

The USA Constitution does not formally recognise the right to education, but several Courts use international standards as guiding principles to interpret the domestic constitutional and legal norms. However, according to Constance de la Vega (1994), "that is not enough. Many of those standards have risen to the level of customary international law and should be considered as such by the courts" (p. 41). In her opinion: "The right to education and the right to enjoy it without discrimination are examples of economic, social and cultural rights that should be considered part of customary international law" (p. 44).

The primacy of the best interests of the child has become Customary Law. This status results, in particular, from the fact that the CRC is a treaty that is already binding for virtually all countries worldwide and whose Article 3 – which is the most far-reaching international formulation of the principle of the primacy of the best interests of the child – has not been subject to reservations. It was also recognised in numerous international legal instruments, Constitutions and Laws, being widely applied by Courts. Well, nobody could doubt that a crucial dimension of the best interests of the child is the right to education.

General Principles of Law

There is no cutting between Customary Law and General Principles of Law. If the "principle of compulsory education free of charge for all" (ICESCR Article 14) has won a so strong legal force, it seems to deserve General Principle of Law status. Also, two Principles of the Ethics of the Right to Education that will be proposed (see 5.2) deserve to be qualified as General Principles of Law, namely:

- Primacy of the best interests of the subject of the right to education
  This principle reflects the principles of the primacy of the human rights subject and, in particular, of the best interests of the child. The primacy of the human rights subject is an undisputable General Principle of the IHRL. Also, the primacy of the best interests of the child "was rightly described as a 'general principle of law'" (Rubellin-Devichi, 1994, p. 260). Joachim Wolf (1992) remarked: "The 'best interests of the child' is a standard without precedent in international legal instruments" (p. 127). It may be included among "the general principles of law recognized by civilized nations" that Article 38.1.c of the Statute of the International Court of Justice considers as being a source of International Law (p. 132).
- Development of the human personality: free, full, harmonious
  The principle of the development of the human personality, in addition to meeting the pedagogical ideal proclaimed by the great authors in the history of the pedagogic thought, necessarily derives from the principle of the primacy of the best interests of the subject of the right to education and is to be found in main international standard-setting instruments and others relating to the right to education, as well as in a large number of Constitutions and General Laws of Education.

Even the third principle of the Ethics of the Right to Education, as thereafter proposed, could be qualified as General Principle of Law, insofar as it reaffirms and renews the traditional primacy of moral education.

Jus Cogens

We know what *Jus Cogens* means (see 2.5.7.2) and will know the consubstantiality between human dignity and the right to education (see 4.5.3). Is there anything else necessary to recognise to the core content of the right to education the normative force of *Jus Cogens*?

4.4 Priority of the Right to Education

4.4.1 *Human Primacy of Education*

The human primacy of education is an idea crossing the history of the pedagogic thought. The metaphors of the human being as soil to be cultivated, or clay to be shaped, or blank slate, or white paper to be written, are recurrent. For example, John Locke wrote in *An Essay Concerning Human Understanding* (1690)[453]: "Let us then suppose the mind to have no ideas in it, to be like white paper with nothing written on it. How then does it come to be written on?" (Chapter I, para. 2). Here are some historical examples of recognition of the primacy of education:

- Plato (1997) wrote in his *Republic*: "You know, don't you, that the beginning of any process is most important, especially for anything young and tender? It's at that time that it is most malleable and takes on any pattern one wishes to impress on it" (377b).
- Aristotle (2000) wrote in his *Politics*: "No one will doubt that the legislator should direct his attention above all to the education of youth, or that the neglect of education does harm to states" (Book VIII, 1337a).
- Comenius wrote in his *Didactica Magna* (The Great Didactic, 1657)[454]: "One of the first lessons the Scriptures gives us is this one: under the sun there is not any other more effective way to correct the human corruptions than the youth's right education" (p. 14).
- Locke (1693) wrote in *Some Thoughts Concerning Education* (§ 1):

> I think I may say that of all the men we meet with nine parts of ten are what they are, good or evil, useful or not, by their education. Tis that which makes the great difference in mankind. The little, or almost insensible impressions on our tender infancies, have very important and lasting consequences.

- Rousseau wrote in the first lines of *Émile* (1762): "All that we lack at birth, all that we need when we come to man's estate, is the gift of education" (Rousseau, 1993, p. 6).
- Danton affirmed during the French Revolution (already quoted): "After the bread, education is the first need of the people".
- Kant (1803) is very often quoted: "Man is the only being who needs education. [...] Man can only become a man by education. He is merely what education makes of him" (para. 1).

The universal conscience of the primacy of education – especially first education and moral education – is reverberated in Proverbs of the wisdom of many peoples and has prominent spokespersons. For example, a Chinese proverb (already quoted) says[455]: "If your plan is for one year, plant rice. If your plan is for ten years, plant trees. If your plan is for one hundred years, educate children" (Kuan Chung, 7th century BC). Lyndon Johnson, who was USA President (1963–1968), is quoted as having said: "At the desk where I sit, I have learned one great truth. The answer for all our national problems – the answer to all the problems of the world – comes to a single word. That word is education".[456] Abraham Lincoln, USA President in the 19th century (1861–1865), is quoted as having said (but the authorship is uncertain): "If you think education is expensive, try ignorance".[457] Nelson Mandela is frequently quoted too: "Education is the most powerful weapon we can use to change the world".[458]

In 1988, a Conference of 75 Nobel Prize Laureates took place in Paris, welcomed by President François Mitterrand and Elie Wiesel (survivor of the concentration camps and Nobel Peace Prize in 1986), to reflect on "Promises and threats at the dawn of the 21st century".[459] One of their conclusions was the following: "Education should become the absolute priority of all budgets and should help to value all aspects of human creativity". Damásio (2018) agrees: "Education, in the broadest sense of the term, is the obvious way forward" (p. 225).

That is why, after the World War II, a UNESCO Report concluded: "The United Nations will not succeed unless the minds of men are moved by new ideas, their hearts stirred by new affections, their wills enlisted to establish a new human unity" (UNESCO, 1947, p. 260). Roger-Pol Droit (2005) remarked:

> Education comes first in the acronym UNESCO [...]. This is not by chance. The order may be taken literally: education comes before all the rest. In a sense, it represents the unique task. It is involved in everything, and everything flows from it. Whatever the goal envisaged, its attainment depends on education. (p. 57)

Summing up: The human primacy of education is an anthropological, moral, psychological, economic, political and legal one.

- *Anthropological* – for human beings are essentially educable. The pedagogical ontology is "ontology of the still-not-being [...] a very utopic ontology" (Ernst Bloch, as cited in Münster, 1997, pp. 142, 144).
- *Moral* – for human beings need moral values to give sense to their lives and to regulating collective living. Each human being feeds on the values and sentiments deposited in the "fount of the being" of its infancy (Bachelard, 1960, p. 98).
- *Psychological* – for we begin by being what education makes of us, for us, with us or without us, or in spite of us, even against us. "Yes, I'm myself as I have resulted from all", said the Portuguese poet Fernando Pessoa.[460]
- *Economic* – for the development is driven by the 'human capital'. Bill Gates has included in its book *The Road Ahead* (1996) a chapter titled *Chapter 9 – Education: The Best Investment.*
- *Political* – for "man is by nature a political animal", as Aristotle (2000) famously wrote. "And since the whole city has one end, it is manifest that education should be one and the same for all, and that it should be public, and not private" (1253a, 1337a).
- *Legal* – for all the previous reasons, so that it has become a human right whose priority is recognised by the IHRL, has been affirmed by the jurisprudence and is supported by doctrine.

4.4.2 *The Priority of the Right to Education Rediscovered*

There are three human rights whose relative priority is generally recognised, namely: the right to life, the right to education and the right to development.

- The right to life is the most fundamental among human rights, insofar as it is the biological condition of all other rights (see 2.6.3).
- The right to development is a right that may be qualified, in accordance with the former UN Independent Expert on the Right to Development (Arjun Sengupta), as a "meta-right", a concept used by Amartya Sen, Nobel Prize of Economy (1998).[461] According to the Independent Expert[462]:

> A meta-right to something x can be defined as the right to have policies p (x), that genuinely pursues the objective of making the right to x realizable. [...] The outcomes of the process of development are human rights while the process of development that leads to these outcomes are also human rights. [...] Therefore, the right to the process of development can be regarded as a meta-right. [...]
>
> It is probably much better to describe the right to development as the right to a process of development, as a "basic right" in the sense in

which Henry Shue used this term (See Henry Shue, *Basic Rights*, Princeton, 1980). A basic right is one the enjoyment of which is essential to the enjoyment of all other rights.

The right to development is, therefore, an individual and collective right to a process of development respecting and favouring the realisation of all human rights for all. The Working Group on the Right to Development established by the former Commission on Human Rights (Resolution 1998/72) elaborated a Draft Convention on the Right to Development (A/HRC/WG.2/21/2)[463] whose first general principle reads: "Human person and people-centred development: the human person and people are the central subjects of development and should be the active participants and beneficiaries of the right to development" (Article 3.a).

In the opinion of Mohammed Bedjaoui, the right to development is "the alpha and omega of human rights, the first and last human right, the beginning and the end, the means and the goal of human rights, in short, it is the *core right* from which all the other stem [...] and its natural foundation is as a corollary of the right to life". It is a right that is, "by its nature, so incontrovertible that it *should* be regarded as belonging to *jus cogens*" (as cited in Steiner & Alston, 2000, pp. 1317, 1321, 1322, 1323).

– Nevertheless, the right to education is of transcendent importance for *human* life and development. It is said to be an unlocking, enabling, multiplier right, an equalising force. It is the key to the motor of human development, understood in the fullness of its individual, collective, cultural, political, economic, ecological dimensions.

That is why the European Parliament, in the "Resolution of 13 November 2018 on EU development assistance in the field of education (2018/2081(INI))",[464] urged "that education be placed at the centre of the development policies of the European Union and its Member States" (para. 2), and called "on the Union and its Member States to devote at least half of their education aid to basic education by 2030" (para. 13).

The Draft Convention on the Right to Development does not highlight the paramountcy of the right to education but, according to the Jomtien Declaration (1990),[465] the "energy and funding directed to basic education are perhaps the most profound investment in people and in the future of a country which can be made" (Article 9.1). Therefore, it is time "to return, after decades of strategies marked by a narrow economism, to the very heart of development, i.e. the human being", which is "the key to any process of empowerment, individual or collective", as wrote UNESCO Director-General (at the time Federico Mayor) in the Preface to its *Medium-term Strategy, 1996–2001* (28 C/4).[466]

The priority of the right to education – that is relative because of the human rights interdependence – was repeatedly invoked during the *travaux préparatoires* of its major international norms. For example, during the drafting of the ICESCR, the Indian Delegation (Hansa Metha) said at the Commission on Human Rights, 7th Session, 226th meeting (E/CN.4/SR.226, 27 June 1951),[467] that: "Education was the most fundamental of all human rights; without education, man was little better than an animal" (p. 21). At the 229th meeting (E/CN.4/SR.229, 28 June 1951),[468] the Greek Delegation (Constantin Eustathiades) said:

> In that respect, free and compulsory primary education was the keystone of all the rights which would be recognized in the Covenant. What would the "adequate standard of living", the "improvement of living conditions" or the "free development of the personality" amount to in a world in which the illiterate were to be counted in millions? (p. 6)

When the draft ICESCR Article 14 was examined by the UN General Assembly Third Committee, at its 12th session, in 1957 (A/C.3/SR.790),[469] UNESCO Director-General (René Maheu) affirmed, in response to some questions arisen about the exceptional character of ICESCR Article 14:

> 12. Finally, it had been maintained that it was unnecessary to include a special implementing article as no such article had been included for the other rights. The right to primary education was, however, a special case. It was a fundamental right, without which the others could hardly be exercised, and it should be given priority over all other.

Other interventions could be quoted, like those of Delegates of Pakistan, Ghana, Greece, Chile, Japan, Afghanistan, Belgium, Ceylon, Egypt, Brazil.

The relative priority of the right to education is recognised by the IHRL that includes among the aims of the right to education "the strengthening of respect for human rights and fundamental freedoms" (UDHR Article 26.2).

At the national level, some national Constitutions determine how much budget the State should allocate to education. For example, Brazil's Constitution (1988, with amendments through 2017)[470] provides: "The Union shall apply annually not less than eighteen per cent of its tax revenues, and the States, Federal District and Counties at least twenty-five per cent of their tax revenues, including revenues resulting from transfers, for maintenance and development of education" (Article 212). As already mentioned, the Constitution of the Republic of Indonesia (1945, with amendments through 2002)[471] commands: "The State shall give priority to the education budget by allocating at least twenty per cent of the State's as well as of regional budgets to meet the requirements of implementing national education" (Article 31.4). In Mexico, according to the *Ley General de Educación* (General Education Act, 2018),[472] the State, at the Federation, States and Municipalities levels – should not allocate less than 8% of the GNP to public education.

The relative priority of the right to education has been reaffirmed by international and national Courts. For example, in 1954, the USA Supreme Federal Court said in *Case Brown v. Board of Education, 347 U.S. 483 (1954)*, its most famous Judgement, which was decisive to put an end to racial segregation[473]:

> Today, education is perhaps the most important function of state and local governments. Compulsory school attendance laws and the great expenditures for education both demonstrate our recognition of the importance of education to our democratic society. It is required in the performance of our most basic public responsibilities, even service in the armed forces. It is the very foundation of good citizenship. Today it is a principal instrument in awakening the child to cultural values, in preparing him for later professional training, and in helping him to adjust normally to his environment. In these days, it is doubtful that any child may reasonably be expected to succeed in life if he is denied the opportunity of an education. Such an opportunity, where the state has undertaken to provide it, is a right which must be made available to all on equal terms.

The same Court said in *Case Wisconsin v. Yoder, 406 U.S. 205 (1972)*[474]:

> There is no doubt as to the power of a State, having a high responsibility for education of its citizens, to impose reasonable regulations for the control and duration of basic education. See, e. g., *Pierce v. Society of Sisters*, 268 U.S. 510, 534 (1925). Providing public schools ranks at the very apex of the function of a State.

In *Case Plyler v. Doe, 457 U.S. 202 (1982)*, the US Supreme Court affirmed[475]:

> Public education is not a "right" granted to individuals by the Constitution. *San Antonio Independent School Dist. v. Rodriguez, 411 U.S. 1, 35 (1973)*. But neither is it merely some governmental "benefit" indistinguishable from other forms of social welfare legislation. Both the importance of education in maintaining our basic institutions, and the lasting impact of its deprivation on the life of the child, mark the distinction. The "American people have always regarded education and [the] acquisition of knowledge as matters of supreme importance". *Meyer v. Nebraska, 262 U.S. 390, 400 (1923)*. We have recognized "the public schools as a most vital civic

institution for the preservation of a democratic system of government", *Abington School District v. Schempp, 374 U.S. 203, 230 (1963)* (BRENNAN, J., concurring), and as the primary vehicle for transmitting "the values on which our society rests". *Ambach v. Norwick, 441 U.S. 68, 76 (1979)*. "[A]s ... pointed out early in our history, ... some degree of education is necessary to prepare citizens to participate effectively and intelligently in our open political system if we are to preserve freedom and independence". *Wisconsin v. Yoder, 406 U.S. 205, 221 (1972)*.

The Supreme Court of Appeals of West Virginia said in *Case Pauley v. Kelly, 255 S.E.2d 859 (W. Va. 1979)*[476]:

> ... education is a fundamental constitutional right in this State [...].
>
> Our basic law makes education's funding second in priority only to payment of the State debt, and ahead of every other State function. Our Constitution manifests, throughout, the people's clear mandate to the Legislature, that public education is a prime function of our State government. We must not allow that command to be unheeded.

Quoting *Brown v. Board of Education*, the Supreme Court of Canada said in *Case The Queen v. Jones, [1986] 2 S.C.R. 284*[477]:

> 22. ... Whether one views it from an economic, social, cultural or civic point of view, the education of the young is critically important in our society. [...] Education is today a matter of prime concern to Government everywhere. [...] Indeed, in modern society, education has far-reaching implications beyond the province, not only at the national but at the international level.

Quoting *Brown v. Board of Education* too, the Supreme Court of India, in *Case Unni Krishnan v State of Andhra Pradesh 1993 AIR 2178; 1993 SCR (1) 594,*[478] in which was at stake the human and political value of education, highlighted "the fundamental significance of education to the life of an individual and the nation" and said: "That the right to education has been treated as one of transcendental importance in the life of an individual has been recognized not only in this country since thousands of years, but all over the world". It further said:

> It is the tyrants and bad rulers who are afraid of spread of education and knowledge among the deprived classes. Witness Hitler railing against universal education. He said: 'Universal education is the most corroding

> and disintegrating poison that liberalism has ever invented for its own destruction' (Rauschning, *The voice of destruction: Hitler speaks*). A true democracy is one where education is universal where people understand what is good for them and nation, and know how to govern themselves.

The Supreme Court of Appeal, South Africa, in *Case Minister of Basic Education v Basic Education for All (20793/2014) [2015] ZASCA 198; [2016] 1 All SA 369 (SCA); 2016 (4) SA 63 (SCA) (2 December 2015)*,[479] quoted Frederick Douglass, a former slave and eminent American human rights leader in the abolitionist movement who said: "Once you learn to read, you will be forever free" ([1]).

Regarding doctrine, here are some examples of recognition of the relative priority of the right to education:

- Commenting on the encyclical *Populorum Progressio* by Pope Paul VI (1967), René Maheu affirmed:

  > ... indeed, from the moment that we understand that there is no development other than that of the human being, by it and for it, we understand that education, science and culture are the foundation and the crowning, the driving principle and the valuing aim of development in its deepest nature [...]. All begins with education, because no appropriation, use or increasing the value of nature or society is possible without it, and that is the reason for the priority universally attached to it.

  These words were quoted by Fasi (1968) who wrote in turn:

  > ... if liberty is the essential and primordial condition for enjoying the other rights, it is certain that education is that that allows – as the Universal Declaration says – to achieve the full development of the human personality; it is the key to the whole development; it gives to the human being the means of being aware of its other rights, of looking for them and gaining them. (pp. 43, 39)

- In 1970, the Report of the Select Committee on Equal Educational Opportunity, United States Senate, titled *Toward Equal Education Opportunity*,[480] read:

  > The costs of inadequate education are, for the most part immeasurable. For the individual, educational failure means a lifetime of lost of opportunities. But the effects are visited on the Nation as well, for society as a whole pays for the under-education of a significant segment of the population. [...]

> Finally, the costs of poor education are not just limited to the present generation. The children of persons with inadequate education are themselves more likely to suffer the same educational and social consequences as their parents. (p. 171)

- Imre Szabo (1974) remarked that the right to education belongs "to the most prominent rights" because, "by interpreting the right to education as a human right the fundamental functions of which comprise *education for preserving and enforcing human rights*, we reach a correlation where human rights, so to say, *revert to themselves* through the medium of the right to education" (p. 36).
- In the opinion of Franciszek Przetacznik (1985):

> Among the individual human rights, the right to education is the most important of those rights, with the only exception of the right to life from which all human rights stem. The right to education is a prerequisite to the genuine enjoyment of almost all other human rights by an individual person. This right is a cornerstone of all human rights because if a person is not properly educated, he or she is unable to enjoy genuinely the other human rights. Accordingly, the realization of the right to education is the most elevating task which is imposed upon each individual as well as upon the State wherein such an individual lives. (p. 257)

- Gustav von Struve considered the right to life, the right to education and the right to the full development of the natural potentialities as "the three eternal and inalienable human rights" (as cited in Perschel, 1984, p. 550).
- Robert Badinter (1990) included the right to instruction in the "core content of human rights" (p. 186).
- James D. Wolfensohn (then World Bank President), Federico Mayor (then UNESCO Director-General), James G. Speth (then UNPD Administrator), Carol Bellamy (then UNICEF Executive Director) and Nafis Sadik (then UNPF Director-Executive) wrote together in 1996:

> We wish to stress our conviction that basic education for all is not only a human right but also the cornerstone of human development. Providing access to high-quality basic education is probably the single most effective means to ensure democracy, sustainable development and peace. (World Bank, 2005, p. 42)

Summing up, quoting CoESCR CG 11 (E/C.12/1999/4)[481]:

2. The right to education, recognized in Articles 13 and 14 of the Covenant, as well as in a variety of other international treaties, such as the Convention on the Rights of the Child and the Convention on the Elimination of All Forms of Discrimination against Women, is of vital importance.

The relative priority of the right to education has been rediscovered, in a way, by the International Community during the last decade of the 20th century, and gained unprecedented visibility on the International Agenda, as witness conferences, declarations, action programmes and other texts and initiatives. Among them (some already mentioned):

- In 1990, the World Conference on Education for All: Meeting Basic Learning Needs, assembled in Jomtien (Thailand),[482] adopted the Jomtien Declaration, according to which, let us recall: "All of society has a contribution to make, recognizing that time, energy and funding directed to basic education are perhaps the most profound investment in people and in the future of a country which can be made" (Article 9.1).
- In 1996, was published the Report *Learning: The treasure within* (Delors Report).
- In 1997, the Sub-Commission on Prevention of Discrimination and Protection of Minorities adopted a Resolution on "The realization of the right to education, including education in human rights", which read:

> *Noting* that the question of the right to education has not been sufficiently dealt with in the framework of the United Nations bodies responsible for the protection of human rights,
>
> *Noting with satisfaction* the developing international awareness of the importance of education, particularly in the field of human rights, for human development, [...]
>
> 2. *Decides* to place the question of the right to education, and particularly human rights education, on the agenda of the Sub-Commission for the duration of the United Nations Decade for Human Rights Education (1995–2004);
>
> 3. *Requests* Mr. Mustapha Mehedi to prepare, without incurring financial obligations, a working paper on the right to education, and particularly human rights education, for submission to the Sub-Commission at its fiftieth session, the purpose of the working paper being to explain the content of the right to education, taking account, in particular, of its social dimension and the freedoms it includes and its dual civil and

political rights and economic, social and cultural rights character, and to identify ways and means of promoting human rights education.

Mehedi remarked:

> The fact that the Sub-Commission on Prevention of Discrimination and Protection of Minorities, the Commission on Human Rights and the Committee on Economic, Social and Cultural Rights decided to study the question of the right to education and the right to human rights education may be considered historic, since this is the first time that this right has been studied in a systematic way by the human rights bodies. (E/CN.4/Sub.2/1999/10, Foreword)[483]

- In 1998, the Commission on Human Rights, following a Resolution concerning the implementation of the economic, social and cultural rights (Resolution 1998/33, 17 April),[484] decided to designate a Special Rapporteur on the Right to Education (Katarina Tomaševski).
- In 1999, the CoESCR devoted to ICESCR Articles 13 and 14, concerning the right to education, the GG 13 (E/C.12/1999/10) and the GC 11 (E/C.12/1999/4), respectively.
- Still in 1999, in the 'Foreword' to the UNICEF's Report on *The State of the World's Children* (UNICEF, 1999),[485] consecrated to education, the UN Secretary-General (at the time Kofi Annan) wrote: "Education is a human right with immense power to transform. On its foundation rest the cornerstones of freedom, democracy and sustainable human development". The UNICEF Report quoted this sentence from Mahbub ul Haq, who was a high official of the World Bank and created the "Human Development (HDI)" used by the United Nations Development Programme (UNDP) Annual Reports since 1993: "Education is the true essence of human development. Without education, development can be neither broad-based nor sustained" (p. 86).
- In 2000, a World Education Forum assembled in Dakar (Senegal), from 26 to 28 April, adopted the Dakar Framework for Action – Education for All: Meeting our Collective Commitments.
- Still, in 2000, the UNESCO devoted to the right to education its World Education Report titled *The right to education – Towards education for all throughout life.*
- In 2001, the UN General Assembly proclaimed "the ten-year period beginning on 1 January 2003 the United Nations Literacy Decade" (A/56/116).
- Still, in 2001, the CoRC devoted its first GC to the right to education (CRC/GC/2001/1, 17/04/2001, The aims of education, Article 29.1).

- In 2004, the UN General Assembly has launched a World Programme for Human Rights Education that is going on (Resolution 59/113).

It is also worth mentioning the World Education Forum launched in 2001 in Porto Alegre (Brazil).

According to the 2014 *My World – The United Nations Global Survey for a Better World – Celebrating 7 Million Voices*[486] (about 1 in 1,000 people on the planet, from 194 countries), which were asked "What would make *your* life better?" and should pick 6 out of 16 priorities:

> The overwhelming majority of the respondents prioritize "A good education". This is the case across all age groups, genders, education levels and HDI rankings. [...]
>
> The prevalence of the issue across different groups, countries and regions suggests that a good education is seen as the foremost issue needed to improve lives and that the lack of a good education has the potential to impede all other progress. While the MDGs have helped increase enrolment in primary school to nine out of every ten children in the world, the *My World* results suggest that access to quality education, including and beyond primary, remains a global priority and shared aspiration. (p. 19)

Someone gave the following justification: "Education allows you to dream, and it's the only thing that no one can take away from you, because it's completely in your mind" (p. 20).

The immediately following top priorities are better health, better jobs opportunities and an honest and responsive government.

Key is a term often used, especially in UN documents, to mean the paramount value of education. Sometimes it is said to be *a key*, other times it is called *the key*. For example:

- The UNICEF 1999 Report on *The State of the World's Children* affirmed: "Education, key to human and social development, needs to assume a place at the centre of nations' lives" (UNICEF, 1999, p. 65).
- In the *Millennium Report*, Kofi Annan (2000) stated: "Education is the key to the new global economy, from primary school on up to life-long learning. It is central to development, social progress and human freedom" (para. 97).
- The 2000 Dakar Framework for Action stated: "Education is a fundamental human right. It is the key to sustainable development and peace and stability within and among countries, and thus an indispensable means for effective participation in the societies and economies of the twenty-first century, which are affected by rapid globalization" (para. 6).

- The first Special Rapporteur on the Right to Education (Katarina Tomaševski) stressed in one of her annual reports: "Education is increasingly defined as the key to development and the right to education as the key to the enjoyment of many other human rights" (E/CN.4/2001/52, para. 79).[487]
- The right to education is "the key to everything", wrote Rosalyn Higgins, who was President of the International Court of Justice (Foreword, in Hausler, Urban, N. & McCorquodale, 2012).

Summing up, the right to education is a priority human right because:
- A human being is not born as the Greek goddess Athena, who came finished and adult out of the head of Zeus. It is the only being having a real aptitude for and a vital need of education.
- Everything in the life of a child, in particular, has educational effects, influencing the development of his/her personality and especially the formation of her/his moral conscience.
- The world is made by human beings, who are what they have in their heads and their hearts, generated by education, through which they learn the rights they have and how to claim, exercise and respect them.
- Education is the most powerful resource in the fight against poverty, oppression and all injustice and violence, as well as for the protection of the identity of indigenous peoples and the rights of all minorities.
- The right to education is the source of autonomy and citizenship, of utopia and rebelness, liberating peoples and the genius inherent in the inexhaustible perfectibility of the human species.

The human resonance of the right to education is condensed in these inspiring words of the Declaration of the Fourth International Conference on Adult Education (UNESCO, Paris, 1985)[488]:

> The right to learn is:
> the right to read and write;
> the right to question and analyze;
> the right to imagine and create;
> the right to read one's own world and to write history;
> the right to have access to educational resources;
> the right to develop individual and collective skills.
>
> The Paris Conference on Adult Education reaffirms the importance of this right.

> The right to learn is not a cultural luxury to be saved for some future date.
>
> It is not a right that will come only after the question of survival has been settled.
>
> It is not the next step to be taken once basic needs have been satisfied.
>
> The right to learn is an indispensable tool for the survival of humanity. [...]
>
> 'Learn' is the keyword.
>
> There can be no human development without the right to learn. [...]
>
> In short, the right to learn is one of the best contributions we can make to solving the crucial problems of humanity today.
>
> But the right to learn is not only an instrument of economic development; it must be recognized as one of the fundamental rights. The act of learning, lying as it does at the heart of all educational activity, changes human beings from objects at the mercy of events to subjects who create their own history.

The international priority accorded to the right to education means that education is no more seen as only a matter falling into the domestic and instrumental forum, but also as an ethical international concern. If the link between education, survival, work and economy has been the most socially and individually valued – and remains the most visible – the right to education is principally the most *humanising* human right.

4.4.3 *Right to Education and Human Dignity*

Human rights have an essential ethical dimension, by definition, because their source and sense is human dignity – the supreme value. The right to education has, however, an incomparable ethical density, for the following main reasons.

The objective foundation of human dignity is the human worth that consists in the species' perfectibility and the educability of its members.
Perfectibility or educability is the most distinctive attribute of the human species, as already explained, requiring the perfecting of its members through education as cultivation of the seeds of the highest aptitudes contained in the human genome, namely: rationality, liberty and creativity – for happier lives and better living together, enjoying our fabulous and powerful diversity.

Resorting to an informatic metaphor, we could say that human dignity is formed by a *hardware* that consists in the biological infrastructure of the perfectibility or educability of the species, genetically *programmed*, and by a *software* that consists in the perfecting of each of its members, culturally *programmable*, through education.

Therefore, we are born 'pre-human', premature, as our essential humanity is brought about by education.
A child is born as a *de-natured animal* that, if he/she is not *humanised*, becomes a *dis-figured human being*, as illustrated by the cases of so-called 'wild children' or 'wolf children'. He/she needs a *second birth* for a *second nature*, through education.

Johannes Giesinger (2012) argued that Kant thought of education as a process of overcoming of the child's animal nature, especially by fostering the development of his/her rational capacity for autonomy that makes human beings ends in themselves – their dignity, a word that appears several times in Kant's posthumous work *Über Pädagogik* (On Pedagogy) (1803, para. 95, 96, 103). This implies an education respecting the categorical imperative under its formulation as Principle of Humanity: never treating a human being merely as a means but always as an end too. Therefore, a child should be absolutely respected, so fostering his/her self-respect that is a condition for learning to respect others. As a consequence, education is an end in itself, whose overall purpose should be the fulfilment of the child's dignity.

Hegel wrote in *Grundlinien der Philosophie des Rechts. Naturrecht und Staatswissenschaft* (Philosophy of Right, 1820):

> Education [*Pädagogik*] is the art of making human beings ethical: it considers them as natural beings and shows them how they can be reborn, and how their original nature can be transformed into a second, spiritual nature so that this spirituality becomes habitual to them. (as cited in Williams 1997, p. 203)

That is why childhood stands out "as the quintessence of the perfectibility or process of enhancement of the naturality by means of which the humankind constitutes itself infinitely in us" (Renaut, 2002, p. 281).

As a consequence, there is no more seminal a right than the right to education for the humanisation of the human species' children. When human life is exhausted in the urgency of daily survival, to satisfy vital needs or to defend against real threats, human beings live and behave like animals, and human dignity is an abstraction …

Hence the consubstantiality of human life, human dignity and the right to education as a right to the full development of the human personality.

Morsink (1999) noticed that within the Commission on Human Rights, during the drafting of the UDHR, "the right to 'the full development of the human personality' was seen by most delegates as a way of summarizing all the social, economic, and cultural rights in the Declaration" (p. 212). All human rights contribute to the development of the human personality, but it is first and foremost the specific object of the right to education. The consubstantial relation between life, human dignity and the right to education has been stressed by the jurisprudence. Examples:

- The Supreme Court of India said in *Case Miss Mohini Jain vs State Of Karnataka And Ors on 30 July, 1992 (1992 AIR 1858, 1992 SCR (3) 658)*,[489] concerning fees charged by private schools, already quoted: "The right to life under Article 21 [of the Constitution] and the dignity of an individual cannot be assured unless it is accompanied by the right to education" (para. 1.07). In *Case Unni Krishnan, J.P. And Ors. Etc. ... vs State Of Andhra Pradesh And Ors. ... on 4 February, 1993 (1993 AIR 2178, 1993 SCR (1) 594)*,[490] it cited an Indian thinker of the first century BC who said: "A man without education is equal to animal" (para. 42).
- The South African Constitutional Court said in *Cases Ferreira v Levin NO and Others; Vryenhoek and Others v Powell NO and Others (CCT5/95) [1995] ZACC 13; 1996 (1) SA 984 (CC); 1996 (1) BCLR 1 (6 December 1995)*,[491] relating to winding-up proceedings, above quoted:

  > [49] Human dignity cannot be fully valued or respected unless individuals are able to develop their humanity, their "humanness" to the full extent of its potential. Each human being is uniquely talented. Part of the dignity of every human being is the fact and awareness of this uniqueness.

- The Constitutional Court of Colombia said, in a Case relating to the violation of the right to education and other rights for alleged breaches of school rules, that "education is the mechanism *par excellence* for the human perfecting" (*Case T-039/16*, para. 4.2).[492] In *Case T-137/15*[493] it addressed the question of whether lack of teachers in a school amounted to a violation of "the right to education and human dignity of a group of children and adolescents" (para. II.2).
- The Constitutional Court of Spain said in *Case 236/2007*,[494] relating to the constitutionality of several rules of a statute on the foreigners' rights, including the right to education, especially post-compulsory: "From the provisions transcribed it can be deduced the unequivocal link of the right to education with the guarantee of human dignity, given its undeniable transcendence for the full and free development of personality and the very living together in society".

– The Inter-American Court on Human Rights said in *Case Xákmok Kásek Indigenous Community v Paraguay* (24 August 2010)[495] (italics added):

186. The Court has indicated that the *right to life* is a fundamental human right, the full enjoyment of which is a precondition for the enjoyment of all the other human rights. If this right is not respected, all the other rights are meaningless. Therefore, *restrictive notions* with regard to this right are not admissible.

187. Consequently, the States are obliged to ensure the creation of the necessary conditions to prevent violations of this right and, in particular, the obligation to prevent its agents from endangering it. The observance of Article 4, in relation to Article 1(1) of the Convention [ACHR], not only presumes that no one be deprived of their life arbitrarily (negative obligation), but also requires the States to take all appropriate measures to protect and preserve the right to life (positive obligation), in keeping with the obligation to ensure the full and free exercise, without discrimination, of the rights of all persons under their jurisdiction. [...]

193. Based on the above, the Court must assess the measures taken by the State to comply with its obligation to guarantee the *right to life* of the members of the Xákmok Kásek Community. To this end, the Court will analyze the alleged violation of this right in two parts: (1) the *right to a decent existence*, and (2) the alleged international responsibility of the State for the alleged deaths. [...]

213. From the evidence gathered, the Court observes that, although some conditions of the State's provision of education have improved, the facilities for the education of the children are inadequate. The State itself provided a series of photographs in which it can be seen that classes take place under a roof, with no walls, in the open air. In addition, the State does not provide any type of program to prevent students from abandoning their studies. [...]

258. This Court has established that the provision of education and health care for children involves different measures of protection and constitutes the fundamental pillars that guarantee the *enjoyment of a decent existence* for children who, owing to their situation, are often without adequate means to defend their rights effectively. [...]

301. Based on the conclusions presented in Chapter VII with regard to Article 4 of the American Convention, the Court orders that, until

> the traditional territory or, if applicable, alternate land is delivered to the members of the Community, the State must take the following measures immediately, periodically, or permanently: [...] (f) provision of the necessary materials and human resources for the school to guarantee the Community's children access to *basic education*, paying special attention to ensuring that the education provided respects their cultural traditions and guarantees the *protection of their own language*. To this end, the State must consult the Community as necessary.

– In 2011, in *Case Abu Libdeh v. Minister of Education* (*HCJ5373/08*),[496] the Supreme Court of Israel Sitting as the High Court of Justice should decide on a petition concerning:

> 1. ... the complaint of five students, residents of East Jerusalem, that the State does not uphold their right to free education in official educational institutions, and that consequently they are forced to study in unofficial institutions, and their parents bear a heavy financial burden. They demand, through their parents, to be reimbursed for their educational costs based on the argument that their basic right to free education under the law is being violated.

The Court significantly ruled as follows (italics added):

> 26. .... The crucial importance of education in the life of the individual and in the formulation of his human existence, the centrality of education in determining a person's way of life and quality of life and the significance of this factor for the realization of his human dignity, ostensibly intertwine the right to education in its basic meaning with the value of human dignity [...]. *It seems, that the right to education forms part of the "hard core" of human dignity, without which the value of personal dignity is materially and severely compromised* [...].
>
> 33. ... Discrimination in general, and when effected in education in particular, creates a sense of deprivation and inferiority, which infringes on a child's dignity as a human being. [...]
>
> 44. ... The violation of equality in this sense also constitutes, by its nature, a violation of dignity, and is inextricably intertwined and integrated in the sphere of human dignity [...].

The Court's President D. Beinisch added in a separate concurring opinion:

> 6. … As I have noted in a previous case, the right to education "is essential for the development of the personality of every child and youth, for their self-realization and the exhaustion of their skills and abilities; the right to education exposes them to a variety of views, which are essential for the formulation of their identities, opinions and choices, as well as for the internalization of the value of human dignity, and particularly, the dignity of the other, the different or the abnormal; the realization of the right to education is their bridge to social integration as autonomous individuals, who can choose their way from various available options, and improve their condition and the condition of the community in which they live".

In sum: The right to education is *the key to the human dignity of life.*

4.5 Right to Education and Liberties of Education

As we know, the recognition of the liberty of education preceded historically that of the right to education. With the proclamation of the human right to education, its relationship with the liberties of education included in its wording has become subject to debate. From the 1980s, education liberalisation and privatisation policies have revived the controversy.

We are next examining the relationship between the right to education and liberties of education, as internationally recognised, to answer two main questions:
- Is children's education a "fundamental right" of parents?
- Is education privatisation compatible with the International Education Law?

4.5.1 *Is Children's Education a 'Fundamental Right' of Parents?*

Family rights have historical roots whose resilience is reflected in the legislation and jurisprudence of many countries, frequently recognising that parents have an (almost) absolute right over their children. They often claim, in particular, a *natural* fundamental right to the religious and moral education of their children, derived from the biological ties, generating a feeling of property.

In the USA, for example, whose Constitution does not mention the right to education, there is significant jurisprudence recognising a fundamental constitutional right of parents to the education of their children, developed for decades through decisions on Cases such as *Meyers v. Nebraska* (1923), *Pierce v. Society of Sisters* (1925), *Prince v. Massachusetts* (1944), *Wisconsin v. Yoder* (1972), *Maher v. Roe* (1977), *Carey v. Population Services International* (1977), *Quilloin* v. *Walcott* (1978), *Parham v. J.R.* (1979), *Santosky v. Kramer* (1982), *Mozert v. Hawkins County Public Schools* (1986). Their jurisprudence was evoked by the Supreme Federal Court in *Case Troxel v. Granville 530 U.S. 57 (2000)*,[497] where it affirmed:

> The liberty interest at issue in this case – the interest of parents in the care, custody, and control of their children – is perhaps the oldest of the fundamental liberty interests recognized by this Court. [...] In light of this extensive precedent, it cannot now be doubted that the Due Process Clause of the Fourteenth Amendment protects the fundamental right of parents to make decisions concerning the care, custody, and control of their children.

This "fundamental right" has a strong religious motivation, as evidenced by the resolution of Republican Senators, in 1995, against the ratification by the USA of the CRC, in which they claimed that the Convention is "incompatible with the God-given right and responsibility of parents to rise their children".[498] It is a right claimed notably by families wanting to teach them at home (home-schooling).

In support of parents' rights concerning education, UDHR[499] Article 26.3 is often invoked, which provides: "Parents have a prior right to choose the kind of education that shall be given to their children". How should this paragraph be interpreted today?

According to Article 32 of the Vienna Convention on the Law of Treaties (1969),[500] by interpreting a treaty there shall be taken into account, *inter alia*: "Any relevant rules of international law applicable in the relations between the Parties" (Article 31.3.c). In addition: "Recourse may be had to supplementary means of interpretation, including the preparatory work [*travaux préparatoires*] of the treaty and the circumstances of its conclusion" (Article 32).

In light of these provisions, let us see how the main relevant norms on parents' liberties of education should be interpreted.

4.5.1.1 Notes from the 'Travaux Préparatoires'

4.5.1.1.1 *International Bill of Human Rights*

UDHR Article 26.3 resulted from proposals of the Delegations of Netherlands and Lebanon and was adopted by the UN General Assembly Third Committee by 17 votes against 13, with 8 abstentions (A/C.3/SR.148, 19 November 1948).[501] The debate resumed during the *travaux préparatoires* of the 1966 International Covenants. For instance, at the 7th Session of the Commission on Human

Rights, 226th meeting (E/CN.4/SR.226, 27 June 1951),[502] the Delegation of Chile (Hernán Santa Cruz), after recalling that Article 26.3 had been adopted by the Third Committee, not by the Commission, expressed his opposition "to the inclusion in the Covenant of the text of Article 26 (3) of the Universal Declaration, which might be construed as giving parents the right to determine the curriculum for their children's education". At the following meeting (E/CN.4/SR.227, 27 June 1951),[503] the Delegation of Denmark (Max Sörensen) said that "he would agree to a provision guaranteeing complete freedom of religious instruction. That was, he would stress, the only aspect of the question on which unlimited freedom could be granted" (p. 9).

The inclusion of a vigorous and broad provision on the parents' right regarding their children's education was always supported by a twofold argument, voiced during the 67th meeting of the Commission on Human Rights (E.CN.4/SR.67, 10 June 1948)[504] by the Consultant of the International Union of Catholic Women's Leagues (Schæfer). After declaring "that the spirit and aims of education should be made clear", she remarked that the draft provisions on the right to education "failed to mention the fundamental right and responsibility incumbent upon parents to educate their children as they saw fit. If that right were not stated in the Declaration, there might very well be a recurrence of situations such as that which prevailed in Germany under Hitler". The two elements of the argument were, therefore, that:

- Parents have a fundamental right regarding the education of their children.
- Children must be protected against a totalitarian political regime like Nazism.

The parents' fundamental right was strongly affirmed by Charles Malik (Lebanon), at the 226th meeting of the Commission on Human Rights (E/CN.4/SR.226, 27 June 1951)[505]: "His country believed that it was the natural right of parents to have the last word in deciding what type of education should be given to their children" (p. 23).

At the 227th meeting (E/CN.4/SR.227, 27 June 1951),[506] the representative of the International Union of Catholic Women's Leagues (Romer):

> ... said that the term "education" involved a much wider concept than the term "instruction". There might be a certain amount of confusion in that connexion, owing to the different meanings of the word "education" in English and French.
>
> When we turned to the educational aspect of the problem one touched upon a point of extreme delicacy, which enabled the real meaning of liberty in the various countries to be assessed. In endeavouring to reconcile authority with freedom, education was faced with a very complex task,

> which it could only accomplish in the sympathetic surroundings of the home. For that reason, it was important to safeguard the essential rights and freedom of choice of parents in respect of the education of their children by maintaining the principle laid down in Article 26(3) of the Universal Declaration. [...]
>
> It was true that teaching was of primary importance, but science could not by itself make the child a real human being; indeed experience had shown that, in the hands of totalitarian States, it might well turn the child into a mechanism devoid of conscience. For that reason, it was absolutely necessary that the Covenant should formally recognize the importance of the part played by parents in the education of the child.
>
> In conclusion, she would ask the Commission to include in the draft Covenant all the three concepts contained in Article 26 of the Universal Declaration, namely: the concept of education as such; the concept of education directed towards the full development of the human personality; and, finally, the concept of the prior right of parents to choose the kind of education that their children should have.

At the 228th meeting (E/CN.4/SR.228, 28 June 1951),[507] the representative of the International Federation of Christian Trade Unions (Georges Eggermann) said that, "as a general rule, the best judges of what was good for the child were its parents" (p. 5).

At the 786th meeting of the UN General Assembly Third Committee (A/C.3/SR.786, 22 October 1957),[508] the Greek Delegation (Zenon Rossides) said that Article 13 paragraphs 3 and 4 "were necessary, if the parents' right to give their children an education conforming to their own convictions was to be protected, in particular in countries with totalitarian regimes and in the Non-Self-Governing Territories. Furthermore, freedom of education must mean freedom of private education as well" (para. 14).

The German Nazism was evoked again and again during the process of establishment of UNESCO and during the *travaux préparatoires* of the IBHR, as well as of Article 2 of the first Protocol to the ECHR.

In the UNESCO Founding Conference (London, 1945),[509] Ellen Wilkinson, Minister of Education of the United Kingdom, recalled in her opening address: "We have seen the service of education – the education of the young – wholly prostituted to the cause of savagery and aggression" (p. 23).

During the drafting process of UDHR Article 26, in the UN General Assembly Third Committee, 146th meeting (A/C.3/SR.146, 19 November 1948),[510] the Delegation of Pakistan (Begum Shaista Ikramullah) said that: "It was essential to guarantee freedom [of parents] to choose education, a principle flagrantly violated by the Nazis". The Delegation of Netherlands (L. J. C. Beaufort) added that: "Nazi Germany, where the Hitler Youth deprived parents of control over their children, had provided an experience which should never be permitted to recur".

During the *travaux préparatoires* of ICESCR Articles 13 and 14, at the 226th meeting of the Commission on Human Rights (E/CN.4/SR.226, 27 June 1951),[511] the representative of the World Jewish Congress (Bienenfeld) observed that UDHR Article 26.2 includes three aims of education:

> ... which had been challenged by the Nazi and Fascist Governments, namely: the full development of the human personality as opposed to the Nazi doctrine ot the deification of the State; the strengthening of respect for human rights in contrast to the Nazi doctrine of the enslavement of inferior races; and the promotion of tolerance between nations, and particularly between racial and religious groups, in contrast to the Nazi doctrine of racial inequality, and the Nazi practice of racial extermination. (p. 19)

Other Delegations paid more attention to the interests of the child, however.

For example, following the report of the 146th meeting of the UN General Assembly Third Committee (A/C.3/SR.147, 19 November 1948),[512] the Australian Delegation (Alan Watt) remarked that:

> The Netherlands and Lebanese amendments touched on a delicate question. Mr. Watt feared that it would be extremely difficult to express the idea contained in those amendments in a way which would be acceptable to everyone. It should not be forgotten that fundamentally the person affected by the right which the Committee wished to establish was the child and that it was above all the child who should be protected.

At the 226th meeting of the Commission on Human Rights (E/CN.4/SR.226, 27 June 1951),[513] Eleanor Roosevelt (USA) said that:

> ... she felt that the draft Covenant should in some way make it clear that the ultimate aim of education was the good of the child. [...] In the interest of the child, therefore, the Government should also specify that, if necessary, the good of the child should take precedence over the wishes of his parents. (p. 24)

At the 229th meeting (E/CN.4/SR.229, 28 June 1951),[514] she repeated "that the ultimate aim of ensuring parental responsibility was to safeguard the rights and interests of the child himself" (p. 11).

During the 786th meeting of the UN General Assembly Third Committee (A/C.3/SR.786, 22 October 1957),[515] the Syrian Delegation (Muhammad H. El-Farra), referring to the draft ICESCR Article 13.3, "pointed out that the ultimate aim of parental responsibility was to safeguard the interests of the child; lack of reference to those interests was unfortunate" (para. 27). The Iraqi Delegation (Bedia Afnan) agreed and noted: "As, unfortunately, parents did not always know best what to choose for their children, the rights of the child should be protected" (para. 42).

4.5.1.1.2 *Article 2 of the First Protocol to the European Convention on Human Rights*

A similar lively debate crossed the *travaux préparatoires* of Article 2 of the ECHR first Protocol (Right to Education)[516] so worded:

> No person shall be denied the right to education. In the exercise of any functions which it assumes in relation to education and to teaching, the State shall respect the right of parents to ensure such education and teaching in conformity with their own religious and philosophical convictions.

This provision resulted from proposals of Pierre-Henri Teitgen, Rapporteur of the Council of Europe Consultative Assembly Committee on Legal and Administrative Questions (whose President was Sir David Maxwell-Fyfe), concerning the rights and freedoms to be guaranteed by the ECHR, presented on 29 August 1949, in Strasbourg. They included: "Rights of parents in regard to the education of their children, in accordance with Article 26 (3) of the United Nations Declaration" (p. 4). Again, many Delegations stressed the rights of parents and recalled Nazi education, but some highlighted the right of the child. Examples:

- *Rights of parents*
  - During the session of the Consultative Assembly on 8 September 1949, the Italian Delegation (Boggiano Pico) said:

    > In founding a family, the man reaches out into space and prolongs in time his own personality. In educating their children according to the dictates of their conscience, parents achieve a task which is simply that of grafting onto the material generation another equally precious, namely the formation of their souls. (p. 23)

  - During the session of the Consultative Assembly on 7–8 December 1951, the Delegation of Netherlands (J. Schmal) said: "As for the fundamental right of parents, all things considered, one point only is important: to make it possible for parents to refuse the compulsory education offered by the State if it is contrary to their conscience" (p. 172). Another Netherlands' Delegate (Bruins Slot) said: "It is a primary right of parents to determine the education and teaching which their children shall have. The right of the State in this respect is purely secondary" (p. 174).

- The German Delegation (Luise Rehling) said:

> It is my religious conviction as a Christian mother that I am responsible for my children, and that no Minister of State can assume this responsibility in my place.
>
> In my view, the rights of parents concerning the upbringing and education of their children are of a fundamental nature, whereas those of the State are subsidiary. (p. 183)

- During the session of the Consultative Assembly on 25 August 1950, the French Delegation (Georges Pernot) had said, mitigating:

> I consider it to be my most natural right, one that is the nearest to my heart, that I should have the control of my children's education, to imbue them in their youth with my personal religious convictions and philosophical beliefs. It will be for them, later on, to make their own personal choices freely.
>
> I will not take up the phrase so often employed and which I find a poor one, which says that the child belongs to its parents. No, a child is a human being and as such cannot be owned. A child, therefore, belongs to nobody. But I do say that both father and mother bear a heavy responsibility with regard to the child. (pp. 84, 85)

- *Nazi education*
  - During the session of the Consultative Assembly on 7–8 December 1951, the German Delegation (Weber) said:

> Under the Third Reich, we in Germany suffered cruelly from the enslavement of conscience to which parents and children were subjected in every school in the matter of education and teaching. All young people, infants and older children, were under the domination of the authoritarian State. (p. 178)

  - Pierre-Henri Teitgen said:

> We have seen the requisitioning, the monopolization of young people by the State, the obligation, enforced upon all children and consequently upon all parents, of joining the State youth organizations for there to receive an abominable totalitarian training. [...] we have seen children brought up from the age of five to worship force, violence, race and hatred. That is what we wish to avoid. (p. 194)

- *Right of the child*
  - During the session of the Consultative Assembly on 8 September 1949, the Delegation of Belgium (Étienne de la Vallée-Poussin) said: "I would prefer that this should not be a right of the parents. I agree that it is a duty of the parents, but the right is that of the child" (p. 11).
  - The French Delegation (Philip) said:

    In this matter, there is, in my opinion, only one right which can be said to be fundamental: that is the right of every child to have access to culture, to be brought up in an atmosphere of freedom and according to methods which do not impose any doctrine or dogma upon him but which appeal to his powers of thinking and of personal research, to his spirit of free enquiry, so that little by little, as he reaches the age of manhood, the child may become a truly mature and free individual. If you insist on enunciating a principle now, the only one which we could consider is the sacred right of a child to be brought up in accordance with methods of free inquiry. That is the function of all educators, in the front rank of whom are certainly the fathers of families – to consider that they have responsibilities and no rights with regard to a child. (p. 16)

  - During the session of the Consultative Assembly on 7–8 December 1951, the Delegation of the United Kingdom (Renton) said that "if in some way the State is commanded to respect the philosophical ideas of the parents, the State might even be asked to place limitations, to a certain extent, upon the education itself of the children" (p. 176).

In this connection, the former European Commission of Human Rights remarked in its Report on *Case Kjeldsen, Busk Madsen and Pedersen against Denmark* (Applications 5095/71, 5920/72 e 5926/72), 21 March 1975)[517]:

> 154. ... It is clear that Art. 2 of Protocol No. 1 poses complicated and many-faceted problems. Its drafting history demonstrates the difficulties

> which the Article presented to the Governments concerned either because various drafts did not go far enough in protecting the right of parents to decide the education of their children or because of the quite contrary concern, namely, that the drafts went too far in giving the parents the decisive voice in their children's educational development. [...] The Committee of Ministers tried to narrow the scope of the Article but was persuaded by the Consultative Assembly to accept the latter's position. Therefore, the final draft does not seem to settle a number of doubts about its application.

Therefore, the purpose of the ECHR Article 2, second sentence, was "first and foremost to grant protection against the interference in the family by totalitarian regimes, as it had occurred during the Second World War", in the interest of children (Smith, 1993, p. 450). In the opinion of Karel Vasak, Article 2 consecrates more the "freedom in education" than the "freedom of education" (as cited in Bannwart-Maurer, 1975, p. 123). Also, Gérard Cohen-Jonathan (1989) observed that, following the European Court of Human Rights, the ECHR "does not expressly proclaim the freedom of education", but according to the former European Commission of Human Rights "State shall permit the parents placing their children in private schools", without any obligation to financing them (pp. 495, 496).

Wildhaber (1976) proposed a balanced and legally consistent interpretation:

> The right to education is a human right which must be guaranteed to all, children and adults, national, foreign and stateless persons. However, the interests of each other are not always compatible. [...] How to decide in these cases? It may be useful to follow the distinction proposed by Opsahl, noting that parents, on the one hand, act as agents of the children in the interest of the children who are not yet fully capable of discernment, while defending, on the other hand, their own interests which may not coincide with those of children. During the *travaux préparatoires* of Article 2, some Delegates argued that it was convenient to mention the rights of children. However, this point of view was not shared by other Delegates who stressed that the rights of parents or even of the father were the expression of a "natural and eternal law". [...] This is why I would put the emphasis on the role of parents as the representatives of the child. The rights of parents must be taken, not as an assertion of a paternalistic philosophy, but as a guarantee against any totalitarian tendency of a State. Despite these rights, "a child shall be given the opportunities to

develop mentally, physically, morally and socially in conditions of freedom and dignity" (Kellberg, Report of the Commission, Case relating to sexual education). (p. 168)

4.5.1.2 Systematic Interpretation and Case Law

Article 31 of the Vienna Convention on the Law of Treaties[518] points to a systematic interpretation, one that aims to promote consistency in the legal order, whose norms should not be interpreted in isolation, but rather together. It is a *principle of harmonious construction* (Supreme Court of India).[519] As said the Inter-American Court of Human Rights (*Case González y otras ("Campo Algodoneiro") vs México*, 2009),[520] "in accordance with the systematic argument, the norms should be interpreted as part of a whole whose meaning and scope should be determined in the light of the legal system to which they belong" (para. 43). Likewise, the Constitutional Court of Spain (*Case 5/1983*)[521] affirmed that the interpretation of the scope and content of a fundamental right "should be done considering the Constitution as a whole where each precept finds its full meaning in its appreciation in relation with others; that is to say, in accordance with a systematic interpretation". A systematic interpretation includes *a fortiori* taking into account each legal instrument itself as a whole. For example, in the *Case "relating to certain aspects of the laws on the use of languages in education in Belgium" v. Belgium* (Applications 1474/62, 1677/62, 1691/62, 1769/63, 1994/63, 2126/64, 23 July 1968),[522] the European Court of Human Rights, referring to the ECHR first Protocol Article 2, said that "the provisions of the Convention and Protocol must be read as a whole" (para. 1).

Following a systematic interpretation, UDHR Article 26, third paragraph, is to be read in conjunction not only with its two first paragraphs and other of its provisions, but also with ICESCR Article 13, paragraphs 3 and 4, and principally in light of the CRC, especially of its Articles 3, 5, 12, 14, 18, 28 and 29. Indeed, the wording of the main provisions on the right to education evolved significantly:

- The scope of UDHR Article 26.3 was limited by ICESCR Article 13.3 under three aspects: it does not take up any more the expression "prior right"; during its drafting, the term 'right' was replaced with 'liberty'; and the scope of the liberty of parents is no longer "to choose the kind of education that shall be given to their children", but only "to ensure the religious and moral education of their children in conformity with their own convictions".

  The Report of the 12th Session of the UN General Assembly Third Committee (A/3764, 5 December 1957)[523] offers the following overview concerning the interpretation of the present ICESCR Article 13, according to the *travaux préparatoires*:

46. Paragraph 3 of the article dealt with the liberty of parents to choose, under certain conditions, the kind of education they wished for their children. The majority of the representatives preferred the word "liberty" to the word "right" since, in their view, the latter word might imply an obligation for the States Parties to grant material assistance to private schools. Much stress was laid upon the minimum educational standards to which those schools should conform. Some fears were expressed that too large a measure of freedom granted to parents with regard to curricula might result in teachings contrary to the principles set forth in paragraph 1. The majority of the representatives were prepared to recognize such freedom as far as "religious and moral education" was concerned (A/C.3/L.625), but it was agreed that paragraph 3 should not be understood as imposing upon States Parties the obligation to provide religious education in public schools.

Commenting ICESCR Article 13.3, Beiter (2006) summarised what is at stake:

> ... the right to education accrues to the child itself. It is in this light that the right of parents must be understood. Parents are accorded a right with regard to their children's education, because children, on account of their immaturity, cannot exercise the right to education themselves. The right of parents is, therefore, an agency right, parents acting as the agents of their children. This has two important implications.
>
> Firstly, the right of parents must not be viewed as a right which parents exercise in their own interest. It is a right which they must exercise in the best interests of the child. The moment they fail to do so, the state must *in lieu* of the parents see to it that the child's best interests are promoted. [...] Parents are accorded a right with regard to their children's education, because it is held that they are best in a position to protect their children's interests vis-à-vis the state and, in the extreme case, against totalitarian tendencies on the part of the state. But parents do not have a right to educate their children "as they please".
>
> Secondly, as children become mature, the justification for parents acting as their children's agents falls away. (pp. 558, 559)

– The CRC no more includes the liberty of parents regarding the education of their children, despite a Netherlands proposal. Some Delegates countered that it "was not directly concerned with the protection of the rights of the child" (E/CN.4/1985/64, 3 April 1985, para. 102).[524]

Sharon Detrick (1999) pointed out: "The CRC does not expressly recognize the liberty of children either to choose schools, other than those established by the public authorities, or to ensure their religious and moral education in conformity with their own convictions", but such liberty may be "indirectly protected by Article 12(1) read in conjunction with Article 14" (p. 524), and taking into account the child's evolving capacities for exercising his/her rights, as provided for in the provision-*chapeau* contained in Article 5. Other authors agree. Bueren (1995), for example:

> Traditionally the interrelationship between the right to education and the right to freedom of conscience has been perceived as a balance between the duties on a state and the rights of the parents. The child, as the beneficiary of education, was perceived by international law as a valuable but silent receptacle of knowledge. [...]
>
> Grouping articles 5, 14, 28(1) and 12 together, children living in states which are Parties to the Convention on the Rights of the Child are provided with the right to participate in decisions to help ensure that their education is in conformity with their religious and moral convictions.
>
> In contrast with other international treaties, the Convention on the Rights of the Child does not contain a provision respecting the parents' right to have their children's education in conformity with the parents' convictions. (pp. 240–243)

Also, Fernando M. Powell (2015) rightly noted that:

> ... the international human rights law treaties that confer parents a right to direct the upbringing of their children predate the Convention on the Rights of the Child. That convention is the result of a paradigm shift regarding the understanding of children's rights within international human rights law. Where children were previously seen as mere objects to protect, they are now recognized as subjects with rights independent of their parents. State obligations emanating from international human rights law provisions concerning parental rights need to be reinterpreted in light of this shift.

At the regional level, the ACHR[525] provides in Article 12 (Freedom of Conscience and Religion): "Parents or guardians, as the case may be, have the right to provide for the religious and moral education of their children or wards that is in accord with their own convictions" (Article 12.4). The Protocol of San Salvador[526] does not replicate this provision in its Article 13 (Right to Education).

As the ECHR is concerned, the first Special Rapporteur on the Right to Education wrote in one of her reports (E/CN.4/2002/60)[527]: "The European Convention on Human Rights is an old document, adopted in 1950, and thus it does not reflect either the right to education as it was subsequently defined in international human rights law nor the even more recent concept of the rights of the child" (para. 48).

The Charter of Fundamental Rights of the European Union (2000)[528] adds "pedagogical" convictions, in its Article 14, but, following the *Explanations on the Charter of Fundamental Rights of the European Union* (2000)[529]: "Regarding the right of parents, it must be interpreted in conjunction with the provisions of Article 24", devoted to the "The rights of the child". This one "is based on the New York Convention on the Rights of the Child signed on 20 November 1989 and ratified by all the Member States [EU], particularly Articles 3, 9, 12 and 13 thereof". Article 24.2 reaffirms that "the child's best interests must be a primary consideration".

The African Charter on the Rights and Welfare of the Child (1990)[530] reflects the wording of ICESCR Article 13, paragraphs 3 and 4, in its Article 11 (Education), paragraphs 4 and 7, but adds that "the religious and moral education of the child" shall be assured "in a manner consistent with the evolving capacities of the child" (Article 11.4). Article 9, after recognising for the child "the right to freedom of thought, conscience and religion" (para. 1), states: "Parents, and where applicable, legal guardians shall have a duty to provide guidance and direction in the exercise of these rights having regard to the evolving capacities and best interests of the child" (para. 2).

The paramountcy of the right to education of the child is confirmed by the jurisprudence, both international and national.

For example, in 1976, the *Case Kjeldsen, Busk Madsen and Pedersen v. Danemark* (Applications 5095/71; 5920/72; 5926/72, 7 December 1976)[531] dealt with a conflict between the liberty of parents to have their children educated according to their convictions, the right of children to education, and the right of the State regarding the curriculum of public school education. At stake was the legitimacy of learning about sexuality as a school subject matter. The European Court of Human Rights decided that the "fundamental right to education" of children should prevail (para. 52). In effect, "the setting and planning of the curriculum fall in principle within the competence of the Contracting States", which includes "imparting through teaching or education information or knowledge of a directly or indirectly religious or philosophical kind" (para. 53). This is also required by "the public interest" as understood in "a democratic State" (para. 54). Indeed, the ECHR is "an instrument designed to maintain and promote the ideals and values of a democratic society" (para. 53).

Other cases could be mentioned where the ECHR organs or the CoHR have decided against parents' claims and in favour of the right to education of children to be protected by States.

At the national level, in *Case The Queen v. Jones [1986] 2 S.C.R. 284,*[532] submitted to the Supreme Court of Canada, a pastor of a fundamentalist church who educated his children in a schooling programme that was religiously minded, refused to send them to a public or approved private school, or even to educate them at home under public control, alleging that this "contravened his religious beliefs that God, rather than the Government, had the final authority over the education of his children, and deprived him of his liberty to educate his children as he pleased, contrary to the principles of fundamental justice". In the Court's opinion, "the appellant's proposition that he has a right to educate his children 'as he sees fit' goes too far" (para. 79). On the one hand, "a religious belief that a person has the right to educate his own children is not as strongly asserted nowadays" (para. 21). On the other hand, quoting the Supreme Court of New Jersey in *Case New Jersey State Board of Higher Education v. Board of Directors of Shelton College, 448 A.2d 988* (1982), the "accommodation of defendants' religious beliefs would entail a complete exemption from State regulation" and "would cut to the heart of the legislation and severely impede the achievement of important State goals" (para. 31).

It should also be noted that the abovementioned Article 17 of the Belgian Constitution on the freedom of education gave rise to two 'school wars' between Catholics and Liberals (the first one from 1879 to 1884, the second one following the parliamentary elections of 1950), involving respect for parents' convictions, the funding of private education and the role of public education. The conflict only ended with the School Pact of 1958, whose principles have been incorporated by the constitutional revision of 1988, following which Article 17 became Article 24, much more elaborated and no longer dominated by freedom of education. In the opinion of Mathias El Berhoumi (2013), the jurisprudence of the Constitutional Court of Belgium "illustrates the strong growth of international tropism: the Constitutional Court imported the abstract preference that the Judge of Strasbourg [European Court] recognises to the rights of the child in relation to the rights of the parents" (p. 699). It is a jurisprudence much influenced also by the PIDESC and the CRC.

4.5.1.3 Religious and Moral Education

The most sensitive issue relating to parents' liberties of education concerns the religious and moral education of their children.

During the drafting of the 1966 International Covenants, at the 7th session of the Commission on Human Rights, 227th meeting (E/CN.4/SR.227, 27 June

1951),[533] the Delegation of Denmark (Sörensen) observed that "many people, when speaking of the right of parents to direct their children's education, had precisely the religious factor in mind". For instance, at the 226th meeting (E/CN.4/SR.226, 27 June 1951),[534] Chief Rabbi Shafran (representative of the Agudas Israel World Organisation) said, in reference to Jewish children escaped to be killed by Nazis and taken into non-Jewish families and institutions: "The Agudas Israel World Organization deeply appreciated such charitable action on behalf of Jewish children, but noted with profound regret that they were being brought up in a religion other than that for which their parents had been put to death" (p. 17).

The human right to freedom of religion was always challenged by the Islamic States, being particularly at stake during the CRC *travaux préparatoires*. For example, on 25 February 1987, in the Working Group on a Draft Convention on the Rights of the Child, the Delegation of Morocco commented (E/CN.4/1987/WG.1/WP.35)[535]:

> On the question of religion, the rule adopted in Moroccan legislation is that the child shall follow the religion of his father. In this case, the child does not have to choose his religion, as the religion of the State is Islam. Islam guarantees freedom of worship to members of other faiths.

At the 44th meeting of the UN General Assembly Third Committee, on 15 November 1989,[536] the Delegation of Yemen (Alhamani):

> 71. … said that Article 14 of the Convention, which provided, *inter alia*, that States Parties should respect the right of the child to freedom of thought, conscience and religion, and under which children would have the right to change their religion, was contrary to Islamic Law, which did not permit Muslims to change their religion. Under the laws of Yemen, a Muslim child must retain his or her Muslim religion. For that reason, Yemen reserved its position on the Article in question.

That is why, after the adoption of the CRC, Article 14 ("right of the child to freedom of thought, conscience and religion") gave rise to the most numerous reservations (18), principally by Islamic States. For example, Iraq introduced the following reservation[537]: "The Government of Iraq has seen fit to accept [the Convention] … subject to a reservation in respect to Article 14, paragraph 1, concerning the child's freedom of religion, as allowing a child to change his or her religion runs counter to the provisions of the *Islamic Shariah*". Also, the Holy See formulated the following reservation: "That it interprets the Articles of the Convention in a way which safeguards the primary and inalienable rights of parents, in particular in so far as these rights concern education (Arts. 13 and 28), religion (Art. 14), association with others (Art. 15) and privacy (Art. 16)". These reservations were recalled in its Initial Report to the CoRC (CRC/C/3/Add.27, para. 16.b)[538] that, in its Concluding Observations (CRC/C/15/Add. 46, 27 November 1995),[539] said:

> 7. The Committee is concerned about reservations entered by the Holy See to the Convention on the Rights of the Child, in particular with respect to the full recognition of the child as a subject of rights. [...]
> 13. The Committee recommends that the position of the Holy See with regard to the relationship between Articles 5 and 12 of the Convention be clarified. In this respect, it wishes to recall its view that the rights and prerogatives of the parents may not undermine the rights of the child as recognized by the Convention, especially the right of the child to express his or her own views and that his or her views be given due weight.

In this respect, at the 786th meeting of the UN General Assembly Third Committee in 1957 (A/C.3/SR.786),[540] the Japanese Delegation (Fujita), expressing its preference for the terms 'the liberty of parents', instead of 'the right of parents', said that "the children themselves might have some say regarding their religious education, and it would be going too far to grant their parents an absolute right in the matter. For those reasons, even if the phrase 'right of parents' should be adopted, her Delegation would interpret it as signifying freedom of choice rather than an unconditional right" (para. 7).

When accepting the CRC (1995), the Netherlands expressed the following interpretative declaration[541]:

> It is the understanding of the Government of the Kingdom of the Netherlands that Article 14 of the Convention is in accordance with the provisions of Article 18 of the International Covenant on Civil and Political Rights of 19 December 1966 and that this Article shall include the freedom of a child to have or adopt a religion or belief of his or her choice as soon as the child is capable of making such choice in view of his or her age or maturity.

The main international standards on freedom of religion or belief are the UDHR Article 18, the ICCPR Article 18 and the Declaration on the Elimination of All Forms of Intolerance and of Discrimination Based on Religion or Belief (UN, 1981). As children are concerned, according to CRC Article 14[542]:

1. States Parties shall respect the right of the child to freedom of thought, conscience and religion.
2. States Parties shall respect the rights and duties of the parents and, when applicable, legal guardians, to provide direction to the child in the exercise of his or her right in a manner consistent with the evolving capacities of the child.

UNESCO Convention against Discrimination in Education (1960),[543] after recognising the liberty of parents, states that "no person or group of persons should be compelled to receive religious instruction inconsistent with his or their convictions" (Article 5.1.b).

Accordingly, the religious and moral education of children should be guided by the following normative framework:

- A child is the absolute holder of his/her human rights.
- A child needs protection and direction by parents.
- A child is a human being with evolving capacities.

These principles inspire the thematic Report "on the rights of the child and his or her parents in the area of freedom of religion or belief" (A/70/286, 5 August 2015)[544] by the former Special Rapporteur on freedom of religion or belief (Heiner Bielefeldt).

The Special Rapporteur remarked: "The Convention on the Rights of the Child combines the recognition of the child as a genuine rights holder with respect for the rights and duties of parents or legal guardians in directing the child in the exercise of his or her human rights" (para. 58). It "operates on the assumption that parents serve as the natural custodians of the best interests of the child" (para. 34). Such an assumption is already patent in the abovementioned 1981 UN Declaration[545] that reads in Article 5:

2. Every child shall enjoy the right to have access to education in the matter of religion or belief in accordance with the wishes of his parents or, as the case may be, legal guardians, and shall not be compelled to receive teaching on religion or belief against the wishes of his parents or legal guardians, the best interests of the child being the guiding principle.

Although "the best interests of the child" is recalled twice in this Article 5, it is indistinguishable from the parents' interest. Well, as the Special Rapporteur notes, "the interests of parents and children are not necessarily identical". The generally prevailing reality is that "children are treated as if they were the property of their parents, families or communities, without having rights in their own capacity" (para. 14).

The relationship between the rights of the child and parental rights and duties is "complex and dynamic" (para. 24). The Special Rapporteur points out: "The decisive term employed in the Convention on the Rights of the Child is 'the evolving capacities of the child' ", as laid down in its Article 5 (para. 23). As the right to freedom of religion is concerned, he noted that "Article 14, paragraph 2, is the only provision in the Convention that reiterates the importance of the evolving capacities of the child" (para. 26).

Although the CRC no longer includes the liberty of parents "to ensure the religious and moral education of their children in conformity with their own convictions", in the opinion of the Special Rapporteur: "Earlier provisions of freedom of religion or belief remain fully valid" (para. 32). Nevertheless: "Respect for the evolving capacities of the child is critical since it reflects the due recognition of the child as a rights holder also within the family context" (para. 39). This means that, while it would be unrealistic to require from parents religious and ideological abstention in order to children to retain their freedom of choice, parents are not entitled to impose religious or other convictions and values to their children, let alone in the case of adolescents. Also, values are a matter in which imposition's attempts are counterproductive.

Therefore, the State may be required to intervene to protect a child "while in the care of parent(s), legal guardian(s) or any other person who has the care of the child" (CRC Article 19.1). For example, against "traditional practices prejudicial to the health of children" (CRC Article 24) or other ones dictated by parents' convictions but not compatible with the respect of the dignity and rights of the child. In this respect, the Special Rapporteur remarked: "There can be situations in which the rights of the child must be safeguarded also against his or her parents. One example is the infliction of harmful practices, such as female genital mutilation or child marriage, sometimes carried out in the name of culture, tradition or religion" (para. 14). Yet, with regard to circumcision:

> 73. … The Special Rapporteur would argue that, if performed by trained practitioners, in sanitary conditions and with the clearly expressed consent of parents or guardians, male circumcision of children who have not yet reached religious maturity should generally be respected as falling within the freedom to manifest one's religion or belief, which includes the ritual initiation of children into religious life.

Isn't circumcision a form of physical violence covered by CRC Article 19?

IHRL protects the right to physical integrity (see: ACHR Article 5 that is one of its non-derogable rights; ACHPR Article 4; Article 3 of the Charter of Fundamental Rights of the European Union). The principle of prohibition of abuse of rights may be applicable too.

In light of the normative framework just considered, the following assertion is more than questionable: "*The first good* that [parents] transmit through education is *the essential good* that constitute *their deepest convictions*, the basis of every lucid conception of a human being's life and the source of his/her moral behaviours" (Riedmatten, 1973, p. 326).

Nevertheless, there are various international and national NGOs upholding the traditional rights of parents, even including the use of corporal punishment, with religious arguments. For instance, in *Case Christian Education South Africa v Minister of Education* (*CCT4/00*) [*2000*] *ZACC 11; 2000* (*4*) *SA 757; 2000* (*10*) *BCLR 1051* (*18 August 2000*), before the Constitutional Court of South Africa[546]:

> [1] The central question in this matter is: when Parliament enacted a law to prohibit corporal punishment in schools, did it violate the rights of parents of children in independent schools who, in line with their religious convictions, had consented to its use? [...]
>
> [4] The appellant [...] contends that corporal punishment is a vital aspect of Christian religion and that it is applied in the light of its biblical context using biblical guidelines which impose a responsibility on parents for the training of their children.
>
> [5] It has further claimed that according to the Christian faith, parents continue to comply with their biblical responsibility by delegating their authority to punish their children to the teachers. [...]
>
> [15] It is clear from the above that a multiplicity of intersecting constitutional values and interests are involved in the present matter — some overlapping, some competing. [...]
>
> [40] The state is further under a constitutional duty to take steps to help diminish the amount of public and private violence in society generally and to protect all people and especially children from maltreatment, abuse or degradation. More specifically, by ratifying the United Nations Convention on the Rights of the Child, it undertook to take all appropriate measures to protect the child from violence, injury or abuse. The Declaration on the Elimination of All Forms of Intolerance and of Discrimination Based on Religion or Belief declares in article 5(5) that: "Practices of a religion or belief in which a child is brought up must not be injurious to his physical or mental health or to his full development ...".

[41] Courts throughout the world have shown special solicitude for protecting children from what they have regarded as the potentially injurious consequences of their parents' religious practices. It is now widely accepted that in every matter concerning the child, the child's best interests must be of paramount importance.

4.5.1.4 In Concluding

Mylène Bidault (2009) warned:

> Thought of as a rampart against State totalitarianism in education, the liberty of parents to ensure the religious and moral education of their children according to their own convictions is an important guarantee of the right to have or adopt a religion or conviction chosen. [...] In the texts, however, it is not the liberty of the child who is consecrated, but that of families, with the risk of allowing other forms of totalitarianism, those of families. (p. 347)

The traditional doctrine of the liberty of education is more concerned with the authority of adults than with the liberty of children, caring more about the liberty of indoctrination than about the autonomy of thinking. As Jost Delbrück (1992) rightly put it:

> Phrased in broader terms, the meaning of the right to education in its dimension of protecting individual freedom may be summarized in the following way: education which makes an individual the object of instruction and/or indoctrination instead of the subject of learning is incompatible with human dignity. (p. 103)

Nowak (2001) thinks along the same lines:

> *Only the children themselves seem to have no right to choose their own education* under present international law. [...]
>
> Nevertheless, from the point of modern educational theories considering the liberation (and not indoctrination) of the child as the major aim of education, it is doubtful whether present international law affords sufficient protection to children to choose their kind of education by themselves. If education aims at fully developing the child's personality and talents and at enabling the child to actively participate in a free society a stronger protection of the rights of the young person to choose his or her education and to participate in the relevant decision-making process would seem highly desirable. [...]

> In most countries of the world education seems to be more directed at indoctrinating national, cultural and religious values than at the ultimate goal of liberating the child, which has been advocated already by Jean-Jacques Rousseau more than two centuries ago. (pp. 262, 263, 271)

In the opinion of the European Court of Human Rights (*Campbell and Cosans v. The United Kingdom*, Application 7511/76; 7743/76, 25 February 1982)[547] (italics added):

> 36. … In its ordinary meaning the word "convictions", taken on its own, is not synonymous with the words "opinions" and "ideas", such as are utilised in Article 10 (Art. 10) of the Convention [ECHR], which guarantees freedom of expression; it is more akin to the term "beliefs" (in the French text: 'convictions') appearing in Article 9 (Art. 9) – which guarantees freedom of thought, conscience and religion – and denotes views that attain a certain level of cogency, seriousness, cohesion and importance. […]
> Having regard to the Convention as a whole, including Article 17 (Art. 17), the expression "philosophical convictions" in the present context denotes, in the Court's opinion, such convictions as are *worthy of respect in a "democratic society"* (see, most recently, the *Young, James and Webster* judgment of 13 August 1981, Series A no. 44, p. 25, par. 63) and are *not incompatible with human dignity*; in addition, *they must not conflict with the fundamental right of the child to education*, the whole of Article 2 (P1-2) being dominated by its first sentence (see the above-mentioned *Kjeldsen, Busk Madsen and Pedersen* judgment, pp. 25–26, par. 52).

Therefore, a "fundamental right" of parents concerning the education of their children would not be compatible with children's "human right" to education. As said the Committee on the Rights of Persons with Disabilities in its GC 4 (CRPD/C/GC/4, 25 November 2016),[548] "education is the right of the individual learner and not, in the case of children, the right of a parent or caregiver. Parental responsibilities in this regard are subordinate to the rights of the child" (Article 10.a). The jurisprudence of the European Court of Human Rights is not different. It recalled in *Case Folgerø and Others v. Norwayb*[549]:

> 84.
> […]
> b. It is on to the fundamental right to education that is grafted the right of parents to respect for their religious and philosophical convictions, and

> the first sentence does not distinguish, any more than the second [of Article 2 of the first Protocol to the ECHR], between State and private teaching.
>
> [...]
>
> e. It is in the discharge of a natural duty towards their children – parents being primarily responsible for the "education and teaching" of their children – that parents may require the State to respect their religious and philosophical convictions. Their right thus corresponds to a responsibility closely linked to the enjoyment and the exercise of the right to education (see *Kjeldsen, Busk Madsen and Pedersen*, ibid.).

Also, according to *A Human Rights-Based Approach to Education for All*:

> The rationale behind parental choice is not to legitimize a denial of their child's rights. Rather, it is to prevent any state monopoly of education and to protect educational pluralism. In the case of conflict between a parental choice and the best interests of the child, however, the child should always be the priority. (UNICEF/UNESCO, 2007, p. 21)

The Constitutional Court of Colombia affirmed in *Case T-293/94*[550] that, following to Constitution Article 86: "A child can take action [*Acción de Tutela*] against his/her parents if they behave against her/his fundamental rights".

Therefore, if conflicts arise between Family and State, regarding children's education, what is really at stake is neither a Family's right nor a State's right, but the right to education of the child. It must be protected both against State, in case of attempted totalitarian appropriation of children, or against Family, if the physical, psychological or moral integrity and the personal development of children are at risk. And not by replacing one totalitarianism with another.

In this connection, let's quote a lucid (and somewhat ironic) remark by Piaget (1949) in a commentary on UDHR Article 26:

> ... it is the same with parents as with everything else: there are excellent parents and others who are not so good, and it is useful to be able to protect the child against the latter's will. [...]
>
> In spite of all these well-known circumstances, Article 26 is not reluctant to confer on parents the "prior" right to decide what type of education shall be given their children. That is because in all known societies, despite structural transformations in the family, it still remains a basic cog in the social structure. [...]
>
> In this respect, if "every person has the right to education", it goes without saying that parents also have this right, and "prior right" as well. (pp. 80, 81, 83)

Children need the protection and guidance of adults, of course, first and foremost of their parents, for growing and learning to exercise their rights. By guiding them, they do it naturally in accordance with their values and convictions, but they do not have the right to impose them. They have only the grave responsibility to be humanely admirable. This is the most legitimate and profound influence adults can exert over children.

4.5.2 *Is Education Privatisation Compatible with the International Education Law?*

The scientific and technological progress in recent decades has caused a digital revolution whose most spectacular outcome is Globalisation, which has been ridden by neoliberalism. In knowledge-based societies and a technology-driven world, the education demand has extraordinarily increased, but the expansion of digital technologies as tools for learning has been explored mainly by private actors.

We are examining closer the relationship between Globalisation, neoliberalism and education, as well as the challenges of the wave of expansion of private education, in light of the IEL.

4.5.2.1 Globalisation, Neoliberalism and Education

Globalisation is a term that emerged in the 1970s, but the phenomenon is not entirely new. Ancient empires, especially the Roman Empire, and the exploits of Portuguese and Spanish sailors in the 15th–16th centuries, meeting new continents and peoples, were already globalising. The new era of Globalisation is, however, an unprecedented inexorable, irreversible process (the genie is out of the bottle). It originated in the generalisation of the applications of the digital revolution virtually in all human life domains, causing a contraction of space and time, by the dissolution of borders and the interconnection of peoples, extraordinarily accelerating the mobility of persons, services, capitals, goods, ideas. Its most visible dimension is economic and financial planetisation, but the phenomenon is much more complex.[551] The motor and symbol of the Globalisation is the INTERNET that, from the beginning of the 1990s, has involved the world in ever-extending interconnectivity, amounting to a re-foundation of Civilisation. "Today, broadband networks are critical infrastructure, as important as roads, railways, water and power networks" (Broadband Commission for Sustainable Development, 2018, p. 12).

Yet, like other historical mutations, Globalisation is an ambivalent phenomenon. So far, the balance seems to be globally negative, with hazardous side effects and outcomes: misery, distress, the revival of communitarianism and fundamentalism, etc. broadening the gap between 'haves and have-nots'. It has been driven by the ideology of neoliberalism.

Classical liberalism was an ideology of liberty, theorised by authors such as John Locke, Montesquieu and Adam Smith, according to which State should be like a night watchman, guaranteeing the freedom and security necessary for the social and economic life.

The term 'neoliberalism', generalised during the 1990s, designates a broad-spectrum ideology with a generally negative connotation. It presents itself as the ideology of the 'free world', of the social progress, advantageous for everybody and democracy. Yet, its true driver is not the value of the liberty and well-being of persons and peoples, but rather the freedom of businesses. "Free fox in a free hen-roost", as says O'Madden Burke in *Ulysses* (James Joyce, 1922).[552] Its ideal world is a market without borders nor moral and environmental scruples, through the submission and weakening of States and the reduction of persons to the condition of labour force and consumers, whose usefulness accounts more than their dignity.

The neoliberal 'commandments' are profit, market freedom and competition, deregulation and privatisation of the economy, minimal State and public disinvestment. It absolutises the economy and relativises politics and social justice, generating inequality and criminality, and may even criminalise poverty. Its objectifying logic is potentially as barbarous as the Nazi biologism. 'Human Capital' is an expression with gloomy resonance …

The crises that have generated the turbulence of the global financial system in the late 1990s and in more recent years have shaken the neoliberal *credo*. Joseph Stiglitz, Nobel Prize Winner of Economics in 2001, noticed that "the intellectual defence of market fundamentalism has largely disappeared", because there is "an understanding of the limitations of markets". Balancing public and private interests "is quintessentially political activity" (Stiglitz, 2006, pp. xiv, 279). The importance of the cultural values, of the public goods and the State's role, is being rediscovered, as the 2020 world pandemic tragically teaches to those who want to learn.

As education is concerned, the neoliberalism advocates market-oriented reforms, through liberalisation and privatisation of education, favoured by the policies of the International Monetary Fund (IMF) and the World Bank (WB), causing underfunding and degradation of public schools, aggravated by the economic and financial difficulties of many countries, which have been exploited by the private sector. The neoliberal arguments are politico-ideological or/and economic-financial: freedom of choice, competition for improving education quality, reduction of public expenditure.

> The concept of education as a basic human right promoted by UNESCO does not fit comfortably with the agenda of the World Bank, the IMF, OECD and the governments of some of the world's richest and most powerful nations. The latter have adopted a revamped version of human

> capital approach to education and development, with a market-driven agenda that still is focused on maximizing the economic returns on investment in education, reducing public expenditure, promoting privatisation, competition, deregulation and the opening up of the growing global trade in education goods and services. (Power, 2015, p. 250)

Neoliberal education policies foster the concentration of the function of school in the more economically profitable learnings and in preparing students for *testing* on which depends the school *ranking*. This may originate practices of performance's manipulation and rejecting or removing underperforming students who might be detrimental to the ranking of the school. Also, rankings may serve business purposes. The first Special Rapporteur on the Right to Education, in her Report of a Mission to the United States of America (E/CN.4/2002/60/Add.1),[553] gave the example of "advertisements for the sale of family houses, which include testing scores of neighbourhood schools as an important marketing item. This process of economic exclusion flouts the common school ideal" (para. 54). In effect:

> It has been well established worldwide that student test scores are correlated with socioeconomic status: the poorer the school district, the lower the test scores (see, e.g., Ladd, 2012). This correlation has been called "The Volvo Effect" (Sacks, 2000); if you count the number of Volvos in a neighbourhood, you can predict with considerable accuracy the standardized test scores of that school district. [...]
>
> In spite of the fact that socioeconomic status is the best predictor of student test scores, the context of educationalization tends to shift responsibility for student test scores from conditions of poverty and inequality to teachers and teaching methods. (Fendler, in Smeyers, 2018, pp. 1176, 1177, 1181)

Therefore, neoliberal education tends to convert economic and social capital into cultural capital, thus increasing segregation and exclusion. As rightly remarks Salim Vally (in Mehendale & Mukhopadhyay, 2018):

> The upshot of neoliberal discourse in education has been to ignore the problems faced by public schools and to promote market solutions through private schools, vouchers, charters, and the like. This proposed 'market solution' to our education crisis, even with State regulation, is less a case of a pragmatic attempt at resolving the problem than a case of ideological wishful thinking. (p. 45)

In short: The neoliberal economistic instrumentalisation of school is reductive of the normative integrity of the right to education, narrowing the personal and social entirety of the school mission and amputating the fullness of the teaching professionality and professionalism.

The neoliberal ideology exploits the frequent tendency to value private education more than public education, which has a double explanation, perhaps: on the one hand, it is associated with the general idea of the superiority of what is 'private', because it is selective; on the other hand, the quality of public education is often very unsatisfactory. Alongside, is the political connotation of 'public' with 'left' and 'private' with 'right'.

4.5.2.2 Public and Private Education

Education has been, since the 19th century, at least in the Western world, a typical function of State, almost a monopoly, through a system of public establishments to implementing, first of all, the expanding constitutional and legal imperative of compulsory schooling, while the liberty of private education was also recognised by Constitutions, having entered the IHRL.

In the IBHR, the liberty to create and manage educational establishments is not found in the UDHR Article 26, but was implicit in its third paragraph, as well as in Article 18, within the scope of "the right to freedom of thought, conscience and religion".[554] It was recognised in the 1960 UNESCO Convention (Article 5) and the ICESCR Article 13.4 (deriving from paragraph 3 too), as well as in the CRC Article 29.2. It is also laid down in the Protocol of San Salvador (Article 13.5) and the African Charter on the Rights and Welfare of the Child (Article 11.7).

States' obligations relating to education appear as being more of result than of behaviour, and the result can be achieved through public or private schools. In the European Social Charter (1996, revised)[555]:

> Article 17 – The right of children and young persons to social, legal and economic protection
>
> With a view to ensuring the effective exercise of the right of children and young persons to grow up in an environment which encourages the full development of their personality and of their physical and mental capacities, the Parties undertake, either directly or *in cooperation with public and private organisations* [emphasis added], to take all appropriate and necessary measures designed:
>
> [...]
>
> 2. to provide to children and young persons a free primary and secondary education as well as to encourage regular attendance at schools.

As Nowak (2001) remarked:

> If there are sufficient private facilities, the state may fulfil its obligations even without its own schools. The government must, however, ensure that all conditions laid down in international law, such as free and compulsory primary education or general and equal access to secondary and higher education, are guaranteed by means of, for example, legislative measures, state supervision, and subsidies. (pp. 257, 258)

The first Special Rapporteur on the Right to Education (E/CN.4/2000/6)[556] noted: "States' practice with regard to ensuring that schools are available for all school-age children reveals a variety of models" (para. 33).

From the late 1980s, a wave of expansion of private education has risen on all continents. In the 1990s, with the General Agreement on Trade in Services (GATS) of the World Trade Organisation (WTO), education policies have entered a somewhat schizophrenic phase:

- States Parties to the ICESCR undertake to act "to achieving the full realization" of the right to education (ICESCR Article 13.2).[557]
- States Members of the WTO undertake "to achieving a progressively higher level of liberalization" (GATS, Article XIX.1).[558]

These two undertakings may come into conflict. As Katarina Tomaševski (2005a) underlined: "International human rights law defines education as a human right; international trade law defines it as a service [...]. Primary and/or compulsory education continues as a public service in most countries, albeit for-fee in many, while post-compulsory education is increasingly sold and purchased for a price", under the liberalisation' pressures. "The pressures originate in requirements to reduce budget deficits, and thus public funding of education, as well as to open the educational markets to exporters of educational services" (pp. 1, 8, 9).

The GATS recognises that education is not a service 'to consumption' like any other, but rather a fundamental right. Therefore, the right to education falls under the responsibility of Governments, at least up to a certain level. The reality is that education has become one of the leading services export markets, including the cloudy world of online courses, in countries such as the USA, the United Kingdom, Canada, Australia and New Zealand. The expansion of private education "is blurring the boundaries between public and private education" (UNESCO, 2015b, p. 77) so that in 2014 the Special Rapporteur on the Right to Education (Kishore Singh, at the time) wrote in his annual report: "Soon, it may not be an exaggeration to say that privatization is supplanting public education instead of supplementing it" (A/69/402, para. 38).[559]

The distinction between public and private school may be made following two criteria: the entity that owns it (public or private) or the source of its funding (public and/or private). Using the first criterion (which is that of UNESCO), a State-funded school, but run by a private entity, is taken as private. Using the second criterion, a school run by a private entity, but funded by State, is taken as public. According to the Glossary of the UNESCO Institute of Statistics (used by the OECD)[560]:

- A public educational institution is an:

> Institution that is controlled and managed directly by a public education authority or agency of the country where it is located or by a government agency directly or by a governing body (council, committee etc.), most of whose members are either appointed by a public authority of the country where it is located or elected by public franchise.

- A private educational institution is an:

> Institution that is controlled and managed by a non-governmental organization (e.g. a church, a trade union or a business enterprise, foreign or international agency), or its governing board consists mostly of members who have not been selected by a public agency.

The world is changing rapidly, altering the way human rights can be exercised and even generating the need for recognition of new rights. States should not ignore or underestimate the expansion of the private sector, all the less that many among them lack the resources needed to maintain and develop a public education system. The Supreme Court of India remarked that "it would be unrealistic and unwise to discourage private initiative in providing educational facilities, particularly for higher education. The private sector should be involved and indeed encouraged to augment the much-needed resources in the field of education, thereby making as much progress as possible in achieving the constitutional goals in this respect". However: "The question is how to encourage private educational institutions without allowing them to commercialise the education? This is the troublesome question facing the society, the government and the courts today" (*Unni Krishnan, J.P. And Ors. Etc. … vs State Of Andhra Pradesh And Ors. … on 4 February, 1993 (1993 AIR 2178, 1993 SCR (1) 594)*.[561] Put another way: How to conceive the public-private relationship in education without complicity or inflexibility in the face of reality, for the benefit of the right to education?

This general question may be split into the following ones:

- Which forms does the privatisation of education take?

- Has private education so far achieved better results than public education?
- Is privatisation of education compatible with IEL?

Answers to these questions are proposed next.

4.5.2.3 Typification and Evaluation of the Privatisation of Education

Public and *private* are terms whose meaning have changed overtime and may vary from country to country. Nowadays, the relationship public-private takes a variety of configurations. Moreover, the causes of the burgeoning of the private sector differs from developed to developing countries: while in the former it serves rather as an alternative to the public sector, for different reasons and purposes, in the latter it often fills an educational gap, due to the absence or impotence of the public supply.

For the sake of clarification, liberty of education, liberalisation of education and privatisation of education should be distinguished. The following distinctions are proposed:

- *Liberty of education* is the traditional liberty of parents relating to the education of children, as well as the liberty to create education establishments as a dimension of the liberty of thought, conscience, religion, expression, to safeguard democratic pluralism and respect for cultural diversity.
- *Liberalisation of education* is a policy of opening up the provision of education services to the private sector, including possible incentives for investment such as land transfers, tax benefits or even funding.
- *Privatisation of education* occurs when public education facilities and services are transferred to the private sector, with possible effects of commercialisation of the right to education.

The UNESCO Report *Rethinking education* contains a broad definition, diluting the precedent distinctions:

> The trend towards the privatization of education is growing at all levels of provision across the world. [...] The privatization of education may be understood as the process of transferring activities, assets, management, functions and responsibilities relating to education from the State or public institutions to private individuals and agencies. In the case of school education, this process takes a variety of forms, including faith schools, low-fee private schools, foreign aid or international schools run by non-governmental organizations (NGOs), Charter, Contract and Vouchers schools, homeschooling and personal tutoring, market-oriented and for-profit schools. (UNESCO, 2015b, p. 73)

Private actors in education may be typified following two main criteria:

- *Their interest: for-profit or not-for-profit?*
  This is the *summa divisio* (the main and most decisive distinction). If an education institution is for-profit, its attendance is paid and may be low-cost or high-fee. Not-for-profit institutions are philanthropic, created by communities, religions or NGOs, independent or publicly funded. Their attendance may also be paid, but only to the extent necessary for its economic sustainability. Both not-for-profit and for-profit institutions may be publicly funded, for different reasons.
- *Their services: core or ancillary?*
  The management of a school is a core service, but the supply of services relating to food, transport of students or the safety of school facilities, for example, are ancillary services.

Other criteria are the nature of the private entity and its scope of activity. Private actors may be individuals or international chains such as Bridge International Academies, owner of over 500 pre-school and primary education institutions in several countries, operating with autonomy or in partnership with public entities.

The relationship between the State and private actors may be of three types:

- *Replacement*
  There is a replacement relationship when the State does not fulfil its obligations, due to lack of resources or other causes, and the public void is filled by private actors.
- *Competition*
  There is some competition relationship when the public sector and the private sector operate in parallel.
- *Collaboration*
  There is collaboration relationship when the State (at the central, regional or local level) hires private supplies and ancillary services for public institutions, or funds private entities for the supplementary provision of essential services through contracts sharing costs, risks and benefits (Public-Private Partnerships: PPPs).

PPPs are sometimes regarded as a kind of 'Columbus egg' combining the best of two worlds: the public and the private. Two typical modalities of public-private relationship are Charter Schools (schools under contract) and Vouchers (education checks).

Charter Schools originated in the USA to improve education quality and to increase families' freedom of choice. They are created through a contract established between a local public entity (usually a School District) and those who propose their creation, which may be private or public entities, including groups of families or of teachers or municipalities. They are privately managed and publicly funded (but can also seek private funding) and, therefore, tuition-free. They are part of the public school system, but often exempt from public regulations. The State holds the power to oversee compliance with the contractual clauses. There are Charter Schools online too. The first American Charter School was established in 1991. Now, they are more than 7000, with over 3 million children.[562]

Charter Schools have been replicated in other countries with different names. For example: Free Schools and Academies (United Kingdom), Independent Schools (Sweden, Denmark, Norway, Australia), Partnership Schools (New Zealand). Similar initiatives have been taken in Chile, Colombia, Germany, South Africa, Czech Republic, China, etc.

Education/School Voucher is a payment title for attendance of a chosen school, delivered to families or directly to schools on their behalf by public authorities (or even by private entities). Voucher programmes may be focused or universal, that is, intended only for a few categories of students or for everyone, and be used in a public or private school.

Vouchers' advocates argue that they provide disadvantaged families, in more degraded city areas or rural areas, with the freedom to choose for their children a private school better than a public school; and that, by stimulating competitiveness between schools (not only between private and public schools, but also between public schools themselves), they also promote the quality of education in general. It is assumed that the better a school, the more students it attracts and more funding it gets.

The main argument of opponents is that Vouchers' policies amount to a form of diversion of public resources into the private sector, to the detriment of improving the quality of public education. Another argument against the Vouchers policy in the USA is that it violates the principle of separation between State and religion (First Amendment of the Constitution), as they are often used to attend religious schools, including those teaching Creationism, which rejects the theory of evolution.

Some USA courts ruled on the unconstitutionality of Voucher programmes, as did the Puerto Rico Supreme Court, in 1994, and an Ohio State District Court in 2000. In 2006, in Florida, several parents of students attending primary and secondary schools, supported by some organisations, claimed the unconstitutionality of the use of Vouchers by an *Opportunity Scholarship Program* (OSP). The State Supreme Court agreed, considering that the OSP violated the Constitution "by devoting the State's resources to the education of children within our State through means other than a system of free public schools" (*Bush v.*

Holmes, N°. SC04-2323, SC-4-2325).[563] The USA Supreme Court admitted the constitutionality of Vouchers Programmes, under certain conditions (*Zelman v. Simmons-Harris*, 2002).

In 2015, the Supreme Court of Washington ruled, in *Case* (*League of Women Voters of Washington v. State of Washington* (N° 89714-0),[564] that funding charter schools is unconstitutional, because Article IX, Section 2, of the Washington Constitution provides: "The legislature shall provide for a general and uniform system of public schools. The public school system shall include common schools, and such high schools, normal schools, and technical schools as may hereafter be established". The Court concluded: "In sum, the Charter School Act violates Article IX, Section 2, because charter schools are not common schools despite the Act's attempt to so designate them".

What conclusions did the reviews reach so far?

The private initiative can have a positive impact on the satisfaction of the right to education: increasing the availability of educational institutions, especially when the public offer is insufficient, can benefit populations from poorer regions; diversification of education on offer is favourable to freedom of choice and can stimulate the participation of families in the education of their children; the presence of credible foreign education institutions can also have benefits.

However, the private provision of education services may have considerable negative effects too, if it is not properly regulated and supervised. In addition to possible effects of commercialisation of the right to education, it may contribute to the creation of a two-track school system: one for the rich (private schools) and another for the poor (public schools), with effects of segregation and stratification.

A report on 22 studies on the assessment of privatisation of education, on all continents, commissioned by the *Ark – Education Partnerships Group* (EPG) – "an education charity that exists to make sure that all children, regardless of their background, have access to a great education and real choices in life"[565] – concluded[566]:

> This review is ultimately somewhat inconclusive; such is the nature of the evidence we have so far. [...]
>
> *There is little evidence that purely private provision will result in substantial learning gains across the entire education system.* (pp. iii, 96)

More precisely, the review concluded that there is:

> ... *insufficient body of evidence* for a positive relationship between contract schools and pupil learning outcomes.

> … a *modest body of evidence* for a weakly positive relationship between subsidies to private or faith-based schools and the learning outcome of their students. […]
>
> The *body of evidence* for the relationship between voucher provision and learning outcomes is mixed and inconclusive, and therefore *insufficient*. […]
>
> This review has highlighted the need for further rigorous research in this area. (pp. vii, viii, 94)

From the diversity of studies conducted in different countries it may be concluded that, overall, privatised education has not achieved the promised success (see UNESCO, 2017, pp. 42, 51, 52).[567]

On 11 October 2017, 152 national, regional and international civil society organisations, trade unions and other' organisations from 45 countries, launched a *Public-Private Partnerships – Global Campaign Manifesto*[568] that deserves to be quoted widely in the present context:

> PPPs are essentially long-term contracts, underwritten by government guarantees, under which the private sector builds (and sometimes runs) major infrastructure projects or services traditionally provided by the state, such as hospitals, schools, roads, railways, water, sanitation and energy. PPPs are promoted by many G20 governments, and some public development banks – such as the World Bank – as the solution to the shortfall in financing needed to achieve the Sustainable Development Goals. […]
>
> The experience of PPPs has been overwhelmingly negative and very few PPPs have delivered results in the public interest. Common problems include:
>
> PPPs are, in most cases, the most expensive method of financing. They cost governments – and hence citizens – significantly more in the long run than if the projects had been directly financed through government borrowing. Yet, they are attractive because they can be hidden 'off balance sheet' so they don't show up in the budget and government debt figures, giving the illusion of 'free money'. Also, despite claims to the contrary, PPPs are often riskier for governments than for the private companies involved, as the government may be required to step in and assume the costs if things go wrong. For example: […]
>
> In Liberia, the PPP contract with Bridge International Academies, a commercial chain of school backed by the World Bank, costs 13 to 21

> times more than government schools, and students were expelled *en masse* from their original schools. […]
>
> Furthermore, PPPs often come with new or increased fees for users of services. […]
>
> PPP contracts are extremely complex. Negotiations are covered by commercial confidentiality, making it hard for civil society and parliamentarians to scrutinise them. This lack of transparency significantly increases the risk of corruption and undermines democratic accountability. […]
>
> In addition, PPP contracts often undermine the right and obligation of the state to regulate in the public interest. […] Under World Bank proposed PPP contracts, the State can even be liable for costs from strikes by workers. […]
>
> Finally, we urge all those concerned with justice, equality, sustainability and human rights to resist the encroachment of PPPs and to push instead for high-quality, publicly-funded, democratically-controlled, accountable public services. The wellbeing of our communities and societies depends on it.[569]

UN Committees have often expressed their concerns and objections to education privatisation policies. For example, in 2016, the CoESCR said in its "Concluding observations on the sixth periodic report of the United Kingdom of Great Britain and Northern Ireland" (E/C.12/GBR/CO/6, 14 July 2016)[570]:

> 14. While welcoming the achievement by the State Party of the international target of allocating 0.7 per cent of gross national product for official development assistance in the framework of international cooperation, the Committee is concerned that in some cases the assistance provided has reportedly been used for activities in contravention of economic, social and cultural rights in the receiving countries. The Committee is particularly concerned about the financial support provided by the State Party to private actors for low-cost and private education projects in developing countries, which may have contributed to undermining the quality of free public education and created segregation and discrimination among pupils and students (Arts. 2, 13 and 14).

The same year, it said in its "Concluding Observations on the combined fifth and sixth periodic reports of the Philippines" (E/C.12/PHL/CO/5-6)[571] that it was concerned about:

55. […]

b. The proliferation of so-called "low-cost private schools" at the primary and secondary levels, owing to inadequacies in the public school system, which have extended to the senior high school level through the Senior High School Voucher Programme;

c. The low quality of education provided by those private schools, the top-up fees to cover the full cost of private education imposed on parents, and the lack of State regulation of those schools, which have led to segregation and discriminatory access to education, particularly for disadvantaged and marginalized children, including children living in rural areas;

The Committee recalled "*that the State has the primary responsibility in ensuring the right to education*" and recommended: "*Review the Education Service Contracting scheme to address its adverse impacts on the right to education of disadvantaged and marginalized children and their parents*" (para. 56.c).

Also, the former Special Rapporteur on the Right to Education (Kishore Singh) devoted some annual reports, in 2014, 2015 and 2016, to the concerns raised by the digital revolution and policies of education privatisation.

4.5.2.4 Some Distinctions

The public-private relationship in education is a truly transcendent issue. It is in the right to education that is most intensely at stake the Kantian categorical imperative of the Principle of Humanity, namely: Never treating a human being (including itself) merely as a *means*, but always simultaneously as an *end*. Some distinctions may contribute to clarifying, highlighting and safeguarding the ethical core of the right to education:

- Education: right and liberties
- Ideological dimension and economic dimension of the liberty of private education
- Commercialisation of 'education services' and commercialisation of the 'right to education'
- The sacred and the profane

4.5.2.4.1 *Education: Right and Liberties*

As we know, the liberty/freedom of education was constitutionalised as an element of "The free communication of ideas and opinions" proclaimed by the 1789 French Declaration,[572] but with the constitutional and international recognition of the human right to education, in the 20th century, their relationship has become controversial.

The main international norms on the right to education include provisions on liberties of education (UDHR Article 26.3, ICESCR Article 13.3 and 13.4, CDE Article 2.c, and CDC Article 29.2), though already during the UDHR *travaux préparatoires* Cassin said that "he wished to see a distinction made between freedom of education and right to education" (E/CN.4/SR.14, 5 February 1947).[573] The inclusion of parents' liberty regarding the education of their children and of the liberty to create and manage educational institutions has always been controversial during the respective drafting, for neither the liberty of parents nor the liberty of private education "is really a component or a constituent element of the right [to education] itself" (Szabo, 1974, p. 38). This happened also with the inclusion of the freedom of private education in CRC Article 29.2, which met with objections alleging that it has no direct relationship with a right of the child.

The incorporation of provisions on liberties of education into the normative content of the right to education is superfluous and not legally logical, for the following main reasons:

- In IHRL, the liberty of education is an element of "the right to freedom of thought, conscience and religion" (ICCPR Article 18), and its exercise must respect all other human rights (ICCPR and ICESCR Article 5, which replicates UDHR Article 30).
- One gets the impression that the incorporation of provisions on liberties of education into the main international norms on the right to education was an attempt of *human-rightisation* of the traditional *right of education* (see 5.1.1) to capturing the *human right to education.*
- The liberties of education are subsidiary of the right to education (see 4.5) to the extent that the satisfaction of the latter is a condition of the exercise of the former, which are instrumental to its realisation as a right that is inherently a right-liberty and can be regarded as the most consubstantial to human dignity (see 4.4.3).

A coherent articulation of the liberties of education with the right to education should sound as follows: The realisation of the right to education is a duty of the family and an obligation of the State, through the direct provision of the necessary public service and, indirectly, private providers duly authorised, regulated and supervised.

As remarked the Special Rapporteur on the Right to Education (Koumba Boly Barry) in her 2019 Report (A/HRC/41/37)[574]: "When the human rights treaties were drafted, the intention was not to protect commercial interests in the area of education or to offer States a way to escape from their responsibilities through the implementation of austerity measures and neoliberal policies" (para. 28). Nor to protect parents' rights against children's rights, as we have seen.

In sum:

- There should be no liberty of education against the right to education.
- The liberty that is truly at stake in education, both at home and in school, public or private, is the liberty of the subject of the right to education as it results from the ethical-juridical principle of his/her primacy: especially, the liberty of children, adolescents and young to learn and to learn liberty with liberty. "That is Education which leads to liberation", as reads an old Sanskrit adage cited by the Supreme Court of India in *Case Unni Krishnan, J.P. And Ors. Etc. ... vs State Of Andhra Pradesh And Ors. ... on 4 February, 1993* (*1993 AIR 2178, 1993 SCR* (*1*) *594*).[575]

4.5.2.4.2 *Ideological Dimension and Economic Dimension of Private Education*

The liberty of education was first recognised as a dimension of the liberty of thought, conscience and religion, as above noted. This is its *ideological* dimension. The *economic* dimension is achieved in the liberty to create for-profit education establishments, particularly in the context of the current flourishing of an international education services market.

These two dimensions were taken into account, for instance, in a Case decided by the Constitutional Court of Turkey in 2016 (Venice Commission, Bulletin 2016, 1, p. 205).[576] It was about the constitutionality of the exclusion of school support centres (*dershane*) from the definition of "private educational establishments", resulting in its closure. The Constitutional Court considered that the closure was a measure infringing on both the right to education and freedom of economic initiative, and its total ban was disproportionate in a democratic society.

The distinction between the ideological and the economic dimensions of private education was also evoked by the Constitutional Court, in Portugal, in its Judgement *398/2008*[577] relating to sanctions imposed on a private college for non-compliance with obligations of a contract of association with the State. The Court said *inter alia* that:

> ... the right to the creation of private schools is something substantially different from the right to private economic initiative. While the latter primarily aims at achieving a juridical-economic good, the first one aims at achieving a different good, which educational freedom – when understood in its unity of meaning – presupposes.

In this respect, the first Special Rapporteur on the Right to Education (E/CN.4/2000/6)[578] remarked:

> 41. … Amongst the existing jurisprudence, the Supreme Court of Colombia has ably clarified why education should not be governed by economic arguments alone:
>
> "… although the Constitution protects economic activities, private initiative and competition, as well as recognizing the right of private entities to establish schools, these liberties cannot negate nor can they diminish the nature of education as public service and its social function; education is also and above all else a fundamental right".

Therefore, the general clause prohibiting the abuse of rights laid down in the final DUDH provision[579] (which is replicated in ECHR Article 17, for example) may apply too. According to it, neither the ideological dimension nor the economic dimension of private education should prevail over the right to education.

4.5.2.4.3 *Commercialisation of 'Education Services' and Commercialisation of the 'Right to Education'*

What distinguishes a *human right* from any other right is essentially its *ethicity*. The ethicity of human rights consists in its inherence to human dignity, from which derives their universality, because all human beings are equal by dignity and rights.

The ethical radicality of the right to education justifies the fact that basic education, whatever its denomination and duration, must be free and compulsory – and this is one of the strongest States' obligations concerning human rights.

Well, the *ethicity, universality, gratuity and imperativity of basic education* are incompatible with its commodification, that is, with children, adolescents, young people and their families being treated as mere consumers. Therefore:

- When the State is unable to ensure the availability of education institutions in sufficient number for its entire school-age population, the private sector can contribute to the universalisation of the right to education.
- Whatever the institution where basic education is provided for, its gratuity must be ensured, as completely as possible, except in case of free option for paid private institutions.
- Whatever the level of school education and nature – public or private – of the respective institutions, the State has an obligation to guarantee its ethicity, that is, the conformity of education with the aims of the right to education.

In light of these principles, education is treated as a consumer good, traded like any other:

- when one has to pay for school education which must be free of charge in full or pay excessively for what must be progressively free;
- where the State does not assume all its obligations relating to the right to education and consents to its commodification and marketisation.

Consequently:
- Education consists of learnings, but not every learning belongs to the 'human right' to education. The foundation of human rights is bio-ethical, but what provides them with a legal guarantee is the agreement founding their international recognition and obligations for States.
- The protection of the right to education is not incompatible with the existence of a 'market' of education services. Nowadays, there is a diversity of learning possibilities going beyond what should be guaranteed as a 'human right' to education and entering the field of options that may entail costs. For example, to pay for attending a language or dance school, does not amount to the commercialisation of the right to education.

4.5.2.4.4 *The Sacred and the Profane*

Considering that the comparative advantages and disadvantages of public and private education are mainly due to differences in means and conditions, an alternative to public education deficiencies and private education inconveniences may be:
- investing in all factors of the availability, accessibility, quality and equity of the right to education;
- integrating into public education the benefits of professional competence and responsible autonomy.

The Finnish school system is an example of the possibility of bonding equality, quality and equity (see Monteiro, 2014b). There are private schools, but the quality of the public school system is such that private education is residual, complies with the National Core Curriculum and is publicly funded. According to its Basic Education Act (628/1998): "Basic education may not be provided in pursuit of financial gain" (Section 7.2).[580]

In this regard, the Supreme Court of India said in *Case Unni Krishnan, J.P. And Ors. Etc. ... vs State Of Andhra Pradesh And Ors. ... on 4 February, 1993 (1993 AIR 2178, 1993 SCR (1) 594)*[581]:

> 63. ... one thing is clear: commercialization of education cannot and should not be permitted. [...]

> 64. ... Imparting of education has never been treated as a trade or business in this country since times immemorial. It has been treated as a religious duty. It has been treated as a charitable activity. But never as trade or business.

Nevertheless, at present, there are:

> ... poisonous weeds in the field of education [...] financial adventurers without morals or scruples. Their only aim is to make money, driving a hard bargain [...]. They could be even called pirates in the high seas of education.

What is at stake is to prevent children and adolescents, in particular, from being treated as mere objects and recipients of the liberties of education, exercised as a refuge of the traditional right of education – amounting to a kind of moral (re)privatisation of human beings – or used as a 'Trojan Horse' for the commercialisation of the right to education.

In the Biblical Gospels, there is a scene where Jesus Christ chases sellers of oxen, sheep, pigeons and money changers from the temple of Jerusalem, telling them: "Don't make my Father's house a business house" (John, 2.14). In education too, there is the sacred and the profane. There is the temple of the human right to education, the holiest place of which is its core normative content, where human dignity is rooted, that must be safeguarded against any transaction. Around, chapels exist that may be approached by diverse services providers, duly accredited. Outside the temple, a variety of knowledge may be freely sold and bought.

4.5.2.5 In Concluding

– *The IEL excludes both a public monopoly and the complete privatisation of education.*

In this regard, the first Special Rapporteur on the Right to Education wrote (E/CN.4/2000/6)[582]:

> 33. ... The extremes of a State's monopoly over education or its complete dissociation from education, neither of which would be consistent with International Human Rights Law, are rare. Between these two extremes, the existing jurisprudence has laid down general principles for the interpretation and application of International Human Rights Law.

– *States have an obligation to establish and to develop a public education system with a free compulsory component, and should give priority to the funding of public education, both at the national level and in their co-operation with other States, as well as in the development aid programmes of international organisations of which they are members.*
The Special Rapporteur on the Right to Education wrote (E/CN.4/2001/52)[583]:

> 5. ... The role of the State in education, affirmed in international and domestic human rights law, provides a powerful antidote against the risk of depleting education of remaining a public good and schooling from remaining a public service. The full mobilization of the existing human rights standards for education can neutralize the negative dimensions of globalization at all levels [...].

In this respect, let us recall what the CoESCR said in GC 13 (E/C.12/1999/10)[584]:

> 56. ... In relation to the negotiation and ratification of international agreements, States Parties should take steps to ensure that these instruments do not adversely impact upon the right to education. Similarly, States Parties have an obligation to ensure that their actions as members of international organizations, including international financial institutions, take due account of the right to education.

– *The IEL does not prescribe or prohibit public funding of private education but, if there is funding, it must be done without discrimination.*
As the CoESCR observed in its GC 13 (E/C.12/1999/10)[585]: "A State Party has no obligation to fund institutions established in accordance with Article 13 (3) and (4); however, if a State elects to make a financial contribution to private educational institutions, it must do so without discrimination on any of the prohibited grounds" (para. 54). It also said:

> 30. ... Given the principles of nondiscrimination, equal opportunity and effective participation in society for all, the State has an obligation to ensure that the liberty set out in Article 13 (4) does not lead to extreme disparities of educational opportunity for some groups in society.

In this regard, the Delors Report (1996) reads:

> Without entering into the complexities of various systems, it [the Commission] holds the view that education is a public good that should be available to all. Once this principle is accepted, public and private funding may be combined, according to different *formulae* that take into account each country's traditions, stage of development, ways of life and income distribution. (p. 32)

For example, in the Kingdom of the Netherlands there is a very high percentage of schools run by private entities, but not-for-profit and subject to strong regulation. The Constitution recognises the right to public funding of private schools (Article 23), which is done through a School Funding System.

The CoHR said in 1990, in its Decision on Communications 298/1988 and 299/1988 (*G. and L. Lindgren and L. Holm; A. and B. Hjord, E. and I. Lundquist, L. Radko and E. Stahl*)[586]:

> 10.3 The State Party's educational system [Sweden] provides for comprehensive public sector schooling and allows for private education as an alternative to public education. [...] The State Party cannot be deemed to be under an obligation to provide the same benefits to private schools; indeed, the preferential treatment given to public sector schooling is reasonable and based on objective criteria. The parents of Swedish children are free to take advantage of the public sector schooling or to choose private schooling for their children. [...] The Committee notes that a State Party cannot be deemed to discriminate against parents who freely choose not to avail themselves of benefits which are generally open to all. The State Party has not violated Article 26 [ICCPR] by failing to provide the same benefits to parents of children attending private schools as it provides to parents of children at public schools.

Within the framework of the European system of protection of human rights, sometimes invoked is a "Resolution on freedom of education in the European Community"[587] adopted by the European Parliament in 1984, following which:

> 9. In accordance with the right to freedom of education, Member States shall be required to provide the financial means whereby this right can be exercised in practice, and to make the necessary public grants to enable schools to carry out their tasks and fulfil their duties under

> the same conditions as in corresponding state establishments, without discrimination as regards administration, parents, pupils or staff;

However, the funding of private schools does not have formal support in the ECHR, nor has its Case Law favourable ruled.
In this regard, the first Special Rapporteur on the Right to Education remarked in one of her reports (E/CN.4/2000/6)[588]:

> 36. The Human Rights Committee found [...] that "the preferential treatment given to public sector schooling is reasonable and based on objective criteria" [*Carl Henrik Blom v. Sweden, Communication No. 191/1985*]. This affirmation of the priority of public over private schools goes beyond funding: the role of education in the socialization of children prioritizes inclusiveness over segregation. In the well-known words of the Supreme Court of the United States, "separate educational facilities are inherently unequal".
>
> 37. The European Commission on Human Rights has during its previous existence affirmed that the State has no obligation to subsidize private schools while it has a right to subject such schools to regulation and supervision because it is responsible for ensuring that all education complies with prescribed standards. Domestic courts have been dealing with this subject matter in different countries and have followed the thrust of international human rights law. The Supreme Court of Canada, having examined a complaint against a denial of public funding to private religious schools, has affirmed that the purpose of public schools is provision of education for all members of the community. The exercise of parents' freedom to educate their children in accordance with their religious beliefs in separate schools (or at home) prevents their children from taking advantage of public schools and creates costs for the parents; such exercise of parental freedom does not entail an entitlement to public funding, however.

The contractualisation of the provision of education services from private actors should be temporary, reversible, and never contribute to sustaining for-profit institutions, becoming a factor of commercialization of the right to education.
In its Resolution 41/16 on the right to education (A/HRC/41/L.26),[589] the CHR affirmed that education is "a public good" (para. 3) and warned against "the wide-ranging impact of the commercialization of education on the enjoyment of the right to education" (para. 4).

In the "Resolution of 13 November 2018 on EU development assistance in the field of education (2018/2081(INI))",[590] the European Parliament declared that the European Union, "in accordance with SDG 4.1 [see below] and Article 26 of the UDHR, must not use ODA [Official Development Assistance] to support private, commercial educational establishments, which do not uphold the Union's principles and values" (para. 12).

As education is a human right and a public good, States are entitled to impose to private actors public service obligations.
The CoESCR said in its GC 24 (E/C.12/GC/24, 10 August 2017)[591]: "Privatization is not *per se* [in itself] prohibited by the Covenant" (ICESCR), but private providers "should be subject to strict regulations that impose on them so-called 'public service obligations'" (para. 21). Referring to education, it said that its provision by private actors may have effects of discrimination, notably:

> 22. ... where private educational institutions lead to high-quality education being made a privilege affordable only to the wealthiest segments of society, or where such institutions are insufficiently regulated, providing a form of education that does not meet minimum educational standards while giving a convenient excuse for States Parties not to discharge their own duties towards the fulfilment of the right to education.

For example, the already mentioned, Indian RTE Act (2009)[592] mandates all private schools to provide free education to at least twenty-five per cent of all children admitted at the entry stage (Section 12). This provision was upheld by the Supreme Court in *Case Society for Un-aided Private Schools of Rajasthan v Union of India & Anr* (12 April 2012).[593] The Court reasoned:

> 89. ... A shift in State's functions, to non-state actors in the field of health care, education, social services etc. has been keenly felt due to liberalization of economy and privatization of state functions. [...]
>
> 93. ... The obligation to protect implies the horizontal right which casts an obligation on the State to see that it is not violated by non-state actors. [...]
>
> 95. Primary responsibility for children's rights, therefore, lies with the State and the State has to respect, protect and fulfil children's rights and has also got a duty to regulate the private institutions that care for children, to protect children from violence or abuse, to protect

> children from economic exploitation, hazardous work and to ensure human treatment of children. Non-state actors exercising the state functions like establishing and running private educational institutions are also expected to respect and protect the rights of the child, but they are not expected to surrender their rights constitutionally guaranteed.

- The Supreme Court of Bangladesh ruled, in 2013, that private schools not respecting the limits of fees charged to students, set by the Ministry of Education, may be sentenced.[594] Another example is provided for by the former Special Rapporteur on freedom of religion or belief (Heiner Bielefeldt), in his Report focussed on school education (A/HRC/16/53, 15 December 2010)[595]:

> 56. … situations in which private denominational schools have a *de facto* monopoly in a particular locality or region, with the result that students and parents have no option to avoid school education based on a denomination different from their own religious or belief conviction. In such situations it falls upon the State, as the guarantor of human rights, to ensure that freedom of religion or belief is effectively respected […].

States should adopt and supervise compliance with regulations ensuring that private provision of education meets international and national standards on the right to education.

A regulation and supervision framework of private education should include:

- the establishment of conditions for the establishment and operation of educational institutions, including their registration, licensing, infrastructure, accessibility, security, resources, programmes, as well as the number, qualification, treatment and conditions of work of its teaching staff;
- the transparency of its management, the participation of stakeholders, disciplinary standards compatible with respect for the right to education and other student rights, the prohibition of discrimination, misleading advertising, excessive costs, parallel business and all kinds of abusive practices;
- availability of a mechanism, well known and accessible by students, their parents and other stakeholders, which be reliable and effective, for

> addressing complaints of infringements to applicable regulations, the sanctions of which should include, if needed, compulsory closure.

The Supreme Court of India said in *Case State Of Maharashtra vs Vikas Sahebrao Roundale And Ors* (1992)[596]:

> In *N.M. Nageshwaramma v. State of Andhra Pradesh & Anr., [1986] (Supp) SCC 166 = AIR 1986 SC 1188* this court held that the private institutions unauthorisedly established were invariably ill housed, ill staffed and ill equipped. If the Govt. is directed to permit the students admitted into those institutions, to appear in the examination, we will practically be encouraging and condoning the establishment of unauthorised institutions.

In 2019, the *Abidjan Principles on the human rights obligations of States to provide public education and to regulate private involvement in education*[597] were adopted, after having been drafted by international experts during approximately three-years, in a process of broad global consultation, with the support of several NGOs. They are 10 "Overarching Principles", more 97 "Guiding Principles", approved by a final Conference in Abidjan (Ivory Coast), on 13 February. The Special Rapporteur on the Right to Education (K. Barry), who was involved in the process, wrote in her 2019 annual report: "The principles provide a landmark consolidation of the norms and jurisprudence on the right to education" (A/HRC/41/37, para. 3).[598]

Summing up:

The 2030 Agenda for Sustainable Development[599] includes: "Encourage and promote effective public, public-private and civil society partnerships" (17.7). According to the Education 2030 Framework of Action (see below):

> 82. The private sector, philanthropic organizations and foundations can play an important role, using their experience, innovative approaches, business expertise and financial resources to strengthen public education. They can contribute to education and development through multi-stakeholder partnerships, investment and contributions that are transparent, aligned with local and national priorities, respect education as a human right and do not increase inequality.

Therefore: "Successful partnerships with the private sector will require effective coordination and regulatory mechanisms to ensure transparency and accountability" (para. 108).

In effect, private education may have effects of discrimination and impoverishment with regard to the universality and integrity of the right to education and the common heritage of the cultural and individual diversity of Humanity.

In *Case Costello-Roberts v. The United Kingdom* (Application 13134/87, 25 March 1993),[600] the European Court of Human Rights agreed "that the State cannot absolve itself from responsibility by delegating its obligations to private bodies or individuals" (para. 27). In its Decision on *Case O'Keeffe v. Ireland* (Application Nº. 35810/09, 28 January 2014),[601] the European Court, sitting as Grand Chamber,[602] reaffirmed:

> 151. … the State cannot be released from its positive obligation to protect simply because a child selects one of the State-approved education options, whether a national school, a fee-paying school or, indeed, home schooling (see *Costello-Roberts*, cited above, § 27). […]
>
> 162. The State was therefore aware of the level of sexual crime by adults against minors. Accordingly, when relinquishing control of the education of the vast majority of young children to non-State actors, the State should also have been aware, given its inherent obligation to protect children in this context, of potential risks to their safety if there was no appropriate framework of protection.

The former Special Rapporteur on the Right to Education emphasised (A/HRC/32/37)[603]: "*Governments should not abdicate their responsibility for ensuring that educational institutions retain their essential public service function. In all circumstances, the State must discharge its responsibility as guarantor and regulator of education as a fundamental human right*" (para. 116).

In sum: States' responsibility for human rights should be never privatised. Their functions are changing, but they remain responsible – legally and politically, individually and collectively – for guaranteeing the respect of IHRL.

4.6 Incheon Declaration (2015) and Education 2030 Agenda

4.6.1 *New Vision*

In 2000, the EFA Movement was launched and MDGs proclaimed. More than 50 million additional children were enrolled in primary school from 2000 to 2010, but there are still about 50 million children of primary school age out of school, most of whom are girls, and dozens of millions do not complete primary education. About 250 million children end their schooling without knowing how to read or write nor do they learn competencies for adult life and decent jobs. The provision of early childhood care and education (ECCE) and reducing adult illiteracy (women account for two thirds of the world's 775 million illiterate adults) have not significantly progressed. Moreover, the EFA and MDGs were narrowly focussed on school access.

A UN Summit gathering all Member States of the United Nations, meeting in New York from 25 to 27 September 2015, as the Organisation celebrated its 70th anniversary, adopted the Resolution "Transforming our World: The 2030 Agenda for Sustainable Development" (A/RES/70/1),[604] with 17 Sustainable Development Goals (SDGs) and 169 targets, to be reached by 2030. They integrate "and balance the three dimensions of sustainable development: the economic, social and environmental" (Preamble), and "build on the Millennium Development Goals and complete what they did not achieve".

At the 2015 UN Summit, the Heads of State and Government and High Representatives adopted a Declaration proclaiming "an Agenda of unprecedented scope and significance" (para. 5) that "is guided by the purposes and principles of the Charter of the United Nations, including full respect for international law", and "is grounded in the Universal Declaration of Human Rights, international human rights treaties, the Millennium Declaration and the 2005 World Summit Outcome", as well as "informed by other instruments such as the Declaration on the Right to Development" (para. 10). Here is the "supremely ambitious and transformational vision" (para. 7) set out by the new Agenda:

> 7. … We envisage a world free of poverty, hunger, disease and want, where all life can thrive. We envisage a world free of fear and violence. A world with universal literacy. A world with equitable and universal access to quality education at all levels, to health care and social protection, where physical, mental and social well-being are assured.
> 8. We envisage a world of universal respect for human rights and human dignity, the rule of law, justice, equality and non-discrimination; of respect for race, ethnicity and cultural diversity; and of equal opportunity permitting the full realization of human potential and contributing to shared prosperity. A world which invests in its children and in which every child grows up free from violence and exploitation. A world in which every woman and girl enjoys full gender equality and all legal, social and economic barriers to their empowerment have been removed. A just, equitable, tolerant, open and socially inclusive world in which the needs of the most vulnerable are met.

In particular:

- "We are committed to ending poverty in all its forms and dimensions, including by eradicating extreme poverty by 2030. All people must enjoy a basic standard of living, including through social protection systems" (para. 24).
- "We pledge to foster intercultural understanding, tolerance, mutual respect and an ethic of global citizenship and shared responsibility" (para. 36).

In order to meet the "shared principles and commitments" restated by the new Agenda (para. 10): "ODA providers reaffirm their respective commitments, including the commitment by many developed countries to achieve the target of 0.7 per cent of gross national income for official development assistance (ODA/GNI) to developing countries and 0.15 per cent to 0.2 per cent of ODA/GNI to least developed countries" (para. 43).

If the SDGs and their 169 associated targets are met by 2030: "We can be the first generation to succeed in ending poverty; just as we may be the last to have a chance of saving the planet" (para. 50), the "Mother Earth" (para. 59). Therefore: "The future of humanity and of our planet lies in our hands" (para. 53).

As a consequence:

> 19. We reaffirm the importance of the Universal Declaration of Human Rights, as well as other international instruments relating to human rights and international law. We emphasize the responsibilities of all States, in conformity with the Charter of the United Nations, to respect, protect and promote human rights and fundamental freedoms for all, without distinction of any kind as to race, colour, sex, language, religion, political or other opinion, national or social origin, property, birth, disability or other status.

Concerning the right to education, in particular:

> 25. We commit to providing inclusive and equitable quality education at all levels – early childhood, primary, secondary, tertiary, technical and vocational training. All people, irrespective of sex, age, race or ethnicity, and persons with disabilities, migrants, indigenous peoples, children and youth, especially those in vulnerable situations, should have access to life-long learning opportunities that help them to acquire the knowledge and skills needed to exploit opportunities and to participate fully in society. We will strive to provide children and youth with a nurturing environment for the full realisation of their rights and capabilities, helping our countries to reap the demographic dividend, including through safe schools and cohesive communities and families.

These challenges are addressed by *Goal 4*, namely: *Ensure inclusive and equitable quality education and promote lifelong learning opportunities for all.* It unfolds in 10 sub-goals, including:

- "ensure that all girls and boys have access to quality early childhood development, care and pre-primary education so that they are ready for primary education" (4.2);
- "ensure that all girls and boys complete free, equitable and quality primary and secondary education leading to relevant and effective learning outcomes" (4.1);
- "increase the supply of qualified teachers" (4.c), as about 69 million teachers are needed to achieve universal primary and secondary education by 2030[605];
- "ensure equal access for all women and men to affordable and quality technical, vocational and tertiary education, including university" (4.3).

In the context of the preparation of the 2030 Agenda for Sustainable Development, UNESCO together with UNICEF, the World Bank and other international entities organised a World Education Forum in Incheon, Republic of Korea, from 19 to 22 May 2015, with about 1600 participants from 160 countries, including 120 Ministers. It was prepared by, among other initiatives, a Global Thematic Consultation on Education in the Post-2015 Development Agenda, co-led by UNESCO and UNICEF (2013)[606] and the already mentioned UNESCO Report *Rethinking education* (2015).

The Incheon World Education Forum adopted the *Incheon Declaration*. On 4 November – therefore, already after the adoption of the 2030 Agenda for Sustainable Development – an *Education 2030 Framework for Action for the implementation of Sustainable Development Goal 4* was adopted by 184 UNESCO's Member States, in Paris, and endorsed by the General Conference.[607] The *Incheon Declaration* and the *Education 2030 Framework for Action*[608] represent the most recent commitments of the International Community, in the medium term, towards the right to education.

The *2015 Incheon Declaration* reads, notably:

> 2. On this historic occasion, we reaffirm the vision of the worldwide movement for Education for All initiated in Jomtien in 1990 and reiterated in Dakar in 2000 – the most important commitment to education in recent decades and which has helped drive significant progress in education. We also reaffirm the vision and political will reflected in numerous international and regional human rights treaties that stipulate the right to education and its interrelation with other human rights. We acknowledge the efforts made; however, we recognize with

great concern that we are far from having reached education for all. [...] ...

5. Our vision is to transform lives through education, recognizing the important role of education as a main driver of development and in achieving the other proposed SDGs. [...] This new vision is fully captured by the proposed SDG 4. [...] It is transformative and universal, attends to the 'unfinished businesses of the EFA agenda and the education-related MDGs, and addresses global and national education challenges. It is inspired by a humanistic vision of education and development based on human rights and dignity; social justice; inclusion; protection; cultural, linguistic and ethnic diversity; and shared responsibility and accountability. We reaffirm that education is a public good, a fundamental human right and a basis for guaranteeing the realization of other rights. It is essential for peace, tolerance, human fulfilment and sustainable development. [...]
6. Motivated by our significant achievements in expanding *access* to education over the last 15 years, we will ensure the provision of 12 years of free, publicly funded, equitable quality primary and secondary education, of which at least nine years are compulsory, leading to relevant learning outcomes. We also encourage the provision of at least one year of free and compulsory quality pre-primary education and that all children have access to quality early childhood development, care and education. [...]
7. *Inclusion* and equity in and through education is the cornerstone of a transformative education agenda, and we therefore commit to addressing all forms of exclusion and marginalization, disparities and inequalities in access, participation and learning outcomes. No education target should be considered met unless met by all. [...]...
9. We commit to *quality* education and to improving learning outcomes, which requires strengthening inputs, processes and evaluation of outcomes and mechanisms to measure progress. We will ensure that teachers and educators are empowered, adequately recruited, well-trained, professionally qualified, motivated and supported within well-resourced, efficient and effectively governed systems. [...]
10. We commit to promoting quality *lifelong learning opportunities* for all, in all settings and at all levels of education. [...]
12. We reaffirm that the fundamental responsibility for successfully implementing this agenda lies with governments. [...]
14. ... We therefore are determined to increase public spending on education in accordance with country context, and urge adherence to the international and regional benchmarks of allocating efficiently

at least 4–6% of Gross Domestic Product and/or at least 15–20% of total public expenditure to education.

15. … We recognize that the fulfilment of all commitments related to official development assistance (ODA) is crucial, including the commitments by many developed countries to achieve the target of 0.7 per cent of gross national product (GNP) for ODA to developing countries. […][609]

[…]

20. Building on the legacy of Jomtien and Dakar, this Incheon Declaration is an historic commitment by all of us to transform lives through a new vision for education, with bold and innovative actions, to reach our ambitious goal by 2030.

The *Education 2030 Framework for Action* reads, notably:

1. The world has made some remarkable progress in education since 2000, when the six Education for All (EFA) Goals and the Millennium Development Goals (MDGs) were established. Those goals were not, however, reached by the 2015 deadline and continued action is needed to complete the unfinished agenda. […]
2. … The Incheon Declaration constitutes the commitment of the education community to SDG4-Education 2030 and the 2030 Agenda for Sustainable Development, recognizing the important role of education as a main driver of development. The *SDG4-Education 2030 Framework for Action*, which provides guidance for implementing SDG4-Education 2030, was discussed at WEF [World Education Forum] 2015, and its essential elements were agreed upon in the Incheon Declaration. […]
4. Education is at the heart of the 2030 Agenda for Sustainable Development and is essential for the success of all SDGs. […] The renewed education agenda encapsulated in Goal 4 is comprehensive, holistic, ambitious, aspirational and universal, and inspired by a vision of education that transforms the lives of individuals, communities and societies, leaving no one behind. […] It is rights-based and inspired by a humanistic vision of education and development, based on the principles of human rights and dignity, social justice, peace, inclusion and protection, as well as cultural, linguistic and ethnic diversity and shared responsibility and accountability. […]
7. The renewed attention to the purpose and relevance of education for human development and economic, social and environmental sustainability is a defining feature of the SDG4-Education 2030 Agenda.

This is embedded in its holistic and humanistic vision, which contributes to a new model of development. That vision goes beyond a utilitarian approach to education and integrates the multiple dimensions of human existence. [...]

10. The principles informing this Framework are drawn from international instruments and agreements [...]. Those principles include:
    - *Education is a fundamental human right and an enabling right.* [...] Education shall aim at the full development of the human personality and promote mutual understanding, tolerance, friendship and peace.
    - *Education is a public good, of which the State is the duty bearer.* [...] The role of the State is essential in setting and regulating standards and norms.
    - *Gender equality is inextricably linked to the right to education for all.* [...]

This *Framework for Action* is coordinated by UNESCO, through a multi-stakeholder Education 2030 Steering Committee (Education 2030 SC), largely representative, Member States forming the majority. An independent team prepares a yearly Global Education Monitoring (GEM) Report that succeeds the EFA Global Monitoring Report. UNESCO has issued a *Quick Guide to Education Indicators for SDG 4*.[610]

The most significant feature of the *2030 Agenda for Sustainable Development* is that it takes an overtly human rights approach (there are 14 references to them). As do the *Incheon Declaration* and the *2030 Education Agenda*. The *Incheon Declaration* formally states, as above quoted, that it "is inspired by a humanistic vision of education and development based on human rights and dignity" (para. 5). Other of the *Declaration* and *Agenda* most important features include:
- They address both developing and developed countries.
- Not losing sight of the hundreds of million children and adolescents still out of school, and of the illiterate persons, the main focus is now on education quality.
- At least one year of free and compulsory quality pre-primary education should be available, and free school education should cover 12 years, 9 of which compulsory.
- The principle of lifelong education is adopted.

The 2030 Agenda does not contain accountability mechanisms, but to the extent that the SDG 4 reflects the normative content of the right to education, the commitments undertaken by States are justiciable.[611]

In the wake of the *Incheon Declaration* and the Oslo Summit on Education for Development (July 2015), an International Commission on Financing Global Education Opportunity was convened by the Prime Minister of Norway, the Presidents of Malawi, Indonesia, and Chile, and the Director-General of UNESCO. The Commission's Report was launched at the UN General Assembly on 18th September 2016. It "builds upon the vision agreed to by world leaders in 2015 with the Sustainable Development Goal for education: *To ensure inclusive and equitable quality education by 2030 and promote lifelong learning opportunities for all.* The aims and actions set out in this report are in line with, and intended to help to deliver this goal" (International Commission on Financing Global Education Opportunity, 2016, p. 6). However, "education is so central for facilitating development that each one of the 17 SDGs includes a target which relates to or depends upon learning and educating" (p. 36).

The International Commission warns that the "gap between what young people want, demand, and believe they have a right to, and what young people can actually access and receive, will grow ever wider. The costs of this learning crisis – unemployment, poverty, inequality, and instability – could undermine the very fabric of our economies and societies" (p. 29).

> The Commission finds that if current trends continue, only seven out of 10 children of school age in low- and middle-income countries will be on track to achieve primary-level skills in 2030. In low-income countries the situation will be worst, with just three out of 10 school age children on track to achieve primary-level skills. It also projects that only four out of 10 children of school age in low- and middle-income countries will be on track to achieve minimum secondary-school level skills in 2030. In low-income countries, less than one in 10 will be on track. This means that, of the 1.4 billion school-age children in low- and middle-income countries in 2030, the Commission estimates that 420 million will not be on track to learn the most basic skills in childhood, and 825 million will not be on track to acquire basic secondary-level skills (see Figure 1). The already vast gap in post-secondary learning between the poorest and richest countries will worsen. Without urgent change, more than 1.5 billion adults will have no education beyond primary school in 2030. (p. 30)

Summing up: "The case for investment is irrefutable. The costs of delay are clear" (p. 32).

We now address the targets stated in Goal 4 of the Agenda for Sustainable Development, namely: quality, inclusive, equity and lifelong education.

4.6.2 *Quality Education*

More than mere right of access to whatever education, the right to education is right to a specific education quality and all that goes with it. The so-called 'Second Bill of Rights'[612] proposed by Franklin Roosevelt in his Message to Congress on the State of the Union, in 1944, included: "The right to good education". Nowadays, *quality education* or *good quality education* is the watchword.

The 2000 UNESCO *World Education Report* observed:

> While it is apparent from the foregoing chapters that there has been a great deal of progress worldwide over the past half-century towards implementation of the right to education in terms of access to education, it nevertheless remains that the vision that came to be embodied in Article 26 of the Universal Declaration of Human Rights was not just a quantitative one. It was also a qualitative one concerning the purposes and hence contents of education. (UNESCO, 2000, p. 74)

The CADE[613] explicitly refers to education quality three times, especially the following one: "For the purposes of this Convention, the term 'education' refers to all types and levels of education, and includes access to education, the standard and quality of education, and the conditions under which it is given" (Article 1.2). Also, in the Recommendation concerning the Status of Teachers (ILO/UNESCO, 1966),[614] the word 'quality' appears six times (referring to education and teachers). It states, in particular: "as an educational objective, no State should be satisfied with the mere quantity, but should seek also to improve quality" (10.g).

Nevertheless, it was only in the 1980s that the word 'quality' became omnipresent in the political-pedagogical discourse, under pressure from economic concerns, following the late 1970s recession. As an OECD Report remarked, "never before the quality of education had aroused so much interest" but, "at the end of the day, behind the current interest in the quality of education are powerful economic and technical imperatives" (OECD, 1989, pp. 15, 21).

At present, we may distinguish two main approaches to education quality:

- *Human capital approach*
  This approach reflects the neoliberal ideology, based on quasi-market principles. It is rooted in the human capital theory elaborated in the 1960s by professors of the University of Chicago (USA), especially Gary Becker and Theodore Schultz.
- *Human right approach*
  This approach is inspired by the normative integrity of the right to education, as internationally agreed, reflecting human rights values and principles and aiming at the free, full and harmonious development of the human personality.

These two approaches were opposed by the first Special Rapporteur on the Right to Education who wrote in her Preliminary Report (E/CN.4/1999/49)[615]:

> 13. ... Human rights law specifies the purpose and objective of education, increasingly calling for the mainstreaming of human rights throughout the contents and process of education. From the human rights viewpoint, education is thus an end in itself rather than merely a means for achieving other ends. Some economists may, however, define education as efficient production of human capital and classify all its human rights dimensions as externalities. A definition of people as human capital obviously differs from defining people as subjects of rights.

Shortly after, she wrote in another Report (E/CN.4/2000/6)[616]:

> 66. The definition of education as a human right does not guide many international or domestic education strategies; the recent emergence of a focus on education as a means for creating human capital and the prospect of education being purchased and sold as service create a great challenge for reaffirming education as a human right and as a public good. [...]
>
> 67 The Special Rapporteur has consistently held that the notion of human capital questions the inherent worth of each human being which underpins human rights, as well as undermining the role of education in the promotion and protection of human rights. [...] The human capital approach molds education solely towards economically relevant knowledge, skills and competence, to the detriment of human rights values. [...] A productivist view of education depletes it of much of its purpose and substance. [...]
>
> 73. ... The Special Rapporteur feels that the vast amounts of data which are being internationally generated within the field of education do not conform to the human rights approach to education, and a conceptual challenge remains for the human rights community to design indicators that would capture the essence of the right to education and human rights in education.

Quality education has become an international leitmotif since the first decade of the 20th century. For example:

- In 2003, during the 32nd Session of the UNESCO's General Conference (from 29 September to 17 October), a Ministerial Round Table on Quality Education took place. It adopted a Final Communiqué[617] that read (I.C.):

> Despite the different contexts, there are many common elements in the pursuit of a quality education, which should equip all people, women and men, to be fully participating members of their own communities and also citizens of the world. Understood like this, quality education requires us to redefine the parameters of education in such a way as to cover certain basic knowledge, values, competencies and behaviours that are specifically attuned to globalization but reflect the beauty and richness of our diversity expressed in different forms of belief, spirituality, culture, and language. The challenge is to develop educational systems that balance local, national and global aspirations in the context of our common humanity.

– In 2004, the theme of the 47th Session of the International Conference on Education taking place in Geneva was "Quality education for all young people: challenges, trends and priorities". It adopted a 'Message' that read[618]:

> 1. Promoting quality education and training [...] is essential to securing a better future and constitutes an essential mechanism for combating social exclusion at the local, national and global levels. As both a basic right and a public good, this education must respond to the needs and interests of all young people with a view to ensuring the realization of their full potential, their successful integration in the world of work, as well as their capacity to participate in active life and as responsible citizens.

In the closing address, UNESCO Director-General (at the time Koïchiro Matsuura) said:

> There has been much discussion of those challenges, which arise within education systems and schools as well as within the broader context that shapes our educational endeavors. The theme of "humanizing globalization" has provided the main framework of the debate. [...]
>
> An education that is perceived and experienced by young people as irrelevant to their needs and interests cannot be education of quality, certainly not in this day and age when other modalities of learning are increasingly available and are often more engaging and more enjoyable.
>
> An education that leaves young people alienated from the challenges and pleasures of learning, or places them in an environment of exclusion, rejection, violence and discrimination, cannot be an education of quality. Nor can an education that leaves young people bewildered, confused and perplexed in their attitudes and beliefs. [...]

> And there is a widely held perception that what counts as "quality education" cannot be divorced from the fundamental problems facing the world, notably those pertaining to peace, sustainable development and respect for basic rights and human dignity everywhere.

- Following a publication by UNESCO (2005a):

> ... quality in education is often perceived and measured as the academic results attained by the pupils through the successful completion of final exams and other quantitative measures. [...] Quality, however, is more than this and entails a school system where all children are welcome and where diversity and flexibility are seen as important ingredients for the development and personal growth of all learners. [...]
>
> If we adopt a holistic perspective of society, it is more relevant to ask about the costs to society when it does *not* provide education for all children. In such a context, it is clear that the most cost-effective solution is to offer education to all children. Education is the fundamental basis upon which the survival of the human race and development of a nation depend; it is an important investment where no compromises should be made. Therefore, systems need to consider minimizing the wastage of resources and using resources optimally in making education cost-effective, rather than focusing on cost-cutting measures. (pp. 17, 18)

- In 2005, the *EFA Global Monitoring Report* was consecrated to "The quality imperative". It stated in Chapter 1:

> Although there is no single definition of quality, two principles characterize most attempts to define the objectives of education. The first, which identifies learners' cognitive development as the major explicit objective of all education systems, sees the success with which systems achieve this as one indicator of their quality. The second emphasizes the role of education in promoting commonly shared values along with creative and emotional development – objectives whose achievement is much more difficult to assess. Common ground is also found in the broadly shared objectives that tend to underpin debates about quality: respect for individual rights, improved equity of access and of learning outcomes, and increased relevance. These principles have been integrated into the aims of education set out in the Convention on the Rights of the Child (1990), which underpins the current positions on quality held by UNESCO and UNICEF. [...]
>
> To reconcile a range of approaches, the Report adopts a framework that takes into account five major factors affecting quality: learners, whose

> diversity must be recognized; the national economic and social context; material and human resources; the teaching and learning process and the outcomes and benefits of education. By focusing on these dimensions and how they interact, it is possible to draw up a comprehensive map for understanding, monitoring and improving quality. (UNESCO, 2005b, p. 19)

- The *UNESCO Medium-Term Strategy, 2014–2021* (37 C/4)[619] includes "supporting Member States to review and update their legal frameworks to reflect the right to quality education for all" (para. 8).

The CoRC first GC (CRC/GC/2001/1)[620] is a landmark for mainstreaming quality education. It reads:

> 2. Article 29 (1) not only adds to the right to education recognized in Article 28 a qualitative dimension which reflects the rights and inherent dignity of the child; it also insists upon the need for education to be child-centred, child-friendly and empowering, and it highlights the need for educational processes to be based upon the very principles it enunciates. [...]
> 3. The child's right to education is not only a matter of access (Art. 28) but also of content. [...] And yet, in the national and international programmes and policies on education that really count, the elements embodied in Article 29 (1) seem all too often to be either largely missing or present only as a cosmetic afterthought. [...]
> 9. ... while Article 28 focuses upon the obligations of State Parties in relation to the establishment of educational systems and in ensuring access thereto, Article 29(1) underlines the individual and subjective right to a specific quality of education. [...].
> 13. ... need for education to be designed and provided in such a way that it promotes and reinforces the range of specific ethical values enshrined in the Convention, including education for peace, tolerance, and respect for the natural environment, in an integrated and holistic manner. This may require a multidisciplinary approach. [...]
> 18. The effective promotion of Article 29 (1) requires the fundamental reworking of curricula to include the various aims of education and the systematic revision of textbooks and other teaching materials and technologies, as well as school policies. Approaches which do no more than seek to superimpose the aims and values of the Article on the existing system without encouraging any deeper changes are clearly inadequate. [...] It is also important that the teaching methods used in schools reflect the spirit and educational philosophy of

the Convention on the Rights of the Child and the aims of education laid down in Article 29 (1). [...]

22. ... Every child has the right to receive an education of good quality which in turn requires a focus on the quality of the learning environment, of teaching and learning processes and materials, and of learning outputs.

There is no single agreed definition of 'quality education', as above noted, but from the CoRC first GC and other normative and programmatic texts, including the *Incheon Declaration* and the *Agenda Education 2030*, it appears that the right to quality education is right to a rightful education (see 5.1.3), that is, right to a human right approach of education meeting the normative integrity of the right to education as internationally agreed. Accordingly, the overarching criterion of education quality should be its *consistency with the radically subjective purpose of the right to education*, namely: the development of the human personality – free, full, harmonious.

The paramountcy of the purpose of education is highlighted, for instance, in the African Youth Charter (African Union, 2006),[621] following which: "Every young person shall have the right to education of good quality" (Article 13.1) that is described through the aims to which education "shall be directed", worded in six subsections of paragraph 3, the first of which reads: "The promotion and holistic development of the young person's cognitive and creative and emotional abilities to their full potential". The purpose of education also stands out in the Recommendation CM/Rec(2012)13 of the Committee of Ministers to Member States on ensuring Quality Education (Council of Europe, 2012),[622] mainly in its paragraph 6, with nine subsections.

In addition to its primordial individual dimension as "both a human right in itself and an indispensable means of realizing other human rights" – as the CoESCR begins by stating in GC 13 (E/C.12/1999/10)[625] – the right to education bears an obvious social dimension as "one of the best financial investments States can make", if not the best (see 4.4.1). Therefore, the conception of quality education has to include a contextually variable perspective, tailored according to particular needs, conditions and possibilities. This implies, notably, to balance the establishment of a national curricular framework consistent with the normative integrity of the right to education with devolving reasonable autonomy to schools, provided that teachers are professionally empowered – that is, adequately selected, duly educated, strongly motivated – to assume it.

This vision of quality education is exemplarily assumed by the Finnish school system, whose inspiring National Core Curriculum, applied from the autumn of 2016, deserves extended quotation (Finnish National Board of Education, 2016):

2.2 *Underlying values of basic education*

The preparation of the national core curriculum was based on the following underlying values.

Uniqueness of each pupil and right to a good education

Basic education is underpinned by the idea of the specific value of childhood. Each pupil is unique and valuable just as he or she is. Each pupil has the right to grow into his or her full potential as a human being and a member of society. [...]

Each pupil has the right to a good education and success in their studies. While learning, the pupils are building their identity, their understanding of humanity, worldview and philosophy of life and finding their place in the world.

[...]

Humanity, general knowledge and ability, equality and democracy

Basic education supports the pupil's growth as a human being who strives for truth, goodness, beauty, justice and peace. [...] Knowledge and ability also means that individuals and communities are capable of making decisions based on ethical reflection, putting themselves in the place of another person, and consideration based on knowledge. The perspectives of ethics and aesthetics guide the pupils to think about what is valuable in life. [...]

Basic education is built on respect for life and human rights. It directs the pupils to defend these values and to appreciate the inviolability of human dignity. [...] Education shall not demand or lead to religious, philosophical or political commitment of the pupils. The school and education may not be used as channels of commercial influence.

Cultural diversity as a richness

[...]

Necessity of a sustainable way of living

[...]

Basic education broadens the pupils' horizons, allowing them to appreciate their cross-generational global responsibility.

Quality education factors and conditions are, therefore, manifold – material and non-material, tangible and intangible, attuned to the individual uniqueness, needs and aspirations, leaving no one behind, as well to the collective well-being – but its deepest and purest sources are the quality of parents' love (see 5.3.1) and the personal qualities of education professionals (see 5.3.8).

This is a humanist, holistic, empowering vision of quality education. Rooted in the ethical core of the human right to education, its unfailing commitment should lie in cultivating the seeds of the highest human aptitudes, which are rationality, liberty and creativity (see 2.6.2.4.4) and sowing the superior values of education, which should be Liberty, Reciprocity and Responsibility (see 5.2.2.3). It is a vision opposed to an education captured by ethnic reflexes, cultural traditions, religious beliefs, partisan indoctrination or neoliberal economism. What should be mostly politically and pedagogically *worthy* is the magnitude of the human personality.

4.6.3 *Inclusive Education*

The term 'exclusion' is not found in the main IHRL instruments, but the Vienna Declaration and Programme of Action (1993)[624] affirms that "extreme poverty and social exclusion constitute a violation of human dignity" (I.25).

Exclusion means discrimination or marginalisation as both consequence and cause of the practical denial of human dignity and rights. This is the objective condition of a great majority of human beings. Its faces and names are numerous, but the reality is always the same: excluded are the human beings diminished in their capacities for surviving and living humanely. When several causes converge, the exclusion becomes multiple and compound, cumulative. For example: to be a girl, disabled, poor, belonging to a minority.

Inclusive education is a concept originating from the special education field, denoting education for children with some disability affecting more or less deeply their aptitude to learning. It was first dominated by a medical welfare approach, concerned with the prevention and the rehabilitation of disability, leading to *separated schooling of the handicapped children*. Later, took place a shift towards the principle of *school integration of children with special education needs*. This approach has developed since the 1960s, within the context of the disability rights movement, culminating with the Convention on the Rights of Persons with Disabilities (UN, 2006). In the meanwhile, some important international normative texts, related to disability, have been adopted. They include:

- Declaration on the Rights of Mentally Retarded Persons (UN, 1971)
- Declaration on the Rights of Disabled Persons (UN, 1975)
- Sundberg Declaration (so named in memory of Nils-Ivar Sundberg, in charge of the UNESCO Programme for Special Education, 1968–1981), adopted by the World Conference on Actions and Strategies for Education, Prevention

and Integration, organised by the Spanish Government in co-operation with UNESCO in Torremolinos, Malaga, in 1981, the International Year of Disabled Persons

- United Nations World Programme of Action Concerning Disabled Persons (1982)
- Standard Rules on the Equalisation of Opportunities for Persons with Disabilities (UN, 1993)
- Salamanca Statement on Principles, Policy and Practice in Special Needs Education, adopted by the World Conference on Special Needs Education organised by the Government of Spain in co-operation with UNESCO, in 1994.[625] The Salamanca Statement proclaimed:

> every child has unique characteristics, interests, abilities and learning needs,
>
> education systems should be designed and educational programs implemented to take into account the wide diversity of these characteristics and needs, [...]
>
> regular schools with this inclusive orientation are the most effective means of combating discriminatory attitudes, creating welcoming communities, building an inclusive society and achieving education for all; moreover, they provide effective education to the majority of children and improve the efficiency and ultimately the cost-effectiveness of the entire education system.

The Salamanca Conference adopted a Framework for Action on Special Needs Education that affirms:

> 3. The guiding principle that informs this Framework is that schools should accommodate all children regardless of their physical, intellectual, social, emotional, linguistic or other conditions. This should include disabled and gifted children, street and working children, children from remote or nomadic populations, children from linguistic, ethnic or cultural minorities and children from other disadvantaged or marginalized areas or groups. These conditions create a range of different challenges to school systems. In the context of this Framework, the term 'special educational needs' refers to all those children and youth whose needs arise from disabilities or learning difficulties. Many children experience learning difficulties and thus have special educational needs at some time during their schooling. Schools have to find ways of successfully educating all children, including those who have serious disadvantages and disabilities. There is an emerging consensus that children and youth with special

educational needs should be included in the educational arrangements made for the majority of children. This has led to the concept of the inclusive school. [...]

4. Special needs education incorporates the proven principles of sound pedagogy from which all children may benefit. [...] A child-centred pedagogy is beneficial to all students and, as a consequence, to society as a whole. [...] Child-centred schools are, moreover, the training ground for a people-oriented society that respects both the differences and the dignity of all human beings.

In the Convention on the Rights of Persons with Disabilities (UN, 2006)[626]: "States Parties recognize the right of persons with disabilities to education" (Article 24.1). The overarching principle of inclusion is supported by the constellation of "General Principles" set out in Article 3. The concept of "reasonable accommodation" is introduced and defined as the "necessary and appropriate modification and adjustments not imposing a disproportionate or undue burden, where needed in a particular case, to ensure to persons with disabilities the enjoyment or exercise on an equal basis with others of all human rights and fundamental freedoms" (Article 2). This concept is largely used by the Committee on the Rights of Persons with Disabilities in its GC 4 on "The right to inclusive education" (CRPD/C/GC/4, 25 November 2016),[627] where the following broad definition is provided for:

10. Inclusive education is to be understood as:

a A fundamental human right of all learners. Notably, education is the right of the individual learner and not, in the case of children, the right of a parent or caregiver. Parental responsibilities in this regard are subordinate to the rights of the child;

b A principle that values the well-being of all students, respects their inherent dignity and autonomy, and acknowledges individuals' requirements and their ability to effectively be included in and contribute to society;

c A means of realizing other human rights. It is the primary means by which persons with disabilities can lift themselves out of poverty, obtain the means to participate fully in their communities and be safeguarded from exploitation. It is also the primary means of achieving inclusive societies;

d The result of a process of continuing and proactive commitment to eliminating barriers impeding the right to education, together with changes to culture, policy and practice of regular schools to accommodate and effectively include all students.

The Committee has made the following distinctions (italics added):

> 11. The Committee highlights the importance of recognizing the differences between exclusion, segregation, integration and inclusion. *Exclusion* occurs when students are directly or indirectly prevented from or denied access to education in any form. *Segregation* occurs when the education of students with disabilities is provided in separate environments designed or used to respond to a particular impairment or to various impairments, in isolation from students without disabilities. *Integration* is the process of placing persons with disabilities in existing mainstream educational institutions with the understanding that they can adjust to the standardized requirements of such institutions. *Inclusion* involves a process of systemic reform embodying changes and modifications in content, teaching methods, approaches, structures and strategies in education to overcome barriers with a vision serving to provide all students of the relevant age range with an equitable and participatory learning experience and the environment that best corresponds to their requirements and preferences. Placing students with disabilities within mainstream classes without accompanying structural changes to, for example, organization, curriculum and teaching and learning strategies, does not constitute inclusion. Furthermore, integration does not automatically guarantee the transition from segregation to inclusion.

Nowadays, the principle of *all children inclusive school* has generalised. As reads a UNESCO publication, inclusion is "*a dynamic approach of responding positively to pupil diversity and of seeing individual differences not as problems, but as opportunities for enriching learning*" (UNESCO, 2005a, p. 12).

In 2017, UNESCO issued *A Guide for ensuring inclusion and equity in education.*[628]

The jurisprudence of the European Court of Human Rights supports the principle of inclusive education, combining Article 2 of the first Protocol to the ECHR with its Article 14, which prohibits indirect discrimination.

Consequently, inclusive education is one that welcomes every child and adolescent, in particular, as he or she is, and strives to meet the diversity of their learning needs and interests. The question is no more how to integrate into school *disabled* children, but rather how *different* shall the school become for not being *disabled* itself, in order to satisfy the right to education of *different* children.[629] Indeed, there are not 'abnormal' children, it is the school that has been 'abnormal'. As said the Constitutional Court of Colombia (*Case*

T-306/11),[630] "the State is obliged to assure that education is adapted to the child, and not that the child adapts to education".

A child or adolescent may need special attention due to physical or intellectual limitations, but also for reasons which, in a particular moment of their life, may affect them materially or emotionally, such as illness or unemployment of the mother or/and father, death of father or mother, brother or sister or other loved ones. If the profound disturbance that such circumstances may cause in their lives does not stay at the door of the school, it must be recognised, respected and spoken inside it. A broad conception of special educational needs is a hallmark of the Finnish school system.

In sum: All human rights are rights against exclusion – the exclusion of discrimination, segregation, poverty, ignorance, unemployment, etc. – but the right to education is the right to inclusion *par excellence*. It is like a vaccine against exclusion. Using the metaphor of the title of the Delors Report – *Education, a treasure within* – excluded people have treasures inside them but are not able to discover them. The right to education is the map and the compass to discover the treasures of our common and diverse Humanity.

4.6.4 *Equity Education*

Equity is an ethical and legal-political notion of Greco-Latin origin. Equity is generally understood as a principle of moderation of the literal, formal legal rigour, inspired by a sense of justice. It is common to the major legal systems and has been used by International Law for many purposes.

According to Aristotle, just and equitable are both good, but "the equitable is superior". The equitable is "not the legally just but a correction of legal justice", when a general principle does not cover a particular case or situation. Therefore, "this is the nature of the equitable, a correction of law where it is defective owing to its universality" (Aristotle, 1925, Book V, 1137b8).

Celsus, one of the most influential Roman jurists, in the 2nd century, offered the following definition (*Libri Digestorum*)[631]: *Jus est ars boni et aequi* (Law is the art of the good and the equitable). In this connection, the Colombian Council of State quoted in its Decision *2000-01823* (2013)[632] another one where it had affirmed in 1967:

> THE SPIRIT OF GEOMETRY CANNOT BE INTRODUCED IN LAW
> Cases as that we are examining are those which make most evident that pruritus of numerical accuracy may be the most incompatible with justice. It happens that rigorisms in judicial processes lead to the most flagrant violations of equity and to ignore the Law, for trying to work with the spirit characteristic of the exact sciences in a field where there are

> no algebraic formulas, nor precision instruments, or machines that provide a true picture of the legal truths. It is what expresses the old proverb saying that to exaggerate the Law is to produce injustice [*summum ius, summa iniuria*], and what is meant today when one says that who administers justice may not work with the spirit of geometry.

In the education field, equity is a principle to struggle against inequalities, discrimination and exclusion. An OECD Report (2012) reads:

> Reducing school failure pays off for both society and individuals. It can also contribute to economic growth and social development. Indeed, the highest performing education systems across OECD countries are those that combine quality with equity. Equity in education means that personal or social circumstances such as gender, ethnic origin or family background, are not obstacles to achieving educational potential (fairness) and that all individuals reach at least a basic minimum level of skills (inclusion). In these education systems, the vast majority of students have the opportunity to attain high level skills, regardless of their own personal and socio-economic circumstances.
>
> *OECD countries face the problem of school failure and dropout*
>
> Across OECD countries, almost one of every five students does not reach a basic minimum level of skills to function in today's societies (indicating lack of inclusion). Students from the low socio-economic background are twice as likely to be low performers, implying that personal or social circumstances are obstacles to achieving their educational potential (indicating lack of fairness). Lack of inclusion and fairness fuels school failure, of which dropout is the most visible manifestation – with 20% of young adults on average dropping out before finalizing upper secondary education.
>
> *Improving equity and reducing school failure pays off*
>
> The economic and social costs of school failure and dropout are high, whereas successful secondary education completion gives individuals better employment and healthier lifestyle prospects resulting in greater contributions to public budgets and investment. More educated people contribute to more democratic societies and sustainable economies and are less dependent on public aid and less vulnerable to economic downturns. Societies with skilled individuals are best prepared to respond to current and future potential crises. Therefore, investing in early, primary and secondary education for all, and in particular for children from disadvantaged backgrounds, is both fair and economically efficient. [...]

> But education policies need to be aligned with other government policies, such as housing or welfare, to ensure student success.

In Mexico, the title of Chapter III of the *Ley General de Educación* (General Education Act, 2004, revised)[633] is "On equity in education". Its first Article (32) affirms:

> The educational authorities shall take measures intended to establish conditions permitting the full exercise by every one of the right to quality education, a more equitable education, as well as achieving effective equality of opportunities of access and permanence in the educational services.

The *Ley Orgánica de Educación Intercultural* of Ecuador (Organic Law of Intercultural Education, 2011)[634] lays down in its Article 2 a set of "Principles" whose number exceeds the number of letters of the alphabet. Among them, are the following:

> v. *Equity and inclusion*
>
>> Equity and inclusion assure to all persons access, permanence and success in the Education System. It guarantees equal opportunities for communities, peoples, nationalities and groups with special educational needs and develops an ethics of inclusion with measures of affirmative action and inclusive school culture, in theory and in practice, on the basis of equity, eradicating all forms of discrimination.
>
> w. *Quality and affection*
>
>> It guarantees the right of persons to quality and warm education, relevant, appropriate, contextualized, updated and articulated in the whole process of education, in their systems, levels, sublevels or modalities; and that includes ongoing assessments. It also ensures to envisaging the student as the centre of the educational process, with flexibility and relevance of contents, processes and methodologies suited to their needs and fundamental realities. It promotes appropriate conditions of respect, tolerance and affection generating a school ambiance conducive to the process of learning.

Summing up: Equity in education should be understood as a principle of guarantee of a minimum/maximum of satisfaction of the right to education, giving more to those most needed through positive discrimination.

4.6.5 *Lifelong Education*

Lifelong education or learning is an ancient insight that has become an international principle (see Elfert, 2016). The *Education 2030 Framework for Action* states: "The right to education begins at birth and continues throughout life; therefore, the concept of *lifelong learning* guides SDG4-Education 2030" (para. 15).[635]

The Final Report of an International Conference on Educational Planning, held in Paris from 6 to 14 August 1968,[636] had already put forwards:

> To be effective, planning must, as many delegates pointed out, be a continuous, integrated flexible process, particularly concerned with obtaining education of the highest quality and the highest efficiency. Planning must be comprehensive in character, both because of the close relationship which must be established with the planning of general development and because it must at the same time embrace all levels and types of education within what should be a process of lifelong education for young and adults alike. (pp. 11, 12)

The Faure Report (1972) proposed two major principles: *Lifelong Education* and *Learning Society*. The title of its Part Three is *Towards a learning society*. It reads: "As Plutarch said, 'the City is the best teacher'" (p. 162).

> "In Athens, education was not a segregated activity, conducted for certain hours, in certain places, at a certain time of life. It was the aim of society. The city educated the man. The Athenian was educated by the culture, by paideia. This was made possible by slavery. [...] Machines can do for every modern man what slavery did for the fortunate few in Athens. [...]
>
> Instead of delegating educative power to one, single, vertical, hierarchical structure constituting a distinct body within society, all groups, associations, unions, local communities and intermediary organizations must take over their share of educative responsibility". [...]
>
> This carries us well beyond simple systematic change, however radical. The very nature of the relationship between society and education is changing. A social configuration which accorded such a place to education and conferred such a status on it deserves a name of its own – the learning society. [...] It implies that every citizen should have the means of learning, training and cultivating himself freely available to him, under all circumstances so that he will be in a fundamentally different position in relation to his own education. Responsibility will replace obligation. [...]

> Is this a utopian vision? Yes, to the extent that any undertaking which aims at changing the fundamental conditions of man's fate necessarily contains a utopian element. (pp. 162, 163)

The Delors Report (1996) consecrates its Chapter 5 to "Learning throughout life".

The title of the UNESCO World Education Report published in 2000 was *The right to education – Towards education for all throughout life*. The Report *Rethinking education* (UNESCO, 2015b) has reaffirmed "the relevance of education that is lifelong and life-wide. The concept is not new, but it maintains its prominence as a means of systematizing and organizing learning in a comprehensive and equitable way. It places the empowerment of learners of all ages at the centre stage" (p. 64). Therefore: "Learning to learn has never been as important as it is today" (p. 41). In reality, it seems demonstrated that "learning may improve one's basic ability to learn more (or 'learning begets learning')".[637]

Lifelong education still bears mainly adult and professional connotations, but the Terminology of European Education and Training Policy of the European Centre for the Development of Vocational Training (CEDEFOP)[638] provides the following definition of lifelong learning: "All learning activity undertaken throughout life, which results in improving knowledge, know-how, skills, competences and/or qualifications for personal, social and/or professional reasons". There is an Institute for Lifelong Learning (UIL, UNESCO), located in Hamburg (Germany) that takes "a holistic and integrated, inter-sectoral and cross-sectoral approach to lifelong learning as the guiding paradigm for 21st-century education".[639] Following a UIL's "Technical Note"[640]:

> In essence, lifelong learning is rooted in the integration of learning and living, covering learning activities for people of all ages (children, young people, adults and the elderly, girls and boys, women and men) in all life-wide contexts (family, school, community, workplace and so on) and through a variety of modalities (formal, non-formal and informal) which together meet a wide range of learning needs and demands. Education systems which promote lifelong learning adopt a holistic and sector-wide approach involving all subsectors and levels to ensure the provision of learning opportunities for all individuals. [...]
>
> Lifelong learning for all is the most appropriate philosophy, conceptual framework and organising principle for learning, education and training in the 21st century.

In 2012, the UIL issued *Guidelines on the Recognition, Validation and Accreditation* (RVA) *of the Outcomes of Non-formal and Informal Learning*.[641]

In 1990, the first International Congress of Educating Cities took place in Barcelona.[642] Their Charter "is based on the Universal Declaration on Human Rights (1948); the International Covenant on Economic, Social and Cultural Rights (1966); the Convention on the Rights of the Child (1989); the World Declaration on Education For All (1990); and the Universal Declaration on Cultural Diversity (2001)". The title of its first principle is "The right to an educating city". It states: "The right to an educating city is understood as an extension of the fundamental right of all to education".

In 2013, the International Conference on Learning Cities, co-organised by UNESCO, the Ministry of Education of China and the Beijing Municipal Government, adopted the "Beijing Declaration on Building Learning Cities: Lifelong Learning for All, Promoting Inclusion, Prosperity and Sustainability in Cities".[643] Considering "that the concept of learning throughout life is not new; it is an integral feature of human development and is deeply rooted in all cultures and civilisations", and that there are many places that "already define themselves as learning cities or regions", the Beijing Declaration called upon "UNESCO to establish a global network of learning cities to support and accelerate the practice of lifelong learning in the world's communities". In 2015, the UIL issued *UNESCO Global Network of Learning Cities – Guiding Documents.*[644]

The *Learning/Educational Society* will have, therefore, spatial and temporal dimensions. It will be a totality where the right to education becomes a right of all, to all learnings, throughout all life, in all places and through all means. The Internet, in particular, is today an incomparable source of lifelong learning.

Consequently, the normative integrity of the right to education is not exhausted in the existing public school systems, designed according to assumptions overtaken by the evolution of societies, knowledge and technologies. However, education systems, in general, are still not up to the principle of lifelong learning. Nowadays, we know that human beings' educability changes, as they mature, but never ceases, and can even increase. The ability, need and desire to learn, have no age or satiety. Education is a human right from cradle to grave.

4.7 Indicators of the Right to Education

The UNHCHR published in 2012, meeting requests of the Human Rights Committees, *Human Rights Indicators: A Guide to Measurement and Implementation.*[645]

Human rights indicators are quantitative/statistical and qualitative/normative references of achievement, in a complex relationship, to assessing their realisation. Following the Glossary of the UNHCHR Guide, an indicator is:

> Information that indicates a state or level of an object, event or activity. It provides an indication of prevailing circumstances at a given place and a given point in time. Often based on some form of quantification (e.g., proportion of children immunized) or qualitative categorization (e.g., a treaty ratified/not ratified). In the context of this work, an indicator can be considered as a *human rights indicator* if it can be related to human rights norms and standards, addresses and reflects human rights principles and concerns, and is used to assess and monitor the promotion and implementation of human rights.

Human rights indicators thus serve to transform the generic and abstract standards of IHRL into operational guidance for their political implementation and assessment, in the context of each State. Following the UNHCHR Guide:

> There are three considerations that guide the identification of the attributes of a human right. These are:
>
> – To the extent feasible, the attributes should be based on an exhaustive reading of the standard, starting with the provisions in the core international human rights treaties, so that no part of the standard is overlooked either in the choice of the attributes of a particular human right or in identifying the indicators for that right;
> – To the extent feasible, the attributes of the human right should collectively reflect the essence of its normative content, be few in number and their articulation should help the subsequent identification of the relevant indicators; and
> – To the extent feasible, the attributes' scope should not overlap. In other words, the selected attributes should be mutually exclusive.

Indicators may be subdivided into structural, process and result indicators, which are not entirely compartmentalizable.

– Structural indicators mainly refer to the international legal instruments that a State has formally committed to implementing.
– Process indicators refer to all decisions taken and implemented by the State to realise human rights.
– Result indicators refer to what has been really achieved at the individual and collective level.

Therefore: The indicators of each human right should reflect its normative content to operationalise the assessment of the achievement of its various elements, condensed in attributes identified on the basis of the provisions of the respective treaties and in accordance with their interpretation by the UN Committees and other protection bodies. Some indicators may be common to some human rights; the same indicator can be valid for more than one attribute of a right; or several indicators may be required for a single attribute. The indicators should be disaggregated to identify situations of discrimination against more vulnerable groups.

One of the rights taken by the UNHCHR Guide to illustrate the application of the conceptual and methodological framework proposed for the selection of indicators is the right to education. Four attributes were chosen:
- Universal primary education
- Accessibility to secondary and higher education
- School programs and resources
- Offer and freedom of education

For each of these attributes, several structural, process and result indicators are selected, each of which must be disaggregated according to non-discrimination criteria. Quantitative indicators are typically public expenditure on education, literacy rates, enrolment ratios, pupil-teacher ratio, completion rates, etc. However, quantitative indicators "are inherently reductive. They strip context and nuances to reduce highly complex information into an easily digestible number" (Fisher, 2017, p. 29). As the right to education is concerned, its qualitative content is unique. In this connection, the US Supreme Court, in *Case Sweatt v. Painter, 339 U.S. 629 (1950)*,[646] referred to "those qualities which are incapable of objective measurement but which make for greatness in a Law School" (339 U. S. 634). Qualitative indicators of the right to education are, for example, the prohibition of corporal punishments, learning in the mother tongue, the inclusion of human rights education programmes, the participation of students in school life, the existence of NGOs concerned with the right to education, the availability of complaint mechanisms in case of its violation, the qualification of educators and teachers.

The Right to Education Initiative published a *Right to Education Monitoring Guide*, based on the UNHCHR Guide, with 150 indicators for monitoring and assessing education policies and identifying violations of the right to education.[647]

4.8 Brief Answers to Some Questions

Every education issue should be examined following a *human right approach*, as we are going to exemplify by highlighting and summing up answers, more or less elaborated, to some familiar issues already addressed elsewhere in this essay and adding some new contents.

- Is there acceptable corporal punishment for the sake of education?
- Does home-schooling meet the whole object of the right to education?
- Do parents have the right to prevent children from attending a school subject matter?
- What may be the place of religion in public schools?
- Is school homework legitimate and beneficial?
- May school regulations include rules on student clothing and appearance?
- Why is education a public or common good?
- Can the digital revolution bring about a real revolution in education?

4.8.1 *Is There Acceptable Corporal Punishment for the Sake of Education?*

In their quoted study, Jonathan Todres and Sarah Higinbotham "found that of the two hundred best-selling children's books of all time, both hardcover and paperback, only seven feature children in intact, supportive families (Todres & Higinbotham, 2016, p. 103). As school is concerned:

> Children's school stories reveal that in previous centuries as now, harassment and fear interfere with children's right to an education.
>
> Charles Dickens immortalized the cruel, tyrannical teacher with the Coketown School administrator, Mr. Gradgrind, and the children's primary teacher, Mr. M'Choakumchild in *Hard Times*. [...] Dickens's narrator describes the children in the school room as "little vessels", "arranged in order, ready to have imperial gallons of facts poured into them until they were full to the brim". Dickens satirizes formal education by centering it not around genuine learning and developing the thinking process, but upon cold memorization of details. The tenor of the school is revealed by the title of Chapter 2: "Murdering the Innocents", and by the infamous example of "Girl Number Twenty" (Sissy) being forced to eschew all imagination and to scientifically "define a horse". Even more grim is Lowood Institution in *Jane Eyre*, where the children's basic needs for warmth and sufficient food go unmet and where the teachers inflict cruel punishments on those girls identified as "sinners". Both of these famous literary children's schools convey more about the harm that teachers and schools can inflict on children rather than the right to education. In fact, they portray *obstacles* to education rights. (p. 151)

The legal defence of assaults of children by parents, caregivers and educators, in general, found support in the Anglo-Saxon "reasonable chastisement" doctrine stemming from a Case dating back to 1860 (*R v Hopley (1860) 2 F&F*

202).[648] Finding a schoolteacher guilty for repeatedly beating a 13-year-old boy for two and a half hours, who died, Chief Justice (Lord Cockburn) said:

> By the law of England, a parent or a schoolmaster (who for this purpose represents the parent and has the parental authority delegated to him), may for the purpose of correcting what is evil in the child inflict moderate and reasonable corporal punishment, always, however, with this condition, that it is moderate and reasonable.

During the 18th century, corporal punishment in schools was abolished in some countries. Poland, for example, abolished it in 1783. In 1957, Swedish Criminal Law removed the legal provisions equivalent to the English "reasonable chastisement", and in 1979 the Swedish Parenthood and Guardianship Code prohibited explicitly the parental corporal punishment. In 1969, Finnish Criminal Law was amended to remove similar provisions, and since 1983 all punishments of children at home have been prohibited (Child Custody and Rights of Access Act). In 1972, Norway followed its neighbours.

The worst forms of violence towards children are already forbidden around the world. The incompatibility of corporal punishment with respect for the dignity and physical and psychological integrity of children is already largely part of the juridical-pedagogical conscience. Corporal punishment in public schools has been forbidden in more than 130 countries, and absolutely in more than 50 countries (22 of which are members of the European Union and 32 of the Council of Europe). Very few are those countries where there is no prohibition.[649] However, corporal punishment continues to be culturally and socially tolerated across geographical and cultural boundaries, in particular at home. Jurisprudence itself still often supports the "right of correction" through *reasonable chastisement.*

Family should not continue to be the only social place where violence is legal. There are no lawful moderate acts of violence upon human beings. When parents hit their children *for love,* children learn that aggression or even killing may be a form of love … The definition of violence "must in no way erode the child's absolute right to human dignity and physical and psychological integrity by describing some forms of violence as legally and/or socially acceptable", said the CoRC in GC 13 (CRC/C/GC/13, para. 17).[650]

The CRC contains an unprecedented provision in conventional International Law (Article 28.2): "State Parties shall take all appropriate measures to ensure that school discipline is administered in a manner consistent with the child's human dignity and in conformity with the present Convention". Article 19.1 lays down a general obligation for States to protect the child from all forms of violence. Referring to CRC Article 37.a (interdiction of "torture or other cruel, inhuman or degrading treatment or punishment"), the UN *Manual on Human Rights Reporting* affirms:

> By presenting it as a general and absolute right, the Convention [on the Rights of the Child] shows that any of the forms of treatment or punishment covered by this article should be prevented and combated at all moments and in all circumstances, including within family life or in the school system. (United Nations, 1997, p. 441)

Some other international instruments include provisions against corporal punishment. For example: Declaration on the Protection of All Persons from Being Subjected to Torture and Other Cruel, Inhuman or Degrading Treatment or Punishment (UN, 1975), United Nations Standard Minimum Rules for the Administration of Juvenile Justice (The Beijing Rules, 1985), United Nations Rules for the Protection of Juveniles Deprived of their Liberty (1990), United Nations Guidelines for the Prevention of Juvenile Delinquency (The Riyadh Guidelines, 1990). In 2004, the Parliamentary Assembly of the Council of Europe adopted the Recommendation 1666 (2004) on 'Europe-wide ban on corporal punishment of children'.

Corporal punishment has been absolutely condemned by the UN Committees.

The CoRC said in its first GC (CRC/GC/2001/1)[651]:

> 8. [CRC Article 29.1] attaches importance to the process by which the right to education is to be promoted. Thus, efforts to promote the enjoyment of other rights must not be undermined and should be reinforced, by the values imparted in the educational process. This includes not only the content of the curriculum but also the educational processes, the pedagogical methods and the environment within which education takes place, whether it be the home, school, or elsewhere. Children do not lose their human rights by virtue of passing through the school gates. Thus, for example, education must also be provided in a way that respects the strict limits on discipline reflected in Article 28 (2) and promotes nonviolence in school. The Committee has repeatedly made clear in its concluding observations that the use of corporal punishment does not respect the inherent dignity of the child nor the strict limits on school discipline. Compliance with the values recognized in Article 29 (1) clearly requires that schools be child-friendly in the fullest sense of the term and that they be consistent in all respects with the dignity of the child.

It repeated: "It is also important that the teaching methods used in schools reflect the spirit and educational philosophy of the Convention on the Rights of the Child and the aims of education laid down in Article 29 (1)" (para. 18). Furthermore, the Committee:

- devoted two General Discussion Days on "State violence against children" (2000) and on "Violence against children, within the family and in schools" (2001), following which an Independent Expert for the Secretary-General Study on Violence against Children was appointed and later a Special Representative of the Secretary-General on Violence against Children[652];
- devoted its GC 8 (CRC/C/GC/8), in 2006, to "The right of the child to protection from corporal punishment and other cruel or degrading forms of punishment (Articles 19, 28(2) and 37, *inter alia*)";
- devoted its GC 13 (CRC/C/GC/13), in 2011, to "The right of the child to freedom from all forms of violence";
- addresses corporal punishment frequently in its Concluding Observations on the Reports of States Parties (see UNICEF, 1998).

The CoHR said in its GC 20 (1992)[653]:

> 5. The prohibition in Article 7 [ICCPR] relates not only to acts that cause physical pain but also to acts that cause mental suffering to the victim. In the Committee's view, moreover, the prohibition must extend to corporal punishment, including excessive chastisement ordered as punishment for a crime or as an educative or disciplinary measure. It is appropriate to emphasize in this regard that Article 7 protects, in particular, children, pupils and patients in teaching and medical institutions.

The CoESCR said in its GC 13 (E/C.12/1999/10)[654]:

> 41. In the Committee's view, corporal punishment is inconsistent with the fundamental guiding principle of international human rights law enshrined in the Preambles to the Universal Declaration of Human Rights and both Covenants: the dignity of the individual. Other aspects of school discipline may also be inconsistent with human dignity, such as public humiliation. Nor should any form of discipline breach other rights under the Covenant, such as the right to food.

In note 18: "The Committee notes that, although it is absent from Article 26 (2) of the Declaration, the drafters of ICESCR expressly included the dignity of the human personality as one of the mandatory objectives to which all education is to be directed (Art. 13 (1))".

Many international and national Courts have strongly condemned children's corporal punishment.

The former European Commission of Human Rights and the European Court of Human Rights have addressed corporal punishment in the following Cases, in particular:

- *Case Tyrer v. the United Kingdom* (1978)
- *Case Campbell and Cosans v. the United Kingdom* (1982)
- *Case A. v. the United Kingdom* (1998)

As a consequence of this Case Law, the United Kingdom abolished corporal punishment successively in all public and private schools, as well as within the family. In 1982, the European Commission of Human Rights rejected an application by a group of Swedish parents alleging a violation of their right to respect for family life, because all parental corporal punishment had been banned in 1979. In 2000, a similar application by individuals associated with a group of Christian private schools in the United Kingdom, who were against the ban on corporal punishment in private schools, was rejected by the European Court. They alleged a breach of their rights to freedom of religion and family life. Corporal punishment also falls into the scope of the European Social Charter (Article 17 of the Revised Charter, 1996) and was addressed by some decisions of the European Committee of Social Rights.

At the national level, examples of High Courts' decisions against corporal punishment of children include:

- *Case Republic of Italy v. Cambria*, decided by the Court of Cassation in Rome (Italy's highest Court) in 1996
- *Criminal Appeal 4596/98 Plonit v. A.G. 54(1) P.D.* [2000], decided by Israel's Supreme Court in 2000
- *Case Naushad Ali v. State*, decided by the Fiji Court of Appeal in 2002

An application by a group of 196 Christian private schools against the ban on corporal punishment in schools was dismissed by the South African Constitutional Court in 2000 (*Case CCT4/00*).

The relationship of corporal punishment with decreased self-esteem, emotional disturbances, malformation of moral conscience, school failure, antisocial behaviour, etc. is well established. Corporal punishment is not only a problem of education but also a matter of public health and security, given its psychological resonances and possible consequences for the entire society.

However, it is important not to understand "corporal punishment" in a fundamentalist way. A seemingly less affectionate physical contact between a mother or father and a little child, occasional and in a context of some tension and turbulence, should not be qualified as bodily harm or assault, as remarked the CoRC in GC 8 (CRC/C/GC/8)[655]:

> 40. The principle of equal protection of children and adults from assault, including within the family, does not mean that all cases of corporal punishment of children by their parents that come to light should lead to the prosecution of parents. The *de minimis* principle – that the Law does not concern itself with trivial matters – ensures that minor assaults between adults only come to court in very exceptional circumstances; the same will be true of minor assaults on children. States need to develop effective reporting and referral mechanisms. While all reports of violence against children should be appropriately investigated and their protection from significant harm assured, the aim should be to stop parents from using violent or other cruel or degrading punishments through supportive and educational, not punitive, interventions.

In any case, breaking the vicious circle of violence against children is not simply a legal issue nor just a pedagogical one. It involves all factors – cultural, social, economic, psychological, etc. – of the reproduction of violence between human beings.

In sum: A sanction is educational only if it does not affect the sentiment of personal value and dignity and carries a sense of reparation and self-revaluation.

4.8.2 *Does Home-Schooling Meet the Whole Object of the Right to Education?*

The IEL does not formally exclude the possibility of basic education to be accomplished at home. In the USA, for example, home-schooling is legal in all States. In Europe, it is legal in some countries. The European Court of Human Rights recognises the Governments' margin of appreciation in this matter.

Home-schooling is obviously justified for children who, for health reasons, cannot attend school, or for children of nomadic families or which, for professional reasons, are frequently moving. Other justifications invoked by parents may be the best quality of instruction at home, gifted children, school insecurity. The most frequent, however, are convictions, religious or other.

Home-schooling is not truly compatible with the normative integrity of the object of the right to education, for these main reasons:

- Even though the instruction of children may be well or even better achieved at home, the human right to education is not only right to instruction (or to whatever education), nor just an individual good, as considered the European Court.
- School is an institution where new generations meet to learn common values, fundamental and other knowledge, as well as for experiencing and learning the coexistence of the cultural, social, individual diversity. As we know, what many children and adolescents most like in school is meeting their friends.

This is why it is generally understood that compulsory schooling means school compulsory attendance. Let us recall that States Parties in the CRC[656] undertake to: "Take measures to encourage regular attendance at schools and the reduction of drop-out rates" (Article 28.1.e). According to the revised European Social Charter (Council of Europe),[657] States Parties undertake "to encourage regular attendance at schools" (Article 17.2).

4.8.3 *Do Parents Have the Right to Prevent Children from Attending a School Subject Matter?*

Some elements of the object of the right to education raise sometimes objections from parents, for religious beliefs, in particular. They generally invoke the third paragraph of UDHR Article 26, interpreted without regard for its preparatory work and disregarding the systematic principle, which takes into account the evolution of Law. In the European framework, Article 2 of the first Protocol to the ECHR is also invoked, disregarding its interpretation by the respective bodies (the former Commission and the European Court of Human (see 4.5.1).

For example, with regard to sexual and reproductive health as a school subject matter, the European Court said in its decision on the *Case Kjeldsen, Busk Madsen and Pedersen against Denmark* (Applications 5095/71, 5920/72 e 5926/72), 21 March 1975)[658]:

> 54. ... The Danish legislator, who did not neglect to obtain beforehand the advice of qualified experts, clearly took as his starting point the known fact that in Denmark children nowadays discover without difficulty and from several quarters the information that interests them on sexual life. The instruction on the subject given in State schools is aimed less at instilling knowledge they do not have or cannot acquire by other means than at giving them such knowledge more correctly, precisely, objectively and scientifically. The instruc-

> tion, as provided for and organised by the contested legislation, is principally intended to give pupils better information; [...]
>
> Even when circumscribed in this way, such instruction clearly cannot exclude on the part of teachers certain assessments capable of encroaching on the religious or philosophical sphere; for what are involved are matters where appraisals of fact easily lead on to value-judgments. [...]
>
> These considerations are indeed of a moral order, but they are very general in character and do not entail overstepping the bounds of what a democratic State may regard as the public interest. Examination of the legislation in dispute establishes in fact that it in no way amounts to an attempt at indoctrination aimed at advocating a specific kind of sexual behaviour. It does not make a point of exalting sex or inciting pupils to indulge precociously in practices that are dangerous for their stability, health or future or that many parents consider reprehensible. Further, it does not affect the right of parents to enlighten and advise their children, to exercise with regard to their children natural parental functions as educators, or to guide their children on a path in line with the parents' own religious or philosophical convictions.

Also, the CoRC said in its GC 4 on "Adolescent health and development in the context of the Convention on the Rights of the Child" (CRC/GC/2003/4, 1 July 2003)[659]:

> 28. In light of Articles 3, 17 and 24 of the Convention, States Parties should provide adolescents with access to sexual and reproductive information, including on family planning and contraceptives, the dangers of early pregnancy, the prevention of HIV/AIDS and the prevention and treatment of sexually transmitted diseases (STDs). In addition, States Parties should ensure that they have access to appropriate information, regardless of their marital status and whether their parents or guardians consent.

There is much international and national jurisprudence converging on this conclusion: There is no valid parents' "conscientious objection" against the right to education of their children, against its internationally recognised and protected normative integrity as a human right. As the Parliamentary Assembly of the Council of Europe has stated in its Resolution 2253 (2019) on "Sharia, the Cairo Declaration and the European Convention on Human Rights",[660] "where human rights are concerned, there is no room for religious or cultural exceptions" (para. 9).

In sum, under IHRL, the guiding principles of parents for their children's education (and not only) should be:
- *The best interest of the child*
- *The evolving capacities of the child*

4.8.4 *What May Be the Place of Religion in Public Schools?*

The separation between political power and religious power is an aspect of the modernisation of societies, when the principle of State secularity emerged. Juridically, secularity means non-confessionality or religious neutrality. "Secularism is a framework for peaceful management in the public space of different denominations and beliefs" (Zuber, 2021, p. 31). It is a typically French principle, instituted by the Law of Separation of Church and State, on 9 December 1905, now commemorated, in France, as the Day of Secularism since 2015.

The IHRL does not oblige to the separation between State and religion, nor does it prohibit a special relationship with a traditional majority religion having deeper cultural roots in a country. It even admits the existence of a State Religion.[661] In any case, indoctrination – religious or anti-religious – is excluded. This is also an imperative of compulsory education.

The principle of non-indoctrination applies not only to religious education but to all curricular contents. According to the canonical formula of the European Court of Human Rights, in its decision on the *Case Kjeldsen, Madsen and Pedersen* (1976)[662]:

> 53. ... the State, in fulfilling the functions assumed by it in regard to education and teaching, must take care that information or knowledge included in the curriculum is conveyed in an objective, critical and pluralistic manner. The State is forbidden to pursue an aim of indoctrination that might be considered as not respecting parents' religious and philosophical convictions. That is the limit that must not be exceeded.

As representatives of State's authority, teachers are subject to a duty of reserve which may entail restrictions on their freedom of expression.

The principle of non-indoctrination is the most widely respectful of the interests at stake in public education, namely:
- the convictions of parents;
- the right to education of students;
- the diversity and pluralism of beliefs, in democracy.

The non-confessionality of public school does not imply the exclusion of religious education. The IHRL admits its inclusion, under certain conditions, particularly the following:

- Religious education in public schools must be taken in charge by the religion concerned. Public school teachers should never be obliged to religious education.
- Religious education in public schools should never be compulsory. Exemption from attending religious education classes may be requested by parents or legal guardians, or by students themselves, from a variable determined age.

It should be noted, however, that the possibility of exemption from attending religious education classes is not free from unwanted or even unacceptable effects of marginalisation, stigmatisation and violation of privacy.

Compulsory instruction about religion as a cultural phenomenon is not incompatible with the principle of non-confessionality of State. In effect, religion is one of the most influential vectors of Civilisation, and the culture of every country has a religious imprint. The knowledge of the religious phenomenon and the plurality of its expressions may be considered as an element of the object of the right to education. It contributes to the formation of the freedom of thought, conscience and religion, as well as to a culture of tolerance. According to the CoESCR (E/C.12/1999/10),[663] ICESCR Article 13.3:

> 28. … permits public school instruction in subjects such as the general history of religions and ethics if it is given in an unbiased and objective way, respectful of the freedoms of opinion, conscience and expression. It notes that public education that includes instruction in a particular religion or belief is inconsistent with Article 13 (3) unless provision is made for non-discriminatory exemptions or alternatives that would accommodate the wishes of parents and guardians.[664]

The Parliamentary Assembly of the Council of Europe stated in its Recommendation 1720 (2005) on "Education and religion"[665]:

> 1. [Religion] is a strictly personal matter. However, this is not inconsistent with the view that a good general knowledge of religions and the resulting sense of tolerance are essential to the exercise of democratic citizenship. […]
>
> 5. Politics and religion should be kept apart. However, democracy and religion should not be incompatible. […]
>
> 8. Knowledge of religions is an integral part of knowledge of the history of mankind and civilisations.

Non-confessionality, in public schools, covers other aspects of school life, about which there is a significant national and international jurisprudence. Although with some variations, its general sense is that are not compatible with the principles of non-confessionality and non-indoctrination in public schools:

- acts or events with religious content, such as mandatory prayers and religious ceremonies;
- presence of religious symbols at school, although admitting that State might have a margin of appreciation;
- use of symbols with clear religious or ideological connotations, such as *hijab*, *kippah*, turbans, crosses, even though teachers' and students' positions are different, and a general ban may not be advisable or even acceptable if the principle of proportionality is disregarded.

For example, the Constitutional Court of South Africa said in *Case Kwazulu-Natal and Others v Pillay* (*CCT 51/06*) [*2007*] *ZACC 21; 2008* (*1*) *SA 474* (*CC*)*; 2008* (*2*) *BCLR 99* (*CC*) (*5 October 2007*),[666] concerned with wearing a nose-ring by a Hindu girl as a religious duty:

> [163] ... the question arises whether the applicant has shown that the failure to afford the learner an exemption to wear the nose-stud imposed a burden on the learner's exercise of her cultural practice that has caused her harm. [...]
>
> [169] In assessing whether the discrimination in this case is unfair, it is necessary to recognise that it arises from the school's refusal to grant an exemption to the learner to wear a nose-stud. [...]
>
> [171] Given that the school had in the past granted exemptions from rules for cultural practices, it has not established that it acted fairly in refusing an exemption in this case on the ground that the applicant had not established that the practice constituted a mandatory requirement of her religion.

The Constitutional Court found that the prohibition was unfairly discriminatory, and concluded by evoking "the vision of the Preamble of our Constitution: a country that is united in its diversity in which all citizens are recognised as being worthy of equal respect" (para. 185).

In its 'Concluding Observations' on the fourth periodic report of France (CCPR/C/FRA/CO/4, 31 July 2008),[667] the CoHR said:

> 23. The Committee is concerned that both elementary and high school students are barred by Act No. 2004/228 of 15 March 2004 from

> attending the public schools if they are wearing so called "conspicuous" religious symbols. [...] The Committee notes that respect for a public culture of *laïcité* would not seem to require forbidding wearing such common religious symbols (Articles 18 and 26).
>
> [...]
>
> *The State Party should re-examine Act No. 2004/228 of 15 March 2004 in light of the guarantees of Article 18 of the Covenant concerning freedom of conscience and religion, including the right to manifest one's religion in public as well as private, as well as the guarantee of equality under Article 26.*

In the opinion of the former Special Rapporteur on freedom of religion or belief (Heiner Bielefeldt), in his Report focussing "freedom of religion or belief and school education" (A/HRC/16/53, 15 December 2010),[668] "there are nevertheless good reasons to start with a general presumption of the students' right to wear religious symbols in the school" (para. 43). Limitations should meet the criteria laid down in the ICCPR Article 18.3.

The use of school facilities for activities of a religious nature, outside of their regular operation, is not, in principle, incompatible with State's non-confessionality.

The non-confessionality of the State does not mean moral neutrality of education, of course. As said the former European Commission of Human Rights in its Report on the admissibility of the *Case Bernard and others against Luxemburg* (Application 17187/90, Decision of 8 November 1993),[669] "the obligation upon the pupils to choose between the religious and moral education course, on the one hand, and the moral and social education course, on the other, allows transmitting to the young people rules of behaviour needed for protecting a democratic society".

The Rule of Law is, nowadays, driven by constitutional values that schools – public and private – must respect and promote. They are, above all, the values of the Ethics of Human Rights. States Parties to IHRL are committed to education for human rights as Common Ethics of Humanity.

4.8.5 *Is School Homework Legitimate and Beneficial?*

The need for school homework is rooted in the most common pedagogical mentality so that the idea of its abolition is not popular. CRC Article 31[670] has implications for school hours and homework, however:

> 1. States Parties recognize the right of the child to rest and leisure, to engage in play and recreational activities appropriate to the age of the child and to participate freely in cultural life and the arts.

2. States Parties shall respect and promote the right of the child to participate fully in cultural and artistic life and shall encourage the provision of appropriate and equal opportunities for cultural, artistic, recreational and leisure activity.

The CoRC said in its first GC (CRC/GC/2001/1)[671]: "It should be emphasized that the type of teaching that is focused primarily on the accumulation of knowledge, prompting competition and leading to an excessive burden of work on children, may seriously hamper the harmonious development of the child to the fullest potential of his or her abilities and talents" (para. 12). This issue is frequently addressed by the Committee when examining States Reports. For example, in 2011, when examining the third and fourth periodic reports of the Republic of Korea (CRC/C/KOR/CO/3-4),[672] it remarked:

62. Despite the efforts made by the State Party to lower the stress of students and the adoption of programs to ensure that children have the opportunity to play and engage in recreational and cultural activities, the Committee is concerned at the severely competitive conditions that are still prevalent in the State Party's education system. The Committee is also concerned at the widespread enrolment of children in additional private tutoring taking place outside the curriculum resulting in, inter alia: children being subject to serious and disproportionate stress and the negative impact on their physical and mental health.

Consequently, in light of the CRC, traditional school homework is an abuse, for the following main reasons:

- It encroaches on other rights, as the rights to rest, to leisure, to play, to cultural life, to private and familial life, etc.
- It may be discriminatory insofar as not all children have 'school at home', i.e. the necessary spaces and resources, as well as parents able and available to help to do it.
- It harms on the harmonious development of children and may become disruptive of the familial life when it is a cause of punishment.
- Other harms include obesity, an increase of diabetes associated with a sedentary lifestyle, and myopia.

In addition, school homework does not have proven usefulness. According to an extensive review of pertinent literature carried out in the decade of 2000,[673] there is very little correlation between it and school results at primary education level, and little at the secondary schooling level. Moreover, in many countries with better school performance, there is little homework, and there is much in countries with the worst performance.

In short: The right to education includes the right to school but does not legitimise *schooling* the entirety of children's and adolescents' lives. The school has an obligation to do everything incumbent on it during the long schooling days and years. This does not prevent a teacher from suggesting activities at home that children or adolescents may be willing to do.

4.8.6 *May School Regulations Include Rules on Student Clothing and Appearance?*

School regulations define the rights and duties of the members of the school community. As far as students are concerned, they sometimes contain rules about their clothing and appearance. For students in private schools, such rules may be consensual, as attendance is free, but in public schools they are controversial.

Let's start with school uniforms. There are arguments for and against. They are frequent in private institutions, but in many USA public schools, for instance, there are Dress Codes including them. President Clinton, in his 1996 State of the Union Address, recommended them as a measure to reduce violence in schools. They have been addressed by judicial litigation over the past decades, but the jurisprudence is not consistent, although decisions are generally favourable to school authorities.

The rules that interfere with individual freedom are more controversial, such as: clothing, use of fashion accessories, haircut or hairstyle, expression of opinions, sexual orientation and private life. There is relevant North American jurisprudence on the matter.

The Constitutional Court of Colombia has pronounced an exceptional and diversified jurisprudence on rules of the *Manuales de Convivencia* (School Regulations) incompatible with the respect of various students' rights. For example, in *Case SU641/98*,[674] dealing with the ban on students wearing long hair and earrings, it summarised:

> As regards clothing, the general rule is the freedom and respect of the various cultures, climate, economic capacity and individual preferences, with the exception being the agreement of the educational community to adopt a uniform, for economic reasons or imposed by a given practical reason. Hair length and hairstyle, makeup and body aesthetic, as well as the use of beauty accessories in general, are part of the right to personal image, endowing everyone with the faculty to decide autonomously how to present itself before others, whether he or she accepts that his or her

> image is captured and disseminated by the media when they are not in a public place or open to the public, whether he grows the beard or the moustache, disguises or highlights a certain characteristic, whether or not he or she is fashionable, etc.

In *Case T-853/04*[675] – relating to a 17 years girl student who, for having married, was prevented from completing her secondary school at the private college she attended (Catholic) – the Court recalled its jurisprudence concerning the respect of students' private life, saying notably:

> [1] student regulations, like all internal rules of private or public entities, must be in accordance, in their content, with the values, principles and rights enshrined in the Colombian Constitution; [...]
>
> [4] School regulations of a college that sanctions "any love manifestation" ignores, without reasonableness, the right to intimacy of students and also affects the rights to freedom and to the free development of their personality;
>
> [5] [...]
>
> Therefore, (i) "the regulations of a college", (ii) "the regulations of educational institutions" and (iii) "the measures of the organs of an educational establishment" should not establish academic or disciplinary sanctions on a student for decisions she may adopt to assert her sexual identity. Even if her behaviours include living in *de facto* union and the consequence of her conscious and free option is to become pregnant; [...]
>
> [8] fundamental rights of a student to due process, to education and to intimacy are violated when he or she is punished for a behaviour that belongs exclusively to his or her intimacy, such as having sex with a married person. [...]
>
> 6.4 In short, for the constitutional jurisprudence, the right of individuals to found confessional institutions of education does not contain the power to suspend or limit, by means of school regulations, the enforcement of the Political Constitution of Colombia for their students, who are subjects of special constitutional protection, nor the power to be unaware of the constitutional rights, the principles and values proper to a Social and Democratic Rule of Law.

The same Court concluded in the *Case T-065/93*,[676] concerning two students who filed a complaint against the school they attended due to the threat of cancellation of enrollment if they did not adjust their haircuts to adhere to school regulations:

> This new constitutional conception also radiates the social scope of education. The subjects participating in the educational process are no longer separated between passive actors receiving knowledge and active actors depositing knowledge. The constitutional principle that protects the free development of personality and the right to participation of the educational community have made the student an active subject with duties and rights, participating in the educational process.

Summing up: The general principle, in these matters, must be the freedom of expression of the personality and the rights it entails.

4.8.7 *Why Is Education a Global Public or Common Good?*

'Public Goods' (PGS) are at the heart of an Ethics of Economy.[677] They are goods possessing such a great value for each and every member of a human community that they must be collectively guaranteed. The concept is not new, but the economic theory of PGS goes back to the 1950s. While 'private goods' are characterised by the excludability (they are not at everyone's disposal) and rivalry (their consumption by some people may reduce the possibility for other people to consume them), PGS exhibit the opposite properties: non-excludability (they are, in principle, accessible to everyone) and non-rivalry (their consumption by some people does not prevent other people from consuming them). PGS may be local, national, regional or global.

'Global Public Goods' (GPGS) are goods that, by their nature, concern every human being and all peoples of the world, or the guarantee of which exceeds, by their characteristics, the capacity of each State. The notion of GPGS is recent, but the reality they denote is not. They include international agreements for the regulation of telecommunications and civil aviation, for example, as well as the common natural elements, such as oceans, and the cultural creations declared to be World Heritage. There are also GPGS caused by global evils, such as vaccines, the protection of the ozone layer, international financial stability and the fight against terrorism. Internet is a new GPG. What were once national PGS are increasingly becoming GPGS, requiring international protection.

It seems undeniable that the criterion for a typology of GPGS should be sought by answering this crucial question: What is the highest category of goods or values? The answer seems obvious: they are the moral or ethical values. Thus, the main criterion for the qualification and hierarchisation of the GPGS should be its ethicity or moral imperativeness. Using this criterion, the GPGS may be divided into two main categories:

- *GPGS with ethical substance*, i.e. the goods inherent in the quality of being human. They are mostly the human genome and human dignity and rights, whose protection rests mainly with the responsibility of States and the International Community.

– GPGs *instrumental in nature*, concerning the varied goods necessary to the protection and realisation of the first ones. They are manifold: institutional, scientific, technological, environmental, aesthetic, preventive.

Human dignity and rights should be considered the highest goods as they constitute an Ethics of Humanity. They are "the common property of all mankind", said the Panamanian Delegation (León) during the 90th meeting of the UN General Assembly Third Committee, on 1 October 1948 (A/C.3/SR.90).[678] Consequently, "the promotion and protection of individual rights are a public good" (Henkin, 1978, p. 2).

The 47th session of the International Conference on Education (Geneva, 2004) reaffirmed in its 'Message' that education is "a basic right and a public good" (para. 1).[679] Likewise, the Jakarta Declaration on "The right to basic education as a fundamental human right and the legal framework for its financing", adopted by the International Conference held in Jakarta (Indonesia) on 2–4 December 2005, has recognised "education, especially basic education, as a public good" (preamble).[680] The Incheon Declaration (2015)[681] has reaffirmed: "*Education is a public good*, of which the State is the duty bearer".

Justifying the preference for 'common good' instead of 'public good', the UNESCO Report *Rethinking education: Towards a global common good?* explains:

> The term *public* often leads to a common misunderstanding that 'public goods' are goods *provided by the public*. On the other hand, *common goods* have been defined as those goods that, irrespective of any public or private origin, are characterized by a binding destination and necessary for the realization of the fundamental rights of all people.
>
> From this perspective, the concept of the 'common good' may prove to be a constructive alternative. […]
>
> Knowledge is the common heritage of humanity. Knowledge, like education, must, therefore, be considered a global common good. If knowledge is considered only a global *public* good, access to it is often restricted. The current trend towards the privatization of knowledge production, reproduction and dissemination is a cause for serious concern. […]
>
> Inspired by the values of solidarity and social justice grounded in our common humanity, the principle of knowledge and education as global common goods has implications for the roles and responsibilities of diverse stakeholders in the collective quest for sustainable and inclusive human and social development. (UNESCO, 2015b, pp. 77, 80, 81)

4.8.8 *Can the Digital Revolution Bring about a Real Educational Revolution?*

The digital revolution and world Globalisation could not fail to have profound repercussions in the education field, some of which undoubtedly fascinating, others disturbingly ambivalent (see, for instance, *The Fourth Education Revolution* by Anthony Seldon, 2020). Internet, in particular:

- is a virtually inexhaustible universal library, making available sources of information that were before only accessible *in loco* (where they are physically placed), thus extraordinarily facilitating research and dissemination of their results, as well as communication and co-operation.
- has become a universal platform of self and distance training, free or paid, the use of which for Massive Open Online Courses (MOOCs) is a sector with increasing weight in the world market of services;
- but it may be used for illicit or even criminal purposes, as we know, also in the academic field, as is the case of plagiarism, whose extent has forced many Universities to the systematic use of specific software for its detection.

The expansion of digital technologies as learning tools has been driven and exploited principally by the education business. Also, there is a great *digital divide*, due to the costs of investment in indispensable technological infrastructures and resources, starting with access to electricity, as noted Kishore Singh, former Special Rapporteur on the Right to Education, in his 2016 annual report, devoted to the "digital revolution in education" (A/HRC/32/37).[682] Also, it was found that the Internet 'speaks' only about 5% of the about 7,000 living languages in the world.

The CHR drew attention to this divide in a Resolution on the right to education adopted in the same year (A/HRC/32/L.33).[683] There are about 3.7 billion of the world's population (52%) still not connected, according to the International Telecommunications Union.[684]

> There is broad agreement that education needs to ensure that people gain four main skills: creativity, communication, collaboration, and critical thinking. Alongside skills such as literacy and numeracy, people should now also gain basic digital skills. They need to have a comprehensive understanding of the rapidly changing world in which they live, as well as their roles and responsibilities within it. [...]
>
> Digital skills are fast becoming vital, in addition to basic literacy and numeracy. (Broadband Commission for Sustainable Development, 2018, pp. 43, 60)

There is also a need for initiatives to reconcile the legitimate rights of intellectual property with the generalisation of access to the benefits of digital creations for educational purposes. In 2019, UNESCO adopted a Recommendation on Open Educational Resources.

The webeducation or webucation can contribute to facilitating and broadening access to education and training but, besides it may be used for commercialisation of the right to education, it is not particularly motivating even for the most interested, as shown by research. What is more, it is not an alternative to the fundamental relational and moral dimension of the educational phenomenon, as pointed out the first Special Rapporteur on the Right to Education (E/CN.4/2001/52, para. 55–59).[685] Therefore, it is an illusion hoping "to find salvation in expensive technological purchases", as stressed the Special Rapporteur (A/HRC/32/37).[686] On the one hand: "There is no real or conclusive evidence that online learning leads to better learning outcomes for students" (para. 50). On the other hand, "the Special Rapporteur considers it important to recognize the limits of the pedagogical value of technology-based and distance education, putting a premium on face-to-face learning and human interactions in education" (para. 58). What is at stake is "the humanistic mission of education" (para. 68), whose first aim, according to the IEL, is not instrumental, but personal, that is, the full, free and harmonious development of the human personality. "*Digital technologies are negatively affecting the cause of education by impairing the ability of students to contemplate and think critically, by scuttling human values in education and by paving the way for the commodification of education*" (para. 112).

Consequently, much has changed in the world with the digital revolution and world Globalisation, for the conceptions, practices and systems of education to continue to be as they have been, but sight should not be lost of the differences between the essential and the incidental. The main challenges that education is facing, at these times, are perhaps the following ones:

- Responding to the new realities and exploring the fabulous possibilities created by scientific and technological progress.[687]
- Creating resistance to the economist, consumerist, predatory and dehumanising totalitarianism of the neoliberal ideology.
- Immunising against the toxic effects of digital technologies and reaffirming that, in education, a truly radical revolution is not one merely instrumental.

Notes

1 https://ec.europa.eu/education/policies/higher-education/bologna-process-and-european-higher-education-area_en

2 PISA is a triennial survey organised by OECD (Organisation for Economic Cooperation and Development) to evaluate education systems worldwide by testing the performance in reading, mathematical and scientific literacy of 15-year-old students.

3 https://ia902306.us.archive.org/17/items/educationalactivooleag/educationalactivooleag.pdf

4 https://www.thenewfederalist.eu/170-years-since-victor-hugo-s-speech-about-the-united-states-of-europe?lang=fr

5 Original French text: https://www.herodote.net/Textes/victor-hugo-discours-du-congres-de-la-paix.pdf

6 See Marie-Adélaïde Zeyer (2006), *Léon Bourgeois, père spirituel de la Société des Nations: solidarité internationale et service de la France, 1899–1919*. Thèse (Leon Bourgeois, spiritual father of the League of Nations: international solidarity and service of France, 1899–1919. Thesis).

7 https://www.loc.gov/law/help/us-treaties/bevans/m-ust000002-0043.pdf

8 P. 15 in: https://ia800905.us.archive.org/1/items/lapremireassembloohyma/lapremireassembloohyma.pdf

9 P. 15 in: https://biblio-archive.unog.ch/Dateien/CouncilMSD/C-25-M-25-1943_EN.pdf

10 https://biblio-archive.unog.ch/Dateien/CouncilMSD/C-99-M-99-1945-V_EN.pdf

11 Annexe 2 in: https://biblio-archive.unog.ch/Dateien/CouncilMSD/C-5-M-5-1947_EN.pdf

12 https://www.unog.ch/C125781000589799/(httpPages)/BA9387B56BFAAFB4C1256F3100418C75?OpenDocument

13 Ibid.

14 P. 44 in: https://unesdoc.unesco.org/ark:/48223/pf0000187142 In 1933, *A League of Minds* was published. (https://ia801600.us.archive.org/13/items/in.ernet.dli.2015.216610/2015.216610.A-League.pdf)

15 https://ia800907.us.archive.org/23/items/leagueofnationsp1922leag/leagueofnationsp1922leag.pdf

16 https://ia902306.us.archive.org/17/items/educationalactivooleag/educationalactivooleag.pdf

17 See: https://archive.org/details/leagueofnationsp1922leag/page/n21/mode/2up

18 See also: https://ia800906.us.archive.org/14/items/firstassemblyofl00worlrich/firstassemblyofl00worlrich.pdf

19 https://ia802303.us.archive.org/28/items/organisationofintooleag/organisationofintooleag.pdf

20 https://ia800303.us.archive.org/19/items/firstassemblystuooleag/firstassemblystuooleag.pdf

21 https://ia800906.us.archive.org/14/items/firstassemblyofl00worlrich/firstassemblyofl00worlrich.pdf

22 https://libraryresources.unog.ch/ld.php?content_id=31291798

23 https://ia802300.us.archive.org/22/items/organisationofinooleag/organisationofinooleag.pdf

24 https://libraryresources.unog.ch/ld.php?content_id=31291797

25 https://libraryresources.unog.ch/ld.php?content_id=31291797

26 http://libraryresources.unog.ch/ld.php?content_id=31402441

27 https://biblio-archive.unog.ch/Dateien/CouncilMSD/C-420-M-260-1922_EN.pdf

28 See: https://archive.org/details/nationalcommitte031498mbp/page/n1/mode/2up

29 https://ia800907.us.archive.org/23/items/leagueofnationsp1922leag/leagueofnationsp1922leag.pdf

30 It is noticeable the political concern in electing a Frenchman and a Britishman for the presidency.

31 https://biblio-archive.unog.ch/Dateien/CouncilDocs/C-688-1923-XII_EN.pdf
32 https://biblio-archive.unog.ch/Dateien/CouncilMSD/C-3-M-3-1924-XII_EN.pdf
33 https://libraryresources.unog.ch/ld.php?content_id=31429171
34 Annexes 1 and 2 in: https://biblio-archive.unog.ch/Dateien/CouncilMSD/C-3-M-3-1924-XII_EN.pdf
35 http://libraryresources.unog.ch/ld.php?content_id=31412309
36 P. 9 in: https://ia801606.us.archive.org/10/items/in.ernet.dli.2015.115676/2015.115676.The-Monthly-Summary-Of-The-League-Of-Nations-January-1924_text.pdf
37 https://biblio-archive.unog.ch/Dateien/CouncilDocs/C-418-1924-XII_EN.pdf
38 https://libraryresources.unog.ch/ld.php?content_id=31429165
39 In effect, this confrontation between the United Kingdom and France crossed the history of international institutions during the first half of the 20th century, since the League of Nations. Under the pretext of financial constraints, it was mainly the concern to restrict the power of international interference in national affairs, as well as the fear of a French cultural imperialism, that was behind the Anglo-Saxon positions in this area.
40 https://libraryresources.unog.ch/ld.php?content_id=31429171
41 https://biblio-archive.unog.ch/Dateien/CouncilMSD/C-825-(1)-M-280-1924-XII_EN.pdf
42 Appendix in: https://biblio-archive.unog.ch/Dateien/CouncilMSD/C-286-M-104-1925-XII_EN.pdf
43 https://biblio-archive.unog.ch/Dateien/CouncilMSD/C-286-M-104-1925-XII_EN.pdf
44 https://biblio-archive.unog.ch/Dateien/CouncilMSD/C-445-M-165-1925-XII_EN.pdf
45 https://biblio-archive.unog.ch/Dateien/CouncilMSD/C-87-M-43-1926-XII_EN.pdf
46 https://biblio-archive.unog.ch/Dateien/CouncilDocs/C-688-1923-XII_EN.pdf
47 https://biblio-archive.unog.ch/Dateien/CouncilMSD/C-342-M-121-1929-XII_EN.pdf
48 https://biblio-archive.unog.ch/Dateien/CouncilMSD/C-533-M-160-1928-XII_EN.pdf
49 https://biblio-archive.unog.ch/Dateien/CouncilDocs/C-63-1928-XII_EN.pdf
50 P. 48 in: https://biblio-archive.unog.ch/Dateien/CouncilMSD/C-287-M-125-1934_EN.pdf
51 https://biblio-archive.unog.ch/Dateien/CouncilDocs/C-573-1928-XII_EN.pdf
52 Appendix 2 in: https://biblio-archive.unog.ch/Dateien/CouncilMSD/C-339-M-156-1934-XII_EN.pdf
53 See: Christel Taillibert (1999), *L'institut international du cinématographe éducatif: Regards sur le rôle du cinéma éducatif dans la politique internationale du fascisme italien.* Paris: Harmattan.
54 https://biblio-archive.unog.ch/Dateien/CouncilMSD/C-424-M-157-1927-XII_EN.pdf
55 https://biblio-archive.unog.ch/Dateien/CouncilMSD/C-533-M-160-1928-XII_EN.pdf
56 https://biblio-archive.unog.ch/Dateien/CouncilMSD/C-424-M-157-1927-XII_EN.pdf
57 https://biblio-archive.unog.ch/Dateien/CouncilMSD/C-533-M-160-1928-XII_EN.pdf
58 Annexe 15 in: https://biblio-archive.unog.ch/Dateien/CouncilMSD/C-342-M-121-1929-XII_EN.pdf
59 https://biblio-archive.unog.ch/Dateien/CouncilMSD/C-428-M-192-1930-XII_EN.pdf
60 P. 38 in: https://biblio-archive.unog.ch/Dateien/CouncilMSD/C-287-M-125-1934_EN.pdf
61 P. 44, ibid.
62 https://biblio-archive.unog.ch/Dateien/CouncilMSD/C-471-M-201-1931-XII_EN.pdf
63 P. 39 in: https://biblio-archive.unog.ch/Dateien/CouncilMSD/C-287-M-125-1934_EN.pdf
64 https://biblio-archive.unog.ch/Dateien/CouncilMSD/C-471-M-201-1931-XII_EN.pdf
65 https://biblio-archive.unog.ch/Dateien/CouncilMSD/C-290-M-154-1935-XII_EN.pdf
66 https://biblio-archive.unog.ch/Dateien/CouncilMSD/C-530-M-369-1937-XII_EN.pdf
67 https://ia801605.us.archive.org/5/items/in.ernet.dli.2015.35191/2015.35191.Proceedings-Of-The-Second-General-Conference-Of-National-Committees-On-Intellectual-Co-operation-Paris-July-5th-1937.pdf

68 https://biblio-archive.unog.ch/Dateien/CouncilDocs/C-145-1938-XII_EN.pdf
69 https://biblio-archive.unog.ch/Dateien/CouncilDocs/C-514-1938_EN.pdf
70 See p. 33 in: https://paperspast.natlib.govt.nz/parliamentary/AJHR1939-I.2.1.2.6#save_as
71 https://biblio-archive.unog.ch/Dateien/CouncilMSD/C-253-M-150-1938-XII_EN.pdf
72 https://biblio-archive.unog.ch/Dateien/CouncilMSD/C-35-M-35-1942_EN.pdf
73 Dumont, J. (2008). *L'Institut International de Coopération Intellectuelle et le Brésil (1924–1946) – Le pari de la diplomatie culturelle*. Éditions IHEAL (Institut des Hautes Études de l'Amérique Latine), pp. 141, 142.
74 https://unesdoc.unesco.org/ark:/48223/pf0000144986
75 https://ia802700.us.archive.org/20/items/geneva1921accoun00harrrich/geneva1921accoun00harrrich.pdf
76 P. 26 in: https://ia800907.us.archive.org/23/items/leagueofnationsp1922leag/leagueofnationsp1922leag.pdf
77 https://biblio-archive.unog.ch/Dateien/CouncilMSD/C-570-M-224-1923-XII_EN.pdf
78 https://biblio-archive.unog.ch/Dateien/CouncilMSD/C-286-M-104-1925-XII_EN.pdf
79 https://biblio-archive.unog.ch/Dateien/CouncilMSD/C-87-M-43-1926-XII_EN.pdf
80 https://biblio-archive.unog.ch/Dateien/CouncilDocs/C-77-1926-XII_EN.pdf
81 https://ia801800.us.archive.org/12/items/BetweenWarAndPeace/BetweenWarAndPeace.pdf
82 See: Maria Montessori, *Education and Peace*, Clio Press, 1992.
83 https://biblio-archive.unog.ch/Dateien/CouncilDocs/C-688-1923-XII_EN.pdf
84 P. 211 in: https://ia801606.us.archive.org/10/items/in.ernet.dli.2015.115676/2015.115676. The-Monthly-Summary-Of-The-League-Of-Nations-January-1924_text.pdf
85 P. 16 in: https://ia801602.us.archive.org/10/items/in.ernet.dli.2015.35719/2015.35719.How-To-Make-The-League-Of-Nations-Known-And-To-Develop-The-Spirit-Of-Internation-Co--operation_text.pdf
Also, Chapter Two in: https://unesdoc.unesco.org/ark:/48223/pf0000063011
86 https://biblio-archive.unog.ch/Dateien/CouncilDocs/C-77-1926-XII_EN.pdf
87 https://biblio-archive.unog.ch/Dateien/CouncilMSD/C-424-M-157-1927-XII_EN.pdf
88 https://biblio-archive.unog.ch/Dateien/CouncilDocs/C-479-1930-XII_EN.pdf
89 https://biblio-archive.unog.ch/Dateien/CouncilMSD/C-428-M-192-1930-XII_EN.pdf
90 https://biblio-archive.unog.ch/Dateien/CouncilMSD/C-602-M-240-1931-IX_EN.pdf
91 Already in 1922, the Fellowship of Reconciliation (USA) had published "The Problem of Moral Disarmament" (in *The Messenger of Peace*).
https://libraryresources.unog.ch/ld.php?content_id=31320509
92 https://libraryresources.unog.ch/ld.php?content_id=31291826
93 P. 43 in: https://biblio-archive.unog.ch/Dateien/CouncilMSD/C-287-M-125-1934_EN.pdf
94 Appendix 2 in: https://biblio-archive.unog.ch/Dateien/CouncilMSD/C-339-M-156-1934-XII_EN.pdf
95 Appendix 1 in: https://biblio-archive.unog.ch/Dateien/CouncilMSD/C-290-M-154-1935-XII_EN.pdf
96 Appendix 10 in: https://biblio-archive.unog.ch/Dateien/CouncilMSD/C-327-M-220-1937-XII_EN.pdf
97 https://biblio-archive.unog.ch/Dateien/CouncilDocs/C-284-1938-XII_EN.pdf
98 Appendix 2 in: https://biblio-archive.unog.ch/Dateien/CouncilMSD/C-290-M-154-1935-XII_EN.pdf
99 https://biblio-archive.unog.ch/Dateien/CouncilMSD/C-328-M-205-1936-XII_EN.pdf
100 https://biblio-archive.unog.ch/Dateien/CouncilDocs/C-371-1937-XII_EN.pdf
101 https://biblio-archive.unog.ch/Dateien/CouncilMSD/C-339-M-156-1934-XII_EN.pdf
102 https://biblio-archive.unog.ch/Dateien/CouncilMSD/C-290-M-154-1935-XII_EN.pdf
103 https://biblio-archive.unog.ch/Dateien/CouncilMSD/C-253-M-150-1938-XII_EN.pdf

104 https://biblio-archive.unog.ch/Dateien/CouncilMSD/C-231-M-153-1939-XII_EN.pdf
105 Appendix 8 in: https://biblio-archive.unog.ch/Dateien/CouncilMSD/C-328-M-205-1936-XII_EN.pdf
106 Appendix 1 in: https://biblio-archive.unog.ch/Dateien/CouncilMSD/C-231-M-153-1939-XII_EN.pdf
107 https://biblio-archive.unog.ch/Dateien/CouncilMSD/C-253-M-150-1938-XII_EN.pdf
108 https://biblio-archive.unog.ch/Dateien/CouncilMSD/C-231-M-153-1939-XII_EN.pdf
109 See: https://libraryresources.unog.ch/ld.php?content_id=31316441
110 Annexe 15 in: https://biblio-archive.unog.ch/Dateien/CouncilMSD/C-471-M-201-1931-XII_EN.pdf
111 See: https://biblio-archive.unog.ch/Dateien/CouncilMSD/C-424-M-157-1927-XII_EN.pdf
112 https://biblio-archive.unog.ch/Dateien/CouncilMSD/C-231-M-153-1939-XII_EN.pdf
113 https://avalon.law.yale.edu/20th_century/leagcov.asp
114 https://biblio-archive.unog.ch/Dateien/CouncilMSD/C-339-M-156-1934-XII_EN.pdf
115 https://biblio-archive.unog.ch/Dateien/CouncilDocs/C-514-1938_EN.pdf
116 https://biblio-archive.unog.ch/Dateien/CouncilMSD/C-224-M-152-1939-XII_EN.pdf
117 https://biblio-archive.unog.ch/Dateien/CouncilMSD/C-231-M-153-1939-XII_EN.pdf
118 (P. 14 in: https://www.unog.ch/80256EDD006B8954/(httpAssets)/36BC4F83BD9E4443C1257AF3004FC0AE/%24file/Historical_overview_of_the_League_of_Nations.pdf)
119 Foundation stablished in 1913 by the American oil baron John D. Rockefeller Sr. (1839–1937) to promote "the well-being of mankind throughout the world". (https://www.encyclopedia.com/social-sciences-and-law/economics-business-and-labor/private-foundations/rockefeller-foundation)
120 Appendix 1 in: https://biblio-archive.unog.ch/Dateien/CouncilMSD/C-253-M-150-1938-XII_EN.pdf
121 See http://www.ibe.unesco.org/sites/default/files/resources/ibe_institutional_documents_0.pdf
122 https://unesdoc.unesco.org/ark:/48223/pf0000247329?posInSet=1&queryId=f402199e-eeb0-4d7b-97fa-b021548b76b3
123 https://nla.gov.au/nla.obj-52879052/view?partId=nla.obj-107700497#page/n4/mode/1up
124 In this connection, Christiaan W.J.M. Alting von Geusau remarked:

> Nazi ideology rejecting the idea of the equal dignity of every human being was not only disseminated through the propaganda of Goebbels, it also entered mainstream education and the academic world in an effort to give it broader support. Gilbert reports the successful 1936 doctoral thesis defense of a student in the German state of Saxony who held that the worth of an individual to the community "is measured by his or her racial personality. Only a racially valuable person has a right to exist in the community. A racially inferior or harmful individual must be eliminated". (p. 153)

(*Human Dignity and the Law in post-War Europe*, Dissertation, 2012, available in June 2020: http://othes.univie.ac.at/20706/1/2012-02-22_0847814.pdf)

125 Created in 1934 as a private agency of diffusion of the British culture, in 1940 it had become an official body of the Foreign Office for international cultural relations.
126 See p. 376 in: http://scholar.harvard.edu/files/kristenghodsee/files/unesco_literacy_and_the_cold_war.pdf
127 See Denis Mylonas, *La Genèse de l'Unesco: La Conférence des Ministres Alliés de l'Education (1942–1945)*, Brussels, Bruylant, 1976.
128 According to Frank R. Cowell (1966): "The first news which the British public had about their labours was a short paragraph in the Daily Telegraph of February 20, 1943" (p. IV).

129 Ralph E. Turner and Hope S.l French, 1944, Department of State, Conference Series 59, p. 3. (https://play.google.com/books/reader?id=Jb8fAAAAMAAJ&hl=pt_PT&pg=GBS.PA1).

130 The Final Report of the Commission of Enquiry on Special Educational Problems in the Liberated Countries, chaired by Joseph A. Lauwerys, was issued in January 1946. https://www.un.org/en/sections/history-united-nations-charter/1941-atlantic-charter/index.html

131 https://www.doaks.org/resources/dumbarton-oaks-conversations/exhibit-items/doconversations-fig46.jpg/view

132 Attention is called for the telegraphic style. General source of these documents: Department of State, Washington, Foreign Relations of the United States – Diplomatic Papers – 1943, General, Volume 1. (https://history.state.gov/historicaldocuments/frus1943v01)

133 Focussed files: https://history.state.gov/historicaldocuments/frus1943v01/comp24 or http://images.library.wisc.edu/FRUS/EFacs/1943v01/reference/frus.frus1943v01.i0028.pdf

134 The general source of the next documents is the following: Department of State, Washington, *Foreign Relations of the United States – Diplomatic Papers – 1944, General, Volume 1* (https://history.state.gov/historicaldocuments/frus1944v01). Focussed files are the following: https://history.state.gov/historicaldocuments/frus1944v01/comp7 or http://images.library.wisc.edu/FRUS/EFacs/1944v01/reference/frus.frus1944v01.i0011.pdf

135 Ralph E. Turner and Hope Sewell French, 1944, Department of State, Conference Series 59. (https://play.google.com/books/reader?id=Jb8fAAAAMAAJ&hl=pt_PT&pg=GBS.PA1).

136 Ralph E. Turner and Hope Sewell French, 1944, Department of State, Conference Series 59, p. 8. (https://play.google.com/books/reader?id=Jb8fAAAAMAAJ&hl=pt_PT&pg=GBS.PA1)

137 The general source of the next American documents is the following: Department of State, Washington, *Foreign Relations of the United States – Diplomatic Papers – 1945, General: The United Nations, Volume 1.* (https://history.state.gov/historicaldocuments/frus1945v01). Focussed files are the following: https://history.state.gov/historicaldocuments/frus1945v01/comp3 or http://images.library.wisc.edu/FRUS/EFacs/1945v01/reference/frus.frus1945v01.i0010.pdf

138 https://www.un.org/en/sections/un-charter/un-charter-full-text/

139 UNIO-Volume-1-E-F.pdf, p. 436, at: https://digitallibrary.un.org/record/1300969?ln=fr#record-files-collapse-header

140 UNIO-Volume-10-E-F.pdf, pp. 94, 95, at: https://digitallibrary.un.org/record/1300969?ln=fr#record-files-collapse-header

141 UNIO-Volume-1-E-F.pdf, p. 717, at: https://digitallibrary.un.org/record/1300969?ln=fr#record-files-collapse-header

142 Pp. 89, 90 in: https://unesdoc.unesco.org/ark:/48223/pf0000117626

143 Ibid., p. 12.

144 https://history.state.gov/historicaldocuments/frus1945v01/d374

145 The Labour Party had formed the Government of Great Britain, after winning elections in July, and Miss Ellen Wilkinson became Minister of Education.

146 P. 21 in: https://unesdoc.unesco.org/ark:/48223/pf0000117626/PDF/117626engo.pdf.multi.page=1&zoom=auto,-16,851

147 Ibid., p. 33.

148 Ibid., p. 55.

149 Ibid., p. 38.

150 Ibid., p. 101.

151 Let us recall that the USSR was not among them, as it suspected the new Organisation of being an arm of American politics. Moreover, the idealism of the Preamble to the UNESCO Constitution did not accord with the scientific materialism. It did not become a member until 1954 (along with Byelorussia and Ukraine). In 1971, following a Resolution of the UN General Assembly, the UNESCO Executive Committee decided that, "from today onwards, the Government of the People's Republic of China is the only legitimate representative of China in UNESCO", replacing the Republic of China (Resolution 88 EX/48 and Add. 1 and 2 and 88 EX/49). (P. 107, in: https://legal.un.org/docs/?path=../unjuridicalyearbook/pdfs/english/volumes/1971.pdf&lang=EF).

152 https://unesdoc.unesco.org/ark:/48223/pf0000117626?posInSet=24&queryId=bd2e57a2-2542-45be-96d4-bfbe5ac46698

153 P. 21 in: https://unesdoc.unesco.org/ark:/48223/pf0000066614

154 P. 22 ibid.

155 P. 24 in: https://unesdoc.unesco.org/ark:/48223/pf0000117626?posInSet=5&queryId=c4961edc-64ea-4b45-9ab9-5a2f12744b10

156 Ibid., p. 99.

157 https://unesdoc.unesco.org/ark:/48223/pf0000114580

158 P. 90 in: https://unesdoc.unesco.org/ark:/48223/pf0000117626/PDF/117626engo.pdf.multi

159 Ibid., p. 22.

160 Ibid., p. 28.

161 Ibid., pp. 132, 133.

162 http://images.library.wisc.edu/FRUS/EFacs/1945v01/reference/frus.frus1945v01.i0010.pdf

163 Ibid., p. 72.

164 https://unesdoc.unesco.org/ark:/48223/pf0000123477/PDF/123477engo.pdf.multi

165 P. I in: https://unesdoc.unesco.org/ark:/48223/pf0000079049

166 The UN logo is born as a pin to identify the Delegates to the San Francisco Conference, designed by a Committee (headed by Oliver Lundquist) nominated by the USA Secretary of State Edward Stettinius, Jr., Chairperson of the American Delegation and President of the Conference. It drew on a design created by the American architect Donal McLaughlin and consisted of a world map surrounded by olive branches. The world map was meant to represent all peoples of the world, and the olive branches were symbols of peace, in white on a blue background. In 1946, a UN Committee proposed the present design, with North America moving away from the centre. It was adopted by the UN General Assembly on 7 December 1946 (A/PV.55), following a Report of the Secretary-General. (https://digitallibrary.un.org/record/552010).

167 https://unesdoc.unesco.org/ark:/48223/pf0000114586

168 The Conservative Party was to return to power and Churchill became Prime Minister again for another four-year term (1951–1955).

169 Built in 1865 by Count Alexander Basilensky, this building was purchased by Isabella II of Spain to live his exile, for 36 years, after the abdication caused by the revolution of September 1868, and renamed 'Palace of Castile'. In 1908, it became a hotel and was used as a military hospital during the World War I. In the 1920s, Marcel Proust, Igor Stravinsky and Pablo Picasso, among other personalities, dined there. In 1936, it was purchased by the French State, having been the headquarters of the German and American authorities during the World War II. It became an international conference centre of the Ministry of Foreign and European Affairs, where were signed the Paris Agreements ending the Vietnam War (1973), the Paris Agreements on Cambodia (1991) and the Kléber Agreements to end the civil war in Côte d'Ivoire (2003). In 2007, it was sold by about 400 million euros

to a Qatari public investment company, which sold it by about 460 million, a few months later, to a Qatari public bank, to be renovated and become again a luxury hotel, *The Peninsula Paris*. A case of selling a piece of history?

170 https://unesdoc.unesco.org/ark:/48223/pf0000120333?posInSet=1&queryId=0117591f-3794-4248-beef-56d309fad435

171 P. 24 in: https://unesdoc.unesco.org/ark:/48223/pf0000066077

172 https://unesdoc.unesco.org/ark:/48223/pf0000053542?posInSet=1&queryId=5cedcec8-e3e4-4a24-9a44-af8f0a40d9b2

173 https://unesdoc.unesco.org/ark:/48223/pf0000114591

174 This French *sagesse* had also been voiced by Henri Bergson at ICIC second session (26 July to 2 August 1923), in his opening speech:

The results which the Committee had obtained up to the present were due not only to the eminent standing of its members but also to the observance from the very beginning of its work of a certain number of tacit conventions. For example, it had been tacitly understood that any vexed question should be avoided – anything, in fact, which would divide the Committee on questions of principle. What was really essential was that there should be agreement on particular decisions and on their application.

175 In this regard, Alison Bashford (2013) wrote:

His humanism and even his transhumanism once he started using that term, was always based on what he called evolutionary humanism. [...]

The evolved capacity to imagine and direct the future should render evolution the new religion, Huxley claimed, an extension of his claims that eugenics might be the religion of the future. Evolutionary humanism, indeed, was to be "the new world faith". [...]

Huxley was a life-long advocate of eugenics, even in the light of the Holocaust, and even though he had authored anti-racist texts like *We, Europeans* and was involved in the UNESCO Statement(s) on Race. He simply didn't perceive eugenics to be necessarily about race at all, nor necessarily about the kind of coercive politics that transhumanist scholars imagine eugenics to have typically or even solely been. Here lies, perhaps, the real usefulness of Huxley for the project of historicizing transhumanism. [...]

Julian Huxley, then, is the direct link between eugenics and contemporary transhumanism, in ways far more complex and interesting than simply his coining of the term. (pp. 169, 161, 166, 167)

176 https://unesdoc.unesco.org/ark:/48223/pf0000125830

177 https://unesdoc.unesco.org/ark:/48223/pf0000114580?posInSet=15&queryId=c5611426-47d1-4a1e-b392-579e6d7082dc

178 1.51, p. 18, in: https://unesdoc.unesco.org/ark:/48223/pf0000114584

179 It was also established an Institute for Education (UIE) – later renamed UNESCO Institute for Lifelong Learning (UIL) – whose governing body met for the first time from 17 to 19 June 1951 in Wiesbaden, Germany, and was attended by Maria Montessori and Jean Piaget. (https://uil.unesco.org/unesco-institute/history)

180 https://unesdoc.unesco.org/ark:/48223/pf0000117626/PDF/117626engo.pdf.multi

181 *The UNESCO Courier*, December 1948, Volume I, N° 11–12. (https://unesdoc.unesco.org/ark:/48223/pf0000262402/PDF/073886engo.pdf.multi.nameddest=262402)

182 Ibid., p. 2

183 https://unesdoc.unesco.org/ark:/48223/pf0000114593

184 https://unesdoc.unesco.org/ark:/48223/pf0000073956
185 https://www2.gwu.edu/~erpapers/myday/displaydoc.cfm?_y=1949&_f=md001244
186 *The UNESCO Courier*, June 1950, Volume III, N° 5. (https://unesdoc.unesco.org/ark:/48223/pf0000081400)
187 https://www2.gwu.edu/~erpapers/myday/displaydoc.cfm?_y=1951&_f=md001903
188 *The UNESCO Courier*, January 1953, Volume VI, N° 1 (https://unesdoc.unesco.org/ark:/48223/pf0000070146)
189 Translation:

May UNESCO one day develop its programme as we who had the privilege of being present at its birth in London, in 1945, dreamed that it might. And notwithstanding all obstacles, may peace assure for the world, through education, science and culture, a destiny worthy of mankind. Ladies and Gentlemen: Goodbye.

190 https://unesdoc.unesco.org/ark:/48223/pf0000009600?posInSet=1&queryId=b9389f01-bcc7-447f-95ea-c8d0b4a5ca8e
191 https://unesdoc.unesco.org/ark:/48223/pf0000114587
192 http://www.revistadelauniversidad.unam.mx/ojs_rum/index.php/rum/article/view/5348
193 https://www.nytimes.com/1974/05/14/archives/dr-jaime-torres-bodet-72-exdirector-of-unesco-dies-dynamic.html
194 https://unesdoc.unesco.org/ark:/48223/pf0000009600?posInSet=1&queryId=b9389f01-bcc7-447f-95ea-c8d0b4a5ca8e
195 Maren Elfert (2016) notes: "According to Iriye (2002, p. 103), it was at a meeting of the newly independent nations in Cairo in 1961 that they defined themselves as 'developing countries'. However, especially in the Cold War years, when the 'developing countries' had formed the 'Non-Aligned movement' and the Group of 77, they often used the term 'Third World countries'" (p. 25, note 11).
196 https://unesdoc.unesco.org/ark:/48223/pf0000160894
197 Maheu was a close friend of Jean-Paul Sartre and Simone de Beauvoir.
198 https://unesdoc.unesco.org/ark:/48223/pf0000049590/PDF/074827engo.pdf.multi.nameddest=49590
199 Published in 1966 with the title *La Civilisation de l'Universel – Inventaire de l'Avenir* (Éditions Laffont, Paris, and Gonthier, Geneva).
200 https://unesdoc.unesco.org/ark:/48223/pf0000066614
201 Director of the IBE between 1929 and 1949, Piaget was also President of the first Swiss National Commission for UNESCO since its creation, in 1949, until 1952, having participated in the General Conferences of 1948 (Beirut), 1949 (Paris), 1950 (Florence), 1951, 1952 (Paris) and 1954 (Montevideo). After resigning as President, he was asked by the Swiss Federal Council to remain a member of the National Commission, having accepted until 1958. He was also a member of the Executive Board of UNESCO between 1950 and 1954. When Torres Bodet resigned, on 22 November 1952, Piaget pronounced a moving speech asking him to stay.
202 Ibid., p. 87.
203 https://biblio-archive.unog.ch/Dateien/CouncilMSD/C-290-M-154-1935-XII_EN.pdf
204 https://unesdoc.unesco.org/ark:/48223/pf0000084008?posInSet=22&queryId=36e251cb-9933-45e3-8e54-f71dd3f815d5
205 http://portal.unesco.org/en/ev.php-URL_ID=15244&URL_DO=DO_TOPIC&URL_SECTION=201.html
206 https://unesdoc.unesco.org/ark:/48223/pf0000114580?posInSet=15&queryId=c5611426-47d1-4a1e-b392-579e6d7082dc

207 See: *The UNESCO Courier – Human Rights: Back to the Future*, October-December 2018 (https://unesdoc.unesco.org/ark:/48223/pf0000265904)

208 See: *The UNESCO Courier*, October-December 2011. (https://en.unesco.org/courier/october-december-2011)

209 P. 6 in: https://unesdoc.unesco.org/ark:/48223/pf0000227855

210 P. 8 ibid.

211 P. 16 ibid.

212 https://en.unesco.org/courier/october-december-2011

213 Introduction in: https://unesdoc.unesco.org/ark:/48223/pf0000227855

214 https://unesdoc.unesco.org/ark:/48223/pf0000231288

215 https://biblio-archive.unog.ch/Dateien/CouncilDocs/C-514-1938_EN.pdf

216 https://unesdoc.unesco.org/ark:/48223/pf0000114580?posInSet=15&queryId=c5611426-47d1-4a1e-b392-579e6d7082dc

217 See: Alice Calaprice (Collected and edited by), *The ultimate quotable Einstein*, Princeton University Press, 2011, p. 293.

218 https://biblio-archive.unog.ch/Dateien/CouncilMSD/C-290-M-154-1935-XII_EN.pdf

219 *Un jour, espérons-le, le globe entier sera civilisé, tous les points de la demeure humaine seront éclairés, et alors sera accompli le magnifique rêve de l'intelligence: avoir pour patrie le monde et pour nation l'humanité.*

220 https://www.jewishvirtuallibrary.org/president-roosevelt-broadcast-to-international-student-assembly-september-1942

221 https://unesdoc.unesco.org/ark:/48223/pf0000114580/PDF/114580engo.pdf.multi

222 https://unesdoc.unesco.org/ark:/48223/pf0000073956

223 https://en.unesco.org/themes/gced

224 Maurel (2010) remarks that the idea of World Government has ceded, especially since the 1990s, to that of *global governance*, imported from the financial and economic world to the field of political science. It implies the obsolescence of the State as the sole ruler of public affairs (nationally and internationally), as it is now challenged by new competing global players.

225 https://history.state.gov/historicaldocuments/frus1943v01/d978

226 https://www.un.org/en/sections/un-charter/un-charter-full-text/

227 http://portal.unesco.org/en/ev.php-URL_ID=15244&URL_DO=DO_TOPIC&URL_SECTION=201.html

228 https://unesdoc.unesco.org/ark:/48223/pf0000114580?posInSet=15&queryId=c5611426-47d1-4a1e-b392-579e6d7082dc

229 *The UNESCO Courier*, December 1948 – January 1949, pp. 4–5. (https://unesdoc.unesco.org/ark:/48223/pf0000073886)

230 https://unesdoc.unesco.org/ark:/48223/pf0000117626/PDF/117626engo.pdf.multi

231 https://pasisahlberg.com/text-test/

232 https://archive.org/details/cu31924031053709/page/n12

233 https://unesdoc.unesco.org/ark:/48223/pf0000117626

234 https://books.google.pt/books?id=yZMUAAAAQAAJ&pg=PA80&lpg=PA80&dq=%22le+plus+consid%C3%A9rable+de+mes+ouvrages,+et+celui+qui+me+tient+plus+au+coeur%22&source=bl&ots=fJfrfhWQT3&sig=ACfU3UoehBDEdaHa6voOOtEU31VoFWqJvg&hl=pt-PT&sa=X&ved=2ahUKEwjmvbWnh-fiAhWPlxQKHd5qBOIQ6AEwAHoECAIQAQ#v=onepage&q=le%20plus%20utile&f=false

235 http://www.ibe.unesco.org/sites/default/files/rousseaue.PDF

236 https://www.conseil-constitutionnel.fr/sites/default/files/as/root/bank_mm/anglais/cst2.pdf

237 https://fr.wikisource.org/wiki/M%C3%A9moires_de_deux_jeunes_mari%C3%A9es/Texte_entier
238 https://www.conseil-constitutionnel.fr/la-constitution/les-constitutions-de-la-france
239 www.conseil-constitutionnel.fr/conseil-constitutionnel/francais/la-constitution/les-constitutions-de-la-france/charte-constitutionnelle-du-14-aout-1830.5104.html
240 http://mjp.univ-perp.fr/constit/be1831.htm
241 https://www.conseil-constitutionnel.fr/les-constitutions-dans-l-histoire/constitution-de-1848-iie-republique
242 Quoted by Ach, N. (2004). *La liberté de l'enseignement face à l'intervention publique.* Université de Metz, Thèse, p. 12. (http://docnum.univ-lorraine.fr/public/UPV-M/Theses/2004/Ach.Nelly.DMZ0401.pdf)
243 https://en.wikiquote.org/wiki/Pope_Pius_VI
244 https://archive.org/stream/QuantaCuraTheSyllabusOfErrors_247/pius_ix_pope_quanta_cura_and_the_syllabus_of_errors_djvu.txt
245 Latin: http://w2.vatican.va/content/pius-ix/la/documents/encyclica-quanta-cura-8-decembris-1864.html
http://w2.vatican.va/content/leo-xiii/fr/encyclicals/documents/hf_l-xiii_enc_20061888_libertas.html
246 http://www.mediterranee-antique.fr/Auteurs/Fichiers/GHI/Guizot/Memoires/T3/Mem_3_00.htm
247 https://www.senat.fr/evenement/archives/D42/1882.html
248 http://www.inp.uw.edu.pl/mdsie/Political_Thought/Hegel%20Phil%20of%20Right.pdf
249 http://www.masshist.org/publications/adams-papers/index.php/view/PJA01d068
250 P. 6 in: Karl Rosenkranz, *Pedagogics as a System* (Transl. from German by Anna C. Brackett). St. Louis, MO: The R. P. Studley Company. (https://archive.org/details/pedagogicsasasy00rosegoog)
251 https://web.archive.org/web/20111217062556/http://sourcebook.fsc.edu/history/constitutionof1791.html
252 https://en.wikisource.org/wiki/Translation:French_Constitution_of_1793#Declaration_of_the_Rights_of_Man_and_Citizen.
253 https://en.wikisource.org/wiki/Translation:Constitution_of_the_Year_III
254 https://en.wikisource.org/wiki/French_Constitution_of_1848
255 http://www.documentarchiv.de/nzjh/verfdr1848.htm
256 https://archive.org/stream/jstor-1013370/1013370_djvu.txt
257 https://www.zum.de/psm/weimar/weimar_vve.php
258 http://soviethistory.msu.edu/1924-2/union-treaty/union-treaty-texts/first-union-constitution/
259 http://pdba.georgetown.edu/Constitutions/Brazil/brazil34.html
260 http://www.departments.bucknell.edu/russian/const/36cons04.html#chap10
261 https://en.wikisource.org/wiki/Constitution_of_Ireland_(original_text)
262 https://www.conseil-constitutionnel.fr/sites/default/files/as/root/bank_mm/anglais/cst3.pdf
263 https://www.senato.it/documenti/repository/istituzione/costituzione_inglese.pdf
264 https://www.un.org/en/ga/search/view_doc.asp?symbol=E/CN.4/AC.1/3/Add.1
265 http://www.oas.org/en/sla/dil/docs/inter_american_treaties_A-41_charter_OAS.pdf
266 See: https://en.unesco.org/themes/higher-education/recognition-qualifications/conventions-recommendations
267 https://undocs.org/E/CN.4/1999/49
268 https://unesdoc.unesco.org/ark:/48223/pf0000369944_eng/PDF/369944eng.pdf.multi

269 See also Yusuf, 2007b.

270 http://www.unesco.org/new/fileadmin/MULTIMEDIA/HQ/BSP/images/ILO.pdf

271 There is also a "Framework Agreement between UNESCO and UNICEF on Collaboration in the Field of Education", signed on 9 February 1999. (http://www.unesco.org/new/fileadmin/MULTIMEDIA/HQ/BSP/images/unicef.pdf)

272 https://www.ilo.org/sector/Resources/codes-of-practice-and-guidelines/WCMS_236528/lang--en/index.htm

273 https://digitallibrary.un.org/record/703061?ln=es

274 http://portal.unesco.org/en/ev.php-URL_ID=12949&URL_DO=DO_TOPIC&URL_SECTION=201.html

275 https://unesdoc.unesco.org/ark:/48223/pf0000160581?posInSet=1&queryId=a1fa7794-05bc-4ed7-a909-593309a3a425

276 https://tbinternet.ohchr.org/_layouts/15/treatybodyexternal/Download.aspx?symbolno=E%2fC.12%2fGC%2f20&Lang=en

277 For further reading, see:
- Hector Gros-Espiell (2005), *Significance of the Convention against Discrimination in Education (1960)*, UNESCO; (https://unesdoc.unesco.org/ark:/48223/pf0000142908)
- Yves Daudet, Pierre Michel Eisemann (2005), *Convention against Discrimination in Education – Commentary*, UNESCO; (https://unesdoc.unesco.org/ark:/48223/pf0000141286)
- UNESCO (2006), *Convention against Discrimination in Education (1960) and Articles 13 and 14 (Right to Education) of the International Covenant on Economic, Social and Cultural Rights: A Comparative Analysis.* (https://unesdoc.unesco.org/ark:/48223/pf0000145922)

278 https://www.refworld.org/docid/49997ae32c.html

279 www.ohchr.org/Documents/HRBodies/HRCouncil/RegularSession/Session23/A.HRC.23.35_en.pdf

280 According to the Comparative Constitutions Project, 149 Constitutions provide, in varying terms, for free education, 127 Constitutions provide for compulsory education, and 66 Constitutions provide for access to higher education. (https://comparativeconstitutionsproject.org/)

281 *Frequently Asked Questions on Economic, Social and Cultural Rights* (UNHCHR, Fact Sheet 33), p. 1. (https://www.ohchr.org/EN/PublicationsResources/Pages/FactSheets.aspx)

282 According to the *UNESCO Education Strategy – 2014–2021*: "About 140 countries have inscribed the right to education in their constitutions and 150 to 160 guarantee it and/or its main components in legislation" (p. 53, note 13: https://unesdoc.unesco.org/ark:/48223/pf0000231288). https://digitallibrary.un.org/record/760549/files/E_CN.4_SR.226-EN.pdf

283 http://ap.ohchr.org/documents/alldocs.aspx?doc_id=7060

284 https://tbinternet.ohchr.org/_layouts/treatybodyexternal/Download.aspx?symbolno=E%2fC.12%2f1999%2f4&Lang=en

285 https://digitallibrary.un.org/record/760549/files/E_CN.4_SR.226-EN.pdf

286 https://digitallibrary.un.org/record/721519/files/E_CN.4_SR.228-EN.pdf

287 http://portal.unesco.org/en/ev.php-URL_ID=12949&URL_DO=DO_TOPIC&URL_SECTION=201.html

288 http://portal.unesco.org/en/ev.php-URL_ID=13088&URL_DO=DO_TOPIC&URL_SECTION=201.html

289 https://hudoc.echr.coe.int/eng#{%22itemid%22:[%22001-57455%22]}

290 http://tbinternet.ohchr.org/_layouts/treatybodyexternal/Download.aspx?symbolno=CRC%2FGC%2F2001%2F1&Lang=en

291 http://portal.unesco.org/en/ev.php-URL_ID=49355&URL_DO=DO_TOPIC&URL_SECTION=201.html

292 http://portal.unesco.org/en/ev.php-URL_ID=49354&URL_DO=DO_TOPIC&URL_SECTION=201.html
At national level, the Supreme Court of Appeals of West Virginia, for instance, said in Case *Pauley v. Kelly, 255 S.E.2d 859 (1979)*: "We may synthesize a definition of education from the cases, encyclopaedias (28 C.J.S. Education, for example), and dictionaries: It is the development of mind, body and social morality (ethics) to prepare persons for useful and happy occupations, recreation and citizenship".
(http://law.justia.com/cases/west-virginia/supreme-court/1979/14036-3.html)

293 The Supreme Court of Washington said, in *Case McCleary et al. v. State of Washington* (N° 84362-7): "The word "education" under Article IX, Section 1 [of the Washington State Constitution] means the basic knowledge and skills needed to compete in today's economy and meaningfully participate in this State's democracy" (¶2). (https://caselaw.findlaw.com/wa-supreme-court/1590607.html)
http://uis.unesco.org/en/topic/international-standard-classification-education-isced

294 https://www.oas.org/dil/access_to_information_human_right_American_Declaration_of_the_Rights_and_Duties_of_Man.pdf

295 https://www.un.org/en/ga/search/view_doc.asp?symbol=A/C.3/SR.146

296 Initially, the French term *élementaire* was translated into English by *fundamental*.

297 http://unesdoc.unesco.org/images/0014/001443/144396mb.pdf

298 https://www.netzwerk-menschenrechte.de/
and
https://www.admin.ch/opc/de/classified-compilation/0.10.html

299 https://www.menschenrechtskonvention.eu/zusatzprotokoll-emrk-9251/

300 https://www.un.org/Depts/german/gv-66/band1/ar66137.pdf

301 https://unesdoc.unesco.org/ark:/48223/pf0000145333

302 http://unesdoc.unesco.org/images/0018/001802/180253e.pdf

303 https://unesdoc.unesco.org/ark:/48223/pf0000219109?posInSet=2&queryId=ed9b97f4-170b-4330-b3c0-c9513a0ffd2f

304 https://tbinternet.ohchr.org/_layouts/treatybodyexternal/Download.aspx?symbolno=E%2FC.12%2F1999%2F10

305 https://www.ohchr.org/en/professionalinterest/pages/crc.aspx

306 *Education Cannot Wait* (ECW) is an NGO concerned with children's education in situations of crisis. It is estimated that there are 75 million children in crisis situations, with low access to primary education and still lower to secondary education.

307 http://ap.ohchr.org/documents/alldocs.aspx?doc_id=9100

308 https://poemforchildren.wordpress.com/2009/06/18/his-name-is-today/

309 See: Joint General Recommendation N° 31 of the Committee on the Elimination of Discrimination against Women/General Comment N° 18 of the Committee on the Rights of the Child on harmful practices.
(https://tbinternet.ohchr.org/_layouts/15/treatybodyexternal/Download.aspx?symbolno=CEDAW%2fC%2fGC%2f31%2fCRC%2fC%2fGC%2f18&Lang=en)
See also the poem by William Ross Wallace (1819–1881) "The Hand That Rocks the Cradle Rules the World". (http://holyjoe.org/poetry/wallace.htm)

310 https://tbinternet.ohchr.org/_layouts/15/treatybodyexternal/Download.aspx?symbolno=CCPR%2fC%2f21%2fRev.1%2fAdd.5&Lang=en

311 http://unesdoc.unesco.org/images/0000/000017/001761fo.pdf

312 http://tbinternet.ohchr.org/_layouts/treatybodyexternal/Download.aspx?symbolno=E%2fC.12%2fGC%2f21&Lang=en

313 http://www.corteconstitucional.gov.co/relatoria/2017/t-085-17.htm

314 https://unesdoc.unesco.org/ark:/48223/pf0000259338

315 https://www.girlsnotbrides.org/

316 https://www.coe.int/en/web/conventions/full-list/-/conventions/treaty/163

317 https://au.int/en/treaties/african-charter-human-and-peoples-rights

318 https://au.int/en/treaties/african-charter-rights-and-welfare-child

319 http://www.oas.org/juridico/english/treaties/a-52.html

320 http://prfjk.org/wp-content/uploads/2018/07/Cairo-Declaration-on-Human-Rights-in-Islam.pdf

321 http://assembly.coe.int/nw/xml/XRef/Xref-XML2HTML-en.asp?fileid=25353

322 http://tbinternet.ohchr.org/_layouts/treatybodyexternal/Download.aspx?symbolno=E%2FC.12%2F1999%2F10

323 http://uis.unesco.org/sites/default/files/documents/international-standard-classification-of-education-isced-2011-en.pdf

324 http://tbinternet.ohchr.org/_layouts/treatybodyexternal/Download.aspx?symbolno=E%2FC.12%2F1999%2F10

325 https://hudoc.echr.coe.int/eng#{„itemid":[„001-57525"]}

326 http://tbinternet.ohchr.org/_layouts/treatybodyexternal/Download.aspx?symbolno=E%2FC.12%2F1999%2F10

327 See: Donald C. Savage and Patricia A. Finn, "The Road to the 1997 UNESCO Statement on Academic Freedom" (Available in May 2020: https://www.caut.ca/sites/default/files/unesco_en_insidepages_final2017-09-11.pdf)

328 http://assembly.coe.int/nw/xml/XRef/Xref-XML2HTML-EN.asp?fileid=17469&lang=en

329 https://hudoc.echr.coe.int/fre#{%22itemid%22:[%22001-144129%22]}

330 See: Céline Romainville, «La liberté académique devant la Cour européenne des droits de l'homme», *Revue trimestrielle des droits de l'homme* (*obs/s. Cour eur. dr. H., Mustafa Erdogan et al. c. Turquie, 27 mai 2014*), Vol. 2015, No. 104, 1021–2051. (https://dial.uclouvain.be/pr/boreal/object/boreal:185955)

331 And could not indicate. As said the Supreme Court of Washington, in *Case McCleary et al. v. State of Washington* (Nº 84362-7): "The program of basic education is not etched in constitutional stone. The legislature has an obligation to review the basic education program as the needs of students and the demands of society evolve" (¶ 2). (https://caselaw.findlaw.com/wa-supreme-court/1590607.html)

332 http://tbinternet.ohchr.org/_layouts/treatybodyexternal/Download.aspx?symbolno=CRC%2FGC%2F2001%2F1&Lang=en

333 https://unesdoc.unesco.org/ark:/48223/pf0000127583

334 https://unesdoc.unesco.org/ark:/48223/pf0000121147

335 http://www.un.org/millennium/declaration/ares552e.htm

336 https://www.undp.org/content/undp/en/home/sdgoverview/mdg_goals.html

337 http://www.assembly.coe.int/nw/xml/XRef/Xref-XML2HTML-en.asp?fileid=15108&lang=en

338 https://unesdoc.unesco.org/ark:/48223/pf0000127583

339 http://tbinternet.ohchr.org/_layouts/treatybodyexternal/Download.aspx?symbolno=E%2fC.12%2f1999%2f10&Lang=en

340 https://www.ohchr.org/en/professionalinterest/pages/crc.aspx

341 https://tbinternet.ohchr.org/_layouts/treatybodyexternal/Download.aspx?symbolno=CRC%2FGC%2F2003%2F5&Lang=en

342 https://www.cidh.oas.org/Basicos/English/Basic2.american%20Declaration.htm
343 www.finlex.fi/fi/laki/kaannokset/1999/en19990731.pdf
344 http://classics.mit.edu/Plotinus/enneads.html
345 See: *Global Education Monitoring Report – 2017/8 – Accountability in education: Meeting our commitments.*
(https://unesdoc.unesco.org/ark:/48223/pf0000259338)
346 https://www.ohchr.org/en/professionalinterest/pages/ccpr.aspx
347 It was at the 779th meeting of the UN General Assembly Third Committee (A/C.3/SR.779) that the Canadian Delegation (Quart) proposed the replacement of the term "it is understood" with "recognise".
(https://digitallibrary.un.org/search?ln=en&p=A%2FC.3%2FSR.779&f=&c=Resource+Type&c=UN+Bodies&sf=&so=d&rg=50&fti=0)
She was, thereafter, supported by other Delegations and the proposal was approved.
(https://digitallibrary.un.org/search?ln=en&p=A%2FC.3%2FSR.787&f=&action_search=Search&c=Resource+Type&c=UN+Bodies&sf=&so=d&rg=50&fti=0)
348 https://www.ohchr.org/en/professionalinterest/pages/cescr.aspx
349 https://www.ohchr.org/en/professionalinterest/pages/crc.aspx
350 https://tbinternet.ohchr.org/_layouts/15/treatybodyexternal/Download.aspx?symbolno=INT%2fCESCR%2fGEC%2f4758&Lang=en
351 https://tbinternet.ohchr.org/_layouts/treatybodyexternal/Download.aspx?symbolno=E%2FC.12%2F1999%2F10
352 https://tbinternet.ohchr.org/_layouts/treatybodyexternal/Download.aspx?symbolno=INT%2fCESCR%2fGEC%2f4758&Lang=en
353 http://tbinternet.ohchr.org/_layouts/treatybodyexternal/Download.aspx?symbolno=E%2fC.12%2f1999%2f10&Lang=en
354 http://tbinternet.ohchr.org/_layouts/treatybodyexternal/Download.aspx?symbolno=E%2FC.12%2F1999%2F10
355 https://www.achpr.org/public/Document/file/English/achpr_instr_guide_draft_esc_rights_eng.pdf
356 https://www.ohchr.org/en/professionalinterest/pages/crc.aspx
357 https://assembly.coe.int/nw/xml/XRef/Xref-XML2HTML-en.asp?fileid=17421&lang=en
358 http://tbinternet.ohchr.org/_layouts/treatybodyexternal/Download.aspx?symbolno=E%2FC.12%2F1999%2F10
359 https://tbinternet.ohchr.org/_layouts/15/treatybodyexternal/Download.aspx?symbolno=INT%2fCESCR%2fGEC%2f4759&Lang=en
360 http://tbinternet.ohchr.org/_layouts/treatybodyexternal/Download.aspx?symbolno=E%2fC.12%2f1999%2f5&Lang=en
361 https://undocs.org/E/CN.4/1999/49
362 http://ap.ohchr.org/documents/alldocs.aspx?doc_id=2880
363 http://tbinternet.ohchr.org/_layouts/treatybodyexternal/Download.aspx?symbolno=E%2FC.12%2F1999%2F10
364 http://tbinternet.ohchr.org/_layouts/treatybodyexternal/Download.aspx?symbolno=E%2fC.12%2f1999%2f10&Lang=en
365 https://tbinternet.ohchr.org/_layouts/15/treatybodyexternal/Download.aspx?symbolno=E%2fC.12%2f1999%2f4&Lang=en
366 http://ap.ohchr.org/documents/alldocs.aspx?doc_id=1920
367 https://www.worldbank.org/en/publication/wdr2018
368 https://undocs.org/E/CN.4/SR.67
369 http://hr-travaux.law.virginia.edu/document/iccpr/ecn4sr285/nid-2005

370 https://undocs.org/en/A/2929
371 https://digitallibrary.un.org/record/863167/files/A_C-3_SR-786-EN.pdf
372 https://www2.gwu.edu/~erpapers/myday/displaydoc.cfm?_y=1951&_f=md001903
373 http://tbinternet.ohchr.org/_layouts/treatybodyexternal/Download.aspx?symbolno=E%2FC.12%2F1999%2F10
374 http://tbinternet.ohchr.org/_layouts/treatybodyexternal/Download.aspx?symbolno=CRC%2fC%2f58&Lang=en
375 http://www.oas.org/en/iachr/mandate/basic_documents.asp
376 http://tbinternet.ohchr.org/_layouts/treatybodyexternal/Download.aspx?symbolno=E%2FC.12%2F1999%2F10
377 https://digitallibrary.un.org/record/863079/files/A_C-3_SR-791-EN.pdf
378 https://tbinternet.ohchr.org/_layouts/treatybodyexternal/Download.aspx?symbolno=E%2fC.12%2f1999%2f4&Lang=en
379 https://unesdoc.unesco.org/ark:/48223/pf0000127583
380 http://www.saflii.org.za/za/cases/ZACC/2011/13.html
381 The first Rapporteur on the Right to Education pointed out: "Available evidence indicates that the key to reducing poverty is secondary rather than primary education" (E/CN.4/2002/60). (https://documents-dds-ny.un.org/doc/UNDOC/GEN/G02/100/12/PDF/G0210012.pdf?OpenElement)
382 www.ilo.org/dyn/normlex/en/f?p=NORMLEXPUB:12100:0::NO::P12100_ILO_CODE:C138
383 http://uis.unesco.org/sites/default/files/documents/education-2030-incheon-framework-for-action-implementation-of-sdg4-2016-en_2.pdf
384 https://hudoc.echr.coe.int/eng#{„itemid":[„001-57525"]}
385 https://www.ecml.at/Portals/1/documents/CoE-documents/CMRec2012-13_quality_EN.pdf?ver=2016-11-29-113145-700
386 https://undocs.org/en/E/C.12/1999/10
387 http://ap.ohchr.org/documents/dpage_e.aspx?si=A/73/53
388 http://www.ohchr.org/EN/Issues/Education/SREducation/Pages/AnnualReports.aspx
389 https://spinternet.ohchr.org/_Layouts/SpecialProceduresInternet/Download.aspx?SymbolNo=E%2fCN.4%2fRES%2f1998%2f33&Lang=en
390 http://ap.ohchr.org/documents/alldocs.aspx?doc_id=9100
391 https://www.ohchr.org/en/issues/education/sreducation/Pages/SREducationIndex.aspx
392 https://digitallibrary.un.org/record/1633463
393 https://www.ilo.org/global/about-the-ilo/how-the-ilo-works/ilo-supervisory-system-mechanism/lang--en/index.htm
394 https://www.icc-cpi.int/nr/rdonlyres/ea9aeff7-5752-4f84-be94-0a655eb30e16/0/rome_statute_english.pdf
395 https://www.right-to-education.org/sites/right-to-education.org/files/resource-attachments/UNESCO_The_Right_To_Education_Monitoring_Standard-Setting_Instruments_of_UNESCO_2008_En.pdf
396 http://portal.unesco.org/en/ev.php-URL_ID=21647&URL_DO=DO_TOPIC&URL_SECTION=201.html
397 Ibid.
398 http://portal.unesco.org/en/ev.php-URL_ID=21647&URL_DO=DO_TOPIC&URL_SECTION=201.html
399 https://unesdoc.unesco.org/ark:/48223/pf0000181839
400 http://portal.unesco.org/en/ev.php-URL_ID=15249&URL_DO=DO_TOPIC&URL_SECTION=201.html
401 Where this autor did an internship for research at the time.

402 In 1952, the Republic of South Africa left the Organisation, because of its *Apartheid* policy. Portugal was excluded from certain meetings in June 1971, because of its colonial policy, and decided to withdraw from the Organisation from 1 January 1973. It returned on 11 September 1974, after the 25 April "Carnation Revolution".
Already during the 1963 International Conference on Public Education, several Delegations of recently independent African nations had protested against the colonial policy of Portugal (although in breach of the IBE Statutes) for offending "human and children's rights and the sacred principles of education" (as cited in Hofstetter & Schneuwly, 2013, note 11).
403 https://www.right-to-education.org/sites/right-to-education.org/files/resource-attachments/ESC_The_Right_to_Education_under_the_European_Social_Charter_2006_en.pdf
404 http://www.oas.org/juridico/english/treaties/a-52.html
405 https://www.oas.org/dil/access_to_information_American_Convention_on_Human_Rights.pdf
406 https://www.eacj.org/
407 https://aichr.org/
408 http://globalsummitryproject.com.s197331.gridserver.com/archive/saarc/saarc-sec.org/areaofcooperation/detail087c.html?activity_id=10#
409 http://lasportal.org/en/humanrights/Committee/Pages/AboutTheCommittee.aspx
410 https://www.oic-oci.org/home/?lan=en
411 https://www.ohchr.org/EN/ProfessionalInterest/Pages/OPCESCR.aspx
412 https://tbinternet.ohchr.org/_layouts/treatybodyexternal/Download.aspx?symbolno=E%2FC.12%2F1998%2F24&Lang=en
413 http://ap.ohchr.org/documents/dpage_e.aspx?si=A/73/53
414 https://www.india.gov.in/my-government/constitution-india
415 http://indiankanoon.org/doc/40715
416 http://indiankanoon.org/doc/1775396
417 http://legislative.gov.in/sites/default/files/The%20Right%20of%20Children%20to%20Free%20and%20Compulsory%20Education%20Act%2C%202009.pdf
418 http://aacc-asia.org/content/landmarkdecisions/13_PUU132008%20-%20Copy.pdf
419 www.corteconstitucional.gov.co/relatoria/2010/c-376-10.htm
420 https://www.enfam.jus.br/wp-content/uploads/2018/11/AP-0150735-64.2008.8.26.0002-TJSP-1.pdf
421 http://www.saflii.org/za/cases/ZAECGHC/2015/67.html
422 For further Case Law, see Appendix 4.
423 http://www.right-to-education.org
424 http://ngoeducation.org
425 www.campaignforeducation.org
426 http://www.hrea.org
427 http://www.oidel.org/presentation-2/?lang=en
428 http://portail-eip.org/En/index.html
429 http://www.forummundialeducacao.org/
430 This author was invited for the first and other FME sessions, as well as for its International Council.
http://www.ngo-unesco.net/en/
431 http://portal.unesco.org/en/ev.php-URL_ID=33137&URL_DO=DO_TOPIC&URL_SECTION=201.html
432 http://tbinternet.ohchr.org/_layouts/treatybodyexternal/Download.aspx?symbolno=E%2fC.12%2f1999%2f10&Lang=en

433 *The Power of Education Foundation* was founded in December 2009 to educate some of the most vulnerable children in Port-au-Prince, Haiti. (https://www.powerofeducationfoundation.org)

434 In this connection, let us note that, in the EU Charter, the right to education only "includes the possibility to receive free compulsory education" (Article 14.2). (https://www.europarl.europa.eu/charter/pdf/text_en.pdf)

435 https://www.ohchr.org/EN/ProfessionalInterest/Pages/CESCR.aspx

436 https://www.ohchr.org/EN/ProfessionalInterest/Pages/ProgressAndDevelopment.aspx

437 https://www.coe.int/en/web/european-social-charter

438 https://unesdoc.unesco.org/ark:/48223/pf0000259338

439 http://www.codices.coe.int/NXT/gateway.dll/CODICES/precis/eng/eur/cze/cze-1995-2-008?f=templates$fn=document-frameset.htm$q=%5Bfield,E_Alphabetical%20Index%3A%5Borderedprox,0%3ASchool%5D%5D%20$x=server$3.0#LPHit1

440 http://www.saflii.org/za/cases/ZAECGHC/2015/67.html

441 https://www.oas.org/es/sla/ddi/docs/acceso_informacion_base_dc_leyes_pais_b_1_en.pdf

442 https://www.achpr.org/public/Document/file/English/achpr_instr_guide_draft_esc_rights_eng.pdf

443 http://www.europarl.europa.eu/doceo/document/TA-8-2018-11-13_EN.html

444 http://www.hamoked.org/files/2013/113481_eng.pdf

445 The term "compulsory" is absent from the European Social Charter (Revised, 1996). (https://www.coe.int/en/web/conventions/full-list/-/conventions/treaty/163)

446 https://www.ohchr.org/EN/ProfessionalInterest/Pages/CEDAW.aspx

447 http://tbinternet.ohchr.org/_layouts/treatybodyexternal/Download.aspx?symbolno=E%2fC.12%2f1999%2f4&Lang=en

448 http://www.corteconstitucional.gov.co/relatoria/1997/C-309-97.htm

449 http://ap.ohchr.org/documents/alldocs.aspx?doc_id=2880

450 *Abgesehen vom internationalen Arbeitsrecht, das dank der jahrzehntelangen gesetzgebenden und rechtsprechenden Tätigkeit der ILO der menschenrechtler Themenbereich mit dem wohl dichtesten völkerrechtlichen Normengeflecht darstellt, weist auch das völkerrechtliche Bildungsrecht heute schon eine beträchtliche Normendichte auf. Insbesondere dank der Rechtsetzungstätigkeit der UNESCO ist in Umrissen heute ein "Internationaler Kodex des Bildungsrecht" zu erkennen.*

451 https://www.ohchr.org/en/professionalinterest/pages/ccpr.aspx

452 https://tbinternet.ohchr.org/_layouts/treatybodyexternal/Download.aspx?symbolno=HRI%2FMC%2F2005%2F5&Lang=en

453 https://www.earlymoderntexts.com/assets/pdfs/locke1690book2.pdf

454 https://archive.org/details/cu31924031053709/page/n12

455 www.jcsintl.org

456 http://thinkexist.com/quotation/at_the_desk_where_i_sit-i_have_learned_one_great/327427.html

457 https://quoteinvestigator.com/2016/05/03/expense/

458 http://www.oxfordreference.com/view/10.1093/acref/9780191843730.001.0001/q-oro-ed5-00007046

459 https://books.google.pt/books?id=Ax4RxBV6n0oC&pg=PA5&lpg=PA5&dq=75+Prix+Nobel,+janvier+1988&source=bl&ots=PnH4Da9WuO&sig=GyF8UVwJQhOPEDEVCSeJhNNr8qg&hl=pt-PT&sa=X&ved=2ahUKEwj-xv2I8cncAhXHxIUKHfblBt8Q6AEwBXoECAMQAQ#v=onepage&q=priorit%C3%A9%20absolue&f=false

460 Campos, Á. (1964). *Poesias* (Obras Completas de Fernando Pessoa). Lisboa: Edições Ática, p. 7.

461 Amartya Sen: "The right not to be hungry", in Alston and Tomaševski (eds.), *The Right to Food*, SIM, Netherlands, 1984.

462 Note 4 of the Fifth Report of the Independent Expert on the Right to Development – Frameworks for development cooperation and the right to development, presented by Arjun Sengupta to the Human Rights Commission (E/CN.4/2002/WG.18/6, September 8, 2002).

463 https://www.ohchr.org/Documents/Issues/Development/Session21/3_A_HRC_WG.2_21_2_AdvanceEditedVersion.pdf

464 http://www.europarl.europa.eu/doceo/document/TA-8-2018-11-13_EN.html

465 https://unesdoc.unesco.org/ark:/48223/pf0000097551/PDF/097551eng.pdf.multi

466 https://unesdoc.unesco.org/ark:/48223/pf0000102501

467 https://digitallibrary.un.org/record/760549/files/E_CN.4_SR.226-EN.pdf

468 https://digitallibrary.un.org/record/721520/files/E_CN.4_SR.229-EN.pdf

469 https://digitallibrary.un.org/record/863010/files/A_C-3_SR-790-EN.pdf

470 https://www.constituteproject.org/constitution/Brazil_2017.pdf?lang=en

471 http://www.unesco.org/education/edurights/media/docs/b1ba8608010ce0c48966911957392ea8cda405d8.pdf

472 https://www.sep.gob.mx/work/models/sep1/Resource/558c2c24-0b12-4676-ad90-8ab78086b184/ley_general_educacion.pdf

473 http://caselaw.lp.findlaw.com/scripts/getcase.pl?court=US&vol=347&invol=483

474 https://www.courtlistener.com/opinion/108530/wisconsin-v-yoder/

475 https://caselaw.findlaw.com/us-supreme-court/457/202.html

476 (http://law.justia.com/cases/west-virginia/supreme-court/1979/14036-3.html)

477 https://scc-csc.lexum.com/scc-csc/scc-csc/en/item/165/index.do

478 https://indiankanoon.org/doc/1775396/

479 http://www.saflii.org/za/cases/ZASCA/2015/198.html

480 https://files.eric.ed.gov/fulltext/ED072153.pdf

481 http://tbinternet.ohchr.org/_layouts/treatybodyexternal/Download.aspx?symbolno=E%2fC.12%2f1999%2f4&Lang=en

482 https://unesdoc.unesco.org/ark:/48223/pf0000097551/PDF/097551eng.pdf.multi

483 http://ap.ohchr.org/documents/alldocs.aspx?doc_id=7060

484 https://spinternet.ohchr.org/_Layouts/SpecialProceduresInternet/Download.aspx?SymbolNo=E%2fCN.4%2fRES%2f1998%2f33&Lang=en

485 See: www.unicef.org/publications/files/pub_sowc99_en.pdf

486 https://myworld2015.files.wordpress.com/2014/12/wethepeoples-7million.pdf

487 http://ap.ohchr.org/documents/alldocs.aspx?doc_id=2360

488 http://www.unesco.org/education/pdf/4TH_E.PDF

489 http://indiankanoon.org/doc/40715

490 http://indiankanoon.org/doc/1775396

491 http://www.saflii.org/za/cases/ZACC/1995/13.html

492 http://www.corteconstitucional.gov.co/relatoria/2016/t-039-16.htm

493 http://www.corteconstitucional.gov.co/relatoria/2015/t-137-15.htm

494 https://www.boe.es/buscar/doc.php?id=BOE-T-2007-21162

495 https://www.corteidh.or.cr/docs/casos/articulos/seriec_214_ing.pdf

496 http://www.hamoked.org/files/2013/113481_eng.pdf

497 https://supreme.justia.com/cases/federal/us/530/57/case.html

498 https://www.congress.gov/bill/104th-congress/senate-resolution/133/text

499 https://www.un.org/en/universal-declaration-human-rights/

500 https://treaties.un.org/doc/publication/unts/volume%201155/volume-1155-i-18232-english.pdf
501 https://www.un.org/en/ga/search/view_doc.asp?symbol=A/C.3/SR.148
502 https://digitallibrary.un.org/record/760549/files/E_CN.4_SR.226-EN.pdf
503 https://digitallibrary.un.org/record/760550/files/E_CN.4_SR.227-EN.pdf
504 http://www.un.org/en/ga/search/view_doc.asp?symbol=E/CN.4/SR.67&referer=http://research.un.org/en/undhr/chr/3&Lang=F
505 https://digitallibrary.un.org/record/760549/files/E_CN.4_SR.226-EN.pdf
506 http://uvallsc.s3.amazonaws.com/travaux/s3fs-public/E-CN_4-SR_227.pdf?null
507 https://digitallibrary.un.org/record/721519/files/E_CN.4_SR.228-EN.pdf
508 https://digitallibrary.un.org/record/863167/files/A_C-3_SR-786-EN.pdf
509 https://unesdoc.unesco.org/ark:/48223/pf0000117626
510 http://www.un.org/en/ga/search/view_doc.asp?symbol=A/C.3/SR.146
511 https://digitallibrary.un.org/record/760549/files/E_CN.4_SR.226-EN.pdf
512 https://www.un.org/en/ga/search/view_doc.asp?symbol=A/C.3/SR.147
513 https://digitallibrary.un.org/record/760549/files/E_CN.4_SR.226-EN.pdf
514 https://digitallibrary.un.org/record/721520/files/E_CN.4_SR.229-EN.pdf
515 https://digitallibrary.un.org/record/863167/files/A_C-3_SR-786-EN.pdf
516 The source of the quotations that follow (to which refer the pages indicated) is the following document: https://www.echr.coe.int/LibraryDocs/Travaux/ECHRTravaux-P1-2-CDH(67)2-BIL2292567.pdf
517 https://hudoc.echr.coe.int/eng#{"fulltext":["\"KJELDSEN, MADSEN AND v. DENMARK\""]}
518 https://treaties.un.org/doc/publication/unts/volume%201155/volume-1155-i-18232-english.pdf
519 https://lawcirca.com/what-is-the-doctrine-of-harmonious-construction/
520 http://www.corteidh.or.cr/docs/casos/articulos/seriec_205_esp.pdf
521 http://hj.tribunalconstitucional.es/en/Resolucion/Show/133
522 https://hudoc.echr.coe.int/eng#{%22display%22:[%220%22],%22languageisocode%22:[%22ENG%22],%22appno%22:[%221474/62%22,%221677/62%22,%221691/62%22,%221769/63%22,%221994/63%22,%222126/64%22],%22documentcollectionid2%22:[%22CHAMBER%22],%22itemid%22:[%22001-57525%22]}
523 https://uvallsc.s3.amazonaws.com/travaux/s3fs-public/A-3764.pdf?null
524 https://digitallibrary.un.org/record/86526
525 https://www.cidh.oas.org/basicos/english/basic3.american%20convention.htm
526 https://www.oas.org/juridico/english/treaties/a-52.html
527 http://ap.ohchr.org/documents/alldocs.aspx?doc_id=2880
528 https://www.europarl.europa.eu/charter/pdf/text_en.pdf
529 www.cvce.eu/obj/note_from_the_praesidium_of_the_convention_explanations_on_the_charter_of_fundamental_rights_of_the_european_union_brussels_11_october_2000-en-3a7f5ec5-c732-4326-8b10-f708e6ba3e07.html
530 http://www.achpr.org/instruments/child/
531 https://hudoc.echr.coe.int/eng#{%22itemid%22:[%22001-57509%22]}
532 https://scc-csc.lexum.com/scc-csc/scc-csc/en/item/165/index.do
533 https://digitallibrary.un.org/record/760550/files/E_CN.4_SR.227-EN.pdf
534 https://digitallibrary.un.org/record/760549/files/E_CN.4_SR.226-EN.pdf
535 https://digitallibrary.un.org/record/128761/files/E_CN.4_1987_WG.1_WP.35-EN.pdf
536 http://uvallsc.s3.amazonaws.com/travaux/s3fs-public/A-C_3-44-SR_44.pdf?null
537 https://treaties.un.org/Pages/ViewDetails.aspx?src=IND&mtdsg_no=IV-11&chapter=4&lang=en#EndDec
538 https://tbinternet.ohchr.org/_layouts/treatybodyexternal/Download.aspx?symbolno=CRC%2FC%2F3%2FAdd.27&Lang=es

539 https://tbinternet.ohchr.org/_layouts/treatybodyexternal/Download.aspx?symbolno=CRC%2FC%2F15%2FAdd.46&Lang=es
540 https://digitallibrary.un.org/record/863167/files/A_C-3_SR-786-EN.pdf
541 https://treaties.un.org/Pages/ViewDetails.aspx?src=IND&mtdsg_no=IV-11&chapter=4&lang=en#EndDec
542 https://www.ohchr.org/en/professionalinterest/pages/crc.aspx
543 http://portal.unesco.org/en/ev.php-URL_ID=12949&URL_DO=DO_TOPIC&URL_SECTION=201.html
544 https://undocs.org/en/A/70/286
545 https://www.ohchr.org/en/professionalinterest/pages/religionorbelief.aspx
546 http://www.saflii.org/za/cases/ZACC/2000/11.html
547 https://hudoc.echr.coe.int/fre#{%22itemid%22:[%22001-57455%22]}
548 https://tbinternet.ohchr.org/_layouts/treatybodyexternal/Download.aspx?symbolno=CRPD/C/GC/4&Lang=en
549 https://hudoc.echr.coe.int/eng#{%22itemid%22:[%22001-81356%22]}
550 http://www.corteconstitucional.gov.co/relatoria/1994/T-293-94.htm
551 See: CoESCR, Day of General Discussion on "Globalization and its impact on the enjoyment of economic, social and cultural rights" (E/1999/22 E/C.12/1998/26). (https://tbinternet.ohchr.org/_layouts/15/treatybodyexternal/Download.aspx?symbolno=E%2fC.12%2f1998%2f26&Lang=en)
552 https://www.gutenberg.org/ebooks/4300
553 http://ap.ohchr.org/documents/alldocs.aspx?doc_id=2880
554 https://www.un.org/en/universal-declaration-human-rights/
555 https://rm.coe.int/CoERMPublicCommonSearchServices/DisplayDCTMContent?documentId=090000168048b059
556 https://ap.ohchr.org/documents/alldocs.aspx?doc_id=1920
557 http://www.ministeriopublico.pt/instrumento/pacto-internacional-sobre-os-direitos-economicos-sociais-e-culturais
558 https://docs.wto.org/dol2fe/Pages/FE_Search/FE_S_S009-SSD.aspx?language=EF&CatalogueIdList=57066&CurrentCatalogueIdIndex=0&FullTextHash=&HasEnglishRecord=True&HasFrenchRecord=True&HasSpanishRecord=True
559 https://undocs.org/en/A/69/402
560 www.uis.unesco.org/Pages/Glossary.aspx
561 http://indiankanoon.org/doc/1775396
562 See: https://charterschoolcenter.ed.gov/publication/state-charter-sector-what-you-need-know-about-charter-sector-today
563 http://caselaw.findlaw.com/fl-supreme-court/1102469.html
564 https://www.courts.wa.gov/opinions/pdf/897140.pdf
565 https://arkonline.org/about-us/what-we-do
566 https://arkonline.org/ppp-review
567 See also: https://static1.squarespace.com/static/5a6e0958f6576ebde0e78c18/t/5bbab9ec7817f7ebddbe1319/1538963964854/EURODAD-history-repppeated-1538666055.pdf
568 https://eurodad.org/files/pdf/1546821-world-bank-must-stop-promoting-dangerous-public-private-partnerships-1549891747.pdf
569 See also: *History RePPPeated – How public-private partnerships are failing* – A report coordinated by Eurodad (European Network on Debt and Development), issued in 2018 (https://eurodad.org/HistoryRePPPeated)
570 https://undocs.org/E/C.12/GBR/CO/6

571 https://tbinternet.ohchr.org/_layouts/treatybodyexternal/Download.aspx?symbolno=E/C.12/PHL/CO/5-6&Lang=En

572 https://www.conseil-constitutionnel.fr/sites/default/files/as/root/bank_mm/anglais/cst2.pdf

573 https://undocs.org/E/CN.4/SR.14

574 https://undocs.org/en/A/HRC/41/37

575 http://indiankanoon.org/doc/1775396

576 https://www.venice.coe.int/files/Bulletin/B2016-1-e.pdf

577 https://dre.pt/pesquisa/-/search/1871231/details/maximized

578 http://ap.ohchr.org/documents/alldocs.aspx?doc_id=1920

579 https://www.un.org/en/universal-declaration-human-rights/

580 https://www.finlex.fi/en/laki/kaannokset/1998/en19980628.pdf

581 http://indiankanoon.org/doc/1775396

582 https://ap.ohchr.org/documents/alldocs.aspx?doc_id=1920

583 http://ap.ohchr.org/documents/alldocs.aspx?doc_id=2360

584 http://tbinternet.ohchr.org/_layouts/treatybodyexternal/Download.aspx?symbolno=E%2fC.12%2f1999%2f10&Lang=en

585 http://tbinternet.ohchr.org/_layouts/treatybodyexternal/Download.aspx?symbolno=E%2fC.12%2f1999%2f10&Lang=en

586 https://www.ohchr.org/Documents/Publications/SDecisionsVol4en.pdf

587 http://www.ceec.be/

588 http://ap.ohchr.org/documents/alldocs.aspx?doc_id=1920

589 https://ap.ohchr.org/documents/dpage_e.aspx?si=A/HRC/41/L.26

590 http://www.europarl.europa.eu/doceo/document/TA-8-2018-11-13_EN.html

591 https://undocs.org/E/C.12/GC/24

592 http://legislative.gov.in/sites/default/files/The%20Right%20of%20Children%20to%20Free%20and%20Compulsory%20Education%20Act%2C%202009.pdf

593 https://indiankanoon.org/doc/154958944/

594 https://www.campebd.org/Details.php?DetId=23

595 https://www.un.org/ga/search/viewm_doc.asp?symbol=A/HRC/16/53

596 https://indiankanoon.org/doc/1439334/

597 https://static1.squarespace.com/static/5c2d081daf2096648cc801da/t/5c933a1be79c70cf6cc27edd/1553152561554/Abidjan-Principles-EN.pdf

598 https://undocs.org/en/A/HRC/41/37

599 https://sustainabledevelopment.un.org/post2015/transformingourworld

600 https://hudoc.echr.coe.int/tur#{%22itemid%22:[%22001-57804%22]}

601 https://hudoc.echr.coe.int/fre#{%22itemid%22:[%22001-140235%22]}

602 https://www.echr.coe.int/Pages/home.aspx?p=court/judges#newComponent_1346152138668_pointer

603 http://ap.ohchr.org/documents/dpage_e.aspx?si=A/HRC/32/37

604 http://undocs.org/en/A/RES/70/1

605 V. http://www.unesco.org/new/fileadmin/MULTIMEDIA/FIELD/Beirut/video/TF.pdf

606 https://unesdoc.unesco.org/ark:/48223/pf0000223025

607 https://unesdoc.unesco.org/ark:/48223/pf0000243325

608 https://unesdoc.unesco.org/ark:/48223/pf0000245656

609 The *Global Education Monitoring Report – 2017/8* informs: "Public education expenditure was 4.7% of GDP and 14.1% of total public expenditure in 2015". (https://unesdoc.unesco.org/ark:/48223/pf0000259338)
The target of 0.7% of GNP for ODA, agreed in 1970, was reached by very few countries.

(https://www.oecd.org/dac/stats/ODA-history-of-the-0-7-target.pdf)
According to the Organisation for Economic Cooperation and Development (OECD): "The following countries met or exceeded the United Nations' ODA as a percentage of GNI [Gross National Income] target of 0.7%: Denmark (0.72%), Luxembourg (1.00%), Norway (0.99%), Sweden (1.01%) and the United Kingdom (0.70%)".
(https://www.oecd.org/development/financing-sustainable-development/development-finance-data/ODA-2017-detailed-summary.pdf)

610 http://uis.unesco.org/sites/default/files/documents/quick-guide-education-indicators-sdg4-2018-en.pdf

611 See: "Accountability from a human rights perspective: The incorporation and enforcement of the right to education in the domestic legal order".
(https://www.right-to-education.org/sites/right-to-education.org/files/resource-attachments/RTE_Accountability_from_a_human_rights_perspective_2017_en.pdf)

612 www.ushistory.org/documents/economic_bill_of_rights.htm

613 http://portal.unesco.org/en/ev.php-URL_ID=12949&URL_DO=DO_TOPIC&URL_SECTION=201.html

614 http://portal.unesco.org/en/ev.php-URL_ID=13084&URL_DO=DO_TOPIC&URL_SECTION=201.html

615 http://ap.ohchr.org/documents/alldocs.aspx?doc_id=1480

616 http://ap.ohchr.org/documents/alldocs.aspx?doc_id=1920

617 http://portal.unesco.org/en/ev.php-URL_ID=16438&URL_DO=DO_TOPIC&URL_SECTION=201.html

618 Final Report: www.ibe.unesco.org/International/ICE47/English/FinalRep/Finalrep_main.htm)

619 https://unesdoc.unesco.org/ark:/48223/pf0000227860

620 https://undocs.org/CRC/GC/2001/1

621 https://au.int/en/treaties/african-youth-charter

622 https://www.ecml.at/Portals/1/documents/CoE-documents/CMRec2012-13_quality_EN.pdf?ver=2016-11-29-113145-700

623 https://tbinternet.ohchr.org/_layouts/treatybodyexternal/Download.aspx?symbolno=E%2FC.12%2F1999%2F10

624 https://www.ohchr.org/en/professionalinterest/pages/vienna.aspx

625 http://www.unesco.org/education/pdf/SALAMA_E.PDF

626 https://www.un.org/development/desa/disabilities/convention-on-the-rights-of-persons-with-disabilities.html

627 https://tbinternet.ohchr.org/_layouts/treatybodyexternal/Download.aspx?symbolno=CRPD/C/GC/4&Lang=en

628 https://unesdoc.unesco.org/ark:/48223/pf0000248254

629 See also: *Inclusive dimensions of the right to education: normative bases – Concept Paper*. UNESCO, 2008.
(https://unesdoc.unesco.org/ark:/48223/pf0000177649)
Another pertinent reference is: https://www.who.int/classifications/icf/icfbeginnersguide.pdf

630 www.corteconstitucional.gov.co/RELATORIA/2011/T-306-11.htm

631 See also: *Applying Right to Education Indicators to the Post-2015 Education Agenda* (www.right-to-education.org/sites/right-to-education.org/files/resource-attachments/RTE_Applying_RTE_Indicators_to_the_Post_2015_Agenda_2015.pdf)
www.histoiredudroit.fr/Documents/Corpus/Digeste%20(Livre%201).pdf

632 http://legal.legis.com.co/document.legis/sentencia-2000-01823-de-octubre-24-de-2013?documento=jurcol&contexto=jurcol_eb7ba534c1cd0078e0430a0101510078&vista=STD-PC#bf1e803c1ad2f504b81ac7a8400382118f7nf9

633 https://mexico.justia.com/federales/leyes/ley-general-de-educacion/
634 http://www.lexis.com.ec/wp-content/uploads/2018/07/LI-LEY-ORGANICA-DE-EDUCACION-INTERCULTURAL.pdf
635 https://unesdoc.unesco.org/ark:/48223/pf0000245656
636 https://unesdoc.unesco.org/ark:/48223/pf0000133484
637 http://www.ibe.unesco.org/sites/default/files/resources/howard-jonestheplasticbrain_0.pdf
638 https://www.cedefop.europa.eu/en/publications-and-resources/publications/4117
639 https://uil.unesco.org/unesco-institute/mandate
640 https://uil.unesco.org/fileadmin/keydocuments/LifelongLearning/en/UNESCOTechNotesLLL.pdf
641 https://uil.unesco.org/lifelong-learning/recognition-validation-accreditation/unesco-guidelines-recognition-validation-and
642 www.edcities.org/wp-content/uploads/2013/10/CARTA-CIUDADES-EDUCADORAS_3idiomas.pdf
643 https://unesdoc.unesco.org/ark:/48223/pf0000226755
644 https://uil.unesco.org/lifelong-learning/learning-cities/key-features-learning-cities
645 https://www.ohchr.org/EN/Issues/Indicators/Pages/documents.aspx
646 https://supreme.justia.com/cases/federal/us/339/629/
647 www.right-to-education.org/resource/measuring-education-human-right-list-indicators
648 http://www.e-lawresources.co.uk/R-v-Hopley.php
649 https://endcorporalpunishment.org
650 https://undocs.org/CRC/C/GC/13
651 http://tbinternet.ohchr.org/_layouts/treatybodyexternal/Download.aspx?symbolno=CRC%2FGC%2F2001%2F1&Lang=en
652 https://violenceagainstchildren.un.org/content/marta-santos-pais
653 https://tbinternet.ohchr.org/_layouts/treatybodyexternal/Download.aspx?symbolno=INT%2fCCPR%2fGEC%2f6621&Lang=en
654 https://tbinternet.ohchr.org/_layouts/treatybodyexternal/Download.aspx?symbolno=E%2fC.12%2f1999%2f10&Lang=en
655 https://undocs.org/CRC/C/GC/8
656 https://www.ohchr.org/en/professionalinterest/pages/crc.aspx
657 https://www.coe.int/en/web/european-social-charter
658 https://hudoc.echr.coe.int/eng#{%22itemid%22:[%22001-57509%22]}
659 https://tbinternet.ohchr.org/_layouts/15/treatybodyexternal/Download.aspx?symbolno=CRC%2fGC%2f2003%2f4&Lang=en
660 http://assembly.coe.int/nw/xml/XRef/Xref-XML2HTML-en.asp?fileid=25353
661 There are more than 40 countries with State religion, the majority being Muslim States in Middle East and North Africa, and about so many favour a religion. More than 50% of the countries of the world has no official or preferred religion, and 5% are hostile to religion. (See: https://dash.harvard.edu/bitstream/handle/1/3710663/Barro_WhichCountries.pdf?sequence=2&isAllowed=y)
662 The Parliamentary Assembly advocates the principle of the separation of State and religion as one of the pillars of a democratic society, for instance, in its Recommendation 1804 (2007) on "State, religion, secularity and human rights". (https://pace.coe.int/pdf/7978a7c3b8d1324c04e9d73314c3928f8f00fcb63326667a8259ffe25682ae848428feba12/recommendation%201804.pdf) https://hudoc.echr.coe.int/eng#{%22itemid%22:[%22001-57509%22]}
663 https://undocs.org/E/C.12/1999/10
664 See: Toledo Guiding Principles on Teaching about Religions and Beliefs in Public Schools (https://www.osce.org/files/f/documents/c/e/29154.pdf)

665 https://assembly.coe.int/nw/xml/XRef/Xref-XML2HTML-en.asp?fileid=17373&lang=en
666 http://www.saflii.org/za/cases/ZACC/2007/21.html
667 https://undocs.org/en/CCPR/C/FRA/CO/4
668 https://www.un.org/ga/search/viewm_doc.asp?symbol=A/HRC/16/53
669 https://hudoc.echr.coe.int/eng#{%22itemid%22:[%22001-86015%22]}
670 https://www.ohchr.org/en/professionalinterest/pages/crc.aspx
671 https://undocs.org/CRC/GC/2001/1
672 http://tbinternet.ohchr.org/_layouts/treatybodyexternal/Download.aspx?symbolno=CRC/C/KOR/CO/3-4&Lang=En
673 www.alfiekohn.org/homework-improve-learning/
674 www.corteconstitucional.gov.co/relatoria/1998/su641-98.htm
675 http://www.corteconstitucional.gov.co/relatoria/2004/T-853-04.htm
676 www.corteconstitucional.gov.co/relatoria/1993/T-065-93.htm
677 See: Hugon, Ph. (2003). *L'Économie Éthique Publique: Biens Publics Mondiaux et Patrimoines Communs*. UNESCO. (https://unesdoc.unesco.org/ark:/48223/pf0000130599/PDF/130599fre.pdf.multi)
678 https://undocs.org/A/C.3/SR.90
679 http://www.ibe.unesco.org/sites/default/files/Finrep_eng.pdf
680 https://unesdoc.unesco.org/ark:/48223/pf0000145333
681 http://www.unesco.org/new/en/brasilia/about-this-office/single-view/news/education_2030_incheon_declaration_and_and_framework_for_ac/
682 http://ap.ohchr.org/documents/dpage_e.aspx?si=A/HRC/32/37
683 http://ap.ohchr.org/documents/alldocs.aspx?doc_id=26740
684 https://www.itu-ilibrary.org/science-and-technology/the-state-of-broadband-2018_pub/810d0472-91fe803b-en
685 http://ap.ohchr.org/documents/alldocs.aspx?doc_id=2360
686 http://ap.ohchr.org/documents/dpage_e.aspx?si=A/HRC/32/37
687 In 2019, was adopted the Beijing Consensus on Artificial Intelligence (AI) and Education. (https://en.unesco.org/news/first-ever-consensus-artificial-intelligence-and-education-published-unesco)

References

Abel, J. F. (1930). National Ministries of Education – A brief history of the development of national Ministries of Education in the Eastern and Western hemispheres. *Bulletin, 12*. Washington, Department of the Interior, Office of Education.

Al-Samman, S. (1987). *The right to education as a human right in international law* (Thesis submitted for the Degree of Doctor of Philosophy). University of Manchester, Faculty of Law.

Aldrich, R. (1995). John Locke (1632–1704). In UNESCO (Ed.), *Penseurs de l'*éducation – Volume 3 (pp. 65–82). UNESCO/BIE.

American Council on Public Affairs. (1943). *Education and the United Nations: A report of a Joint Commission of the Council for Education in World Citizenship and the London*

International Assembly. Washington. https://nla.gov.au/nla.obj-52879052/view?partId=nla.obj-107700497#page/n4/mode/1up

Angenot, M. (2012). *Le rationnel et le raisonnable: Sur un distinguo de Chaïm Perelman* (Discours Social, Vol. 42). Université McGill.

Ariès, Ph. (1960). *L'enfant et la vie familiale sous l'Ancien Régime* (Trad. em Relógio d'Água). Seuil.

Aristotle. (1925). *The Nicomachean ethics* (Translated with an Introduction by D. Ross, Revised by J. L. Ackrill & J. O. Urmson). Oxford University Press (1998).

Aristotle. (1998). *The metaphysics* (Translated with an introduction by H. Lawson-Tancred). Penguin Books.

Aristotle. (2000). *Politics* (Translated by B. Jowett, with Introduction, Analysis and Index by H. W. C. Davis). Dover Publications, Incl.

Avanzini, G. (2003). Scientificité, axiologie et argumentation chez les théoriciens de l'Éducation Nouvelle. *Revue Française de Pédagogie* (INRP), *143*, avril–mai–juin, 53–59.

Bachelard, G. (1960). *La poétique de la rêverie*. PUF.

Baczko, B. (Prés.). (2000). *Une éducation pour la démocratie – Textes et projets de l'époque révolutionnaire*. Droz.

Badinter, E. (1980). *L'amour en plus – Histoire de l'amour maternel (XVIIIe-XXe siècle)*. Flammarion.

Badinter, R. (1990). Rapport final. In *Universalité des droits de l'homme dans un monde pluraliste – Actes du Colloque organisé par le Conseil de l'Europe en collaboration avec l'Institut international des droits de l'homme, Strasbourg, 17–19 avril 1989* (pp. 181–188). Conseil de l'Europe/Éditions N. P. Engel.

Bashford, A. (2013). Julian Huxley's transhumanism. In M. Turda (Ed.), *Crafting humans: From genesis to eugenics and beyond* (pp. 153–167). V&R Unipress. https://www.academia.edu/6086492/Julian_Huxleys_Transhumanism

Bannwart-Maurer, E. (1975). *Das Recht auf Bildung und das Elternrecht – Art.2 des ersten Zusatzprotokolls zur Europäischen Menschenrechtskonvention*. Herbert Lang & Peter Lang.

Beiter, K. D. (2006). *The protection of rhe Right to education by international law – Including a systematic analysis of Article 13 of the International Covenant on Economic, Social and Cultural Rights* (International Studies in Human Rights, Vol. 82). Martinus Nijhoff Publishers. https://www.researchgate.net/publication/305428961_The_protection_of_the_right_to_education_by_international_law_Including_a_systematic_analysis_of_article_13_of_the_international_covenant_on_economic_social_and_cultural_rights

Bekri, Ch. (1991). *L'UNESCO – Une "entreprise erronée"?* Éditions Publisud.

Bidault, M. (2009). *La protection internationale des droits culturels* (Collection du Centre des Droits de l'Homme de l'Université Catholique de Louvain, Vol. 10). Bruylant. https://www.academia.edu/36199058/La_protection_internationale_des_droits_culturels?auto=download

Bonneau, D. (1975). Le droit de l'enfant à l'éducation dans le monde grec, du IIIe siècle avant notre ère au IIIe siècle de notre ère. In AAVV, *Recueil de la Société Jean Bodin pour l'histoire comparative des institutions, XXXIX – L'enfant – Cinquième partie: Le droit à l'éducation* (pp. 101–115). Bruxelles.

Bossuyt, M. (1975). La distinction juridique entre les droits civils et politiques et les droits économiques, sociaux et culturels. *Revue des droits de l'homme/Human rigths journal – Droit international et Droit comparé/International and Comparative Law, VIII*(4), 783–820.

Broadband Commission for Sustainable Development. (2018). *The state of broadband: Broadband catalyzing sustainable development.* ITU (International Telecommunications Union)/UNESCO. https://www.itu.int/dms_pub/itu-s/opb/pol/S-POL-BROADBAND.19-2018-PDF-E.pdf

Bueren, G. (1995). *The international law on the Rights of the Child* (International Studies in Human Rights, Vol. 35). Martinus Nijhoff Publishers.

Buisson, F. (Sous la direction de). (1887a). *Dictionnaire de Pédagogie et d'Instruction Primaire.* https://archive.org/stream/dictionnairedep21buis#page/1468/mode/2up/search/nettet%C3%A9

Capello, H. H. K. de. (1970). The creation of the United Nations Educational, Scientific and Cultural Organization. *International Organization, 24*(1), Winter, 1–30.

Cassin, R. (1953). La Déclaration universelle et les droits culturels de l'homme. *Les Dialogues, 6*, janvier, 1–12.

Château, J. (1980). *Les Grands Pédagogues.* Presses Universitaires de France.

Chatton, G. T. (2013). *Vers la pleine reconnaissance des droits économiques, sociaux et culturels.* Schulthess.

Čížek, J. (2016). *The conception of man in the works of John Amos Comenius.* Peter Lang.

Cohen-Jonathan, G. (1989). *La Convention européenne des droits de l'homme.* Economica/Aix-en-Provence, Presses Universitaires d'Aix-Marseille.

Compayré, J.-G. (1897). *Cours de Pédagogie théorique et pratique.* Librairie Classique Paul Delaplane. http://michel.delord.free.fr/comp-cptp-tdm.html

Compayré, J.-G. (1911). Pédagogie (Histoire de la). In F. Buisson (Dir.), *Nouveau dictionnaire de pédagogie et d'instruction primaire.* www.inrp.fr/edition-electronique/lodel/dictionnaire-ferdinand-buisson/document.php?id=3354

Compernolle, R. (1975). Le droit à l'éducation dans le monde grec aux époques archaïque et classique – Résumé. In *Recueil de la Société Jean Bodin pour l'histoire comparative des institutions, XXXIX – L'enfant – Cinquième partie: Le droit à l'**éducation*** (pp. 95–99). Bruxelles.

Cowell, F. R. (1966). Planning the organization of UNESCO, 1942–1946: A personal record. *Journal of World History, 10*(1), 'International Intellectual Cooperation' (on the occasion of the twentieth anniversary of UNESCO), 210–236. https://unesdoc.unesco.org/ark:/48223/pf0000145580

Crampe-Casnabet, M. (1985). *Condorcet, lecteur des Lumières*. PUF.

Damásio, A. (1994). *O erro de Descartes – Emoção, razão e cérebro humano* [*Descartes' error – Emotion, reason and human brain*] (Trad. de Dora Vicente e Georgina Segurado). Publicações Europa-América.

Damásio, A. (2018). *The strange order of things – Life, feeling, and the making of cultures*. Pantheon Books.

Daudet, Y., & Singh, K. (2001). *The right to education: An analysis of UNESCO's standard-setting instruments*. UNESCO. https://unesdoc.unesco.org/ark:/48223/pf0000123817

Delbrück, J. (1992). *The right to education as an international human right. Articles by Maurer Faculty*. https://www.repository.law.indiana.edu/facpub/2824

Delors, J. et al. (1996). *Learning: The treasure within – Report to UNESCO of the International Commission on Education for the Twenty-first Century*. UNESCO Publishing.

French version: http://unesdoc.unesco.org/images/0011/001159/115930f.pdf

Detrick, Sh. (1999). *A commentary on the United Nations Convention on the Rights of the Child*. Kluwer Law International.

Dobinson, C. H. (Ed.). (1970). *Comenius and contemporary education: An international symposium*. UNESCO Institute for Education, Hamburg. https://unesdoc.unesco.org/ark:/48223/pf0000131996?posInSet=8&queryId=c09fbb1b-e835-4c63-8c4f-7bcd76c090fa

Donnelly, J., & Howard, Rh. E. (1988). Assessing national human rights performance: A theoretical framework. *Human Rights Quarterly*, *10*(2), 214–248.

Dorn, Ck. (2006). 'The world's schoolmaster': Educational reconstruction, Grayson Kefauver, and the founding of UNESCO, 1942–46. *History of Education*, *35*(3), 297–320. https://www.academia.edu/23737061/_The_World_s_Schoolmaster_Educational_Reconstruction_Grayson_Kefauver_and_the_Founding_of_UNESCO_1942_46

Dreyfus, F.-G. (1975). Les politiques de l'enseignement dans les États allemands au XVIIIe siècle. In *Recueil de la Société Jean Bodin pour l'histoire comparative des institutions, XXXIX – L'enfant – Cinquième partie: Le droit à l'**éducation*** (pp. 253–264). Éditions de la Librairie Encyclopédique.

Droit, R.-P. (2005). *Humanity in the making: overview of the intellectual history of UNESCO: 1945–2005*. UNESCO. https://unesdoc.unesco.org/ark:/48223/pf0000142076

Dronamraju, K. R. (1993). *If I am to be remembered – The life and work of Julian Huxley with selected correspondence*. World Scientific Publishing.

Dupuy, P.-M. (2007). The impact of legal instruments adopted by UNESCO on General International Law. In *Standard-setting in UNESCO – Volume I: Normative Action in Education, Science and Culture. Essays in Commemoration of the Sixtieth Anniversary of UNESCO* (pp. 351–363). UNESCO Publishing/Martinus Nijhoff Publishers.

Eggersdorfer, F. X. (1962). Bildung. In Deutschen Institut für Wissenschaftliche Pädagogik, Münster, und dem Institut für Vergleichende Erziehungswissenschaft, Salzburg (Herausgegeven vom), *Lexikon der Pädagogik in vier Bänden – I. Band: ABB-Fertigkeit* (dritte Auflage, pp. 476–484). Herder.

Eisemann, P. M. (2007). Introduction (to Panel 5 – Fostering Access to Education and Knowledge). In *Standard-setting in UNESCO – Volume I: Normative action in education, science and culture. Essays in commemoration of the sixtieth anniversary of UNESCO*. UNESCO Publishing/Martinus Nijhoff Publishers.

Elfert, M. (2016). *UNESCO's utopia of lifelong learning: An intellectual history of UNESCO's humanistic approach to education, 1945–2015* (Thesis). University of British Columbia (Canada). Published (2018) by Routledge, Routledge Research in Lifelong Learning and Adult Education Series. https://open.library.ubc.ca/cIRcle/collections/ubctheses/24/items/1.0228054

Elvin, L. (1972). Education. In AAVV (Ed.), *In the minds of men – UNESCO: 1946 to 1971* (pp. 53–67). UNESCO/PUF. https://unesdoc.unesco.org/search/0576314b-6646-43ba-afc1-a4b19e9431e5

European Court of Human Rights/Cour Européenne des Droits de l'Homme. (2020). *Guide on Article 2 of Protocol N° 1 to the European Convention on Human Rights – Right to Education*. Council of Europe. https://www.echr.coe.int/Documents/Guide_Art_2_Protocol_1_ENG.pdf

Faure, E. et al. (1972). *Apprendre à être*. UNESCO/Fayard. http://unesdoc.unesco.org/images/0013/001329/132982f.pdf (English edition: http://unesdoc.unesco.org/images/0000/000018/001801e.pdf).

Fasi, M. El. (1968). Droit à l'éducation et à la culture. *Revue de la Commission Internationale de Juristes*, *IX*(1), juin, 38–46.

Finnish National Board of Education. (2016). *National Core Curriculum for Basic Education 2014* (transl. by Lingsoft Oy). Next Print Oy.

Freire, P. (1975). *Educação política e conscientização*. Sá da Costa.

Garin, E. (1957). *Éducation de l'homme moderne – La pédagogie de la Renaissance (1400–1600)* (Trad. de l'italien par Jacqueline Humbert). Fayard.

Gebert, P. (1996). *Das Recht auf Bildung nach Art. 13 des UNO-Paktes über wirtschaftliche, soziale und kulturelle Rechte – und seine Auswirkungen auf das schweizerische Bildungswesen – Dissertation – zur Eerlangung der Würde eines Doktors beider Rechte vorgelegt der Rechtswissenschaftlichen Fakultät der Universität Freiburg in der Schweiz* [The right to education according to the UN International Covenant on the Economic, Social and Cultural Rights – and its outcomes in the Switzerland's system of education] (Univ. Diss.). Freiburg (Schweiz)

Ginneken, A. H. M. van. (2006). *Historical dictionary of the league of nations* (Historical Dictionaries of International Organizations, Vol. 23). The Scarecrow Press, Inc.

Grandjean, M. (2108). *Les réseaux de la coopération intellectuelle. La Société des Nations comme actrice des échanges scientifiques et culturels dans l'entre-deux-guerres* (Thesis). University of Lausanne. https://halshs.archives-ouvertes.fr/tel-01853903

Griffin, J. (2008). *On human rights*. Oxford University Press.

Gynther, P. (2007). *Beyond systemic discrimination: Educational rights, skills acquisition and the case of Roma*. Brill.

Hábl, J. (2017). *On being human(e) – Comenius' pedagogical humanization as an anthropological problem*. Pickwick Publications.

Hausler, K., Urban, N., & McCorquodale, R. (2012). *Protecting education in insecurity and armed conflict – An international law handbook*. British Institute of International and Comparative Law/Education Above All.

Hofstetter, R., & Schneuwly, B. (2013). The International Bureau of Education (1925–1968): A platform for designing a 'chart of world aspirations for education'. *European Educational Research Journal, 12*(2), 215–230. https://pdfs.semanticscholar.org/c943/9453707f7c6168e083b0eeae978a478cc005.pdf?_ga=2.147394423.1325542556.1588445171-1425538599.1588445171

Huxley, J. (1944). *On living in a revolution*. Chatto & Windus. https://ia801605.us.archive.org/24/items/in.ernet.dli.2015.208592/2015.208592.On-Living_text.pdf

Huxley, J. (1946). *UNESCO – Its purpose and its philosophy*. Preparatory Commission of the United Nations Educational, Scientific and Cultural Organisation. https://unesdoc.unesco.org/ark:/48223/pf0000068197

International Commission on Financing Global Education Opportunity. (2016). *The learning generation – Investing in education for a changing world*. https://report.educationcommission.org/downloads/

Jacob, F. (1981). *Le Jeu des possibles*. Fayard.

Jenkner, S. (Hrsg.). (1994). *Das Recht auf Bildung und die Freiheit der Erziehung in Europäischen Verfassungen* [*The right to education and the freedom of education in European constitutions*]. Info3 – Verlag.

Kant, I. (1803). *Traité de pédagogie* (Tr. de J. Barni, revue et actualisée, Introduction et notes par Pierre-José About). Hachette (1981). Original text: https://de.wikisource.org/wiki/%C3%9Cber_P%C3%A4dagogik
An English translation: https://oll.libertyfund.org/titles/kant-kant-on-education-uber-padagogik

Kershaw, I. (2015). *À beira do abismo: A Europa – 1914–1949* [*To hell and back: Europe – 1914–1949*]. Publicações Dom Quixote.

Kiss, A.-Ch. (1975). La protection du droit à l'éducation dans le cadre de la protection internationale des droits de l'homme depuis 1948. In *Recueil de la Société Jean Bodin pour l'histoire comparative des institutions, XXXIX – L'enfant – Cinquième partie: Le droit à l'éducation* (pp. 417–439). Éditions de la Librairie Encyclopédique.

Kuhn, Th. S. (1962). *La structure des révolutions scientifiques* [*The structure of scientific revolutions*] (Trad. par Laure Meyer). Flammarion. (Original text: https://projektintegracija.pravo.hr/_download/repository/Kuhn_Structure_of_Scientific_Revolutions.pdf)

Latapí, P. (1992). El pensamiento educativo de Torres Bodet: una apreciación crítica. *Revista Latinoamericana de Estudios Educativos (México), XXII*(3), 13–44. https://www.cee.edu.mx/rlee/revista/r1991_2000/r_texto/t_1992_3_02.pdf

Lecercle, J.-L. (1958). Émile dans l'histoire. In J.-J. Rousseau (Ed), Émile ou de l'éducation – Introduction par Henri Wallon, Études et notes par J.-L. Lecercle (pp. 62–79). Éditions Sociales.

Locke, J. (1693). *Some thoughts concerning education.* https://ia801406.us.archive.org/16/items/somethoughtsconcoolockuoft/somethoughtsconcoolockuoft.pdf

Maheu, R. (1972). Serving the mind as a force in history. In AAVV (Ed.), *In the minds of men – UNESCO: 1946 to 1971* (pp. 281–319). UNESCO/PUF. https://unesdoc.unesco.org/ark:/48223/pf0000002246?posInSet=6&queryId=74f92898-bf9a-4126-86ef-62971b78dd86

Marrou, H.-I. (1948). *Histoire de l'éducation dans l'antiquité. Éditions du Seuil.*

Maurel, Ch. (2006). *L'UNESCO de 1945 à 1974. Histoire.* Université Panthéon-Sorbonne, Paris I. https://tel.archives-ouvertes.fr/tel-00848712/document

Maurel, Ch. (2010). Le rêve d'un 'gouvernement mondial' des années 1920 aux années 1950. L'exemple de l'UNESCO. *Histoire@Politique. Politique, culture, société, 10*, janvier–avril. https://www.cairn.info/revue-histoire-politique-2010-1-page-9.htm

Mechlem, K. (2009). Treaty bodies and the interpretation of human rights. *Vanderbilt Journal of Transnational Law, 42*, 905–947. Retrieved October 2018, from https://www.vanderbilt.edu/wp-content/uploads/sites/78/mechlem-cr_final_final.pdf

Mehendale, A., & Mukhopadhyay, R. (Eds.). (2018). *The right to education – Movements and policies: Promises and realities.* NORRAG – Network for International Policies and Co-operation in Education and Training, Special Issue 01. https://resources.norrag.org/resource/124/the-right-to-education-movements-and-policies-promises-and-realities

Merle, M. (Textes choisis et présentés par). (1966). *Pacifisme et internationalisme: XVIIe-XXe siècles.* Armand Colin.

Miller, A. (1980). *C'est pour ton bien – Racines de la violence dans l'**éducation de** l'enfant* [*Am Anfang war Erziehung*] (Trad. de Jeanne Etoré). Éditions Aubier Montaigne.

Miller, D. H. (1928). *The drafting of the covenant, Volumes 1 and 2.* G. P. Putnam's Sons. https://books.google.pt/books?id=YRiPAAAAMAAJ&hl=pt-PT&source=gbs_book_other_versions and https://books.google.pt/books/about/The_Drafting_of_the_Covenant.html?id=YxyPAAAAMAAJ&redir_esc=y

Monchablon, A. (Coord.). (1989). *L'esprit de 1789 et des droits de l'homme – Textes et documents (1725–1986) – Préface de Claude Nicolet.* Coédition CNDP/Larousse.

Monteiro, A. R. (2014b). *O Segredo da Finlândia: Direito à Educação* [*Finland's secret: Right to education*]. https://www.academia.edu/35854488/O_Segredo_da_Finl%C3%A2ndia_Direito_%C3%A0_Educa%C3%A7%C3%A3o_docx

Morange, J. (1985). *Libertés publiques*. Presses Universitaires de France.

Morsink, J. (1999). *The Universal Declaration of Human Rights: Origins, drafting, and intent*. University of Pennsylvania Press.

Moschella, M. (2016). *To whom do children belong? – Parental rights, civic education and children's autonomy*. Cambridge University Press.

Mulliez, J. (1989). 'Pater ist...' – La source juridique de la puissance paternelle du droit révolutionnaire au Code civil. In I. Théry & Ch. Biet (Textes réunis et présentés pas), *La famille, la loi, l'*État – de la Révolution au Code civil (pp. 412–431). Éditions du Centre Georges Pompidou/Imprimerie Nationale-Éditions.

Münster, A. (1997). *Le principe dialogique – De la réflexion monologique vers la pro-flexion intersubjective (Essais sur M. Buber, E. Lévinas, F. Rosenzweig, G. Scholem et E. Bloch)*. Éditions Kimé.

Nartowski, A. (1975). The UNESCO system of protection of the Right to Education (as an example of the most rational model of the protection of human rights by an international organisation). In *Annuaire Polonais de Droit International,* VI, 1974, éd. par Académie Polonaise des Sciences/Institut des Sciences Juridiques, 289–309. Maison d'Édition de l'Académie Polonaise des Sciences.

Néraudau, J.-P. (1984). *Être enfant à Rome*. Éditions Payot & Rivages.

Neveux, J. (1975). École et société en Saxe au XVIe et au XVIIe siècle (1550–1700). In *Recueil de la Société Jean Bodin pour l'histoire comparative des institutions, XXXIX – L'enfant – Cinquième partie: Le droit à l'éducation* (pp. 237–252). Editions de la Librairie Encyclopédique.

Nowak, M. (1995). The right to education. In A. Eide, C. Krause, & A. Rosas (Eds.), *Economic, social and cultural rights – A textbook* (pp. 189–211). Martinus Nijhoff Publishers.

Nowak, M. (2001). The right to education. In A. Eide, C. Krause, & A. Rosas (Eds.), *Economic, social and cultural rights – A textbook* (pp. 245–271). Kluwer Law International.

Nowak, M. (2003). *Introduction to international human rights regime*. Martinus Nijhoff Publishers.

Nuria, S., & Tejada, C. (2016). *México y la UNESCO, la UNESCO y México: historia de una relación*. UNESCO Publishing, UNESCO Office Mexico. https://unesdoc.unesco.org/ark:/48223/pf0000234777?posInSet=2&queryId=0037a7ed-759d-4771-afb3-c48598abbebe

OECD. (1989). *Les écoles et la qualité – Un rapport international.*

OECD. (2012). *Equity and quality in education: Supporting disadvantaged students and schools*. OECD. https://www.oecd.org/education/school/50293148.pdf

Olmeda, G. J. (1989). El derecho a la educación en los textos internacionales de derechos humanos. *Revista española de pedagogía, XLVI*(180), 281–303.

Opocensky, J. (1950). *The beginnings of UNESCO: 1942–1948*. UNESCO.

https://unesdoc.unesco.org/ark:/48223/pf0000085521?posInSet=2&queryId=72fe6647-0264-4241-a610-c3fdee1c4d64

Paiva, J. (1911). *Apontamentos para o Manual pacifista das escolas primárias* [*Notes for the Pacifist manual of primary schools*]. Parceria António Maria Pereira.

Partsch, K. J. (1966). *Die Rechte und Freiheiten der Europäischen Menschenrechtskonvention.* Dunker-Humblot.

Partsch, K. J. (1991). La mise en œuvre des droits de l'homme par l'UNESCO – Remarques sur un système particulier. In *Annuaire Français de Droit International* (pp. 482–506). Éditions du Centre National de la Recherche Scientifique, XXXVI.

Perelman, Ch. (1979). The rational and the reasonable. *Philosophic Exchange, 10*(1), Article 5, 29–34. http://digitalcommons.brockport.edu/phil_ex/vol10/iss1/5

Perelman, Ch. (1982). *The realm of rhetoric* [*L'Empire Rhétorique: Réthorique at Argumentation*, 1977] (Transl. by W. Kluback). University of Notre Dame Press.

Perelman, Ch. (1989). Argumentation. In *Encyclopaedia Universalis – Corpus, 2* (pp. 937–938).

Pernet, C. A. (2014). Twists, turns and dead alleys: The league of nations and intellectual cooperation in times of war. *Journal of Modern European History, 12*(3), 342–358. https://www.academia.edu/8426989/Twists_Turns_and_Dead_Alleys_The_League_of_Nations_and_Intellectual_Cooperation_in_Times_of_War

Perschel, W. (1984). Recht auf Bildung. In D. Lenzen (Herausgegeben von), *Enzyklopaedie Erziehungswissenschaft – Handbuch und Lexikon der Erziehung in 11 Bänden und einem Registerband. Band 5: Organisation, Recht und Oekonomie des Bildungswesens* (Herausgegeben von Martin Baethge, Knut Nevermann) (pp. 549–553). Klettt-Cotta.

Petitjean, P. (2006). Needham and UNESCO: Perspectives and realizations. In AAVV (Ed.), *Sixty years of science at UNESCO: 1945–2005* (pp. 43–47). UNESCO Publishing. https://vdocuments.site/download/sixty-years-of-science-at-unesco

Piaget, J. (1949). *Le droit à l'éducation dans le monde actuel – N°1 Collection 'Droits de l'Homme'* (Publiée par l'Organisation des Nations Unies pour l'Éducation, la Science et la Culture) (UNESCO). Sciences et Lettres/Librairie du Recueil Sirey. http://unesdoc.unesco.org/images/0013/001392/139216fo.pdf (English and Spanish translations: unesdoc.unesco.org/images/0000/000061/006133Eo.pdf)

Piaget, J. (1957). L'actualité de Jan Amos Comenius. In J. Prévot (Ed.), *L'utopie éducative – Coménius* (pp. 265–283). UNESCO.

Plato. (1997). *Plato – Complete works* (J. M. Cooper & D. S. Hutchinson, Ed.). Hackeht Publishing Company.

Powell, F. M. (2015). Prohibition of indoctrination in education – A look at the case law of the European Court of Human Rights. *Brigham Young University Education and Law Journal, 2015*(2), Article 11, 597–629. Retrieved July 2019, from http://digitalcommons.law.byu.edu/cgi/viewcontent.cgi?article=1376&context=elj

Power, C. (2015). *The power of education – Education for all, development, globalisation and UNESCO.* Springer. doi:10.1007/978-981-287-221-0

Prévot, J. (1981). *L'utopie éducative – Coménius.* Belin.

Przetacznik, F. (1985). *Cultural rights*. A. W. Sijthoff.

Przetacznik, F. (1985). The philosophical concept of the right to education as a basic human right. *Revue de Droit International de Sciences Diplomatiques et Politiques (The International Law Review)*, *LXIII*, 257–288.

Puig, C. M. V. (1979). Regulación internacional del derecho à la educación. In *Estudios de derecho internacional – Homenaje al Profesor Miaja de la Muela, I+II* (pp. 553–580). Editorial Tecnos.

Renaut, A. (2002). *La libération des enfants – Contribution philosophique à une histoire de l'enfance*. Calmann-Lévy.

Riedmatten, R. P. H. (1973). La Convention et le droit au respect de la vie familiale spécialement en ce qui concerne l'unité de la famille et la protection des droits des parents et tuteurs familiaux dans l'éducation des enfants. In AAVV, *Vie privée et droits de l'homme – Actes du Troisième Colloque International sur la Convention Européenne des Droits de l'Homme* (*Bruxelles, 30 septembre – 3 octobre 1970*) (pp. 323–336). Établissements Émile Bruylant.

Ringelheim, J. (2016). La discrimination dans l'accès à l'éducation: les leçons de la jurisprudence de la Cour Européenne des Droits de l'Homme. *Revue Trimestrielle des Droits de l'Homme*, *105*, 77–96. Retrieved July 2019, from https://www.academia.edu/22169305/J._Ringelheim_La_discrimination_dans_lacc%C3%A8s_%C3%A0_l%C3%A9ducation_les_le%C3%A7ons_de_la_jurisprudence_de_la_Cour_europ%C3%A9enne_des_droits_de_lhomme_Rev._trim._dr._h._N_105_janvier_2016

Rivero, J. (1980). Les droits de l'homme: Droits individuels or droits collectifs ? – Rapport général introductif. In *Les droits de l'homme: Droits individuels ou droits collectifs ?* (pp. 17, 25). Librairie Générale de Droit et de Jurisprudence, Actes du Colloque de Strasbourg des 13 et 14 mars 1979.

Rivero, J. (1981). *Les libertés publiques – 1/Les droits de l'homme*. Presses Universitaires de France, Col. Thémis-Droit.

Rosselló, P. (1979). Aperçu Historique. In *Conférence Internationale de l'Éducation: Recommandations, 1934–1977* (pp. xi–xxi). UNESCO. http://www.ibe.unesco.org/fileadmin/user_upload/Publications/Institutional_Docs/Rossello_historical_note_en.pdf

Rousseau, J.-J. (1762a). *Émile ou de l'éducation* (Chronologie et introduction par Michel Launay). Garnier-Flammarion (1966). http://gallica.bnf.fr/ark:/12148/bpt6k5786957n/f12.image (An English translation: https://oll.libertyfund.org/titles/rousseau-emile-or-education).

Rousseau, J.-J. (1913). *The social contract and discourses* (Translated and introduced by G.D.H. Cole). Everyman. (An English translation: https://oll.libertyfund.org/titles/rousseau-the-social-contract-and-discourses).

Rousseau, J.-J. (1993). Émile (Translated by B. Foxley, Introduction by P. D. Jimack). Everyman.

Rubellin-Devichi, J. (1994). The best interests principle in French law and practice. In P. Alston (Ed.), *The best interests of the child – Reconciling culture and human rights* (pp. 259–290). Clarendon Press, UNICEF-International Child Development Center, Florence.

Saikawa, T. (2014). *From intellectual cooperation to international cultural exchange: Japan and China in the International Committee on Intellectual Cooperation of the League of Nations, 1922–1939* (Doctoral thesis). University of Heidelberg, Faculty of Philosophy. Retrieved May 2020, from https://archiv.ub.uni-heidelberg.de/volltextserver/20294/

Saladin, J.-Ch. (2021). On ne naît pas homme, on le devient. *Les grands dossiers des Sciences Humaines – La grande histoire de l'humanisme: naissance, apogée, désillusions et renouveau, 61*, 18–19.

Sargent, P. (1945). *Between two wars – The failure of education: 1920–1940*. Porter Sargent Publishers. https://babel.hathitrust.org/cgi/pt?id=mdp.39015039754877&view=1up&seq=582

Saul, B. (Ed.). (2016). *The International Covenant on Economic, Social and Cultural Rights: Travaux Préparatoires, 1948–1966* (Vol. 1). Oxford University Press.

Seeckaert, G. P. (1970). A glance at sixty years of activity (1910–1970) of the Union of International Associations. In *Union of international associations – 1910–1970 – Past, present, future* (pp. 19–52). Extracted from the *International Review "Syntheses", 288*, June 1970, Brussels – Paris. https://www.laetusinpraesens.org/uia/docs/anniv60/60_eng_all.pdf

Sicard, G. (1975). La Révolution française et l'éducation. In *Recueil de la Société Jean Bodin pour l'histoire comparative des institutions, XXXIX – L'enfant – Cinquième partie: Le droit à l'éducation* (pp. 265–295). Société Jean Bodin.

Smeyers, P. (Ed.). (2018). *International handbook of philosophy of education*. Springer International Handbooks of Education.

Smith, L. (1993). Children, parents and the European Human Rights Convention. In J. Eekelaar & P. Sarcevic (Eds.), *Parenthood in modern society – Legal and social issues for the twenty-first century* (pp. 447–462). Martinus Nijhoff Publishers, The International Society of Family Law.

Soëtard, M. (1995). Jean-Jacques Rousseau. In UNESCO, *Penseurs de l'éducation – Volume 4* (pp. 443–456). UNESCO.

Soëtard, M. (1997). La pédagogie entre pensée de la fin et science des moyens. *Revue Française de Pédagogie, 120*, juillet–août–septembre, 99–104.

Steiner, H. J., & Alston, Ph. (2000). *International human rights in context – Law, politics, morals*. Oxford University Press.

Stiglitz, J. (2006). *Making globalization work*. W. W. Norton & Company.

Symonides, J. (2000). Cultural rights. In J. Symonides (Ed.), *Human rights: Concept and standards* (pp. 175–227). UNESCO/Ashgate/Dartmouth.

Szabo, I. (1974). *Cultural rights*. A. W. Sijthoff.

Thomas, J. (1962). *U.N.E.S.C.O.* (Problèmes et Documents). Gallimard.

Todres, J., & Higinbotham, S. (2016). *Human rights in children's literature: imagination and the narrative of law*. Oxford University Press.

Tomaševski, K. (2001b). *Human rights obligations: Making education available, accessible, acceptable and adaptable*. Lund: Raoul Wallenberg Institute, Right to Education Primers No. 3. www.right-to-education.org/sites/right-to-education.org/files/resource-attachments/Tomasevski_Primer%203.pdf

Tomaševski, K. (2005a). Globalizing what: Education as a human rights or as a traded service? *Indiana Journal of Global Legal Studies*, *12*(1), Article 1, 1–78. Retrieved March 2019, from https://www.repository.law.indiana.edu/cgi/viewcontent.cgi?referer=https://www.google.pt/&httpsredir=1&article=1289&context=ijgls

Tomaševski, K. (2005b). Has the right to education a future within the United Nations? A behind-the-scenes account by the Special Rapporteur on the Right to Education 1998–2004. *Human Rights Law Review*, *5*(2), 205–237. Retrieved July 2019, from https://academic.oup.com/hrlr/article/5/2/205/789450

Toye, J., & Toye, R. (2010). One world, two cultures? Alfred Zimmern, Julian Huxley and the ideological origins of UNESCO. *History – The Journal of the Historical Association*, *95*(319), 308–331. https://johntoyedotnet.files.wordpress.com/2012/02/one-worldtwo-cultures2010.pdf

Töws, H.-J. (1970). Rechtsgrundlagen der Schule. In J. Speck & G. Wehle (Herausgegeben von), *Handbuch Pädagogischer Grundbegriffe – Band II*. Kösel-Verlag.

UNESCO. (1947). *Fundamental education: Common ground of all peoples*. Report (EDU/9, EDU/10). https://archive.org/stream/ERIC_ED105181/ERIC_ED105181_djvu.txt

UNESCO. (1948). *Human Rights – Comments and interpretations – A symposium edited by UNESCO, with an Introduction by Jacques Maritain*. UNESCO/PHS3(rev.). Paris, 25 July 1948. https://unesdoc.unesco.org/ark:/48223/pf0000155042

UNESCO. (1979). *Conférence Internationale de l'*Éducation – Recommandations (1934–*1977*). http://www.unesco.org/education/pdf/34_77_F.PDF

UNESCO. (2000). *World Education Report – 2000 – The Right to Education: Towards education for all throughout life*. UNESCO. www.unesco.org/education/information/wer/PDFeng/wholewer.PDF

UNESCO. (2005a). *Guidelines for inclusion – Ensuring access to education for all*. http://unesdoc.unesco.org/images/0014/001402/140224e.pdf

UNESCO. (2005b). *EFA Global Monitoring Report – 2005 – Education for All – The quality imperative*. http://unesdoc.unesco.org/images/0013/001373/137333e.pdf

UNESCO. (2005c). *60 ans d'Histoire de l'UNESCO: Actes du Colloque International, Paris, 16–18 Novembre 2005*. https://unesdoc.unesco.org/ark:/48223/pf0000154122

UNESCO. (2008). *EFA Global Monitoring Report – 2008*. UNESCO Publishing/Oxford University Press. https://fr.unesco.org/gem-report/node/490?q=report/2008/education-all-2015-will-we-make-it

UNESCO. (2014). *EFA Global Monitoring Report 2013/4 – Teaching and learning: Achieving quality for all.* https://fr.unesco.org/gem-report/node/832

UNESCO. (2015a). *EFA Global Monitoring Report 2015 – Education for All 2000–2015: Achievements and challenges.* http://unesdoc.unesco.org/images/0023/002322/232205e.pdf

UNESCO. (2015b). *Rethinking education: Towards a global common good?* https://unesdoc.unesco.org/ark:/48223/pf0000232555

UNESCO. (2017). *Global Education Monitoring Report 2017/8 – Accountability in education – Meeting our commitments.* https://en.unesco.org/gem-report

UNESCO/Right to Education Initiative. (2019). *Right to education handbook.* https://unesdoc.unesco.org/ark:/48223/pf0000366556/PDF/366556eng.pdf.multi

UNICEF. (1998). *Implementation handbook for the Convention on the Rights of the Child* (prepared for UNICEF by Rachel Hodgkin and Peter Newell). (2007: Fully rev. 3rd ed.). https://www.unicef.org/publications/index_43110.html

UNICEF. (1999). *The state of the world's children – 1999 – education.* https://www.unicef.org/publications/index_7358.html

UNICEF/UNESCO. (2007). *A human rights-based approach to education for all – A framework for the realization of children's right to education and rights within education.* https://unesdoc.unesco.org/ark:/48223/pf0000154861/PDF/154861eng.pdf.multi

Valderrama, F. (1995). *Histoire de l'UNESCO.* UNESCO. https://unesdoc.unesco.org/ark:/48223/pf0000189844

Vega, C. (1994). The right to equal education: Merely a guiding principle or customary international legal right? *Harvard Blackletter Journal, 11*, 37–60. Retrieved March 2019, from http://papers.ssrn.com/sol3/papers.cfm?abstract_id=1149880

Verdoodt, A. (1964). *Naissance et signification de la Déclaration universelle des droits de l'homme (Préface de René Cassin).* Éditions Nauwelaerts.

Volio, F. (1979). The child's right to education: A survey. In G. Mialaret (Ed.), *The child's right to education* (pp. 19–33). UNESCO. https://unesdoc.unesco.org/ark:/48223/pf0000032391

Wanner, R. E. (2015). *UNESCO's origins, achievements, problems and promises: An inside/outside perspective from the US.* The University of Hong Kong, Faculty of Education, Comparative Education Research Centre (CERC). http://cerc.edu.hku.hk/wp-content/uploads/M12-Whole-Web.pdf

Wildhaber, L. (1976). Dans quelle mesure le droit à l'instruction a-t-il subit une évolution? – Rapport. In Conseil de l'Europe, *Actes du quatrième colloque international sur la Convention européenne des droits de l'homme*, Organisé par le Ministère des Affaires étrangères de la République italienne/Secrétariat Général du Conseil de l'Europe, à Rome, 5–8 novembre 1975, Strasbourg.

Wildhaber, L. (1993). Right to education and parental rights. In R. St. J. MacDonald, F. Matscher, & H. Petzold (Eds.), *The European system for the protection of human rights* (pp. 531–551). Martinus Nijhoff Publishers.

Wilson, F. (1928). *The origins of the League Covenant – Documentary history of its drafting*. Leonard and Virginia Woolf. https://ia801604.us.archive.org/33/items/in.ernet.dli.2015.167271/2015.167271.The-Origins-Of-The-League-Covenant-Documentary-History-Of-Its-Drafting.pdf

Wolf, J. (1992). The concept of the 'best interest' in terms of the UN Convention on the Rights of the Child. In M. Freeman & P. Veerman (Eds.), *The ideologies of children's rights* (pp. 125–134) (International Studies in Human Rights, Vol. 23). Martinus Nijhoff Publishers,

World Bank. (2005). *Voice for the world's poor – Selected speeches and writings of World Bank President James D. Wolfensohn, 1995–2005*. The International Bank for Reconstruction and Development/The World Bank. https://www.gfdrr.org/sites/default/files/publication/Voices%20for%20the%20World%27s%20Poor.pdf

World Commission on Culture and Development. (1995). *Our creative diversity*. https://unesdoc.unesco.org/ark:/48223/pf0000101651

Yusuf, A. A. (Ed.). (2007a). *Standard-setting in UNESCO – Volume I: Normative action in education, science and culture. Essays in commemoration of the Sixtieth Anniversary of UNESCO*. UNESCO Publishing/Martinus Nijhoff Publishers.

Yusuf, A. A. (Ed.). (2007b). *Standard-setting in UNESCO – Volume II: Conventions, recommendations, declarations and charters adopted by UNESCO (1948–2006)*. UNESCO Publishing/Martinus Nijhoff Publishers.

Zuber, V. (2021). Aux sources des droits humains. *Les grands dossiers des Sciences Humaines – La grande histoire de l'humanisme: naissance, apogée, désillusions et renouveau, 61*, 30–31.

CHAPTER 5

Towards a Rightful Education

Abstract

1. For the traditional educational mindset, the individual 'right' to education is a mere reflex of the family and social right to educate children according to dominant domestic beliefs and interests. This amounts to a right of education (an expression absent from International Human Rights Law).
2. It was against the traditional holistic political-pedagogical paradigm of the right of education that emerged, in the late 19th century, in the American and European continents, the most powerful wave of renewal in the history of education: New Education Movement.
3. The ideal of the New Education Movement is reflected and universalised in the right to education that is indeed a new right to new education, i.e. to a human right or rights-based approach of education conducive to a Rightful Education.
4. Rightful Education, as here understood, is education consistent with the normative integrity of the right to education that may be condensed in Principles of the Ethics of the Right to Education, from which stem Educational Rights.
5. The Ethics of the Right to Education may be summed up in the following principles:
   - *Primacy of the best interests of the subject of the right to education*
   - *Development of the human personality: free, full, harmonious*
   - *Priority of human rights education as an ethical, civic, international education*
6. Educational Rights may be summed up as follows:
   - Right to pedagogical responsibility
   - Right to be different
   - Right to respect for human dignity and rights in education
   - Right to learn the and in the mother tongue
   - Right to the whole object of the right to education
   - Right to a right to education school
   - Right to admirable education professionals
   - Right to an effective remedy
7. Rightful Education needs to be translated into a Right to Education Policy and a Right to Education Pedagogy. Furthermore, education may be improved by the recognition and study of new 'Sciences of Education', such as: International Edu-

 | DOI: 10.1163/9789004462465_006

cation Law, Neuroscience of Education, Semiotics of Education, Aesthetics of Education.

5.1 New Paradigm

In his commentary on the Universal Declaration Article 26, Piaget (1949) pointed out "The gap [*abîme*] that still separates education as it now exists from what is implied by the right to education" (p. 58). Referring to its international dimension, he wrote that, when the education will become the right it ought to be, "peoples themselves will hesitate to allow to be led exactly like schoolchildren – we want to say like the schoolchildren of the 'Old Regime', those who never benefited from the transformations in teaching that are postulated in Article 26" (p. 142).

At the beginning of the 1980s, in a synthesis of the proceedings of the 37th International Conference of Education (1979), requested by the IBE, Daniel Haag (1982) cited a study (*The World Educational Crisis*) published in 1968 by P. H. Coombs, at the time Director of the UNESCO International Institute for Educational Planning, following which: "In the early 1950's, educational systems the world over began a process of expansion without precedent in human history". However: "Twelve years later, we have to note that our hopes have been dashed. Never have education systems been the object of so many reforms; never, however, have they been the target of so much criticism" (pp. 11, 12). He suggested "that there should be an epistemological reversal: think of the whole before thinking of its parts: go from the microscopic to the macroscopic". Otherwise, "the results of an education system will always be piecemeal. They will simply be added on to the old system without their being any effort to rethink it, thus frustrating any attempt to change it in the desired direction" (p. 27). And concluded: "In the final analysis, education is suffering from the lack of coherence between its goals and its management. The pathways to action start from the meaning given to the right to education" (p. 124). Well, he was "surprised to note how vague this concept often is: it can cover accepted meanings which vary greatly from one context to another and can even go so far – we do not hesitate to say – as to be self-contradictory" (p. 9).

Two decades later, the first UN Special Rapporteur on the Right to Education (E/CN.4/1999/49)[1] wrote: "The prevailing linguistic variety reflects different visions of what education should be" (para. 13). That is why she announced in her Preliminary Report, as already quoted: "A simple but crucial question

– what does full realization of the right to education entail? – will thus orientate the work of the Special Rapporteur" (para. 8).

The full realisation of the right to education resounds as a paradigm shift.

Following the classic theorisation of Thomas Kuhn (1962), *paradigm* or *normal science* means "the criteria determining the legitimacy both of problems and of proposed solutions" (p. 109). Scientific revolutions are "those non-cumulative developmental episodes in which an older paradigm is replaced, in whole or in part, by an incompatible new one" (p. 92). The most famous scientific revolution was perhaps the astronomic revolution of the 16th century. To integrate the movements of new celestial bodies in the old heaven of the geocentric paradigm of Ptolemy, circumferences (epicycles) were invented, for centuries, up to saturation. The heliocentric hypothesis has brought about an astronomic revolution that has associated Copernicus's name, for ever, to all theoretical revolutions.

The term 'paradigm' (and 'revolution') has been often used (and abused) in the education field – perhaps due to a voluntaristic impulse motivated by the feeling of the urgency to change – but the Reference Document[2] of the 47th session of the International Conference on Education, in 2004, whose theme was "Quality education for all young people: Challenges, trends and priorities", affirmed:

> Many observers consider that a "new paradigm" is needed for education in the world since it would appear that, continuing along current lines, the problem really lies in the solution. Continuing to do "more of the same", even though there might be improvements, might be self-defeating. (p. 25)

5.1.1 *The Traditional Right of Education*

Traditionally, education is a familial reserved area, strongly supported by religions, as we know. The religious and moral education of children – taken as education strictly speaking – keeps often claimed as an exclusive parents' right, the intellectual education or instruction being considered a subsidiary function of State.

In Western culture, the greatest religious reference of traditional education was the Encyclical *Divini Illius Magistri* of Pope Pius XI (1922–1939), issued in 1929, motivated by Mussolini policy. The Catholic doctrine on education was explained in an Encyclopaedia published in the 1960s and may be summarised as follows:

- The human being shares with other animals the inclination for "the *generation of the offspring*", but it must be achieved "*according to reason*". There is no human life without "the use of the specifically human faculties of the intelligence and the free will and the *ability to the moral life*, which appear much later and not without a long and patient work of education" (Braido, 1962, p. 172, ff.). In fact, "before having the use of reason, the child is not different from the animal".

- Education is a "proper and exclusive *function*" of the progenitors, "total and absolute", their right-duty as a "*continued generation*". A child, in the Scholastic Theology, is "like a thing of parents" (*quaedam res parentum*), continuing, after its birth, "as if it was in a spiritual womb" (*sub quodam spirituali womb*). The "rights of the child" come from a secular inspiration and a false or fool concept of rights and freedoms.
- Therefore, other intervenients in education, "whatever the claims of freedom and autonomy on the part of the class of educators and teachers, should not exceed the precise limits of representation and service in relation to the family", which represents the Church regarding the religious and moral education. Public education is only a subsidiary right of civil society, derived, delegated by the primary right of the family and based in State responsibility for the common good. The right of the State in this area is, on the one hand, a right of supervision, "so that in the exercise of their natural rights-duties the progenitors do not adopt purposes, methods and means contrary to the common good"; on the other, it is a right to require from the individual "everything that, although in relation with education and even so considered, is not education in a strict and formal sense, such instruction, culture, certain psychic and technical qualities, *to the extent* that they are postulated by the *common good*".

This doctrine was updated in 1965 by the Council Vatican II (1962–1965), in its Declaration *Gravissimum Educationis*, and restated by Pope John-Paul II especially in the Apostolic Exhortation *Familiaris Consortio*, in 1981. The Catholic doctrinal framework concerning education is laid down in the Code of Canonical Law promulgated by Pope John-Paul II in 1983, Book III, Title III, Canons 793 to 803 (*De educatione catholica*).

A typical defence of the traditional and still largely shared educational principles (in the USA, for instance) is found in an essay bearing the suggestive title *To whom do children belong?*, with the subtitle *Parental rights, civic education and children's autonomy*. Its author explains: "When we ask the question 'To whom do children belong?' what we really mean is: Who has primary responsibility for children and decision-making authority over them?" (Moschella, 2016, p. 1). The essay develops as "a robust defence of parental rights in education" (p. 4) whose "metaphysical and ethical presuppositions" are drawn from

Aristotle and Aquinas (p. 9), as well as the "new natural law theory". These presuppositions are central to the author's "defence of the moral relevance of the biological tie between parent and child, which in turn is central to my view of parental authority as natural and original, rather than conventional and derivative of the authority of the larger political community" (p. 10).

Accordingly, parents have an "absolute obligation to love their children" (p. 44) and "are the primary educators of children particularly in moral and religious matters" (p. 167) that "is at the very centre of parents' rightful sphere of authority" p. 157). Their educational rights are "a subset of conscience rights" (p. 167) and, therefore, "discretionary by their very nature" (p. 61). Being so, to what extent should the State be involved in education? In particular, should it run schools at all? If so, should there be a monopoly on public education funding? Moreover, should the State regulate home-schooling and private schools? If so, to what extent?

In the author's opinion:

- The family is "a pre-political authoritative community" (p. 45) and "children directly and primarily 'belong' to – i.e. are members of and under the care of – their families, and only indirectly and secondarily 'belong' to the larger political community" (p. 179). Parents "are the ones with the primary responsibility to provide for their children's physical, psychological, moral and intellectual development" (p. 59). Therefore, they "are the ones with the authority to make controversial decisions about what type of education is in the best interests of their children", including "to decide whether or not the child's wishes on any particular matter should be followed or not" (p. 158). In effect, they are "in the best position to know the difference between a child's sincere and mature moral convictions, on the one hand, and, on the other hand, spurious rationalizations or judgments reflecting a lack of experience and insight regarding what really matters" (p. 157).
- Parents should not, therefore, be prevented "from educating their children as they think best, particularly with respect to moral and religious values" (p. 59), nor compelled "to allow their children to be taught something that the parents think is harmful, or to place their children in an educational environment that parents believe will be detrimental" (p. 61).
- Consequently, parents "have a right to exempt their children from the offensive aspect of the curriculum, to educate them at home" (p. 61), which implies that "respecting the primacy of parental authority and the conscience rights of parents" requires "some form of school choice policy", such as "charter school and voucher programs" (p. 172).
- To the extent that the role of the State is subsidiary to that of parents, it should limit itself to supporting the primary authority of parents concern-

> ing the overall well-being of the child, "except in cases that involve abuse, neglect or a significant threat to the public order" (p. 180), which can justify the direct coercive and direct intervention of the State on behalf of the child or the common good.

The author admits that "parental educational authority is not absolute or exclusive" (p. 48), that "there is a truly compelling State interest in what I call education for minimally decent citizenship" (p. 117), and "that an ideal education would involve teaching critical thinking skills and exposing students to the best arguments in favour of competing views (at the right time and in the right way)" (p. 160). However, the State lacks authority "to coercively enforce any particular educational ideal" (p. 8). In addition:
- "fostering a critical attitude toward the values taught by parents may on balance be more harmful than helpful to children" (p. 8);
- "to shelter one's children from diverse conceptions of the good life is neither abusive nor neglectful", and "may even be beneficial" (p. 145);
- therefore, "concern for the development of children's autonomy need not be incompatible with robust parental discretionary rights over education – including the right to deny children sympathetic exposure to alternative ways of life" (p. 146), which "may be more harmful than helpful to children who have not yet achieved a sufficient level of moral maturity, and parents are the ones who are in the best position to know when children have reached that point" (p. 160).

The author affirms that she takes an approach to parental rights that is "primarily philosophical in nature" (p. 8). It is a *naturalistic and religious approach*, bypassing the *human right* to education (see also, for instance, *The School Revolution* by Paul Ron, 2013).

Under the traditional political-pedagogical paradigm, both the parent-child relation and the teachers-students relation were seen as "a *special power relation* that took place in a space amply non-juridical" (Brenner & Töpper, 1997, p. 2). The institutional status of *son* or *daughter* and *pupil* or *student* amounted to a *capitis diminutio* (undermined legal status) allowing to treat the child as "a mere object of the Law, a piece entirely subjected to an institutional montage" (Supiot, 1990, p. 489). This paradigm is holistic in the sense that the Whole (community) prevails over the parts (individuals). In this connection, Néraudau (1984) wrote:

> Ancient societies are organised into functional age groups that – at various points in their lives – welcome the individual, set his place in the

> social body and define his role. The transition from one class to another takes place at an age that the custom or political constitution determines, bending more or less the physiological reality, if needed. This passage is accompanied by rituals that customs often fade to the point of making them disappear or relegating their formalism into gestures not always understood by those who perform them. [...]
>
> Apart from the folklore, it remains the principle, however, that is clear: it is based on the usefulness of the individual to the society, its preservation, its functioning and its continuity. (pp. 21, 22)

The classic reference of the holistic political-pedagogical paradigm is Plato's *Republic,* which was evoked by the USA Supreme Court in the *Case Meyer v. Nebraska, 262 U.S. 390 (1923)*,[3] relating to the legality of the use in school of a language other than English.

> In order to submerge the individual and develop ideal citizens, Sparta assembled the males at seven into barracks and intrusted their subsequent education and training to official guardians. Although such measures have been deliberately approved by men of great genius, their ideas touching the relation between individual and State were wholly different from those upon which our institutions rest, and it hardly will be affirmed that any legislature could impose such restrictions upon the people of a State without doing violence to both letter and spirit of the Constitution.

The traditional educational mindset was eloquently expressed in the *Case "relating to certain aspects of the laws on the use of languages in education in Belgium" v. Belgium* (Applications 1474/62, 1677/62, 1691/62, 1769/63, 1994/63, 2126/64),[4] decided by the European Court of Human Rights in 1968. Belgium has four language areas: Flemish, French, German and the Brussels Region. The principle of linguistic territoriality had been adopted for education purposes. Several families of the Francophone region, living in the Flemish region, complained that the State did not guarantee them the right of their children to be educated in the French language. They alleged, *inter alia,* that the head of the family "has also the right to maintain the homogeneity and the integrity of the home, including '*the personal, absolute and inalienable right that his children should resemble him intellectually and culturally*'" (A.3) (italics added).

This traditional parental right regarding the education of children was juridified in the German Weimar Constitution (1919) under the term *Erziehungsberechtichte* (those who possess the right of education). Bernhard Bergmann (1962) remarked: "Since the Constitution of Weimar, the concept of

Erziehungsberechtigte has become usual as the legal formulation of this primary family right of education" (p. 1027). The individual 'right' to education was a mere reflex of the family and social right to educate according to the dominant domestic beliefs and interests.

The typical paradigm of the *right of education* – an expression absent from the IHRL – has the following main features:

- The overarching aims of education were often summed up in the Latin Cicero trilogy *Pietas erga deos, patriam et parentes* (Duties towards God, Motherland and Parents).
- Its anthropological foundation is the representation of the child as a *being naturally bad*, justifying education as a process of making him/her a *being socially good.*
- Education is envisaged as an endeavour of submission of the *minors* (children, students) to the *majors* (parents, teachers), whose principle of legitimacy is the *power* of the strongest, imposing to the weakest the duty of *obedience.*[6] In *Antigone* (Sophocles),[7] Creon says that "disobedience is the worst of evils".
- Its principle of method is *punishment*, always *for your good.* "You torment the poor thing for his good" (*On tourmente le malheureux, pour son bien*) – lamented Rousseau (1762a, p. 92). *C'est pour ton bien* (It is for your good) – reads the title of the French edition of a book by Miller (1980). The methodological tones may vary:
  - *Black Pedagogy* (*Schwarze Pädagogik*) is the title of a work by Katharina Rutschky (1977) that, in Miller's opinion, is "a collection of texts about education in which all the traditional techniques of conditioning the subject, so that he is not aware of what actually is done to him, are so clearly described that they confirm, taken from the reality, reconstructions I had succeeded in the course of the long analytical work" (pp. 21, 22).
  - *White Pedagogy* is that of smiling and seducing for motivating (see Lobrot, 1966, 1992; Charlot, 1976), with sweet methods, but whose effects are not necessarily psychologically less bitter …
  - *Scottish Shower Pedagogy* – maybe the most frequent – is that Rousseau (1762a) called "*tantôt … tantôt …*" (sometimes … sometimes …), which makes "insolent or timid […] performing monkeys or noisy little rascals" (pp. 50, 536) that will become "big children" and "little men" (p. 76).

In this connection, the worldwide "enquiry into the theoretical problems raised by the elaboration of an International Declaration of the Rights of Man" conducted by UNESCO in 1947, following a Resolution of the first UNESCO General Conference, which gathered dozens of contributions, also deserves to be mentioned. One of them was entirely concerned with education. Its author was Isaac L. Kandel, Professor at the Teachers' College of Columbia University, New York, who offered insightful reflections. He said:

> A study of recent statements on Human Rights reveals the curious paradox that the one condition which is essential to their realization and proper use is hardly ever mentioned. Perhaps the omission of any reference to education can be explained on the assumption that it is taken for granted as a human right and as the essential foundation for the enjoyment of human rights. The history of education, however, provides ample evidence that education has not been regarded as a human right nor has it been used as an instrument for developing an appreciation of the importance of human rights for the fullest development of each individual as a human being. Historically, two motives have dominated the provision of education. The first and the earliest motive was directed to indoctrinating the younger generation in the religious beliefs of their particular denominations. The second motive, which came with the use of the national State, was to develop a sense of loyalty to the political group or nation. In both cases, the ends that were sought emphasized acquiescent discipline rather than education for freedom as a human being.
>
> ... The recognition of education as a human right is, however, only one aspect of the problem as it concerns the Rights of Man. Free access to education at all levels may be provided without affecting either the content or the methods of instruction. (UNESCO, 1948, pp. 231, 232)

It was against the traditional holistic political-pedagogical paradigm of the right of education that emerged, in the late 19th century, in the American and European continents, the most powerful wave of renewal in the history of education: the New Education Movement that reached its apogee between the two World Wars.

5.1.2 *The New Education Movement*

The New Education Movement's (NEM) major source of inspiration was Rousseau and was greatly influenced by the British New Education Fellowship (NEF), founded in 1921 by Beatrice Ensor, originated from the Theosophical Fraternity in Education.[8] Theosophy was a syncretic religious belief with Buddhist, Hinduist, Christian and other inspirations. Other names for NEM were New School, Progressive Education, *École Active, Escuela Nueva, Reformpädagogic ...*

The NEM is a fascinating chapter of the History of Education. It evolved as a true Education International gathering education professionals from all continents, as well as personalities from other professional and scientific areas. Among them: Adolphe Ferrière, Maria Montessori, John Dewey, Alexander Neill, Georg Kerschensteiner, Faria de Vasconcelos, Rudolf Steiner, Paul Geheeb, Beatrice Ensor, Anton Makarenko, Roger Cousinet, Célestin Freinet, Robert Dottrens, Édouard Claparède, Jean-Ovide Decroly, Pierre Bovet, Paul Langevin, Henri Piéron, Henri Wallon, Jean Piaget, etc.

The NEM held several long congresses, in the decades of 1920 and 1930, in Europe, South Africa, Australia and New Zealand, with an ever-increasing number of participants and countries represented. The first one took place in 1921 in Calais (France), where the *Ligue Internationale pour l'Éducation Nouvelle* (L.I.E.N. – New Education International Fellowship) was created and its purpose and principles adopted. In 1932, the Congress of Nice (France) adopted new principles, which suffered inflexions with the publication of three *Manifestos* at the end of the same decade (in France, United Kingdom and the USA), motivated by the deterioration of the international atmosphere that preceded the outbreak of the Second World War.

The NEM was very heterogeneous, 'new education' being a term with different assumptions. What was most unifying of their trends were reformism, child-centrism and pacifism. What was most dividing were two classic questions, interconnected, which cross the history of the pedagogic thought and crossed its congresses: nature of the child and freedom in education. Given the NEM diversity, Béatrice Haenggeli-Jenni (2011) observed, not surprisingly: "The reading of the PEN [*Pour l'Ère Nouvelle,* NEM magasin] highlights a recurrent word in speeches of their authors, both in the 1920s and in the 1930s, scientists or practitioners, in the North or the South: The word 'synthesis'" (p. 321). For example, in the Congress of Elseneur (Denmark, 1929), Hélène Radlinska, from the Free University of Warsaw (Poland), said that the New Education had become "chaos of ideas […]. The total synthesis is difficult" (*Pour l'Ère Nouvelle,* N° 55, 1930).[9]

The NEM did not have a profound impact on school realities, but it may be said what Francine Dubreucq (1994) said of one of its most notable personalities, Ovide Decroly: "The sad paradox of the failure of his work, so daring and so simple, at the same time, is that it still appears as avant-garde!" (p. 275).

In NEM documents and the speeches of its militants, there are references to human rights, the rights of the child and the right to education, its values and principles. Referring to the first Declaration of the Rights of the Child (Geneva, 1923), Adolphe Ferrière – maybe the NEM most influential personality – remarked (*Pour l'Ère Nouvelle,* N° 10, 1924)[10]: "It should be noted, moreover, that this Declaration is similar, on the essential points, to that our New Education International Fellowship adopted in 1921" (in the Calais Congress).

In 1942, the New Education Fellowship convened an Inter-Allied Conference, on 11–12 April, in London, that requested:

> ... the Governments of the Allied Nations to approve and adopt the following Charter for Children as a statement of the basic and minimum rights of children to be secured and guarded, above and beyond all considerations of sex, race, nationality, creed or social position.
>
> 1. The personality of the child is sacred; and the needs of the child must be the foundation of any good educational system.
> 2. The right of every child to proper food, clothing and shelter shall be accepted as a first charge on the resources of the nation.
> 3. For every child there shall always be available medical attention and treatment.
> 4. All children shall have equal opportunity of access to the nation's stores of knowledge and wisdom.
> 5. There shall be full-time schooling for every child.
> 6. Religious training should be available for all children.
>
> (Veerman, 1992, Appendix XIII)

Percy Nunn, Professor of the University of London, President of the Congress of Cheltenham (United Kingdom, 1936) – the last great NEM Congress – pointed to "the growing trend to consider education, not as a privilege reserved for a few, but as a right of everyone, a trend which modifies many ideas" (in *Pour l'Ère Nouvelle*, 1936, 121, p. 231).[11] In this respect, there is some historical interest in noting that one of the speakers in the Congress of Cheltenham was Peng Chun Chang, Professor of the University of Nankai, Tianjin (China), a Confucian philosopher, writer and diplomat, who would come to be one of the *Big Five* of the UN Commission on Human Rights that drafted the UDHR (1947–1948), as Nationalist China's Delegate.

The NEM collaborated with the League of Nations in fostering international understanding, and some of UNESCO's first high officials came from NEM.[12]

It may be concluded that the right to education reflects and universalised the ideal that, during nearly two decades, between the two World Wars, gathered so many educators and other militants of the renewal of education.

5.1.3 *Rightful Education*

IHRL is rooted in the subversion triggered by the *New Law* of the French Revolution, as we saw (see 2.7.1).

Regarding the right to education, Nehemiah Robinson (1958) noted, commenting on the UDHR: "Art. 26 (especially para. 2) is, no doubt, innovation in International Law" (p. 137). The right to education has evolved, reaching a higher coherence in the CRC (1989) that "reconceptualised the existing international education rights law from the child's perspective" (Verheyde, 2006, p. 9). This evolution amounts to a very "reconstructing of the right to education" (Bueren, 1995, p. 256).

In effect, as remarked the first Special Rapporteur on the Right to Education in her "Preliminary Report" (E/CN.4/1999/49)[13]: "The 1959 Declaration of the Rights of the Child laid down the entitlement of the child to receive education, articulating the vision of the child of the time as a passive recipient of education rather than the principal subject of the right to education" (para. 75). In another Report (E/CN.4/2001/52),[14] she pointed out that the IHRL "has changed education law, which traditionally treated children as the object of education" (para. 76).

Indeed, the right to education is not whichever right to whichever education, it is a *new right* to a *new education.*

The right to education is a *new right* for its *subjectivity, universality* and *exigibility*, as a *human right*, but specifically for its *normativity.*

- *Subjectivity*
  Subjectivity means that the primary subject of the right to education is each human being.[15] As children are concerned, parents' and State's rights are merely 'functional' rights, as above noted (see 4.2.2.1).
- *Universality*
  Universality means that every human being holds a right to education. As we know, the first and still the main international legal instrument on the right to education is the Convention against Discrimination in Education.
- *Exigibility*
  Exigibility means that the right to education is not a mere moral and social right, depending on parents' and collectivities' needs and good will, but an individual right legally opposable to States as the principal duty-bearers of the human rights.
- *Normativity*
  Normativity means that the human right to education is not simply a right to 'an education' (whatever), but to education quality in accordance with the agreed international norms.

The right to education is, therefore, right to *new education.*

Already the Faure Report (1972) had concluded that "a radical change in educational practices" was needed (p. 157). In effect, "for the right to education to have any meaning as a human right, education in any context should follow as closely as possible the human rights idea", wrote Kate Halvorsen (1990, p. 363). In other words: The right to education calls for a *human right* or *rights-based approach.*

UNICEF and UNESCO published *A Human Rights-Based Approach to Education for All: A framework for the realisation of children's right to education and rights within education* (2007), drawing on the "UN Statement of Common Understanding on a Human Rights-Based Approach to Development Cooperation", an outcome of the United Nations Programme for Reform, launched in 1997 by UN Secretary-General (Kofi Annan, at the time),[16] and on the *Manual on Rights-Based Education: Global human rights requirements made simple* by Katarina Tomaševski (2004). According to it:

> Full realization of the right to education is not merely a question of access. A rights-based approach to Education for All is a holistic one, encompassing access to education, educational quality (based on human rights values and principles) and the environment in which education is provided. (UNICEF/UNESCO, 2007, p. xi)

Hans-Jürgen Töws (1970) wrote, for around half a century: "Children and young are not mere pedagogical objects. Since a long time ago, the bearers of education and training are legally bound to the minor's good; he is himself recognised, more and more, as a holder of own legal positions" (p. 377). At the time, also Hans Heckel (1970) remarked that "the moving of the pupil from the condition of an object without rights towards the status of the holder of own rights and duties, moved the school from an authoritarian institution into a democratic one, ruled by Law". However: "At present, a central problem consists in the enforcement of the principles of the Rule of Law in school" (pp. 363, 365).

If "education is not exempt from the rule of law" – as wrote the first Special Rapporteur (E/CN.4/2000/6, para. 27)[17] – then it is necessary "to emphasizing differences between *education* and the *right to education* so as to create a background for advocating changes within education aimed at conformity with the human rights requirements", as she announced in her "Preliminary Report" (E/CN.4/1999/49, para. 13),[18] as already quoted. This means that a *human right approach* of education is one conducive, under the true Rule of Law, to a *Rightful Education*. It meets a critical concern so expressed by Tomaševski (2001a):

> Conceptualization of the right to education has not advanced a great deal as is evidenced in the absence of a clear-cut answer to a simple question: when is the right to education fully realized? Our failure to secure schooling for all children tends to focus all attention on the needed but lacking schools, funds, and teachers. This keeps attention focused on the means. Securing them does not automatically mold education towards desired ends, provided that there was a global agreement on what education is for. (p. 8)

Summing up:

The right to education is right to a *human right approach of education* that, in the Rule of Law, means *Right to a Rightful Education*, understood as an education consistent with the *normative integrity of the right to education*, which can be systematised in *Principles of the Ethics of the Right to Education* from which stem *Educational Rights*.

Drawing on the foregoing chapters, a conception of Rightful Education is being proposed

5.2 Ethics of the Right to Education

The right to education carries an ethical significance fundamentally because it is no longer a *right over the human being*, but a *right of the human being*. Right to a Rightful Education that should be the criterion of quality education or *good education*.

The major theories in the history of education are conceptions of a good education – through which "all the good in the world arises" (Kant, 1803, para. 16)[19] – structured, at least implicitly, by the already mentioned conceptual trilogy inspiring its main definitions: *Perfectibility, Perfection, Perfecting*.

The first great theory of education, in the Western world, is due to Plato, whose *Republic* is *le plus beau traité d'éducation qu'on ait jamais fait* ("the finest treatise on education ever written"), as famously said Rousseau (1762a, p. 40). In Plato's opinion, the good, the 'correct' education is that that "is capable of making our souls and bodies as fine and as handsome as they can be" (Plato, 1997, *Laws*, 788c). It is an ideal condensed in the well-known saying that, in the 2nd century, the Roman poet Juvenal used in the satire X: *Mens sana in corpore sano* (A healthy mind in a healthy body)[20] that is still today the *motto* (maxim) of many institutions of education. Kant called Rousseau the "Newton of the moral world" for having placed "the character of the species" in the "capacity and necessity of receiving an education" for "perfecting itself according to aims chosen by himself [man]" (Renaut, 2002, pp. 231, 232).

We know how paramount the aims of education – the overarching issue of the pedagogic thought – were for the UNESCO's founding fathers (see 4.1.2.5.4.1). The purpose of education is the core of the normative integrity of the right to education, evoking the sublimity of the Kantian *Kingdom of Ends*. The CoRC said in its first GC (CRC/GC/2001/1)[21] that CRC Article 29.1, stating the aims of education, "highlights the need for educational processes to be based upon the very principles it enunciates" (para. 2). The EFA 2005 Global Monitoring Report (UNESCO, 2005b), consecrated to "The quality imperative", already quoted, referred to the principles "integrated into the aims of education set out in the Convention on the Rights of the Child (1990), which underpins the current positions on quality held by UNESCO and UNICEF" (Chapter 1). According to the UNESCO Report *Rethinking education*: "A humanistic vision reaffirms a set of universal ethical principles that should be the foundation for an integrated approach to the purpose and organization of education for all" (UNESCO, 2015b, p. 37).

As set out in the main international provisions on the right to education (see 4.2.2.2.1), the purpose of education may be summed up in the following Principles of the Ethics of the Right to Education:

- *Primacy of the best interests of the subject of the right to education*
  It is a principle deriving from the general primacy of the subject of human rights and generalising the primacy of the best interests of the child in education.
- *Development of the human personality: free, full, harmonious*
  It is a principle identifying the specific value of the right to education and the sense of all learnings necessary for its realisation.
- *Priority of human rights education as an ethical, civic, international education*
  It is a principle reaffirming and renewing the traditional primacy of moral education and synthesizing the amplitude of its present conception.

These principles are justified next.

5.2.1 *Primacy of the Best Interests of the Subject of the Right to Education*

The primacy of the best interests of the subject of the right to education is rooted in the very nature of human rights, as recalled the Vienna Declaration and Programme of Action (1993),[22] in the second paragraph of its preamble:

> *Recognizing and affirming* that all human rights derive from the dignity and worth inherent in the human person and that the human person is the central subject of human rights and fundamental freedoms, and consequently should be the principal beneficiary and should participate actively in the realization of these rights and freedoms,

The child is obviously the subject of the right to education *par excellence*. The primacy of "the best interests of the child" in education was first internationally stated by the 1959 Declaration (Principle 7). The 1989 Convention[23] restated (Article 18.1):

> 1. States Parties shall use their best efforts to ensure recognition of the principle that both parents have common responsibilities for the

> upbringing and development of the child. Parents or, as the case may be, legal guardians, have the primary responsibility for the upbringing and development of the child. The best interests of the child will be their basic concern.

The principle of the primacy of the best interests of the subject of the right to education, besides reflecting the principle of the primacy of the human rights subject, generalises the principle of the primacy of the best interests of the child, in education. It is increasingly recognised in national legal systems. For example, the *Ley General de Educación de Uruguay* (General Education Act of Uruguay, 2008)[24] recalls in its Article 5 (On the subject of the right to education): "The holders of the enjoyment and effective exercise of the right to education are students". And devotes a Title (V), with a sole Article (120), to the following "Specific Principle of Interpretation and Integration of the Act":

> For the interpretation and integration of this Act, it should be taken into account the best interests of the student, which consists in the recognition and respect for the rights inherent in his/her quality as a human person. Consequently, this principle shall not be invoked in prejudice of such rights.

The primacy of the best interests of the subject of the right to education has been also recognised by Case Law, at international and national levels. For example:

- The former European Commission of Human Rights observed in its Report on the admissibility of the *Case Bernard and others against Luxemburg* (Application 17187/90, Decision of 8 November 1993)[25]:

  > … parents' convictions, for the purpose of Article 2 of Protocol Nº 1 [to the ECHR], are convictions which do not conflict with the child's fundamental right to education. Where, instead of supporting the child's right to education, the parents' rights come into conflict with it, the child's rights must prevail. (see Nº 13887/88, Dec 5 2 90, DR 64, p. 158)

- The CoESCR affirmed, in its GC 13 (E/C.12/1999/10),[26] that "the best interests of the student shall be a primary consideration" (para. 7).
- Tomaševski (2001a) mentioned, in this respect, a decision of a Tribunal of Brussell (Belgian) on the *Case A.M. (16 ans) v. K.N., O.M. et l'asbl Institut d'enseignement secondaire général La Retraite du Sacré Cœur* (98/1510/c, 3 février 1999):

> In a rare case where a child, sixteen years old, has been accorded the right to challenge parental disagreements about the choice of school for her, justice Dalcq in Bruxelles has acknowledged that the best interest of the child should prevail. The case involved a girl whose divorced parents disagreed as to which school she should attend. The girl had ultimately refused to attend the school chosen by the mother (who exercised parental rights) and ended up attending no school, to then legally challenge the mother's attempt to force her to attend the school which her mother had chosen. The child's choice of school was judicially vindicated so as to prevent further jeopardy of the child's right to education. (p. 44)

The primacy of the best interests of the subject of the right to education should be held as the supreme principle of the IEL. And what interest could be higher than the development of his/her personality?

5.2.2 *Development of the Human Personality: Free, Full, Harmonious*

Human dignity is like the backbone of the ethical subject underlying all the differences and contingencies of the empirical subjects, conferring equal rights whose ultimate sense is the development of the human personality, without arbitrary or unjust limitations.

5.2.2.1 Principle of the Free Development of the Human Personality

Already in *The Communist Manifesto,*[27] Friedrich Engels and Karl Marx envisaged a society without classes as "an association, in which the free development of each is the condition for the free development of all". It is not unlikely that this sentence had inspired the ILO Recommendation concerning the Development of Facilities for the Utilisation of Workers' Spare Time (R021)[28] where the notion of "the full development of the human personality" emerged in International Law. In it are used expressions such as "full and harmonious development of the individual and the family", and "moral, intellectual and physical development of the workers" (IV), which is "of great value from the point of view of the progress of civilization" (preamble). It is thus not surprising that, when the UDHR drafting began, the only proposal before the Commission on Human Rights to include the right to "full development" was that submitted by the American Federation of Labour. According to its preamble:

> The State has no good other than the good of its individual members, present and prospective – its supreme test is the way in which it provides for the full and free development of each individual. The more rights

> enjoyed by individuals and the more individuals for whom these rights of free development are safeguarded, the more democratic any society will be (E/CN.4/W.8). (in Schabas, 2013, p. 73)

The draft of the Division of Human Rights of the UN Secretariat didn't expressly enunciate the right to "the full development of his personality". It was added by the draft of René Cassin in the Commission on Human Rights.

In the UDHR, the word 'development' is used three times in relation to the human personality, the development of which should be "free" (Article 22), "full" (Article 26.2), "free and full" (Article 29.1). According to the 1959 Declaration and the 1989 Convention, the development of the child should be "full and harmonious" (Principle 6 and Preamble, respectively).

The development of the human personality is referred to in many IHRL instruments, at the universal and regional levels. In the Constitutional Law posterior to World War II, it is recognised by many Constitutions as right or principle. In other cases, it was decisions of Higher Courts which derived the right or principle of the development of the personality from constitutional provisions.

Just as, human dignity is recognised, sometimes, as a right, but is generally regarded as the principle-source of all human rights, also should the development of the human personality, more than one right among others, be taken as a principle consubstantial with human dignity, virtually condensing all rights inherent in it. The German Federal Constitutional Court said in *Case BVerfGE 7, 198 (Lüth)*[29]:

> ... far from being a value-free system (BVerfGE 2, 1 [12]; 5, 85 [134 ff., 197 ff.]; 6, 32 [40 f.]), the [German] Constitution erects an objective system of values in its section on basic rights, and thus expresses and reinforces the validity of the basic rights (Klein-v. Mangoldt, Das Bonner Grundgesetz, Vorbem. B III 4 vor Art. 1 S. 93). This system of values, *centring on the freedom of the human being to develop in society*, must apply as a constitutional axiom throughout the whole legal system: it must direct and inform legislation, administration, and judicial decision. (para. 27)

The Constitutional Court of Peru said almost literally the same (*EXP. N.º 06113-2008-PA/TC*)[30]: "This Court considers that dignity and the free development of the personality are central axes of the value system recognised by the Constitution, being the support of all fundamental rights".

In accordance with the jurisprudence of the European Court of Human Rights and the Constitutional Court of Colombia, in particular, the essence of the right-principle of the free development of the human personality lies in the autonomy inherent in the dignity of every human being, which express themselves in their power for self-determination, i.e. the freedom to choose the ends and the means that give meaning and shape to their existence. It implies the right to private life, provided that it respects the rights of others and other values of the Public Order.

5.2.2.2 Development of the Human Personality and Right to Education

The development of the human personality is most often associated with the right to education, of course.

In this regard, Rita Hofstetter and Bernard Schneuwly (2013) pointed out, referring to the IBE International Conferences on Public Education: "In all recommendations on teaching, the aspects 'intellectual, moral, social, manual, physical and aesthetic' are mentioned in one way or another, with the target of 'complete and harmonious development'" (p. 224). Let us recall the Faure Report (1972):

> We find this pedagogic ideal throughout history, in almost all countries, among philosophers and moralists, and among most theoreticians and visionaries of education. It has been one of the fundamental themes for humanist thought in all times. It may have been applied imperfectly, but it has been fruitful and helped to inspire many of the noblest educational enterprises. […]
>
> *The separation of its intellectual, physical, aesthetic, moral and social components is an indication of alienation, undervaluation and mutilation of the human person.* (pp. 156, 69)

Therefore, reads another Report of UNESCO (2000):

> An old idea in one form or another in most philosophies of education, the principle that 'Education shall be directed to the full development of the human personality' was adopted almost without debate when Article 26 was drawn up. There only was some brief discussion of whether terms like 'physical', 'intellectual', 'spiritual' and 'moral' should be added to 'personality', but in the interest of keeping the Declaration as concise as possible, they were left out. (pp. 82, 83)

The minor discrepancies in the description of the dimensions of the development of the human personality have been overcome with their subsumption in the term "full".

When the draft ICESCR was examined by the UN General Assembly Third Committee, in 1957 (12th Session), the UNESCO Director-General (René Maheu), answering a question about the wording of the present Article 13.1 (A/C.3/SR.783)[31]:

> 66. ... said that UNESCO regarded the first aim, the full development of the human personality, as essential. The second, the strengthening of respect for human rights, was equally important, for it introduced a notion of responsibility which would eliminate the possibility of the first objective being interpreted as forced individualism. The third aim, the suppression of all incitement to racial hatred, was also of great importance.

The Chinese Delegation (Lin) said that (A/C.3/SR.781)[32]: "The Chinese educational system, which had been regulated in the fifth century B.C. during the time of Confucius, was based on the sage's teaching that the purpose of education was to perfect the human personality" (para. 4). The Delegation of Venezuela (Rojas) affirmed (A/C.3/SR.782)[33]: "As the essential purpose of education was to encourage the full development of the human personality, it would be well to give that aim more emphasis by stating it in a separate paragraph" (para. 38). The Delegation of Pakistan (Chaudhuri) affirmed (A/C.3/SR.781)[34]:

> 38. ... "The right of education" therefore meant the right of every individual to develop his potentialities to the utmost and implied an obligation on the part of the community to ensure that he did so.
> 39. The role of education was to prepare individuals for the obligations of citizenship, which were not only personal but national and international. Power belonged to those who could formulate and grasp ideas, and there was a minimum level of education below which no one should be permitted to fall if he was not to be a slave to others.

The CoESCR underlined in its GC 13 (E/C.12/1999/10)[35]: "Of those educational objectives which are common to Article 26 (2) of the Universal Declaration of Human Rights and Article 13 (1) of the Covenant, perhaps the most fundamental is that 'education shall be directed to the full development of the human personality'" (para. 4).

The CRC uses the term 'development' or other with the same etymology 21 times: 10 concerning the development of the child and 11 referring to different matters. Those relating to the development of the child are in Preamble (2) and Articles 6.2, 18.1, 23.3, 27.1, 27.2, 29.1.a and 32.1. The CoRC highlighted in its first GC (CRC/GC/2001/1)[36]:

> 9. ... Consistent with the Convention's emphasis on the importance of acting in the best interests of the child, this Article [29.1] emphasizes the message of child-centred education: that the key goal of education is the development of the individual child's personality, talents and abilities, in recognition of the fact that every child has unique characteristics, interests, abilities, and learning needs.

In GC 5 (CRC/GC/2003/05)[37], it remarked:

> 12. ... The Committee expects States to interpret 'development' in its broadest sense as a holistic concept, embracing the child's physical, mental, spiritual, moral, psychological and social development. Implementation measures should be aimed at achieving optimal development for all children.

It is pertinent to quote, here, the commentary on the UDHR Article 26 asked by UNESCO to Jean Piaget after its proclamation:

> Affirming the right of all human beings to education is to take on a far greater responsibility than simply to assure to each one reading, writing, and arithmetic capabilities; it is to guarantee fairly to each child the entire development of his mental faculties and the acquisition of knowledge and of ethical values corresponding to the exercise of these faculties until adaptation to actual social life. Moreover, it is to assume the obligation – keeping in mind the aptitudes and constitution that each person possesses – of not destroying or spoiling those possibilities that he may have that would benefit society first of all, or of allowing the loss of important abilities, or the smothering of others. [...]
>
> The right to education, therefore, is neither more nor less than the right of an individual to develop normally, in accord with all the potential he possesses, and the obligation that society has to transform this potential into useful and effective fulfilment. [...]
>
> The right to education that it [UDHR Article 26] outlines so explicitly is not only the right to attend schools but it is also, insofar as it pursues the full development of the personality, the right to find in these schools all that is necessary to the building of a questioning mind and a dynamic moral conscience. (Piaget, 1949, pp. 54, 56, 92)

The principle of the full development of the human personality is laid down in many General Education Acts worldwide.

5.2.2.3 Liberty, Reciprocity, Responsibility: Superior Values of Education

In his essay on the UDHR Article 26, Piaget (1949) asked:

> But what is the development of the personality? And by what educational methods can it be attained, since "full development" is never the end goal of all the known forms of education, but rather, it represents a demand that is contrary to the usual goals of conformist education and an ideal that must be reconciled with the collective goals of education?

Here is his answer:

> The text of Article 26 gives no definition of "personality". However, it does state that its development is accompanied by a return to the respect for the rights and freedoms that belong to other personalities. Such precision seems almost tautological, but it is really important; an entire concept of personality could be defined by terming it a reciprocal "rapport". From a psychological point of view as well as from the sociological, it is essential to distinguish the individual and the personality. In the degree that the individual is self-centred, he creates an obstacle by his moral or intellectual egocentrism to the inherent relations of reciprocity that all evolved social living contains. Whereas, on the contrary, the part of an individual that is a "person" freely accepts some kind of discipline, or contributes to its creation, by voluntarily subjecting himself to a system of mutual "norms" that subordinate his liberty in respect to that of others. Personality, therefore, means a certain form of intellectual and moral conscience, as removed from the anomie that is part of egocentrism as from the heteronomy of outside pressure, since it attains its autonomy by regulating it through reciprocity. [...] To sum up, that "education shall be directed to the full development of the human personality and to the strengthening of respect for human rights and fundamental freedoms" is really to create individuals capable of intellectual and moral autonomy and of respecting this autonomy in others by applying the rule of reciprocity that makes it legitimate for themselves. (pages in the English version: 89, 90, 91, 110, 111)

In this quotation, two values stand out: Liberty and Reciprocity. With Responsibility, they may be considered the highest expressions of a humanely developed personality and, therefore, the superior values of education.

- *Liberty*

  As wrote Rousseau (1762a), "liberty, not authority, is the greatest good" (p. 99). Therefore: "Prepare at the earliest the reign of its [the child] liberty" (p. 71). Rousseau "inscribes the distinction between being human and only animal in these two qualities: perfectibility and liberty" (Soëtard & Hétier, 2003, p. 62). Compayré (1897) taught in his *Cours de Pédagogie Théorique et Pratique* (Course of Theoretical and Practical Pedagogy) that "the object of education, at all levels, is to make free men" (Lesson XII of the Second Part).

  Liberty or freedom should be the central value of education for the following main reasons:
  - it is the ethical substance of human dignity;
  - it is the principle of legitimacy of the value of the authority;
  - it is the psychological and methodological condition of every true learning.

  Liberty is not a *liberty-anomie* (without rules) nor a *liberty-heteronomy* (subordinated), but a *liberty-autonomy* (self-determining).

  Respecting personal autonomy is to respect the ethical condition of every human being, i.e. his or her absolute dignity, but in a broad sense autonomy encompasses all the conditions of independent existence, especially the capacity and possibility to meet the subsistence needs and others necessary for a life with dignity.

  Moral autonomy is the superior form of human liberty.[38]
- *Reciprocity*

  There is no human liberty without reciprocity, i.e. the recognition of the equal dignity and liberty of others. It is a principle underlying the Golden Rule and the Ethics of Human Rights as an Ethics of Recognition, as we know. In the opinion of Charles Foster (2011): "Reciprocity isn't just one of the rules of the human game: it is the game itself" (p. 13). The geneticist Axel Kahn said[39]: "Individuals humanise one another".

  Reciprocity should be regarded as the most humanising dimension of the development of the personality of a human being.
- *Responsibility*

  Liberty and reciprocity imply responsibility. According to the UNESCO Constitution (1945),[40] to realise its purpose, the Organisation will suggest "educational methods best suited to prepare the children of the world for the responsibilities of freedom" (Article I.2.b). CRC Article 29.1.d[41] affirms: "States Parties agree that the education of the child shall be directed to [...] the preparation of the child for responsible life in a free society". Kahn[42] thinks that in the responsibility lies our "irreducible humanity" (in AAVV, 2012, p. 72). It is the responsibility to behave humanely and, in its maximum exigence, responsibility for the other human beings.

> In the opinion of Dieter-Jürgen Löwisch (1995): "*An Ethics of the pedagogical action should be only a discourse on the Ethics of Responsibility.* [...] *Who acts pedagogically must form the capacity to be responsible with the capacity to be responsible*" (pp. 105–111).[43]
> Responsibility is the highest expression of moral conscience as a sentiment of recognition of the common fragility and destiny, calling for empathy and solidarity.

In concluding:
- The development of the human personality is a complex right-principle, both for its scope and the restrictions it admits to safeguarding the rights of others and other values of the Public Order.
- Liberty, Reciprocity and Responsibility lie at the core of the pedagogical responsibility. The main responsibility of parents and education professionals is to help children, adolescents and the young, with words and attitudes of affectionate and firm serenity, to learn thinking, acting and reacting rationally and ethically.

5.2.3 *Priority of Human Rights Education as an Ethical, Civic, International Education*

The Roman poet Horace wrote (Book III, Ode 24)[44]: *Quid leges sine moribus* (What good are laws when there are no morals)? Law can *write* laws in *codes*, but only education can *engrave* values in *hearts*.

Education is a term etymologically axiologically neutral, but when one says that someone is 'an educated person' one wants to mean *well-educated*, that is, educated according to a collective moral ideal. Indeed, if the perfection at which education should aim includes all the potential inherent in the perfectibility or educability of every human being, it bears a fundamentally moral connotation. "Beginning with the Renaissance, but with increasing confidence in the seventeenth century", perfection "came gradually to be further particularized as 'doing the maximum of good'" (Passmore, 1970, p. 260).

Hence the traditional primacy of moral education.

5.2.3.1 Primacy of Moral Education

The human primacy of moral education has been recognised by the major authors of the history of pedagogic thought (and not only). Some examples follow:
- Plato (1997) wrote in *Protagoras*:

> Starting when they are little children and continuing as long as they live, they [good men] teach them and correct them. As soon as a child understands what is said to him, the nurse, mother, tutor, and the father himself

> fight for him to be as good as he possibly can, seizing on every action and word to teach him and show him that this is just, that is unjust, this is noble, that is ugly, this is pious, that is impious, he should do this, he should not do that. If he obeys willingly, fine; if not, they straighten him out with threats and blows as if he were a twisted, bent piece of wood. After this, they send him to school and tell his teachers to pay more attention to his good conduct than to his grammar or music lessons. (325 d,e)

And in *Laws*:

> Any living creature that flourishes in its first stages of growth gets a tremendous impetus towards its natural perfection and the final development appropriate to it, and this is true of both plants and animals (tame and wild), and men too. Man is a 'tame' animal, as we put it, and of course if he enjoys a good education and happens to have the right natural disposition, he's apt to be a most heavenly and gentle creature; but his upbringing has only to be inadequate or misguided and he'll become the wildest animal on the face of the earth. (765e)

- Kant (1803) echoed somewhat Plato:

> 3. Discipline changes animal nature into human nature. Animals are by their instinct all that they ever can be; some other reason has provided everything for them at the outset. But man needs a reason of his own. Having no instinct, he has to work out a plan of conduct for himself. Since, however, he is not able to do this all at once but comes into the world undeveloped, others have to do it for him. [...]
>
> 4. Unruliness consists in the independence of law. By discipline, men are placed in subjection to the laws of mankind and brought to feel their constraint. This, however, must be accomplished early. Children, for instance, are first sent to school, not so much with the object of their learning something, but rather that they may become used to sitting still and doing exactly as they are told. And this to the end that in later life they should not wish to put actually and instantly into practice anything that strikes them. [...]
>
> 7. ... Neglect of discipline is a greater evil than the neglect of culture, for this last can be remedied later in life, but unruliness cannot be done away with, and a mistake in discipline can never be repaired.

- According to Herbart (1835), educability is mainly "educability of the will for morality" that constitutes "the entire purpose of man and education" (§ 1, § 8).[45]

- In *Anna Karénina* (Tolstoy), Lvov says referring to the education of his children (Part 7, Chapter 4): "If only they're better than I! That's all I desire. [...] The great thing is the education of character".[46]

The human primacy of moral education was often evoked during the *travaux préparatoires* (elaboration) of the creation of UNESCO and of the main international standards of the IHRL that recognises the crucial moral importance of human rights education.

5.2.3.2 Origins and Evolution of Human Rights Education

In the UN Charter (1945),[47] "the peoples of the United Nations" are determined "to reaffirm faith in fundamental human rights, in the dignity and worth of the human person, in the equal rights of men and women and of nations large and small" (Preamble). Accordingly:

> Article 1
>
> The Purposes of the United Nations are:
>
> [...]
>
> 3. To achieve international cooperation in solving international problems of an economic, social, cultural, or humanitarian character, and in promoting and encouraging respect for human rights and for fundamental freedoms for all without distinction as to race, sex, language, or religion;
>
> Article 13
>
> The General Assembly shall initiate studies and make recommendations for the purpose of:
>
> [...]
>
> b. promoting international co-operation in the economic, social, cultural, educational, and health fields, and assisting in the realization of human rights and fundamental freedoms for all without distinction as to race, sex, language, or religion.
>
> Article 55
>
> With a view to the creation of conditions of stability and well-being which are necessary for peaceful and friendly relations among nations based on respect for the principle of equal rights and self-determination of peoples, the United Nations shall promote:

> [...]
> c. universal respect for, and observance of, human rights and fundamental freedoms for all without distinction as to race, sex, language, or religion.
>
> Article 56
>
> All Members pledge themselves to take joint and separate action in cooperation with the Organization for the achievement of the purposes set forth in Article 55.

UNESCO's Constitution[48] Article I states:

> Purposes and functions
> 1. The purpose of the Organization is to contribute to peace and security by promoting collaboration among the nations through education, science and culture in order to further universal respect for justice, for the rule of law and for the human rights and fundamental freedoms which are affirmed for the peoples of the world, without distinction of race, sex, language or religion, by the Charter of the United Nations.

In the Working Group on the Declaration created by the Commission on Human Rights at its second session (Geneva, 1947), the World Jewish Congress representative (Alexis Easterman) said about the draft of the present Article 26.2 (E/CN.4/AC.2/SR.8)[49]:

> Article 31 [present Article 26] as drafted provided a technical framework of education but contained nothing about the spirit governing education which was an essential element. Neglect of this principle in Germany had been the main cause of two catastrophic wars. He proposed the following wording: 'This education shall be directed to the full development of the human personality [and] to strengthening respect for human rights and fundamental freedoms, and shall combat the spirit of intolerance and hatred against other nations or racial or religious groups everywhere'.

The reference to the mission of the United Nations in Article 26.2 was added at the Third Committee stage, originated from proposals of Mexico and USA.

In the UDHR text, as adopted, the paramount importance of human rights education is recognised since its Preamble that mentions "teaching and education to promote respect for these rights and freedoms". Cassin called attention to the following:

> The Preamble of the [Universal] Declaration mentions "the progressive measures of national and international order" only in the second line. [...]
>
> Indeed, the influence of education is previous to the "measures" and conditions its respect. Furthermore, it is mainly up to it to prepare the spirits for the great national or international transformations, necessary for the human rights to be better respected, as the International Community consolidates itself morally and legally. (in Verdoodt, 1964, pp. 325, 327)

Article 26 formally includes human rights education in its second paragraph, which "is a directive to the State and every other school authority. It relates to *all* education, whether compulsory or elective, paid or free, elementary, higher, or professional" (Robinson, 1958, p. 139). Morsink (1999) remarked: "Article 26 (on education) is one of the articles most clearly shaped by the experience of the war" (p. 90). In his opinion, the UDHR has "an open and explicit educational goal and a hidden legislative one" (p. 324).

> It is not just that the Declaration is an authoritative exposition of the principles enunciated in the Charter, and not just that Article 26 of the Declaration makes human rights an educational goal. Human rights education itself is the first and primary purpose of the Universal Declaration as a whole. (p. 326)

Immediately after the proclamation of the Universal Declaration, the UN General Assembly approved a Resolution on the 'Publicity to be given to the Universal Declaration of Human Rights' (A/RES/217(III)D),[50] recommending to the Member States its dissemination through every means, "principally in schools and other educational institutions". Specialised UN agencies and NGOs were also invited to do so. To this effect, the Secretary-General was requested to make the Declaration available in the greatest possible number of languages (more than 520, at present).

In 1950, the General Assembly approved a Resolution on a "Human Rights Day" (A/RES/423(V)).[51] "*Considering* that the Declaration marks a distinct forward step in the march of human progress", it invited:

> ... all States and interested organizations to adopt 10 December of each year as Human Rights Day, to observe this day to celebrate the proclamation of the Universal Declaration of Human Rights by the General Assembly on 10 December 1948, and to exert increasing efforts in this field of the human progress.

Here are the main events, documents and standards in the evolution of human rights education:

- In 1959, the UN General Assembly adopted the Declaration of the Rights of the Child[52] whose Principle 10 reads:

  > The child shall be protected from practices which may foster racial, religious and any other form of discrimination. He shall be brought up in a spirit of understanding, tolerance, friendship among peoples, peace and universal brotherhood, and in full consciousness that his energy and talents should be devoted to the service of his fellow men.

- In 1966, the ICESCR Article 13.1, taking up the UDHR Article 26.2, reaffirmed that human rights education is an element of the right to education.[53]
- In 1974, UNESCO adopted the Recommendation on Education for International Understanding and Co-operation and Peace and Education relating to Human Rights and Fundamental Freedoms[54] that continues to be the main international legal instrument in this field. It drew on the Recommendation on "Education for International Understanding as an integral part of the curriculum and life of the school" adopted by the International Conference on Public Education in 1968.
- In 1987, an International Congress on Human Rights Teaching, Information and Documentation[55] took place in Malta and approved several Recommendations.
- In 1988, following the Malta Recommendations, the UN General Assembly decided (A/43/128)[56] to launch "a World Public Information Campaign on Human Rights".
- In 1989, the CRC Article 29.1 restated that human rights education should be an element of the purpose of education.[57] Article 42 provides: "States Parties undertake to make the principles and provisions of the Convention widely known, by appropriate and active means, to adults and children alike". This is a unique provision in conventional IHRL.
- In 1993, an International Congress on Education for Human Rights and Democracy took place in Montreal (Canada), convened by UNESCO and the former UN Centre for Human Rights, in collaboration with the Canadian Commission for UNESCO. It adopted a World Plan of Action on Education for Human Rights and Democracy.[58]
- In the same year, the World Conference on Human Rights adopted the Vienna Declaration and Programme of Action,[59] in which the word education appears 28 times. Section II-D (para. 78–82) is devoted to "Human rights education". Janusz Symonides wrote: "From the UNESCO's point of

view, one of the main results of the World Conference on Human Rights concerns the recognition of the importance of human rights education" (in Johnson & Symonides, 1998, p. 106).

- In 1994, following a recommendation of the Vienna Conference, the UN General Assembly proclaimed "the ten-year period beginning on 1 January 1995 the United Nations Decade for Human Rights Education" (A/RES/49/184).[60]
- Also, in 1994 – the year of the 20th anniversary of the 1974 Recommendation – the 44th session of the International Conference on Education took place, convened in Geneva under the theme "Appraisal and perspectives of education for international understanding". It adopted a Declaration and an Integrated Framework of Action on Education for Peace, Human Rights and Democracy, which have been endorsed by the 28th Session of UNESCO's General Conference in 1995.[61] The Integrated Framework proposed "an up-to-date and integrated view of problems and strategies concerning education for peace, human rights and democracy [...] in order to chart new directions for the education of citizens in every country" (para. 4).
  The same General Conference adopted a Declaration of Principles on Tolerance and a Follow-Up Plan of Action for the United Nations Year for Tolerance.[62]
- In 1999, the UN General Assembly adopted a Declaration and Programme of Action on a Culture of Peace (A/RES/53/243).[63]
- In 2001, the World Conference against Racism, Racial Discrimination, Xenophobia and Related Intolerance, held in Durban, South Africa, adopted the Durban Declaration and Programme of Action.
- According to the CoRC, in its first GC (CRC/GC/2001/1):

> 15. Article 29 (1) [CRC] can also be seen as a foundation stone for the various programs of human rights education called for by the World Conference on Human Rights, held in Vienna in 1993, and promoted by international agencies. Nevertheless, the rights of the child have not always been given the prominence they require in the context of such activities. Human rights education should provide information on the content of human rights treaties. But children should also learn about human rights by seeing human rights standards implemented in practice, whether at home, in school, or within the community. Human rights education should be a comprehensive, lifelong process and start with the reflection of human rights values in the daily life and experiences of children.

- In 2002, the UN General Assembly proclaimed "the ten-year period beginning on 1 January 2005 the United Nations Decade of Education for Sustainable Development" (A/RES/57/254).[64]

- In 2004, the UN General Assembly took note of "the achievements and shortcomings of the United Nations Decade for Human Rights Education, 1995–2004" and proclaimed "the World Programme for Human Rights Education, structured in consecutive phases, scheduled to begin on 1 January 2005, in order to advance the implementation of human rights education programmes in all sectors" (Resolution 59/113).[65] The fourth phase is ongoing (2020–2024).[66]
- In 2011, the UN General Assembly adopted the United Nations Declaration on Human Rights Education and Training (A/RES/66/137).[67]
- In 2012, the UN General Assembly adopted a Resolution on Education for Democracy (A/RES/67/18)[68] where: "*Strongly encourages* Member States to integrate education for democracy, along with civic education and human rights education, into national education standards".

Therefore, the universal and most general normative framework of human rights education is formed by the following legal instruments and provisions:
- UN Charter, 1945 (especially Articles 1.3, 55.a and 56)
- UNESCO's Constitution, 1945 (especially Preamble and Article 1.1)
- UDHR, 1948 (especially Preamble and Article 26.2)
- ICESCR, 1966 (especially Article 13.1)
- CRC, 1989 (especially Articles 29.1 and 42)

The main universal specific normative framework of human rights education is developed in the following instruments:
- Recommendation on Education for International Understanding and Co-operation and Peace and Education relating to Human Rights and Fundamental Freedoms (UNESCO, 1974)
- Declaration and Integrated Framework of Action on Education for Peace, Human Rights and Democracy (UNESCO, 1995)
- United Nations Declaration on Human Rights Education and Training (2011)

In the European continent, the umbrella-concept, common to the European Union and the Council of Europe, has been *European dimension of education*.[69] In 2010, a Council of Europe Charter on Education for Democratic Citizenship and Human Rights Education[70] was adopted.

The legislative and programmatic activities of the UN and other IGOs in the field of human rights education is perhaps the most extensive chapter of IEL.[71]

5.2.3.3 Broad Conception

Despite its title, the scope and content of the UNESCO 1974 Recommendation are far-reaching. It refers to "international education", "international dimension" of education, "international and inter-cultural understanding", "study of the major problems of mankind", "solving the world problems affecting the individuals' and communities' life", "ethical and civic aspects", "cultural aspects" of learning, training and action.

According to the UNESCO 1995 Integrated Framework: "Strategies relating to education for peace, human rights and democracy must [...] be comprehensive and holistic, which means addressing a very broad range of factors" (para. 14.a).

The former UNESCO Advisory Committee on Education for Peace, Human Rights, Democracy, International Understanding and Tolerance affirmed in the Final Report of its Fifth Session (2000)[72]:

> 3. ... The Committee addressed the question of the holistic concept of education for a culture of peace in the widest sense of the term. Global education covered education for human rights, peace, international understanding, tolerance and non-violence. It also covered all aspects of education relating to the principles of democracy and multicultural and intercultural education. Turning more specifically to human rights education, the Committee noted that those rights, based on human dignity, were not only principles but also ethical values which were at the very core of any strategy for a culture of peace. It was not enough merely to list or learn them; it was an everyday practical application that made those values a reality, soundly anchored in society. [...]
>
> The different approaches to the subject (such as "global" education, education for peace, education for human rights and democracy, civics education, education with an international/intercultural vocation, education for tolerance or non-violence, etc.) and the link existing between that education and an integrated development concept, were examined.

The Final *Communiqué* of the Ministerial Round Table on Quality Education which took place during the 32nd Session of the UNESCO General Conference (2003),[73] read:

> 2. We understand that the concept of quality education is necessarily dynamic but, through our discussions, we agree that the following perspectives need to be taken into account:
>
> [...]
>
> b. There is a need to stress democratic citizenship, values, and solidarity as important outcomes of holistic education. Education for human rights and sustainable development is essential.

[...]

5. Steering education systems towards greater quality is a complex endeavor involving a number of processes of change. [...] States have found that various initiatives contribute to overall quality improvement:

   [...]

   e. Equipping all children with universally shared ethical and moral values in order to enable them to learn and practice these values of empathy, compassion, honesty, integrity, non-violence, respect for diversities, thus learning to live together in peace and harmony.

According to the Plan of Action for the First Phase (2005–2007) of the World Programme for Human Rights Education[74]:

3. ... human rights education can be defined as education, training and information aiming at building a universal culture of human rights through the sharing of knowledge, imparting of skills and molding of attitudes directed to:
   a. The strengthening of respect for human rights and fundamental freedoms;
   b. The full development of the human personality and the sense of its dignity;
   c. The promotion of understanding, tolerance, gender equality and friendship among all nations, indigenous peoples and racial, national, ethnic, religious and linguistic groups;
   d. The enabling of all persons to participate effectively in a free and democratic society governed by the rule of law;
   e. The building and maintenance of peace; and
   f. The promotion of people-centred sustainable development and social justice.

4. Human rights education encompasses:
   a. *Knowledge and skills* – learning about human rights and mechanisms for their protection, as well as acquiring skills to apply them in daily life;
   b. *Values, attitudes and behaviour* – developing values and reinforcing attitudes and behavior which uphold human rights;
   c. *Action* – taking action to defend and promote human rights.

Following the "Guidelines for the Preparation of Reports by Member States on the Application of Recommendation on Education for International Understanding and Cooperation and Peace and Education relating to Human Rights and Fundamental Freedoms (1974)", issued by UNESCO Executive Board in 2016 (199 EX/14 PART I IV, Annexe, A.3)[75]:

> The 1974 Recommendation is applicable to formal, non-formal and informal education and to all levels, from pre-primary to higher and adult education and lifelong learning. It concerns areas such as civics and ethics education, education for international understanding, solidarity and cooperation and/or other related subjects, such as peace education, human rights education or other areas of study that focus or include the teaching and learning of the above principles. Over time, these areas have evolved to include other topics related to education on sustainable development, climate change, global citizenship, preventing violent extremism, or others, which are also closely related to the original principles of the 1974 Recommendation.

Therefore, the conception of human rights education has evolved, and its content has ramified, diversified, expanded. At the times of the League of Nations, Heerdt-Quarles (1929), Dutch pacifist, referred to the need of a "practical system of *moral, civic and international education* for youth" (p. 6). The present holistic conception of human rights education may be described as an ethical education with civic and international dimensions, covering individual, social and international life.

- It is an ethical education aimed at knowing and adhering to the Ethics of Human Rights as Common Ethics of Humanity that may be summarised in the rights-principles highlighted above (see 2.6.2).
- It has a civic dimension, as human rights are the most fundamental rights of citizens, in democracies, with implications for all forms and places of daily citizenship, making necessary various learnings, including education for global citizenship.
- It has an international dimension, as the respect of human rights is the condition of peace and leaven of justice, as stated by the founding texts of the contemporary international legal order that are the UN Charter (1945) and the UDHR (1948).

This broad, holistic conception of human rights education may be figured as a set of concentric circles, whose centre is the right to education.

Human rights education, as an ethical, civic, international education, consists of values, knowledge, competencies, sentiments, attitudes, behaviours, that is, it has cognitive, emotional and praxeological dimensions. It should be experiential, transdisciplinary, but also requires specific learning. While each subject matter of human rights education has its own history and thematic specificity, there is a substratum common to them. To put it into practice, all creativity is welcome, but it is not necessary to "try to reinvent the wheel" (Alfredsson, 2001, p. 278). There are international normative and programmatic texts with methodological guidelines. They allow for a conception of a Pedagogy of ethical, civic and international education conceived as a theory of its necessity, aims, contents, methodology (principles, activities, resources) and organisation.

5.2.3.4 A Crucial Right

President Truman said at the Closing Session of the San Francisco Conference, on 26 June 1945, let us recall: "It is easier to remove tyrants and destroy concentration camps than it is to kill the ideas which gave them birth and strength".[76] Therefore: "Knowledge of human rights law and the values on which it rests should be a required element of everyone's education" (Mayerfeld, 2009, p. 80). However: "Many lawyers across the globe still pass through law school without obtaining any education in human rights law" (Marks, 2011, p. 55), particularly about their international dimension (see Boerefijn, 2009, p. 591). Where education is concerned, the situation is worse.

As stated, the "Sexennial report on the progress achieved in the implementation of the Recommendation concerning Education for International Understanding, Co-operation and Peace and Education relating to Human Rights and Fundamental Freedoms (1974)" (26 C/32),[77] in 1991, "apart from the international legal validity of human rights, they may be considered as the basis of a universal ethics to be known and conformed to by everyone who receives a formal education", because it is about the "ethical foundations of human life at personal, group, national, international and global levels" (para. 46). That is why "many of the major international human rights instruments actually establish a right to human rights education" (Alfredsson, 2001, p. 273). It has been reaffirmed by many international texts. Examples:

- In the introduction to the Resolution proclaiming the UN Decade for Human Rights Education, 1995–2004 (A/RES/49/184),[78] the General Assembly mentioned the World Plan of Action of Montreal, "according to which education for human rights and democracy is itself a human right and a prerequisite for the realization of human rights, democracy and social justice". The first general principle of its Guidelines affirmed: "Education in and for human rights is a fundamental human right" (II-A, para. 16).[79]
- The Plan of Action for the First Phase (2005–2007) of the World Programme for Human Rights Education (Resolution A/59/113 B)[80] recalled: "Human rights education is widely considered to be an integral part of the right to education" (para. 15).

- The United Nations Declaration on Human Rights Education and Training (2011)[81] begins by proclaiming (Article 1.1): "Everyone has the right to know, seek and receive information about all human rights and fundamental freedoms and should have access to human rights education and training".

Because "preventing a fire is always cheaper than having to extinguish one", Nowak (2003) wrote: "Human rights should be imprinted on the hearts and minds of everyone in a process of life-long learning as well as being practiced in our day-to-day behaviour towards our fellow human beings" (pp. 30, 347). In effect, human rights are foremostly learnt in the daily experience of their respect at home, in school, in other institutions and social life in general. Eleanor Roosevelt pointed out on 27 March 1958, presenting *IN YOUR HANDS: A Guide for Community Action for the Tenth Anniversary of the Universal Declaration of Human Rights*, in the UN Headquarters (New York)[82]:

> Where, after all, do universal human rights begin? In small places, close to home – so close and so small that they cannot be seen on any maps of the world. Yet they are the world of the individual person; the neighborhood he lives in; the school or college he attends; the factory, farm or office where he works. Such are the places where every man, woman, and child seek equal justice, equal opportunity, equal dignity without discrimination. Unless these rights have meaning there, they have little meaning anywhere. Without concerned citizen action to uphold them close to home, we shall look in vain for progress in the larger world.

In the text presenting the Delors Report (1996), titled "Education: the necessary Utopia", Jacques Delors wrote:

> ... the Commission has put greater emphasis on one of the four pillars that it proposes and describes as the foundations of education: *learning to live together* [...]. Utopia, some might think, but it is a necessary Utopia [...]. It is no exaggeration on the Commission's part to say that the survival of humanity depends thereon.

The present reality, however, is not very different from that which was confirmed by a survey published for more than three decades by UNESCO (1985): "The general impression resulting from the answers given is that, in spite of the numerous recommendations, resolutions and commitments, human rights continue to be the poor relative in the world of education" (para. 15). All countries are more or less underdeveloped in this respect. States, in general, do not even do the minimum: circulating key international human rights instruments, particularly in schools.

The texts adopted by the International Community on the matter recommend with growing insistence the inclusion of human rights education in family and school education, as well as in other education and training institutions and places, for all ages, especially for some professions more sensitive in regard to the respect of human rights – such as the military, judges, lawyers, law enforcement officers, physicians, education professionals, social workers, etc. According to the Declaration on the Right and Responsibility of Individuals, Groups and Organs of Society to Promote and Protect Universally Recognized Human Rights and Fundamental Freedoms (UN, 1998)[83]:

> Article 15
>
> The State has the responsibility to promote and facilitate the teaching of human rights and fundamental freedoms at all levels of education and to ensure that all those responsible for training lawyers, law enforcement officers, the personnel of the armed forces and public officials include appropriate elements of human rights teaching in their training program.

Referring to education and training for those working with children, the CoRC said in its GC 5 (CRC/GC/2003/5)[84]:

> 53. ... The purpose of training is to emphasize the status of the child as a holder of human rights, to increase knowledge and understanding of the Convention and to encourage active respect for all its provisions. The Committee expects to see the Convention reflected in professional training curricula and codes of conduct and educational curricula at all levels. [...]
> 54. ... The Convention highlights the importance of the family in its Preamble and in many articles. It is particularly important that the promotion of children's rights should be integrated into preparation for parenthood and parenting education. [...]
> 66. Individuals need to know what their rights are. Traditionally in most, if not all, societies children have not been regarded as rights holders. So, Article 42 acquires particular importance. If the adults around children, their parents and other family members, teachers and careers do not understand the implications of the Convention, and above all its confirmation of the equal status of children

> as subjects of rights, it is most unlikely that the rights set out in the Convention will be realized for many children.

Human rights education, as an ethical, civic, international education, lies at the heart of quality education. "The acquisition of knowledge about human rights values should be at the forefront of any discourse on quality education", wrote the former (Kishore Singh) Special Rapporteur on the Right to Education (A/HRC/20/21, 2012, para. 18).[85] It is not less important than to learn reading, writing, mathematics or informatics. It is a matter of learning universal values and principles of good and evil, right and wrong, the desirable and the undesirable, giving sense to the individual life and regulating living in communities, with their plurality and diversity. It is about closing the gap between scientific and moral progress. The scientific and technological progress are fabulous creations of the human genius that are extraordinarily and increasingly enhancing our longevity, wellbeing, happiness, but how many and unspeakable evils do they cause when applied without the highest moral conscience?

In sum: Human rights education, as an ethical, civic, international education, is an element of the right to education that is crucial for every human being, all societies and the whole Humanity, because:

- The powers that the human species has conquered over nature and itself are already so powerful that their misuse may violate its very essence and threaten its survival.
- It is in their values and sentiments that lives the *soul* of human beings and cultures and lies the *immortality* of the species …
- Human rights education means a kind of implantation of the symbolic prosthesis of the species' very *humanness.*

In the era of Globalisation and of so many threats for the present and future, a vital and irreplaceable mission of the school is the communication to the new generations of fundamental values for the protection and reproduction of the ethical identity and unity of the human species while respecting the real, legitimate and rich diversity of its members. It is a matter of preventing, nowadays, that "the Stone Age returns upon the gleaming wings of science", as Winston Churchill warned (quoted by John Polanyi, in Danieli & Stamatopoulou & Dias, 1999: xi). Indeed, it is an "eternal truth that barbarity is never behind us but under us", as recalled Sir David Maxwell-Fyfe (who participated as Prosecutor in the Nuremberg trials and the creation of the Council of Europe), during the *travaux preparatoires* of the ECHR (as cited in Modinos, 1975, p. 699). Auschwitz "was a great machine to reduce us to beasts", wrote Primo Levi (1958), who spent about a year there (p. 39). It has become the symbol of *Absolute Evil*. That is why Theodor Adorno (1984) emphasised dramatically:

> The premier demand upon all education is that Auschwitz not happen again. [...] Every debate about the ideals of education is trivial and inconsequential compared to this single ideal: never again Auschwitz.

Nie Wieder!/Never Again!/Plus Jamais! – reads a monument erected in the first Nazi concentration camp, in Dachau, Bavaria, opened by Heinrich Himmler in 1933. It is an imperative resounding as the epitaph of a Modernity without meta-political values and principles of legitimacy and goodness. As proclaimed Charles Chaplin in the final speech of *The Great Dictator*, in 1940[86]:

> Machinery that gives abundance has left us in want.
> Our knowledge has made us cynical; our cleverness, hard and unkind.
> We think too much and feel too little.
> More than machinery, we need humanity.
> More than cleverness, we need kindness and gentleness.
> Without these qualities, life will be violent, and all will be lost.

5.3 Educational Rights

Educational Rights are rights of "every person" – child, youth, adult, man or woman – formally recognised or implicit or relating to conditions of realisation of the right to education. They are foremostly the rights of children and adolescents within the two main institutions of education that are family and school.

Educational rights are often placed under three headings: rights *to*, *in* and *through* education. They may be summed up as follows:

- Right to pedagogical responsibility
- Right to be different
- Right to respect for human dignity and rights in education
- Right to learn the and in the mother tongue
- Right to the whole object of the right to education
- Right to a right to education school
- Right to admirable education professionals
- Right to an effective remedy

These rights are more or less briefly justified next.

5.3.1 *Right to Pedagogical Responsibility*

The first right of the subject of the right to education, as a child, is the right to the responsibility of adults, primarily of mother and father. It is right to protection, of course, but also right both to pedagogical love and to pedagogical authority.

There is not a 'right to love', as we know (see 3.3.2). However, insofar as the educational relation has an axial affective dimension, it can be argued that there is a *pedagogical right* to a *pedagogical love*. How to love pedagogically?

Parents' love is unique, but may be problematic. They are generally deemed to want good for their children, but what is best for children may not be what parents deem to be so. They love them in the way they know, they need, they can ... When they treat children as biological 'property', it is a possessive love that may be repressive or permissive:

- Repressive love is a symptom of immaturity of adults in need of exercising power over *minors* to feel themselves *majors*, or a feeling founded in religious or other convictions legitimising the 'appropriation' of children by parents. This authoritarian love has been the perfect *alibi* (almost always sincere) of the *pedagogical violence* crossing the history of education as a chain of reproduction of violence among human beings.
- Permissive love is that motivated by psychological weakness or fear of losing children, making mothers and fathers 'hostages' of their whims and insolence. Some parents treat their child "as an object, a beloved domestic animal, if not even as a circus animal" (Dolto, 1985, p. 379) or as "object of erotic possession" (Dolto, 1984, p. 274).

Whenever parents try to moor their children by means of repression or permissiveness, it may happen that they break the moorings and go out, do not come back, and sink. The sole legitimate and secure moorings are those of a liberating affection. Loving children, adolescents and young is to give them the best we know and have; to desire that they know what we did not know; that they have what we had not; that they are what we could not be; to allow them to drink from the bowl of the nectar of their age; to let them go so that they return ...

A child has a vital need for adults' love that it be an *adult love*, that is, not a drive of property, but passion for liberty. The right to be treated as equal and different by adults who are equal, but different. In effect, if the principle of the legitimacy of education, as a human right, should not be the *law of the strongest*, it should not be the *law of the weakest*, either. Education is not a matter of knacks, however, it is a deep moral responsibility. The right to education is the right both to the *yes* and to the *no* – said by respectable and respected adults

– which are indispensable to the child's protection and learning liberty, reciprocity and responsibility that implies the exercise of authority.

An authoritarian educator does not educate, but neither does one who is not respected. The alternative to authoritarianism is not laxity without borders and horizons. And when the results of the dissolution of the dialectic of love-authority are increasingly appearing – especially when children publicly exhibit uncontrolled capricious or insolent behaviours that they are allowed in private – one often hears: "children are thus", "he has been so since a baby" ... *Thus* are children who have learnt to be *thus* with fathers and mothers who are *thus* ... In this connection, Rousseau (1762a) remarked that adults responsible for these "ordinary educations" (p. 481) do what they do "and then they tell us seriously: 'Such is the man'. Yes, such is man, as you have made him" (p. 110).

When parents do not assume the authority necessary to carry out their responsibility, they lose credibility and respectability. Then, there is a sole alternative: either continuing to increasingly become hostages of the child they did not know to help to be autonomous; or to try to correct past mistakes and to control the child hostage to himself/herself, but at the expense of principles whose application, at the appropriate time, would have been preventive. Children may be punished for behaviours resulting from the irresponsibility of adults ...

The main resource of the pedagogical authority should be words, from the very beginning. For that, it is necessary that educators learn to say the right word, at the opportune moment, and respect their words. Otherwise, this induces a kind of psychological deafness which obliges to multiply and even to shout the words. And when adults get involved in Homeric discussions with children the scene is pathetic ...

The most rational and humanising communication is dialogue, demanded by the essential fact of human intersubjectivity, because human beings are relational and communicational beings. Dialogue is all the more authentic when it respects and values the alterity and transcends reciprocity. It is also the most educational communication to the extent that it harmonises the value of authority with the value of liberty. All education should be dialogic for ethical, psychological, epistemological, methodological and political reasons.

However, words are not the last word in education ... Everything is significant for a child, in particular, nothing is indifferent to him/her in the behaviours of surrounding adults. It is the everyday attitudes of mothers and fathers and other educators that sow the values and principles of education.

According to Jonas (1979), political and pedagogical responsibilities, which are principally the governmental and parental responsibilities, "share some properties wherein the essence of responsibility appears most completely, putting them before all other". The most important of such properties is *totality* that means, as already noticed by Aristotle, that it involves "the whole being of their objects, that is to say, all their aspects, from the mere existence until the highest interests". Also, governmental and parental responsibilities are oriented towards the *future*, individual and collective as well, deeply interpenetrated. Yet, it is the parental responsibility "that is really – in time and by essence – the archetype of any responsibility [...]. Its object is the totality of the child with all his/her possibilities" (pp. 145–151).

Paul Ricoeur (1994) agreed: "The pattern of the parental responsibility is obviously exemplary. The child I take the charge of protecting, of making to grow, is a fragile being, and my responsibility is to lead him/her to maturity, so that he/she can be able later, in turn, of becoming responsible and taking somebody in charge. The idea of charge is, here, absolutely central" (p. 25). Jean-Marie Domenach (1994) expressed a similar opinion:

> In any case, whoever assumes a risk should know that he or she assumes two: the first one regards the consequences of their actions; the second one regards their imitation by others [...]. Some professions are more exposed to such a risk than others: those of teacher, priest, statesman ..., and even more the parents. 'The risk is the example', said Victor Hugo. Example, that is to say, the influence a personality exerts, often against one's will. Such is really the most frightening responsibility: that that we assume with a phrase, a gesture, in relation to persons that, sometimes, we do not even know. [...] The parental responsibility is, no doubt, the heaviest one, and it is understandable that it frightens so many parents, which refuse it or pass it to others. (p. 19)

Pedagogical responsibility is, therefore, the responsibility of educators for the right of children to education with its affective and normative dimensions, i.e. as a right both to pedagogical love and to pedagogical authority.

In sum:

- Pedagogical is the *love* that knows the need children have of authority for the formation of their personality. It is perhaps *the most difficult love.*
- Pedagogical is the *authority* that, being respectful, is felt as an expression of love. Knowing how to exercise it is perhaps *the most important knowledge for educators.*

5.3.2 *Right to Be Different*

After the right to the pedagogical responsibility of adults, as a child, the most *nourishing* right of the subject of the right to education, as a human being, is the right to be different. It was first proclaimed, at the universal level, in the

Declaration on Race and Racial Prejudice (UNESCO, 1978),[88] whose Article 1.2 reads: "All individuals and groups have the right to be different, to consider themselves as different and to be regarded as such". Its international legal basis is still rather soft, however.

The right to be different has a collective and an individual dimension, but the first one is so far the most juridically recognised, as in the following international instruments[89]:

- Declaration on the Rights of Persons Belonging to National or Ethnic, Religious and Linguistic Minorities (UN, 1992),[90] Article 1.1:

> States shall protect the existence and the national or ethnic, cultural, religious and linguistic identity of minorities within their respective territories and shall encourage conditions for the promotion of that identity.

- Universal Declaration on Cultural Diversity (UNESCO, 2001),[91] Article 1:

> Culture takes diverse forms across time and space. This diversity is embodied in the uniqueness and plurality of the identities of the groups and societies making up humankind. As a source of exchange, innovation and creativity, cultural diversity is as necessary for humankind as biodiversity is for nature. In this sense, it is the common heritage of humanity and should be recognized and affirmed for the benefit of present and future generations.

- United Nations Declaration on the Rights of Indigenous Peoples (UN, 2007)[92]: "Indigenous peoples have the right to determine their own identity or membership in accordance with their customs and traditions" (Article 33.1). Therefore: "Indigenous peoples have the right to the dignity and diversity of their cultures, traditions, histories and aspirations which shall be appropriately reflected in education and public information" (Article 15.1).

Because human dignity may be captured by collective representations not compatible with the respect of human rights, and also because the right to be different may be invoked to justify violations of others' human rights, its recognition is always accompanied by a clause safeguarding the primacy of its individual dimension and thus the respect for human rights, reverberating the canonical clause laid down in the DUDH Article 30[93]: "Nothing in this Declaration may be interpreted as implying for any State, group or person any right to engage in any activity or to perform any act aimed at the destruction of any of the rights and freedoms set forth herein". For example:

- Declaration on the Rights of Persons Belonging to National or Ethnic, Religious and Linguistic Minorities (UN, 1992),[94] Article 8.2: "The exercise of the rights set forth in the present Declaration shall not prejudice the enjoyment by all persons of universally recognized human rights and fundamental freedoms".
- Universal Declaration on Cultural Diversity (UNESCO, 2001),[95] Article 4: "No one may invoke cultural diversity to infringe upon human rights guaranteed by international law, nor to limit their scope".
- Convention on the Protection and Promotion of the Diversity of Cultural Expressions (UNESCO, 2005),[96] Article 2.1: "No one may invoke the provisions of this Convention in order to infringe human rights and fundamental freedoms as enshrined in the Universal Declaration of Human Rights or guaranteed by international law, or to limit the scope thereof".
- Protocol to the African Charter on Human and People's Rights on the Rights of Women in Africa (African Union, 2003),[97] Article 5: "States Parties shall prohibit and condemn all forms of harmful practices which negatively affect the human rights of women and which are contrary to recognised international standards".

The individual differences are not chosen and chosen:
- Differences not chosen are principally the inborn ones, including physical or mental handicaps, and many cultural ones.
- Differences chosen are those resulting from the free development of the aptitudes, interests and options of each one.

The clearest and bold recognition of the individual right to be different is found in two of the "General principles" laid down in the Convention on the Rights of Persons with Disabilities (UN, 2006),[98] Article 3:

> d. Respect for difference and acceptance of persons with disabilities as part of human diversity and humanity;
> [...]
> h. Respect for the evolving capacities of children with disabilities and respect for the right of children with disabilities to preserve their identities.

As it results from the above quoted provisions, the right to be different implies the right to the identity formed by differences.

The collective and individual dimensions of differences and identity are interwoven because the family, community and culture within which a human being is born moulds the individual identity. The family, inscription in a lineage, is the source, the foundation of its construction. It is the *genealogical imperative* (Pierre Légendre). Vincent de Gaulejac (2001) wrote:

> The individual identity consists of a family name, sign of filiation, and the forename, a sign of singularity, but bearer, however, of the traits of the aspirations of parents and ascendants. [...]
>
> In fact, there is a permanent dialectic between the inherited identity and the acquired identity, between diachrony and synchrony [...]. In this sense, the individual is the product of a story of which it strives to become subject. (p. 358)

The right to be different and to the corresponding identity are, therefore, twin-rights. Their foundation is clearly stated in the following international instruments:

- Universal Declaration on the Human Genome and Human Rights (UNESCO, 1997),[99] Article 1: "The human genome underlies the fundamental unity of all members of the human family, as well as the recognition of their inherent dignity and diversity. In a symbolic sense, it is the heritage of humanity". Therefore, "dignity makes it imperative not to reduce individuals to their genetic characteristics and to respect their uniqueness and diversity" (Article 2.b).
- International Declaration on Human Genetic Data (UNESCO, 2003),[100] Article 3 (Person's identity):

> Each individual has a characteristic genetic make-up. Nevertheless, a person's identity should not be reduced to genetic characteristics, since it involves complex educational, environmental and personal factors and emotional, social, spiritual and cultural bonds with others and implies a dimension of freedom.

The individual identity is, thus multifaceted and then a trans/interdisciplinary concept. The Universal Declaration on Bioethics and Human Rights (UNESCO, 2005)[101] recalls "that a person's identity includes biological, psychological, social, cultural and spiritual dimensions" (Preamble). In effect, each human being is a bundle of identities, with physical and symbolic markers, objective and subjective, which cause the *first impression* ... They are mainly the following ones:

- *Biological identity* is the identity *possessed* by the human species' children. It has a common genetic content and a singular genealogic one.

- *Ethical identity* is the identity *recognised* to every human being, just for being human. It consists in the recognition of his/her dignity and rights.
- *Cultural identity* is the identity *learnt* within the culture where each one grows. It is simultaneously spontaneous and compulsive learning.
- *Civic identity* is the identity *attributed* to each newborn by parents and the respective society (essentially the name, filiation, and nationality).

Consequently, in addition to its civic dimension – that is the most legally recognised (CRC Articles 7 and 8: name, nationality, parents) – the individual identity has an objective dimension (biological), an intersubjective dimension (ethical), a trans-subjective dimension (cultural) and a subjective dimension (psychological). The psychological identity is the crystallisation of the individual identity as a composition of multiple identities, resulting from a diachronic and dialectic construction of socialisation and autonomisation. It is a feeling of uniqueness, unity and continuity – a dynamic and evolutionary identity, variable with the ages of life and social positions.

Education – as a right to free, full and harmonious development of the human personality – lies at the heart of the right to be different. In its comments on the first draft Convention on the Rights of the Child (E/CN.4/1324, 27 December 1978),[102] UNESCO proposed that the Convention should: "Mention, in particular, the right to be different as defined in Article 1, paragraph 2, of the draft Declaration on Race and Racial Prejudice". Nevertheless, Santos Pais wrote, referring to the CRC, as above quoted: "The child is therefore recognized in his or her fundamental dignity and individuality, with the right to be different and differ in his or her assessment of reality" (United Nations, 1997, p. 446). As the right to education is concerned, the first Special Rapporteur on the Right to Education commented in her last Report (E/CN.4/2004/45)[103]:

> 54. ... International human rights law demands substitution of the previous requirement upon children to adapt themselves to whatever education was available by adapting education to the best interests of each child. In our imperfect world, the right of each child to be regarded – and respected – as different remains a distant dream.

The right to education should include, in particular:
- the right of the child to the difference of his/her age, first and foremost, that is the right to enjoy the happiness and irresponsibility of childhood;
- the right of every subject of the right to education to respect for their differences not chosen and the differences they should be allowed to choose, lifelong.

In their study on *Human rights in children's literature,* Jonathan Todres and Sarah Higinbotham, after having reviewed more than five hundred children's books, and drawing on research on literary studies and human rights education, make "the case that children's literature can be a powerful means of explicating human rights norms and educating children on their own rights and their responsibilities toward others in a democratic society", thus contributing to a human rights culture (Todres & Higinbotham, 2016, pp. xviii, 16, 19). An example is *The Story of Ferdinand,* a young bull that preferred smelling flowers to the violence of bullfighting. This book, translated into more than sixty languages and adapted as a short Disney animated and prized film in 1938, was admired by such great personalities as Thomas Mann, H. G. Wells, and Gandhi, but was banned by the Spanish dictator Francisco Franco and Nazi Germany. "Ferdinand functions as a metaphor for a child's right to develop her own distinct identity, even when that identity does not conform to the mainstream or further the national agenda" (p. 96).

The school teacher Louis Germain, writing the last letter to his "little Camus", from Algiers, on 30 April 1959, said: "I believe that throughout my career I have respected what is most sacred in a child: the right to seek out his own truth".[104]

In conclusion:

- Cultures are not isolated, homogeneous, static units, but dynamic and increasingly interacting complexes of beliefs, values, ways of living (see World Commission on Culture and Development, 1995).
- A culture is a collective enduring cradle, music unforgettable, symbolic milk, but not a frontier, a destiny, imposing an obligation of identification and making human beings hostages of the culture in which they are born.
- The inevitability of learning a cultural identity should not prevent the liberty to create an original personal identity, open to the universal treasure of the fabulous human diversity.
- The right to be different is crucial for Humanity in the making, because it is by means of education that it is reborn and can perfect itself, through their children, if they are not dispossessed of their right to be different and better.

5.3.3 *Right to Respect for Human Dignity and Rights in Education*

The right to be different is inseparable from the principle of equality by dignity and rights.

In the IEL we find rare references to teaching methods, but it is very concerned with the educational discipline both in family and school. In education, as in social life in general, rules are needed whose non-observance justifies sanctions. They are legitimate to the extent that they do not harm the values to be promoted.

The exercise of human rights in schools – both by pupils/students and by teachers – may be subject to legitimate restrictions, but their regulations should recognise and respect the individual rights whose exercise is not incompatible with the respect for the rights of others, the security of the school settings and the accomplishment of the school mission.

In *Case Çölgeçen and Others v. Turkey* (Applications 50124/07, 53082/07, 53865/07, 399/08, 776/08, 1931/08, 2213/08 e 2953/08), in 2017,[105] the European Court of Human Rights underlined:

> 50. … that the right to education does not in principle exclude recourse to disciplinary measures such as suspension or expulsion from an educational institution in order to ensure compliance with its internal rules. […]
>
> 51. However, such regulations must not injure the substance of the right or conflict with other rights enshrined in the Convention or its Protocols (see *İrfan Temel and Others*, cited above, § 45).

Therefore, school sanctions should not disproportionately affect the right to education or violate other rights of students. For example, the temporary suspension of school attendance is legitimate if its duration is not excessive and difficult to overcome, but the definitive expulsion of a student of compulsory schooling breaches the right to education if he or she cannot attend another school. This is the opinion of the CoRC that, in its Concluding Observations on a New Zealand report (CRC/C/15/Add.216, 27 October 2003),[106] recommended: "*Enforce legislation on compulsory education and prohibit exclusions on arbitrary grounds such as pregnancy, and ensure that students of the age of compulsory education who have legitimately been excluded from a school are enrolled elsewhere*" (para. 44.b). And even in a Case where the constitutionality of a ban imposed on students expelled from a higher education institution for disciplinary reasons prevented them from enrolling in another one was at stake, the Constitutional Court of Turkey considered, in 2011, that a sanction so absolute violated the very essence of the right to education and was disproportionate (Venice Commission, Bulletin 2011, 2, p. 381).[107]

Examples of sanctions involving the violation of other rights include deprivations of lunch or of rest time and recreation. And, typically, the traditional corporal punishment that has been the most traditional and general methodological principle of education, recommended from generation to generation through well-known proverbs (see 4.8.1).[108]

In addition to these and other abusive and disrespectful sanctions, other violence may contribute to making schools fearful and even dangerous places:

taunting, humiliation, harassment, aggression, whose frequent targets include children from poor backgrounds and other more vulnerable, such as children with disability, Roma children and minority children. Following the *School Violence and Bullying: Global Status Report*, issued by UNESCO in 2017[109]:

> School violence, which includes physical, psychological and sexual violence and bullying, occurs in all countries. The root causes include gender and social norms and wider structural and contextual factors such as income inequality, deprivation, marginalisation and conflict. It is estimated that 246 million children and adolescents experience school violence in some form every year. Available data from Europe, North America and Australasia suggests that bullying is the most common form of school violence and, hence, this report considers bullying as a separate issue. However, physical violence, including corporal punishment by teachers, is common in many countries in other regions. (p. 12)

Moreover, children and young people have a right not merely to formally 'participate' in what adults decide for them, but also to be involved in decision-making itself concerning their right to education, both at home and school, as provided for by CRC Article 12, in particular. Real participation rights include the right to freedom of thought, expression, association, including the expressions of their personality not incompatible with respect for school institutional dignity, safety and well-functioning, and other public values (see 5.2.2). As already quoted, the CoRC pointed out in its first GC (CRC/GC/2001/1)[110]: "Children do not lose their human rights by virtue of passing through the school gates" (para. 8). These words evoke those of the US Supreme Court in *Case Tinker v. Des Moines Independent Community School District 393 U.S. 503, 1969*)[111]:

> First Amendment rights, applied in light of the special characteristics of the school environment, are available to teachers and students. It can hardly be argued that either students or teachers shed their constitutional rights to freedom of speech or expression at the schoolhouse gate. This has been the unmistakable holding of this Court for almost 50 years. [...]
>
> In our system, State-operated schools may not be enclaves of totalitarianism. School officials do not possess absolute authority over their students. Students in school, as well as out of school, are "persons" under our Constitution. They are possessed of fundamental rights which the State must respect, just as they themselves must respect their obligations to the State. (506, 511)

Disrespect for children's and young persons' dignity and rights at school is not only a potential cause of learning disaffection, underperformance, school dropout, early marriage, but also a factor of risk and disruptive behaviour, including tobacco, alcohol and drug consumption, aggressivity against peers and teachers, social delinquency, as well as vulnerability to various forms of exploitation, such as sexual abuse, prostitution, forced labour, enrolment and use in armed conflict, etc.

5.3.4 *Right to Learn the and in the Mother Tongue*

As already noted, the major international provisions on the right to education do not entail a linguistic dimension. The linguistic accessibility (see 4.2.2.3.3.2) deserves to be included in its core content (see 4.2.2.3.3.1), however.

Following the already mentioned Global Campaign for Education Police Brief[112]:

> In developing countries, an estimated 221 million children enter the classroom unable to understand the language they are taught in. Many countries teach in the old colonial language, or in a dominant national or international language, which young children do not speak at home. [...]
>
> It is now well-established through research that children who receive schooling in their mother tongue language in early grades have better learning outcomes overall and, in particular, significantly better literacy levels. Despite increasingly overwhelming evidence of the value and benefits of early education in mother-tongue, few countries invest in it.

The mother tongue is one of the deepest elements of cultural identity, "for a people's language is perhaps its most fundamental cultural attribute" (World Commission on Culture and Development, 1995, p. 59). ICCPR[113] Article 27 recognises to "ethnic, religious or linguistic minorities" the right "to use their own language" that implies learning the and in the mother tongue. CRC[114] Article 30 recognises to "a child belonging to such a minority or who is indigenous" the right "to use his or her own language". In Article 29.1.c: "States Parties agree that the education of the child shall be directed to: [...] The development of respect for [...] his or her cultural identity, language and values". The United Nations Declaration on the Rights of Indigenous Peoples (2006)[115] states: "Indigenous peoples have the right to establish and control their educational systems and institutions providing education in their own languages, in a manner appropriate to their cultural methods of teaching and learning" (Article 14.1).

However, other provisions are vague, flexible, and with loopholes, leaving to States a wide margin of discretion, as the following instruments show (italics added):

- The CADE[116] provides: "It is essential to recognize the right of members of national minorities to carry on their own educational activities, including the maintenance of schools and, *depending on the educational policy of each State*, the use or the teaching of their own language [...]" (Article 5.1.c).
- According to the Convention concerning Indigenous and Tribal Peoples in Independent Countries (ILO, C169, 1989),[117] Article 28:

> 1. Children belonging to the peoples concerned shall, *wherever practicable*, be taught to read and write in their own indigenous language or in the language most commonly used by the group to which they belong. When this is not practicable, the competent authorities shall undertake consultations with these peoples with a view to the adoption of measures to achieve this objective.

- Following the Declaration on the Rights of Persons Belonging to National or Ethnic, Religious and Linguistic Minorities (UN, 1992),[118] Article 4.3: "States should take appropriate measures so that, *wherever possible*, persons belonging to minorities may have adequate opportunities to learn their mother tongue or to have instruction in their mother tongue".
- In the European Social Charter (Revised),[119] States Parties undertake "to promote and facilitate, *as far as practicable*, the teaching of the migrant worker's mother tongue to the children of the migrant worker" (Article 19.12).

As reads the "Commentary of the working group on minorities to the United Nations Declaration on the rights of persons belonging to national or ethnic, religious and linguistic minorities" (E/CN.4/Sub.2/AC.5/2005/2, 4 April 2005)[120]:

> 28. ... Denying minorities the possibility of learning their own language and of receiving instruction in their own language, or excluding from their education the transmission of knowledge about their own culture, history, tradition and language, would be a violation of the obligation to protect their identity.

As other minority groups without national minority status, are concerned, the International Convention on the Protection of the Rights of All Migrant Workers and Members of Their Families (UN, 1990),[121] ratified only by 55 States so far (as of November 2020), provides: "States of employment *may* provide special schemes of education in the mother tongue of children of migrant workers, if necessary in collaboration with the States of origin" (Article 45.4).

In the European region, there are the European Charter for Regional or Minority Languages (Council of Europe, 1992) and the Framework Convention for the Protection of National Minorities (Council of Europe, 1995). The European Charter affirms "that the right to use a regional or minority language in private and public life is an inalienable right" (Preamble).[122]

Practice does not always follows.

The European Court of Human Rights said in the classic *Case "relating to certain aspects of the laws on the use of languages in education in Belgium v. Belgium"* (Applications 1474/62; 1677/62; 1691/62; 1769/63; 1994/63; 2126/64),[123] "that Article 14 [ECHR], even when read in conjunction with Article 2 of the [first] Protocol (Art. 14+P1-2), does not have the effect of guaranteeing to a child or to his parent the right to obtain instruction in a language of his choice" (B.11). However, the European Court admitted that "the right to education would be meaningless if it did not imply in favour of its beneficiaries, the right to be educated in the national language or in one of the national languages, as the case may be" (B.3).

The same may be said of the mother tongue when it has not national language status.

In any case, the general principle of non-discrimination is applicable. Paivi Gynther (2007), after having conducted a study to seek "from international standards the quintessence, the very core, of a sound, non-discriminatory and inclusive legal framework on education", concluded that, "seeing that universal anti-discrimination clauses recognize language relatively often as an unreasonable ground to justify discrimination, the study suggests the reading of the non-discrimination clauses and the substantive provisions together, and on that basis demands equal recognition of rights-holders from diverse language groups before the law of education" (pp. 295, 299).

On 6 June 1996, a World Conference on Linguistic Rights, gathering in Barcelona more than 200 people from more than 90 States, in all 5 continents, proclaimed a Universal Declaration of Linguistic Rights.[124]

International and national judicial or quasi-judicial bodies may pave the way to the recognition of the right to learn, not only the mother language but in the mother language too (see, for example, the decision of the European Court of Human Rights on *Case Cyprus v. Turkey*). Learning in the mother tongue, at least in early childhood and primary school, is a powerful factor of equality of opportunities. Moreover, in such a globalised world and multilingual societies, the right to education should include the right to a trilingual education: to both learn the mother tongue and in the mother tongue, at least at the first levels; to learn the or one of the national languages, if this is the case; and to learn one or more international languages. There is accumulated "evidence for the mental advantages of growing up in a bilingual or multilingual environment".[125]

In sum, the strongest and irrefutable arguments in support of the right to learn in the mother tongue, when it is different from the official language(s), are twofold:

- Mother tongue is not a choice, it is an identity inheritance.
- *If you don't understand, how can you learn?* – reads an international policy paper.[126]

5.3.5 *Right to the Whole Object of the Right to Education*

The object of the right to education covers all elements of its full and expanded content, as here understood (see 4.2.2.3.3). It follows some highlights of its wholeness.

Pre-school education

The main international provisions on the right to education do not formally include pre-school education. This is especially surprising regarding the CRC, despite proposals made during its *travaux préparatoires*, especially the following one by UNESCO:

> 1. (The) States Parties (to the present Convention) recognize the right of the child to all forms of education and, with a view to achieving the full realization of this right on the basis of equal opportunity and equal chances of success, they shall, in particular:
>
> (a) facilitate the provision of early childhood care and education, using all possible means, in particular for the disadvantaged child, in order to contribute to the young child's growth, development and to enhance his or her later success at other levels of education,[127]

In GC 7 (2005) on "Implementing child rights in early childhood", the CoRC said (CRC/C/GC/7/Rev.1)[128] CRC Article 6.2 provides[129]: "States Parties shall ensure to the maximum extent possible the survival and development of the child":

> 4. *Definition of early childhood.* Definitions of early childhood vary in different countries and regions, according to local traditions and the organization of primary school systems. In some countries, the transition from preschool to school occurs soon after 4 years old. In other countries, this transition takes place at around 7 years old. In

> its consideration of rights in early childhood, the Committee wishes to include all young children: at birth and throughout infancy; during the preschool years; as well as during the transition to school. Accordingly, the Committee proposes as an appropriate working definition of early childhood the period below the age of 8 years; States Parties should review their obligations towards young children in the context of this definition.

Where the right to education is concerned: "The Committee interprets the right to education during early childhood as beginning at birth and closely linked to young children's right to maximum development (Art. 6.2)" (para. 28).

Pre-school education is referred to in various international conventional and declaratory instruments. For instance, in Article 10.a of the Convention on the Elimination of All Forms of Discrimination against Women (UN, 1979), in Article 30 of the International Convention on the Protection of the Rights of All Migrant Workers and Members of Their Families (UN, 1990), in Article 1.3 of the International Charter of Physical Education, Physical Activity and Sport (UNESCO, 2015), other international non-binding instruments and other texts such as: World Declaration on Education for All (Jomtien, Thailand, 1990), Copenhagen Declaration on Social Development (UN, 1995), Recommendation 1286 (1996) on a 'European Strategy for Children' (Parliamentary Assembly of the Council of Europe, 1996). The first goal agreed in the Dakar Framework for Action (2000)[130] was: "expanding and improving comprehensive early childhood care and education, especially for the most vulnerable and disadvantaged children".

The UNESCO Committee on Conventions and Recommendations includes preschool education in its consultations on the implementation of the 1960 Convention. According to the "Principles and Guidelines on the Implementation of Economic, Social and Cultural Rights in the African Charter on Human and Peoples' Rights"[131] adopted by the African Commission on Human and Peoples' Rights: "The right to education encompasses pre-school, primary, secondary, tertiary, adult education and vocational training" (para. 70).

The *Global Education Monitoring Report – 2017/8*[132] informed: "In 2015, 69% of children participated in organized learning at the pre-primary or primary level one year before the official primary entry age".[133]

The resonance and value of pre-school education are now well established. According to neurobiological research: "Our first learning experiences are foundational for our later education, and experiences *in the early years of life can greatly impact on later achievement*".[134]

Higher education

Higher education is an element of the object of the right to education (see Kotzmann, 2018). In that regard, it is worth quoting what the European Court of Human Rights (Grand Chamber) said in *Case Leyla Şahin v. Turkey* (Application 44774/98, 10 November 2005)[135]:

> 134. The first sentence of Article 2 of Protocol N°. 1 [ECHR] provides that no one shall be denied the right to education. Although the provision makes no mention of higher education, there is nothing to suggest that it does not apply to all levels of education, including higher education. [...]
>
> 136. The Court does not lose sight of the fact that the development of the right to education, whose content varies from one time or place to another according to economic and social circumstances, mainly depends on the needs and resources of the community. [...] While the first sentence of Article 2 essentially establishes access to primary and secondary education, there is no watertight division separating higher education from other forms of education. [...]
>
> 137. Consequently, it would be hard to imagine that institutions of higher education existing at a given time do not come within the scope of the first sentence of Article 2 of Protocol N° 1. Although that Article does not impose a duty on the Contracting States to set up institutions of higher education, any State doing so will be under an obligation to afford an effective right of access to them. [...]
>
> 141. In the light of all the foregoing considerations, it is clear that any institutions of higher education existing at a given time come within the scope of the first sentence of Article 2 of Protocol N°. 1, since the right of access to such institutions is an inherent part of the right set out in that provision. This is not an extensive interpretation forcing new obligations on the Contracting States: it is based on the very terms of the first sentence of Article 2 of Protocol N°. 1 read in its context and having regard to the object and purpose of the Convention, a law-making treaty (see, *mutatis mutandis, Golder v. the United Kingdom*, judgment of 21 February 1975, Series A no. 18, p. 18, § 36).

States Parties' obligations concerning higher education are formally less strong, since they do not include, differently from secondary education, making education "generally available". The access may be restricted (*numerus clausus*: closed number), but it "shall be made equally accessible to all, on the basis of capacity" (see ICESCR Article 13.2c, Appendix 1), that is, regardless of economic resources and according to appropriate and objective criteria, taking into account knowledge and experience other than those certified by school diplomas.

Higher education is part of tertiary education that includes all post-secondary education, in universities, polytechnics, and other similar institutions. Tertiary education is a term used in the Convention on the Rights of Persons with Disabilities (UN, 2006), Article 24.5 (see Appendix B), and is also to be found in the *2030 Agenda for Sustainable Development* (A/RES/70/1),[136] whose *Goal 4: Ensure inclusive and equitable quality education and promote lifelong learning opportunities for all* reads (4.3): "By 2030, ensure equal access for all women and men to affordable and quality technical, vocational and tertiary education, including university".

Tertiary education has been the main target of neoliberalism in education. Many States, supported by the World Bank, have withdrawn from funding it, favouring private taking over. Others have implemented 'cost-sharing' policies, economically and socially selective. Now, a shift seems to be on the way, as the *World Development Report 2018: Learning to Realise Education's Promise*[137] notices:

> Starting in the 1950s, the Republic of Korea focused on ensuring quality primary education for the vast majority of its population before shifting to a similar emphasis on secondary and ultimately higher education – with excellent learning results. The success of this strategy shows it is possible to ensure quality education even while rapidly expanding schooling. The key ingredient is a persistent emphasis on the needs of the poor and disadvantaged. (p. 73)

Vocational education

Vocational education is an element of the object of the right to education that has gained relevance in contemporary societies.

In its Resolution 41/16 (A/HRC/41/L.26),[138] the CHR: "*Calls* upon States to promote holistic technical vocational education and training" (para. 6), i.e. not merely instrumental, without humanist and cultural perspectives and competences. The Glossary of *UNESCO Guidelines on the Recognition, Validation and Accreditation of the Outcomes of Non-formal and Informal Learning*[139] provides this definition of 'competences': "*Competences* indicate a satisfactory state of knowledge, skills and attitudes and the ability to apply them in a variety of situations". According to the Recommendation Concerning Technical and Vocational Education and Training (UNESCO, 2015)[140]:

> ... technical and vocational education and training (TVET) is understood as being part of both the universal right to education and the right to work, [...]
>
> TVET contributes towards the promotion of understanding and respect for human rights; inclusion and equity; gender equality and cultural diversity; and to the fostering of a desire and capacity for lifelong learning and learning to live together, all of which are essential to social and economic participation and to the realization of lasting peace, responsible citizenship, and sustainable development, [...]
>
> 2. TVET, as part of lifelong learning, can take place at secondary, post-secondary and tertiary levels and includes work-based learning and continuing training and professional development which may lead to qualifications. TVET also includes a wide range of skills development opportunities attuned to national and local contexts. Learning to learn and the development of literacy and numeracy skills, transversal skills and citizenship skills are integral components of TVET.

There is a UNESCO-UNEVOC International Centre for Technical and Vocational Education and Training, set up in 1999 in Bonn (Germany), following a UNESCO General Conference Resolution.[141]

Controversial and other learnings

The object of the right to education should be personally and socially relevant, not excluding controversial matters as is, for example, sexual and reproductive health education, to which the CoESCR devoted its GC 22 (E/C.12/GC/22, 2 May 2016).[142] According to the Committee:

> 9. The realization of the right to sexual and reproductive health requires that States Parties also meet their obligations under other provisions of the Covenant. For example, the right to sexual and reproductive health, combined with the right to education (Articles 13 and 14) and the right to non-discrimination and equality between men and women (Articles 2 (2) and 3), entails a right to education on sexuality and reproduction that is comprehensive, non-discriminatory, evidence-based, scientifically accurate and age appropriate.

The most uncontroversial example, perhaps, of learning required by the evolving nature of the object of the right to education is digital literacy, including to learn how to navigate the Internet's virtually infinite but dangerous ocean. In 2020, the CoESCR adopted the GC 25 "on science and economic, social and cultural rights (Article 15 (1) (b), (2), (3) and (4) of the International Covenant on Economic, Social and Cultural Rights)" (E/C.12/GC/25),[143] already quoted. It recalls that "UNESCO, declarations made at international conferences and summits, the Special Rapporteur on cultural rights, and eminent scientific organizations and publications have upheld the 'human right to science', referring to all the rights, entitlements and obligations related to science" (para. 1), which "include education policies, grants, participation tools, dissemination, providing access to the Internet and other sources of knowledge, participation in international cooperation programmes and ensuring appropriate financing" (para. 45). According to the Committee:

> 52. Core obligations related to the right to participate in and to enjoy the benefits of scientific progress and its applications require States Parties to:
> [...]
> – Ensure that people have access to the basic education and skills necessary for the comprehension and application of scientific knowledge and that scientific education in both public and private schools respects the best available scientific knowledge;
> [...]
> 63. The right to participate in and to enjoy the benefits of scientific progress and its applications is a human right with an intrinsic value, but it also has an instrumental value, as it constitutes an essential tool for the realization of other economic, social and cultural rights, particularly the right to food and the right to health.

Other learnings increasingly topical in our times include health education in general, education for global citizenship or the "ethic of global citizenship and shared responsibility" referred to in the Agenda for Sustainable Development (para. 36). And even, for instance, "the right to philosophy" (*droit à la philosophie*) to learn to endlessly question (Derrida, 1990).[144] All the questions that children can ask in classroom belong to the school curriculum, as wisely remarked the Colombian Constitutional Court (*Sentencia T-337/95*)[145]: "Questions students ask in the classroom and teachers' answers belong to the education process".

5.3.6 *Right to a Right to Education School*

School attendance is so relevant for the implementation of the right to education that it is frequently confused with the right to school. It is eminently right to school, but not to whichever school.

School is an institution that has configured modern times but, while the world and most societies have changed profoundly, its 'soul' remains in the 19th century. It falls short of meeting the demands of the challenges of our times, having become a cemetery of reforms, an incinerator of pedagogical literature ... This is why it is criticised so much, especially since the 1960s. The most disturbing criticism of school is that of its principal 'clients' – children and adolescents – reflecting their *malaise* (unease) and even revolt. They *feel* that they are entitled to another school. And they are right.

When children go to school, for the first time, their eyes twinkle but, from year to year, the desire blanches ... giving way to disliking school. School underperformance and indiscipline are chronic symptoms of the authoritarian, homogenising, reductive, and anachronistic logic of the most schools we know. The 'school success' costs, to a large extent, the renouncement of the sense of learning, and may induce the habit of renouncing to sense in general, generating conformism and passiveness, so that its human costs are no less disturbing than the individual and social costs of 'school failure'.

Here is the 'mortal sin' of school: it tends to undermine the desire and joy to learn, so denying its *raison d'être* (reason to be). As wrote Rousseau (1762a), the best method for teaching-learning is but "one which is generally overlooked, it consists in the desire to learn. Arouse this desire in your scholar and [...] any method will serve" (p. 145).[146]

School is illegitimate, irrational, pathological, when:

- it keeps working following scientific assumptions invalidated by the progress of knowledge, ignoring or devaluing, in particular, the importance of sensitivity, diversity and creativity in learning as a cultural, social, emotional phenomenon;
- it does not meet the normative integrity of the right to education, if it does not do everything it should do and does wrong much of what it does;
- it is more *suffered* as an obligation and necessary evil than *beloved* as a right and desired good;
- it contributes to the frivolousness of existence, the civic indifference, the alienating mimetism and even delinquent behaviours;
- it is unable to compete with the media and other influences;
- it shares responsibility for so many personal and social evils.

This criticism is not a manifestation of a gratuitous and sterile radicalism, it was expressed in documents adopted by Ministers of Education, as well as in international and national reports published in recent decades. For example, the 13th Session of the Standing Conference of European Ministers of

Education (Dublin, 1983) adopted a "Statement on the compulsory secondary school adolescents and the curriculum" that reads (Conseil de l'Europe, 1995):

> 3. The problem of lack of motivation at school may be part of a more general sense of alienation: the absenteeism, the violence at school, the juvenile delinquency, the alcohol and other substances abuse among young people should often be considered related problems. For many young people, an underlying cause of this alienation may be the prospect of prolonged unemployment, which they face.

The CoRC first GC (CRC/GC/2001/1)[147] underlined:

> 12. ... Article 29 (1) [CRC] insists upon a holistic approach to education which ensures that the educational opportunities made available reflect an appropriate balance between promoting the physical, mental, spiritual and emotional aspects of education, the intellectual, social and practical dimensions, and the childhood and life-long aspects. The overall objective of education is to maximize the child's ability and opportunity to participate fully and responsibly in a free society. It should be emphasized that the type of teaching that is focused primarily on accumulation of knowledge, prompting competition and leading to an excessive burden of work on children, may seriously hamper the harmonious development of the child to the fullest potential of his or her abilities and talents. Education should be child-friendly, inspiring and motivating the individual child. Schools should foster a humane atmosphere and allow children to develop according to their evolving capacities.

Furthermore, school is, in general, an institution designed exclusively to children and adolescents, closing after regular teaching hours. This is a waste of facilities and resources.

A school like this is not yet fully a school of the right to education and may even be an obstacle to its satisfaction.

Does the school have a future?

One hardly conceives of societies without an institution such as school, which remains necessary to Civilisation. For having a future, however, it must undergo a transfiguration. A right to education school is a community, welcoming, humanist, empowering school:

- *Community school*
  A right to education school is an institution transfigured by the principle of lifelong education, where new generations meet, with their diversity, to learn fundamental and other values and knowledge, but also where adult people may willingly go, outside their working hours, to learn whatever they need or like, with available and able professionals. It should offer to parents, for example, the possibility to learn how to better love and educate their children.
  This is a broad sense of an inclusive school as a school open to the diversity of ages, needs and interests of the plurality of the subjects of the right to education.
- *Welcoming school*
  A right to education school is a safe, healthy, comfortable, beautiful setting, concerned with what each child and adolescent is and can be, as well as with all aspects and conditions of their ability and willingness to learn. A setting where those who get there like to be, because they feel respected and valued in their worth, dignity and uniqueness.
  A respectful, child-friendly, school environment is a place of desire, life and future.
- *Humanist school*
  A right to education school is an institution entirely consistent with its civilisational mission, where children, adolescents, young and adults can enjoy learning all that matters for a life with dignity, the development of their personality and the fullness of their citizenship, in democratic societies and a globalised world.
  A non-humanist school, on the contrary, is an institution of alienation, depersonalization, desolation.
- *Empowering school*
  "Schooling is more about conformity than empowerment, about control rather than freedom" (Power, 2015, p. 5). A right to education school is inspired by the value of liberty and driven by the cultivation of autonomy, and no more commanded by the principle of authority and oriented to the virtue of obedience. Liberty cannot be learnt without liberty, without the risks of liberty. "When one chooses the liberty, it should not be feared", said the Constitutional Court of Colombia in *Case C-221/94*.[148]
  An empowering school is not, therefore, a school one-size-fits-all, skills-results-based, impoverishing the richness of individual and cultural diversity.

In such a meaningful school, could there be dislike, underperformance, indiscipline, violence? The Finnish school is probably the closest to become a right to education school.

5.3.7 *Right to Admirable Education Professionals*

The right to school requires education professionals that are mainly teachers.

For children, mothers and fathers are persons *unique* in the world, but they may not be the best persons of the world ... They are not chosen but can learn to love and to educate. Their unique role, rights and responsibilities are recognised in several international legal provisions and other documents, notably in CRC Articles 5 and 18, but parents are mentioned 33 times in the Convention. Their need for education is addressed too. For example:

- Recommendation on Education for International Understanding and Co-operation and Peace and Education relating to Human Rights and Fundamental Freedoms (UNESCO, 1974)[149]: "In this respect, the attitude of parents should be deemed to be an essential factor for the education of children, and the adult education referred to in paragraph 30 should pay special attention to the preparation of parents for their role in pre-school education" (para. 24).
- Recommendation 874 (1979) on a "European Charter on the Rights of the Child" (Parliamentary Assembly of the Council of Europe)[150]: "Education for parenthood should be given during the last years at school both for boys and girls" (III.a).
- World Declaration on Education for All (Jomtien, Thailand, 1990),[151] Article 6:

  > ... Knowledge and skills that will enhance the learning environment of children should be integrated into community learning programs for adults. The education of children and their parents or other caretakers is mutually supportive, and this interaction should be used to create, for all, a learning environment of vibrancy and warmth.

- CoRC, GC 5 (CRC/GC/2003/5)[152]:

  > 54. ... The Convention highlights the importance of the family in its Preamble and in many articles. It is particularly important that the promotion of children's rights should be integrated into preparation for parenthood and parenting education.

- CoRC, GC 7 (CRC/C/GC/7/Rev.1, 2005)[153]: "Assistance to parents will include the provision of parenting education" (20.c).

Be things as they may be, one can choose, educate and train education professionals who incarnate the best that society and humankind have to give to their children.

At UNESCO's General Conference 1st Session (1946), in "Other Projects and Activities" concerning "Education" was included the following[154]:

> 3. Teachers' Charter
>
> Promote the drafting of a teachers' charter by appointing a committee which will invite drafts of such a charter from interested persons and groups, with a view to improving the status of teachers. (p. 273)

Only twenty years later the Recommendation concerning the Status of Teachers (UNESCO/OIT, 1966) was adopted. It did not include higher education, whose professionals were addressed by the Recommendation concerning the Status of Higher-Education Teaching Personnel (UNESCO, 1997). In 2013, the "ILO Policy Guidelines on the promotion of decent work for early childhood education personnel" were adopted. There are pertinent provisions in other international legal instruments, such as the CADE and the ICESCR. The CoESCR said in its GC 13 (E/C.12/1999/10)[155]:

> 27. ... The Committee also notes the relationship between Articles 13 (2) (e), 2 (2), 3 and 6–8 of the Covenant, including the right of teachers to organize and bargain collectively; draws the attention of States Parties to the joint UNESCO-ILO Recommendation Concerning the Status of Teachers (1966) and the UNESCO Recommendation Concerning the Status of Higher-Education Teaching Personnel (1997); and urges States Parties to report on measures they are taking to ensure that all teaching staff enjoy the conditions and status commensurate with their role.

The CoRC said in its first GC (CRC/GC/2001/1)[156]:

> 18. ... The relevant values cannot be effectively integrated into, and thus be rendered consistent with, a broader curriculum unless those who are expected to transmit, promote, teach and, as far as possible, exemplify the values have themselves been convinced of their importance. Pre-service and in-service training schemes which promote the principles reflected in Article 29 (1) are thus essential for teachers, educational administrators and others involved in child education.

In 2019, a Global Framework of Professional Teaching Standards[157] was adopted jointly by UNESCO and Education International.

However, the education profession, teachers in particular, suffer from a chronic problem of identity. In other publications, this author has addressed the Sociology of Professions and the situation of the teaching profession worldwide (especially Monteiro, 2015a, 2015b). In the present context, only some general concepts are recalled: profession, professional identity, professional ethics, professional self-regulation, professionality, professionalism.

- *Profession* is every lawful occupation, by means of which individuals earn their principal regular income, with its corresponding utility and dignity, whatever its reality. It consists of a knowing-well-doing something, i.e. in applying more or less skilled expertise to addressing human needs and problems.
- *Professional identity* is determined by the density of the identity content of a profession understood as the composition of what distinguishes it and should distinguish its professionals, namely: *knowledge* to be applied, *values* to be respected, *qualities* to be cultivated. They are often laid down in Professional Standards.
- *Professional Ethics* is a normative framework adopted by a profession, at the national and/or international level, formally and publicly proclaiming its core values, which are the source of professional responsibilities, expressed in principles and duties (and implying rights too).
- *Professional self-regulation* means that a profession is entrusted with self-governing statutory powers, in return for its commitment to its clients' and public interest, by complying with high Professional Standards. Traditionally, it was a privilege of the so-called 'liberal professions'.
- *Professionality* and professionalism are terms whose definitions are not consensual in sociological literature, sometimes being confused. Professionality may be used to mean the global profile of a profession, that is, everything distinguishing it from other occupational groups.
- *Professionalism* is a term that may be used with two main meanings: it consists barely in doing well what one does (whatever it may be, even a crime) or in doing well something lawful one is supposed to know how to do. According to the latter, superior professionalism amounts to the unity of science, conscience and excellence.

Consequently, defining the teaching profession should be, basically, to make clear what should distinguish their professionals from the parents most capable of educating their children, as well as from other professionals holding common academic background. The scope of the teaching profession being education, defining its identity implies grasping the nature of the educational phenomenon.

It may be argued that the teachers' knowing-well-doing something should consist in *knowing-to-be-and-to-communicate-pedagogically*, that is, in their being the persons they should be, knowing who their students are and how they develop and learn, as well as knowing about education both as a human right and as a process of communication.

Therefore, the identity of the teaching profession does not truly lie in the 'knowledge to be taught' or 'to know how to teach', that is, it does not consist only in *what teachers are expected to know and be able to do*, but also in *the persons they should be, not only to do things right but also to do the right things.* They should consider themselves and be considered as *professionals of the right to education and of the pedagogical communication*, the centre of gravity of their professionalism being their *personality*.

Given its largely degraded professional and social status, as well as the revolution of technologies of information and communication, an issue is emerging: Does the teaching profession have a future? If the school has a future, it has a future as well, but what kind of professionals should teachers become to live up to the challenges of the whole human resonance of education and the mission of the school?

The answer may follow the three famous questions of the Paul Gauguin painting, which teachers should also ask themselves, nowadays: *Where do we come from? What are we? Where are we going?*

It is submitted that:

- At the beginnings, teachers were *professionals of knowledge.*
- At present, they are becoming rather *professionals of learning how to learn.*
- In the future school institution, they will be primarily *professionals of learning to be.*

The educational relation – especially during childhood and the first years of compulsory education – is always eminently interpersonal. Teachers are more than *transmitters of knowledge* and should be more than *enablers of learning*. A teacher 'teaches' more the person he or she is than what she or he knows, as one reads in pedagogical literature. This is his or her most unforgettable lesson. In this respect, let us recall the letter Albert Camus wrote to his schoolteacher on 19 November 1957, when he heard that he had been awarded the Nobel Prize for Literature[158]:

> Dear Mr Germain
>
> I let the flurry around me these last few days die down somewhat before writing to you from the depths of my heart. I have just been paid a great

> honour indeed, which I neither sought nor solicited. But when I heard the news, my first thought, after my mother, was for you. Without you, without the affectionate hand that you held out to the poor child that I was, without your teaching and your example, none of this would have happened. I do not like making a big fuss over this kind of event, but this one is at least an opportunity to tell you what you meant and will always mean to me and to assure you that your efforts, your work and the generous heart that you put into it are still alive in one of your little pupils who, despite his age, has not ceased to be a grateful one. I hug you with all my might.

As a consequence, here is a vision of the quintessence and future of the teaching profession: Teachers – and education professionals in general – will be *professionals of example*. Example – a classical theme in the history of the pedagogic thought – lies at the core of the teaching professionalism. It begins with the way of being, speaking, treating, and has multiple resonances: moral, intellectual, civic, aesthetic, etc. Manners matter. The example stands for education professions as empathy for health professions, and the feeling of justice for legal professions. In no other profession is the example so inherently central, essential and professional. Teachers' professional exemplarity should be understood as an exceptional incarnation of a blend of qualities, values and knowledge. This is their most profound and distinct professional identity.

Therefore, in education there is not professional quality without personal qualities: emotional, moral, intellectual qualities – of affectivity, kindness, attention to the alterity, openness to the diversity and the historicity of Humanity. They are qualities that arouse respect and admiration, exerting a profound and resonant influence. That is why an educator is not whoever, but who is it, who communicates and communicates himself or herself affectively, freely, truly, serenely, luminously, admirably, unforgettably ...

For the teaching profession to be what it should be, two factors are decisive: the cultivation of its ethical dimension and professional self-regulation.

- *Professional Ethics is the soul of professionalism.* It expresses the quintessence of a professional culture. A high ethical profile affirms the identity and cultivates the dignity, honorability, credibility and prestige of a profession. Is there a higher professional priority? And who better than teachers should know, and more interest should have, in taking care of the Value and the Values of their profession, which may be considered as the most ethical one?
- *Self-regulation is an insignia of professionality.* It can have decisive repercussions on the conception of the identity and attractiveness of the profession; on the selection, education, training and evaluation of teachers; on their

> professional and social status, self-esteem and motivation; on the mission of the school as an institution of humanisation; and on the quality of education. Professional self-regulation may be a bridge between the present and future of the teaching profession.

At the end of the day, the right to education should be understood as the right to learn to be human with the best of human beings.

5.3.8 *Right to an Effective Remedy*

As reads UDHR Article 8[159]: "Everyone has the right to an effective remedy by the competent national tribunals for acts violating the fundamental rights granted him by the constitution or by law". In its Resolution 38/9 of 5 July 2018,[160] already quoted, the CHR: "*Encourages* States to consider justiciability when determining the best way to give domestic legal effect to the right to education" (para. 15).

According to *Human Rights Indicators: A Guide to Measurement and Implementation*[161] issued by the UNHCHR:

> Accountability and rule of law are closely related to the notion of access to remedy, which is a critical element in the human rights framework. In the event of a violation or denial of rights, the human rights approach emphasizes the need to have available appropriate means to seek and support redress, including by invoking the right to remedy and to due process, and the right to information. (p. 13)

The *Right to Education Monitoring Guide* issued by *Right to Education Initiative*, with 150 indicators for monitoring and assessing education policies and identifying violations of the right to education,[162] includes the "right to a complaint mechanism".

As reads UNICEF/UNESCO (2007) *A Human Rights-Based Approach to Education for All: A framework for the realisation of children's right to education and rights within education* (2007): "In order to claim rights, people need to know what their rights are and how they are being addressed, how decisions are made and by whom, and what mechanisms, if any, exist to seek redress in cases of violations" (p. 17).

The CoRC recommended in its first GC (CRC/GC/2001/1)[163]: "States Parties should also consider establishing a review procedure which responds to complaints that existing policies or practices are not consistent with Article 29 (1)" (para. 25). The Committee devoted its GC 2 to "The Role of Independent National Human Rights Institutions [NHRIS] in the Protection and Promotion of the Rights of the Child" (CRC/GC/2002/2, 15/11/2002).[164] It reads:

2. The Committee issues this general comment in order to encourage States Parties to establish an independent institution for the promotion and monitoring of implementation of the Convention [...]. Where such institutions have already been established, the Committee calls upon States to review their status and effectiveness for promoting and protecting children's rights, as enshrined in the Convention on the Rights of the Child and other relevant international instruments.

In particular, Children's Ombudspersons or Child's Rights Commissions or similar independent bodies are welcome.

Students' Ombudspersons have been established in many Universities.[165] It would be highly desirable to have National Students' Ombudspersons with a broad and extended mandate to include the whole school population.

5.4 Further Outcomes

A Rightful Education demands a Right to Education Policy and a Right to Education Pedagogy, so understood:
- Right to Education Policy is a policy of the priority of the right to education, aimed at implementing its normative integrity and taking due account of human rights interdependence.
- Right to Education Pedagogy is a theoretical-practical conception of education illuminated by a rightful education and the most advanced knowledge about the educational phenomenon.

A Right to Education Pedagogy includes Principles of General Methodology. Indeed, in addition to the methods specific to each learning subject and appropriate to age, there are general methodological principles, valid in all learning contexts. The overarching ones are maybe the following:
- The educators' personality is the principle of all methods.
- The great educational principle of method should be recognition and understanding:
  - Recognition of the human value and personal uniqueness of each child and adolescent: this is the deepest desire of a human being.
  - Understanding as a moral and scientific attitude: if all behaviours have reasons, it is necessary to know them for reacting fairly and well.

A Right to Education Pedagogy should be the core of the professional culture of education professionals. Furthermore, if 'Sciences of Education' are all knowledge disciplines which can contribute to the comprehension of the educational phenomenon and the improvement of education, they should include notably the following ones: International Education Law, Neuroscience of Education, Semiotics of Education, Aesthetics of Education:

- *International Education Law*
  As we know, IEL has become the highest source in the hierarchy of the contemporary normativity on education, to which should conform the Education Law of States Parties to it. Therefore, it is but logical that it be recognised and studied as a new legal and educational discipline amounting to the science of the principles of legitimacy and quality of education.
- *Neuroscience of Education*
  Neuroscience studies the nervous system. It's a multidisciplinary field.
  Neuroscience of Education may be defined as a branch of neuroscience whose object is the application to education of the findings of the neuroscientific revolution ongoing since the last decade of the 20th century. According to Immordino-Yang and Fischer (2010), it is "a branch of neuroscience that deals with educationally relevant capacities in the brain" (pp. 2, 3) enabling, as reads an OECD Report, "the move from correlation to causation" (OECD, 2007, p. 17). It confirms ancient intuitions, overcomes some classical debates and raises new questions. In particular, it dissolves the classic controversies nature-culture and reason-emotion, revealing the foundation of the human educability.
  In 2007, the International Mind, Brain and Education Society (IMBES, USA) has launched the journal *Mind, Brain, and Education*. IMBES' mission "is to facilitate cross-cultural collaboration in biology, education and the cognitive and developmental sciences".[166]
- *Semiotics of Education*
  Semiotics is the general science of signs and of semiosis or processes of meaning making. Human semioticity consists in the aptitude for the creation, interpretation and use of signs or symbols, especially language. Man is so much a being of communication, that this is perhaps his best definition, as above said: Man is a semiotic or symbolic animal. It is because of being a *semiotic animal* that the human being is a *pedagogical animal*, that is, essentially educable. Human beings *are born to be reborn through education* as a communication phenomenon.
  The Semiotics of Education deals with the application of the findings of the Sciences of Communication to the theory and practice of education. Therefore, as Jan Anward (1997) wrote:

  > Since education, like all social activities, is crucially a sign-mediated activity, semiotics has an obvious bearing on the study of educational phenomena. Educational semiotics can easily be defined as the study of

the life of signs and the fundamental varieties of semiosis within education. (p. 106)

- *Aesthetics of Education*
Aesthetics is a discipline whose object is the art and the values involved in the appreciation of its works. Aesthetics of Education should deal with the resonances of beauty in education for the cultivation of sensitivity as the basis of the formation of personality.
Aesthetics of Education includes artistic education, but all mediations of education have an inescapable and influential aesthetical dimension. They are human and material, from the family spaces and environments through the location, architecture, decoration and equipment of schools, to textbooks, to the appearance, communication, behaviour and personality of educators.[167] Their aesthetic quality has silent and multiple influences, especially in children and adolescents.
The relationship between the beautiful and the good, contributing to form the moral conscience, is a recurrent theme in the history of philosophical thought.

Let's conclude with Kant's resounding words:

8. The prospect of a theory of education is a glorious ideal [...]
11. Education is an art which can only become perfect through the practice of many generations. Each generation, provided with the knowledge of the foregoing one, is able more and more to bring about an education which shall develop man's natural gifts in their due proportion and in relation to their end, and thus advance the whole human race towards its destiny. [...]
14. Since the development of man's natural gifts does not take place of itself, all education is an art. [...] All education which is merely mechanical must carry with it many mistakes and deficiencies, because it has no sure principle to work upon. If education is to develop human nature so that it may attain the object of its being, it must involve the exercise of judgment. [...] The mechanism of education must be changed into a science, otherwise there will never be a united effort, and one generation may have to pull down what another had built up.
15. One principle of education which those men especially who form educational schemes should keep before their eyes is this – children ought to be educated, not for the present, but for a possibly improved condition of man in the future; that is, in a manner which is adapted to the idea of humanity and the whole destiny of man.

Notes

1 http://ap.ohchr.org/documents/alldocs.aspx?doc_id=1480
2 https://unesdoc.unesco.org/ark:/48223/pf0000140735_spa
3 https://supreme.justia.com/cases/federal/us/262/390/
4 https://hudoc.echr.coe.int/eng#{%22fulltext%22:[%22linguistique%20belge%22],%22documentcollectionid2%22:[%22GRANDCHAMBER%22,%22CHAMBER%22],%22itemid%22:[%22001-62083%22]}
5 https://undocs.org/E/CN.4/1999/49
6 In *The Magic Mountain* by Thomas Mann (2005), Naphta says:

> All institutions dedicated to genuine education have always known that there can be only one central truth in any pedagogy, and that is: absolute authority and an ironclad bond – discipline and sacrifice, renunciation of the ego and coercion of the personality. It is ultimately a cruel misunderstanding of youth to believe it will find its heart's desire in freedom. Its deepest desire is to obey.

7 http://classics.mit.edu/Sophocles/antigone.html
8 See: Kevin J. Brehony, A new education for a new era: the contribution of the conferences of the New Education Fellowship to the disciplinary field of education 1921–1938. *Paedagogica Historica*, 2004, 40:5–6, 733–755, DOI: 10.1080/0030923042000293742 (https://doi.org/10.1080/0030923042000293742)
9 http://www.unicaen.fr/recherche/mrsh/sites/all/modules/ereNouvelle/pdf/1930-55.pdf
10 www.unicaen.fr/recherche/mrsh/sites/all/modules/ereNouvelle/pdf/1924-10.pdf
11 www.unicaen.fr/recherche/mrsh/sites/all/modules/ereNouvelle/pdf/1936-121.pdf
12 See: Christopher James Clews, *The New Education Fellowship and the reconstruction of education: 1945 to 1966* (2009) – Doctoral Thesis, Institute of Education, University of London. (https://discovery.ucl.ac.uk/id/eprint/10020592)
13 https://undocs.org/E/CN.4/1999/49
14 http://ap.ohchr.org/documents/alldocs.aspx?doc_id=2360
15 It means "individualisation […] understood as allowance of individual rights independently of the belonging to a community or to a determined institution. From this point of view, it should be distinguished of 'subjectivation' that consists in recognising individual rights in the frame of a community or institution" (Supiot, 1990, p. 489).
16 https://unsdg.un.org/sites/default/files/6959-The_Human_Rights_Based_Approach_to_Development_Cooperation_Towards_a_Common_Understanding_among_UN.pdf
17 http://ap.ohchr.org/documents/alldocs.aspx?doc_id=1920
18 http://ap.ohchr.org/documents/alldocs.aspx?doc_id=1480
19 *Gute Erziehung gerade ist das, woraus alles Gute in der Welt entspringt.*
20 http://www.thelatinlibrary.com/juvenal/10.shtml
21 https://undocs.org/CRC/GC/2001/1
22 https://www.ohchr.org/EN/ProfessionalInterest/Pages/Vienna.aspx
23 https://www.ohchr.org/en/professionalinterest/pages/crc.aspx
24 https://www.ineed.edu.uy/images/pdf/-18437-ley-general-de-educacion.pdf
25 https://hudoc.echr.coe.int/eng#{%22itemid%22:[%22001-86015%22]}
26 http://tbinternet.ohchr.org/_layouts/treatybodyexternal/Download.aspx?symbolno=E%2fC.12%2f1999%2f10&Lang=en
27 https://www.gutenberg.org/ebooks/61

28 https://www.ilo.org/dyn/normlex/en/f?p=NORMLEXPUB:12100:0::NO::P12100_ILO_CODE:R021
29 http://www.servat.unibe.ch/dfr/bv007198.html
Translation: https://germanlawarchive.iuscomp.org/?p=51
30 http://www.tc.gob.pe/jurisprudencia/2009/06113-2008-AA.pdf
31 https://digitallibrary.un.org/record/863093/files/A_C-3_SR-783-EN.pdf
32 https://digitallibrary.un.org/record/862944/files/A_C-3_SR-781-EN.pdf
33 https://digitallibrary.un.org/record/863020/files/A_C-3_SR-782-EN.pdf
34 https://digitallibrary.un.org/record/862944/files/A_C-3_SR-781-EN.pdf
35 http://tbinternet.ohchr.org/_layouts/treatybodyexternal/Download.aspx?symbolno=E%2fC.12%2f1999%2f10&Lang=en
36 http://tbinternet.ohchr.org/_layouts/treatybodyexternal/Download.aspx?symbolno=CRC%2FGC%2F2001%2F1&Lang=en
37 https://tbinternet.ohchr.org/_layouts/treatybodyexternal/Download.aspx?symbolno=CRC%2fGC%2f2003%2f5&Lang=en
38 http://www.corteconstitucional.gov.co/RELATORIA/1994/C-221-94.htm
39 Interview in *Le Point – Références – Le Bien et le Mal – Textes Fondamentaux*, Décembre 2016-Janvier 2017, p. 99–101.
40 http://portal.unesco.org/en/ev.php-URL_ID=15244&URL_DO=DO_TOPIC&URL_SECTION=201.html
41 https://www.ohchr.org/en/professionalinterest/pages/crc.aspx
42 Ibid.
43 *Eine Ethik für pädagogisches Handeln sollte nur eine diskursverfahrende Verantwortungsethik sein.* [...] *Mit verantwortungswahrnehmungskompetenz hat der pädagogisch Handelnde verantwortungswahrnehmungskompetenz zu bilden.*
44 www.perseus.tufts.edu/hopper/text?doc=Perseus%3Atext%3A1999.02.0024%3Abook%3D3%3Apoem%3D24
45 *Der Grundbegriff der Pädagogik ist die Bildsamkeit des Zöglings.* [...] *Von der Bildsamkeit des Willens zeigen sich Spuren in den Seelen der edlern Thiere. Aber Bildsamkeit des Willens zur Sittlichkeit kennen wir nur beim Menschen.* [...] *Tugend is der Name für das Ganze des pädagogischen Zwecks.*
46 https://www.gutenberg.org/files/1399/1399-h/1399-h.htm#chap07
47 https://www.un.org/en/sections/un-charter/un-charter-full-text/
48 http://portal.unesco.org/en/ev.php-URL_ID=15244&URL_DO=DO_TOPIC&URL_SECTION=201.html
49 https://digitallibrary.un.org/search?ln=en&p=E%2FCN.4%2FAC.2%2FSR.8&f=&c=Resource+Type&c=UN+Bodies&sf=&so=d&rg=50&fti=0
50 www.un-documents.net/a3r217d.htm
51 https://undocs.org/en/A/RES/423(V)
52 www.abanet.org/humanrights/central/declaration_child.pdf
53 https://www.ohchr.org/en/professionalinterest/pages/cescr.aspx
54 http://portal.unesco.org/en/ev.php-URL_ID=13088&URL_DO=DO_TOPIC&URL_SECTION=201.html
55 http://unesdoc.unesco.org/images/0007/000741/074172eb.pdf
56 https://www.un.org/en/ga/search/view_doc.asp?symbol=A/RES/43/128
57 https://www.ohchr.org/en/professionalinterest/pages/crc.aspx
58 http://unesdoc.unesco.org/images/0016/001610/161096e0.pdf
59 www.ohchr.org/EN/ProfessionalInterest/Pages/Vienna.aspx
60 https://undocs.org/en/A/RES/49/184

61 http://www.unesco.org/education/pdf/34_69.pdf
62 http://portal.unesco.org/en/ev.php-URL_ID=13175&URL_DO=DO_TOPIC&URL_SECTION=201.html
63 https://undocs.org/A/RES/53/243
64 https://undocs.org/en/A/RES/57/254
65 https://undocs.org/A/RES/59/113
66 https://www.ohchr.org/EN/Issues/Education/Training/Pages/Programme.aspx
67 https://undocs.org/en/A/RES/66/137
68 https://undocs.org/en/A/RES/67/18
69 See, for example: https://ec.europa.eu/epale/en/content/reinforcing-european-dimension-education-commission-launches-future-learning-package
70 https://rm.coe.int/CoERMPublicCommonSearchServices/DisplayDCTMContent?documentId=09000016803034e3
71 See: https://www.ohchr.org/EN/Issues/Education/Training/Compilation/Pages/Listofcontents.aspx
or: https://www.ohchr.org/Documents/Publications/RightHReducationen.pdf
72 http://unesdoc.unesco.org/images/0012/001202/120250e0.pdf
73 https://unesdoc.unesco.org/ark:/48223/pf0000134972
74 https://www.ohchr.org/EN/Issues/Education/Training/Compilation/Pages/PlanofActionforthefirstphase(2005–2007)oftheWorldProgrammeforHumanRightsEducation(2005).aspx
75 http://unesdoc.unesco.org/images/0024/002438/243899e.pdf
76 https://www.presidency.ucsb.edu/documents/address-san-francisco-the-closing-session-the-united-nations-conference
77 unesdoc.unesco.org/images/0008/000893/089326eo.pdf
78 https://undocs.org/en/A/RES/49/184
79 https://www.ohchr.org/EN/Issues/Education/Training/Compilation/Pages/GuidelinesforNationalPlansofActionforHumanRightsEducation(1997).aspx
80 https://www.ohchr.org/en/publicationsresources/pages/trainingeducation.aspx
81 https://www.ohchr.org/EN/Issues/Education/Training/Pages/UNDHREducationTraining.aspx
82 https://www.carnegiecouncil.org/publications/100_for_100/in-your-hands-a-guide-for-community-action
83 https://www.ohchr.org/en/professionalinterest/pages/rightandresponsibility.aspx
84 https://tbinternet.ohchr.org/_layouts/treatybodyexternal/Download.aspx?symbolno=CRC%2FGC%2F2003%2F5&Lang=en
85 https://undocs.org/en/A/HRC/20/21
86 https://lyricstranslate.com/fr/final-speech-great-dictator-sir-charles-chaplin-le-discours-final-du-grand-dict.html
87 https://undocs.org/E/CN.4/1999/49
88 https://unesdoc.unesco.org/ark:/48223/pf0000123862
89 http://www.unesco.org/culture/culturaldiversity/docs_pre_2007/unesco_diversity_review_strategy_1946_2004_en.pdf
90 https://www.ohchr.org/en/professionalinterest/pages/minorities.aspx
91 http://portal.unesco.org/en/ev.php-URL_ID=13179&URL_DO=DO_TOPIC&URL_SECTION=201.html
92 https://www.un.org/development/desa/indigenouspeoples/declaration-on-the-rights-of-indigenous-peoples.html

93 https://www.un.org/development/desa/disabilities/convention-on-the-rights-of-persons-with-disabilities.html
94 https://en.unesco.org/creativity/convention
95 https://www.ohchr.org/EN/ProfessionalInterest/Pages/Minorities.aspx
96 http://portal.unesco.org/en/ev.php-URL_ID=13179&URL_DO=DO_TOPIC&URL_SECTION=201.html
97 http://portal.unesco.org/en/ev.php-URL_ID=31038&URL_DO=DO_TOPIC&URL_SECTION=201.html
98 https://www.refworld.org/docid/3f4b139d4.html
99 https://www.un.org/en/universal-declaration-human-rights/index.html
100 http://www.unesco.org/new/en/social-and-human-sciences/themes/bioethics/human-genome-and-human-rights/
101 http://www.unesco.org/new/en/social-and-human-sciences/themes/bioethics/human-genetic-data/
102 http://portal.unesco.org/en/ev.php-URL_ID=31058&URL_DO=DO_TOPIC&URL_SECTION=201.html
103 https://digitallibrary.un.org/search?ln=en&p=E%2FCN.4%2F1324&f=&action_search=Search&rm=&ln=en&sf=&so=d&rg=50&c=United+Nations+Digital+Library+System&of=hb&fti=0&fti=0
104 http://ap.ohchr.org/documents/alldocs.aspx?doc_id=9100
105 Appendix to Albert Camus book The First Man (Thorndike Press, 1996).
106 https://hudoc.echr.coe.int/eng#{%22itemid%22:[%22001-179408%22]}
107 https://tbinternet.ohchr.org/_layouts/15/treatybodyexternal/Download.aspx?symbolno=CRC%2FC%2F15%2FAdd.216&Lang=en
108 https://www.venice.coe.int/WebForms/pages/?p=02_02_Bulletins
109 https://unesdoc.unesco.org/ark:/48223/pf0000246970
110 http://tbinternet.ohchr.org/_layouts/treatybodyexternal/Download.aspx?symbolno=CRC%2FGC%2F2001%2F1&Lang=en
111 https://supreme.justia.com/cases/federal/us/393/503
112 https://www.campaignforeducation.org/docs/reports/GCE%20Mother%20Tongue_EN.pdf
113 https://www.ohchr.org/en/professionalinterest/pages/ccpr.aspx
114 https://www.ohchr.org/en/professionalinterest/pages/crc.aspx
115 https://www.un.org/development/desa/indigenouspeoples/declaration-on-the-rights-of-indigenous-peoples.html
116 http://portal.unesco.org/en/ev.php-URL_ID=12949&URL_DO=DO_TOPIC&URL_SECTION=201.html
117 https://www.ilo.org/dyn/normlex/en/f?p=NORMLEXPUB:12100:0::NO::P12100_ILO_CODE:C169
118 https://www.ohchr.org/Documents/Publications/GuideMinoritiesDeclarationen.pdf
119 https://www.coe.int/en/web/conventions/full-list/-/conventions/treaty/163
120 https://undocs.org/en/E/CN.4/Sub.2/AC.5/2005/2
121 https://www.ohchr.org/en/professionalinterest/pages/cmw.aspx
122 https://www.coe.int/en/web/european-charter-regional-or-minority-languages
123 https://hudoc.echr.coe.int/eng#{„itemid":[„001-57525"]}
124 https://culturalrights.net/descargas/drets_culturals389.pdf
125 http://www.ibe.unesco.org/sites/default/files/resources/howard-jonestheplasticbrain_0.pdf

126 https://en.unesco.org/gem-report/if-you-don%E2%80%99t-understand-how-can-you-learn

127 *Report of the Working Group on a Draft Convention on the Rights of the Child* (E/CN.4/1989/48, 2 March 1989). (https://digitallibrary.un.org/record/57437)

128 https://tbinternet.ohchr.org/_layouts/15/treatybodyexternal/Download.aspx?symbolno=CRC%2fC%2fGC%2f7%2fRev.1&Lang=en

129 https://www.ohchr.org/en/professionalinterest/pages/crc.aspx

130 https://unesdoc.unesco.org/ark:/48223/pf0000120240

131 https://www.achpr.org/public/Document/file/English/achpr_instr_guide_draft_esc_rights_eng.pdf

132 https://unesdoc.unesco.org/ark:/48223/pf0000259338

133 See *Case Movimento Creche para Todos vs Municipality of São Paulo* (Nº 0150735-64.2008.8.26.0002, 16/12/2013), quoted above (https://www.enfam.jus.br/wp-content/uploads/2018/11/AP-0150735-64.2008.8.26.0002-TJSP-1.pdf)

134 http://www.ibe.unesco.org/sites/default/files/resources/howard-jonestheplasticbrain_0.pdf

135 https://hudoc.echr.coe.int/fre#{%22fulltext%22:[%22sahin%22],%22documentcollectionid2%22:[%22GRANDCHAMBER%22,%22CHAMBER%22],%22itemid%22:[%22001-70956%22]}

136 http://undocs.org/en/A/RES/70/1

137 https://www.worldbank.org/en/publication/wdr2018

138 https://ap.ohchr.org/documents/dpage_e.aspx?si=A/HRC/41/L.26

139 https://uil.unesco.org/lifelong-learning/recognition-validation-accreditation/unesco-guidelines-recognition-validation-and

140 http://portal.unesco.org/en/ev.php-URL_ID=49355&URL_DO=DO_TOPIC&URL_SECTION=201.html

141 https://unevoc.unesco.org/home/UNESCO-UNEVOC+-+What+we+do

142 https://tbinternet.ohchr.org/_layouts/15/treatybodyexternal/Download.aspx?symbolno=E%2fC.12%2fGC%2f22&Lang=en

143 https://tbinternet.ohchr.org/_layouts/15/treatybodyexternal/Download.aspx?symbolno=E%2fC.12%2fGC%2f25&Lang=en

144 https://redaprenderycambiar.com.ar/derrida/frances/droit_philosophie.pdf

145 www.corteconstitucional.gov.co/relatoria/1995/T-337-95.htm

146 In *Of Human Bondage* (W. Somerset Maugham, 1915, XXXIX), Philip wants to give up his apprenticeship, in London, to be an account, and desires to go study painting in Paris. Mrs. Carey, his aunt, asks the solicitor Albert Nixon' advice, who answered: "I am naturally very disappointed, but as you know you can take a horse to the water, but you can't make him drink" (https://www.gutenberg.org/ebooks/351).

Célestin Freinet, a French pedagogue, prominent figure of the New Education Movement (see 5.1.2), echoed in *Les dits de Mathieu* (1949):

> And do you know that you don't make the horse that is not thirsty drink? [...]
> Any method is regrettable that tries to make the horse drink that is not thirsty. Any method is good that opens the appetite for knowledge and sharpens the powerful need for work.
> *Et savez-vous qu'on ne fait point boire le cheval qui n'a pas soif ?* [...]
> *Toute méthode est regrettable qui prétend faire boire le cheval qui n'a pas soif. Toute méthode est bonne qui ouvre l'appétit de savoir et aiguise le besoin puissant de travail.*
> (https://www.icem-freinet.fr/archives/educ/55-56/11/2.pdf)

147 http://tbinternet.ohchr.org/_layouts/treatybodyexternal/Download.aspx?symbolno=CRC%2FGC%2F2001%2F1&Lang=en
148 http://www.corteconstitucional.gov.co/RELATORIA/1994/C-221-94.htm
149 http://portal.unesco.org/en/ev.php-URL_ID=13088&URL_DO=DO_TOPIC&URL_SECTION=201.html
150 http://assembly.coe.int/nw/xml/XRef/Xref-XML2HTML-en.asp?fileid=14908&lang=en
151 https://unesdoc.unesco.org/ark:/48223/pf0000127583
152 https://tbinternet.ohchr.org/_layouts/treatybodyexternal/Download.aspx?symbolno=CRC%2FGC%2F2003%2F5&Lang=en
153 https://tbinternet.ohchr.org/_layouts/15/treatybodyexternal/Download.aspx?symbolno=CRC%2fC%2fGC%2f7%2fRev.1&Lang=en
154 https://unesdoc.unesco.org/ark:/48223/pf0000114580?posInSet=15&queryId=c5611426-47d1-4a1e-b392-579e6d7082dc
155 https://undocs.org/E/C.12/1999/10
156 http://tbinternet.ohchr.org/_layouts/treatybodyexternal/Download.aspx?symbolno=CRC%2FGC%2F2001%2F1&Lang=en
157 Available in June 2020: https://issuu.com/educationinternational/docs/2019_ei-unesco_framework?fr=sYTQ5MDQxMzY3Ng
158 Appendix to his book *The First Man* (Thorndike Press, 1996).
159 https://www.un.org/en/udhrbook/pdf/udhr_booklet_en_web.pdf
160 http://ap.ohchr.org/documents/dpage_e.aspx?si=A/73/53
161 https://www.ohchr.org/EN/Issues/Indicators/Pages/documents.aspx
162 www.right-to-education.org/resource/measuring-education-human-right-list-indicators
163 https://undocs.org/CRC/GC/2001/1
164 https://tbinternet.ohchr.org/_layouts/treatybodyexternal/Download.aspx?symbolno=CRC%2FGC%2F2002%2F2&Lang=en
165 See: *Being an Ombudsman in Higher Education – A Comparative Study.* (http://www.enohe.net/wp-content/uploads/2017/06/Being-an-ombudsman.pdf)
166 https://imbes.org/
167 The French Code of Education reads in its Article L521-4: "The school architecture has an educational function. It is an indispensable element of the pedagogy, contributes to the transmission of knowledge and the discovery of the cultures and fosters the development of the autonomy and the artistic sensitivity of the students". (https://www.legifrance.gouv.fr/affichCode.do;jsessionid=86D2FD706967B9C89D00B2533E019094.tplgfr29s_1?idSectionTA=LEGISCTA000006166645&cidTexte=LEGITEXT000006071191&dateTexte=2019060)

References

AAVV. (2012). Qu'est-ce que l'Homme? – 100 scientifiques répondent. *Sciences et Avenir*, janvier.

Abi-Saab, G. (2007). General Conclusions. In *Standard-setting in UNESCO – Volume I: Normative action in education, science and culture. Essays in commemoration of the sixtieth anniversary of UNESCO* (pp. 395–401). UNESCO Publishing/Martinus Nijhoff Publishers.

Adorno, Th. W. (1984). *Modèles critiques – Interventions-Répliques* [*Eingriffe. Neun kritische Modelle*, 1963; *Stichworte. Kritische Modelle 2*, 1965] (Trad. par Eliane Kaufholz de l'allemand). Payot. http://www.staff.uni-giessen.de/~g31130/PDF/polphil/ErziehungAuschwitzOffBrief.pdf (An English version: https://signale.cornell.edu/text/education-after-auschwitz)

Alfredsson, G. (2001). The right to human rights education. In A. Eide, C. Krause, & A. Rosas (Eds.), *Economic, social and cultural rights – A textbook* (2nd rev. ed., pp. 273–288). Kluwer Law International.

Anward, J. (1997). Semiotics in educational research. In J. P. Keeves (Ed.), *Educational research, nethodology, and measurement: An international handbook* (pp. 106–111). Pergamon Press. Retrieved June 2019, from https://liu.se/ikk/medarbetare/jan-anward/filarkiv-publikationer/1.209695/ja-1994a-semiotics.pdf

Aristotle. (1998). *The metaphysics* (Translated with an introduction by H. Lawson-Tancred). Penguin Books.

Aristotle. (2000). *Politics* (Translated by B. Jowett, with Introduction, Analysis and Index by H. W. C. Davis). Dover Publications, Incl.

Bart, J. (1989). L'individu et ses droits. In I. Théry & Ch. Biet (Textes réunis et présentés par), *La famille, la loi, l'État – de la Révolution au Code civil* (pp. 351–362). Éditions du Centre Georges Pompidou/Imprimerie Nationale – Éditions.

Bergmann, B. (1962). Erzieher, Persönlichkeit des Erziehers. In Deutschen Institut für wissenschaftliche Pädagogik, Münster, und dem Institut für Vergleichende Erziehungswissenschaft, Salzburg (Herausgegeven vom), *Lexikon der Pädagogik in vier Bänden – I. Band: ABB-Fertigkeit* (pp. 1026–1029). Herder.

Berhoumi, M. (2013). *Le régime juridique de la liberté d'enseignement à l'épreuve des politiques scolaires*. Bruylant. https://dial.uclouvain.be/pr/boreal/object/boreal:136205

Braido, P. (A cura di). (1962). *Enciclopedia delle Scienze dell'educazione – 1. Educare – Sommario di Scienze Pedagogiche – Volume primo: Storia, filosofia e metodologia dell'educazione. Metodologia didattica e problemi della scuola*. Pas-Verlag.

Brenner, M., & Töpper, B. (1997). *Meine Rechte in der Schule* (dtv, Vol. 1490). Deutscher Taschenbuch Verlag, Beck-Rechtsberater.

Bueren, G. (1995). *The international law on the Rights of the Child* (International Studies in Human Rights, Vol. 35). Martinus Nijhoff Publishers.

Charlot, B. (1976). *A mistificação pedagógica* (*La mystification pédagogique*, trad. de Ruth Rissin Josef). Zahar Editores.

Coomans, F. (2002). In search of the core content of the right to education. In A. Chapman & S. Russell (Eds.), *Core obligations: Building a framework for economic, social and cultural rights* (pp. 217–246). Intersentia.

Coomans, F. (2004). Exploring the normative content of the right to education as a human right: Recent approaches. *Persona y Derecho, Revista de fundamentación de las instituciones jurídicas y de derechos humanos*, *50*, 61–100.

Compayré, J.-G. (1897). *Cours de Pédagogie théorique et pratique.* Librairie Classique Paul Delaplane. http://michel.delord.free.fr/comp-cptp-tdm.html

Conseil de l'Europe. (1995). *Conférence permanente des ministres européens de l'Éducation – Résolutions de la Conférence permanente – Recueil des textes adoptés – 1959–1994.* Secrétariat du Conseil de l'Europe.

Danieli, Y., Stamatopoulou, E., & Dias, C. J. (Eds.). (1999). *The Universal Declaration of Human Rights: Fifty years and beyond.* United Nations/Baywood Publishing Company, Inc.

Delors, J. et al. (1996). *Learning: The treasure within – Report to UNESCO of the International Commission on Education for the Twenty-first Century.* UNESCO Publishing. French version: http://unesdoc.unesco.org/images/0011/001159/115930f.pdf

Dolto, F. (1984). *L'image inconsciente du corps.* Seuil.

Dolto, F. (1985). *La cause des enfants.* Éditions Robert Laffont.

Domenach, J.-M. (1994). *La responsabilité – Essai sur le fondement du civisme.* Hatier.

Dubreucq, F. (1994). Jean-Ovide Decroly (1871–1932). In UNESCO (Ed.), *Penseurs de l'éducation – Volume 1* (pp. 251–276).

Elfert, M. (2016). *UNESCO's utopia of lifelong learning: An intellectual history of UNESCO's humanistic approach to education, 1945–2015* (Thesis). University of British Columbia (Canada). (Published in 2018 by Routledge, Routledge Research in Lifelong Learning and Adult Education Series) https://open.library.ubc.ca/cIRcle/collections/ubctheses/24/items/1.0228054

Faure, E. et al. (1972). *Learning to be: The world of education today and tomorrow.* UNESCO and George G. Harrap & Co. Ltd. http://unesdoc.unesco.org/images/0000/000018/001801e.pdf

Fisher, A. (2017). *Minimum core and the right to education.* World Bank. https://openknowledge.worldbank.org/handle/10986/29142

Foster, Ch. (2011). *Human dignity in bioethics and law.* Hart Publishing.

Gaulejac, V. (2001). Sociologues en quête d'identité. *Cahiers internationaux de sociologie, 2*(111), 355–362. https://www.cairn.info/revue-cahiers-internationaux-de-sociologie-2001-2-page-355.htm

Giesinger, J. (2012). Kant on dignity and education. *Educational Theory, 62*(6), 609–620.

Haag, D. (1982). *The right to education: What kind of management?* UNESCO/BIE. https://unesdoc.unesco.org/ark:/48223/pf0000045428/PDF/045428engo.pdf.multi

Hænggeli-Jenni, B. (2011). *Pour l'Ere Nouvelle: une revue-carrefour entre science et militance (1922–1940)* (Thèse de Doctorat). Université de Genève. https://archive-ouverte.unige.ch/unige:18162

Hænggeli-Jenni, B., & Hofstetter, R. (2011). Pour l'Ère nouvelle (1922–1940). La science convoquée pour fonder une "internationale de l'éducation". *Carrefours de l'éducation, 1*(31), 137–159.

Halvorsen, K. (1990). Notes on the realization of the human right to education. *Human Rights Quarterly – A Comparative and International Journal of the Social Sciences, Humanities and Law, 12*(3), August, 341–364.

Heckel, H. (1970). Rechtsgrundlagen der Schule. In J. Speck & G. Wehle (Herausgegeben von), *Handbuch Pädagogischer Grundbegriffe – Band II* (pp. 362–381). Kösel-Verlag.

Heerdt-Quarles, Comtesse P. (1929). *Un Monde Nouveau réclame une Éducation Nouvelle*. Editions de 'La Paix par le Droit'.

Henkin, L. (1978). *The rights of man today*. Stevens and Sons.

Herbart, J. F. (1835). *Umriss pädagogischer Vorlesungen* [*Summary of lessons on pedagogy*]. Dieterichshen Buchhandlung. https://archive.org/details/umrisspdagogiscooherbgoog

Immordino-Yang, M., & Fischer, K. (2010). Neuroscience bases of learning. In V. G. Aukrust (Ed.), *International encyclopedia of education* (3rd ed., pp. 310–316). Elsevier. Retrieved July 2019, from www.bcf.usc.edu/~immordin/papers/Immordino-Yang+Fischer_2009_NeuroscienceBasesofLearning.pdf

Johnson, M. G., & Symonides, J. (1998). *The Universal Declaration of Human Rights: A history of its creation and implementation – 1948–1998*. UNESCO.

Jonas, H. (1979). *Le principe responsabilité – Une éthique pour la civilisation technologique* [*Das Prinzip Verantwortung – Versuch einer Ethik für die technologische Zivilisation*] (Trad. de Jean Greisch). Les Éditions du Cerf.

Kant, I. (1803). *Traité de pédagogie* (tr. de J. Barni, revue et actualisée, Introduction et notes par Pierre-José About). Hachette. Original text: https://de.wikisource.org/wiki/%C3%9Cber_P%C3%A4dagogik An English translation: https://oll.libertyfund.org/titles/kant-kant-on-education-uber-padagogik

Kotzmann, J. (2018). *The human rights-based approach to higher education: Why human rights norms should guide higher education law and policy*. Oxford University Press.

Kuhn, Th. S. (1962). *The structure of scientific revolutions*. The University of Chicago Press.

Levi, P. (1958). *If this is a man* (Transl. by Stuart Woolf). Orion Press.

Lobrot, M. (1966). *A pedagogia institucional* [*La pédagogie institutionnelle*] (Trad. de José Gonçalves]. Iniciativas Editoriais.

Lobrot, M. (1992). *À quoi sert l'école?* Armand Colin.

Löwisch, D.-J. (1995). *Einführung in Pädagogishe Ethic – Eine Handlungsorientierte Anleitung für die Durchführung von Verarantwortungsdiskursen*. Wissenschaftliche Buchgesellschaft.

Mehendale, A., & Mukhopadhyay, R. (Eds.). (2018). *The right to education – Movements and policies: Promises and realities*. NORRAG – Network for International Policies and Co-operation in Education and Training, Special Issue 01. https://resources.norrag.org/resource/124/the-right-to-education-movements-and-policies-promises-and-realities

Mann, Th. (2005). *The magic mountain* [*Der Zauberberg*, 1924] (Transl. by John E. Woods). Everyman's Library.

Miller, A. (1980). *C'est pour ton bien – Racines de la violence dans l'éducation de l'enfant* [*Am Anfang war Erziehung*] (Trad. de Jeanne Etoré). Éditions Aubier Montaigne.

Modinos, P. (1975). Dialogue avec les droits de l'homme/Introduction à l'étude des droits de l'homme/La Convention européenne des droits de l'homme – Ses origines, ses objectifs, ses réalisations. *Revue des droits de l'homme/Human rights journal – Droit international et Droit comparé/International and Comparative Law – 25e Anniversaire de la Convention Européenne des Droits de l'Homme (4 Novembre 1950–4 Novembre), VIII* (A. Pedone, Nº Spécial). pp. 631–636, 648–658, 689–716.

Monchablon, A. (Coord.). (1989). *L'esprit de 1789 et des droits de l'homme – Textes et documents (1725–1986) – Préface de Claude Nicolet.* Coédition CNDP/Larousse.

Monteiro, A. R. (2015a). *Profissão Docente – Profissionalidade e Auto-regulação* [*Teaching profession – professionality and self-regulation*]. Cortez Editora.

Monteiro, A. R. (2015b). *The teaching profession – Present and future.* Springer International Publishing.

Monteiro, A. R. (2017). *Uma Teoria da Educação* [*A theory of education*]. Edições Piaget.

Morsink, J. (1999). *The Universal Declaration of Human Rights: Origins, drafting, and intent.* University of Pennsylvania Press.

Néraudau, J.-P. (1984). *Être enfant à Rome.* Éditions Payot & Rivages.

Nowak, M. (2003). *Introduction to international human rights regime.* Martinus Nijhoff Publishers.

OECD. (2007). *Understanding the brain: The birth of a learning science.* Centre for Educational Research and Innovation. http://www.narhu.org/wp-content/uploads/2016/02/understanding_the_brain.pdf

Passmore, J. (1970). *The perfectibility of man* (3rd ed.). Liberty Fund. Retrieved July 2019, from http://files.libertyfund.org/files/670/0092_LFeBk.pdf

Piaget, J. (1949). *Le droit à l'éducation dans le monde actuel – Nº1 Collection 'Droits de l'Homme'* (Publiée par l'Organisation des Nations Unies pour l'Éducation, la Science et la Culture) (UNESCO). Sciences et Lettres/Librairie du Recueil Sirey). http://unesdoc.unesco.org/images/0013/001392/139216fo.pdf (English and Spanish translations: unesdoc.unesco.org/images/0000/000061/006133Eo.pdf)

Plato. (1997). *Plato – Complete works* ((Ed. by John M. Cooper & D. S. Hutchinson). Hackeht Publishing Company.

Renaut, A. (2002). *La libération des enfants – Contribution philosophique à une histoire de l'enfance.* Calmann-Lévy.

Robinson, N. (1958). *The Universal Declaration of Human Rights – Its origin, significance, application and interpretation.* Institute of Jewish Affairs, World Jewish Congress.

Rousseau, J.-J. (1762a). *Émile ou de l'éducation* (Chronologie et introduction par Michel

Launay). Garnier-Flammarion (1966). http://gallica.bnf.fr/ark:/12148/bpt6k5786957n/f12.image (An English translation: https://oll.libertyfund.org/titles/rousseau-emile-or-education)

Rousseau, J.-J. (1762b). *Du contrat social* (Édition établie par Pierre Burgelin). GF-Flammarion. https://www.rousseauonline.ch/pdf/rousseauonline-0004.pdf (An English translation: https://www.earlymoderntexts.com/assets/pdfs/rousseau1762.pdf).

Schabas, W. A. (2013). *The Universal Declaration of Human Rights – The 'travaux préparatoires'*. Cambridge University Press. Retrieved July 2019, from http://documents.law.yale.edu/sites/default/files/UDHR2013FullText.pdf

Soëtard, M., & Hétier, R. (2003). L'éducation entre fin, finalité et finalisme. Le sens de la pédagogie: repères philosophiques, résonances pédagogiques. *Revue Française de Pédagogie, 143*, 61–68.

Supiot, A. (1990). Pourquoi un droit du travail?. *Droit social, 6*, juin, 485–492.

Todres, J., & Higinbotham, S. (2016). *Human rights in children's literature: imagination and the narrative of law*. Oxford University Press.

Tomaševski, K. (2001a). *Human rights in education as prerequisite for human rights education* (Right to Education Primers, Vol. 4). Raoul Wallenberg Institute. www.nonformality.org/wp-content/uploads/2006/10/rte-primer-4.pdf

Tomaševski, K. (2004). *Manual on rights-based education: Global human rights requirements made simple*. UNESCO. https://unesdoc.unesco.org/ark:/48223/pf0000135168

Töws, H.-J. (1970). Rechtsgrundlagen der Schule. In J. Speck & G. Wehle (Herausgegeben von), *Handbuch Pädagogischer Grundbegriffe – Band II* (pp. 362–366). Kösel-Verlag.

UNESCO. (1947). *Fundamental education: Common ground of all peoples*. Report (EDU/9, EDU/10). https://unesdoc.unesco.org/ark:/48223/pf0000125830

UNESCO. (1948). *Human Rights – Comments and interpretations – A symposium edited by UNESCO, with an Introduction by Jacques Maritain*. UNESCO/PHS3(rev.). Paris, 25 July 1948. https://unesdoc.unesco.org/ark:/48223/pf0000155042

UNESCO. (1985). *Consultation informelle pour apprécier les progrès accomplis dans la mise en œuvre du Plan pour le développement de l'enseignement des droits de l'homme – Analyse des réponses au questionnaire visant à évaluer l'état d'avancement du Plan pour le développement de l'enseignement des droits de l'homme – Rapport élaboré par Martin Ennals et Elizabeth Jenkins*. Paris, le 18 juin 1985 (SHS-85/CS.10/3). http://unesdoc.unesco.org/images/0006/000671/067127fb.pdf

UNESCO. (2000). *Rapport mondial sur l'éducation – 2000 – Le droit à l'éducation: Vers l'éducation pour tous tout au long de la vie*. Éditions UNESCO. http://unesdoc.unesco.org/images/0011/001197/119745f.pdf (English edition: www.unesco.org/education/information/wer/PDFeng/wholewer.PDF)

UNESCO. (2015a). *EFA Global Monitoring Report 2015 – Education for All 2000–2015: Achievements and challenges*. http://unesdoc.unesco.org/images/0023/002322/232205e.pdf

UNESCO. (2015b). *Rethinking education: Towards a global common good?* UNESCO Publishing. https://unesdoc.unesco.org/ark:/48223/pf0000232555

UNESCO. (2017). *Global Education Monitoring Report 2017/8 – Accountability in education – Meeting our commitments*. UNESCO Publishing. https://en.unesco.org/gem-report

UNICEF. (1998). *Implementation handbook for the Convention on the Rights of the Child* (prepared for UNICEF by Rachel Hodgkin and Peter Newell). Xxx. (2007: Fully rev. 3rd ed.). https://www.unicef.org/publications/index_43110.html

United Nations. (1997). *Manual on Human Rights reporting – Under six major international human rights instruments*. Geneva, HR/PUB/91/1 (Rev. 1). https://www.ohchr.org/documents/publications/manualhrren.pdf

Verdoodt, A. (1964). *Naissance et signification de la Déclaration universelle des droits de l'homme (Préface de René Cassin)*. Éditions Nauwelaerts.

Verheyde, M. (2006). *A commentary on the United Nations Convention on the Rights of the Child – Article 28 – The Right to Education*. Martinus Nijhoff Publishers.

Williams, R. (1997). *Hegel's ethics of recognition*. University of California Press.

World Commission on Culture and Development. (1995). *Our creative diversity*. https://unesdoc.unesco.org/ark:/48223/pf0000101651

CONCLUSION

One Day, the Humankind …

Abstract

1. The Revolution of the Right to Education is ultimately about solving the Gordian Knot of the humankind having to educate itself and singling out the right to education as Right to Possible.
2. It is submitted that this is perhaps the *secret* for solving the Gordian Knot of education: it will begin to be decisively disentangled only when children might *learn to be* with *the best human beings.*
3. How do we get the best human beings to become educators? They should be chosen by rulers. And who chooses the rulers?
4. The best education is one ethically illuminated by the best idea of human perfection, scientifically enlightened by the best knowledge on the human nature, and politically entrusted to the best human beings by better rulers elected by better educated citizens. The dissolution of the education Gordian Knot will thus take a lasting temporal magnitude …

   What is the best humankind has ever envisioned for becoming better?
5. The answer seems indisputable: it is the Ethics of Human Rights and, in particular, the Ethics of the Right to Education. Human rights institute limits that it is necessary to learn and open possibilities that should be explored and brought about. The right to education is the right to learn both the *limits* of the human finitude, which inscribe in the species' children their ethical identity, and the *Possible* as the ontological *utopia* of the infinite human perfectibility …
6. The Revolution of the Right to Education means the political-pedagogical breaking of the vicious circle of the historical and psychological 'cloning' of the coming generations by the older ones, driven by the human compulsion and 'divine' temptation to 'create' children in their image and likeness. The *pedagogical reason* is no longer the *biological reason* of the Family nor the *political reason* of the State, but the *Ethical Reason* of the Subject, opening to full human flourishing.
7. Now that we know why education is the greatest power and the greatest responsibility of the human species, maybe it will be able to reach – in time – the full awareness that the right to education is the *abracadabra* to find the Holy Grail of its destiny …
8. *To be or not to be a human right* – here's the question regarding the future of education and our Humanity.

•••

 | DOI: 10.1163/9789004462465_007

The Revolution of the Right to Education is ultimately about solving the Gordian Knot of the humankind having to educate itself and singling out the right to education as Right to Possible.

Solving the Gordian Knot of education
Education is a phenomenon of cultural and social integration of the coming generations, so that the new members of each community become good and useful, according to its values and needs. This implies a representation of human nature and the role of education.

In light of the best present knowledge, human nature is dual, as we saw: it is inextricably biological (innate) and cultural (acquired):
- The biological nature is the objective substratum of the educability, that is, of the possibility and need of education.
- The cultural nature results from education as a formal, non-formal and informal phenomenon of a lifelong configuration of every human being.

The biological foundation of educability lies, as above explained, in the perfectibility contained in the genome of the species that, brought about by the brain plasticity, originates the semiotic aptitude or semioticity and the human mental world, generating rationality and inexhaustible ability to learn.

A cultural conception of education answers, explicitly or implicitly, as we know, to the following main questions: *What for?* (the aims of education), *What?* (the corresponding learnings), *How?* (the educational mediations: persons, institutions, methods ...). These are political-pedagogical questions because they are mostly decided by rulers, assisted by experts.

Education is, therefore, linked to politics by an umbilical cord that cannot be ignored without the risk of sterile idealism. It cannot be thought of and improved in isolation, that is, as if it were not a culturally and socially embedded phenomenon. Nor can society be thought of and improved without considering the educational phenomenon as the cradle of reproduction of the material and mental conditions of its existence. Also, politics and education have been considered not only the main arts but also the most difficult ones, because they end up by facing a Gordian Knot,[1] making them 'impossible' (Aristotle, Comenius, Locke, Rousseau, Kant, Freud).

The political Gordian Knot is meant in the question formulated by the Roman poet Juvenal (Satire VI, 346)[2]: *Quis custodiet ipsos custodes*? (Who will guard the guards themselves?). The pedagogical Gordian Knot has been coined following the *Theses on Feuerbach* (Thesis III) first published by Karl Marx as an appendix to *Ludwig Feuerbach and the End of Classical German Philosophy* (1888),[3] where he affirmed that "it is essential to educate the educator himself".

It was highlighted by Jean Baechler (1994), for instance, when he wrote that politics has been the "first motor" of modernity as "a gigantic historical process of transcription of democracy into the different orders", but each of them "must adapt itself to a democratic regime by combining, the best it can, the democratic demands with its own rationality". However, "such transcription is not yet over", and children are "a grave exception".

> Just as they are not free to not be born, so they are not free to choose their parents. [...] There is no technical solution to mitigate or eliminate the failure because, in this field, any solution will always be confronted with the invincible argument: "Who will educate the educators?" (pp. 82, 84)

In effect, as Kant (1803) remarked: "It is noticeable that man is only educated by man – that is, by men who have themselves been educated" (para. 7). Therefore, "one man whose education has been spoilt will only repeat his own mistakes in trying to educate others" (para. 14). The improvement of education "demands a great deal of insight on the part of parents and teachers" (para. 77), but "insight depends on education, and education in its turn depends on insight" (*Einsicht hängt von der Erziehung und Erziehung hängt wieder von der Einsicht ab*) (para. 12). Moreover: "Parents care for the home, rulers for the State. Neither have as their aim the universal good and the perfection to which man is destined, and for which he has also a natural disposition" (para. 16).

In this connection, the American educationist Porter Sargent (1945) wrote in the already quoted Dedication of his book *Between Two Wars – The Failure of Education: 1920–1940*:

> To those who courageously strive to change what we do to children under the guidance of the dead hand. For what we have done to children in the name of education has planted the seeds of resentment and frustration – has made all of us what we are today. So, war begins in the nurseries, and in the chancelleries the choicest product of our system in perplexed predicament promote and provoke future wars.

This political-pedagogical Gordian Knot generates a vicious circle of reproduction of several human evils. How to solve it?

As politics is concerned, according to Plato (1997), here is "the smallest change that would enable our city to reach our sort of constitution [...]. It's certainly neither small nor easy, but it is possible":

> Until philosophers rule as kings or those who are now called kings and leading men genuinely and adequately philosophize, that is, until

> political power and philosophy entirely coincide, while the many natures who at present pursue either one exclusively are forcibly prevented from doing so, cities will have no rest from evils, Glaucon, nor, I think, will the human race. (*Republic*, 473b-d)

This was echoed by Rousseau (1762b):

> In order to discover the rules of society best suited to nations, a superior intelligence beholding all the passions of men without experiencing any of them would be needed. This intelligence would have to be wholly unrelated to our nature, while knowing it through and through; its happiness would have to be independent of us, and yet ready to occupy itself with ours; and lastly, it would have, in the march of time, to look forward to a distant glory, and, working in one century, to be able to enjoy in the next. It would take gods to give men laws. (Book II, Chapter VII)

Things being as they are, "the best and most natural arrangement is for the wisest to govern the multitude when it is assured that they will govern for its profit and not for their own" (Book III, Chapter V). Democracy is so far the best political regime as it allows citizens to elect rulers. They are supposed to choose the best for ruling in accordance with the General Will, but citizens are often misguided and deceived. "Were there a people of gods, their government would be democratic. So perfect a government is not for men" (Book III, Chapter IV).

Concerning education, Kant (1803) – Rousseau's reader and admirer – similarly said: "Were some being of higher nature than man to undertake our education, we should then be able to see what man might become" (*Wenn einmal ein Wesen höherer Art sich unserer Erziehung annähme, so würde man doch sehen, was aus dem Menschen werden könne*) (para. 7).

No God or Alexander the Great will come to break the circle of the Gordian Knot of education. Yet, it might become increasingly less vicious and more virtuous. How?

Am Anfang war Erziehung – is the original title of the work by the psychoanalyst Alice Miller (1980) already quoted, whose literal translation is 'At the beginning was education'. This was Plato's vision, following which the principles for building an ideal city are few and simple, provided its rulers "guard the one great thing, though I'd rather it sufficient than great", namely: "Good education and upbringing" (Plato, 1997, *Republic*, 424b). Accordingly, "when one or more true philosophers come to power in a city" (540d) – Plato goes on – "the quickest and easiest way for the city and constitution we've discussed to be established" would be to "send everyone in the city who is over ten years old into the country. Then they [philosophers] will take possession of the children, who are now free from the ethos of their parents, and bring them up in their own customs and laws, which are the ones we've described" (541). More realistically, in *Laws*, Plato recommended that "the legislator should not treat the education of children cursorily or as a secondary matter; he should regard the right choice of the man who is going to be in charge of the children as something of crucial importance, and appoint as their Minister the best all-round citizen in the State" (*Laws*, 766a), because "this is by far the most important of all the supreme offices in the State" (765a).

In line with the foregoing historical insights, it is submitted that this is perhaps the *secret* for solving the Gordian Knot of education: it will begin to be decisively disentangled only when children might *learn to be* with *the best human beings*. Taking a luminous Platonic insight, it is about "fostering their best part with our own" (Plato, 1997, *Republic*, 590e).

More recently, the American Report *Tomorrow's Teachers* affirmed: "Only the best and brightest should be entitled to teach" (The Holmes Group, 1986, p. 25). Lee Iacocca (a famous American businessman) is quoted as having said: "In a completely rational society, the best of us would be teachers, and the rest would have to settle for something less" (as cited in Hinds, 2002, p. 4). The prevailing rhetoric on quality education emphasises the need to attract the best for the teaching profession.

How do we get the best human beings to become educators? They should be chosen by rulers. And who chooses the rulers?

Civilisation is driven by many factors: higher values, the advancement of knowledge, individual and collective struggles, exceptional human beings, etc. Their interaction is the subject of Tolstoy's meditation ending his literary cathedral *War and Peace* (Second Part of the Epilogue).[4] Considering that "history has for its object the study of the movement of the nations and of humanity", Tolstoy asked: "What force moves" them? His answer: it is power. Being so, this is "history's essential question: what is power?". Answer: "Power is the collective will of the people transferred, by expressed or tacit consent, to their chosen rulers. […] This relation of the men who command to those they command is what constitutes the essence of the conception called power". However:

> The theory of the transference of the will of the people to historic persons is merely a paraphrase – a restatement of the question in other words.
>
> What causes historical events? Power. What is power? Power is the collective will of the people transferred to one person. Under what condition is the will of the people delegated to one person? On condition that that

> person expresses the will of the whole people. That is, power is power: in other words, power is a word the meaning of which we do not understand.

In effect, it is not possible to "imagine the action of a man quite devoid of freedom". Therefore: "Whatever presentation of the activity of many men or of an individual we may consider, we always regard it as the result partly of man's free will and partly of the law of inevitability". Consequently:

> All that we know of the life of man is merely a certain relation of free will to inevitability [...].
>
> So also in history what is known to us we call laws of inevitability, what is unknown we call free will. Free will is for history only an expression for the unknown remainder of what we know about the laws of human life.

Therefore, if "every human action appears to us as a certain combination of freedom and inevitability", the increasing of freedom causes the decreasing of inevitability.

Here comes into play education paramountcy that crosses another literary monument: *The Magic Mountain* by Thomas Mann (2005). Considering that "everything is politics", Settembrini – Mann's voice – affirms that the purpose of politics should be: "The well-crafted social edifice, the perfection of humanity, the new Jerusalem". This is the goal of the 'International League for the Organization of Progress', whose founding principles form an evolutionary philosophical conception following which "humankind's innermost natural purpose is its own self-perfection". This is the classic humanist ideal. "But what was humanism? Love of humankind, nothing more, and so it, too, was political, it, too, was a rebellion against everything that had soiled and degraded the ideal of humanity". Humanism is a historically recent conquest. "The achievements that the Renaissance and the Enlightenment wrested from the past – and may I emphasize, my dear sir, the struggles contained in that verb – were individual human personality, human rights, and human freedom".

Well, the humanist ideal – the humankind's self-perfecting – is essentially an educational struggle. *The Magic Mountain* is a kind of *Bildungsroman* (novel of education, formation) of Hans Castorp. "Gentlemen, the historical connection between humanism and pedagogy only proves the psychological basis of that connection. One should not deny the humanist his position as an educator – indeed it cannot be denied to him, for he alone preserves the tradition of man's dignity and beauty".[5] Indeed, "without education you cannot prevail before humanity, and there is only *one* kind of education – you call it bourgeois, but in fact it is human". It is about creating the *Homo humanus*. Humanity and dignity are words which appear in Mann's masterpiece more than 60 and 50 times, respectively, including the term "altar of humanity".

Already for Locke "the pedagogical issue appears, not under the mere form of a subsidiary extension of the legal-political question, but, on the contrary, as a hyperbolic version of the problem of the government of human beings" (Renaut, 2002, p. 207). This is a "subversion that makes the educational issue appearing as more fundamental than the political one" (p. 208). In Renaut's opinion:

> In this way, the relation between education and politics asserts itself as a relation of condition (education) to conditioned (politics). […]
>
> Consequently, it is between the failure and the success of education that the political dimension takes root: a powerful thesis, impressive, on the horizon of which stands out the conviction that all the more success one has in education, more one may avoid waiting all from the politics and its power. (pp. 219, 220)

This is the powerful role of education as the most profound source of individual and collective liberation and transformation. Kant (1803) believed: "It may be that education will be constantly improved and that each succeeding generation will advance one step towards the *perfecting* of mankind; for with education is involved the great secret of the perfection of human nature" (… *hinter der Edukation steckt das große Geheimnis der Vollkommenheit der menschlichen Natur*) (para. 7).

If every human being is essentially configured by education, at the beginning is education. However, education is socially influenced and politically decided. Education and politics are Siamese sisters not susceptible to separation, as pointed out by J.-P. Rabaut Saint-Étienne, presenting his "National Education Project" at the French National Convention, on 21 December 1792:

> The need for a good theory of education is based on these truths: that it was the Enlightenment that made the revolution and broke the irons of the slaves; that man is susceptible to indefinite perfection; that perfection depends on the Enlightenment he gets; that the more enlightened men are, the better Governments will become; that the more enlightened they are, the more they will know the price of liberty and will know how to keep it; that the more the Enlightenment is available to all, the more equality between men will be maintained. So, you owe the people the Enlightenment, the surest Enlightenment and the means of education most suitable to extend it to infinity. (in Baczko, 2000, p. 296)

To the extent that education becomes better, human beings become better persons, better citizens and more able to better educate their children and to elect rulers able to design better education policies, for better societies and better human beings. "We can therefore only expect progress to be brought about by rulers if their education has been of a higher kind than that of their subjects" (Kant, 1803, para. 14).

Getting the best human beings to become educators is, therefore, an inextricable political-pedagogical responsibility. There is no realistic and humanist way to make the vicious circle of education less vicious and more virtuous other than the 'natural' but cultural and dialectical selection of the best for governing and educating, producing something like what Patrick Tort (2004) called the *evolution reversed effect*: "Natural selection selects then the *civilisation*, which *opposes* to natural selection" (p. 43).

In sum: The best education is one ethically illuminated by the best idea of human perfection, scientifically enlightened by the best knowledge on the human nature, and politically entrusted to the best human beings by better rulers elected by better educated citizens. The dissolution of the education Gordian Knot will thus take a lasting temporal magnitude ...

What is the best that humankind has ever envisioned for becoming better?

Thomas Paine, English writer and politician of the 18th century, a supporter of the American Independence and the French Revolution, author of *The Rights of Man*, wrote: "We have it in our power to begin the world over again".[6] It is the revolutionary power of the human rights ideal, especially of the rights of the child and, in particular, the right to education as Right to Possible.

Right to Possible

In *Candide* (Voltaire, 1759),[7] the philosopher and preceptor Pangloss, disciple of Leibnitz, professes the belief that we live in the "best of all possible worlds", but during the miraculous adventures and misfortunes of his travels, Candide saw and suffered the material and moral miseries of the humankind. He found himself in the *Eldorado*, ancient realm of the Incas, where gold and precious stones were vulgar things, there were no priests, no prisons, no palace of justice, but there was a palace of the sciences. This was a better world, geographically almost inaccessible. It remains for us to "cultivate our garden", concludes Candide. The Garden of the Possible.

As Jean Rivero (1981) taught, every right must have "a precise and possible object" (p. 133). He meant a realistic object, but the possible can transcend the reality. Human rights institute limits that it is necessary to learn and open possibilities that should be explored and brought about. The right to education is the right to learn both the *limits* of the human finitude, which inscribe in the species' children their ethical identity, and the *Possible* as the ontological *utopia* of the infinite human perfectibility. It can be said of the humankind what Don Quixote said of his Dulcinea: that it "is the daughter of her own works, and that virtues rectify blood"; so that it virtually "has in herself higher fortunes".[8]

In Milan Kundera's novel *Identity* (1997), Chantal reads in a letter she had just received from Jean-Marc:

> You have reawakened the obsession of my early youth: I would imagine life before me like a tree. I used to call it the tree of possibilities. We see the life that way for only a brief time. Thereafter, it comes to look like a track laid out once and for all, a tunnel one can never get out of. Still, the old spectre of the tree stays with us in the form of an ineradicable nostalgia. (p. 75)

Many of us probably feel the nostalgia of our infancy and youth lost possibilities ... The human ontogenetic need for ethical *limits* has often been a pretext for the imposition of arbitrary *limitations*. As Rousseau wrote (1762b): "The bounds of possibility, in moral matters, are less narrow than we imagine: it is our weaknesses, our vices and our prejudices that confine them" (Book III, Chapter XII). This idea resounds in the speech Robespierre made at the French National Convention on 13 August 1793: "It is the imagination that usually lays the foundations for the possible and the impossible. But when one has the will to do well one must have the courage to cross the lines" and to move "the boundaries separating the possible from the impossible" (as cited in Baczko, 2000, pp. 27, 37).

Possible is a philosophical multifaceted category. There is the Possible *enclosed* in the real, as mere non-impossibility, less than the real, and the Possible *open* to the imagination, more than the real, as a better reality.

There is, first and foremost, the *Genetic Possible*, both enclosed and open, evoked in the Universal Declaration on the Human Genome and Human Rights (UNESCO, 1997),[9] Article 3:

> The human genome, which by its nature evolves, is subject to mutations. It contains potentialities that are expressed differently according to each individual's natural and social environment, including the individual's state of health, living conditions, nutrition and education.

The *Political Possible* is one enclosed in the real, called upon by Joseph E. Stiglitz (2006), Nobel Prize Winner of Economics in 2001, when he wrote that "another world is possible [...] another world is necessary and inevitable" (p. 24).

Open to the imagination are the Ethical Possible, the Aesthetic Possible and the Pedagogical Possible.

- The *Ethical Possible* is that meant by Richard Kearney (1984) in his doctoral thesis titled *Poétique du Possible* (Poetry of the Possible), where he argued that the human being is a *figuring* being. He/she "figures and is figured, at the same time", creates and is created (p. 98). To exist humanly is being figured, and "we are simultaneously *already figured* and *always to be figured*; older and younger than ourselves" (p. 97). That is why "to live in the world ethically means that nothing goes without saying" (p. 142), that "every institution may be other than it is at present" (p. 156), that man himself, as Hegel said, "is what he is not and is not what he is" (p. 148), or that, in Husserl's words, being human "is an ought to be" (p. 201).[10]
- The *Aesthetic Possible* is that referred to by Picasso when he said: "Everything that can be imagined is real", "I aim at representing a real more real than the real".[11] Marcel Proust: There are "a series of verities pertaining to a world more real than that in which I lived".[12] According to Denis Huisman (1954), "the real is what both art and science are founded on, but one to investigate it, the other to overcome it" (p. 105).
- The *Pedagogical Possible* is rooted in the Genetic Possible, calls for the Political Possible, believes in the Ethical Possible and dreams of the Aesthetic Possible. It draws on the perfectibility of the human species and the uniqueness of each human being. We could say that education is a poetic action, not in the Aristotelian sense of action carried out in view of a finished product, ready to be used, but in the sense of Kearney's *Poétique du Possible.*

The Possible is, therefore, the inexhaustible harvest of the human species' unique perfectibility and fabulous diversity. It does not become real, however, without being struggled for.

Struggling for Possible

In *The Struggle for Law* – the title under which a famous lecture given in the Juridical Society of Vienna, in 1872, was published – Rudolf von Jhering (1872) said: "All the law in the world has been obtained by strife. […] the struggle for law, the battle for one's legal rights, is the poetry of character" (pp. 60, 138). Struggling for Law is struggling for power, most importantly the power of human rights, which are empowering, by definition, as above seen (see 4.4.2). The right to education may be considered the most empowering human right, to the extent that it is about the *power to be,* to be human. This will be a long-lasting struggle, because:

- Basic human rights are still lacking for the great majority of human beings, especially children.

- Schools are lacking and tens of millions of children are lacking in school because they must work, or are forced to be involved in the wars of adults, or because of other disgraceful causes.
- The right to education is lacking at home and in schools, because loving children is necessary, but not any love is pedagogical; education is necessary, but not any education is legitimate; school is necessary, but it is not yet, in general, fully a right to education school.

The right to education is then “a big struggle”, as the extraordinary girl Malala Yousafzai said. She wrote: “I don’t want to be thought of as ‘the girl who was shot by the Taliban’ but ‘the girl who fought for education’. This is the cause to which I want to devote my life”. It’s a fight for the liberating “weapon of knowledge”.

> Peace in every home, every street, every village, every country – this is my dream. Education for every boy and every girl in the world. To sit down on a chair and read my books with all my friends at school is my right. To see each and every human being with a smile of happiness is my wish. (Yousafzai, 2013, pp. 369, 372, 374)

In the novel *The Pearl* by John Steinbeck (1945),[12] a fisherman (Kino) found an exceptionally valuable pearl, “the greatest pearl in the world”, that became a “dream of the future”. Kino says: “This pearl has become my soul. If I give it up, I shall lose my soul”. He tells his wife (Juana): “This is our one chance. Our son [Coyotito] must go to school. He must break out of the pot that holds us in”. However, feeling more and more surrounded by the greediness of the pearl buyers and fearing for his life, the fisherman had no choice but to throw the “Pearl of the World” back into the sea ...

Education is like a pearl hidden in a shell, the treasure evoked by the title of the Delors Report (1996) *Learning: The treasure within.* Ferdinand Buisson (1882) had already written: “Education does not create *ex nihilo* [from nothing] but it really creates. The treasures it draws from the very depths of the child’s nature ...” (p. 807). The Supreme Court of India, in *Case Unni Krishnan, J.P. And Ors. Etc. ... vs State Of Andhra Pradesh And Ors. ... on 4 February, 1993 (1993 AIR 2178, 1993 SCR (1) 594)*,[13] cited an Indian thinker of the first century BC who said: “Education is the special manifestation of man; Education is the treasure which can be preserved without the fear of loss” (para. 42).

Struggling for the Pedagogic Possible is to struggle for the pearl, the treasure of our humanity that, the better distributed, the richer humankind gets.

Summing up

Education is a genetic human need vested with human right status. This fundamentally means that, without education, human beings are not fully human, i.e. are not empowered to accomplish their unique worth and dignity.

Revolution is a term frequently used to qualify the advent of human rights, as we know. Revolution of the Right to Education is not, therefore, a voluntarist title, a rhetorical proclamation. We know why human rights and the rights of the child are revolutionary advancements: The human person has become the ethical-juridical supreme value and the child has been fully recognised as a human person. The Revolution of the Right to Education is simply the corollary of the revolutionary significance of the normative integrity of the right to education. It may be clear-cut summarised this way:

- *The right to education is not:*
  - a right of parents over children, because children are not their parents' property;
  - a right of States over citizens, because citizens are not States' property.
- *The right to education is:*
  - a right of every human being, regardless of age, gender, family, national and cultural belongings, each and every one having his/her own right – son and daughter, mother and father, student and teacher;
  - a right to an education as agreed in IEL and incorporated in numerous Constitutions and General Education Acts, concerning its values, aims, contents, methods, conditions, both in families and schools, public and private.

It may be that the revolutionary significance of these sentences is not evident to everyone, but if we take a lucid look at the realities and perversities of family and school education all over the world … at education amounting to spiritual sequestration of children and peoples … at the indecent leaders people may elect … at what humans can do to each other … at violence and even atrocities committed in the name of Gods … How long can the human species survive such wastage of *possibles* for its perfecting?

Consequently, the Revolution of the Right to Education consists not just of making education available and accessible to all, both children and adults, everywhere. This is great and still a distant goal, especially for girls and dozens of million children striving to survive on all continents. However, for education to be the most empowering human right – as it can be – it must effectively aim at the personal flourishing through free, full, and harmonious development of the human personality. This is a far more distant, uncertain goal, but the sole hope for the humankind …

Revolution of the Right to Education: The key is liberty and responsibility for what *human* liberty means..

In this respect, let us quote Jean-Paul Sartre who, in tune with what he said speaking at the inaugural session of UNESCO's first General Conference (see 4.1.2.5.5), in those days famously stated in his conference on *Existentialism Is a Humanism* (1946)[14] "that *existence* comes before *essence* [...]. What do we mean by saying that existence precedes essence? We mean that man first of all exists, encounters himself, surges up in the world – and defines himself afterwards". As a consequence, "one will never be able to explain one's action by reference to a given and specific human nature; in other words, there is no determinism – man is free, man *is* freedom". Nonetheless, there is "a human universality of *condition*", that is, "all the *limitations* which *a priori* define man's fundamental situation in the universe".

> I cannot make liberty my aim unless I make that of others equally my aim. Consequently, when I recognise, as entirely authentic, that man is a being whose existence precedes his essence, and that he is a free being who cannot, in any circumstances, but will his freedom, at the same time I realize that I cannot not will the freedom of others. [...]
>
> If, however, it is true that existence is prior to essence, man is responsible for what he is. [...] And, when we say that man is responsible for himself, we do not mean that he is responsible only for his own individuality, but that he is responsible for all men. [...] For in effect, of all the actions a man may take in order to create himself as he wills to be, there is not one which is not creative, at the same time, of an image of man such as he believes he ought to be. To choose between this or that is at the same time to affirm the value of that which is chosen; [...] Our responsibility is thus much greater than we had supposed, for it concerns mankind as a whole. [...] In fashioning myself I fashion man.

This *humanitas* seems to be out of reach of any *cyborg* ...

The right to education is, therefore, a new paradigm, that is, a normative-theoretical framework that reconstitutes the sense and success of education, dissolving chronic problems, pointing to solutions for others, and raising new ones.

In the history of the pedagogic thought, the new-born was sometimes compared to a clean slate or blank canvas where education writes the text of much of his/her destiny. Education should be the *Ars Magna* (Great Art) of dreaming, loving, reading and writing the *human text*.

A Theory of Education illuminated by the Ethics of the Right to Education and our best knowledge distinguishes itself by its radicalness and utopian dialecticity, but when *normal thinking* becomes circular, sterile and even perverse, thinking radically and utopianly is the only ethical, rational and practical alternative.

In line with its *Medium-Term Strategy, 2014–2021* (37 C/4),[15] following which "UNESCO will continue to serve as a laboratory of ideas and innovations in education, and [...] will inspire new ways of conceptualizing education and learning" (para. 38), it launched in September 2019 the Global Initiative *Futures of Education – Learning to Become*. It is steered by an Independent International Commission comprised of 18 members from the worlds of politics, academia, arts, science, business, and education. The Initiative is so presented[16]:

> This project uses the concept of futures in the plural in order to recognize that there is a rich diversity of ways of knowing and being around the world. [...]
>
> The goal is to generate discussion and action on the role of education, knowledge and learning in view of the predicted, possible and preferred futures of humanity and the planet. [...]
>
> The concept of *Learning to Become* points to a philosophy of education and an approach to pedagogy that views learning as a process of continual unfolding that is ongoing and lifelong. To think in terms of "becoming" is to invoke a line of thought that emphasizes potentials, rejects determinism and expresses a flexible openness to the new. [...]
>
> As we come to terms with human-caused changes to the planet and face the possibilities of fundamental transformations in social organization, human consciousness and human identity, humanity needs to devote attention to the question: what do we want to become? Knowledge and learning are at the core of transformations in human minds and societies. *Learning to Become* invites us to become something we have not yet become. [...]
>
> Education is a key piece of the *2030 Agenda for Sustainable Development*. Despite the scope of these global commitments and the expected achievements, there is still an urgent need to look beyond this fast-approaching horizon. While the *Education 2030 Incheon Declaration and Framework for Action* lays out a roadmap for the transformation of education systems and affirms a central commitment to inclusion and equity, we must still ask what education might yet become – and what education might yet enable us to become. UNESCO's *Futures of Education* initiative

uses the horizon of 2050 and beyond in order to anticipate and shape both nearer and more distant futures.

The *UNESCO Medium-term Strategy – 2002–2007* (31 C/4)[17] included (para. 63):

- Intensified international public debate about the right to education
- Development of guidelines and shared norms, including the proposal of a consolidated normative instrument on the right to education

This idea has not been fruitful so far, but a *consolidated international normative instrument on the right to education*, enhancing the consistency, unity, readability and effectivity of its normativity, would serve as Constitution of the Revolution of the Right to Education.[18]

In sum:

- The moral and intellectual progress of humankind is protagonised by great personalities – prophets, heroes, martyrs, creators, etc. – spokespersons of peoples' conscience and aspirations, as were the Big Five who have most influenced the drafting of the UDHR: Eleanor Roosevelt (EUA), René Cassin (France), Charles Malik (Lebanon), Peng Chun Chang (Chine) and John P. Humphrey (Canada).
- The world will not be an empire of human rights while States are not realms of human rights, but States will not be realms of human rights while families and schools are not homelands of the rights of the child. Violations of human rights chain themselves in a vicious circle of reproduction of poverty, ignorance, suffering, exclusion, violence, between generations, through children.
- One says that the wealth of nations lies in their peoples. The treasure of peoples are their children. It is in the bodies, hearts and minds of children that parents and all peoples should sow the joys of their future. Children are the Utopia of Humankind. The map and the compass of this Utopia is the right to education as a right to learn, to learn to learn, to learn to be human – equal, free, different, better. Every human being can learn to *imprint* into the world his/her love for Humanity.
- The human species has of itself a positively or negatively exaggerated image. A human being is born without a *raison d'être* (a reason for being) but has many reasons to be as he or she is. Of how many needs and influences, sentiments and thoughts, distresses and revolts, desires and dreams, a human being is made up ... It is for being so radically educable that human beings are able both to ascend to the heights of the sublimity of moral, intellectual or artistic genius, and to descend to the depths and darkness of cruelty of which no other animal is capable.

- Education is the greatest power and the greatest responsibility of the human species because human beings are their names, their faces, their bodies and everything education and life can generate inside themselves. The species' children become truly *human* insofar as their basic needs are satisfied and they are neuronally endowed – through words, silences, looks, gestures – with a symbolic interiority nurtured by sentiments of recognition, self-esteem, otherness, goodness, kindness.[19] This is why the humankind is not the worst animal species: it can be infinitely better.
- Inasmuch as morality may be considered the most distinguishing faculty of the human perfectibility, the primacy of moral education should be imperative and consist of learning the values the species has invented for being and living better: human dignity and rights. Learning, first and foremost, to put oneself in the shoes of others, in order to strive to understand their feelings, thoughts, behaviours, and to act accordingly. The essence of the pedagogical responsibility lies in the cultivation of Liberty, Reciprocity and Responsibility – Edenic flowers and fruits whose colours, smells and flavours are the Promised Land of our infinite humanisation …
- Globally regarded, the world of education still looks like the Ptolemaic astronomical system in the late Middle Ages: In the galaxy of education, the sun keeps moving around the earth … Saturated with reforms, the paradigm of the traditional right of education is exhausted. The human right to education is the telescope of a Copernican Revolution that will mean the political-pedagogical breaking of the vicious circle of the historical and psychological 'cloning' of the coming generations by the older ones, driven by the human compulsion and 'divine' temptation to 'create' children in their image and likeness.
- The Revolution of the Right to Education – in resonance with the Revolution of Human Rights and the Revolution of the Rights of the Child – could be summarised in this astronomic metaphor: Education should not be centred either in the *earth of the adults* or in the *sun of the childhood*, but rather projected into the *universe of the human rights* where there are not majors and minors, parents and children, teachers and pupils, but rather *persons* equal by dignity and rights. As a consequence, the *pedagogical reason* is no longer the *biological reason* of the Family nor the *political reason* of the State, but the *Ethical Reason* of the Subject, opening to full human flourishing.

H. G. Wells wrote in *Outline of History* (1920, Part II, 40.4)[20]: "Human history becomes more and more a race between education and catastrophe". Now that we know why education is the greatest power and the greatest responsibility of the human species, maybe it will be able to reach – in time – the full awareness that the right to education is the *abracadabra* to find the Holy Grail of its destiny …

To be or not to be a human right – here is the question regarding the future of education and our Humanity.

Notes

1 Gordian Knot is a seemingly intractable issue, given its complexity. On the Greek legend of the Gordian Knot, protagonised by Alexander the Great, see: https://en.wikipedia.org/wiki/Gordian_Knot

2 https://en.wikisource.org/wiki/The_Satires_of_Juvenal

3 https://www.marxists.org/archive/marx/works/1845/theses/theses.htm

4 https://web.archive.org/web/20160404072503/http://www.jus.uio.no/sisu/war_and_peace.leo_tolstoy/portrait.a5.pdf

5 *Man soll dem Humanisten das Amt der Erziehung nicht nehmen – man kann es ihm nicht nehmen, denn nur bei ihm ist die Überlieferung von der Würde und Schönheit des Menschen.*

6 https://oll.libertyfund.org/titles/paine-the-writings-of-thomas-paine-vol-i-1774-1779#Paine_0548-01_319

7 http://www.gutenberg.org/ebooks/19942

8 http://www.spanisharts.com/books/quijote/2chapter32.htm
In Spanish: *A eso puedo decir – respondió don Quijote – que Dulcinea es hija de sus obras, y que las virtudes adoban la sangre*" y *virtualmente tiene en sí encerradas mayores venturas.* (https://cvc.cervantes.es/literatura/clasicos/quijote/edicion/parte2/cap32/cap32_03.htm).

9 http://www.unesco.org/new/en/social-and-human-sciences/themes/bioethics/human-genome-and-human-rights/

10 Referring to Julian Huxley, Alison Bashford (2013) notes: "The 'Need for a Science of Human Possibilities' was his special plea" (p. 161).

11 https://www.babelio.com/auteur/Pablo-Picasso/16890/citations

12 https://archive.org/stream/ThePearlJohnSteinbeck/The-Pearl-John-Steinbeck_djvu.txt

13 http://indiankanoon.org/doc/1775396

14 https://www.marxists.org/reference/archive/sartre/works/exist/sartre.htm

15 https://unesdoc.unesco.org/ark:/48223/pf0000227860

16 https://en.unesco.org/futuresofeducation/initiative

17 http://unesdoc.unesco.org/images/0012/001254/125434e.pdf

18 This is an idea shared by the late Alfred Fernandez (to whom I pay homage), who believed "that it is perhaps time to work within UNESCO on developing a consolidated normative instrument on the right to education. [...] It would be a specific instrument with an effective monitoring mechanism and should be the linchpin of all UNESCO work in the field of education, placing education matters firmly in a rights-based context" (Fernandez, 2007, p. 321).

19 See https://mgiep.unesco.org/the-blue-dot-issue-11

20 https://archive.org/details/OutlineOfHistory

References

Bæchler, J. (1994). *Précis de la démocratie.* Calman-Lévy/Éditions UNESCO.

Baczko, B. (Prés.). (2000). *Une éducation pour la démocratie – Textes et projets de l'époque révolutionnaire*. Droz.

Bashford, A. (2013). Julian Huxley's transhumanism. In M. Turda (Ed.), *Crafting humans: From genesis to eugenics and beyond* (pp. 153–167). V&R Unipress. https://www.academia.edu/6086492/Julian_Huxleys_Transhumanism

Buisson, F. (1882). Éducation. In F. Buisson (Sous la direction de), *Dictionnaire de Pédagogie et d'Instruction Primaire* – 1ère Partie, Tome Premier. https://gallica.bnf.fr/ark:/12148/bpt6k24232h/f1.image

Crampe-Casnabet, M. (1985). *Condorcet, lecteur des Lumières*. PUF.

Delors, J. et al. (1996). *Éducation – Un trésor est caché dedans*. Éditions UNESCO. http://unesdoc.unesco.org/images/0011/001159/115930f.pdf (Highlights in English: www.unesco.org/education/pdf/15_62.pdf).

Fernandez, A. (2007). Ensuring Equal Opportunities in Education. In *Standard-setting in UNESCO – Volume I: Normative action in education, science and culture. Essays in commemoration of the sixtieth anniversary of UNESCO* (pp. 313–321). UNESCO Publishing/Martinus Nijhoff Publishers.

Hinds, M. (2002). *Teaching as a clinical profession: A new challenge for education*. Carnegie Corporation of New York. Retrieved July 2018, from https://www.carnegie.org/publications/teaching-as-a-clinical-profession-a-new-challenge-for-education

Huisman, D. (1954). *L'esthétique* (Que-sais-je?, Vol. xxx), PUF.

Jhering, R. (1872). *Der Kampf um's Recht – Zum hundertsten Todesjahr des Autors herausgegeben von Felix Ermacora*. Prophyläen Verlag. www.koeblergerhard.de/Fontes/JheringDerKampfumsRecht_hgvErmacora1992.pdf (An English translation: https://archive.org/details/cu31924021172832/page/n8).

Kant, I. (1803). *Traité de pédagogie* (tr. de J. Barni, revue et actualisée, Introduction et notes par Pierre-José About). Hachette (1981). Original text: https://de.wikisource.org/wiki/%C3%9Cber_P%C3%A4dagogik (An English translation: https://oll.libertyfund.org/titles/kant-kant-on-education-uber-padagogik).

Kearney, R. (1984). *Poétique du possible – Phénoménologie herméneutique de la figuration*. Beauchesne.

Kundera, M. (1997). *Identity* (Transl. by Linda Asher). HarperCollins Publishers.

Mann, Th. (2005). *The magic mountain* [*Der Zauberberg*, 1924] (Transl. by J. E. Woods). Alfred A. Knopf, Everyman's Library.

Miller, A. (1980). *C'est pour ton bien – Racines de la violence dans l'éducation de l'enfant* (*Am Anfang war Erziehung*, trad. de Jeanne Etoré). Éditions Aubier Montaigne.

Plato. (1997). *Plato – Complete works* (J. M. Cooper & D. S. Hutchinson, Ed.). Hackeht Publishing Company.

Renaut, A. (2002). *La libération des enfants – Contribution philosophique à une histoire de l'enfance*. Calmann-Lévy.

Rivero, J. (1981). *Les libertés publiques – 1/Les droits de l'homme* (3rd éd.). Presses Universitaires de France, Col. Thémis-Droit.

Rousseau, J.-J. (1762a). *Émile ou de l'éducation* (Chronologie et introduction par Michel Launay). Garnier-Flammarion (1966). http://gallica.bnf.fr/ark:/12148/bpt6k5786957n/

f12.image (An English translation: https://oll.libertyfund.org/titles/rousseau-emile-or-education).

Rousseau, J.-J. (1762b). *Du contrat social* (Édition établie par Pierre Burgelin). GF-Flammarion. https://www.rousseauonline.ch/pdf/rousseauonline-0004.pdf (An English translation: https://www.earlymoderntexts.com/assets/pdfs/rousseau1762.pdf).

Rousseau, J.-J. (1913). *The social contract and discourses* (Translated and introduced by G. D. H. Cole). Everyman (1993). (An English translation online: https://oll.libertyfund.org/titles/rousseau-the-social-contract-and-discourses).

Sargent, P. (1945). *Between two wars – The failure of education: 1920–1940*. Porter Sargent Publishers. https://babel.hathitrust.org/cgi/pt?id=mdp.39015039754877&view=1up&seq=582

Stiglitz, J. (2006). *Making globalization work*. W. W. Norton & Company.

The Holmes Group. (1986). *Tomorrow's teachers*. New York.

Tort, P. (2004). La généalogie darwinienne de la morale. *Sciences et Avenir – Hors-Série, 139*, 43.

Yousafzai, M. (with C. Lamb). (2013). *I am Malala – The girl who stood up for education and was shot by the Taliban*. Weidenfeld & Nicolson (ebook).

Appendices

APPENDIX A

Universal Most General Normative Framework of the Right to Education

A.1 Universal Declaration of Human Rights, UN, 1948

Article 26

1. Everyone has the right to education. Education shall be free, at least in the elementary and fundamental stages. Elementary education shall be compulsory. Technical and professional education shall be made generally available and higher education shall be equally accessible to all on the basis of merit.
2. Education shall be directed to the full development of the human personality and to the strengthening of respect for human rights and fundamental freedoms. It shall promote understanding, tolerance and friendship among all nations, racial or religious groups, and shall further the activities of the United Nations for the maintenance of peace.
3. Parents have a prior right to choose the kind of education that shall be given to their children.

A.2 Convention against Discrimination in Education, UNESCO, 1960

The General Conference of the United Nations Educational, Scientific and Cultural Organization, meeting in Paris from 14 November to 15 December 1960, at its eleventh session,

Recalling that the Universal Declaration of Human Rights asserts the principle of non-discrimination and proclaims that every person has the right to education,

Considering that discrimination in education is a violation of rights enunciated in that Declaration,

Considering that, under the terms of its Constitution, the United Nations Educational, Scientific and Cultural Organization has the purpose of instituting collaboration among the nations with a view to furthering for all universal respect for human rights and equality of educational opportunity,

Recognizing that, consequently, the United Nations Educational, Scientific and Cultural Organization, while respecting the diversity of national educational

 | DOI: 10.1163/9789004462465_008

systems, has the duty not only to proscribe any form of discrimination in education but also to promote equality of opportunity and treatment for all in education,

Having before it proposals concerning the different aspects of discrimination in education, constituting item 17.1.4 of the agenda of the session,

Having decided at its tenth session that this question should be made the subject of an international convention as well as of recommendations to Member States,

Adopts this Convention on the fourteenth day of December 1960.

Article 1

1. For the purpose of this Convention, the term "discrimination" includes any distinction, exclusion, limitation or preference which, being based on race, colour, sex, language, religion, political or other opinion, national or social origin, economic condition or birth, has the purpose or effect of nullifying or impairing equality of treatment in education and in particular:

a Of depriving any person or group of persons of access to education of any type or at any level;

b Of limiting any person or group of persons to education of an inferior standard;

c Subject to the provisions of article 2 of this Convention, of establishing or maintaining separate educational systems or institutions for persons or groups of persons; or

d Of inflicting on any person or group of persons conditions which are incompatible with the dignity of man.

2. For the purposes of this Convention, the term "education" refers to all types and levels of education, and includes access to education, the standard and quality of education, and the conditions under which it is given.

Article 2

When permitted in a State, the following situations shall not be deemed to constitute discrimination, within the meaning of article 1 of this Convention:

a The establishment or maintenance of separate educational systems or institutions for pupils of the two sexes, if these systems or institutions offer equivalent access to education, provide a teaching staff with qualifications of the same standard as well as school premises and equipment of the same quality, and afford the opportunity to take the same or equivalent courses of study;

b The establishment or maintenance, for religious or linguistic reasons, of separate educational systems or institutions offering an education which is in keeping with the wishes of the pupil's parents or legal guardians, if participation in such systems or attendance at such institutions is optional and if the education provided conforms to such standards as may be laid down or approved by the competent authorities, in particular for education of the same level;

c The establishment or maintenance of private educational institutions, if the object of the institutions is not to secure the exclusion of any group but to provide educational facilities in addition to those provided by the public authorities, if the institutions are conducted in accordance with that object, and if the education provided conforms with such standards as may be laid down or approved by the competent authorities, in particular for education of the same level.

Article 3

In order to eliminate and prevent discrimination within the meaning of this Convention, the States Parties thereto undertake:

a To abrogate any statutory provisions and any administrative instructions and to discontinue any administrative practices which involve discrimination in education;

b To ensure, by legislation where necessary, that there is no discrimination in the admission of pupils to educational institutions;

c Not to allow any differences of treatment by the public authorities between nationals, except on the basis of merit or need, in the matter of school fees and the grant of scholarships or other forms of assistance to pupils and necessary permits and facilities for the pursuit of studies in foreign countries;

d Not to allow, in any form of assistance granted by the public authorities to educational institutions, any restrictions or preference based solely on the ground that pupils belong to a particular group;

e To give foreign nationals resident within their territory the same access to education as that given to their own nationals.

Article 4

The States Parties to this Convention undertake furthermore to formulate, develop and apply a national policy which, by methods appropriate to the circumstances and to national usage, will tend to promote equality of opportunity and of treatment in the matter of education and in particular:

a To make primary education free and compulsory; make secondary education in its different forms generally available and accessible to all; make higher education equally accessible to all on the basis of individual capacity; assure compliance by all with the obligation to attend school prescribed by law;

b To ensure that the standards of education are equivalent in all public education institutions of the same level, and that the conditions relating to the quality of education provided are also equivalent;

c To encourage and intensify by appropriate methods the education of persons who have not received any primary education or who have not completed the entire primary education course and the continuation of their education on the basis of individual capacity;

d To provide training for the teaching profession without discrimination.

Article 5

1. The States Parties to this Convention agree that:
   a Education shall be directed to the full development of the human personality an d to the strengthening of respect for human rights and fundamental freedoms; it shall promote understanding, tolerance and friendship among all nations, racial or religious groups, and shall further the activities of the United Nations for the maintenance of peace;
   b It is essential to respect the liberty of parents and, where applicable, of legal guardians, firstly to choose for their children institutions other than those maintained by the public authorities but conforming to such minimum educational standards as may be laid down or approved by the competent authorities and, secondly, to ensure in a manner consistent with the procedures followed in the State for the application of its legislation, the religious and moral education of the children in conformity with their own convictions; and no person or group of persons should be compelled to receive religious instruction inconsistent with his or their conviction;
   c It is essential to recognize the right of members of national minorities to carry on their own educational activities, including the maintenance of schools and, depending on the educational policy of each State, the use or the teaching of their own language, provided however:
      i. That this right is not exercised in a manner which prevents the members of these minorities from understanding the culture and language of the community as a whole and from participating in its activities, or which prejudices national sovereignty;
      ii. That the standard of education is not lower than the general standard laid down or approved by the competent authorities; and
      iii. That attendance at such schools is optional.
2. The States Parties to this Convention undertake to take all necessary measures to ensure the application of the principles enunciated in paragraph 1 of this article.

Article 6

In the application of this Convention, the States Parties to it undertake to pay the greatest attention to any recommendations hereafter adopted by the General Conference of the United Nations Educational, Scientific and Cultural Organization defining the measures to be taken against the different forms of discrimination in education and for the purpose of ensuring equality of opportunity and treatment in education.

Article 7

The States Parties to this Convention shall in their periodic reports submitted to the General Conference of the United Nations Educational, Scientific and Cultural Organization on dates and in a manner to be determined by it, give information on the legislative and administrative provisions which they have adopted and other action which they have taken for the application of this Convention, including that taken for the formulation and the development of the national policy defined in article 4 as well as the results achieved and the obstacles encountered in the application of that policy.

Article 8

Any dispute which may arise between any two or more States Parties to this Convention concerning the interpretation or application of this Convention which is not settled by negotiations shall at the request of the Parties to the dispute be referred, failing other means of settling the dispute, to the International Court of Justice for decision.

Article 9

Reservations to this Convention shall not be permitted.

Article 10

This Convention shall not have the effect of diminishing the rights which individuals or groups may enjoy by virtue of agreements concluded between two or more States, where such rights are not contrary to the letter or spirit of this Convention.

Article 11

This Convention is drawn up in English, French, Russian and Spanish, the four texts being equally authoritative.

Article 12

1. This Convention shall be subject to ratification or acceptance by States Members of the United Nations Educational, Scientific and Cultural Organization in accordance with their respective constitutional procedures.
2. The instruments of ratification or acceptance shall be deposited with the Director-General of the United Nations Educational, Scientific and Cultural Organization.

Article 13

1. This Convention shall be open to accession by all States not Members of the United Nations Educational, Scientific and Cultural Organization which are invited to do so by the Executive Board of the Organization.
2. Accession shall be effected by the deposit of an instrument of accession with the Director-General of the United Nations Educational, Scientific and Cultural Organization.

Article 14

This Convention shall enter into force three months after the date of the deposit of the third instrument of ratification, acceptance or accession, but only with respect to those States which have deposited their respective instruments on or before that date. It shall enter into force with respect to any other State three months after the deposit of its instrument of ratification, acceptance or accession.

Article 15

The States Parties to this Convention recognize that the Convention is applicable not only to their metropolitan territory but also to all non-self-governing, trust, colonial and other territories for the international relations of which they are responsible; they undertake to consult, if necessary, the governments or other competent authorities of these territories on or before ratification, acceptance or accession with a view to securing the application of the Convention to those territories, and to notify the Director-General of the United Nations Educational, Scientific and Cultural Organization of the territories to which it is accordingly applied, the notification to take effect three months after the date of its receipt.

Article 16

1. Each State Party to this Convention may denounce the Convention on its own behalf or on behalf of any territory for whose international relations it is responsible.

2. The denunciation shall be notified by an instrument in writing, deposited with the Director-General of the United Nations Educational, Scientific and Cultural Organization.
3. The denunciation shall take effect twelve months after the receipt of the instrument of denunciation.

Article 17

The Director-General of the United Nations Educational, Scientific and Cultural Organization shall inform the States Members of the Organization, the States not members of the Organization which are referred to in article 13, as well as the United Nations, of the deposit of all the instruments of ratification, acceptance and accession provided for in articles 12 and 13, and of notifications and denunciations provided for in articles 15 and 16 respectively.

Article 18

1. This Convention may be revised by the General Conference of the United Nations Educational, Scientific and Cultural Organization. Any such revision shall, however, bind only the States which shall become Parties to the revising convention.
2. If the General Conference should adopt a new convention revising this Convention in whole or in part, then, unless the new convention otherwise provides, this Convention shall cease to be open to ratification, acceptance or accession as from the date on which the new revising convention enters into force.

Article 19

In conformity with Article 102 of the Charter of the United Nations, this Convention shall be registered with the Secretariat of the United Nations at the request of the Director-General of the United Nations Educational, Scientific and Cultural Organization.

DONE in Paris, this fifteenth day of December 1960, in two authentic copies bearing the signatures of the President of the eleventh session of the General Conference and of the Director-General of the United Nations Educational, Scientific and Cultural Organization, which shall be deposited in the archives of the United Nations Educational, Scientific and Cultural Organization, and certified true copies of which shall be delivered to all the States referred to in articles 12 and 13 as well as to the United Nations.

The foregoing is the authentic text of the Convention duly adopted by the General Conference of the United Nations Educational, Scientific and Cultural Organization during its eleventh session, which was held in Paris and declared closed the fifteenth day of December 1960.

IN FAITH WHEREOF we have appended our signatures this fifteenth day of December 1960.

A.3 International Covenant on Economic, Social and Cultural Rights, UN, 1966

Article 13

1. The States Parties to the present Covenant recognize the right of everyone to education. They agree that education shall be directed to the full development of the human personality and the sense of its dignity, and shall strengthen the respect for human rights and fundamental freedoms. They further agree that education shall enable all persons to participate effectively in a free society, promote understanding, tolerance and friendship among all nations and all racial, ethnic or religious groups, and further the activities of the United Nations for the maintenance of peace.
2. The States Parties to the present Covenant recognize that, with a view to achieving the full realization of this right:
   a Primary education shall be compulsory and available free to all;
   b Secondary education in its different forms, including technical and vocational secondary education, shall be made generally available and accessible to all by every appropriate means, and in particular by the progressive introduction of free education;
   c Higher education shall be made equally accessible to all, on the basis of capacity, by every appropriate means, and in particular by the progressive introduction of free education;
   d Fundamental education shall be encouraged or intensified as far as possible for those persons who have not received or completed the whole period of their primary education;
   e The development of a system of schools at all levels shall be actively pursued, an adequate fellowship system shall be established, and the material conditions of teaching staff shall be continuously improved.
3. The States Parties to the present Covenant undertake to have respect for the liberty of parents and, when applicable, legal guardians to choose for their children schools, other than those established by the public authorities, which conform to such minimum educational standards as may be laid down or approved by the State and to ensure the religious and moral education of their children in conformity with their own convictions.

4. No part of this article shall be construed so as to interfere with the liberty of individuals and bodies to establish and direct educational institutions, subject always to the observance of the principles set forth in paragraph I of this article and to the requirement that the education given in such institutions shall conform to such minimum standards as may be laid down by the State.

Article 14

Each State Party to the present Covenant which, at the time of becoming a Party, has not been able to secure in its metropolitan territory or other territories under its jurisdiction compulsory primary education, free of charge, undertakes, within two years, to work out and adopt a detailed plan of action for the progressive implementation, within a reasonable number of years, to be fixed in the plan, of the principle of compulsory education free of charge for all.

A.4 Convention on the Rights of the Child, UN, 1989

Article 1

For the purposes of the present Convention, a child means every human being below the age of eighteen years unless under the law applicable to the child, majority is attained earlier.

Article 5

States Parties shall respect the responsibilities, rights and duties of parents or, where applicable, the members of the extended family or community as provided for by local custom, legal guardians or other persons legally responsible for the child, to provide, in a manner consistent with the evolving capacities of the child, appropriate direction and guidance in the exercise by the child of the rights recognized in the present Convention.

Article 18

1. States Parties shall use their best efforts to ensure recognition of the principle that both parents have common responsibilities for the upbringing and development of the child. Parents or, as the case may be, legal guardians, have the primary responsibility for the upbringing and development of the child. The best interests of the child will be their basic concern.

2. For the purpose of guaranteeing and promoting the rights set forth in the present Convention, States Parties shall render appropriate assistance to parents and legal guardians in the performance of their child-rearing responsibilities and shall

Article 28

1. States Parties recognize the right of the child to education, and with a view to achieving this right progressively and on the basis of equal opportunity, they shall, in particular:
   a Make primary education compulsory and available free to all;
   b Encourage the development of different forms of secondary education, including general and vocational education, make them available and accessible to every child, and take appropriate measures such as the introduction of free education and offering financial assistance in case of need;
   c Make higher education accessible to all on the basis of capacity by every appropriate means;
   d Make educational and vocational information and guidance available and accessible to all children;
   e Take measures to encourage regular attendance at schools and the reduction of drop-out rates.
2. States Parties shall take all appropriate measures to ensure that school discipline is administered in a manner consistent with the child's human dignity and in conformity with the present Convention.
3. States Parties shall promote and encourage international cooperation in matters relating to education, in particular with a view to contributing to the elimination of ignorance and illiteracy throughout the world and facilitating access to scientific and technical knowledge and modern teaching methods. In this regard, particular account shall be taken of the needs of developing countries.

Article 29

1. States Parties agree that the education of the child shall be directed to:
   a The development of the child's personality, talents and mental and physical abilities to their fullest potential;
   b The development of respect for human rights and fundamental freedoms, and for the principles enshrined in the Charter of the United Nations;
   c The development of respect for the child's parents, his or her own cultural identity, language and values, for the national values of the country in

which the child is living, the country from which he or she may originate, and for civilizations different from his or her own;

d The preparation of the child for responsible life in a free society, in the spirit of understanding, peace, tolerance, equality of sexes, and friendship among all peoples, ethnic, national and religious groups and persons of indigenous origin;

e The development of respect for the natural environment.

2. No part of the present article or article 28 shall be construed so as to interfere with the liberty of individuals and bodies to establish and direct educational institutions, subject always to the observance of the principle set forth in paragraph 1 of the present article and to the requirements that the education given in such institutions shall conform to such minimum standards as may be laid down by the State.

APPENDIX B

Provisions on the Right to Education of Some More Vulnerable Categories of Persons

B.1 Convention on the Elimination of all Forms of Discrimination against Women, UN, 1979

Article 10

States Parties shall take all appropriate measures to eliminate discrimination against women in order to ensure to them equal rights with men in the field of education and in particular to ensure, on a basis of equality of men and women:

a The same conditions for career and vocational guidance, for access to studies and for the achievement of diplomas in educational establishments of all categories in rural as well as in urban areas; this equality shall be ensured in pre-school, general, technical, professional and higher technical education, as well as in all types of vocational training;

b Access to the same curricula, the same examinations, teaching staff with qualifications of the same standard and school premises and equipment of the same quality;

c The elimination of any stereotyped concept of the roles of men and women at all levels and in all forms of education by encouraging coeducation and other types of education which will help to achieve this aim and, in particular, by the revision of textbooks and school programmes and the adaptation of teaching methods;

d The same opportunities to benefit from scholarships and other study grants;

e The same opportunities for access to programmes of continuing education, including adult and functional literacy programmes, particularly those aimed at reducing, at the earliest possible time, any gap in education existing between men and women;

f The reduction of female student drop-out rates and the organization of programmes for girls and women who have left school prematurely;

g The same opportunities to participate actively in sports and physical education;

h Access to specific educational information to help to ensure the health and well-being of families, including information and advice on family planning.

 | DOI: 10.1163/9789004462465_009

B.2 Convention on the Rights of Persons with Disabilities, UN, 2006

Article 24
Education

1. States Parties recognize the right of persons with disabilities to education. With a view to realizing this right without discrimination and on the basis of equal opportunity, States Parties shall ensure an inclusive education system at all levels and lifelong learning directed to:
   a The full development of human potential and sense of dignity and self-worth, and the strengthening of respect for human rights, fundamental freedoms and human diversity;
   b The development by persons with disabilities of their personality, talents and creativity, as well as their mental and physical abilities, to their fullest potential;
   c Enabling persons with disabilities to participate effectively in a free society.
2. In realizing this right, States Parties shall ensure that:

a Persons with disabilities are not excluded from the general education system on the basis of disability, and that children with disabilities are not excluded from free and compulsory primary education, or from secondary education, on the basis of disability;

b Persons with disabilities can access an inclusive, quality and free primary education and secondary education on an equal basis with others in the communities in which they live;

c Reasonable accommodation of the individual's requirements is provided;

d Persons with disabilities receive the support required, within the general education system, to facilitate their effective education;

e Effective individualized support measures are provided in environments that maximize academic and social development, consistent with the goal of full inclusion.

3. States Parties shall enable persons with disabilities to learn life and social development skills to facilitate their full and equal participation in education and as members of the community. To this end, States Parties shall take appropriate measures, including:

a Facilitating the learning of Braille, alternative script, augmentative and alternative modes, means and formats of communication and orientation and mobility skills, and facilitating peer support and mentoring;

b Facilitating the learning of sign language and the promotion of the linguistic identity of the deaf community;

c Ensuring that the education of persons, and in particular children, who are blind, deaf or deafblind, is delivered in the most appropriate languages and modes and means of communication for the individual, and in environments which maximize academic and social development.

4. In order to help ensure the realization of this right, States Parties shall take appropriate measures to employ teachers, including teachers with disabilities, who are qualified in sign language and/or Braille, and to train professionals and staff who work at all levels of education. Such training shall incorporate disability awareness and the use of appropriate augmentative and alternative modes, means and formats of communication, educational techniques and materials to support persons with disabilities.

5. States Parties shall ensure that persons with disabilities are able to access general tertiary education, vocational training, adult education and lifelong learning without discrimination and on an equal basis with others. To this end, States Parties shall ensure that reasonable accommodation is provided to persons with disabilities.

B.3 International Convention on the Protection of the Rights of All Migrant Workers and Members of their Families, UN, 1990

Article 30

Each child of a migrant worker shall have the basic right of access to education on the basis of equality of treatment with nationals of the State concerned. Access to public pre-school educational institutions or schools shall not be refused or limited by reason of the irregular situation with respect to stay or employment of either parent or by reason of the irregularity of the child's stay in the State of employment.

B.4 Convention relating to the Status of Refugees, UN, 1951

Article 22
Public education

1. The Contracting States shall accord to refugees the same treatment as is accorded to nationals with respect to elementary education.
2. The Contracting States shall accord to refugees treatment as favourable as possible, and, in any event, not less favourable than that accorded to aliens generally in the same circumstances, with respect to education other than elementary education and, in particular, as regards access to studies, the recognition of foreign

school certificates, diplomas and degrees, the remission of fees and charges and the award of scholarships.

B.5 Declaration on the Rights of Persons Belonging to National or Ethnic, Religious and Linguistic Minorities, UN, 1992

Article 4

1. States shall take measures where required to ensure that persons belonging to minorities may exercise fully and effectively all their human rights and fundamental freedoms without any discrimination and in full equality before the law.
2. States shall take measures to create favourable conditions to enable persons belonging to minorities to express their characteristics and to develop their culture, language, religion, traditions and customs, except where specific practices are in violation of national law and contrary to international standards.
3. States should take appropriate measures so that, wherever possible, persons belonging to minorities may have adequate opportunities to learn their mother tongue or to have instruction in their mother tongue.
4. States should, where appropriate, take measures in the field of education, in order to encourage knowledge of the history, traditions, language and culture of the minorities existing within their territory. Persons belonging to minorities should have adequate opportunities to gain knowledge of the society as a whole.
5. States should consider appropriate measures so that persons belonging to minorities may participate fully in the economic progress and development in their country.

B.6 Declaration on the Rights of Indigenous Peoples, UN, 2007

Article 14

1. Indigenous peoples have the right to establish and control their educational systems and institutions providing education in their own languages, in a manner appropriate to their cultural methods of teaching and learning.
2. Indigenous individuals, particularly children, have the right to all levels and forms of education of the State without discrimination.
3. States shall, in conjunction with indigenous peoples, take effective measures, in order for indigenous individuals, particularly children, including those living outside their communities, to have access, when possible, to an education in their own culture and provided in their own language.

APPENDIX C

Main Regional Framework of the Right to Education

Europe

C.1 First Protocol to the European Convention on Human Rights, Council of Europe, 1952

Article 2
Right to education

No person shall be denied the right to education. In the exercise of any functions which it assumes in relation to education and to teaching, the State shall respect the right of parents to ensure such education and teaching in conformity with their own religious and philosophical convictions.

C.2 Charter of Fundamental Rights of the European Union, European Union, 2000

Article 14
Right to education

1. Everyone has the right to education and to have access to vocational and continuing training.
2. This right includes the possibility to receive free compulsory education.
3. The freedom to found educational establishments with due respect for democratic principles and the right of parents to ensure the education and teaching of their children in conformity with their religious, philosophical and pedagogical convictions shall be respected, in accordance with the national laws governing the exercise of such freedom and right.

 | DOI: 10.1163/9789004462465_010

Article 24
The rights of the child

1. Children shall have the right to such protection and care as is necessary for their well-being. They may express their views freely. Such views shall be taken into consideration on matters which concern them in accordance with their age and maturity.
2. In all actions relating to children, whether taken by public authorities or private institutions, the child's best interests must be a primary consideration. Every child shall have the right to maintain on a regular basis a personal relationship and direct contact with both his or her parents, unless that is contrary to his or her interests.

Americas

C.3 Additional Protocol to the American Convention on Human Rights in the Area of Economic, Social and Cultural Rights ("Protocol of san Salvador"), Organisation of American States, 1988

Article 13
Right to education

1. Everyone has the right to education.
2. The States Parties to this Protocol agree that education should be directed towards the full development of the human personality and human dignity and should strengthen respect for human rights, ideological pluralism, fundamental freedoms, justice and peace. They further agree that education ought to enable everyone to participate effectively in a democratic and pluralistic society and achieve a decent existence and should foster understanding, tolerance and friendship among all nations and all racial, ethnic or religious groups and promote activities for the maintenance of peace.
3. The States Parties to this Protocol recognize that in order to achieve the full exercise of the right to education:
   a Primary education should be compulsory and accessible to all without cost;
   b Secondary education in its different forms, including technical and vocational secondary education, should be made generally available and accessible to all by every appropriate means, and in particular, by the progressive introduction of free education;

c Higher education should be made equally accessible to all, on the basis of individual capacity, by every appropriate means, and in particular, by the progressive introduction of free education;

d Basic education should be encouraged or intensified as far as possible for those persons who have not received or completed the whole cycle of primary instruction;

e Programs of special education should be established for the handicapped, so as to provide special instruction and training to persons with physical disabilities or mental deficiencies.

4. In conformity with the domestic legislation of the States Parties, parents should have the right to select the type of education to be given to their children, provided that it conforms to the principles set forth above.

5. Nothing in this Protocol shall be interpreted as a restriction of the freedom of individuals and entities to establish and direct educational institutions in accordance with the domestic legislation of the States Parties.

Article 16
Rights of children

Every child, whatever his parentage, has the right to the protection that his status as a minor requires from his family, society and the State. Every child has the right to grow under the protection and responsibility of his parents; save in exceptional, judicially recognized circumstances, a child of young age ought not to be separated from his mother. Every child has the right to free and compulsory education, at least in the elementary phase, and to continue his training at higher levels of the educational system.

Africa

C.4 African Charter on Human and Peoples' Rights, Organisation of African Unity, 1981

Article 17

1. Every individual shall have the right to education.
2. Every individual may freely, take part in the cultural life of his community.
3. The promotion and protection of morals and traditional values recognized by the community shall be the duty of the State.

C.5 African Charter on the Rights and Welfare of the Child, Organisation of African Unity, 1990

Article 11
Education

1. Every child shall have the right to an education.
2. The education of the child shall be directed to:
   a the promotion and development of the child's personality, talents and mental and physical abilities to their fullest potential;
   b fostering respect for human rights and fundamental freedoms with particular reference to those set out in the provisions of various African instruments on human and peoples' rights and international human rights declarations and conventions;
   c the preservation and strengthening of positive African morals, traditional values and cultures;
   d the preparation of the child for responsible life in a free society, in the spirit of understanding tolerance, dialogue, mutual respect and friendship among all peoples ethnic, tribal and religious groups;
   e the preservation of national independence and territorial integrity;
   f the promotion and achievements of African Unity and Solidarity;
   g the development of respect for the environment and natural resources;
   h the promotion of the child's understanding of primary health care.
3. States Parties to the present Charter shall take all appropriate measures with a view to achieving the full realization of this right and shall in particular:
   a provide free and compulsory basic education;
   b encourage the development of secondary education in its different forms and to progressively make it free and accessible to all;
   c make the higher education accessible to all on the basis of capacity and ability by every appropriate means;
   d take measures to encourage regular attendance at schools and the reduction of drop-out rates;
   e take special measures in respect of female, gifted and disadvantaged children, to ensure equal access to education for all sections of the community.
4. States Parties to the present Charter shall respect the rights and duties of parents, and where applicable, of legal guardians to choose for their children's schools, other than those established by public authorities, which conform to such minimum standards may be approved by the State, to ensure the religious and moral education of the child in a manner with the evolving capacities of the child.

5. States Parties to the present Charter shall take all appropriate measures to ensure that a child who is subjected to schools or parental discipline shall be treated with humanity and with respect for the inherent dignity of the child and in conformity with the present Charter.
6. States Parties to the present Charter shall have all appropriate measures to ensure that children who become pregnant before completing their education shall have an opportunity to continue with their education on the basis of their individual ability.
7. No part of this Article shall be construed as to interfere with the liberty of individuals and bodies to establish and direct educational institutions subject to the observance of the principles set out in paragraph I of this Article and the requirement teal the education given in such institutions shall conform to such minimum standards as may be laid down by the States.

APPENDIX D

List of Case Law and Other Interpretative Materials on the Right to Education (Systematised)

This is an essay of systematisation of around 120 judgements of international and national Courts and Tribunals, as well as about 30 General Comments of the United Nations Human Rights Committees (for the sake of the normative development), organised following the various elements of the integrity of the right to education. A judgement or document may appear more than once under different heads.

Considering the increasing intercommunication of the international and national jurisprudence, in a so connected world, and also taking into account the temporal factor in the evolution and interpretation of the legal norms, the list is presented in descending chronological order, regardless of the hierarchy of its sources.

D.1 Value and Priority of the Right to Education as a Human Right and Public Good

- European Court of Human Rights, 2016, *Case Ozan Barış Sanlisoy v. Turkey* (Application 77023/12)[1] concerning a child with autism (in French).
- South Africa, Supreme Court of Appeal, 2015, *Case Minister of Basic Education v Basic Education for All (20793/2014) [2015] ZASCA 198; [2016] 1 All SA 369 (SCA); 2016 (4) SA 63 (SCA) (2 December 2015)*[2] concerning free textbooks.
- USA, Supreme Court of Florida, 2006, *Case Bush v. Holmes, N°. SC04-2323 to SC-4-2325*[3] concerning a vouchers programme.
- European Court of Human Rights, 2005, *Case Timichev v. Russia* (Applications 55762/00 and 55974/00)[4] concerning the refusal of school admission of two children.
- India, Supreme Court, 1993, *Case Unni Krishnan, J.P. And Ors. Etc. … vs State Of Andhra Pradesh And Ors. … on 4 February, 1993 (1993 AIR 2178, 1993 SCR (1) 594)*[5] concerning the human and political value of education.
- Human Rights Committee, 1990, *Communications 298/1988 and 299/1988*[6] concerning funding private education.
- India, Supreme Court, 1984, *Case Bandhua Mukti Morcha vs Union of India & Others [1984] 2 S.C.R. 67*[7] concerning serious breaches of the right to education of some workers.

 | DOI: 10.1163/9789004462465_011

- USA, Supreme Court, 1982, *Case Plyler v. Doe (No. 80-1538)(1982)*[8] concerning the right to education of immigrant children in Texas.
- USA, Supreme Court, 1954, *Case Brown v. Board of Education*[9] concerning racial segregation in schools.
- USA, Supreme Court of Appeals of West Virginia, 1979, *Case Pauley v. Kelly, 255 S.E.2d 859 (W. Va. 1979)*[10] concerning insufficient funding of public schools.

D.2 Right of Every Human Being

D.2.1 *Basic Education – Accessible, Free, Obligation, Quality*

D.2.1.1 Access

- European Court of Human Rights, 2015, *Case Memlika v. Greece* (Application 37991/12)[11] concerning two children excluded from school for having been wrongly diagnosed with leprosy (in French).
- South Africa, Constitutional Court, 2011, *Case Governing Body of the Juma Musjid Primary School & Others v Essay N.O. and Others* (*CCT 29/10*) [*2011*] *ZACC 13; 2011* (*8*) *BCLR 761* (*CC*)[12] concerning an order to evict a school located on private land.
- Inter-American Court of Human Rights, 2005, *Case Niñas Yean y Bosico vs República Dominicana*[13] concerning the refusal to issue birth certificates to two girls, required to access primary education, due to their parents' status (in Spanish).
- Constitutional Court of Colombia, 2003, *Case T-170/03*[14] concerning the right to attend a school near a child's home (in Spanish).
- United Kingdom, Queen's Bench Division, 1990, *Case R v Inner London Education Authority, Ex parte Ali and Another*[15] relating to lack of school places.

D.2.1.2 Free

- USA, Kansas Supreme Court, 2016, *Case Gannon v. State, 304 Kan. 490* (*Kan. 2016*) (*Gannon III*)[16] concerning equity funding of poor school districts required by Kansas Constitution.
- South Africa, Supreme Court of Appeal, 2015, *Case Minister of Basic Education v Basic Education for All* (*20793/2014*) [*2015*] *ZASCA 198;* [*2016*] *1 All SA 369* (*SCA*)*; 2016* (*4*) *SA 63* (*SCA*) (*2 December 2015*)[17] concerning free textbooks.
- South Africa, Eastern Cape High Court, Grahamstown, 2015, *Case Tripartite Steering Committee and Another v Minister of Basic Education and Others* (*1830/2015*) [*2015*] *ZAECGHC 67; 2015* (*5*) *SA 107* (*ECG*)*;* [*2015*] *3 All SA 718* (*ECG*) (*25 June 2015*)[18] concerning free transport to and from school for those children who live a distance from their schools.
- Bangladesh, Supreme Court, High Court Division, 2014, *Case Campaign for Popular Education* (*CAPE*) *and another v Secretary of the Ministry of Education and Others*[19] concerning fees charged by various private educational institutions.

- Community Court of Justice of the Economic Community of West African States (ECOWAS), 2012, Case *SERAP* [*Socio-Economic Rights and Accountability Project*] *v Federal Republic of Nigeria and Universal Basic Education Commission* (ECW/CCJ/APP/12/07; Judgement N° ECW/CCJ/JUD/07/10)[20] concerning violations of several human rights by Nigeria.
- USA, Washington Supreme Court, 2012, *Case McCleary v State 269 P.3d 227* (*Wash. 2012*)[21] concerning the constitutional obligation to fund education.
- Colombia, Constitutional Court, 2010, *Case C-376-10*[22] concerning the right to free compulsory school (in Spanish).
- USA, Court of Appeals of New York, 2003, *Case Campaign for Fiscal Equity et al. v State of New York et al.* (*2003*)[23] concerning the constitutional obligation to finance public schools.
- USA, Supreme Court of Texas, 1989, *Case Edgewood Independent School District v Kirby* (777 S.W.2d 391 (1989))[24] concerning the constitutional obligation to fund public schools.
- USA, Supreme Court, 1973, *Case San Antonio Independent School District et al. v. Demetrio P. Rodriguez et al, 411 U.S. 1* (*1973*)[25] relating to the financing of public elementary and secondary schools in Texas.

D.2.1.3 Obligation

- Switzerland, Federal Court, 2020, *Case 2C_1005/2018* (22.08.2019)[26] concerning home-schooling (in German).
- Spain, Constitutional Court, 2010, *Case 133/2010*[27] concerning home-schooling (in Spanish).
- USA, Court of Appeal, Second District, Division 3, California, 2008, *Case Rachel L. et al., Persons Coming Under the Juvenile Court Law. Jonathan L. and Mary Grace L., Petitioners, v. Superior Court of the State of California for the County of Los Angeles, No. B192878*[28] concerning home-schooling.
- European Court of Human Rights, 2006, *Case Konrad v. Germany* (Application 35504/03)[29] concerning home-schooling.
- Canada, Supreme Court, 1986, *Case La Reine c. Jones,* [*1986*] *2 R.C.S. 284*[30] concerning a refusal to send schools to school.

D.2.1.4 Quality

- India, Supreme Court, 2012, *Case Environmental & Consumer Protection Foundation v Delhi Administration & Others* [*2012*] *INSC 584*[31] concerning schools' quality.
- UN, Committee on the Rights of the Child, 2001, *General Comment 1* (CRC/GC/2001/1),[32] "Article 29(1): The aims of education".

D.2.2 *Secondary Education*

- European Court of Human Rights, 2011, *Case Ponomaryovi v. Bulgary* (Application 5335/05)[33] concerning access to secondary education for non-nationals.

D.2.3 *Higher Education*

- European Court of Human Rights, 2013, *Case Tarantino and Others v. Italy* (Applications 25851/09, 29284/09 and 64090/09)[34] concerning the legality of an obligatory entrance exam and *numerus clausus*.
- European Court of Human Rights, 2013, *Case Leyla Şahin v. Turkey* (Application 44774/98)[35] concerning the wearing of Islamic headscarves in higher education institutions.
- African Commission on Human and People's Rights, 1995, *Case Free Legal Assistance Group and Others v. Zaire* (Communication 25/89-47/90-56/91-100/93)[36] concerning, among other things, the violation of the right to education because of the closure of universities and secondary schools.
- Portugal, Constitutional Court, 1994, *Case 148/94*[37] concerning the constitutionality of increasing public higher education fees (in Portuguese).

D.2.4 *Teachers*

- Canada, Supreme Court, 2016, *Case British Columbia Teachers' Federation v British Columbia*[38] concerning the right to collective bargaining for teachers' union.
- UN, Committee on the Elimination of Racial Discrimination, 2015, *Communication 56/2014*[39] concerning the discrimination of a Roma teacher.
- UN, Human Rights Committee, 2000, *Communication 736/1997*[40] concerning the sanction imposed on a teacher motivated by the frequent public expression of beliefs of religious intolerance.
- Canada, Supreme Court, 1996, *Case Ross v. New Brunschwig School District N° 15 [1996] 1 SCR 825*[41] concerning a teacher of Alberta charged for promoting hatred against Jews.
- Canada, Supreme Court, 1990, *Case R.V. v. Keegstra [1990] 3 S.C.R. 697*[42] concerning a teacher charged for promoting hatred against Jews.

D.3 Without Discrimination

D.3.1 *General Principle*

- UN, Committee on Economic, Social and Cultural Rights, 2009, *General Comment 20*, "Non-discrimination in economic, social and cultural rights (Art. 2, para. 2, of the International Covenant on Economic, Social and Cultural Rights) (E/C.12/GC/20)[43].

- UN, Human Rights Committee, 1989, *General Comment 18*,[44]"Non-discrimination".

D.3.2 *Girls*

- UN, Committee on the Elimination of Discrimination against Women, 2017, *General Recommendation 36* "on the right of girls and women to education" (CEDAW/C/GC/36).[45]
- UN, Committee on Economic, Social and Cultural Rights, 2005, *General Comment 16*, "The equal right of men and women to the enjoyment of all economic, social and cultural rights (Art. 3 of the International Covenant on Economic, Social and Cultural Rights)" (E/C.12/2005/4).[46]
- UN, Human Rights Committee, 2000, *General Comment 28*, "Article 3 (The Equality of Rights Between Men and Women)" (CCPR/C/21/Rev.1/Add.10).[47]

D.3.3 *Persons with Disabilities*

- European Court of Human Rights, 2016, *Case* Çam v. Turkey (Application 51500/08)[48] concerning the refusal of a blind person to attend a music conservatory.
- UN, Committee on the Rights of Persons with Disabilities, 2016, *General Comment 4*, (CRPD/C/GC/4) "on the right to inclusive education".[49]
- European Committee of Social Rights, 2013, *Case European Action of the Disabled (AEH) v. France* (Complaint 81/2012)[50] concerning the right to education of children and adolescents with autism.
- European Committee of Social Rights, 2008, *Case Mental Disability Advocacy Center (MDAC) v. Bulgaria* (Complaint 41/2007)[51] concerning the right to education of children living in homes for intellectually disabled children.
- UN, Committee on the Rights of the Child, 2006, *General Comment 9*, "The rights of children with disabilities" (CRC/C/GC/9).[52]
- Australia, Federal Court, 2003, *Case Clarke v Catholic Education Office & Anor [2003] FCA 1085*[53] relating to indirect discrimination of a boy with congenital profound deafness.
- European Committee of Social Rights, 2003, *International Association Autism-Europe v. France* (Complaint No. 13/2002)[54] concerning the right to education of children with disabilities.
- UN, Committee on Economic, Social and Cultural Rights, 1995, *General Comment 5*, "Persons with disabilities" (E/1995/22).[55]

D.3.4 *Persons Living with HIV/AIDS*

- Inter-American Court of Human Rights, 2015, *Case Gonzales Lluy y Otros vs Ecuador, Sentencia de 1 de septiembre de 2015 (Excepciones Preliminares, Fondo, Reparaciones*

y Costas)[56] concerning a little girl expelled from a public school because of HIV/AIDS (in Spanish).
- UN, Commission on the Rights of the Child, 2003, *General Comment 3*, "HIV/AIDS and the rights of the child" (CRC/GC/2003/3).[57]

D.3.5 *Persons with Different Sexual Orientation*

- Colombia, Constitutional Court, 2015, *Case T-478/15*[58] concerning the suicide of an adolescent because of the discrimination suffered at school because of his sexual orientation (in Spanish).
- European Committee of Social Rights, 2009, Case *International Centre for the Legal Protection of Human Rights* (*INTERIGHTS*) *v. Croatia* (Complaint 45/2007)[59] concerning sexual and reproductive health school education.

D.3.6 *Blacks and Ethnic Groups*

- European Court of Human Rights, 2013, *Case Horváth and Kiss v. Hungary* (Application 11146/11)[60] concerning the placement of Roma children in "special schools" for disabled children.
- African Committee of Experts on the Rights and Welfare of the Child, 2011, *Case Institute for Human Rights and Development in Africa* (*IHRDA*) *and Open Society Justice Initiative on behalf of Children of Nubian Descent in Kenya v. the Government of Kenya* (Com/002/2009)[61] concerning the statelessness of children of Nubian origin in Kenya, affecting the enjoyment of their rights, including the right to education.
- European Court of Human Rights, 2010, *Case Oršuš and Others v. Croatia* (Application 15766/03)[62] concerning the placement of Roma children in "special schools" for disabled children.
- European Court of Human Rights, 2009, *Case Sejdić and Finci v. Bosnia and Herzegovina* (Applications 27996/06 and 34836/06)[63] concerning ethnic discrimination.
- European Court of Human Rights, 2008, *Case Sampanis and Others v. Greece* (Application N° 32526/05)[64] relating to the education of Roma/Gypsies children.
- European Court of Human Rights, 2007, *Case D.H. and Others v. The Czech Republic* (Application 57325/00)[65] concerning the placement of Roma children in "special schools" for disabled children.
- UN, Committee on the Elimination of Racial Discrimination, 2007, Complaint *Murat Er v. Denmark* (Communication 40/20072007)[66] concerning school's discriminatory practice, based on ethnicity.
- European Court of Human Rights, 2004, *Case Gorzeliket and Others v. Poland* (Application 44158/98)[67] concerning the right to ethnic identity.
- USA, Supreme Court, 1954, *Case Brown v. Board of Education*[68] concerning racial segregation in schools.

D.3.7 *Linguistic and Other Minorities*

- European Court of Human Rights, 2012, *Case Catan and Others v. Moldova and Russia* (Applications 43370/04, 8252/05 and 18454/06)[69] concerning the closure of three Moldovan language schools in Transdniestria.
- UN, Human Rights Committee, 1994, *General Comment 23*, on the rights of ethnic, religious or linguistic minorities (CCPR/C/21/Rev.1/Add.5).[70]
- Canada, Supreme Court, 1990, *Case Mahe v. Alberta* [*1990*] *1 S.C.R. 342*[71] relating to management and control over minority language instruction and facilities.
- European Court of Human Rights, 1968, *Case "relating to certain aspects of the laws on the use of languages in education in Belgium v. Belgium"* (Applications 1474/62; 1677/62; 1691/62; 1769/63; 1994/63; 2126/64)[72] concerning the impossibility of hundreds of children to receive education in French because of their territory of residence.

D.3.8 *Indigenous Peoples*

- Inter-American Court of Human Rights, 2010, *Case Comunidad Indígena Xákmok Kásek vs Paraguay* (Fondo, Reparaciones y Costas)[73] concerning the lack of guarantee of the right to ancestral ownership of the Indigenous Community Xákmok Kosek, with implications for the right to education (in Spanish).
- UN, Committee on the Rights of the Child, 2009, *General Comment 11*, "Indigenous children and their rights under the Convention" (CRC/C/GC/11).[74]
- Inter-American Court of Human Rights, 2005, *Case Yakye Axa Indigenous Community v. Paraguay* (Merits, Reparations and Costs) (2005)[75] concerning the right to education of indigenous peoples.

D.3.9 *Migrants*

- UN, Committee on the Protection of the Rights of All Migrant Workers and Members of Their Families and Committee on the Rights of the Child, 2017, Joint *General Comment 3 and General Comment 22*, respectively, "on the general principles regarding the human rights of children in the context of international migration" (CMW/C/GC/3-CRC/C/GC/22).[76]
- Inter-American Court of Human Rights, 2014, *Advisory Opinion OC-21/14*, "Rights and Guarantees of Children in the Context of Migration and/or in Need of International Protection".[77]
- CoHR, 2014, "Views" on a Communication (348/2014) by *Nell Toussaint v. Canada* (CCPR/C/123/D/2348/2014)[78] alleging violation of human rights because of his irregular migrant situation.
- European Court of Human Rights, 2005, *Case Timichev v. Russia* (Applications 55762/00 and 55974/00)[79] concerning the refusal of school admission of two children.

D.3.10 *Refugees/Displaced Persons*

- UN, Committee on Economic, Social and Cultural Rights, 2016, *Communication 003/2014* (E/C.12/58/D/3/2014)[80] concerning discrimination of a refugee child.
- UN, Committee on the Rights of the Child, 2005, *General Comment 6*, "Treatment of unaccompanied and separated children outside their country of origin" (CRC/GC/2005/6).[81]

D.3.11 *Detainees*

- European Court of Human Rights, 2014, *Case Velyo Velev v. Bulgaria* (Application 16032/07)[82] concerning an inmate's right to attend the prison school.
- Inter-American Court of Human Rights, 2004, *Case of the "Juvenile Reeducation Institute" v. Paraguay* (Preliminary Objections, Merits, Reparations and Costs)[83] concerning the rights of detained children, including their right to education.
- UN, Human Rights Committee, 1992, *General Comment 21*, "Article 10 (Humane treatment of persons deprived of their liberty)".[84]

D.4 Different Treatment for Other Reasons

- India, Supreme Court, 2012, *Case Society for Un-Aided P. School Of ... vs U.O.I & Anr on 12 April*[85] concerning the constitutionality of the imposition on schools, both public and private, of a quota for disadvantaged groups.
- UN, Committee on Economic, Social and Cultural Rights, 2009, *General Comment 20*, "Non-discrimination in economic, social and cultural rights (Art. 2, para. 2, of the International Covenant on Economic, Social and Cultural Rights) (E/C.12/GC/20).[86]
- UN, Committee on Economic, Social and Cultural Rights, 2005, *General Comment 16*, "The equal right of men and women to the enjoyment of all economic, social and cultural rights (Art. 3 of the International Covenant on Economic, Social and Cultural Rights)" (E/C.12/2005/4).[87]
- Supreme Court of Mauritius, 2002, *Case S. Tengur v. The Minister of Education & Scientific Research and the State of Mauritius* (2002 SCJ 48)[88] concerning discrimination related to education on religious grounds.

D.5 General Obligations of the State

D.5.1 *Public Education System*

- South Africa, Eastern Cape High Court, Grahamstown, 2015, *Case Linkside v Minister of Basic Education and Others (3844/2013)* [*2015*] *ZAECGHC 36* (26 January 2015)[89] concerning the appointment and funding of teachers.

- South Africa, Eastern Cape High Court, Mthatha, 2014, *Case Madzodzo and Others v Minister of Basic Education and Others* (2144/2012) [2014] ZAECMHC 5; [2014] 2 All SA 339 (ECM); 2014 (3) SA 441 (ECM) (20 February 2014)[90] concerning the provision of essential school furniture to public schools.
- UN, Committee on Economic, Social and Cultural Rights, 1999, *General Comment 13*, "The right to education (Article 13 of the Covenant)" (E/C.12/1999/10).[91]
- UN, Committee on Economic, Social and Cultural Rights, 1999, *General Comment 11*, "Plans of action for primary education (Article 14 of the International Covenant on Economic, Social and Cultural Rights)" (E/C.12/1999/4).[92]
- African Commission on Human and Peoples' Rights, 1995, *Communications 25/89-47/90-56/91-100/93: Free Legal Assistance Group, Lawyers' Committee for Human Rights, Union Interafricaine des Droits de l'Homme, Les Témoins de Jehovah/DRC*[93] concerning violations of human rights in the Democratic Republic of the Congo.

D.5.2 *Regulation and Supervision of Public and Private Education*

- Colombia, Constitutional Court, 1997, *Case C-560/97*[94] concerning the constitutionality of a provision of the General Education Act relating to the tuition fees in private institutions (in Spanish).
- Former European Commission of Human Rights, 1982, *X, Y and Z v. the Federal Republic of Germany* (Application 9411/81)[95] concerning a parents' complaint that school curricula direct children towards an ideology based on the pre-eminence of science, which they do not share.

D.5.3 *Controversial Learnings*

D.5.3.1 Sexual and Reproductive Health Education

- European Court of Human Rights, 2017, *Case R. and L. R. v. Switzerland* (Application 22338/15)[96] concerning an elementary school's rejection of an application to exempt a 7-year-old child from sex education lessons.
- UN, Committee on Economic, Social and Cultural Rights, 2016, *General Comment 22* "on the right to sexual and reproductive health (Article 12 of the International Covenant on Economic, Social and Cultural Rights)" (E/C.12/GC/22).[97]
- USA, Court of Appeals, Ninth Circuit., 2005, Case *James FIELDS; Tammany Fields; Stuart Haberman; Robert Hoaglin; Kathie Hoaglin; Vanessa Shetler, Plaintiffs-Appellants, v. PALMDALE SCHOOL DISTRICT (PSD); Michael Geisser; Arland Atwood, Defendants-Appellees (No. 03-56499)*[98] concerning an enquiry about sexuality in a public school.
- UN, Committee on the Rights of the Child, 2003, *General Comment 4*, "Adolescent health and development in the context of the Convention on the Rights of the Child" (CRC/GC/2003/4).[99]

- UN, Committee on Economic, Social and Cultural Rights, 2000, *General Comment 14*, "The right to the highest attainable standard of health (Article 12 of the International Covenant on Economic, Social and Cultural Rights)" (E/C.12/2000/4).[100]
- European Court of Human Rights, 2000, *Case Alejandro Jimenez Alonso and Pilar Jimenez Merino v. Spain* (Application 51188/99)[101] concerning a sexual education course in a public college.
- USA, Court of Appeals, Third Circuit, 1998, *Case Parents United for Better Sch., Inc. v. Sch. Dist. of Pa. Bd. of Educ., 148 F.3d 260, 270 (3d Cir. 1998)*[102] concerning a voluntary programme to distribute condoms in Philadelphia schools.
- USA, Court of Appeals, First Circuit, 1995, *Case Brown v. Hot, Sexy and Safer Productions INC. (No. 95-1275)*[103] concerning the obligation to participate in a sexual and reproductive education programme in a public school.
- European Court of Human Rights, 1976, *Case Kjeldsen, Busk Madsen and Pedersen v. Denmark* (Applications 5095/71; 5920/72; 5926/72)[104] concerning the legitimacy of sexual education in Danish public schools.

D.5.3.2 Moral Education and Instruction on Religions

- European Court of Human Rights, 2009, *Case Johanna Appel-Irrgang and Others v. Germany* (Application 45216/07)[105] concerning the legitimacy of an amendment to the School Act of January 26, 2004 (*Erstes Gesetz zur Änderung des Schulgesetzes*).
- Romania, Constitutional Court, 1997, *Case 72/1995*[106] concerning the obligation of education about religions in elementary school (in French).
- UN, Human Rights Committee, 1993, *General Comment 21* on ICCPR Article 18 (CCPR/C/21/Rev.1/Add.4).[107]
- Former European Commission of Human Rights, 1993, *Case Bernard and Others v. Luxembourg* (Application 17187/90)[108] concerning the obligation to attend "religious and moral education lessons" or "moral and social education lessons" in secondary education.
- Former European Commission of Human Rights, 1986, *Case Lena and Anna-Nina Angeleni v. Sweden* (Application 10491/83)[109] concerning religious education in schools.
- UN, Human Rights Committee, 1981, *Case Erkki Juhani Hartikainen v. Finland* (Communication 40/1978)[110] concerning the obligation to take religious history and morals courses in schools in Finland.

D.5.3.3 Creationism

- USA, Supreme Court, 1987, *Case Edwards v. Aguillard*, 482 U.S. 578; 107 (1987)[111] concerning the constitutionality of the *Balanced Treatment of Creation-Science and Evolution-Science in Public Schools Instruction Act* (*Creationism Act*) of Louisiana, prohibiting the teaching of the theory of evolution unaccompanied by the narrative of creation.

In this regard, see:

- *Science, Evolution, and Creationism* (National Academy of Sciences and Institute of Medicine of the National Academies, USA, 2008).[112]
- *Guidance on the Place of Creationism and Intelligent Design in Science Lessons* (Department for Children, Schools and Families, UK, 2007).[113]

D.6 Liberties of Education

D.6.1 *Liberty/Primacy of the Child*

- UN, Committee on the Rights of the Child, 2013, *General Comment 14* "on the right of the child to have his or her best interests taken as a primary consideration (Art. 3, para. 1)" (CRC/C/GC/14).[114]
- Inter-American Court of Human Rights, 2002, *Advisory Opinion OC-17/2002*, "Juridical Condition and Human Rights of the Child".[115]
- Former European Commission of Human Rights, 1993, *Case Bernard and Others v. Luxembourg* (Application 17187/90)[116] concerning the obligation to attend "religious and moral education lessons" or "moral and social education lessons" in secondary education.
- UN, Human Rights Committee, 1989, *General Comment 17*, "Article 24 (Rights of the child)".[117]
- European Court of Human Rights, 1976, *Case Kjeldsen, Busk Madsen and Pedersen v. Denmark* (Applications 5095/71; 5920/72; 5926/72)[118] concerning the legitimacy of sexual education in Danish public schools.
- USA, 1972, *Case Wisconsin v. Yoder, 406 U.S. 205 (1972)*[119] dissenting opinion of Judge Douglas concerning the refusal of the religious community to allow their children to attend compulsory school beyond grade eight, invoking the freedom of religion (Free Exercise Clause) of the First Amendment to the Constitution.

D.6.2 *Parental Liberty*

- European Court of Human Rights, 2010, *Case Grzelak v. Poland* (Application 7710/02)[120] concerning a child left alone during religious classes he did not attend, in accordance with the wishes of his parents.
- European Court of Human Rights, 2007, *Case Hasan and Eylem Zengin v. Turkey* (Application 1448/04)[121] concerning the refusal to exempt a student from compulsory classes on religious culture and moral knowledge in a public school.
- European Court of Human Rights, 1996, *Case Valsamis v. Greece* (Application 21787/93)[122] concerning a suspension of school attendance for Jehovah's Witness students who refused to participate in a parade.

- Former European Commission of Human Rights, 1984, *Case W. and D. M., M. and H. I. v. The United Kingdom* (Applications 10228/82 and 10229/82)[123] concerning two couples who claimed to register, one their daughter and the other their son, in a high school only for girls and for boys, respectively.
- Former European Commission of Human Rights, 1977, *Case 40 Mothers v. Sweden* (Application 6853/74)[124] concerning respect for the religious and philosophical beliefs of mothers of 53 children in public kindergartens and the funding of private schools.

D.6.3 *Liberty of Creation and Direction of Private Schools*

- Former European Commission of Human Rights, 1987, *Ingrid Jordebo Foundation of Christian Schools and Ingrid Jordebo v. Sweden* (Application 11533/85)[125] concerning the denial of permission to set up a private school.

D.6.4 *Academic Freedom*

- European Court of Human Rights, 2014, *Case Mustafa Erdoğan and Others v. Turkey* (Applications 346/04, 39779/04, Judgement of 27 May 2014)[126] concerning freedom of expression.
- European Court of Human Rights, 2010, *Case Sapan v. Turkey* (Application 44102/04)[127] concerning the seizure of a book based on a doctoral thesis, because it was infringing on the image and personality of a singer.
- African Commission on Human and Peoples' Rights, 2010, *Case Kenneth Good v. Botswana* (Communication 313/05)[128] concerning the deportation of a university professor.
- European Court of Human Rights, 2009, *Case Sorguç v. Turkey* (Application 17089/03)[129] concerning a university professor's freedom of expression.

D.6.5 *Public Funding of Private Education*

- USA, Washington Supreme Court, 2015, *Case League of Women Voters of Wash. v State 355 P.3d 1131 (Wash. 2015)*[130] concerning the constitutionality of funding charter schools.
- USA, Supreme Court, 2002, *Case Zelman v. Simmons-Harris, 536 U.S. 639* (2002 [131] concerning the constitutionality of a school vouchers programme in Ohio.
- Colombia, Constitutional Court, 1997, *Case C-560/97*[132] concerning the constitutionality of a provision of the General Education Act relating to the fees in private institutions (in Spanish).
- Former European Commission of Human Rights, 1992, *Case Rudolf Bachmann, Michael Hofreiter and Beatrix Gulyn against Austria* (Application 19315/92)[133] concerning the denial of public funding of private education.
- Former European Commission of Human Rights, 1989, *Case André Simpson v. The United Kingdom* (Application 14688/89)[134] concerning the right to education of a dyslexic child.

- UN, Human Rights Committee, 1985, *Case Carl Henrik Blom c. Sweden* (Communication 191/1985)[135] concerning the denial of a grant to attend a private school.

D.6.6 *Commercialisation of Education*

- Colombia, Constitutional Court, 1997, *Case C-560/97*[136] concerning the constitutionality of a provision of the General Education Act relating to the fees in private institutions (in Spanish).
- India, Supreme Court, 1993, *Case Unni Krishnan, J.P. And Ors. Etc. ... vs State Of Andhra Pradesh And Ors. ... on 4 February, 1993 (1993 AIR 2178, 1993 SCR (1) 594)*[137] concerning State's obligations towards the right to education.

D.7 Public School and Religion

D.7.1 *Principle of Non-Indoctrination*

- Colombia, Constitutional Court, 2011, *Case T-832/11*[138] concerning a clothing rule in a higher education institution (in Spanish).
- European Court of Human Rights, 2004, *Case Ciftçi v. Turkey* (Application 71860/01)[139] concerning the legality of imposing a minimum age for attending a religious course.
- European Court of Human Rights, 1976, *Case Kjeldsen, Busk Madsen and Pedersen v. Denmark* (Applications 5095/71; 5920/72; 5926/72)[140] concerning the legitimacy of sexual education in Danish public schools.

D.7.2 *State or Majority Religion*

- UN, Human Rights Committee, 1993, *General Comment 22*, "Article 18" (CCPR/C/21/Rev.1/Add.4).[141]

D.7.3 *Interdiction of Compulsory Religious Education*

- European Court of Human Rights, 2007, *Case Folgerø and Others v. Norway* (Application 15472/02)[142] concerning the respect for the convictions of three Norwegian couples relating to their children' education.

D.7.4 *Acts or Events of a Religious Nature*

- USA, Supreme Court, 1963, *Case School District of Abington Tp. v. Schempp 374 US 203 (1963)*[143] concerning the constitutionality of Bible reading or praying at the beginning of the school day.
- USA, Supreme Court, 1962, *Case Engel v. Vitale, 370 U.S. 421, 1962*[144] concerning the constitutionality of prayer at the beginning of the school day.

D.7.5 *Presence of Religious Symbols*

- European Court of Human Rights, 2011, *Case Lautsi and Others v. Italy* (Application 30814/06)[145] concerning the presence of crucifixes on the wall of every classroom.
- Germany, Federal Constitutional Court, 1995, *Case BVerfGE 93 11*[146] concerning the presence of crucifixes in the classrooms of the State of Bavaria.
- USA, Supreme Court, 1980, *Case Stone v. Graham, 449 U.S. 39, 1980*[147] concerning the constitutionality of a State of Kentucky law ordering the display of a copy of the Ten Commandments on the wall of each public classroom.

D.7.6 *Wearing Religious or Other Ideological Symbols*

- Canada, Supreme Court, 2006, *Case Singh Multani v. Commission Scolaire Marguerite-Bourgeoy* ([2006] 1 S.C.R. 256, 2006 SCC 6)[148] concerning the prohibition of wearing the *kirpan* at school, which is a dagger-like religious object worn by Sikh believers.

D.7.7 *Garments with a Religious Connotation*

D.7.7.1 Worn by Students

- UN, Human Rights Committee, 2012, *Communication 1852/2008*[149] concerning the expulsion of a student from a school motivated by wearing religious clothing.

D.7.7.2 The Case of the Islamic Veil

D.7.7.2.1 *Worn by Students*

- Belgium, Constitutional Court, 2020, *Case 81/2020* (4 June 2020)[150] concerning the banning of wearing of clothes or other items with ideological or religious connotations on the premises of a public higher education institution
- European Court of Human Rights, 2014, *Case S.A.S. v. France* (Application 43835/11)[151] concerning the compliance with the ECHR of the French *Loi n° 2010–1192 du 11 octobre 2010 interdisant la dissimulation du visage dans l'espace public* (*1*) (Act No. 2010-1192 of October 11, 2010, prohibiting the concealment of the face in public space (1)).
- European Court of Human Rights, 2008, *Case Dogru v. France* (Application 27058/05)[152] concerning the refusal of two girls to remove the Islamic headscarf in physical and sports education classes.
- European Court of Human Rights, 2006, *Case Şefika Köse and Other 93 v. Turkey* (Application 26625/02)[153] concerning the prohibition of wearing the Islamic headscarf within the school.
- House of Lords, 2006, *Case R(SB) v Governors of Denbigh High School*[154] concerning the use of religious symbols and dress instead of a school uniform.
- European Court of Human Rights, 2005, *Case Leyla Şahin v. Turkey* (Application 44774/98)[155] concerning the prohibition of female students of the Faculty of Medicine of the University of Istanbul from wearing the Islamic veil.

- UN, Human Rights Committee, 2004, *Communication 931/2000*[156] concerning the exclusion of a university student because of her refusal to stop wearing an Islamic headscarf.

D.7.7.2.2 *Worn by Teachers*

- European Court of Human Rights, 2006, *Case Sevgi Kurtulmus v. Turkey* (Application 65500/01)[157] concerning the prohibition from wearing the Islamic headscarf by a professor at the University of Istanbul.
- Germany, Federal Constitutional Court, 2003, *Case BvR 1436/028*[158] concerning the wearing of the Islamic headscarf by a teacher (in German).
- European Court of Human Rights, 2001, *Case Lucia Dahlab v. Switzerland* (Application 42393/98)[159] concerning the prohibition of wearing an Islamic veil in class by a Swiss teacher who converted to Islamism.

D.8 School Regulations and Student Rights

D.8.1 *Liberty of Expression*

D.8.1.1 Hair Length and Style

- Colombia, Constitutional Court, 1998, *Case SU641/98*[160] concerning the prohibition of attending classes by a student without cutting hair (in Spanish).
- Colombia, Constitutional Court, 1998, *Case T-124/98*[161] concerning a school disciplinary sanction because of the hair length (in Spanish).
- Colombia, Constitutional Court, 1993, *Case 065/93*[162] concerning school hair length regulations (in Spanish).
- USA, Court of Appeals, Fourth Circuit, 1972, *Case Massie v. Henry* (*455 F.2d 779, 4th Cir. 1972*)[163] concerning the suspension of high school students in North Carolina for refusing to obey a school rule on long hair and sideburns.
- USA, District Court for the Central District of California, 1970, *Case King v. Saddleback Junior College District* (*318 F. Supp.89, 1970*)[164] concerning the refusal to high school admission of several students because their hairstyle did not comply with school regulations.
- USA, District Court for the Western District of Wisconsin, 1969, *Case Breen v. Kahl 296 F. Supp. 702 1969*)[165] concerning the refusal to high school admission of several students because their hairstyle did not comply with school regulations.

D.8.1.2 Clothing

- Colombia, Constitutional Court, 2011, *Case T-832/11*[166] concerning a rule on clothing in a higher education institution (in Spanish).

- USA, District Court, E. D. Arkansas, W. D., 1972, *Case Wallace v. Ford* (*Nº LR-71-C-242*[167] concerning the suspension of several students, boys and girls, from a secondary school for failing to comply with school rules regarding clothing.

D.8.1.3 School Uniforms

- Former European Commission of Human Rights, 1986, *Case Stevens v. The United Kingdom* (Application 11674/85)[168] concerning rules on school clothing.

D.8.1.4 Opinions

- USA, Supreme Court, 1969, *Case Tinker v. Des Moines Independent Community School District 393 U.S. 503, 1969*[169] concerning the suspension of three public school students in Des Moines, Iowa, who wore armbands to protest against EU policy in Vietnam.

D.8.1.5 Affectivity and Sexuality

- Colombia, Constitutional Court, 2004, *Case T-853/04*[170] concerning a 17-year-old student who, having married civilly and become pregnant, was prevented from completing secondary school at the Catholic college she attended (in Spanish).
- Colombia, Constitutional Court, 1999, *Case T-015/99*[171] concerning the expulsion of a girl from an educational institution because she decided to live with her boyfriend (in Spanish).
- Colombia, Constitutional Court, 1999, *Case T-412/99*[172] concerning the requirement by a college Director to present a medical certificate stating that she was not pregnant as a condition of college attendance (in Spanish).
- Colombia, Constitutional Court, 1997, *Case T-225/97*[173] concerning a rule sanctioning any amorous expression at school (in Spanish).

D.8.2 *Disciplinary Sanctions*

- European Court of Human Rights, 2009, *Case Irfan Temel and Others v. Turkey* (Application 36458/02)[174] concerning the claim for a Kurdish language course at the University.
- European Court of Human Rights, 1982, *Case Campbell and Cosans v. The United Kingdom* (Application 7511/76; 7743/76)[175] concerning two mothers complaining against corporal punishment as a disciplinary measure in public schools attended by their children.
- USA, Supreme Court, 1975, *Case Goss v. Lopez 419 U.S. 565, 1975*)[176] concerning the suspension for 10 days of nine students from a public school in Ohio for bad behaviour, without being heard.

D.8.3 *Interdiction of Corporal Punishment*

- UN, Committee on the Rights of the Child, 2011, *General Comment 13*, "The right of the child to freedom from all forms of violence" (CRC/C/GC/13).[177]
- UN, Committee on the Rights of the Child, 2006, *General Comment 8*, "The right of the child to protection from corporal punishment and other cruel or degrading forms of punishment (Arts. 19; 28, para. 2; and 37, inter alia)" (CRC/C/GC/8).[178]
- UN, Committee on the Rights of the Child, 2001, *General Comment 1*, "Article 29 (1): The aims of education" (CRC/GC/2001/1).[179]
- Fiji, Supreme Court, 2002, *Case Naushad Ali v. State (Criminal Appeal N° HAA 0083 of 2001 (C. P. N° 0001 of 2001L, 21 March 2002*)[180] concerning a judicial condemnation to corporal punishment.
- Israel, Supreme Court, 2000, *Case Criminal Appeal 4596/98 Plonit v. A.G. 54(1) P.D.* [*2000*][181] concerning corporal punishment of two children by their mother.
- UN, Committee on Economic, Social and Cultural Rights, 1999, *General Comment 13*, "The right to education (Article 13 of the Covenant)" (E/C.12/1999/10).[182]
- European Court of Human Rights, 1998, *Case A. v. The United Kingdom* (100/1997/884/1096)[183] concerning corporal punishment of children in the family.
- UN, Human Rights Committee, 1992, *General Comment 20*, "Article 7 (Prohibition of torture, or other cruel, inhuman or degrading treatment or punishment)".[184]
- European Court of Human Rights, 1982, *Case Campbell and Cosans v. The United Kingdom* (Application 7511/76; 7743/76)[185] concerning two mothers complaining against corporal punishment as a disciplinary measure in public schools attended by their children.
- Former European Commission of Human Rights, 1982, *Case Seven Individuals v. Sweden* (Application 8811/79)[186] concerning the prohibition of corporal punishment of children.
- European Court of Human Rights, 1978, *Case Tyrer v. The United Kingdom* (Application 5856/72)[187] concerning the application of corporal punishment to a schoolboy.

D.8.4 *Rights of Defence*

- USA, Supreme Court, 1975, *Case Wood v. Strickland, 420 U.S. 308, 1975*[188] concerning the expulsion from an Arkansas school of two girls who had violated school rules prohibiting the consumption or carrying certain beverages to school, without being heard.

D.9 Protection of Children/Students against Sexual Abuse and Other Ill-Treatment in Public and Private Schools

- European Court of Human Rights, 2014, *Case O'Keeffe v. Ireland* (Application 35810/09)[189] concerning State responsibility for the protection of children/pupils from sexual abuse and other ill-treatment in public and private schools.

- African Committee of Experts on the Rights and Welfare of the Child, *Decision N° 003/Com/001/2012 on the Talibés Children Case*[190] which are children aged 4–12 years (known as *talibés*) attending private Qur'anic schools (*daaras*) in Senegal but forced by some teachers to beg in the streets to fund their education.

D.10 Examples of Remedies for Violations of the Right to Education

- Inter-American Court of Human Rights, 2015, *Case Gonzales Lluy y Otros vs Ecuador, Sentencia de 1 de septiembre de 2015* (*Excepciones Preliminares, Fondo, Reparaciones y Costas*)[191] concerning a little girl expelled from a public school because she was HIV/AIDS positive (in Spanish).
- Colombia, Constitutional Court, 2015, *Case T-478/15*[192] concerning a 17-year-old student who committed suicide because of discrimination at school because of his or her sexual orientation (in Spanish).
- European Court of Human Rights, 2014, *Case O'Keeffe v. Ireland* (Application 35810/09)[193] concerning State responsibility for the protection of children/pupils from sexual abuse and other ill-treatment in public and private schools.
- Committee on the Elimination of Racial Discrimination, 2015, *Communication 56/2014*[194] regarding discrimination of a female teacher.
- Colombia, Constitutional Court, 2004, *Case T-853/04*[195] concerning a 17-year-old student who, having married civilly and become pregnant, was prevented from completing secondary school at the Catholic college she attended (in Spanish).
- Fiji, Supreme Court, 2002, *Case Naushad Ali v. State* (*Criminal Appeal N° HAA 0083 of 2001* (*C. P. N° 0001 of 2001L, 21 March 2002*)[196] concerning a judicial condemnation to corporal punishment.
- Inter-American Commission on Human Rights, *Case Mónica Carabantes Galleguillos, Petition 12, 046, Chile, March 12 2002* (*Report No. 33/02 – Friendly Settlement*)[197] concerning a student expelled from a private school for being pregnant (in Spanish).

Notes

1 http://hudoc.echr.coe.int/fre?i=001-169450
2 http://www.saflii.org/za/cases/ZASCA/2015/198.html
3 http://caselaw.findlaw.com/fl-supreme-court/1102469.html
4 https://hudoc.echr.coe.int/fre#{%22itemid%22:[%22001-71627%22]}
5 http://indiankanoon.org/doc/1775396
6 https://www.ohchr.org/Documents/Publications/SDecisionsVol4en.pdf
7 http://indiankanoon.org/doc/595099
8 www.law.cornell.edu/supct/html/historics/USSC_CR_0457_0202_ZO.html

9 http://caselaw.findlaw.com/us-supreme-court/347/483.html
10 http://law.justia.com/cases/west-virginia/supreme-court/1979/14036-3.html
11 https://hudoc.echr.coe.int/eng#{«fulltext»:[«\»MEMLIKA c. GRÈCE\»»],»itemid»:[«001-157529»]}
12 www.saflii.org/za/cases/ZACC/2011/13.html
13 http://www.corteidh.or.cr/docs/casos/articulos/seriec_130_esp.pdf
14 https://www.corteconstitucional.gov.co/relatoria/2003/T-170-03.htm
15 http://www.hrcr.org/safrica/education/R_InnerLondonEducationAuthority.htm
16 http://www.kscourts.org/Cases-and-Opinions/opinions/SupCt/2016/20160527/113267.pdf
17 http://www.saflii.org/za/cases/ZASCA/2015/198.html
18 http://www.saflii.org/za/cases/ZAECGHC/2015/67.html
19 https://www.blast.org.bd/content/writ/Writ-312-2012-CAMPE-Judgment.pdf
20 http://www.worldcourts.com/ecowasccj/eng/decisions/2010.11.30_SERAP_v_Nigeria.htm
21 https://www.courtlistener.com/opinion/2351814/mccleary-v-state/
22 www.corteconstitucional.gov.co/relatoria/2010/c-376-10.htm
23 https://caselaw.findlaw.com/ny-court-of-appeals/1084567.html
24 https://nces.ed.gov/edfin/pdf/lawsuits/Edgewood_v_Kirby_TX.pdf
25 https://www.law.cornell.edu/supremecourt/text/411/1
26 https://www.bger.ch/ext/eurospider/live/de/php/aza/http/index.php?highlight_docid=aza%3A%2F%2Faza%3A%2F%2F22-08-2019-2C_1005-2018&lang=de&zoom=YES&type=show_document&
27 http://hj.tribunalconstitucional.es/HJ/docs/BOE/BOE-A-2011-275.pdf
28 http://caselaw.findlaw.com/ca-court-of-appeal/1086131.html
29 https://hudoc.echr.coe.int/eng#{„languageisocode":[„ENG"],"appno":[„35504/03"],"documentcollectionid2":[„ADMISSIBILITY"],"itemid":[„001-76925"]}
30 https://scc-csc.lexum.com/scc-csc/scc-csc/en/item/165/index.do
31 www.ielrc.org/content/e1213.pdf
32 http://tbinternet.ohchr.org/_layouts/treatybodyexternal/Download.aspx?symbolno=CRC%2fGC%2f2001%2f1&Lang=en
33 https://hudoc.echr.coe.int/fre#{„itemid":[„001-105295"]}
34 https://hudoc.echr.coe.int/fre#{„itemid":[„001-118477"]}
35 https://hudoc.echr.coe.int/eng#{„languageisocode":[„ENG"],"appno":[„44774/98"],"documentcollectionid2":[„GRANDCHAMBER"],"itemid":[„001-70956"]}
36 https://www.escr-net.org/caselaw/2008/free-legal-assistance-group-and-others-v-zaire-comm-no-2589-4790-5691-10093
37 http://www.tribunalconstitucional.pt/tc/acordaos/19940148.html
38 https://www.escr-net.org/caselaw/2016/british-columbia-teachers-federation-v-british-columbia-2016-scc-49
39 https://digitallibrary.un.org/record/833654
40 http://juris.ohchr.org/Search/Details/902
41 https://scc-csc.lexum.com/scc-csc/scc-csc/en/item/1367/index.do
42 https://scc-csc.lexum.com/scc-csc/scc-csc/en/item/695/index.do
43 http://tbinternet.ohchr.org/_layouts/treatybodyexternal/Download.aspx?symbolno=E%2fC.12%2fGC%2f20&Lang=en
44 http://tbinternet.ohchr.org/_layouts/treatybodyexternal/Download.aspx?symbolno=INT%2fCCPR%2fGEC%2f6622&Lang=en
45 http://tbinternet.ohchr.org/_layouts/treatybodyexternal/Download.aspx?symbolno=CEDAW/C/GC/36&Lang=en
46 http://tbinternet.ohchr.org/_layouts/treatybodyexternal/Download.aspx?symbolno=E%2fC.12%2f2005%2f4&Lang=en

47 https://www.refworld.org/docid/45139c9b4.html
48 https://hudoc.echr.coe.int/fre#{%22languageisocode%22:[%22ENG%22],%22appno%22:[%2251500/08%22],%22documentcollectionid2%22:[%22CHAMBER%22],%22itemid%22:[%22001-161149%22]}
49 http://tbinternet.ohchr.org/_layouts/treatybodyexternal/Download.aspx?symbolno=CRPD/C/GC/4&Lang=en
50 https://hudoc.esc.coe.int/eng/#{%22ESCDcIdentifier%22:[%22cc-81-2012-dmerits-en%22]}
51 http://hudoc.esc.coe.int/fre/#{„fulltext":[„41/2007"]}
52 http://tbinternet.ohchr.org/_layouts/treatybodyexternal/Download.aspx?symbolno=CRC%2fC%2fGC%2f9&Lang=en
53 https://jade.io/article/107700
54 https://www.coe.int/en/web/european-social-charter/processed-complaints/-/asset_publisher/5GEFkJmH2bYG/content/no-13-2002-international-association-autism-europe-iaae-v-france?inheritRedirect=false
55 http://tbinternet.ohchr.org/_layouts/treatybodyexternal/Download.aspx?symbolno=INT%2fCESCR%2fGEC%2f4760&Lang=en
56 www.corteidh.or.cr/docs/casos/articulos/seriec_298_esp.pdf
57 http://tbinternet.ohchr.org/_layouts/treatybodyexternal/Download.aspx?symbolno=CRC%2fGC%2f2003%2f3&Lang=en
58 http://www.corteconstitucional.gov.co/relatoria/2015/t-478-15.htm
59 https://hudoc.esc.coe.int/eng/#{„fulltext":[„45/2007"],"ESCDcType":[„FOND","Conclusion","Ob"],"ESCDcIdentifier":[„cc-45-2007-dmerits-en"]}
60 https://hudoc.echr.coe.int/eng#{„itemid":[„001-116124"]}
61 http://www.ihrda.org/wp-content/uploads/2011/09/002-09-Nubian-children-v-Kenya-Eng.pdf
62 https://hudoc.echr.coe.int/eng#{„languageisocode":[„ENG"],"appno":[„15766/03"],"documentcollectionid2":[„GRANDCHAMBER"],"itemid":[„001-97689"]}
63 https://hudoc.echr.coe.int/eng#{„languageisocode":[„ENG"],"appno":[„27996/06","34836/06"],"documentcollectionid2":[„GRANDCHAMBER"],"itemid":[„001-96491"]}
64 https://hudoc.echr.coe.int/fre#{%22itemid%22:[%22001-86798%22]}
65 https://hudoc.echr.coe.int/eng#{„itemid":[„001-83256"]}
66 https://juris.ohchr.org/Search/Details/1734
67 https://hudoc.echr.coe.int/fre#{„languageisocode":[„ENG"],"appno":[„44158/98"],"documentcollectionid2":[„GRANDCHAMBER"],"itemid":[„001-61637"]}
68 http://caselaw.findlaw.com/us-supreme-court/347/483.html
69 https://hudoc.echr.coe.int/eng#{„languageisocode":[„ENG"],"appno":[„43370/04","18454/06","8252/05"],"documentcollectionid2":[„GRANDCHAMBER"],"itemid":[„001-114082"]}
70 http://tbinternet.ohchr.org/_layouts/treatybodyexternal/Download.aspx?symbolno=CCPR%2fC%2f21%2fRev.1%2fAdd.5&Lang=en
71 https://scc-csc.lexum.com/scc-csc/scc-csc/en/item/580/index.do
72 https://hudoc.echr.coe.int/eng#{„itemid":[„001-57525"]}
73 http://www.corteidh.or.cr/docs/casos/articulos/seriec_214_esp.pdf
74 http://tbinternet.ohchr.org/_layouts/treatybodyexternal/Download.aspx?symbolno=CRC%2fC%2fGC%2f11&Lang=en
75 http://www.corteidh.or.cr/docs/casos/articulos/seriec_125_ing.pdf
76 http://tbinternet.ohchr.org/_layouts/treatybodyexternal/Download.aspx?symbolno=CRC%2fC%2fGC%2f22&Lang=en
77 https://www.refworld.org/cases,IACRTHR,54129c854.html
78 https://tbinternet.ohchr.org/_layouts/15/treatybodyexternal/Download.aspx?symbolno=CCPR%2FC%2F123%2FD%2F2348%2F2014&Lang=en

79 https://hudoc.echr.coe.int/eng#{%22itemid%22:[%22001-71627%22]}
80 http://juris.ohchr.org/Search/Details/2137
81 http://tbinternet.ohchr.org/_layouts/treatybodyexternal/Download.aspx?symbolno=CRC%2fGC%2f2005%2f6&Lang=en
82 https://hudoc.echr.coe.int/fre#{„languageisocode":[„ENG"],"appno":[„16032/07"],"documentcollectionid2":[„CHAMBER"],"itemid":[„001-144131"]}
83 http://www.corteidh.or.cr/docs/casos/articulos/seriec_112_ing.pdf
84 http://tbinternet.ohchr.org/_layouts/treatybodyexternal/Download.aspx?symbolno=INT%2fCCPR%2fGEC%2f4731&Lang=en
85 https://indiankanoon.org/doc/154958944
86 http://tbinternet.ohchr.org/_layouts/treatybodyexternal/Download.aspx?symbolno=E%2fC.12%2fGC%2f20&Lang=en
87 http://tbinternet.ohchr.org/_layouts/treatybodyexternal/Download.aspx?symbolno=E%2fC.12%2f2005%2f4&Lang=en
88 http://www.codices.coe.int/NXT/gateway.dll/CODICES/full/afr/mri/eng/mri-2002-a-002?fn=document-frame.htm$f=templates$3.0
89 http://www.saflii.org/za/cases/ZAECGHC/2015/36.html
90 http://www.saflii.org/za/cases/ZAECMHC/2014/5.html
91 http://tbinternet.ohchr.org/_layouts/treatybodyexternal/Download.aspx?symbolno=E%2fC.12%2f1999%2f10&Lang=en
92 http://tbinternet.ohchr.org/_layouts/treatybodyexternal/Download.aspx?symbolno=E%2fC.12%2f1999%2f4&Lang=en
93 http://www.achpr.org/communications/decision/25.89-47.90-56.91-100.93/
94 www.corteconstitucional.gov.co/relatoria/1997/C-560-97.htm
95 https://hudoc.echr.coe.int/eng#{„languageisocode":[„ENG"],"appno":[„9411/81"],"documentcollectionid2":[„DECCOMMISSION"],"itemid":[„001-74471"]}
96 https://hudoc.echr.coe.int/eng#{„itemid":[„001-180402"]}
97 http://tbinternet.ohchr.org/_layouts/treatybodyexternal/Download.aspx?symbolno=E%2fC.12%2fGC%2f22&Lang=en
98 http://caselaw.findlaw.com/us-9th-circuit/1051665.html
99 http://tbinternet.ohchr.org/_layouts/treatybodyexternal/Download.aspx?symbolno=CRC%2fGC%2f2003%2f4&Lang=en
100 http://tbinternet.ohchr.org/_layouts/treatybodyexternal/Download.aspx?symbolno=E%2fC.12%2f2000%2f4&Lang=en
101 https://hudoc.echr.coe.int/eng#{%22languageisocode%22:[%22ENG%22],%22appno%22:[%2251188/99%22],%22documentcollectionid2%22:[%22ADMISSIBILITY%22],%22itemid%22:[%22001-5973%22]}
102 https://casetext.com/case/parents-united-better-sch-v-school-district
103 http://caselaw.findlaw.com/us-1st-circuit/1014792.html
104 https://hudoc.echr.coe.int/eng#{%22itemid%22:[%22001-57509%22]}
105 https://hudoc.echr.coe.int/eng#{%22languageisocode%22:[%22ENG%22],%22appno%22:[%2245216/07%22],%22documentcollectionid2%22:[%22ADMISSIBILITY%22],%22itemid%22:[%22001-112539%22]}
106 http://www.codices.coe.int/NXT/gateway.dll/Codices/Precis/FRA/EUR/ROM/ROM-1995-S-010?f=templates$fn=document-frameset.htm$q=$uq=$x=$up=1#0-0-0-38779
107 http://tbinternet.ohchr.org/_layouts/treatybodyexternal/Download.aspx?symbolno=CCPR%2fC%2f21%2fRev.1%2fAdd.4&Lang=en
108 https://www.strasbourgconsortium.org/common/document.view.php?docId=4657
109 https://hudoc.echr.coe.int/eng#{„itemid":[„001-78933"]}

110 https://www.ohchr.org/Documents/Publications/SelDec_1_en.pdf
111 https://supreme.justia.com/cases/federal/us/482/578
112 https://www.nap.edu/read/11876/chapter/1#iv
113 https://humanism.org.uk/wp-content/uploads/1sja-creationism-guidance-180907-final.pdf
114 http://tbinternet.ohchr.org/_layouts/treatybodyexternal/Download.aspx?symbolno=CRC%2fC%2fGC%2f14&Lang=en
115 https://www.refworld.org/cases,IACRTHR,4f59d6432.html
116 https://www.strasbourgconsortium.org/common/document.view.php?docId=4657
117 http://tbinternet.ohchr.org/_layouts/treatybodyexternal/Download.aspx?symbolno=INT%2fCCPR%2fGEC%2f6623&Lang=en
118 https://hudoc.echr.coe.int/eng#{%22itemid%22:[%22001-57509%22]}
119 https://supreme.justia.com/cases/federal/us/406/205/case.html
120 https://hudoc.echr.coe.int/eng#{„languageisocode":[„ENG"],"appno":[„7710/02"],"documentcollectionid2":[„CHAMBER"],"itemid":[„001-99384"]}
121 https://hudoc.echr.coe.int/eng#{%22languageisocode%22:[%22ENG%22],%22appno%22:[%221448/04%22],%22documentcollectionid2%22:[%22CHAMBER%22],%22itemid%22:[%22001-82580%22]}
122 https://hudoc.echr.coe.int/eng#{%22languageisocode%22:[%22ENG%22],%22appno%22:[%2221787/93%22],%22documentcollectionid2%22:[%22CHAMBER%22],%22itemid%22:[%22001-58011%22]}
123 https://hudoc.echr.coe.int/eng#{„itemid":[„001-73774"]}
124 https://hudoc.echr.coe.int/eng#{„itemid":[„001-74529"]}
125 https://hudoc.echr.coe.int/eng#{%22languageisocode%22:[%22ENG%22],%22appno%22:[%2211533/85%22],%22documentcollectionid2%22:[%22DECCOMMISSION%22],%22itemid%22:[%22001-386%22]}
126 https://hudoc.echr.coe.int/eng#{%22itemid%22:[%22001-144615%22]}
127 https://hudoc.echr.coe.int/eng#{„itemid":[„001-99160"]}
128 http://www.achpr.org/fr/communications/decision/313.05/
129 https://hudoc.echr.coe.int/eng#{%22languageisocode%22:[%22ENG%22],%22appno%22:[%2217089/03%22],%22documentcollectionid2%22:[%22CHAMBER%22],%22itemid%22:[%22001-93161%22]}
130 http://www.courts.wa.gov/opinions/pdf/897140.pdf
131 https://caselaw.findlaw.com/us-supreme-court/536/639.html
132 http://www.corteconstitucional.gov.co/relatoria/1997/C-560-97.htm
133 http://echr.ketse.com/doc/19315.92-en-19950906/view
134 https://hudoc.echr.coe.int/eng#{„itemid":[„001-82186"]}
135 https://www.ohchr.org/Documents/Publications/SelDec_2_en.pdf
136 http://www.corteconstitucional.gov.co/relatoria/1997/C-560-97.htm
137 http://indiankanoon.org/doc/1775396
138 www.corteconstitucional.gov.co/relatoria/2011/T-832-11.htm
139 https://hudoc.echr.coe.int/eng#{%22languageisocode%22:[%22ENG%22],%22appno%22:[%2271860/01%22],%22documentcollectionid2%22:[%22ADMISSIBILITY%22],%22itemid%22:[%22001-68089%22]}
140 https://hudoc.echr.coe.int/eng#{%22itemid%22:[%22001-57509%22]}
141 http://tbinternet.ohchr.org/_layouts/treatybodyexternal/Download.aspx?symbolno=CCPR%2fC%2f21%2fRev.1%2fAdd.4&Lang=en
142 https://hudoc.echr.coe.int/eng#{%22languageisocode%22:[%22ENG%22],%22appno%22:[%2215472/02%22],%22documentcollectionid2%22:[%22GRANDCHAMBER%22],%22itemid%22:[%22001-81356%22]}

143 https://supreme.justia.com/cases/federal/us/374/203/case.html
144 www.law.cornell.edu/supremecourt/text/370/421
145 https://hudoc.echr.coe.int/eng#{%22languageisocode%22:[%22ENG%22],%22appno%22:[%2230814/06%22],%22documentcollectionid2%22:[%22GRANDCHAMBER%22],%22itemid%22:[%22001-104040%22]}
146 www.utexas.edu/law/academics/centers/transnational/work_new/german/case.php?id=615
147 https://supreme.justia.com/cases/federal/us/449/39/case.html
148 https://scc-csc.lexum.com/scc-csc/scc-csc/en/item/15/index.do
149 http://juris.ohchr.org/Search/Details/1655
150 https://www.unia.be/files/Documenten/2020-081f.pdf
151 https://hudoc.echr.coe.int/eng#{%22languageisocode%22:[%22ENG%22],%22appno%22:[%2243835/11%22],%22documentcollectionid2%22:[%22GRANDCHAMBER%22],%22itemid%22:[%22001-145466%22]}
152 https://hudoc.echr.coe.int/eng#{%22languageisocode%22:[%22ENG%22],%22appno%22:[%2227058/05%22],%22documentcollectionid2%22:[%22CHAMBER%22],%22itemid%22:[%22001-90039%22]}
153 https://hudoc.echr.coe.int/eng#{%22languageisocode%22:[%22ENG%22],%22appno%22:[%2226625/02%22],%22documentcollectionid2%22:[%22ADMISSIBILITY%22],%22itemid%22:[%22001-90405%22]}
154 https://publications.parliament.uk/pa/ld200506/ldjudgmt/jd060322/begum-1.htm
155 https://hudoc.echr.coe.int/eng#{%22languageisocode%22:[%22ENG%22],%22appno%22:[%2244774/98%22],%22documentcollectionid2%22:[%22GRANDCHAMBER%22],%22itemid%22:[%22001-70956%22]}
156 http://juris.ohchr.org/Search/Details/977
157 https://hudoc.echr.coe.int/eng#{„itemid":[„001-72337"]}
158 http://www.bundesverfassungsgericht.de/SharedDocs/Entscheidungen/DE/2003/09/rs20030924_2bvr143602.html
159 https://hudoc.echr.coe.int/fre#{%22languageisocode%22:[%22ENG%22],%22appno%22:[%2242393/98%22],%22documentcollectionid2%22:[%22ADMISSIBILITY%22],%22itemid%22:[%22001-22643%22]}
160 www.corteconstitucional.gov.co/relatoria/1998/su641-98.htm
161 www.corteconstitucional.gov.co/relatoria/1998/t-124-98.htm
162 www.corteconstitucional.gov.co/relatoria/1993/T-065-93.htm
163 https://law.resource.org/pub/us/case/reporter/F2/455/455.F2d.779.15325.html
164 http://law.justia.com/cases/federal/district-courts/FSupp/318/89/1480832
165 https://law.justia.com/cases/federal/district-courts/FSupp/296/702/1982747/
166 www.corteconstitucional.gov.co/relatoria/2011/T-832-11.htm
167 www.leagle.com/decision/1972502346FSupp156_1470.xml/WALLACE%20v.%20FORD
168 https://hudoc.echr.coe.int/eng#{%22languageisocode%22:[%22ENG%22],%22appno%22:[%2211674/85%22],%22documentcollectionid2%22:[%22DECCOMMISSION%22],%22itemid%22:[%22001-593%22]}
169 https://supreme.justia.com/cases/federal/us/393/503
170 http://www.corteconstitucional.gov.co/relatoria/2004/T-853-04.htm
171 www.corteconstitucional.gov.co/relatoria/1999/T-015-99.htm
172 www.corteconstitucional.gov.co/relatoria/1999/t-412-99.htm
173 www.corteconstitucional.gov.co/relatoria/1997/t-225-97.htm
174 https://hudoc.echr.coe.int/eng#{%22languageisocode%22:[%22ENG%22],%22appno%22:[%2236458/02%22],%22documentcollectionid2%22:[%22CHAMBER%22],%22itemid%22:[%22001-91532%22]}

175 https://hudoc.echr.coe.int/eng#{%22itemid%22:[%22001-57455%22]}
176 https://supreme.justia.com/cases/federal/us/419/565
177 http://tbinternet.ohchr.org/_layouts/treatybodyexternal/Download.aspx?symbolno=CRC%2fC%2fGC%2f13&Lang=en
178 http://tbinternet.ohchr.org/_layouts/treatybodyexternal/Download.aspx?symbolno=CRC%2fC%2fGC%2f8&Lang=en
179 http://tbinternet.ohchr.org/_layouts/treatybodyexternal/Download.aspx?symbolno=CRC%2FGC%2F2001%2F1&Lang=en
180 http://www.globalhealthrights.org/wp-content/uploads/2014/09/Fiji-2002-Naushad-Ali-v-State.pdf
181 http://versa.cardozo.yu.edu/sites/default/files/upload/opinions/A.%20v.%20State%20of%20Israel.pdf
182 http://tbinternet.ohchr.org/_layouts/treatybodyexternal/Download.aspx?symbolno=E%2fC.12%2f1999%2f10&Lang=en
183 https://hudoc.echr.coe.int/eng#{%22languageisocode%22:[%22ENG%22],%22appno%22:[%2225599/94%22],%22documentcollectionid2%22:[%22CHAMBER%22],%22itemid%22:[%22001-58232%22]}
184 http://tbinternet.ohchr.org/_layouts/treatybodyexternal/Download.aspx?symbolno=INT%2fCCPR%2fGEC%2f6621&Lang=en
185 https://hudoc.echr.coe.int/eng#{%22itemid%22:[%22001-57455%22]}
186 http://hudoc.echr.coe.int/app/conversion/pdf/?library=ECHR&id=001-73804&filename=001-73804.pdf
187 https://hudoc.echr.coe.int/eng#{%22itemid%22:[%22001-57587%22]}
188 https://supreme.justia.com/cases/federal/us/420/308
189 https://hudoc.echr.coe.int/fre#{%22languageisocode%22:[%22ENG%22],%22appno%22:[%2235810/09%22],%22documentcollectionid2%22:[%22GRANDCHAMBER%22],%22itemid%22:[%22001-140235%22]
190 https://www.escr-net.org/sites/default/files/caselaw/decision_on_the_communication.pdf
191 www.corteidh.or.cr/docs/casos/articulos/seriec_298_esp.pdf
192 http://www.corteconstitucional.gov.co/relatoria/2015/t-478-15.htm
193 https://hudoc.echr.coe.int/fre#{%22languageisocode%22:[%22ENG%22],%22appno%22:[%2235810/09%22],%22documentcollectionid2%22:[%22GRANDCHAMBER%22],%22itemid%22:[%22001-140235%22]
194 http://juris.ohchr.org/Search/Details/2091
195 http://www.corteconstitucional.gov.co/relatoria/2004/T-853-04.htm
196 http://www.globalhealthrights.org/wp-content/uploads/2014/09/Fiji-2002-Naushad-Ali-v-State.pdf
197 http://cidh.org/annualrep/2002eng/Chile12046.htm

APPENDIX E

International Chronology of Human Rights in General and of the Right to Education in Particular

Note: Titles only concerned with education are put in *italics*

1945

- Charter of the United Nations
  Conference of San Francisco, USA
- Constitution of the United Nations Educational, Scientific and Cultural Organisation (UNESCO)
  United Kingdom, Conference at London

1946

- Commission on Human Rights
  United Nations

1948

- Universal Declaration of Human Rights
  United Nations
- Convention on the Prevention and Punishment of the Crime of Genocide
  United Nations
- *Recommendation N° 24 Concerning the Development of International Understanding Among Young People and Teaching About International Organisations*
  UNESCO/IBE, International Conference on Public Education
- Agreement for Facilitating the International Circulation of Visual and Auditory Materials of an Educational, Scientific and Cultural character with Protocol of Signature and model form of certificate provided for in Article IV of the above-mentioned Agreement ("Beirut Agreement")
  UNESCO Diplomatic Conference of Plenipotentiaries, Beirut, Lebanon
- Charter of the Organisation of American States
  International Conference of American States, Bogota, Colombia

 | DOI: 10.1163/9789004462465_012

- American Declaration of the Rights and Duties of Man
  International Conference of American States, Bogota, Colombia

1949

- Convention for the Suppression of the Traffic in Persons and of the Exploitation of the Prostitution of Others
  United Nations
- Vocational Guidance Recommendation
  International Labour Organisation (R87)
- Geneva Convention relative to the Protection of Civilian Persons in Time of War
  Diplomatic Conference for the Establishment of International Conventions for the Protection of Victims of War, Geneva
- Statute of the Council of Europe

1950

- High Commissioner for Refugees
  United Nations
- Human Rights Day: 10 December
  United Nations
- Agreement on the Importation of Educational, Scientific and Cultural Materials (Florence Agreement)
  UNESCO
- Convention for the Protection of Human Rights and Fundamental Freedoms (European Convention on Human Rights)
  Council of Europe
- Geneva Convention (III) Relative to the Treatment of Prisoners of War
  Diplomatic Conference
- Geneva Convention (IV) Relative to the Protection of Civilian Persons in Time of War
  Diplomatic Conference

1951

- Convention relating to the Status of Refugees
  United Nations

1952

- Convention on the Political Rights of Women
  United Nations
- Protocol to the Convention for the Protection of Human Rights and Fundamental Freedoms
  Council of Europe

1953

- European Commission and European Court of Human Rights
  Council of Europe

1954

- Convention relating to the Status of Stateless Persons
  United Nations
- European Cultural Convention
  Council of Europe

1955

- Standard Minimum Rules for the Treatment of Prisoners
  First United Nations Congress on the Prevention of Crime and the Treatment of Offenders, Geneva

1956

- Supplementary Convention on the Abolition of Slavery, the Slave Trade, and Institutions and Practices of Slavery
  Geneva Conference of Plenipotentiaries convened by the UN Economic and Social Council

1957

- Convention on the Nationality of Married Women
  United Nations

- Standard Rules for the Minimum Treatment of Prisoners
  United Nations
- Abolition of Forced Labour Convention
  International Labour Organisation (C105)

1958

- *Revised Recommendation concerning the International Standardization of Educational Statistics*
  UNESCO
- Convention concerning Discrimination in Respect of Employment and Occupation
  International Labour Organisation (C111)

1959

- Declaration on the Rights of the Child
  United Nations

1960

- Declaration on the Granting of Independence to Colonial Countries and Peoples
  United Nations
- *Convention* [*and Recommendation*] *against Discrimination in Education*
  UNESCO
- Recommendation concerning the Most Effective Means of Rendering Museums Accessible to Everyone
  UNESCO
- Inter-American Commission on Human Rights
  Organisation of American States

1961

- Declaration on the Prohibition of the Use of Nuclear and Thermo-Nuclear Weapons
  United Nations
- European Social Charter
  Council of Europe

- Amnesty International

1962

- Convention on Consent to Marriage, Minimum Age for Marriage and Registration of Marriages
  United Nations
- *Protocol Instituting a Conciliation and Good Offices Commission to be responsible for seeking a settlement of any disputes which may arise between States Parties to the International Covenant on Economic, Social and Cultural Right*
  UNESCO
- Social Policy (Basic Aims and Standards) Convention
  International Labour Organisation (C117)

1963

- Declaration on the Elimination of Racial Discrimination
  United Nations
- Organisation of African Unity (OAU)

1965

- International Convention on the Elimination of all Forms of Racial Discrimination
  United Nations
- Declaration on the Promotion among Youth of the Ideals of Peace, Mutual Respect and Understanding between Peoples
  United Nations

1966

- International Covenant on Economic, Social and Cultural Rights
  United Nations
- International Covenant on Civil and Political Rights
  United Nations
- International Convention on the Elimination of all Forms of Racial Discrimination
  United Nations

- Declaration on the Elimination of All Forms of Discrimination against Women
  United Nations
- *Recommendation concerning the Status of Teachers*
  UNESCO
- Declaration of Principles of International Cultural Co-operation
  UNESCO
- European Social Charter (Revised)
  Council of Europe

1967

- Declaration on the Elimination of Discrimination against Women
  United Nations

1968

- Convention on the Non-Applicability of Statutory Limitations to War Crimes and Crimes against Humanity
  United Nations
- Proclamation of Tehran
  United Nations, International Conference on Human Rights, Teheran, Iran
- *Resolution XX on Education of Youth in the Respect for Human Rights and Fundamental Freedoms*
  United Nations, International Conference on Human Rights, Teheran, Iran
- *Recommendation nº 64 to the Ministries of Education concerning Education for International Understanding as an Integral Part of the Curriculum and Life of the School*
  UNESCO/IBE, International Conference on Public Education

1969

- Vienna Convention on the Law of Treaties
  United Nations Conference
- Declaration on Social Progress and Development
  United Nations
- American Convention on Human Rights (Pact of San José)
  Inter-American Specialised Conference on Human Rights, San José, Costa Rica

1970

- Declaration of Principles of International Law Concerning Friendly Relations and Co-operation Among States in Accordance with the Charter of the United Nations
  United Nations

1971

- Declaration on the Rights of Mentally Retarded Persons
  United Nations

1972

- Stockholm Declaration
  United Nations Conference on the Environment
- Convention Concerning the Protection of the World Cultural and Natural Heritage
  UNESCO
- Declaration of Guiding Principles on the Use of Satellite Broadcasting for the Free Flow of Information, the Spread of Education and Greater Cultural Exchange
  UNESCO

1973

- Principles of international co-operation in the detection, arrest, extradition and punishment of persons guilty of war crimes and crimes against humanity
  United Nations
- International Convention on the Suppression and Punishment of the Crime of Apartheid
  United Nations
- Minimum Age of Employment (Convention)
  International Labour Organisation (C138)

1974

- Declaration on the Protection of Women and Children in Emergency and Armed Conflict
  United Nations

- Declaration on the Establishment of a New International Economic Order
  United Nations
- Charter of Economic Rights and Duties of States
  United Nations
- *Recommendation on Education for International Understanding and Co-operation and Peace and Education relating to Human Rights and Fundamental Freedoms*
  UNESCO
- Declaration on the Protection of Women and Children in Emergency and Armed Conflict
  United Nations
- Paid Educational Leave Convention
  International Labour Organisation (C140)
- Paid Educational Leave Recommendation
  International Labour Organisation (R148)
- *Regional Convention on the Recognition of Studies, Diplomas and Degrees in Higher Education in Latin America and the Caribbean*
  Mexico City, Mexico

1975

- Declaration on the Rights of Disabled Persons
  United Nations
- Declaration on the Protection of All Persons from Being Subjected to Torture and Other Cruel, Inhuman or Degrading Treatment or Punishment
  United Nations
- Declaration on the Use of Scientific and Technological Progress in the Interests of Peace and for the Benefit of Mankind
  United Nations
- Human Resources Development Convention
  International Labour Organisation (C142)
- Human Resources Development Recommendation
  International Labour Organisation (R150)
- Conference on Security and Co-operation in Europe Final Act
  Helsinki, Finland

1976

- *Recommendation on the Development of Adult Education*
  UNESCO

- Recommendation on Participation by the People at Large in Cultural Life and their Contribution to It
  UNESCO
- *International Convention on the Recognition of Studies, Diplomas and Degrees in Higher Education in the Arab and European States bordering on the Mediterranean*
  Nice, France
- Cultural Charter for Africa
  African Union

1977

- Additional Protocol to the Geneva Conventions of 12 August 1949, relating to the Protection of Victims of International Armed Conflicts (Protocol I)
  Diplomatic Conference on the Reaffirmation and Development of International Humanitarian Law applicable in Armed Conflicts, Geneva
- Additional Protocol to the Geneva Conventions of 12 August 1949, relating to the Protection of Victims of Non-International Armed Conflicts (Protocol II)
  Diplomatic Conference on the Reaffirmation and Development of International Humanitarian Law applicable in Armed Conflicts, Geneva

1978

- Declaration on the Preparation of Societies for Life in Peace
  United Nations
- Declaration on Race and Racial Prejudice
  UNESCO
- *Principles for the Teaching of Human Rights*
  UNESCO, International Congress on the Teaching of Human Rights, Vienna, Austria
- Declaration on Fundamental Principles concerning the Contribution to the Mass Media to Strengthening Peace and International Understanding, to the Promotion of Human Rights and to Countering Racialism, Apartheid and Incitement to War
  UNESCO
- *Revised Recommendation concerning the International Standardization of Educational Statistics*
  UNESCO
- *Convention on the Recognition of Studies, Diplomas and Degrees in Higher Education in the Arab States*
  Paris, France

- 104 EX/Decision 3.3 of the Executive Board of UNESCO on Complaints concerning violations of Human Rights in UNESCO's Fields of Competence
  UNESCO, Executive Board
- Human Rights Watch

1979

- Convention on the Elimination of All Forms of Discrimination against Women
  United Nations
- Code of Conduct for Law Enforcement Officials
  United Nations
- *Convention on the Recognition of Studies, Diplomas and Degrees concerning Higher Education in the States belonging to the Europe Region*
  Paris, France
- Recommendation 874 (1979) on a European Charter on the Rights of the Child
  Council of Europe, Parliamentary Assembly
- Inter-American Court of Human Rights

1980

- International Agreement for the Establishment of the University for Peace and Charter of the University for Peace
  United Nations
- Recommendation concerning the Status of the Artist
  UNESCO, 1980

1981

- Declaration on the Elimination of All Forms of Intolerance and of Discrimination Based on Religion or Belief
  United Nations
- African Charter on Human and Peoples' Rights
  Organisation of African Unity
- *Regional Convention on the Recognition of Studies, Certificates, Diplomas, Degrees and other Academic Qualifications in Higher Education in the African States*
  Arusha, Tanzania
- Universal Islamic Declaration of Human Rights
  Islamic Council, Paris

1982

- Principles of Medical Ethics relevant to the Role of Health Personnel, particularly Physicians, in the Protection of Prisoners and Detainees against Torture and Other Cruel, Inhuman or Degrading Treatment or Punishment
  United Nations
- World Charter for Nature
  United Nations
- Protocol Nº 6 to the Convention for the Protection of Human Rights and Fundamental Freedoms concerning the Abolition of the Death Penalty
  Council of Europe

1983

- *Regional Convention on the Recognition of Studies, Diplomas and Degrees in Higher Education in Asia and the Pacific*
  Bangkok, Thailand
- *Statement on the Compulsory Secondary School: Adolescents and the Curriculum*
  Council of Europe, Standing Conference of Ministers of Education
- Charter on the Rights of the Arab Child
  League of Arab States

1984

- Convention against Torture and Other Cruel, Inhuman or Degrading Treatment or Punishment
  United Nations
- Declaration on the Right of Peoples to Peace
  United Nations
- *Recommendation Nº R (84) 18 on The Training of Teachers in Education for Intercultural Understanding, Notably in a Context of Migration*
  Council of Europe

1985

- International Convention against Apartheid in Sports
  United Nations

- United Nations Standard Minimum Rules for the Administration of Juvenile Justice (The Beijing Rules)
  United Nations
- Declaration on the Human Rights of Individuals Who are not Nationals of the Country in which They Live
  United Nations
- Declaration of Basic Principles of Justice for Victims of Crime and Abuse of Power
  United Nations
- Basic Principles on the Independence of the Judiciary
  United Nations, Congress on the Prevention of Crime and the Treatment of Offenders
- United Nations Standard Minimum Rules for the Administration of Juvenile Justice (The Beijing Rules)
  United Nations, Committee on Economic, Social and Cultural Rights
- *Recommendation N° R (85) 7 on Teaching and Learning about Human Rights in Schools*
  Council of Europe
- Inter-American Convention to Prevent and Punish Torture
  Organisation of American States

1986

- Declaration on the Right to Development
  United Nations
- Declaration on Social and Legal Principles relating to the Protection and Welfare of Children, with special reference to Foster Placement and Adoption Nationally and Internationally
  United Nations
- The Seville Statement on Violence
  UNESCO
- Limburg Principles on the Implementation of the International Covenant on Economic, Social and Cultural Rights
  Group of International Experts in International Law

1987

- *Malta Recommendations on Human Rights Teaching, Information and Documentation*
  UNESCO, International Congress on Human Rights Teaching, Information and Documentation, Malta

- European Convention for the Prevention of Torture and Inhuman or Degrading Treatment or Punishment
  Council of Europe

1988

- Body of Principles for the Protection of All Persons under Any Form of Detention or Imprisonment
  United Nations
- Additional Protocol to the American Convention on Human Rights in the Area of Economic, Social and Cultural Rights (Protocol of San Salvador)
  General Assembly of States Parties to the American Convention on Human Rights, San Salvador, El Salvador
- African Commission on Human and Peoples' Rights
  Organisation of African Unity

1989

- Convention on the Rights of the Child
  United Nations
- Optional Protocol to the International Covenant on Civil and Political Rights Aiming at the Abolition of the Death Penalty
  United Nations
- Principles on the Effective Prevention and Investigation of Extra-legal, Arbitrary and Summary Executions
  United Nations, Economic and Social Council
- *Convention on Technical and Vocational Education*
  UNESCO
- Recommendation on the Safeguarding of Traditional Culture and Folklore
  UNESCO
- Yamoussoukro Declaration on Peace in the Minds of Men
  UNESCO, International Congress on Peace in the Minds of Men, Yamoussoukro, Côte d'Yvoire
- Convention Concerning Indigenous and Tribal Peoples in Independent Countries
  International Labour Organisation (C169)
- Community Charter of the Fundamental Social Rights of Workers
  European Union
- Fall of the Berlin Wall
- Tiananmen Square Protests

1990

- World Summit for Children
  United Nations, New York
- International Convention on the Protection of the Rights of All Migrant Workers and Members of Their Families
  United Nations
- Basic Principles for the Treatment of Prisoners
  United Nations
- United Nations Guidelines for the Prevention of Juvenile Delinquency (The Riyadh Guidelines)
  United Nations
- United Nations Rules for the Protection of Juveniles Deprived of their Liberty
  United Nations
- Basic Principles on the Role of Lawyers
  United Nations, Congress on the Prevention of Crime and the Treatment of Offenders
- Guidelines on the Role of Prosecutors
  United Nations, Congress on the Prevention of Crime and the Treatment of Offenders
- Guidelines for the Regulation of Computerized Personal Data Files
  United Nations
- World Declaration on the Survival, Protection and Development of Children, and Plan of Action for Implementing the World Declaration on the Survival, Protection and Development of Children in the 1990s
  World Summit for Children, New York
- *World Declaration on Education for All: Meeting Basic Learning Needs, and Framework for Action to Meet Basic Learning Needs: Guidelines for implementing the World Declaration on Education for All*
  World Conference on Education for All, Jomtien, Thailand
- Recommendation 1121 (1990) on the Rights of the Child
  Council of Europe, Parliamentary Assembly
- Protocol to the American Convention on Human Rights to Abolish the Death Penalty
  Organisation of American States
- African Charter on the Rights and Welfare of the Child
  Organisation of African Unity
- Cultural Charter for Africa
  African Union
- Cairo Declaration on Human Rights in Islam
  Organisation of Islamic Co-operation
- Charter of Paris for a New Europe

Conference on Security and Co-operation in Europe (CSCE)
- Nelson Mandela released after 27 years in prison

1991

- United Nations Principles for Older Persons
  United Nations
- Principles for the protection of persons with mental illness and the improvement of mental health care
  United Nations

1992

- Declaration on the Rights of Persons Belonging to National or Ethnic, Religious and Linguistic Minorities
  United Nations
- European Charter for Regional or Minorities Languages
  Council of Europe
- Treaty on European Union
  Maastricht, Nedtherlands
- *Sinaia Statement on Academic Freedom and University Autonomy*
  International Conference, Sinaia, Romania

1993

- Declaration on the Elimination of Violence against Women
  United Nations
- Vienna Declaration and Programme of Action
  United Nations, World Conference on Human Rights
- Principles relating to the Status of National Institutions for the Promotion and Protection of Human Rights (Paris Principles)
  United Nations
- High Commissioner for Human Rights
  United Nations (UNHCHR)
- International Criminal Tribunal for the Former Yugoslavia
  United Nations, Security Council
- *World Plan of Action on Education for Human Rights and Democracy, and Contributions to the Preparation of a Declaration on Academic Freedom*

UNESCO, International Congress on Education for Human Rights and Democracy, Montreal, Canada
- *Recommendation on the Recognition of Studies and Qualifications in Higher Education*
  UNESCO
- Declaration on the Elimination of Violence against Women
  United Nations
- Standards Rules on the Equalisation of Opportunities for Persons with Disabilities
  United Nations
- Bangkok NGOs Declaration on Human Rights
  Conference of Non-Governmental Organisations (NGOs)

1994

- Programme of Action of the International Conference on Population and Development
  United Nations, Cairo, Egypt
- *The Salamanca Statement and Framework for Action on Special Needs Education*
  UNESCO, World Conference on Special Needs Education: Access and Quality, Salamanca, Spain
- Framework Convention for the Protection of National Minorities
  Council of Europe
- Inter-American Convention on the Prevention, Punishment and Eradication of Violence Against Women (Convention of Belém do Pará)
  Organisation of American States
- Arab Charter on Human Rights (Revised)
  League of Arab States
- International Criminal Tribunal for Rwanda
  United Nations, Security Council

1995

- Copenhagen Declaration and Programme of Action on Social Development
  United Nations, World Summit for Social Development, Copenhagen, Denmark
- Beijing Declaration and Platform for Action
  United Nations, Fourth World Conference on Women, Beijing, China
- *Plan of Action of the United Nations Decade for Human Rights Education*
  United Nations
- *Declaration and Integrated Framework of Action on Education for Peace, Human Rights, and Democracy*
  UNESCO

- Declaration of Principles on Tolerance
  UNESCO
- Framework Convention for the Protection of National Minorities
  Council of Europe
- Additional Protocol to the European Social Charter Providing for a System of Collective Complaints
  Council of Europe
- Commonwealth of Independent States Convention on Human Rights and Fundamental Freedoms
  Minsk, Belarus
- Organisation for Security and Co-operation in Europe (OSCE)
  Replacing the Conference on Security and Co-operation in Europe (CSCE)

1996

- International Code of Conduct for Public Officials
  United Nations
- European Social Charter (Revised)
  Council of Europe

1997

- Guidelines for Action on Children in the Criminal Justice System
  United Nations, ECOSOC
- Declaration on the Responsibilities of the Present Generations Towards Future Generations
  UNESCO
- Universal Declaration on the Human Genome and Human Rights
  UNESCO
- *Recommendation concerning the Status of Higher-Education Teaching Personnel*
  UNESCO
- *The Hamburg Declaration on Adult Learning, and Agenda for the Future*
  UNESCO, Fifth International Conference on Adult Education, Hamburg, Germany
- Universal Declaration on the Human Genome and Human Rights
  UNESCO
- Declaration on the Responsibilities of the Present Generations Towards Future Generations
  UNESCO

- *Convention on the Recognition of Qualifications concerning Higher Education in the European Region*
  Lisbon, Portugal
- Convention for the Protection of Human Rights and Dignity of the Human Being with regard to the Application of Biology and Medicine: Convention on Human Rights and Biomedicine
  Council of Europe
- Universal Declaration on Democracy
  Inter-Parliamentary Council
- Maastricht Guidelines on Violations of Economic, Social and Cultural Rights
  Group of International Experts in International Law

1998

- Declaration on the Right and Responsibility of Individuals, Groups and Organs of Society to Promote and Protect Universally Recognized Human Rights and Fundamental Freedoms
  United Nations
- Declaration on Fundamental Principles and Rights at Work
  International Labour Organisation
- *World Declaration on Higher Education for the Twenty-first Century: Vision and Action, and Framework for priority Action for Change and Development in Higher Education*
  UNESCO, World Conference on Higher Education, Paris, France
- Rome Statute of the International Criminal Court
  United Nations, Diplomatic Conference of Plenipotentiaries on the Establishment of an International Criminal Court, Rome

1999

- Optional Protocol to the Convention on the Elimination of All Forms of Discrimination against Women
  United Nations
- Declaration and Programme of Action on a Culture of Peace
  United Nations
- Worst Forms of Child Labour (Convention)
  International Labour Organisation (C182)

- *Technical and Vocational Education and Training: A Vision for the twenty-first Century*
  UNESCO, Recommendations of the Second International Congress on Technical and Vocational Education, Seoul, Republic of Korea
- Inter-American Convention on the Elimination of all Forms of Discrimination against Persons with Disabilities
  Organisation of American States

2000

- Millennium Declaration (with Millennium Development Goals)
  United Nations
- Optional Protocol to the Convention on the Rights of the Child on the Involvement of Children in Armed Conflict
  United Nations
- Optional Protocol to the Convention on the Rights of the Child on the sale of children, child prostitution and child pornography
  United Nations
- Convention against Transnational Organised Crime
  United Nations
- Protocol to Prevent, Suppress and Punish Trafficking in Persons, Especially Women and Children, supplementing the United Nations Convention against Transnational Organised Crime
  United Nations
- *The Dakar Framework for Action – Education for All: Meeting our Collective Commitments*
  World Education Forum, Dakar, Senegal
- Human Rights Defenders: Support for the Individuals, Groups and Organisations of Civil Society Working to Promote and Protect Human Rights in the Americas
  Organisation of American States
- Charter of Fundamental Rights of the European Union
  European Union

2001

- World Conference against Racism, Xenophobia and all Forms of Discrimination
  Durban, South Africa
- *Revised Recommendation concerning Technical and Vocational Education*
  UNESCO

- Universal Declaration on Cultural Diversity, and Main Lines of an Action plan for the Implementation of the UNESCO Universal Declaration on Cultural Diversity
  UNESCO
- Inter-American Democratic Charter
  Organisation of American States
- Macchu Picchu Declaration on Democracy, the Rights of Indigenous Peoples and the War against Poverty
  Organisation of American States
- African Union
  Replacing the Organisation of African Unity (OAU)
- Attacks on the World Trade Centre and the Pentagon (September 11)

2002

- Optional Protocol to the Convention against Torture and other Cruel, Inhuman or Degrading Treatment or Punishment
  United Nations
- A World Fit For Children – Declaration and Plan of Action
  United Nations, General Assembly, Special Session on Children

2003

- Convention against Corruption
  United Nations
- The Human Rights Based Approach to Development Co-operation – Towards a Common Understanding Among UN Agencies
- Recommendation concerning the Promotion and Use of Multilingualism and Universal Access to Cyberspace
  UNESCO
- Convention for the Safeguarding of the Intangible Cultural Heritage
  UNESCO
- Charter on the Preservation of Digital Heritage
  UNESCO
- International Declaration on Human Genetic Data
  UNESCO
- *Declaration on Intercultural Education in the New European Context*
  Council of Europe, Standing Conference of European Ministers of Education, Athens, Greece

- Declaration on freedom of communication on the Internet
  Council of Europe, Committee of Ministers
- Convention on Preventing and Combating Corruption
  African Union
- Protocol to the African Charter on Human and Peoples' Rights on the Rights of Women in Africa
  African Union

2004

- *World Programme for Human Rights Education*
  United Nations
- *Declaration of Amsterdam on the Right to and the Rights in Education*
  World Conference on the Right to and the Rights in Education, Amsterdam, Netherlands
- African Court on Human and Peoples' Rights
  African Union

2005

- World Summit
  United Nations
- Declaration on Human Cloning
  United Nations
- Basic Principles and Guidelines on the Right to a Remedy and Reparation for Victims of Gross Violations of International Human Rights and Serious Violations of International Humanitarian Law
  United Nations
- Convention on the Protection and Promotion of the Diversity of Cultural Expressions
  UNESCO
- International Convention against Doping in Sport
  UNESCO
- Universal Declaration on Bioethics and Human Rights
  UNESCO
- *Jakarta Declaration on the Right to Basic Education as a Fundamental Human Right and the Legal Framework for its Financing*
  UNESCO

- Additional Protocol (III) to the Geneva Conventions
  Diplomatic Conference
- Convention on Action against Trafficking in Human Beings
  Council of Europe
- Covenant of the Rights of the Child in Islam
  Organisation of Islamic Co-operation

2006

- International Convention on the Rights of Persons with Disabilities, with an Optional Protocol
  United Nations
- International Convention for the Protection of All Persons from Enforced Disappearance
  United Nations
- Council of Human Rights
  United Nations, replacing the Commission on Human Rights
- African Youth Charter
  African Union

2007

- Declaration on the Rights of Indigenous Peoples
  United Nations
- African Charter on Democracy, Elections and Governance
  African Union
- Treaty of Lisbon
  European Union

2008

- Optional Protocol to the International Covenant on Economic, Social and Cultural Rights
  United Nations

2009

- Asian Intergovernmental Commission on Human Rights
  Association of Southeast Asian Nations (ASEAN)

2010

- *Charter on Education for Democratic Citizenship and Human Rights Education*
  Council of Europe

2011

- Optional Protocol to the Convention on the Rights of the Child on a communications procedure
  United Nations
- Guiding Principles on Business and Human Rights: Implementing the United Nations 'Protect, Respect and Remedy' Framework
  United Nations
- *United Nations Declaration on Human Rights Education and Training*
  United Nations
- *Asia-Pacific Regional Convention on the Recognition of Qualifications in Higher Education*
  Tokio, Japan
- Council of Europe Convention on preventing and combating violence against women and domestic violence
  Council of Europe, Istanbul
- Maastricht Principles on Extraterritorial Obligations of States in the area of Economic, Social and Cultural Rights
  Group of International Experts in International Law

2012

- Social Charter of the Americas
  Organisation of American States
- African Court of Justice and Human Rights
  African Union
- ASEAN Human Rights Declaration
  Association of Southeast Asian Nations (ASEAN)

2013

- *ILO Policy Guidelines on the promotion of decent work for early childhood education personnel*
  International Labour Organisation (ILO)

2014

- *Convention on the Recognition of Studies, Certificates, Diplomas, Degrees and Other Academic Qualifications in Higher Education in African States (revised)*
  Addis Ababa, Ethiopia

2015

- 2030 Agenda for Sustainable Development
  United Nations
- *Incheon Declaration*
  World Education Forum, Incheon, Republic of Korea
- *Education 2030 Framework for Action*
  High-level Meeting at UNESCO
- *International Charter of Physical Education, Physical Activity and Sport*
  UNESCO
- *Recommendation concerning Technical and Vocational Education and Training (TVET)*
  UNESCO
- *Recommendation on Adult Learning and Education*
  UNESCO
- *Declaration on Promoting Citizenship and the Common Values of Freedom, Tolerance and Non-Discrimination Through Education*
  European Union, Education Ministers

2016

- Declaration on the Right to Peace
  United Nations

2017

- Recommendation on Science and Scientific Researchers
  UNESCO

2018

- Protocol to the African Charter on Human and Peoples' Rights on the Rights of Persons with Disabilities in Africa
  African Union

2019

- *Global Convention on the Recognition of Qualifications Concerning Higher Education*
  UNESCO
- *Recommendation on Open Educational Resources*
  UNESCO
- *Regional Convention on the Recognition of Studies, Diplomas and Degrees in Higher Education in Latin America and the Caribbean*
  Buenos Aires, Argentina

APPENDIX F

Glossary

This little glossary is limited to the main technical terms of the Treaty Law. It borrows from the Vienna Convention on the Law of Treaties (1969),[1] the UN *Treaty Handbook*[2] and the *Glossary of terms relating to treaty actions.*[3] It is not organised alphabetically, but rather according to a certain temporal logic. A larger and more specific glossary on human rights may be found, for instance, in *Ethics of Human Rights* (Back Matter).[4]

Treaty/Convention/Protocole, etc.
Adoption
Contracting State
Final clauses
Authentic language
Depositary
Entry into force
Signature
Ratification/Acceptation/Approval/Accession
State Party
Third State
Interpretative declaration
Reservation
Amendment/Modification
Other terms

– *Treaty/Convention/Protocole, etc.*
  According to the Vienna Convention (Article 2):

  a "Treaty" means an international agreement concluded between States in written form and governed by international law, whether embodied in a single instrument or in two or more related instruments and whatever its particular designation;

  According to the UN *Treaty Handbook*:

 | DOI: 10.1163/9789004462465_013

Treaty

Treaty is a generic term embracing all instruments binding under international law, regardless of their formal designation, concluded between two or more international juridical persons. [...]

The application of the term treaty, in the generic sense, signifies that the Parties intend to create rights and obligations enforceable under International Law.

...

No international rules exist as to when an international instrument should be entitled a treaty. However, usually the term treaty is employed for instruments of some gravity and solemnity.

...

Bilateral treaty

A bilateral treaty is a treaty between two subjects of international law.

Multilateral treaty

A multilateral treaty is a treaty between more than two subjects of international law

Convention

Whereas in the twentieth century the term "convention" was regularly employed for bilateral agreements, it is now generally used for formal multilateral treaties with a broad number of Parties. Conventions are normally open for participation by the international community as a whole, or by a large number of States. Usually instruments negotiated under the auspices of an international organization are entitled conventions. The same holds true for instruments adopted by an organ of an international organization.

Protocol

A Protocol, in the context of treaty law and practice, has the same legal characteristics as a treaty. The term protocol is often used to describe agreements of a less formal nature than those entitled treaty or convention. Generally, a protocol amends, supplements or clarifies a multilateral treaty. A protocol is normally open to participation by the parties to the parent agreement. However, in recent times States have negotiated a number of protocols that do not follow this principle. The advantage of a protocol is that, while it is linked to the parent agreement, it can focus on a specific aspect of that agreement in greater detail.

– *Adoption*

According to the UN *Treaty Handbook*:

Adoption is the formal act by which negotiating Parties establish the form and content of a treaty. The treaty is adopted through a specific act expressing the will of the States and the international organizations participating in the negotiation of that treaty, for example, by voting on the text, initialling, signing, etc. Adoption may also be the mechanism used to establish the form and content of amendments to a treaty, or regulations under a treaty.

Treaties that are negotiated within an international organization are usually adopted by resolution of the representative organ of that organization. For example, treaties negotiated under the auspices of the United Nations, or any of its bodies, are adopted by a resolution of the General Assembly of the United Nations.

Where an international conference is specifically convened for the purpose of adopting a treaty, the treaty can be adopted by a vote of two thirds of the States present and voting, unless they have decided by the same majority to apply a different rule.

See Article 9 of the Vienna Convention 1969.

- *Contracting State*
  According to the Vienna Convention (Article 2):

  f. "Contracting State" means a State which has consented to be bound by the treaty, whether or not the treaty has entered into force;

  According to the UN *Treaty Handbook*:

  A contracting State is a State that has expressed its consent to be bound by a treaty where the treaty has not yet entered into force or where it has not entered into force for that State.

  See Article 2 (1) (f) of the Vienna Convention 1969.

- *Final clauses*
  According to the UN Treaty Handbook:

  Final clauses are provisions typically found at the end of a treaty, dealing with such topics as signature, ratification, acceptance, approval, accession, denunciation, amendment, reservation, entry into force, settlement of disputes, depositary matters and authentic texts. [...]

- *Authentic language*
  According to the UN *Treaty Handbook*:

  A treaty typically specifies its authentic languages – the languages in which the meaning of its provisions is to be determined.

- *Depositary*
  According to the UN *Treaty Handbook*:

  > The depositary of a treaty is the custodian of the treaty and is entrusted with the functions specified in Article 77 of the Vienna Convention 1969. [...] A depositary can be one or more States, an international organization, or the chief administrative officer of the organization, such as the Secretary-General of the United Nations. [...] The Secretary General, at present, is the depositary for over 550 multilateral treaties.
  >
  > See Articles 76 and 77 of the Vienna Convention 1969.

- *Entry into force*
  According to the UN *Treaty Handbook*:

  > Entry into force of a treaty is the moment in time when a treaty becomes legally binding on the Parties to the treaty. The provisions of the treaty determine the moment of its entry into force. This may be a date specified in the treaty or a date on which a specified number of ratifications, approvals, acceptances or accessions have been deposited with the depositary. The date when a treaty deposited with the Secretary-General enters into force is determined in accordance with the treaty provisions. [...]

- *Signature*
  According to the UN *Treaty Handbook*:

  > Definitive signature occurs where a State expresses its consent to be bound by a treaty by signing the treaty without the need for ratification, acceptance or approval. A State may definitively sign a treaty only when the treaty so permits. A number of treaties deposited with the Secretary-General permit definitive signature.
  >
  > See article 12 of the Vienna Convention 1969.
  >
  > ...
  >
  > Simple signature applies to most multilateral treaties. This means that when a State signs the treaty, the signature is subject to ratification, acceptance or approval. The State has not expressed its consent to be bound by the treaty until it ratifies, accepts or approves it. [...]
  >
  > See Articles 14 and 18 of the Vienna Convention 1969.

- *Ratification/Acceptation/Approval/Accession*
  According to the Vienna Convention (Article):

> b. "Ratification", "acceptance", "approval" and "accession" mean in each case the international act so named whereby a State establishes on the international plane its consent to be bound by a treaty;

According to the UN *Treaty Handbook*:

> Ratification, acceptance and approval all refer to the act undertaken on the international plane, whereby a State establishes its consent to be bound by a treaty. [...]
>
> Ratification, acceptance or approval at the international level indicates to the international community a State's commitment to undertake the obligations under a treaty.
>
> See Articles 2 (1) (b), 11, 14 and 16 of the Vienna Convention 1969
>
> Accession is the act whereby a State that has not signed a treaty expresses its consent to become a Party to that treaty by depositing an "instrument of accession". Accession has the same legal effect as ratification, acceptance or approval. The conditions under which accession may occur and the procedure involved depend on the provisions of the relevant treaty. Accession is generally employed by States wishing to express their consent to be bound by a treaty where the deadline for signature has passed. However, many modern multilateral treaties provide for accession even during the period that the treaty is open for signature.
>
> See Articles 2 (1) (b) and 15 of the Vienna Convention 1969.

– *State Party*
 According to the Vienna Convention (Article 2):

> g. "Party" means a State which has consented to be bound by the treaty and for which the treaty is in force;
>
> According to the UN *Treaty Handbook*:
>
> A Party to a treaty is a State or other entity with treaty-making capacity that has expressed its consent to be bound by that treaty by an act of ratification, acceptance, approval or accession, etc., where that treaty has entered into force for that particular State. This means that the State is bound by the treaty under international law.
>
> See Article 2 (1) (g) of the Vienna Convention 1969

– *Third State*
 According to the Vienna Convention (Article 2):

> h. "Third State" means a State not a Party to the treaty;

In accordance with its Article 38, a rule set forth in a treaty may become "binding upon a third State as a customary rule of international law, recognized as such".

- *Interpretative declaration*
  According to the UN *Treaty Handbook*:

  An interpretative declaration is a declaration by a State as to its understanding of some matter covered by a treaty or its interpretation of a particular provision. Unlike reservations, declarations merely clarify a State's position and do not purport to exclude or modify the legal effect of a treaty. [...]

- *Reservation*
  According to the Vienna Convention (Article 2):

  d. "Reservation" means a unilateral statement, however phrased or named, made by a State, when signing, ratifying, accepting, approving or acceding to a treaty, whereby it purports to exclude or to modify the legal effect of certain provisions of the treaty in their application to that State;

  According to the UN *Treaty Handbook*:

  A reservation is a statement made by a State by which it purports to exclude or alter the legal effect of certain provisions of a treaty in their application to that State. A reservation may enable a State to participate in a multilateral treaty that it would otherwise be unable or unwilling to participate in. States can make reservations to a treaty when they sign, ratify, accept, approve or accede to it. When a State makes a reservation upon signing, it must confirm the reservation upon ratification, acceptance or approval. [...]

  See Articles 2 (1) (d) and 19–23 of the Vienna Convention 1969

- *Amendment/Modification*
  According to the UN *Treaty Handbook*:

  Amendment, in the context of treaty law, means the formal alteration of the provisions of a treaty by its Parties. [...]

  Modification, in the context of treaty law, refers to the variation of certain provisions of a treaty only as between particular Parties to that treaty. As between other Parties, the original provisions apply. [...]

- *Other terms*
  According to the UN *Treaty Handbook*:

The term memorandum of understanding (M.O.U.) is often used to denote a less formal international instrument than a typical treaty or international agreement. It often sets out operational arrangements under a framework international agreement. It is also used for the regulation of technical or detailed matters. [...]

A Final Act is a document summarizing the proceedings of a diplomatic conference. It is normally the formal act by which the negotiating Parties bring the conference to a conclusion. It is usually part of the documentation arising from the conference, including the treaty, the resolutions and interpretative declarations made by participating States. [...]

Notes

1 https://treaties.un.org/doc/Publication/UNTS/Volume%201155/volume-1155-I-18232-English.pdf
2 https://treaties.un.org/Pages/Resource.aspx?path=Publication/TH/Page1_en.xml
3 https://treaties.un.org/pages/Overview.aspx?path=overview/glossary/page1_en.xml
4 http://link.springer.com/book/10.1007%2F978-3-319-03566-6

APPENDIX G

Revolution of the Right to Education

Global Summary

Introduction: Advent of the International Education Law

Throughout centuries, education has often, somewhat paradoxically, been blamed for being the main cause of human evils and prized as the main remedy for correcting them. This proves the primacy commonly recognised to education, but what a *good education* should be has always been a rather controversial issue.

An educational revolution or paradigm shift has been claimed principally since the end of the 19th century. A very educational revolution is, first and foremost, a normative one, concerning the truly inspiring values and the aims effectively guiding education, which is purposeful, by definition. It's about what we want to become as human beings.

There is no timeless ideal education, but there is a universal pedagogic heritage indefinitely open to the lights of the advancements of science and conscience, for the historical perfecting of the humankind. It is condensed in the right to education proclaimed by the Universal Declaration of Human Rights.

The birth of the *human right* to education, after a millennial-long gestation, has opened a new chapter in the History of Education. What is more, its normative, jurisprudential, doctrinal, and programmatic developments are constituents of an International Education Law that is now the highest source in the hierarchy of the contemporary normativity on education, to which should conform the Education Law in States Parties to it. Therefore, it should be recognised and studied as a new legal and educational discipline, source of the principles of legitimacy and quality of education.

This book offers a very interdisciplinary and topical introduction to the International Education Law, broadly defined. It submits that the normative integrity of the right to education carries far-reaching revolutionary significance, a corollary of the Revolution of Human Rights and the Revolution of the Rights of the Child.

Chapter 1: Education, Power and Law

A juridical approach of education as a human right raises a preliminary challenge: How to introduce it into the theorisation of the educational phenomenon?

Education is a complex theoretical-practical field of research because it is a multiform, multidimensional, multidisciplinary phenomenon, crossed by multiple interests

 | DOI: 10.1163/9789004462465_014

and stakes. There are 'sciences of education', but their plurality makes necessary a specific discipline whose scope should be *only but the whole education* to bring about a *fundamental and global theorisation* consisting of identifying and trying to answer the essential questions involved in the educational phenomenon. Such a discipline should be, on the one hand, the centre of gravity of the *professional culture* of teachers and other educators to learn to reflect on education, and on the other hand, a *conceptual grid* of observation and interpretation to know how to act and react well in every situation. After all, there is nothing more practical than a good theory ...

Education is ultimately a form of power. Well, every power of human beings over human beings raises the question of its legitimacy. The question of the legitimacy of education is that of the foundation, sense and control of the power it exerts through the contents and forms of the communication it accomplishes. It was sparked by some precursors, in the modern and contemporary history of education, but it has been, in general, *unthinkable*. For the traditional pedagogical mindset, educating is so *natural* that the question of the legitimacy of education is dissolved in this postulate: (if) education is necessary, (whatever) education is legitimate. This is fallacious reasoning, as it does not distinguish between necessity and legitimacy.

The question of the legitimacy of education amounts to determining the very criterion of the *pedagogic* that is the traditional signifier of all validity claims concerning education. All in all, it is a matter of answering the following bold question: *By what right to educate?* This is the *meta-question* of education insofar as it underlies and overdetermines the subsequent ones.

Education having been elevated to *human right* status – the highest one of the contemporary ethical-juridical normativity – the most legitimate response to the meta-question of its legitimacy should be researched in the *right to education*.

In order to grasp the revolutionary novelty of the right to education, we need first to understand the revolutionary significance of human rights and, in particular, of the rights of the child.

Chapter 2: Human Rights

Every community needs rules to regulate living together. Law is a social regulatory device that has become the most powerful driver of Civilisation. It has expanded as a normative network framing the international, social and individual life. In the contemporary world, there is no other alternative for the peaceful coexistence of cultures, peoples and the whole human diversity. The superior expression of the civilisational power of Law are human rights.

The human rights sentiment and ideal are as ancient and cross-cultural as human suffering and ideals, but the term, with its present meaning, has generalised only at the end of the 18th century, in the Western world. We may distinguish three main stages in the modern and contemporary history of human rights:

- Philosophical elaboration of the 'natural rights' idea in the 17th–18th centuries
- Declarations of 'rights of man' and their constitutionalisation since the second half of the 18th century, especially the French Declaration of the Rights of Man and the Citizen (1789)
- Internationalisation and codification of human rights after World War II

The belief in the correspondence between what is 'right' and what is 'natural' underlies the 'Natural Law' and 'natural rights' ideas, which were groundbreaking insights in the genealogy of the human rights concept.

International Law does not provide a definition of 'human rights'. They are said to be inherent in the 'human dignity', but there is no legal definition of human dignity either. Following the most elementary and common one, human rights are rights recognised to every human being simply because of being a member of the human species. They aim at protecting the weakest against the strongest – especially the State – as well as guaranteeing to everyone minimum conditions for a dignified life. As a consequence, human rights are universal, by definition, and are qualified as "equal and inalienable".

- They are *equal* because they are held by every human being, without any discrimination, everywhere.
- They are *inalienable* because they are never lost, i.e. they cannot forcibly be taken away (by expropriation) or voluntarily given up (by transaction).

Although 'human rights' is the most common term in International Law, the most used in constitutional texts is 'fundamental/basic rights', which include other exclusive citizens' rights, such as the right to vote. There is also the term 'fundamental freedoms', but no conceptual distinction can be drawn between human rights and fundamental freedoms. There are still the term 'civil rights' and the French term *libertés publiques* (public liberties/freedoms).

The history of human rights' juridification – i.e. of their moral claims becoming Law – is frequently presented as a 'generations' succession, reflecting the trilogy of the French Revolution: *Liberté* (Liberty: first generation), *Égalité* (Equality: second generation), *Fraternité* (Fraternity: third generation). This is controversial, however, because it is neither historically nor conceptually accurate and may be misleading.

The United Nations Charter (1945) was the first universal treaty to proclaim the principle of respect for the human dignity and rights, which were given name and content in the Universal Declaration of Human Rights (1948). In 1966, two major human rights treaties were adopted: International Covenant on Civil and Political Rights and International Covenant on Economic, Social and Cultural Rights. The Universal

Declaration and the two International Covenants, adopted by the United Nations General Assembly, form together the so-called International Bill of Human Rights that constitutes the universal most general framework of International Human Rights Law. Its *Corpus Juris* (Body of Law) includes seven other universal core human rights treaties and some hundreds of instruments, conventional or declaratory, with general, specific or categorical content, and universal or regional in scope.

Determining the structure and normative content of a human right amounts to answering the following main interrogations: Who holds the right (entitlement: right-holder)? In what does it consist (object: to what is it a right)? Who has the corresponding obligations (exigibility/opposability: duty-bearers)?

- Holders of human rights are, by definition, "everyone", "every human being", "all persons", except when a legal instrument addresses a more vulnerable category of persons (children or women, for example).
- The object of a human right provides what the right-holder is entitled to. Each right aims at protecting and fostering a fundamental universal human value by laying down the interdictions it commands and/or positive measures it requires.
- Duty-bearers are those obliged to fulfil the object's normative content. They are principally States, individually and collectively, as they are the authors and direct addressees of the International Law to which they oblige themselves.

The specificity of each right is essentially determined by its object, the content of which may be described as a normative complex composed of three layers, as it were: minimum content, full content and expanded content, to which correspond as many States' obligations levels.

The protection of human rights displays two faces: one turned to the inside, to national legal orders, the other one turned to the outside, to International Law. In effect, this is the double paradox of human rights: they are born against the State, against the abuses of public powers, but need protection and provisions by State; however, if States should be their main guarantors, they are often their main violators. Therefore, the protection of human rights is also a responsibility of the International Community, as the last resort.

There are international systems/regimes for the protection of human rights at the universal and regional levels. The United Nations universal system is made up of twofold mechanisms: Charter-based and Treaty-based. At the regional level, there are three systems: European (Council of Europe), American (Organisation of the American States), African (Organisation of African Unity – African Union since 2000). There are still other regional organisations and instruments.

When the victims of violation (or threat of violation) of their rights (or someone on their behalf) can submit a complaint to an independent and impartial instance to repair (or to prevent) it, the right is said to be justiciable. Justiciability, in a strict sense, is accomplished by Tribunals, which are the organs typically competent to take binding decisions based on laws and facts. Their jurisprudence (interpretations) contributes, to a large extent, to define and develop the normative content of human rights.

As a World Court of Human Rights is still lacking, there is no veritable Case Law on human rights at the universal level, but there are regional Courts (European, American, African). The most comprehensive regional Case Law is due to the organs of the European Convention on Human Rights (the former European Commission of Human Rights and European Court of Human Rights, now merged in a permanent Court).

The protection and promotion of human rights begin with each and every person, howeve: to know, to claim and to exercise one's human rights is a duty towards the personal dignity, the communities in which we live and our common Humanity.

There are tens of thousands of Non-Governmental Organisations, international and national, devoted to human rights.

The interpretation and implementation of human rights treaties should be made according to general rules of International Law and other principles specific to the International Human Rights Law. The latter may be systematised into the following categories: ethical principles, most general legal principles, other legal principles, jurisprudential principles, political principles. They form a whole whose overall sense is the guarantee of all human rights for all, as fully as possible.

The ethical principles are paramount. They form an Ethics of Human Rights that should be highlighted.

The history of human rights is the history of the invention of the Human Being by human beings. Of the revelation of *Human Being in human beings.* The Human Being is the ethical subject transcending the empirical subjects – ethnic, cultural, national, social, familial, psychological and other ones – with their roots, memberships, cradles, situations and other particularities. The *ethical subject* stands for the field of values and the forum of conscience as the *epistemic subject* for the field of knowledge and the realm of science (as well as the *citizen* for the social diversity).

Human rights constitute an Ethics because their source and sense are the worth and dignity of the human person, whose absolute primacy they consecrate. The Ethics of Human Rights concentrates the juice of the best fruits of the cultural plurality of the humankind, expressing the quintessence of the evolution of its conscience. It is, therefore, an intercultural Ethics with legal force and political, economic, pedagogical and other exigencies. Adding a universal moral heritage to the genetic heritage of the human species and the cultural heritages of peoples, human rights vest every human being with a common ethical identity, making him/her a citizen of the world.

Here is the most profound and transcendent significance of the Ethics of Human Rights: The Human Being should be a *God* for human beings. His temple *sanctum sanctorum* (the most sacred place) is Human Dignity.

Human Dignity is the most brilliant star in the human rights firmament, the highest lighthouse in the ocean of the human species' indefinite destiny. It lies at the heart of the Human Rights Philosophy and is the spinal column of the International Human Rights Law, the axiological core of a New Constitutionalism, the supreme value of the Rule of Law, the embryo of a Law of Humanity. The Human Dignity Principle may be considered as the quintessence of Civilisation.

It may be said that human dignity and rights are fruits of a double Historical Consensus:

- The moral consensus of religious traditions and philosophical wisdom crystallised in the Golden Rule as a principle of reciprocity, empathy and compassion that distinguishes *humanity* from *animality*.
- The legal consensus laid down in the Universal Declaration of Human Rights, whose values and principles have expanded, becoming the Law of Law, that is, a superior and indisposable Law.

While human dignity is said to be the source of human rights, it remains, paradoxically, a foundation lacking to be founded ... An account of the human dignity and rights foundation/justification is submitted that consists in arguing the following sentences:

- Human dignity is the principle and the sense of human rights
- Human dignity hallmarks the belonging to the human species
- Human dignity is an ethical invention with genetic foundation
- Human dignity consists in perfectibility calling for perfecting
- Human dignity is inviolable and indisposable
- Human dignity is vulnerable and variable

It may be concluded that human dignity is composed of three layers, as it were:

- *Objective layer*, formed by the 'first human nature'. It can be *known*.
- *Intersubjective layer*, concerned with the 'second human nature'. It must be *recognised.*
- *Subjective layer*, depending on each one's merits and behaviours. It should be *deserved.*

Summing up: Human dignity is a *natural attribute*, a *moral status* and a *personal responsibility.*

There are other values-rights-principles constituents of the Ethics of Human Rights, allowing for the following definition: *The Ethics of Human Rights is an Ethics of the Recognition of Human Dignity as a Principle-Right to have Rights – rights of a living human being – which are fundamentally the Rights-Principles of Liberty, Equality, Diversity, with the consequent Responsibility.*

The Ethics of Human Rights has become the Ethics of Humanity, the Common Temple of the *secular faith* of the Rule of Law. And as human dignity will never be definitively protected and enhanced, the Human Rights Temple is an endless building, open to the *Possible* ...

Revolution is a term frequent in human rights literature. Three moments and documents may be highlighted in the history of the Revolution of Human Rights:
- Declaration of the Rights of Man and the Citizen (France, 1789)
- Universal Declaration of Human Rights (United Nations, 1948)
- Convention on the Rights of the Child (United Nations, 1989)

The Revolution of Human Rights may be summarised as follows:
- Consecration of the Individual as the highest ethical-juridical value
- Transformation of the International Law and renovation of the Constitutional Law
- Reconstruction of the Rule of Law
- Inception of a Law of Humanity

The Revolution of Human Rights is an everyday individual, collective, endless struggle ...

Chapter 3: Rights of the Child

The recognition of the rights of the child has meant a historical deepening of the logic and ideal of human rights.

The history of childhood is crossed by the ambivalence of its representation and treatment by adults. A pessimistic mindset has long prevailed, underlying the lasting violence over children. It is submitted that the evolution of the attitudes towards children may be historically schematically divided into the following three eras, at least as the Western culture is concerned:
- *Unawareness* of the childhood specificity and despise of children, regarded as humanly inferior and reduced to the condition of being objects of property and violence (for millennia).
- *Awareness* of the value of childhood and dawn of a new sensitivity regarding children as developing human beings, arousing feelings of compassion and love and demanding protection and care (since the Renaissance).
- *Recognition* of the child as a human person equal by dignity and rights, in the Convention on the Rights of the Child, which has become the source of a new International Law of the Child.

The International Law of the Child deals with her/his human rights internationally recognised and protected, at the universal and regional levels. It is inseminating national legal orders.

Parents are *naturally* the first responsible for the rights of their children, but *legally* the main responsible are States. There are Committees on the Rights of the Child at the universal and regional levels. At the national level, there are varied institutions devoted to the rights of the child. They are also the *cause* of thousands of international and national Non-Governmental Organisations.

We know why human rights constitute an Ethics of Humanity. The rights of the child have an ethical content too, fundamentally because they outlaw the discrimination of children on account of their age, and command their special protection by virtue of their age. They recognise, therefore, both the ethical-legal equality and the bio-psychological difference of children, i.e. they protect the fullness of their dignity and rights, as human beings, and their immaturity, vulnerability and perfectibility, as children.

The Ethics of the Rights of the Child – inscribed in the Ethics of Human Rights – may be summarised into the following principles:

- *Primacy of the "best interests of the child"*
- *Love, respect and responsibility for the child*
- *Evolving autonomy of the child*
- *Priority of children*

The New International Law of the Child meant a movement from the traditional (naturalist) representation of the *child-object of Law* towards a new (ethical) vision of the *child-subject of rights*. It is the culmination of an evolution that means a revolution, as it is generally acknowledged by both its defenders and detractors. The Revolution of the Rights of the Child is, however, the most candid and peaceful one: it consists simply in fully recognising and treating children as human persons. It is an ethical and juridical revolution, but above all, it is the principle of a deeper, slow and long cultural revolution because it must transform mentalities and customs.

The Convention on the Rights of the Child is a visionary text. That is why the idea of 'rights of the child' remains resisted. Underlying most resistance is this misunderstanding: to recognise rights to children is to take them away from parents. The rights of children are not rights against adults, they make them better human beings, instead. If they are respected, children will be adults more developed, conscious, creative, happy, responsible, better citizens and better educators of their children.

The right to education is the Bastille of the Revolution of the Rights of the Child.

Chapter 4: Right to Education

In the history of education, three eras may be roughly distinguished, before its recognition as a human right:

- Education as mostly a familial matter, the longest era.
- Education as a national interest, from five centuries or so ago.
- Education as an international concern too, from the late 19th century.

Along millennia, education has been taken as a *natural* extension of parents' power over their progeny-property, supported by religions and surrounded by community's needs, interests and pressures.

The economic, political and ideological value of education was discovered, in the Western world, since the end of the Middle Ages, as instrumental for Nation-State building. The idea of *national education* emerged, competing with the centuries-long Christian 'monopoly' of education. The ideology of the Enlightenment put the public interest in education ahead of other ones.

Because of it being the main resource for the cultivation of a nation's identity (and for other not good motives), education is maybe the dimension of peoples' life most resistant to internationalisation. The principles of State's sovereignty and non-intervention in domestic affairs – cornerstones of the classic International Law – have been the strongest obstacles to the internationalisation of education until (and after) it was proclaimed a 'human right'.

It is submitted that the major precursors of the normative distinctiveness of the human right to education, at least within the Western culture, were Comenius (17th century) and Rousseau (18th century), for these main reasons: Comenius pointed to the universality of education as imperative of the anthropological educability, Rousseau questioned the legitimacy of the educational power, alongside with that of the political power.

Education is a word absent from the French Declaration of the Rights of Man and the Citizen (1789), as well as from the precedent American Bills of Rights. The constitutional recognition of a 'right to education' occurred, for the first time, likely in the Brazilian Constitution of 1934.

At the international level, education was first recognised as a human right in the American continent by the Charter of the Organisation of American States and the American Declaration of the Rights and Duties of Man (1948). At the universal level, it was first proclaimed, some months later, by the Universal Declaration of Human Rights.

Therefore, although in the history of great concepts there is dawn when it is no longer night but day is not yet fully born either, talking about the recognition of a very 'right to education', before the 20th century, sounds anachronism. Indeed, the right to education:

- is not just a (*natural*) *right* of children, morally opposable to parents;
- is not only a (*social*) *right* increasingly vital for the existence, subsistence and progress of a nation, justifying compulsory schooling;

– is rather an (*individual*) *right* internationally and nationally recognised and protected as a *human right* essential for the personal flourishing of beings endowed with perfectibility and the aptitude for rationality, morality, creativity and responsibility.

The Universal Declaration Article 26 has become the source of an International Education Law that comprises provisions in much more than one hundred legal texts. Its universal most general normative framework is the International Bill of Human Rights. The principal universal conventional categorical provisions are laid down in the Convention on the Rights of the Child. The Convention against Discrimination in Education remains its main specific instrument.

In accordance with the titles of the International Covenants on human rights, they fall into five categories: civil, political, economic, social and cultural. While the right to education has a cross-cutting content, it is generally included in 'cultural rights'.

Education means a process and the outcome of the process. There are tens of definitions in the history of the pedagogic thought, varying from broader to narrower conceptions. We also find definitions in International Education Law instruments and Case Law, as well as in international glossaries.

The international terminology on the right to education and the respective translations are voluble and variable. Since the 1970s, the term "basic education" has begun to generalise, but there is no international consensus about its scope. It means, in general, the segment of a school system that is compulsory and should be free.

Like all human rights, the right to education is a right of "everyone", children and adults, women and men, white, black or whatever their colour and belongings, differences and other circumstances.

As the educational phenomenon consists in learning, right to education fundamentally means right to learn. Therefore, determining its object amounts to answering the following main interrogations: Learning ... for what? ... what? ... how? ... It is described principally in the following provisions: Article 26 of the Universal Declaration, Articles 13 and 14 of the International Covenant on Economic, Social and Cultural Rights, Articles 28 and 29 of the Convention on the Rights of the Child.

The learnings to be ensured in order to meet the aims of the right to education internationally agreed are not determined, but there are indications in other international texts. They are frequently summed up in the so-called "four pillars" of education, namely: learning to know, to do, to live together and to be.

The exigibility of the right to education concerns persons or entities with obligations or responsibilities regarding its satisfaction, i.e. to which it is opposable. They are families, first and foremost, but the realisation of the whole object of the right to education exceeds their means. States are the principal responsible, legally and politically, for guaranteeing human rights, as we know. The International Community bears a subsidiary responsibility, by means of intergovernmental organisations. The right to education is self-opposable too, i.e. a duty of each one towards himself/herself. Education is a right-duty, more than any other human right because in it is at stake the *humanisation* itself.

There are many Non-Governmental Organisations devoted to the right to education.

States' obligations being paramount, they should be highlighted. They are general and specific.

States have general obligations to the International Law they agree. Their specific legal obligations concerning the right to education correspond to its triple normative content, following the distinction proposed. Therefore, they may be represented as three concentric circles: minimum, full, and expanded content/obligations.

- Minimum content/obligations consist of free primary education, without discrimination, while developing a complete education system, progressively free, with respect for the liberties of education; and of assuring that public and private education meet the aims set out in the international provisions on the right to education and conform to other national norms.
- Full content/obligations comprise all the formal elements of the object of the right to education, to which applies the so-called '4-A Scheme', namely: availability, accessibility, acceptability, adaptability. Considering that acceptability and adaptability are largely overlapping and sometimes confused notions, and given the timeliness and comprehensiveness of the principle of quality education – which can subsume its acceptability and adaptability – as well as the overarching significance of the equity principle, in its relation with the principles of non-discrimination, equality and diversity, the *4-A Scheme* could become: *Availability, Accessibility, Quality, Equity*.
- Expanded content/obligations, as here understood, cover the full content, all commitments internationally assumed by States concerning education, and other obligations derived from the principle of human rights interdependence and the dialectical relationship education-society.

Three paramount specific States' obligations are the following ones: all education shall be directed to the purpose of the right to education; everyone shall be guaranteed basic free compulsory schooling; private education shall be regulated and supervised.

The international protection of the right to education comes under general mechanisms common to other human rights, at the universal and regional levels, as well as special mechanisms within the UNESCO framework (and the International Labour Organisation, concerning the professional element of its normative content).

There is a worldwide considerable Case Law on the right to education. The most important one is that of the organs of the European Convention on Human Rights, whose jurisprudence is the most significant contribution of the European Education Law to the International Education Law.

The right to education displays some distinguishing characteristics:
- It is the most complex human right
- It is the most empowering human right
- It is the only human right with a formally free element
- It is the only human right with a compulsory component
- Its content is among the most internationally developed
- Its content includes elements from all international legal sources

The human primacy of education is an idea crossing the history of education, reverberated in proverbs of the wisdom of many peoples, and has prominent spokespersons. It is an anthropological, moral, psychological, economic, political and legal primacy.

The priority of the right to education – that is relative because of the human rights interdependence – was often invoked during the *travaux préparatoires* of its major international provisions, is recognised by the International Human Rights Law, has been affirmed by jurisprudence and is supported by doctrine. It has been rediscovered, in a way, by the International Community, and the right to education has gained unprecedented visibility on the International Agenda, as witness conferences, declarations, action programmes and other texts and initiatives. Indeed, while all human rights have an essential ethical dimension, by definition, because their source and sense is human dignity – the supreme value – the right to education has an incomparable ethical radicality, because of its consubstantiality with the human dignity.

The recognition of the liberty of education preceded historically that of the right to education, as an element of the liberty of expression proclaimed by the French Declaration of the Rights of Man and the Citizen (1789). With the proclamation of the human right to education, the relationship with the liberties of education included in its wording has become debated. Education liberalisation and privatisation policies, from the 1980s, have revived the controversy. What is at stake is answering two main questions:
- Is children's education a "fundamental right" of parents?
- Is education privatisation compatible with the International Education Law?

Family rights have historical and cultural roots whose resilience is reflected in the legislation and jurisprudence of many countries, frequently recognising to parents an (almost) absolute right over their children. The most sensitive issue relating to parents' liberties of education concerns the religious and moral education of their children.

The recognition of a "fundamental right" of parents concerning the education of children would not be compatible with their "human right" to education. If conflicts arise between Family and State in this respect, what is really at stake is neither a Family's right nor a State's right, but the right to education of the child. It must be protected both against the State, in case of attempted totalitarian appropriation of children, or against Family, if the physical, psychological or moral integrity and the personal development of children are at risk. And not by replacing one totalitarianism with another.

As education privatisation is concerned, International Education Law excludes both a public monopole and the complete privatisation of education. States have an obligation to establish and to develop a public education system with a free compulsory component, as well as to adopt and supervise compliance with regulations ensuring that private provision of education meets international and national standards on the right to education.

The most recent international commitments towards the implementation of the right to education are the *Incheon Declaration* together with the *2030 Education Agenda,* adopted in the context of the United Nations *2030 Agenda for Sustainable Development.* They draw a *new vision* pointing to an education qualified by the following attributes: *human right approach, humanistic, holistic, child-friendly, child-centred, empowering.* It is a vision opposed, therefore, to an education captured by ethnic reflexes, religious beliefs, partisan indoctrination or neoliberal economism.

Human rights indicators are quantitative/statistical and qualitative/normative references of achievement, in a complex relationship. The right to education indicators should *a fortiori* (for a still stronger reason) be both quantitative and qualitative.

Every education issue should be examined following a *human right approach,* according to which the right to education is Right to a Rightful Education.

Chapter 5: Towards a Rightful Education

For the traditional educational mindset, the individual 'right' to education is a mere reflex of the family and social right to educate children according to dominant domestic beliefs and interests. This political-pedagogical paradigm – that was dominant *de jure* and *de facto* (by Law and in fact) until modern times – is holistic in the sense that the Whole (community) prevails over the parts (individuals). This amounts to a *right of education* (an expression absent from the International Human Rights Law).

It was against the traditional holistic political-pedagogical paradigm of the right of education that emerged, in the late 19th century, in the American and European continents, the most powerful wave of renewal in the history of education: the New Education Movement, which reached its apogee between the two World Wars. It evolved as a true Education International gathering education professionals from all continents, as well as personalities from other professional and scientific areas. However, 'new education' was a term with varying assumptions. What was most unifying of its heterogeneity were reformism, child-centrism and pacifism.

In the documents and speeches of militants of the New Education Movement, there are references to human rights, the rights of the child and the right to education, its values and principles. The normative content of the right to education reflects and universalised the ideal that, during nearly two decades, gathered so many actors of this fascinating chapter of the History of Education.

Indeed, the right to education is a *new right* to *new education.*

The International Human Rights Law is rooted in the subversion triggered by the *New Law* of the French Revolution. As regards the right to education, in particular, it is a *new right* for two main reasons:

- Education was recognised as a *human right*, i.e. a right qualified by its *subjectivity*, *universality* and *exigibility*, but specifically for its *normativity.*
- The right to education has evolved at the normative, jurisprudential and doctrinal levels, reaching a higher coherence in the Convention on the Rights of the Child.

The right to education is, therefore, right to a *new education*, i.e. to a *human right* or *rights-based approach* of education, that is, conducive, under the Rule of Law, to a Rightful Education understood as education consistent with the normative integrity of the right to education that may be condensed in Principles of the Ethics of the Right to Education, from which stem Educational Rights.

The right to education has an ethical significance – inscribed in the Ethics of Human Rights and the Ethics of the Rights of the Child – fundamentally because it is not a *right over the human being*, but a *right of the human being*. Right to a Rightful Education that should be the criterion of a *good education.*

The major theories in the history of education are conceptions of a good education, structured, at least implicitly, by the already mentioned conceptual trilogy inspiring its main definitions: *Perfectibility, Perfection, Perfecting.* This is reflected in the transcendence always recognised to the purpose of education – the Kantian *Kingdom of Ends.* As set out in the main international provisions on the right to education, its purpose may be summed up in the following Principles of the Ethics of the Right to Education:

- *Primacy of the best interests of the subject of the right to education*
  This is a principle deriving from the general primacy of the subject of human rights and generalising the primacy of the best interests of the child in education.
- *Development of the human personality: free, full, harmonious*
  This is a principle identifying the specific value of the right to education that should be the sense of all school learnings.
- *Priority of human rights education as an ethical, civic, international education*
  This is a principle reaffirming and renewing the traditional primacy of moral education and synthesizing the scope of its present conception.

From the Ethics of the Right to Education stem Educational Rights that are, foremostly, the rights of children and adolescents within the two main institutions of education which are family and school. They may be summed up as follows:

- Right to pedagogical responsibility
- Right to be different
- Right to respect for human dignity and rights in education
- Right to learn the and in the mother tongue
- Right to the whole object of the right to education
- Right to a right to education school
- Right to admirable education professionals
- Right to an effective remedy

A Rightful Education demands a Right to Education Policy and a Right to Education Pedagogy. Furthermore, if 'Sciences of Education' are all knowledge disciplines which can contribute to the comprehension of the educational phenomenon and the improvement of education, they should include notably the following ones: International Education Law, Neuroscience of Education, Semiotics of Education, Aesthetics of Education.

Conclusion: One Day, the Humankind …

The Revolution of the Right to Education is ultimately about solving the Gordian Knot of the humankind having to educate itself and singling out the right to education as Right to Possible.

It is submitted that this is perhaps the *secret* for solving the Gordian Knot of education: it will begin to be decisively disentangled only when children might *learn to be* with *the best human beings*.

How do we get the best human beings to become educators? They should be chosen by rulers. And who chooses the rulers?

The best education is one ethically illuminated by the best idea of human perfection, scientifically enlightened by the best knowledge on the human nature, and politically entrusted to the best human beings by better rulers elected by better educated citizens. The dissolution of the education Gordian Knot will thus take a lasting temporal magnitude …

What is the best humankind has ever envisioned for becoming better?

The answer seems indisputable: it is the Ethics of Human Rights and, in particular, the Ethics of the Right to Education as Right to Possible. Human rights institute limits that it is necessary to learn and open possibilities that should be explored and brought about. The right to education is the right to learn both the *limits* of the human finitude, which inscribe in the species' children their ethical identity, and the *Possible* as the ontological *utopia* of the infinite human perfectibility …

In sum:

Education is a genetic human need vested with human right status. This fundamentally means that, without education, human beings are not fully human, i.e. are not empowered to accomplish their unique worth and dignity.

The Revolution of the Right to Education means the political-pedagogical breaking of the vicious circle of the historical and psychological 'cloning' of the coming generations by the older ones, driven by the human compulsion and 'divine' temptation to 'create' children in their image and likeness. The *pedagogical reason* is no longer the *biological reason* of the Family nor the *political reason* of the State, but the *Ethical Reason* of the Subject, opening to full human flourishing.

Now that we know why education is the greatest power and the greatest responsibility of the human species, maybe it will be able to reach – in time – the full awareness that the right to education is the *abracadabra* to find the Holy Grail of its destiny ...

To be or not to be a human right – here is the question regarding the future of education and our Humanity.

Name Index